T0212478

Lecture Notes in Computer Science 10613

Commenced Publication in 1973
Founding and Former Series Editors:
Gerhard Goos, Juris Hartmanis, and Jan van Leeuwen

Editorial Board

David Hutchison
Lancaster University, Lancaster, UK
Takeo Kanade
Carnegie Mellon University, Pittsburgh, PA, USA
Josef Kittler
University of Surrey, Guildford, UK
Jon M. Kleinberg
Cornell University, Ithaca, NY, USA
Friedemann Mattern
ETH Zurich, Zurich, Switzerland
John C. Mitchell
Stanford University, Stanford, CA, USA
Moni Naor
Weizmann Institute of Science, Rehovot, Israel
C. Pandu Rangan
Indian Institute of Technology, Madras, India
Bernhard Steffen
TU Dortmund University, Dortmund, Germany
Demetri Terzopoulos
University of California, Los Angeles, CA, USA
Doug Tygar
University of California, Berkeley, CA, USA
Gerhard Weikum
Max Planck Institute for Informatics, Saarbrücken, Germany

More information about this series at http://www.springer.com/series/7407

Alessandra Lintas · Stefano Rovetta
Paul F.M.J. Verschure · Alessandro E.P. Villa (Eds.)

Artificial Neural Networks and Machine Learning – ICANN 2017

26th International Conference on Artificial Neural Networks
Alghero, Italy, September 11–14, 2017
Proceedings, Part I

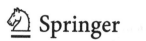 Springer

Editors

Alessandra Lintas
University of Lausanne
Lausanne
Switzerland

Stefano Rovetta
University of Genoa
Genoa
Italy

Paul F.M.J. Verschure
Universitat Pompeu Fabra
Barcelona
Spain

Alessandro E.P. Villa
University of Lausanne
Lausanne
Switzerland

ISSN 0302-9743   ISSN 1611-3349   (electronic)
Lecture Notes in Computer Science
ISBN 978-3-319-68599-1   ISBN 978-3-319-68600-4   (eBook)
https://doi.org/10.1007/978-3-319-68600-4

Library of Congress Control Number: 2017955786

LNCS Sublibrary: SL1 – Theoretical Computer Science and General Issues

© Springer International Publishing AG 2017
This work is subject to copyright. All rights are reserved by the Publisher, whether the whole or part of the material is concerned, specifically the rights of translation, reprinting, reuse of illustrations, recitation, broadcasting, reproduction on microfilms or in any other physical way, and transmission or information storage and retrieval, electronic adaptation, computer software, or by similar or dissimilar methodology now known or hereafter developed.
The use of general descriptive names, registered names, trademarks, service marks, etc. in this publication does not imply, even in the absence of a specific statement, that such names are exempt from the relevant protective laws and regulations and therefore free for general use.
The publisher, the authors and the editors are safe to assume that the advice and information in this book are believed to be true and accurate at the date of publication. Neither the publisher nor the authors or the editors give a warranty, express or implied, with respect to the material contained herein or for any errors or omissions that may have been made. The publisher remains neutral with regard to jurisdictional claims in published maps and institutional affiliations.

Printed on acid-free paper

This Springer imprint is published by Springer Nature
The registered company is Springer International Publishing AG
The registered company address is: Gewerbestrasse 11, 6330 Cham, Switzerland

Preface

This volume is part of the two-volume proceedings of the 26th International Conference on Artificial Neural Networks (ICANN-2017), held during September 11–14, 2017 in Alghero, Italy. ICANN 2017 was organized with the support of the Department of Architecture of the University of Sassari, the Neuroheuristics Research Group of the University of Lausanne, and the European Neural Network Society (ENNS).

The ICANN conference is the flagship annual conference of the European Neural Network Society. The ICANN series of conferences was initiated in 1991 and soon became the major European gatherings of experts in the field of neural networks and related areas. The unique character of this conference is its transdisciplinarity, beyond the interdisciplinarity of machine learning, bringing together researchers from all horizons, i.e., mathematics, physics, information and computer sciences, engineering, as well as theoretical and experimental neurosciences. The conference is organized in partnership with ENNS with its governance fully committed to not-for-profit procedures that allow us to keep the congress fees low compared with international standards. This policy granted the participation of a significant number of undergraduate and master students, who accounted for 18% of the scientific delegates. The ICANN governance model consolidated the practice to include membership of ENNS, valid through December of the calendar year of the conference, for all ICANN participants who present a scientific communication. Last, but not least, two best paper awards are distributed, along with ten travel grants sponsored by ENNS.

Following the practice of the ICANN conference series since 2011, the ICANN 2017 conference was organized following a dual-track stream of oral talks lasting 20 minutes each, one track including seven sessions of mainly ANN and machine-learning-inspired presentations, and one track including seven sessions of mainly bio-inspired presentations. A tutorial on the capabilities of shallow and deep networks supported by ENNS President Vera Kurkova and a special session organized on the topic of neural networks and applications to environmental sciences were organized on the first day of the conference, before the opening of the main program. Poster sessions have always played a key role in successful ICANN conferences. This year, the time and space allocated to nine poster sessions was further expanded, and posters were left on display throughout the entire duration of the conference. The scientific program was completed by five keynote lectures from world-renowned scholars: Professor Moshe Abeles talking about temporal information in neural coding; Professor Marco Gori about the computational framework associated with the emergence of inference rules; Professor Elisabeth André about emotional intelligence in human–computer interaction; Professor David Ríos about adversarial machine learning; and Professor Michele Giugliano about information transmission in weakly coupled large-scale neural ensembles.

Out of approximately 270 papers submitted to ICANN 2017, the Program Committee selected 128 full and 63 short papers. It is interesting to note that about half of the accepted short papers were initially submitted as full papers. Although these papers did not get through the strict reviewing process for full papers, their authors prepared a short paper version for presentation at ICANN. Because of its reputation as a high-level conference, ICANN rarely receives papers of poor quality, and the fact that one third of the scientific delegates chose to submit short papers is certainly a proof of the vitality and attractiveness of the ICANN conference. The type of submission was not the ultimate criterion in assigning the submitters to an oral or a poster presentation. Short papers account for 19/79 oral presentations and 44/112 poster presentations.

The number of accepted papers necessitated publishing the proceedings in two volumes. The contributions (oral and posters) were grouped following the respective track: Volume I for Artificial Neural Networks and Biological Inspiration and Volume II for Formal Models and Their Applications. The proceedings of the short papers have been grouped, following the rules of the publisher, at the end of each volume. The presenting authors came from 33 countries all over the world: 87 from Europe, 74 from Asia, 26 from the Americas, three from Oceania and one from Africa. China (39) and Germany (33) were the most represented countries.

It is our pleasure to express our gratitude to everybody who contributed to the success of the conference and the publication of the proceedings. In particular, we thank the members of the Executive Committee of the ENNS and the president, Vera Kurkova, for entrusting us with the organization of the conference. We would like to express our sincere gratitude to the members of the Program Committee and all the reviewers, who did a tremendous job under time constraints during the review process. We thank all members of the local Organizing Committee and the local staff for the great effort and assistance in the organization of the conference, in particular, Antonello Monsù Scolaro (Department of Architecture in Alghero of the University of Sassari), Eugenio Lintas (Sassari), and Anna Mura (SPECS, Universitat Pompeu Fabra, Barcelona). We are greatly indebted to Dr. Paolo Masulli for his commitment as ENNS interim secretary and ICANN communication chair along all phases of the organization. We would also like to thank the publisher, Springer, for their cooperation during the publishing process that was under strict time limitations. Finally, we thank all authors who contributed to these volumes for sharing their ideas, their results, and their spirit with the community during the scientific and social programs of the conference. We are sure that the participants of ICANN 2017 maintained the enthusiasm of the founders of ENNS and initial organizers of the ICANN conferences and that they will continue to generate new ideas and innovative results in the field of neural networks and related areas.

August 2017

Alessandra Lintas
Stefano Rovetta
Paul F.M.J. Verschure
Alessandro E.P. Villa

Organization

General Chair

Alessandro E.P. Villa   University of Lausanne, Switzerland

General Co-chair

Alessandra Lintas   University of Lausanne, Switzerland

Local Co-chairs

Stefano Rovetta   University of Genoa, Italy
Paul F.M.J. Verschure   SPECS-Universitat Pompeu Fabra, Spain

Communication Chair

Paolo Masulli   University of Lausanne, Switzerland

Local Organizing Committee

Paolo Enrico   University of Sassari, Italy
Alessandra Lintas   University of Lausanne, Switzerland
Eugenio Lintas   Sassari
Antonello Monsù Scolaro   University of Sassari, Italy
Anna Mura   SPECS-Universitat Pompeu Fabra, Barcelona, Spain

Scientific and Reviewing Committee

Jérémie Cabessa   Université Panthéon-Assas - Paris 2, France
Petia Koprinkova-Hristova   Bulgarian Academy of Sciences, Sofia, Bulgaria
Věra Kůrková   Czech Academy of Sciences, Prague, Czech Republic
Alessandra Lintas   University of Lausanne, Switzerland
Paolo Masulli   University of Lausanne, Switzerland
Francesco Masulli   University of Genoa, Italy
Paul F.M.J. Verschure   SPECS-Universitat Pompeu Fabra, Spain
Antonio Javier Pons Rivero   Universitat Politècnica de Catalunya, Spain
Yifat Prut   Hebrew University Jerusalem, Israel
Stefano Rovetta   University of Genoa, Italy
Antonino Staiano   University of Naples Parthenope, Italy
Igor V. Tetko   Helmholtz Zentrum München, Germany
Alessandro E.P. Villa   University of Lausanne, Switzerland

Program Committee

Lydia Fischer	Honda Research Institute Europe, Germany
Věra Kůrková	Czech Academy of Sciences, Prague, Czech Republic
Alessandra Lintas	University of Lausanne, Switzerland
Francesco Masulli	University of Genoa, Italy
Stefano Rovetta	University of Genoa, Italy
Antonino Staiano	University of Naples Parthenope, Italy
Alessandro E.P. Villa	University of Lausanne, Switzerland

Secretariat and Communication

Alessandra Lintas	University of Lausanne, Switzerland
Paolo Masulli	University of Lausanne, Switzerland

ENNS Travel Grant Committee

Cesare Alippi	Politecnico di Milano, Italy
Jérémie Cabessa	Université Panthéon-Assas - Paris 2, France
Barbara Hammer	University of Bielefeld, Germany
Petia Koprinkova-Hristova	Bulgarian Academy of Sciences, Sofia, Bulgaria
Věra Kůrková	Czech Academy of Sciences, Prague, Czech Republic
Paolo Masulli	University of Lausanne, Switzerland
Jaakko Peltonen	University of Tampere, Finland
Antonio Javier Pons Rivero	Universitat Politècnica de Catalunya, Spain
Yifat Prut	Hebrew University Jerusalem, Israel
Igor V. Tetko	Helmholtz Zentrum München, Germany
Paul F.M.J. Verschure	SPECS-Universitat Pompeu Fabra, Spain
Francisco Zamora-Martínez	University of Pamplona, Spain

Additional Reviewers

Tayfun Alpay	University of Hamburg, Knowledge Technology, WTM, Germany
Pablo Barros	University of Hamburg, Germany
Lluis Belanche	Universitat Politècnica de Catalunya, Spain
Michael Biehl	University of Groningen, The Netherlands
Giacomo Boracchi	Politecnico di Milano, Italy
Hans Albert Braun	University of Marburg, Germany
Li Bu	China
Guido Bugmann	Plymouth University, UK
Jérémie Cabessa	Université Panthéon-Assas, Paris 2, France
Francesco Camastra	University of Naples Parthenope, Italy
Angelo Cangelosi	Plymouth University, UK
Giovanna Castellano	University of Bari, Italy
Marta Castellano	Institute of Cognitive Sciences, Germany

Davide Chicco	University of Toronto, Canada
Angelo Ciaramella	University of Naples Parthenope, Italy
Jorg Conradt	TU München, Germany
David Coufal	Insitute of Computer Science AS CR, Czech Republic
Jose Enrique De Tomas	University of Alicante, Spain
Marc Deffains	Hebrew University Jerusalem, Israel
Sergey Dolenko	D.V. Skobeltsyn Institute of Nuclear Physics, M.V. Lomonosov Moscow State University, Russia
Jose Dorronsoro	Universidad Autonoma de Madrid, Spain
Wlodzislaw Duch	Nicolaus Copernicus University, Poland
David Díaz-Vico	Universidad Autónoma de Madrid, Spain
Lambros Ekonomou	City University London, UK
Anna Maria Fanelli	University of Bari, Italy
Andreas Fischer	University of Fribourg, Switzerland
Lydia Fischer	Honda Research Institute Europe
Giorgio Gnecco	IMT Lucca, Italy
José Luis González-de-Suso	das-Nano, Spain
Claudius Gros	Goethe University of Frankfurt, Germany
Ankur Gupta	University of British Columbia, Canada
Tatiana V. Guy	Institute of Information Theory and Automation, Czech Republic
Frantisek Hakl	Institute of computer Science, Czech Republic
Barbara Hammer	Bielefeld University, Germany
Stefan Heinrich	Universität Hamburg, Germany
Katsuhiro Honda	Osaka Prefecture University, Japan
Brian Hyland	University of Otago, New Zealand
Lazaros Iliadis	Democritus University of Thrace, Greece
Maciej Jedynak	University Grenoble Alpes, Grenoble Institute of Neuroscience, France
Marika Kaden	HS Mittweida, Germany
Fotis Kanellos	National Technical University of Athens, Greece
Juha Karhunen	Aalto University, Finland
Matthias Kerzel	Universität Hamburg, Germany
Mario Koeppen	Kyushu Institute of Technology, Japan
Stefanos Kollias	National Technical University of Athens, Greece
Ján Koloda	das-Nano, Spain
Petia Koprinkova-Hristova	Bulgarian Academy of Sciences, Bulgaria
Irena Koprinska	University of Sydney, Australia
Vera Kurkova	Institute of Computer Science, Academy of Sciences of the Czech Republic, Czech Republic
Giancarlo La Camera	SUNY Stony Brook, USA
Alessandra Lintas	University of Lausanne, Switzerland
Ling Luo	University of Sydney, Australia
Iván López-Espejo	University of Granada, Spain
Sven Magg	Universität Hamburg, Germany
Miroslaw Malek	USI-Lugano, Switzerland

Petr Marsalek	Charles University in Prague, Czech Republic
Francesco Masulli	University of Genoa, Italy
Paolo Masulli	University of Lausanne, Switzerland
Joshua Mati	Hebrew University Jerusalem, Israel
Corrado Mencar	University of Bari A. Moro, Italy
George Mengov	Sofia University, Bulgaria
Valeri Mladenov	Technical University of Sofia, Bulgaria
Juan Manuel Moreno	Universitat Politecnica de Catalunya, Spain
Anna Mura	SPECS-UPF Barcelona, Spain
Roman Neruda	Institute of Computer Science, ASCR, Czech Republic
Nathan Netanyahu	Bar-Ilan University, Israel
Francesca Odone	University of Genoa, Italy
Luca Oneto	University of Genoa, Italy
Sebastian Otte	University of Tübingen, Germany
Joan Pastor Pellicer	Universitat Politècnica de València, Spain
Riccardo Pecori	eCampus, Italy
Jaakko Peltonen	Aalto University, Finland
Vincenzo Piuri	University of Milan, Italy
Mirko Polato	University of Padova, Italy
Antonio Javier Pons Rivero	Universitat Politècnica de Catalunya, Barcelona, Spain
Yifat Prut	Hebrew University Jerusalem, Israel
Federico Raue	University of Kaiserslautern, Germany
Francesco Regazzoni	Università della Svizzera Italiana, Switzerland
Marina Resta	University of Genoa, Italy
Jean Roaut	University of Québec Sherbrooke, Canada
Manuel Roveri	Politecnico di Milano, Italy
Stefano Rovetta	University of Genoa, Italy
Alessandro Rozza	Waynaut, Italy
Marcello Sanguineti	University of Genoa, Italy
Wolfram Schenck	Bielefeld University of Applied Sciences, Germany
Friedhelm Schwenker	University of Ulm, Germany
Jordi Soriano	Universitat de Barcelona, Spain
Alessandro Sperduti	University of Padova, Italy
Antonino Staiano	University of Naples Parthenope, Italy
Michael Stiber	University of Washington Bothell, USA
Aubin Tchaptchet	Philipps University of Marburg, Germany
Igor Tetko	HMGU, Germany
Yancho Todorov	Aalto University, Finland
Alberto Torres-Barrán	Universidad Autónoma de Madrid, Spain
Jochen Triesch	Frankfurt Institute for Advanced Studies, Germany
Francesco Trovo	Politecnico di Milano, Italy
Georgi Tsvetanov Tsenov	Technical University Sofia, Bulgaria
Antonio Vergari	University of Bari, Italy
Paul F.M.J. Verschure	SPECS-Universitat Pompeu Fabra, Spain
Petra Vidnerová	Czech Academy of Sciences, Czech Republic
Alexander Vidybida	Bogolyubov Institute for Theoretical Physics, Ukraine

Alessandro E.P. Villa	University of Lausanne, Switzerland
Thomas Villmann	UAS Mittweida, Germany
Roseli Wedemann	Universidade do Estado do Rio de Janeiro, Brazil
Thomas Wennekers	Plymouth University, UK
Heiko Wersing	Honda Research Institute Europe, Germany
Baptiste Wicht	University of Applied Sciences of Western Switzerland, Switzerland
Francisco Zamora-Martinez	das-Nano SL, Spain
Jianhua Zhang	East China University of Science and Technology, China
Dongbin Zhao	China

Contents – Part I

From Neurons to Networks

Brain Imaging

Recurrent Neural Networks

Neuromorphic Hardware

Brain Topology and Dynamics

Synaptic Plasticity and Learning

Neural Networks Meet Natural and Environmental Sciences

Short Papers

Contents – Part II

Convolutional Neural Networks

Games and Strategy

Boltzmann Machines and Phase Transitions

Context Information Learning and Self-Assessment in Advanced Machine Learning Models

Representation and Classification

Clustering

Learning from Data Streams and Time Series

Image Processing and Medical Applications

Advances in Machine Learning

From Perception to Action

Semi-supervised Phoneme Recognition
with Recurrent Ladder Networks

Marian Tietz$^{(\boxtimes)}$, Tayfun Alpay, Johannes Twiefel, and Stefan Wermter

Department of Informatics, Knowledge Technology Institute, Universität Hamburg,
Vogt-Kölln-Str. 30, 22527 Hamburg, Germany
{tietz,alpay,twiefel,wermter}@informatik.uni-hamburg.de
http://www.informatik.uni-hamburg.de/WTM/

Abstract. Ladder networks are a notable new concept in the field of semi-supervised learning by showing state-of-the-art results in image recognition tasks while being compatible with many existing neural architectures. We present the recurrent ladder network, a novel modification of the ladder network, for semi-supervised learning of recurrent neural networks which we evaluate with a phoneme recognition task on the TIMIT corpus. Our results show that the model is able to consistently outperform the baseline and achieve fully-supervised baseline performance with only 75% of all labels which demonstrates that the model is capable of using unsupervised data as an effective regulariser.

Keywords: Semi-supervised learning · Recurrent neural networks · Ladder networks · Phoneme recognition

1 Introduction

There is no doubt that the recent success of deep learning is tied to the rising availability of labelled data. While tasks such as image or text classification have greatly benefited from this availability, there are still a number of domains, e.g. speech recognition, where the majority of the research community has no free access to large amounts of labelled data. One promising approach towards this problem is semi-supervised learning where models trained with *labelled* data can be further improved by training with *unlabelled* data.

Recent methods, such as graph-supported training [10], sparse autoencoders ([4]; SSSAE) and especially the Ladder Network (LN) [11], a stacked Denoising Autoencoder (DAE) with shortcut connections, show promising results for semi-supervised training of feed-forward neural networks. The LN has been shown to deliver state-of-the-art results in semi-supervised image classification while still being compatible with many existing feed-forward neural networks [11].

However, this novel architecture has not yet been explored on more complex sequential tasks, such as speech recognition, where Recurrent Neural Network (RNN) architectures, like Gated Recurrent Units (GRU; [1]), are the current state of the art. We therefore propose a novel Recurrent Ladder Network (RLN)

© Springer International Publishing AG 2017
A. Lintas et al. (Eds.): ICANN 2017, Part I, LNCS 10613, pp. 3–10, 2017.
https://doi.org/10.1007/978-3-319-68600-4_1

architecture and evaluate it on the TIMIT phoneme recognition benchmark [5]. We introduce a novel recurrent layer for the LN decoder in order to find better-suited abstractions for semi-supervised learning and test two noise injection schemes tailored to support recurrent dynamics to increase the regularising nature of the RLN. Our results show that after hyper-parameter optimization the model is able to significantly outperform the baseline in all experiments using unsupervised data as a regulariser and achieves fully-supervised baseline performance while training only on 75% of the labelled data.

2   The Ladder Network Architecture

The basic idea of the LN architecture [11], depicted in Fig. 1, is to make autoencoders more expressive by adding shortcut connections from the encoder to the decoder. Each decoder layer is then able to combine the preactivation of the encoder layer with the reconstruction of the previous decoder layer by means of a combinator function $g(\cdot, \cdot)$. Therefore, the encoder does not have to carry all reconstruction information since the shortcuts can compensate for it. Since the shortcuts allow perfect reconstruction by simply copying the encoder input to the decoder output, Gaussian noise $\mathcal{N}(0, \sigma^2)$ is added to prevent the direct usage of these short-circuits and enforce learning in the intermediate layers, i.e. we use a denoising autoencoder. To ensure that the noise can be removed, the decoder's (noisy) reconstruction $\hat{\mathbf{z}}^{(l)}$ is compared to the encoder's (clean) preactivation $\mathbf{z}^{(l)}$ and added to the unsupervised objective function:

$$C_{\text{DAE}} = \sum_{l}^{n} \lambda_l C_d^{(l)} \text{ with } C_d^{(l)} = \| \mathbf{z}^{(l)} - \hat{\mathbf{z}}^{(l)} \|^2, \tag{1}$$

where n is the total amount of layers, $\mathbf{z}^{(l)}$ is the preactivation vector of the l-th encoder layer without noise and $\hat{\mathbf{z}}^{(l)}$ the l-th decoder layer reconstruction from noisy input. The hyper-parameter λ_i controls the targeted similarity between the encoder and decoder layers and prevents short-circuits by punishing direct copies of the noisy data by weighting the difference between the layers. For semi-supervised learning the encoder path is also used for the supervised task, i.e. its output is evaluated with a supervised objective function C_{sup} and combined with the unsupervised objective function C_{DAE}: $C_{\text{semsup}} = C_{\text{sup}} + C_{\text{DAE}}$. When using the encoder in a supervised task the shortcuts help with reconstruction as the needed information may also be retrieved over the shortcuts [11].

The combinator function $g(\cdot, \cdot)$ models $p(\mathbf{z}^{(l)} \mid \mathbf{z}^{(l+1)})$ and is responsible for creating the reconstruction of the l-th layer $\hat{\mathbf{z}}^{(l)}$ with the help of the reconstruction of the previous layer $\hat{\mathbf{z}}^{(l+1)}$ and the shortcut value of the l-th layer $\tilde{\mathbf{z}}^{(l)}$, i.e., $\hat{\mathbf{z}}^{(l)} = g(\tilde{\mathbf{z}}^{(l)}, \hat{\mathbf{z}}^{(l+1)})$. The function may attempt to remove the noise from $\tilde{\mathbf{z}}^{(l)}$ with the help of the previous reconstruction, infer the inverse mapping $\hat{\mathbf{z}}^{(l+1)} \rightarrow \hat{\mathbf{z}}^{(l)}$ or do a combination of both.

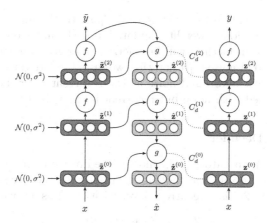

Fig. 1. Illustration of the non-recurrent LN architecture with one hidden and one output layer. The encoder and decoder paths are highlighted in green and yellow, respectively. (Color figure online)

3   Recurrent Ladder Networks

In this section, we will elaborate our modelling choices for the RLN. In order to extend the original LN to support recurrence in the encoder, both the noise injection scheme and the decoder have to be adapted since recurrent layers use additional context layers. Overall, we are proposing two noise injection methods and two decoder variants (see Fig. 2). Our supervised baseline model will be the encoder of the RLN since it encodes the task closely to the full RLN but has no means of using unsupervised data. The resulting six model combinations are No-Decoder with Feed-Forward Noise (ND-FFN), No-Decoder with Recurrent Noise (ND-RN), Recurrent Decoder with Feed-Forward Noise (RD-FFN) and Recurrent Noise (RD-RN) as well as a Feed-Forward Decoder with Feed-Forward Noise (FFD-FFN) and Recurrent Noise (FFD-RN).

3.1   Noise Injection

In the *feed-forward* case, noise is applied directly to the preactivations so that the output of the layer and the shortcut are affected, i.e. $\tilde{\mathbf{z}} = W\tilde{\mathbf{x}} + \mathbf{n}$ with $\mathbf{n} \sim \mathcal{N}(0, \sigma^2)$. This would, however, introduce noise into the context memory of recurrent layers even *after* receiving the noisy output from the previous layer, effectively amplifying the noise even further. Therefore, we apply noise only to the preactivation and the shortcut without direct perturbation of the context memory. A hidden layer $\mathbf{h}_t$ and its noisy counterpart $\tilde{\mathbf{h}}_t$ are therefore updated as follows:

$$\mathbf{h}_t = f(\mathbf{z}_t) = f(W\tilde{\mathbf{x}}_t + U\mathbf{h}_{t-1}), \tag{2}$$

$$\tilde{\mathbf{h}}_t = f(\tilde{\mathbf{z}}_t) = f(\mathbf{z}_t + \mathbf{n}), \tag{3}$$

where $f(\cdot)$ is the activation function, $\mathbf{x}_t$ the input, W the input weight matrix, and U the hidden-to-hidden weights, updated at each time step t.

This noise injection method will be referred to as *recurrent noise* from here on. Another method of noise injection that we tested, referred to as *feed-forward noise*, is to not inject additional noise at the recurrent layer, i.e. feed-forward layers will be injected with noise but recurrent layers will not.

3.2   Recurrent Decoder

The decoder path in an autoencoder models the inverse information flow of the encoder path. We propose two modelling options for the decoder path in an RLN. The first (Fig. 2c) is a recurrent layer with $g(\cdot, \cdot)$ as activation function:

$$\mathbf{u}_t^{(l)} = V\hat{\mathbf{z}}_t^{(l+1)} + O\hat{\mathbf{z}}_{t-1}^{(l)}, \tag{4}$$

$$\hat{\mathbf{z}}_t^{(l)} = g(\tilde{\mathbf{z}}_t^{(l)}, \mathbf{u}_t^{(l)}), \tag{5}$$

where V are the input weights, O the hidden-to-hidden weights, $\mathbf{u}_t^{(l)}$ the pre-activation of the recurrent decoder and $\tilde{\mathbf{z}}_t^{(l)}$ the noisy preactivation of the l-th encoder layer at time-step t from the shortcut. The second modelling option is to simply use a feed-forward network (Fig. 2d) in the decoder [11].

Batch normalisation is heavily used in the LN both for normalisation of the layer-wise reconstruction cost and for normalisation of layer activations. It was considered problematic with recurrent networks until the introduction of recurrent batch normalisation [2]. Since it potentially requires tuning of another hyper-parameter we decided to model the RLN without batch normalisation with the exception of the layer-wise reconstruction cost function $C_d^{(l)}$ which is computed exactly as described by Rasmus et al. [11].

4   Experiments

We evaluate the RLN on the TIMIT phoneme recognition benchmark [5], a widely used test corpus which allows comparing our architecture to previous approaches. The audio samples of the corpus are reduced in dimensionality by using libROSA[1] to compute 13 Mel Frequency Cepstral Components (MFCC) [3] and their first and second derivative with 20ms frames and 10ms frame skip, similar to related work [4]. The 39-dimensional feature vectors are normalised to have zero mean and unit variance. We grouped easily confused phonemes of the English phoneme alphabet as described by Halberstadt [8] resulting in 39 phoneme classes to predict.

We use Connectionist Temporal Classification (CTC) [6] for the supervised cost C_{sup} to solve the problem of label alignment. Phoneme Error Rate (PER) is used for evaluation and computed using the Levenshtein distance of all label sequences to the predictions, normalised to the total length of all label sequences.

---

[1] https://librosa.github.io.

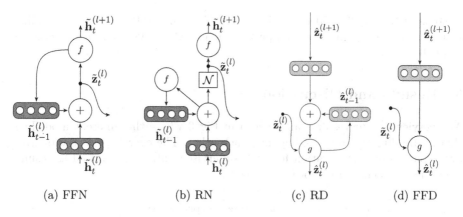

(a) FFN   (b) RN   (c) RD   (d) FFD

Fig. 2. Overview of (a) feed-forward noise (FFN) and (b) recurrent noise (RN) injection schemes for the encoders (green) introduced in Subsect. 3.1 as well as (c) recurrent decoder (RD) and (d) feed-forward decoder (FFD) layouts (yellow) introduced in Subsect. 3.2. Combining all encoder and decoder layouts gives a total of six model variants including the two no-decoder (ND) baselines ND-RN and ND-FFN. (Color figure online)

The predictions are obtained by using best path decoding [6], i.e. choosing the phoneme class with the highest probability at each time step.

To build the supervised and unsupervised training sets we keep all input data for unsupervised training and reduce the supervised set by drawing samples from the full dataset until the least represented phonemes are drawn a minimum number of times to prevent under-representing a class while keeping the distribution intact. We cycle the supervised dataset to match sizes with the unsupervised set, similar to the implementation by Rasmus et al. [11].

4.1 Training Procedure

All networks have been trained using Adam [9] with a learning rate of 0.002 for at least 100 epochs until the validation error stopped improving. The models are four-layer networks consisting of one GRU layer with 192 units with $\tanh(\cdot)$ activation and one feed-forward output layer with softmax activation, as well as the inverse layers in the decoder. The noisy softmax output is used to classify phonemes during training for additional regularisation. Since the performance of the encoder is likely to correlate with RLN performance, hyper-parameters, including layer sizes and learning rate, were determined empirically by a grid search using the encoder described in Sect. 3, i.e. an RLN with $\lambda_i = 0$, which also serves as the baseline. DAE cost weights $(\lambda_0, \lambda_1, \lambda_2) = (1000, 10, 0.1)$ and the MLP combinator $g(\cdot, \cdot)$ were both adopted from Rasmus et al. [11].

We test the semi-supervised learning capabilities of the six RLN variants from Sect. 3, by varying the labels for the supervised part of the architecture in steps of 25% (940), 50% (1856), 75% (2754), and 100% (3696) of labelled sequences while the unsupervised part of the model always receives all available unlabelled data.

5   Results and Discussion

An overview of our results can be seen in Fig. 3 where the different modelling choices are directly compared against each other. The overall best results after hyper-parameter optimization for each supervised data split, as well as results of other approaches, are shown in Table 1.

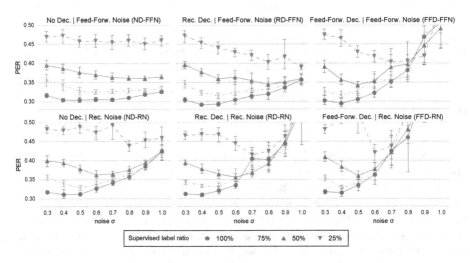

Fig. 3. Comparison of PER achieved by the RLN variants with varying amount of labelled data (25%–100%) and noise standard deviation σ. Each data point represents the mean, the whiskers cover a 95% confidence interval. Higher σ are needed for fewer labels to prevent overfitting.

As can be seen in Table 1, the RLN consistently outperforms the baseline configuration, even in fully-supervised training and is able to achieve the same performance as the baseline with 25% less labelled data which shows that the RLN complements the encoder well and demonstrates the compatibility of the LN with existing models. On average, the RD models perform better than the FFD models for most σ, more so with fewer labels, suggesting that the recurrent decoder is better at filtering noise. This also explains why the RD models work better with higher σ compared to FFD.

The noise injection method and the chosen σ greatly impact the overall performance. The performance curves are roughly concave and shift towards stronger noise with less available labels because the network overfits easily with fewer labels which is prevented by the higher noise. Performance degrades for higher σ because the network needs to be trained significantly longer to remove the noise which the chosen training parameters do not allow.

Recurrent noise injection was expected to achieve better regularisation due to the additional noise at the recurrent layer but does not. By observing the encoder layers we found that their outputs often differed significantly which causes unre-coverable perturbations in the recurrent layers when applying equally strong noise to all layers instead of noise relative to each layer's output. Employing batch normalisation might solve this, as hypothesised in related work [12]: nor-malising the preactivation of each layer to unit variance before adding noise makes the change in variance relative to the preactivation, therefore coupling noise and layer activation strength with the benefit of reducing the search space for σ significantly. We predict that this will lead to an increase in performance when using fewer labels.

Even though our best results for the RLN are slightly lower ranked when compared with related approaches, our model has significantly fewer parameters (e.g. differing by a factor of 160 when compared to SSSAE [4]). We therefore hypothesise that an increase of parameters and more complex layer architec-tures will result in even better performance. This is indicated by our best RLN achieving similar results (31.66% PER, 175k parameters) as the Bi-directional Long Short-Term Memory (BLSTM) ([6]; 31.25% PER, 114k parameters) while using only half of the labels.

Table 1. Best results in phoneme error rate (PER), achieved by the proposed RLN modelling options: No decoder (ND, baseline), recurrent decoder (RD), feedforward decoder (FFD), feedforward noise (FFN), and recurrent noise (RN). †: linear inter-polation between 10% and 30% labels. ††: Graves et al. [7] have shown significantly improved results with more parameters (17.7% PER, 4.3 m param.).

Labels	ND-FFN	RD-FFN	FFD-FFN	ND-RN	RD-RN	FFD-RN	SSSAE [4]	BLSTM [6]
25%	40.65	**36.40**	37.13	39.90	38.82	**36.41**	31.0†	–
50%	34.22	**31.66**	32.06	34.07	**33.07**	33.39	–	–
75%	30.96	**29.16**	30.31	31.17	30.84	**30.42**	–	–
100%	29.11	**28.02**	28.08	29.26	29.67	**29.26**	–	31.25††
Param	0.134 m	0.177 m	0.159 m	0.134 m	0.177 m	0.159 m	28.7 m	0.114 m

6   Conclusion

We have shown that the recurrent ladder network is able to perform as good as similarly parametrised BLSTM models while using only 50% of the labelled data, demonstrating the RLN's ability to effectively regularise itself using unsupervised training data. Current state-of-the-art methods performed better overall but this does not come as a surprise given that these models use up to 160 times more parameters. We argue that this gap could potentially be closed by scaling up our models, as demonstrated for BLSTM models by Graves et al. [7].

The proposed recurrent decoder proved to be better at denoising than the feed-forward decoder. Additionally, we found that recurrent noise injection does not perform as expected and we hypothesise that it needs the help of normali-sation (e.g. batch normalisation) to work efficiently.

In the future, we would also like to take advantage of the semi-supervised learning abilities of the RLN in conjunction with more complex recurrent mod-els such as bidirectional and attention-based RNNs to utilise unlabelled data even more effectively and explore how the learning framework scales with more complex temporal dynamics in more challenging tasks such as end-to-end speech recognition or question answering.

Acknowledgments. The authors gratefully acknowledge partial support from the German Research Foundation DFG under project CML (TRR 169), the European Union under project SECURE (No 642667), and the Hamburg Landes-forschungsförderungsprojekt CROSS.

References

1. Cho, K., Van Merriënboer, B., Gülçehre, Ç., Bahdanau, D., Bougares, F., Schwenk, H., Bengio, Y.: Learning phrase representations using RNN encoder-decoder for statistical machine translation. arXiv preprint (2014). arXiv:1406.1078
2. Cooijmans, T., Ballas, N., Laurent, C., Gülçehre, Ç., Courville, A.: Recurrent batch normalization. arXiv preprint (2016). arXiv:1603.09025
3. Davis, S., Mermelstein, P.: Comparison of parametric representations for mono-syllabic word recognition in continuously spoken sentences. IEEE Trans. Acoust. Speech Signal Process. **28**(4), 357–366 (1980)
4. Dhaka, A.K., Salvi, G.: Semi-supervised learning with sparse autoencoders in phone classification. arXiv preprint (2016). arXiv:1610.00520
5. Garofolo, J.S., Lamel, L.F., Fisher, W.M., Fiscus, J.G., Pallett, D.S.: DARPA TIMIT acoustic-phonetic continous speech corpus CD-ROM. NIST speech disc 1–1.1. NASA STI/Recon Technical Report N 93 (1993)
6. Graves, A., Fernández, S., Gomez, F., Schmidhuber, J.: Connectionist temporal classification: labelling unsegmented sequence data with recurrent neural networks. In: Proceedings of ICML-2006, pp. 369–376 (2006)
7. Graves, A., Mohamed, A., Hinton, G.E.: Speech recognition with deep recurrent neural networks. In: Proceedings of ICASSP-2013, pp. 6645–6649 (2013)
8. Halberstadt, A.K.: Heterogeneous acoustic measurements and multiple classifiers for speech recognition. Ph.D. thesis, Massachusetts Institute of Technology (1998)
9. Kingma, D.P., Ba, J.: Adam: A method for stochastic optimization. arXiv preprint (2014). arXiv:1412.6980
10. Liu, Y., Kirchhoff, K.: Graph-based semi-supervised learning for phone and seg-ment classification. In: Proceedings of INTERSPEECH-2013, pp. 1840–1843 (2013)
11. Rasmus, A., Berglund, M., Honkala, M., Valpola, H., Raiko, T.: Semi-supervised learning with ladder networks. In: Proceedings of NIPS-2015, pp. 3532–3540 (2015)
12. Zhang, Y., Lee, K., Lee, H.: Augmenting supervised neural networks with unsuper-vised objectives for large-scale image classification. In: Proceedings of ICML-2016, pp. 612–621 (2016)

Mixing Actual and Predicted Sensory States Based on Uncertainty Estimation for Flexible and Robust Robot Behavior

Shingo Murata[1]([✉]), Wataru Masuda[1], Saki Tomioka[1], Tetsuya Ogata[2], and Shigeki Sugano[1]

[1] Department of Modern Mechanical Engineering, Waseda University, Tokyo, Japan
murata@sugano.mech.waseda.ac.jp
[2] Department of Intermedia Art and Science, Waseda University, Tokyo, Japan

Abstract. In this paper, we propose a method to dynamically modulate the input state of recurrent neural networks (RNNs) so as to realize flexible and robust robot behavior. We employ the so-called stochastic continuous-time RNN (S-CTRNN), which can learn to predict the mean and variance (or uncertainty) of subsequent sensorimotor information. Our proposed method uses this estimated uncertainty to determine a mixture ratio for combining actual and predicted sensory states of network input. The method is evaluated by conducting a robot learning experiment in which a robot is required to perform a sensory-dependent task and a sensory-independent task. The sensory-dependent task requires the robot to incorporate meaningful sensory information, and the sensory-independent task requires the robot to ignore irrelevant sensory information. Experimental results demonstrate that a robot controlled by our proposed method exhibits flexible and robust behavior, which results from dynamic modulation of the network input on the basis of the estimated uncertainty of actual sensory states.

Keywords: Recurrent neural networks · Uncertainty · Robot · Neurorobotics

1 Introduction

Flexible and robust behavior is crucial for autonomous robots that are expected to work in the same environments as people. Flexibility enables robots to generate context-dependent behavior that is suitable for the current situation. As a complement, robustness enables robots to generate behavior without being affected by perturbations, such as unknown irregularities and unrelated or noisy sensory information. Flexibility can be realized by accepting sensory information about the current environment, and robustness by ignoring the information or assessing its relative importance. From this viewpoint, flexibility and robustness are conflicting demands, which makes it non-trivial to achieve both at the same time. We aim to tackle this issue in terms of predictive learning of sensorimotor

© Springer International Publishing AG 2017
A. Lintas et al. (Eds.): ICANN 2017, Part I, LNCS 10613, pp. 11–18, 2017.
https://doi.org/10.1007/978-3-319-68600-4_2

information with uncertainty estimation, which has been widely accepted as a key computational principle for cognitive functions, including action, perception, and attention [1].

In the context of robot learning, Noda et al. [2] demonstrated that a small humanoid robot with a connectionist framework using a recurrent neural network with parametric biases (RNNPB) [3] can dynamically generate and switch its object-handling behavior. Their RNNPB was trained to predict sensorimotor information by receiving current information and integrating it with contextual information stored in the network. The key point is that the network received a mixture of actual and predicted sensorimotor states as network input. Modulation of network input is an important aspect of using RNNs. For example, in the studies [4,5], the performance of RNNs was improved by replacing the predicted states with the actual (true) states for network input in the training phase. In the study by Noda et al. [2], mixing the actual and predicted states together results in both flexibility in the face of environmental change and robustness against noise. However, the usefulness of this method as presented is limited because the mixture ratio must be hand-tuned for each target task, after which the tuned ratio was static through the task.

In the present study, we speculate that the uncertainty of sensory information can be used to dynamically modulate the input state of RNNs so as to realize flexible and robust robot behavior. Specifically, we propose a method in which the uncertainty of a future actual sensory state is estimated by a so-called stochastic continuous-time RNN (S-CTRNN) [6]. The estimated uncertainty is used as a factor in determining the mixture ratio between actual and predicted sensory states for the network input. The proposed method is validated by a robot-learning experiment that compares its results with those from a conventional method.

2   Computational Framework

2.1   Overview of S-CTRNN

S-CTRNN is an extension of conventional CTRNNs [7], and it consists of input, context, output, and variance layers. The distinguishing characteristic of this network is the newly added variance layer, which is used to estimate the uncertainty of target states. As a generative model, the network learns to predict the mean y_t and variance (uncertainty) v_t of a target state $\hat{y}_t$ given the input state x_t and the context c_t stored in the network, where the target state at time step t characterizes the input state at the next time step $t+1$. The internal state of the ith neural unit at time step t ($u_{t,i}$) in each layer other than the input layer is described by

$$
u_{t,i} = \begin{cases} \left(1 - \dfrac{1}{\tau_i}\right) u_{t-1,i} + \dfrac{1}{\tau_i}\left(\displaystyle\sum_{j=1}^{N_I} w_{ij} x_{t,j} + \sum_{j=1}^{N_C} w_{ij} c_{t-1,j} + b_i\right) & (i \in I_C), \\[4mm] \displaystyle\sum_{j=1}^{N_C} w_{ij} c_{t,j} + b_i & (i \in I_O \cup I_V), \end{cases}
\tag{1}
$$

where I_C, I_O, and I_V are the index sets for the context, output, and variance layers, respectively; N_I, N_C, N_O, and I_V are the numbers of the input, context, output, and variance units, respectively; $x_{t,j}$ is the jth input state at time step t; $c_{t-1,j}$ is the state of the jth context at time step $t-1$; τ_i is the time constant of the ith context unit; w_{ij} is the synaptic weight of the connection from the jth to the ith unit; and b_i is the bias of the ith unit. The activation state for the context and output states is computed by $\tanh(u_{t,i})$; that for the variance state is computed by $\exp(u_{t,i})$.

The goal of predictive learning is to maximize the likelihood $L(\boldsymbol{\theta})$, which is derived from the Gaussian assumption:

$$L(\boldsymbol{\theta}) = \prod_{t=1}^{T}\prod_{i=1}^{N_O} \frac{1}{\sqrt{2\pi v_{t,i}}} \exp\left(-\frac{(\hat{y}_{t,i} - y_{t,i})^2}{2 v_{t,i}}\right), \tag{2}$$

where $\boldsymbol{\theta}$ is a set of network parameters (w_{ij}, b_i), T is the length of the time series, and $\hat{y}_{t,i}$ is the ith target state corresponding to the next input state $x_{t+1,i}$. The network parameters are optimized by using the gradient ascent method with back-propagation through time (BPTT), as detailed in [6].

2.2   Mixing Actual and Predicted States Using S-CTRNN

Conventionally, forward computation of RNNs is performed via open-loop generation or closed-loop generation. In open-loop generation, shown in Fig. 1 (left), the input layer receives the actual state, such as recorded or online sensory data, at time step $t+1$, and the state is taken as the target state at the previous time step t ($x_{t+1,i} = \hat{y}_{t,i}$). In closed-loop generation, shown in Fig. 1 (center), in contrast, the input layer receives the output state generated at the previous time step t, which corresponds to the prediction of the input state at the current time step $t+1$ ($x_{t+1,i} = y_{t,i}$).

Here, we propose to mix these operations according to the variance predicted by the S-CTRNN, which represents the uncertainty of the next input state. This is done as follows:

$$x_{t+1,i} = (1 - \alpha(v_{t,i}))\,\hat{y}_{t,i} + \alpha(v_{t,i})y_{t,i}, \tag{3}$$

where $0 \leq \alpha(v_{t,i}) \leq 1$ is the mixture ratio, represented by a monotonically increasing function of the uncertainty. This equation is derived from the idea that actual states with high uncertainty, which may perturb the network dynamics, should not be input to the network and should, instead, be replaced with predicted states for stability. When $\alpha(v_{t,i})$ is a fixed value that does not depend on the time step t and the element i, Eq. (3) corresponds to the method used in the study by Noda et al. [2]. The generation method, which can be called *mixture-loop* generation, is illustrated in Fig. 1 (right). In the figure, as an example, the S-CTRNN generates low uncertainty for the first dimension and high uncertainty for the second. The first dimension of the input layer at the next time step receives the actual state (which has a relatively certain estimate) in

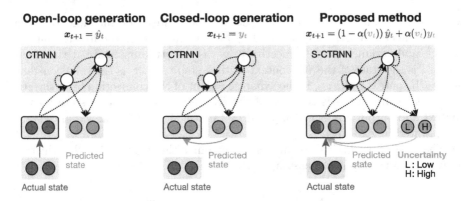

Fig. 1. Different generation methods. Left: open-loop generation with a conventional CTRNN in which the actual state $\hat{y}_t$ (magenta) is fed into the input layer. Center: closed-loop generation with a conventional CTRNN in which the predicted state y_t (cyan), instead of the actual state, is fed into the input layer. Right: proposed method (mixture-loop generation) with an S-CTRNN in which the actual and predicted states are mixed according to the mixture ratio $\alpha(v_t)$, where v_t is a vector representing uncertainty or variance (orange) as estimated by the S-CTRNN. (Color figure online)

greater proportion than the predicted state. In contrast, the second dimension receives the predicted state in greater proportion than the actual state (which has an uncertain estimate). This mixture method, which is specific to each time step and dimension, is expected to contribute to the flexibility and robustness of robot behavior.

3   Robot Experiment

3.1   Task Setting

We performed a robot learning experiment to evaluate the proposed method. In the experiment, a small humanoid robot "NAO" (Aldebaran Robotics) was used and interacted with a human experimenter, who was wearing a red glove to ease visual processing. The robot was required to perform an interactive task with the experimenter. The required task consisted of two phases: a sensor-dependent task and a sensor-independent task, as shown in Fig. 2.

In the first phase (the sensor-dependent task), the experimenter moved his hand to the left or right relative to the home position, and the robot was required to raise its corresponding hand. The direction of the human hand movement was randomly selected with equal probability by generating a sequence in advance. This phase was repeated until the experimenter cued a task transition by putting his hand up. Whether to continue the current task or transition to the other task was also determined with equal probability.

In the second phase (the sensor-independent task), after the demonstration of the transition cue, the robot was required to alternately raise its right and

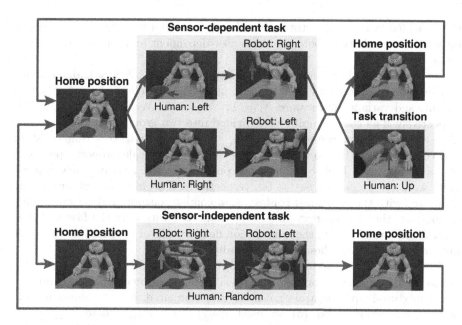

Fig. 2. Interactive task between a human experimenter and a small humanoid robot "NAO". The task has sensor-dependent and sensor-independent tasks.

left hands once, independent of the human hand movement. During this phase, the experimenter made hand movements as distractions, such as by randomly moving the hand or keeping the hand at a specific position. That is, in this phase, the robot needed to ignore unrelated sensory states (visual information from the human hand movement) and perform its own task. After finishing this phase, the task returned to the first phase again without giving any cue that task transition had occurred.

3.2   Experimental Procedure

The robot learning experiment consisted of three phases: recording of training data, training the S-CTRNN, and testing the performance of the robot. In what follows, each phase is briefly introduced.

In the first phase (data recording), training data were collected through kinesthetic teaching, with the robot controlled by directly guiding its arm movements. The recorded training data consisted of 3-dimensional visual information and 8-dimensional motor information. The visual information comprises time-series data of the center of gravity and area ratio of the red glove as extracted from a visual image obtained by a camera mounted on the robot. The motor information comprises time-series data of the four joint angles of each arm of the robot. In this data recording phase, the sensor-dependent task was repeated several times and then the task switched to the sensor-independent task. The entire procedure was repeated twice, and in total 10 training data were recorded, each of which included two transitions between the sensor-dependent and sensor-independent tasks.

In the second phase (network training), the S-CTRNN was trained offline by using the recorded data from the first phase. The numbers of input, context, output, and variance units were $N_I = 11$, $N_C = 55$, $N_O = 11$, and $N_V = 11$, respectively. The context units were divided into two groups, fast context units ($N_{FC} = 50$) and slow context units ($N_{SC} = 5$), on the basis of a time constant and connection setting to introduce the multiple timescale property proposed by Yamashita and Tani [8]. The time constants of the fast and slow context units were $\tau_{FC} = 5$ and $\tau_{SC} = 50$, respectively. The fast context units were connected with the input, fast context, slow context, output, and variance units. In contrast, the slow context units were connected with only the fast and slow context units to constrain the information flow. Details of the multiple timescale property derived from these settings are discussed in [8].

In the third phase (performance testing), the trained S-CTRNN was installed in the robot, and the actions generated via the conventional open-loop and proposed mixture-loop generation methods were compared. For the monotonically increasing function in Eq. (3), we used $\alpha(v_{t,i}) = v_{t,i}/v_{max}$, where $v_{max} = 0.01$ is a predefined parameter representing an upper bound of the estimated uncertainty. In this testing phase, the sensor-dependent task was repeated twice and then the processing was switched to the sensor-independent task. This set of procedures was repeated twice, meaning that, in all, each trial included four sensor-dependent tasks and two sensor-independent tasks.

4   Results and Discussion

In the sensor-dependent task, both the robot with open-loop generation and that with the proposed mixture-loop generation were able to perform flexible behavior corresponding to demonstrated human hand movements. However, in the sensor-independent task, only the robot with mixture-loop generation succeeded in generating learned behavior robustly; the robot with open-loop generation failed.

Examples of the time-series data during action generation with each method are shown in Fig. 3. In the sensor-dependent task, the experimenter first moved the hand to the right side and then to the left side. The network outputs show the corresponding movement of both the left and right robot arms. In the sensor-independent task with open-loop generation, although the robot needed to first raise its right hand and then its left hand, it moved the left arm first (represented by the gray ellipse). After this failure, the robot moved the left arm again for the latter part of the sensor-independent task. However, the movement was not enough large relative to the other movements. In contrast, no failures occur with the proposed mixture-loop generation: both the sensor-dependent and sensor-independent tasks are successfully completed. It should be noted that the ratio of actual states used for the network inputs dynamically changes at around time step 300, which corresponds to the moment after the task transition. This dynamic modulation of the mixture ratio between actual and predicted sensory

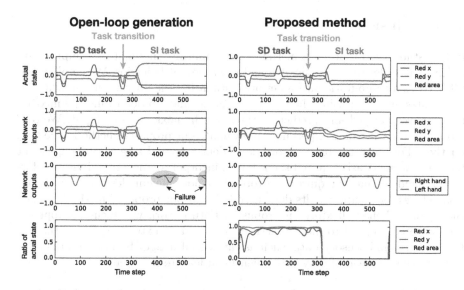

Fig. 3. Time-series data of actual states, network inputs, network outputs, and the ratio of actual states with open-loop generation and the proposed mixture-loop generation. Task transition points from the sensor-dependent (SD) task to the sensor-independent (SI) task are indicated by orange arrows. Failures are indicated by the gray ellipses in the sensor-independent task with open-loop generation.

states on the basis of estimated uncertainty enables the robot to perform flexible and robust behavior by accounting for necessary visual states in the sensor-dependent task and ignoring unnecessary visual states in the sensor-independent task.

We characterized the success of the proposed method by taking success rates for generated movements in both methods. Specifically, we set a threshold for the shoulder roll angles each necessary depending on the situation. If the angle value exceeded the threshold within a certain period, the generated movement was considered successful. Table 1 shows the success rates for generated movements with the conventional open-loop generation and with the proposed mixture-loop generation in each task. The results demonstrate that the proposed method outperforms the open-loop generation on both tasks.

Table 1. Success rates for generated movements out of 160 trials

	Open-loop generation		Proposed method	
	SD task	SI task	SD task	SI task
Number of successes	145	106	157	154
Success rates	0.906	0.663	0.981	0.963

5   Conclusions

In this study, we proposed a method to dynamically modulate the input state of RNNs in order to realize flexible and robust robot behavior. We employed S-CTRNN as a computational framework, estimating the uncertainty of next sensory states and then using the estimated uncertainty to determine the mixture ratio between actual and predicted states for the next network input. We performed a robot learning experiment to evaluate our proposed method. The task for the robot consisted of a sensory-dependent task and a sensory-independent task. The former task required the robot to incorporate meaningful visual information, and the latter required the robot to ignore meaningless visual information. The experimental results demonstrated that our proposed method enabled the robot to behave flexibly and robustly. Future work will focus on applying the proposed method to more practical tasks and on extending the method to high-dimensional sensory data, such as raw visual images by using state of the art data sets, instead of only low-dimensional feature information.

Acknowledgement. This work was supported in part by JST CREST Grant Number: JPMJCR15E3, Japan;JSPS KAKENHI Grant Numbers: 25220005, 17K12754, Japan and the "Fundamental Study for Intelligent Machine to Coexist with Nature" program of the Research Institute for Science and Engineering at Waseda University, Japan.

References

1. Clark, A.: Surfing Uncertainty: Prediction, Action, and the Embodied Mind. Oxford University Press, Oxford (2015)
2. Noda, K., Ito, M., Hoshino, Y., Tani, J.: Dynamic generation and switching of object handling behaviors by a humanoid robot using a recurrent neural network model. In: Nolfi, S., Baldassarre, G., Calabretta, R., Hallam, J.C.T., Marocco, D., Meyer, J.-A., Miglino, O., Parisi, D. (eds.) SAB 2006. LNCS, vol. 4095, pp. 185–196. Springer, Heidelberg (2006). doi:10.1007/11840541_16
3. Tani, J., Ito, M.: Self-organization of behavioral primitives as multiple attractor dynamics: a robot experiment. IEEE Trans. Syst. Man Cybern. - Part A Syst. Hum. **33**(4), 481–488 (2003)
4. Williams, R.J., Zipser, D.: A learning algorithm for continually running fully recurrent neural networks. Neural Comput. **1**(2), 270–280 (1989)
5. Bengio, S., Vinyals, O., Jaitly, N., Shazeer, N.: Scheduled sampling for sequence prediction with recurrent neural networks. arXiv 19994575, pp. 1–9 (2015)
6. Murata, S., Namikawa, J., Arie, H., Sugano, S., Tani, J.: Learning to reproduce fluctuating time series by inferring their time-dependent stochastic properties: application in robot learning via tutoring. IEEE Trans. Auton. Ment. Dev. **5**(4), 298–310 (2013)
7. Doya, K., Yoshizawa, S.: Adaptive neural oscillator using continuous-time back-propagation learning. Neural Netw. **2**(5), 375–385 (1989)
8. Yamashita, Y., Tani, J.: Emergence of functional hierarchy in a multiple timescale neural network model: a humanoid robot experiment. PLoS Comput. Biol. **4**(11), e1000220 (2008)

Neurodynamical Model for the Coupling of Action Perception and Execution

Mohammad Hovaidi-Ardestani[1,2]([✉]), Vittorio Caggiano[3], and Martin Giese[1]

[1] Section of Computational Sensomotorics, Department of Cognitive Neurology,
CIN and HIH, University Clinic Tübingen, Ottfried-Müller-Str. 25,
72076 Tübingen, Germany
Mohammad.Hovaidi-Ardestani@uni-tuebingen.de
[2] IMPRS for Cognitive and Systems Neuroscience, Tübingen, Germany
[3] Computational Biology Center, IBM T.J. Watson Research Center, 1101
Kitchawan Road, Route 134, Room 30-048, 10598 Yorktown Heights, USA

Abstract. In cortical representations action perception and action execution are closely linked, as indicated by the presence of mirror neurons. Experiments show that concurrent action execution and action perception influence each other. We have developed a physiologically-inspired neural model that accounts for the neural encoding of perceived actions and motor plans, and their interactions. The core of the model is a set of coupled neural fields that represent either perceived actions or motor programs. We demonstrate that this model reproduces the results of a variety of quite different experiments investigating the interaction between action perception and execution. It also predicts the emergence and stability of synchronized coordinated behavior of two individuals that observe each other during action execution.

Keywords: Action perception · Motor program · Neural field · Recurrent neural network · Mirror neurons

1 Introduction

Perceptual and motor representations of actions are tightly coupled (e.g. [1]). This is supported by many results from behavioral and functional imaging studies, and physiologically by the existence of mirror neurons, e.g. in premotor and parietal cortex [2,3]. Behavioral and functional imaging studies show influences of motor execution on simultaneous action perception as well as influences in the opposite direction (e.g. [4–6]). Physiological data provides insights in the basis of the encoding of actions at the single-cell level [2,7,8]. This has motivated the development of neural models that account for action perception (e.g. [9,10]) as well as for the neural encoding of motor programs (e.g. [11]). Multiple conceptual models have been proposed that discuss the interaction between action perception and execution (e.g. [12–14]). Some implemented models have been proposed for these interactions in the context of robot systems (e.g. [15]).

© Springer International Publishing AG 2017
A. Lintas et al. (Eds.): ICANN 2017, Part I, LNCS 10613, pp. 19–26, 2017.
https://doi.org/10.1007/978-3-319-68600-4_3

We describe here a model that is based on electrophysiologically plausible mechanisms. It combines mechanisms from previous models that accounted separately for electrophysiological results from action recognition and the neural encoding of motor programs [9,16,17]. We demonstrate that our model provides a unifying account for multiple experiments on the interaction between action execution and action perception. The model might thus provide a starting point for the detailed quantitative investigation how motor plans interact with perceptual action representations at the level of single-cell mechanisms.

2   Model Architecture

The architecture of our model is illustrated in Fig. 1. The core of the model is a set of dynamically coupled neural fields that encode visually perceived actions and motor programs (Fig. 1B). Each encoded action is represented by a pair of neural fields, a *motor field* encoding the associated motor program, and a *vision field* that represents the visually perceived action. Within these fields the evolving action is represented by a stable traveling pulse solution that runs along the field. The different fields are dynamically coupled in a way that enforces a synchronization of the traveling peaks between the vision and motor field that encode the same action. Fields encoding different actions inhibit each other. The vision fields receive a feed-forward input from a visual pathway that recognizes shapes from gray-level images (Fig. 1A). The motor fields are read out by a neural network that models the motor pathway and produces joint angle trajectories that correspond to the evolving action. These angles are used to animate an avatar, which is rendered to produce an image sequence or movie that shows the action (C). The architecture thus models motor execution as well as action recognition. The following sections describe the individual components of the model in further detail.

2.1   Neural Vision and Motor Fields

The model assumes that individual actions can be encoded as visual patterns, or as motor program. Neurally, the patterns are encoded as stable traveling pulse solutions in dynamic neural fields. For the simulations in this paper these fields are defined over periodic spaces ($x, y \in [-\pi, \pi]$). We assume the encoding of M different actions (where M was 2 for the simulations). The vision field that encodes the precept of action m (assuming $1 \leqslant m \leqslant M$) is driven by an input signal distribution $s^m(x, t)$, which is produced by the output neurons of the visual pathway that are tuned for body postures of the action pattern m. The temporal evolution of the activation $u^m(x, t)$ of this visual field is determined by the neural field equation [18]:

$$\frac{\tau \partial u^m(x, t)}{\partial t} = -u^m(x, t) - h + w_u(x) * F(u^m(x, t)) + s^m(x, t) + c_u^m(x, t) \quad (1)$$

with the nonlinear saturationg threshold function $F(u) = d_0 \left(1 - \exp(u^2/2d_1)\right)$ for $u > 0$, and $F(u) = 0$ otherwise, and $h > 0$ determining the resting level activity. As interaction kernel we chose the asymmetric function: $w_u(x) = -a_0 + a_1(\frac{1+\cos(x-a_3)}{2})^\gamma$ with $\gamma > 0$. The convolution operator is defined by $f(x) * g(x) = \int_{-\pi}^{\pi} f(x')g(x - x')dx'$. With this kernel for appropriate choice of the parameters, a traveling-pulse input signal $s^m(x,t)$ induces a traveling pulse equilibrium solution that moves synchronously with the input. This solution breaks down if the frames of the input movies appear in inverse or random temporal order [9]. The term $c_u^m(x,t)$ summarizes the inputs from the other fields and is further specified below.

The corresponding motor program is encoded by another neural field without feed forward input. It is defined by the equation:

$$\frac{\tau \partial v^m(y,t)}{\partial t} = -v^m(y,t) - h + w_v(y) * F(v^m(y,t)) + c_v^m(y,t). \qquad (2)$$

The form of the interaction kernel w_v is identical to the one of w_u with slightly different parameters, resulting in stronger recurrent feedback. As consequence, once a local activation is established by a 'go signal' a self-stabilizing traveling peak solution emerges that propagates with constant speed along the y-dimension [19]. We associate the values of y with the body poses (joint angles) that emerge during the action, so that the traveling pulse encodes the temporal evolution of a motor program. The term $c_v^m(x,t)$ again specifies inputs from the other fields.

2.2 Coupling Structure

The cross connections between the vision and motor fields encoding the same actions were defined by the kernel function:

$$w_{uv}(x,y) = -b_0 + b_1 \left(\frac{1+\cos(x-y)}{2}\right)^\gamma = w_{vu}(y,x). \qquad (3)$$

This kernel results in a tendency of the activation peaks in both fields to propagate synchronously. The fields encoding different actions are coupled by the cross-inhibition kernel $w_I(x,y) = -c_0$ with $c_0 > 0$. As consequence the different encoded actions compete in the neural representation. Summarizing, the corresponding interaction terms in Eqs. 1 and 2 are given by the relationships

$$c_u^m(x,t) = w_{uv}(x,y) *_y F(v^m(y,t)) + \sum_{m' \neq m} w_I(x,y) *_y (F(u^{m'}(y,t) + F(v^{m'}(y,t)))$$

$$c_v^m(x,t) = w_{vu}(x,y) *_y F(u^m(y,t)) + \sum_{m' \neq m} w_I(x,y) *_y (F(u^{m'}(y,t) + F(v^{m'}(y,t)))$$

where the operator $*_y$ indicates the convolution with respect to the variable y.

2.3 Vision and Motor Pathway

The input module of our model is given by a vision pathway that recognizes shapes from image sequences (Fig. 1A). This module is taken over form a previous model without motor pathway (see [9] for details). In brief, the vision

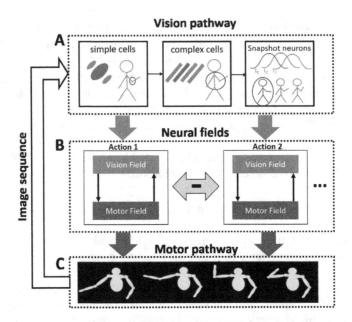

Fig. 1. Overview of the model architecture. **A** The form pathway taken over from a previous neural model [9] drives the input signals for the vision fields from image sequences. **B** The core of the model consists of coupled pairs of vision and motor fields that encode the same action. **C** Motor pathway that reads out the motor fields and generates joint angle trajectories, which are used to animate an avatar, which then can be rendered to produce visual input movies.

pathway consists of a hierarchy of neural shape detectors. The complexity of the extracted features and the position and scaling invariance increase along the hierarchy. The highest level of this pathway is composed from radial basis function (RBF) units that have been trained with snapshots of the learned action movies. These neurons thus detect instantaneous body shapes in image sequences, where the underlying neural network is trained in a supervised manner. Dropping for a moment the index m, assume that the vector $\mathbf{z}(t)$ is formed by the activations of the shape-selective RBF units that encode one particular action pattern at time t, and that the vector $\mathbf{s}(t)$ signifies input signal $s(x,t)$, sampled at a sufficient number of discrete points along the variable x. We learned a linear mapping of the form $\mathbf{s}(t) = \mathbf{R}\mathbf{z}(t)$ between these vectors using sparse regression. Training data pairs consisted of vectors $\mathbf{z}(t)$ of the RBF outputs for equidistantly sampled key frames from the training action movies. Vectors $\mathbf{s}(t)$ were derived from appropriately positioned idealized Gaussian input signals. For learned training patterns the outputs of this linear network define a moving positive input peak, while the input signal $s(x,t)$ remains very small for actions that deviate from the training action. In total, we learned M separate linear mappings from the RBF outputs of the units encoding the keyframes of action m to the corresponding input signal distributions $s^m(x,t)$.

The motor pathway computes joint angles from the position of the activation peak in the motor field along the variable y. This variable parameterizes the temporal evolution of the action. Dropping again the index m, we learned by Support Vector Regression a mapping of the position of the activation peaks $y_{\max}(t) = \arg\max_y v(y, t)$ onto the joint angles of the corresponding body postures. The motor fields encoding different actions compete in a winner-takes-all fashion, and we used only the output of the most activated motor field for the computation of the joint angles. In order to close the loop between action control and perception we used the joint angles to animate an avatar, which then was rendered to produce input movies for the visual pathway.

3   Simulations in Comparison with Experimental Data

We simulated the results of four experiments that studied the interaction between action perception and execution. In the following, simulation results from the model are presented side-by-side with the original data, always using the same model parameters.

(i) **Influence of action execution on action perception:** In the underlying experiment arm actions were presented as point-light stimuli in noise while the observers performed the same action in a virtual reality setup. The spatiotemporal coherence between the executed and the visually observed action was systematically varied, either by delaying the observed action in time or by rotating it in the image plane relative to the executed action. (See [6] for further details.) Fig. 2A shows a recognition index (RI) that measures the facilitation ($RI > 0$) or inhibition ($RI < 0$) of the visual detection by concurrent motor execution in comparison with a baseline without motor execution. For increasing spatial (Fig. 2A) as well as temporal (Fig. 2B) incoherence between the executed and observed actions the facilitation by concurrent motion execution goes over into an inhibitory interaction. The same behavior is reproduced by our model, simulating the masked point-light stimulus by a noisy traveling input peak (Fig. 2 C, D).

(ii) **Influence of action perception on action execution:** The underlying experiment measured the variability of motor execution when participants moved their arms periodically in on direction while they saw another person performing a periodic arm movement in the same or in orthogonal direction [4]. As illustrated in Fig. 3A, compared to a baseline without concurrent visual stimulation, the variability of the motor pattern increases when the visually observed arm movement is inconsistent (orthogonal) to the executed pattern. The same increase in variability is obtained from the model (Fig. 3B) (quantified as variability of the timing of the corresponding activation peak in the motor field).

(iii) **Spontaneous coordination in multi-person interaction:** A classical experiment in interactive sensorimotor control [20] shows that two people that observe each other during the execution of a periodic leg movement tend spontaneously to synchronize their movements. In addition, the variability of the

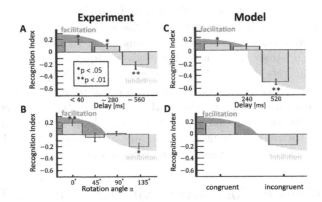

Fig. 2. Influence of concurrent motor execution on the visual detection of action patterns. The experimentally measured Recognition Index (RI) indicates transitions from facilitation to inhibition of visual detection by concurrent motor execution, when the temporal coherence (panel **A**) or the spatial congruence (panel **B**) of the visual pattern with the executed patterns are progressively reduced ([6]). Similar RI computed from the model output shows qualitatively the same behavior (panels **C** and **D**).

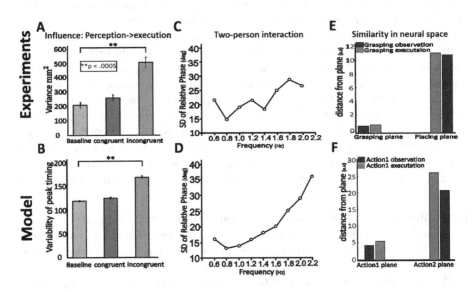

Fig. 3. Reproduction of experimental effects: **A** Motor variability of executed actions increases during observation of incongruent actions [4]. **B** Timing variability of motor peak in the model shows similar behavior. **C** Frequency dependence of standard deviation (SD) of relative phase for the spontaneous synchronization of two agents who observe each other [20]. **D** Corresponding model result derived from activity in motor fields. **E** Neural trajectories for grasping execution and observation are close to 'grasping' plane, but far away from 'placing' plane [8]. **F** Same behavior is observed for the neural trajectories computed from the model neurons. (Details see text.)

relative phase of the synchronized movements is frequency-dependent. Figure 3C shows the original data for the frequency dependence. In order to simulate this interactive behavior of two agents, we implemented two separate models and defined the visual input of either model by the movie that was generated by the motor output of the other. Like in the experiment, the two simulated agents spontaneously synchronize. Figure 3D shows that, in addition, the model predicts correctly frequency dependence of the variability of the relative phase (as consequence of the selectivity of the neural fields for the propagation speed of the moving peaks).

(iv) Reproduction of the population dynamics of F5 mirror neurons: Our last simulation reproduces electrophysiological data from action-selective (mirror) neurons in area F5 [8]. To generate this data, the responses of 489 mirror neurons, relative to the baseline activity, were combined into a population activity vector that varies over time. Using principle components analysis, the dimensionality of the 'neural state space' that is spanned up by these vectors was reduced to three. (Higher-dimensional approximations led to very similar results; see [8] for details.) In this neural state space the trajectories for the execution and observation of a first action ('grasping') were lying close to the same plane, while the trajectory for the observation of another action ('placing') evolved in an orthogonal pane. This is quantified in Fig. 3 E, which illustrates the average distances of the neural trajectories from the planes that fit best the trajectories for the observation of 'grasping' and 'placing'. A very similar topology of the neural trajectories emerges for our model, if we concatenate the activities of all neural field neurons into a population vector and apply the same techniques for dimension reduction (Fig. 3F). Thus neural trajectories for the perception and the execution of the same action are close to the same plane, while neural trajectories for different actions evolve in orthogonal subspaces.

4   Conclusion

The proposed model is consistent with the behavior of action-selective neurons in the superior temporal sulcus and mirror neurons in area F5 of monkeys ([16,17]). It provides a unifying account for a whole spectrum of experiments on the interaction between action perception and execution. Future work needs to give up the strict separation of visual and motor fields, potentially exploiting inhomogeneous neural field models.

Acknowledgments. We thank A. Christensen for helpful comments. Funded by EC, HBP FP7-ICT-2013-FET-F/ 604102, HFSP RGP0036/2016, German Federal Ministry of Education and Research: BMBF, FKZ: 01GQ1002A; Deutsche Forschungsgemeinschaft: DFG GI 305/4-1, DFG GZ: KA 1258/15-1.

References

1. Prinz, W.: Perception and action planning. Eur. J. Cogn. Psychol. **9**, 129–154 (1997)
2. Rizzolatti, G., Fogassi, L., Gallese, V.: Neurophysiological mechanisms underlying the understanding and imitation of action. Nat. Rev. Neurosci. **2**, 661–670 (2001)
3. Giese, M.A., Rizzolatti, G.: Neural and computational mechanisms of action processing: Interaction between visual and motor representations. Neuron **88**, 167–180 (2015)
4. Kilner, J.M., Paulignan, Y., Blakemore, S.J.: An interference effect of observed biological movement on action. Curr. Biol. **13**, 522–525 (2003)
5. Calvo-Merino, B., Grèzes, J., Glaser, D.E., Passingham, R.E., Haggard, P.: Seeing or doing? Influence of visual and motor familiarity in action observation. Curr. Biol. **16**, 1905–1910 (2006)
6. Christensen, A., Ilg, W., Giese, M.A.: Spatiotemporal tuning of the facilitation of biological motion perception by concurrent motor execution. J. Neurosci. **31**, 3493–3499 (2011)
7. Barraclough, N.E., Keith, R.H., Xiao, D., Oram, M.W., Perrett, D.I.: Visual adaptation to Goal-directed hand actions. J. Cogn. Neurosci. **21**, 1805–1819 (2009)
8. Caggiano, V., Fleischer, F., Pomper, J.K., Giese, M.A., Thier, P.: Mirror neurons in monkey premotor area F5 show tuning for critical features of visual causality perception. Curr. Biol. **26**, 3077–3082 (2016)
9. Giese, M.A., Poggio, T.: Neural mechanisms for the recognition of biological movements. Nat. Rev. Neurosci. **4**, 179–192 (2003)
10. Jhuang, H., Serre, T., Wolf, L., Poggio, T.: A biologically inspired system for action recognition. In: IEEE International Conference on Computer Vision, vol. 1, pp. 1–8 (2007)
11. Chersi, F., Ferrari, P.F., Fogassi, L.: Neuronal chains for actions in the parietal lobe: a computational model. PLoS ONE **6**, e27652 (2011)
12. Hommel, B., Müsseler, J., Aschersleben, G., Prinz, W.: Codes and their vicissitudes. Behav. Brain Sci. **24**, 910–926 (2001)
13. Wolpert, D.M., Doya, K., Kawato, M.: A unifying computational framework for motor control and social interaction. Philos. Trans. Royal Soc. London B Biol. Sci. **358**, 593–602 (2003)
14. Kilner, J.M., Friston, K.J., Frith, C.D.: The mirror-neuron system: a Bayesian perspective. Neuroreport **18**, 619–623 (2007)
15. Erlhagen, W., Bicho, E.: The dynamic neural field approach to cognitive robotics. J. Neural Eng. **3**, R36 (2006)
16. Cisek, P., Kalaska, J.F.: Neural mechanisms for interacting with a world full of action choices. Annu. Rev. Neurosci. **33**, 269–298 (2010)
17. Fleischer, F., Caggiano, V., Thier, P., Giese, M.A.: Physiologically inspired model for the Visual recognition of transitive hand actions. J. Neurosci. **33**, 6563–6580 (2013)
18. Amari, S.: Dynamics of pattern formation in lateral-inhibition type neural fields. Biol. Cybern. **27**, 77–87 (1977)
19. Zhang, K.: Representation of spatial orientation by the intrinsic dynamics of the head-direction cell ensemble: a theory. J. Neurosci. **16**, 2112–2126 (1996)
20. Schmidt, R.C., Carello, C., Turvey, M.T.: Phase transitions and critical fluctuations in the visual coordination of rhythmic movements between people. J. Exp. Psychol. Hum. Percept. Perform. **16**, 227–247 (1990)

Neural End-to-End Self-learning of Visuomotor Skills by Environment Interaction

Matthias Kerzel$^{(\boxtimes)}$ and Stefan Wermter

Department of Informatics, Knowledge Technology Institute,
Universität Hamburg, Vogt-Kölln-Str. 30, 22527 Hamburg, Germany
{kerzel,wermter}@informatik.uni-hamburg.de

Abstract. Deep learning with neural networks is dependent on large amounts of annotated training data. For the development of robotic visuomotor skills in complex environments, generating suitable training data is time-consuming and depends on the availability of accurate robot models. Deep reinforcement learning alleviates this challenge by letting robots learn in an unsupervised manner through trial and error at the cost of long training times. In contrast, we present an approach for acquiring visuomotor skills for grasping through fast self-learning: The robot generates suitable training data through interaction with the environment based on initial motor abilities. Supervised end-to-end learning of visuomotor skills is realized with a deep convolutional neural architecture that combines two important subtasks of grasping: object localization and inverse kinematics.

Keywords: Visuomotor policies · Humanoid robot grasping · Deep learning · Self-learning

1 Introduction

Acquiring visuomotor skills is vital for robots that act as assistants and companions in complex domestic environments. Grasping is an essential capability for such a robot as it enables manipulation and multimodal inspection of objects. However, grasping is a challenging task. Even in a non-cluttered environment with an easy-to-grasp object, the robot must be able to localize its target in 3D-space and then use visuomotor skills to move its end-effector to this position.

Conventional frameworks solve this problem with modular approaches, which employ computer vision algorithms for determining the 3D-position of an object and inverse kinematics solvers to reach for the object, see [7] for example. These approaches rely on expert human knowledge and accurate data about the kinematic model of the robot.

Developmental robotics seeks to solve this challenge through learning and teaching. According to Cangelosi and Schlesinger [1], robots should autonomously develop increasingly sophisticated sensorimotor abilities. This paradigm opens up intuitive human-robot interaction scenarios, where a non-expert user can act as an instructor, much in the same way a human would

© Springer International Publishing AG 2017
A. Lintas et al. (Eds.): ICANN 2017, Part I, LNCS 10613, pp. 27–34, 2017.
https://doi.org/10.1007/978-3-319-68600-4_4

teach a child. Moreover, developmental robotics benefits from the exchange with neuro-cognitive science [10], as robotic models can be inspired by and evaluate findings about ontogenetic development.

Following the idea of developmental robotics, we present a deep convolutional architecture for self-learning of robotic grasping skills through interaction with the environment. We perform supervised end-to-end training of a deep convolutional neural network architecture with training data that the robot acquired through interaction with the environment with minimal human involvement.

2   Related Work

Convolutional neural networks (CNNs), inspired by the visual system of mammals, have been successful in various visual and also nonvisual tasks including object localization [6]. Supervised training of CNNs relies on the availability of annotated training data. These annotations are represented as object bounding boxes [16] or coordinates of object centers [15]. Oquab et al. [12] have circumvented the necessity of spatial annotations to learn object localization by using labeled images.

To avoid the need for annotated data, deep reinforcement learning, introduced by Mnih et al. [11], combines a CNN architecture for visual processing with a neural realization of reinforcement learning to develop sensorimotor skills through trial and error. This and similar approaches [4] have been extended for continuous control problems. For instance, Lillicrap et al. [9] developed the Deep Deterministic Policy Gradient algorithm by coupling deep learning with a continuous actor-critic approach.

Deep reinforcement learning proved to be strong in virtual environments where collecting training data can happen fast, without human assistance and without danger of damaging the learning agent, e.g. [13]. But when applying trial-and-error methods to real robots in complex environments, the time needed for training increases dramatically. Pinto and Gupta [14] showed how a robot can learn grasping positions and angles in 700 h. They employed staged learning where continuously improving neural networks were used to collect samples for the next iteration of training. The large number of required trials makes this approach unsuitable for non-industrial, domestic robots. To solve this challenge, Levine et al. [8] proposed a guided policy search method that transforms motor policy search into supervised learning. To achieve this transformation, Levine et al. used visuomotor training setups in which the state of the environment was fully observable at training time, thus generating sufficiently annotated data for supervised learning by exploiting the known forward kinematics of the robot.

In summary, existing approaches rely either on human-annotated training data, extensive learning phases that are not suitable for domestic robots, or information about the kinematic model of the robot. We extend the state of the art by presenting an approach that circumvents all of these necessities by letting the robot randomly generate annotated training samples through autonomous interaction with its environment.

3   Self-learning to Grasp by Randomly Placing Objects

For the supervised learning of visuomotor grasping skills with a neural architecture, training samples are required that associate the state of the environment, represented by an image, with the desired action, represented as a joint configuration that places the robot's end-effector in a grasp position. With extensive human effort, these samples could be generated by repeatedly placing an object in front of the robot at different positions and manually guiding the robot's end-effector into a grasping position.

We present a novel approach to acquiring training samples through self-learning with minimal human intervention by inverting the grasping task. The robot autonomously places objects at random positions in front of itself, memorizes the joint configuration that led to this state of the environment and then associates an image with the joint configuration. The rationale behind this approach is the reversibility of the grasping action: When the robot places an object on a surface from a given joint configuration, the same configuration is likely to be suitable for grasping the object.

3.1   Experimental Setup

Experiments were carried out on NICO (Neuro-Inspired Companion) [5], a child-sized developmental robot that we designed as a multimodal research platform for neural architectures, see Fig. 1. NICO's arms have six degrees of freedom; its Seed Robotics[1] hands have three segmented fingers. All joints provide proprioceptive information. The head is equipped with two cameras and is able to perform pitch and yaw movements. We used a 3D-printed grasping object that has a broad base for stability and is rotation-invariant along its upright axis for easy grasping, see Fig. 1.

3.2   Initial Motor Skills

To enable the robot to place objects on the table during its self-learning phase, it requires initial motor skills. The robot needs to explore the surface of the table to learn joint configurations that bring its hand close to the table surface for placing the object for grasping. We used human demonstration to train this skill: For easy handling, the robot closes its hand around the grasping object. A human demonstrator then moves the object around on the table surface. The motors of the robot's arm have no torque during this time and are only used to record joint angles. Only 30 s of demonstration time were needed to record 600 samples.

3.3   Self-learning by Gathering Training Samples

In the main training phase, the robot repeats a training cycle to gather pairs of images of the object on the table and matching joint configurations.

---

[1] http://www.seedrobotics.com.

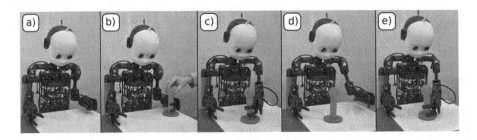

Fig. 1. NICO (Neuro-Inspired COmpanion) performing a self-learning cycle with the grasping object. (a) The robot begins with its hand in the home position. (b) A human experimenter places the grasping object in the robot's hand. (c) The robot moves to a random position from the initial motor training. (d) The robot releases the object, removes the hand and records an image. (e) The robot moves back to the last joint configuration to grasp the object again. The self-learning cycle repeats steps (c) to (e).

The training begins with the robot's hand in the home position, see Fig. 1 (a). A human experimenter puts the grasping object into the robot's hand, Fig. 1 (b). The robot moves to a randomly selected joint configuration from the initial motor training, thus moving its hand and the object on the table, Fig. 1 (c). The robot releases the object, and moves the hand to a predefined position outside its field of vision to record an image along with the previously selected joint configuration, Fig. 1 (d). The hand is moved away to avoid interference with the training of the visual system. After recording the image, the robot moves its hand back to the previously selected joint configuration, thus attempting to grasp the previously placed object, Fig. 1 (e). After closing its hand, the robot repeats its training cycle with a new random position from the initial motor training.

The robot uses proprioceptive haptic information from its hand motors to determine if a grasping attempt during the self-learning phase has been successful. The attempt can fail if the grasping object tumbles during release or is accidentally moved while the robot retracts its hand. In this case, the training cycle is automatically stopped and the last collected sample is deleted, as it might lead to learning wrong visuomotor policies. The robot moves its hand back to the home position and requests human assistance. Once the object is placed back into the robot's hand the self-learning is resumed.

3.4   Neural Architecture

A deep neural architecture is used for end-to-end learning of grasping skills from the collected samples. The architecture consists of convolutional layers for object localization and dense layers for learning motor policies, see Fig. 2. The input layer of the architecture takes a downsampled cutout of the RGB image that shows the area directly in front of the robot with a dimensionality of 3*80*60. The input is processed by two convolutional layers with 16 filters of size 3×3 and 4×4 that are moved over the input with a stride of 1. The filter size and number

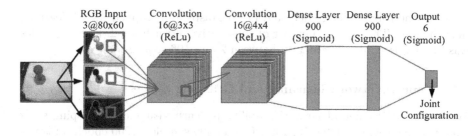

Fig. 2. Neural architecture for end-to-end learning of grasping.

is empirically determined. The convolutional layers are not followed by pooling, as these layers would realize translational invariance, which is detrimental for localization tasks (compare [11]). Two dense layers with 900 neurons each follow the convolution layers. Finally, the output layer consists of 6 neurons, one for each degree of freedom of the robot arm. The neurons in the convolutional layers use the rectified linear activation function introduced by Hahnloser et al. [3] to prevent the exploding or vanishing-gradient effect. The dense layers and output layer use sigmoid activation function to ensure an output in the [0..1] interval. Joint configurations are accordingly normalized to the same interval, with 0 being the minimum and 1 being the maximum joint value from the set of training samples. The network architecture and its hyper-parameters, as shown in Fig. 2, were empirically determined. We chose a set of parameters that performed best on the average of the different experimental conditions described below.

4   Experimental Results

We conducted a full training and evaluation of the system that encompassed the initial motor training, a self-learning phase, neural network learning, grasping evaluation and an experiment on autonomous recovery during self-learning.

4.1   Self-learning

During the self-learning phase, the robot autonomously collects training samples. Each training cycle takes ~30 s to perform. 500 samples were collected. We analyzed three factors during the self-learning phase: Did collisions occur that required urgent intervention by the experimenters, did the robot recognize failed grasping attempts, and how often did grasping attempts fail?

During the 500 self-learning cycles, no self-collision of the robot or a forceful collision of the robot with the environment occurred, because all joint configurations selected during self-learning stem from the initial motor training which is inherently collision free. Compared to trial-and-error methods like Deep Deterministic Policy Gradient [9] or multi-staged learning [14] the robot performs no explorative actions that could lead to harmful states.

Also, the robot reliably detected failed grasps and stopped its self-learning in such cases. The average number of consecutive, error-free self-learning cycles was 31.24 with a high fluctuation between 2 and 106 sequential cycles.

4.2   Neural Network Learning and Grasping Success

We evaluated the neural network's ability to learn visuomotor grasping skills from training sets of 10, 25, 50, 100, 200 and 400 samples. 2000 epochs of training were performed with stochastic gradient descent with Nesterov momentum [17] (learning rate = 0.01, momentum = 0.9). The batch size depended on the size of the training set. We used a batch size of 10 for the 10-sample condition, a batch size of 20 for the 25-sample condition and a batch size of 40 for all other conditions. The squared error was used as a loss function. Glorot uniform initialization, also known as Xavier initialization, was used for all layers to stabilize the strength of the input signal throughout the deep network [2].

Each experimental condition was repeated ten times to minimize the influence of randomization. For each trial, 50 validation and 50 test samples were randomly chosen from the sample set along with the desired number of training samples. Figure 3 (left) shows the results of training. As expected, the squared error in the test set decreased steadily with increasing training set size.

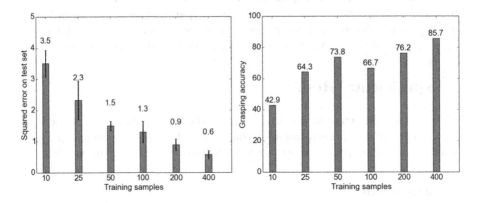

Fig. 3. Results of training with different numbers of samples. Left: Squared error of learned joint configurations from ten trails per experimental condition. Right: Percentage of successful grasps from 42 grasping tasks using the neural model that performed best on its test set.

As different joints contribute differently to the grasping action, it is difficult to predict grasping success of the neural models from the squared error. Therefore, we performed standardized grasping experiments to evaluate the best model for each training condition. We subtly marked 42 positions in a six by seven grid on the table in front of the robot and manually placed the object in these positions for the robot to grasp. The results are shown in Fig. 3 (right). After 400 samples, the robot is reliably grasping with over 85% success rate. The most common error was that the robot's hand was slightly too low, pushing the object away instead of grasping it.

4.3 Autonomous Recovery During Self-learning

The results indicate that a low number of training samples are sufficient to achieve a reasonable grasp chance. We adapted the idea of multi-staged learning [14] to automate the self-learning phase further. In the case of a failed grasp, the already collected samples are used to train the neural architecture which then controls up to ten further grasp attempts before human assistance is requested.

We repeated the collection of 500 grasping samples. Slightly exceeding the result reported above, the average number of continuous grasping trials was 45.5. Ten grasping attempts failed, mostly due to displacing the object while removing the hand. Except for the first two failed grasps, the robot could recover from the error state. On average, 1.6 grasping attempts using the trained neural architecture were needed.

5 Conclusion

The presented approach extends the state of the art by facilitating self-learning of robotic visuomotor skills for grasping without the need for annotated training data or information about the kinematics of the robot. In contrast to trial and error methods that can take hundreds of training hours, the presented approach continuously improves its performance in a time span of several minutes to a few hours. Human assistance is only needed for 30 s of initial motor training and occasionally during the self-learning phase. The self-learning phase does not require monitoring, as there is no danger of harmful collisions. The robot will request help if needed.[2]

Our approach enables a domestic developmental robot to learn to grasp in a modest amount of time. We have shown how complex visuomotor skills can develop through interaction with the environment based on more simple initial motor skills. End-to-end visuomotor learning offers opportunities to research the emergence of spatial representations in hidden layers as well as the benefits of end-to-end learning compared to the separate training of components. In future work, our approach will be extended to multiple objects with different grasping geometries and bimanual grasping. Self-organization will be used to select samples from the initial motor training in a more principled way. Also, we will evaluate how well our self-learning method is suited to generate pre-trained networks for continuous deep reinforcement learning.

Acknowledgments. This work was partially funded by the German Research Foundation (DFG) in project Crossmodal Learning (TRR-169) and the Hamburg Landesforschungsförderungsprojekt.

---

[2] Visit nico.knowledge-technology.info for further information and video material.

References

1. Cangelosi, A., Schlesinger, M.: Developmental Robotics. From Babies to Robots. MIT Press/Bradford Books, Cambridge (2014)
2. Glorot, X., Bengio, Y.: Understanding the difficulty of training deep feedforward neural networks. In: Proceedings of Aistats, vol. 9, pp. 249–256 (2010)
3. Hahnloser, R.H., Sarpeshkar, R., Mahowald, M.A., Douglas, R.J., Seung, H.S.: Digital selection and analogue amplification coexist in a cortex-inspired silicon circuit. Nature **405**(6789), 947–951 (2000)
4. van Hasselt, H., Guez, A., Silver, D.: Deep reinforcement learning with double q-learning. arXiv preprint 2015. arXiv:1509.06461
5. Kerzel, M., Strahl, E., Magg, S., Navarro-Guerro, N., Heinrich, S., Wermter, S.: NICO - Neuro-inspired companion: a developmental humanoid robot platform for multimodal interaction. In: RO-MAN 2017 (2017, accepted)
6. LeCun, Y., Bengio, Y., Hinton, G.: Deep learning. Nature **521**(7553), 436–444 (2015)
7. Leitner, J., Harding, S., Förster, A., Corke, P.: A Modular software Framework for eyehand coordination in humanoid robots. Front. Robot. AI **3** (2016)
8. Levine, S., Finn, C., Darrell, T., Abbeel, P.: End-to-end training of deep visuomotor policies. J. Mach. Learn. Res. **17**(39), 1–40 (2016)
9. Lillicrap, T.P., Hunt, J.J., Pritzel, A., Heess, N., Erez, T., Tassa, Y., Silver, D., Wierstra, D.: Continuous control with deep reinforcement learning. arXiv preprint arXiv:1509.02971 (2015)
10. Lungarella, M., Metta, G., Pfeifer, R., Sandini, G.: Developmental robotics: a survey. Connection Sci. **15**(4), 151–190 (2003)
11. Mnih, V., Kavukcuoglu, K., Silver, D., Rusu, A.A., Veness, J., Bellemare, M.G., Graves, A., Riedmiller, M., Fidjeland, A.K., Ostrovski, G., Petersen, S., et al.: Human-level control through deep reinforcement learning. Nature **518**(7540), 529–533 (2015)
12. Oquab, M., Bottou, L., Laptev, I., Sivic, J.: Is object localization for free?-weakly-supervised learning with convolutional neural networks. In: Proceedings of the IEEE Conference on Computer Vision and Pattern Recognition, pp. 685–694 (2015)
13. Peng, X.B., Berseth, G., Panne van de, M.: Terrain-adaptive locomotion skills using deep reinforcement learning. ACM Trans. Graph. **35**(4) (2016). 81
14. Pinto, L., Gupta, A.: Supersizing self-supervision: learning to grasp from 50k tries and 700 robot hours. In: 2016 IEEE International Conference on Robotics and Automation (ICRA), pp. 3406–3413. IEEE Press (2016)
15. Speck, D., Barros, P., Weber, C., Wermter, S.: Ball localization for robocup soccer using convolutional neural networks. In: RoboCup Symposium, Leipzig, Germany (2016)
16. Sermanet, P., Eigen, D., Zhang, X., Mathieu, M., Fergus, R., LeCun, Y.: Overfeat: integrated recognition, localization and detection using convolutional networks. arXiv preprint arXiv:1312.6229 (2013)
17. Sutskever, I., Martens, J., Dahl, G.E., Hinton, G.E.: On the importance of initialization and momentum in deep learning. In: Proceedings of The 30th International Conference on Machine Learning, pp. 1139–1147 (2013)

Learning of Labeling Room Space for Mobile Robots Based on Visual Motor Experience

Tatsuro Yamada[1], Saki Ito[1], Hiroaki Arie[2], and Tetsuya Ogata[1(✉)]

[1] Department of Intermedia Art and Science, Waseda University, Tokyo, Japan
ogata@waseda.jp
[2] Department of Modern Mechanical Engineering, Waseda University, Tokyo, Japan

Abstract. A model was developed to allow a mobile robot to label the areas of a typical domestic room, using raw sequential visual and motor data, no explicit information on location was provided, and no maps were constructed. The model comprised a deep autoencoder and a recurrent neural network. The model was demonstrated to (1) learn to correctly label areas of different shapes and sizes, (2) be capable of adapting to changes in room shape and rearrangement of items in the room, and (3) attribute different labels to the same area, when approached from different angles. Analysis of the internal representations of the model showed that a topological structure corresponding to the room structure was self-organized as the trajectory of the internal activations of the network.

Keywords: Symbol grounding · Mobile robots · Deep autoencoder · Recurrent neural network · Indoor scene labeling

1 Introduction

In recent years, service robots that share our home environment (e.g., living room, kitchen) have become more widespread. They must be designed to work flexibly and alongside humans in such complex environments. This requires them to recognize and identify different areas within the room. For example, in order for a robot vacuum cleaner to follow instructions from a human, it must understand the relationship between human's vocabulary and areas identified by the words, such as "in front of the refrigerator" or "around the dining table".

In this study, we consider the task in which a robot operating within a room labels the area it currently occupies. One approach to this is to learn the relationships between labels and areas represented by 2D coordinates. Taniguchi et al. [1] trained a Bayesian model to learn the probabilistic dependencies between spoken words and the areas they denoted. Their approach has the advantage of allowing the robot to infer its own location from a spoken sentence, and vice versa. However, the application of such a model (or other methods that make use of 2D coordinates or room maps) to the task addressed in this study faces three challenges. (1) First, whereas Taniguchi et al. [1] assumed that the areas

© Springer International Publishing AG 2017
A. Lintas et al. (Eds.): ICANN 2017, Part I, LNCS 10613, pp. 35–42, 2017.
https://doi.org/10.1007/978-3-319-68600-4_5

indicated by human words can be represented as a two-dimensional Gaussian distribution, they in fact have a wide diversity of shapes and sizes (ovals, rectangles, etc.). (2) Second, the references made in human language are dependent on the environment being referred to. Rooms have a wide variety of layouts, and the furniture within a single room may be rearranged. Models that make use of 2D coordinates to learn the relationships between labels and areas are unable to deal with such variation. (3) Finally, human language is often able to identify the same area using different words, according to the context. For example, "in front of the refrigerator" and "the side of the sink" might refer to the same area, reflecting the intentions of the speaker or changes in physical perspective. These issues are part of the symbol grounding problem [2]: how to capture a dynamic and continuous world using discrete words or symbols.

In the field of image processing, previous studies have involved constructing large datasets of images taken indoors, then using these to classify and label indoor scenes [3–5]. However, these approaches have only attempted to build classifications of static images, and are also unable to take account of contextual information.

In this study, we investigate area recognition of a living room by a mobile robot. We address the three problems noted above, using a neural network model. Our proposed model does not require explicit knowledge of the 2D coordinates of the robot's location, and does not build maps. Instead, it learns the relationships between labels and areas directly from the sequential visual and motor data.

2   Task Setting

In the task used in this study, a mobile robot was required to label its current area in a simulated room. More precisely, the label was predicted for the following time step (200 ms later). The correspondence between labels and areas was given in advance, as shown in Fig. 1. The robot used in the experiment was RULO, a robot vacuum cleaner made by Panasonic. At each time step t, the robot captured an image using its mounted camera V_t, motor perceptions m_t, and motor command inputs c_t. m_t consists of the angular velocity around the z-axis measured by its inertial measurement unit and the rotational speed of its wheels measured by rotary encoders. c_t consists of commands of linear and rotation velocity given by a joystick device. The history of these was used to predict the label to be assigned in the following time step l_{t+1}. The training function F was therefore as follows:

$$l_{t+1} = F(V_{0:t}, m_{0:t}, c_{0:t}). \tag{1}$$

Three complexities were added to the task. (1) First, areas with different geometries (ovals, rectangles, L-shapes) were included. (2) Second, the back wall was made movable in the depth direction. Simultaneously, items placed in the room, including the refrigerator, kitchen counter, boxes, and the television stand, could be moved. Areas, including REFRIGERATOR, TV were also moved (area names are written in capital letters). Five rooms were built of +60 cm, +20 cm,

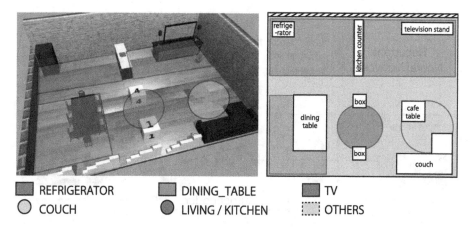

REFRIGERATOR   DINING_TABLE   TV
COUCH   LIVING / KITCHEN   OTHERS

Fig. 1. [Left] The room in a simulation environment built for the evaluation experiment. Areas are colored differently from each other. [Right] Rough 2D sketch of the room. Three complexities were added to the task. (1) First, areas with different geometries (ovals, rectangles, L-shapes) were included. (2) Second, the back wall (shaded area) was made movable in the depth direction. Simultaneously, items placed in the room, including the refrigerator, kitchen counter, boxes, and the television stand, could be moved together with the back wall. Areas, including REFRIGERATOR, TV were also moved. (3) Finally, The purple area was given a label based on the path history. When the robot approached from the left side of the room, the area was labeled LIVING; when approached from the right side, the same space was labeled KITCHEN. (Color figure online)

−20 cm, −60 cm, and ±0 cm. These were coded as Rooms 1–5. (3) Finally, The purple area shown in Fig. 1 was given a label based on the path history. When the robot approached from the left side of the room, the area was labeled LIVING; when approached from the right side, the same space was labeled KITCHEN.

3   Proposed Neural Network Model

3.1   Forward Dynamics

A neural network model was developed for task learning. The working of the model after training is described as its forward propagation. As shown in Fig. 2, the model comprises two sub networks, a deep autoencoder (DAE) [6], and a recurrent neural network (RNN) [7]. At each time step t, the DAE is used to extract visual features by compressing high-dimensional raw image V_t data into a lower-dimensional vector v_t. All the connections between layers are fully connected and their activation function is given by tanh. Next, v_t is fed into the RNN, together with the motor perceptions m_t, commands c_t, and previous output from the model y_{t-1}. These inputs are fed into a long short-term memory (LSTM) layer [8]. In this layer, the past movement context is encoded as the state of the memory cells. The current output of the LSTM layer is then determined by

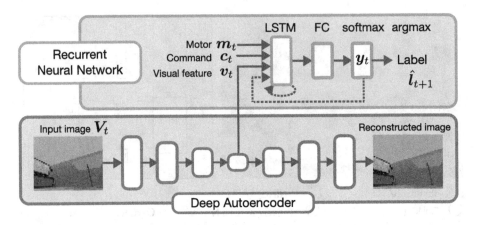

Fig. 2. Model overview. The model comprises two sub networks, a DAE and an RNN. The DAE is used to extract visual features by compressing high-dimensional raw image into a lower-dimensional vector. RNN predicts a area label for the next time step by integrating the current visual motor inputs and their contextual information encoded as the state of memory cells of LSTM layer.

integrating the contextual information with the current input, and transformed by a fully connected (FC) layer into a vector with seven dimensions. This number of dimensions is the same as the number of labels. A softmax function is applied, such that y_t represents the probability distribution of labels predicted for the next time step $P(\hat{l}_{t+1})$. Finally, the argmax index in y_t is treated as the label predicted by the model. This model does not receive the explicit information on the robot's location. Nor does it make any explicit maps. It learns the relationship between labels and corresponding areas just from raw sequential visual motor experiences.

3.2 Learning Procedure

First, training of the DAE is conducted, in which the loss function to be minimized is the mean squared error between the original images and the images reconstructed by the model. The RNN is next trained, using the sequential data recorded by the robot when in motion. The loss function is the cross entropy between the predicted probability distribution of areas and the correct label. The correct label is represented as a one-hot vector in which the element corresponding to the correct area takes a value of one and all others take a value of zero. The losses in all the time steps were back-propagated to all past states using the back-propagation through time algorithm [9].

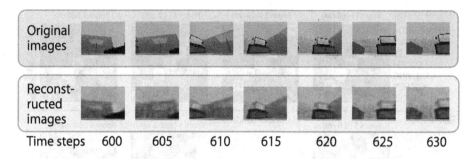

Fig. 3. Examples of reconstruction of camera images by the trained DAE. Although the reconstructed images were blurred, the global structure was broadly reconstructed.

4 Experiment

4.1 Data for Learning

To evaluate the proposed model, a learning experiment was conducted. The robot was walked through the rooms, controlled by a joystick. Sequential data was recorded, including camera images, motor feedback, input commands, and area labels. In each room data for 10000 steps was collected, at a rate of five steps per second. Only data collected in Room 1–4 was used for training.

4.2 Results of Training the DAE

In this section, we report the results of training the DAE. The layer configuration was [9216 (Width:64, Height:48, Color:3), 1280, 640, 320, 160, 10, 160, 320, 640, 1280, 9216], and a batch normalization layer [10] was inserted in all layers. The number of learning iterations was 50000, with a batch size of 100. Adam algorithm [11] was used as an optimizer, with a learning rate of 0.001. Figure 3 compares the original images captured by the robot camera with those reconstructed by the trained DAE. Although the reconstructed images were blurred, the global structure was broadly reconstructed. The ten-dimensional features extracted by the model were therefore used as the input to the RNN.

4.3 Results of Training the RNN

We next report the training of the RNN. This had 30 LSTM units, and an optimizer was Adam with a learning rate of 0.001. Learning was halted when the loss function fell below 0.1. This occurred after 3116 parameter updatings. Figure 4 shows the results for label prediction after training. As the confusion matrices show, in the trained rooms, the network was able to generate correct labels more than 85% of the time in each area. Although the accuracy was lower in the test room than in the trained rooms, the network still scored above 83% in all areas. Most cases of confusion were ones with the OTHERS area.

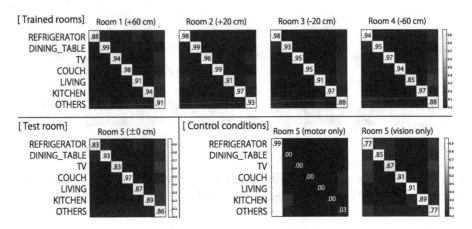

Fig. 4. The results of the area label predictions. (a) In the trained rooms, the network was able to generate correct labels more than 85% of the time in each area. (b) Although the accuracy was lower in the test room than in the trained rooms, the network still scored above 83% in all areas. (c) In the motor only condition, in which the noise data were supplied to the model as visual inputs in place of the original images, the model was unable to predict the correct labels at all. In contrast, in the vision only condition, the model had a limited ability to assign labels correctly, but its performance was worse than when given the original motor inputs.

This may be because only OTHERS area is adjacent to the other areas, and in this task the borders between areas were set arbitrarily, making confusion with the OTHERS area inevitable.

The three specific problems set in the task were successfully addressed. (1) Label prediction was accurate across areas with different geometries and sizes. (2) When the shape of the room was changed, the model was able to label the areas appropriately from visual and motor information, without constructing maps or requiring explicit information on location. (3) The model was able to apply different labels (KITCHEN or LIVING) to the same area, based on its angle of approach.

4.4   Control Experiments

To identify which information had been used for label prediction, some of the original inputs were replaced by Gaussian noise. First, the noise data were supplied to the model as visual inputs, in place of the original images. The mean and variance of the noise were the same as those of the original data. As shown in Fig. 4 (annotated as "motor only"), when given this blind condition, the model was unable to predict the correct labels, and instead output REFRIGERATOR in almost all cases. Next, noise was used to replace motor perceptions and commands (annotated as "vision only"). In this case, the model had a limited ability to assign labels correctly, but its performance was worse than when given the original motor inputs. This suggested that, while visual information played the

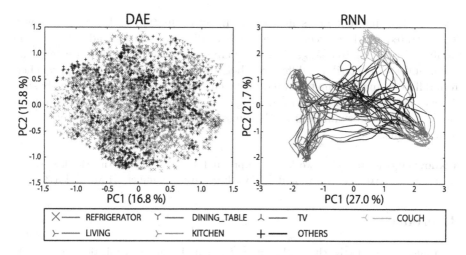

Fig. 5. The internal representations during moving the test room visualized by principal component analysis. [Left] DAE. each point corresponds to the state at one time step and is colored to match the area. No cluster structures correspond to specific areas. [RIGHT] RNN. the trajectory of LSTM layer's activation during movement. It is shown that the transitions in the activation space correspond to transitions between areas within the room.

most important role in task completion, motor information also contributed to the assignment of correct labels. The model learned to recognize its current areas by integrating the visual and motor sequential information.

4.5   Internal Representations in the Networks

Finally, we visualized the internal representations made by the model when executing the task. The left panel in Fig. 5 shows the internal states of the middle layer of the DAE when moving through Room 5. These were projected onto two-dimensional space using principal component analysis (PCA). Here each point corresponds to the state at one time step and is colored to match the area. It can be seen that no cluster structures correspond to specific areas. The right panel shows the trajectory of LSTM layer activation during movement, again visualized using PCA. In contrast with the DAE representations, those in the activation space can be seen to correspond to transitions between areas. This suggests that, in the process of learning relationships between labels and sequential visual and motor perceptions, a topological structure corresponding to the room structure was self-organized as a trajectory in the RNN's activation space.

5   Conclusions

In this study, a neural network model was applied to the sequential visual and motor perceptions of a mobile robot, with the goal of allowing it to learn to recognize the different areas in a room. In an evaluation task, the model was demonstrated to (1) correctly label areas of different shapes and sizes, (2) be capable of adapting to changes in room shape and rearrangement of items in the room, and (3) to attribute different labels to the same area, when approached from different angles. The task used in the current study was comparatively simple one; in future work, we will investigate the extension of the model to more complex tasks, for example involving unseen rooms or more radical rearrangement of items.

Acknowledgments. This work was supported by JSPS Grant-in-Aid for Young Scientists (A) (No. 16H05878), and JST CREST Grant Number: JPMJCR15E3.

References

1. Taniguchi, A., Taniguchi, T., Inamura, T.: Spatial concept acquisition for a mobile robot that integrates self-localization and unsupervised word discovery from spoken sentences. IEEE Trans. Cogn. Dev. Syst. **8**(4), 285–297 (2016)
2. Harnad, S.: The symbol grounding problem. Physica D **42**(1–3), 335–346 (1990)
3. Quattoni, A., Torralba, A.: Recognizing indoor scenes. In: Computer Vision and Pattern Recognition, pp. 413–420 (2009)
4. Xiao, J., Hays, J., Ehinger, K.A., Oliva, A., Torralba, A.: SUN database: large-scale scene recognition from abbey to zoo. In: 2010 IEEE Conference on Computer Vision and Pattern Recognition (CVPR), pp. 3485–3492 (2010)
5. Zhou, B., Lapedriza, A., Xiao, J., Torralba, A., Oliva, A.: Learning deep features for scene recognition using places database. In: Advances in Neural Information Processing Systems, pp. 487–495 (2014)
6. Hinton, G.E., Salakhutdinov, R.: Reducing the dimensionality of data with neural networks. Science **313**(5786), 504–507 (2006)
7. Elman, J.L.: Finding structure in time. Cogn. Sci. **14**(2), 179–211 (1990)
8. Gers, F.A., Schmidhuber, J.: Recurrent nets that time and count. IN: Proceedings of the IEEE-INNS-ENNS International Joint Conference on Neural Networks, vol. 3, pp. 189–194 (2000)
9. Rumelhart, D.E., Hinton, G.E., Williams, R.J.: Learning internal representations by error propagation. In: Parallel Distributed Processing: Explorations in the Microstructure of Cognition, pp. 318–362. MIT Press (1986)
10. Ioffe, S., Szegedy, C.: Batch normalization: accelerating deep network training by reducing internal covariate shift. Arxiv arXiv:1502.03167 (2015)
11. Kingma, D., Ba, J.: Adam: a method for stochastic optimization. In: International Conference on Learning Representations, December 2015

Towards Grasping with Spiking Neural Networks for Anthropomorphic Robot Hands

J. Camilo Vasquez Tieck[✉], Heiko Donat, Jacques Kaiser, Igor Peric,
Stefan Ulbrich, Arne Roennau, Marius Zöllner, and Rüdiger Dillmann

FZI Research Center for Information Technology, 76131 Karlsruhe, Germany
{tieck,donat,jkaiser,peric,ulbrich,roennau,zoellner,dillmann}@fzi.de

Abstract. Representation and execution of movement in biology is an active field of research relevant to neurorobotics. Humans can remember grasp motions and modify them during execution based on the shape and the intended interaction with objects. We present a hierarchical spiking neural network with a biologically inspired architecture for representing different grasp motions. We demonstrate the ability of our network to learn from human demonstration using synaptic plasticity on two different exemplary grasp types (pinch and cylinder). We evaluate the performance of the network in simulation and on a real anthropomorphic robotic hand. The network exposes the ability of learning finger coordination and synergies between joints that can be used for grasping.

Keywords: Grasp motion representation · Spiking networks · Neurorobotics · Motor primitives

1 Introduction

The way movement is represented and executed in biology is an active field of research. The human hand is a complex system that can perform a wide range of motions with great flexibility and adaptation, for example, playing the piano or grasping unknown objects. Humans can remember grasp motions and modify them during execution based on the shape and the interaction with objects. However, studies show that only a small grasp repertoire is actually used [6]. Furthermore, a principle component analysis revealed that the first two components determine the 80% of the variance of all grasps [15]. A generally accepted hypothesis is that the central nervous system (CNS) uses motor building blocks when performing motion tasks [1]. These building blocks are called *motor primitives* [4] and are formed by *muscle synergies* [7]. In this context, the term synergy refers to the coupling of motor activation. A common assumption is that these primitives are linearly combined by the CNS in a hierarchical manner to compose complex motions [2]. These insights have been successfully transfered in robotics, for instance in the concepts of *eigengrasps* [5] and *dynamic movement primitives* [11].

Spiking neural networks (SNN) focus on biological plausibility [14]. Plasticity is used for learning by changing the synaptic weights. In a neuro-robotics context, there are approaches of SNNs using spike time dependent plasticity (STDP).

© Springer International Publishing AG 2017
A. Lintas et al. (Eds.): ICANN 2017, Part I, LNCS 10613, pp. 43–51, 2017.
https://doi.org/10.1007/978-3-319-68600-4_6

For instance, to learn transformations of spatio-temporal data between coordinate systems [8,16]. Inspired by this research, approaches for learning robot kinematics in simulation [18] and with a real robotic arm [3] were developed.

In this work, we present a model of a hierarchical SNN with a biologically inspired architecture that is able to learn and perform different grasp motions. Our model combines two different network types, one for the fingers and one for the hand. The finger networks learn different motor primitives as synergies between the joints. The hand network efficiently represents different grasp types coordinating the finger networks reusing the learned motor primitives. Both, the hand and the finger networks, are trained independently using STDP. Finally, we incorporate a mechanism for tactile feedback in the finger networks to stop the motion on contact. We evaluate our model with two different grasp types, i.e. pinch and cylinder [6]. After learning from human demonstration, the SNN is evaluated in simulation and on a real anthropomorphic robot hand.

2   Approach

Our SNN approach is inspired by the biological concepts of hierarchical motion representation [2] and motor primitives [1] for grasping using muscle synergies [7]. We make the following assumptions for the fingers and for the hand. The hand makes different types of grasp motions when picking a pen from a table (pinch) than when holding a tennis racket (cylinder). The motion of a single finger, in the examples above, is represented by the synergies between its joints and defines a motor primitive. Consequently, the motion representation and control movements are modeled using two types of networks, one for the fingers and one for the hand (see Fig. 1). The finger networks control the movements of single fingers independent of the task, while the hand network coordinates the activation of the finger networks to resemble a specific grasp motion. Training data is recorded from human demonstration to train the SNN.

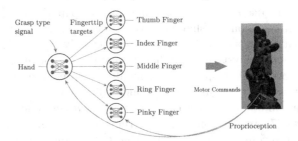

Fig. 1. Complete architecture. The hand network (*left*) receives the proprioception of all fingers and a grasp type signal to generate fingertip targets. Each finger network (*middle*) receives its proprioception and fingertip target to generate motor commands.

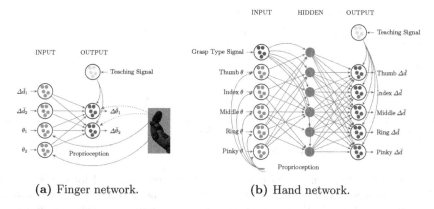

(a) Finger network.   **(b)** Hand network.

Fig. 2. SNN. Input and output layers are divided in populations. For learning, a teaching signal is connected one-to-one to the output layer. (a) The Finger network learns to associate the proprioception (θ_1, θ_2) and the fingertip target $(\Delta \bar{d}_1, \Delta \bar{d}_2)$, with the joint changes $(\Delta \bar{\theta}_1, \Delta \bar{\theta}_2)$. The input and output layers are all-to-all connected with plastic synapses. Each finger has a single neuron to receive tactile feedback (*dotted*). (b) The Hand network learns to generate the fingertip targets $\Delta \bar{d}$ to coordinate the finger networks. The inputs are the proprioception of all fingers θ and the grasp type. Each input layer is sparse projected to the hidden layer (*middle*) with static synapses. The hidden and output layers are connected all-to-all with plastic synapses.

2.1 Finger Networks

A single finger motion is abstracted to be planar (2D) and performed by two joints, proximal and distal. A finger network (see Fig. 2a) learns the synergies between the joints to represent a motor primitive. The network has an input layer and an output layer all-to-all connected with plastic synapses that are learned with associative learning (see Sect. 2.4). The input layer is divided into four populations. Two encode the joint angles θ_1 and θ_2 from the finger proprioception, and two represent the fingertip target as a normalized direction vector of the spatial changes with $\Delta \bar{d}_1$ and $\Delta \bar{d}_2$ in finger coordinates (Cartesian). The output layer is divided into two populations $\Delta \theta_1$ and $\Delta \theta_2$, for the angular changes of each joint.

2.2 Hand Network

The hand network (see Fig. 2b) represents the different grasp types as the coordination of the finger networks reusing the learned primitives. The network learns to associate the proprioception of all fingers and the grasp type with the corresponding fingertip targets. Here, we introduce a signal coming from higher brain areas to determine grasp type. For example, this signal could be generated in another network to represent grasp affordances from vision [12]. A simple two layer architecture as in the finger networks was not suited to learn multiple motions, due to the high number of input and output populations with

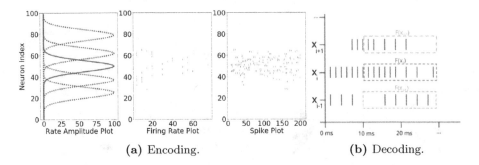

(a) Encoding.   (b) Decoding.

Fig. 3. Neural coding scheme. In the input, (a) the receptive field for a given value (*left*), the different activation frequencies (*middle*), and the spike activity of the neurons (*right*). In the output (b) the voting schema $F(x)$ determines the central neuron x_i.

correlations local attractors were created by the STDP. To overcome this, a higher dimensional hidden layer was added to reduce correlations and get an sparse representation of the input. Each input population is projected with static synapses to the hidden layer with a small out-degree creating only a few static synapses between the input and the hidden layers. The hidden and the output layer are connected all-to-all with plastic synapses, that are learned with associative learning (see Sect. 2.4).

2.3   Encoding and Decoding

We call this mechanism, stochastic population position Gaussian coding. This scheme relates values of consecutive states by sharing part of the activation. For the encoding, values are converted into spikes using a mixture of Gaussian kernels to tune the firing rate of a population (Fig. 3a). Different receptive fields encode values in a normalized interval. The populations are sub-divided to quantize the interval with multiple duplicates. For decoding, a voting schema is applied to determine the central activation of the Gaussian (Fig. 3b).

2.4   Learning

We use a supervised associative learning mechanism based on STDP inspired by [3]. During learning, a teaching signal is connected one-to-one to the output layer. For noise reduction in the output layer a winner-takes-all approach is applied. The hand and the finger networks are independently trained. The plastic synapses are initialized with random weights $\in (0, 1]$. With the training data we calculate the motion direction vector for each fingertip and the desired motor commands to feed the hand and finger networks respectively. The teaching signal encodes the desired activation. It raises the membrane potential of specific output neurons just below the firing threshold, and inhibits all other. Thus, the activation of input neurons trigger STDP for the desired activation. This approach is called *selective disinhibition* [17] and is used to prevent input and teaching signals from competing. After learning, the SNN associates the input with the desired output and reproduces the teaching signal. To regulate STDP, each neuron in the output layer has incoming synapses from two corresponding neurons in the input layer, one excitatory and inhibitory. These two neurons work as one having complementary activation (the sum of their firing rates is constant). For excitatory synapses an anti-symmetric STDP learning rule and a weight-dependence rule are used [9]. The inhibitory synapses use an anti-symmetric anti-Hebbian STDP rule using additive weight-dependence. Jointly tuned excitatory and inhibitory STDP in feed-forward SNNs lead to a local synaptic balance to make the network sensitive to learning new synapses and prevent fast increase of the weights [13].

2.5 Tactile Feedback

A signal to represent tactile feedback is added to stop the motion on contact with an object. Each finger network has a single tactile neuron connected with very strong inhibitory synapses to the output layer (see Fig. 2a). The firing frequency of this neuron is higher than the maximal activation frequency of the output neurons. Once active, it will the membrane potential of the output neurons low, to prevent them from firing and stop the motion as a reflex.

3 Evaluation

In this section, we evaluate the capabilities of the SNN with two different grasp motions. In Fig. 4, the experimental setup is presented. The system architecture is depicted in Fig. 4a. The SNN was implemented with Nest 2.10. The world simulation is made with Gazebo physics simulator using a model of the robot hand. As middleware for modular design and inter-component communication we use ROS. To control the hand, we use the *schunk_svh_driver* [10]. This architecture allows an easy transition from simulation to the real robot.

In a basic setup the SNN is implemented with a total of 5100 neurons. We define each input or output populations to have 100 neurons. Each finger network has 7 input and output populations (see Fig. 2a), making of a total of 700 neurons. The hand network has 12 input and output populations (see Fig. 2b), and a hidden layer, that is desired to be larger than all the input layers together, with 1400 neurons, making of a total of 2600 neurons. We use mainly the leaky integrate-and-fire (LIF) neuron model with alpha-function shaped post-synaptic currents. For the grasp type input population a variant of LIF with spike-time adaptive neuron model is used to stabilize the constant spiking activity. The mean squared error (MSE) of the SNN output with and without adaptive neurons in the grasp type population is shown in Fig. 5. Adaption leads to a more stable weight development as shown later in Fig. 9a.

The data service selects the samples to train the SNN. A motion capture system (*LeapMotion*) is used to record training data from human demonstration using a 3D visualization tool (see Fig. 4b). Two types of grasps were recorded:

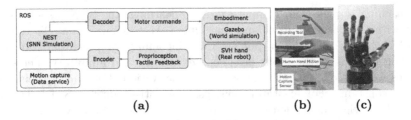

Fig. 4. (a) System architecture. ROS is the middleware for inter-component communication. The world physic simulation is made in Gazebo. Motor commands are send form the SNN to the hand. Proprioception and tactile feedback are send back to the SNN. The spike encoder and decoder are described in Sect. 2.3. (b) Motion capture system to record human hand motion. (c) The SNN is evaluated on the real Schunk SVH hand.

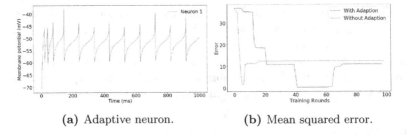

(a) Adaptive neuron.   (b) Mean squared error.

Fig. 5. With adaptation in the grasp type population, (a) a neuron's membrane potential adapts to continuous input, (b) and SNN learns faster and more stable.

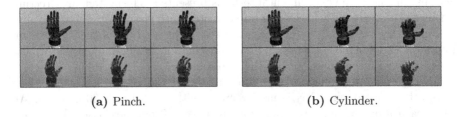

(a) Pinch.   (b) Cylinder.

Fig. 6. Frame sequences of different grasp motions, (a) pinch and (b) cylinder, executed by the SNN in both simulation (*row 1*) and the real robot (*row 2*) respectively.

cylinder and pinch. Each grasp type has 2 different examples. The sensor operates at 115 Hz, and was down-sampled to 22 Hz to increase the differences between consecutive samples. Each sample is presented to the network for 40 ms, followed by 50 ms of pause to relax the neuron potentials and stabilize the output.

The SNN is evaluated in simulation and on the real robotic hand (see Fig. 4c), and the activity was recorded during the execution of two different grasp motions (pinch and cylinder). A frame sequence presenting the generated grasp motions is shown in Fig. 6, and it can be observed, that the simulated model and real robot performed similar grasp motions (Fig. 7).

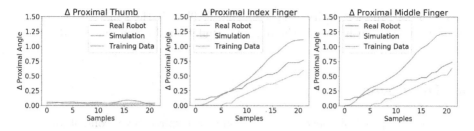

Fig. 7. A comparison between training data, simulation and robot of the proximal joint proprioception (*thumb, index and middle fingers*) during a cylinder grasp motion. The SNN is capable of resembling the motion tendency by learning joint synergies.

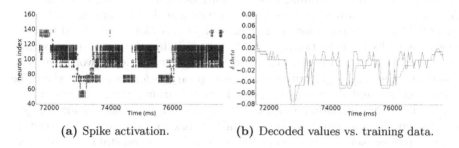

(a) Spike activation.   (b) Decoded values vs. training data.

Fig. 8. A segment of spike activation from the SNN for the proximal joint of the index finger. (a) The spike trains and (b) the SNN output decoded values vs. training data.

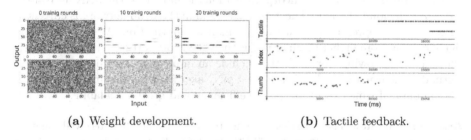

(a) Weight development.   (b) Tactile feedback.

Fig. 9. (a) Weight development of the index finger network during learning. (b) The simulated tactile signal inhibits the activation of the two fingers at different times.

We also compared the training data joint values, with the proprioception obtained from the simulation and the real robot (see Fig. 7). Both resembled the same behavior as the demonstrated data, which translates in a similar motion using similar joint synergies. In Fig. 9, a segment of the SNN activation for the index finger's proximal joint is shown. The spike trains from the SNN are presented and the decoded values are compared against the training data. It can be seen that the SNN output resembles the training data. While performing a cylinder grasp motion, tactile feedback was simulated in two fingers to trigger the inhibitory mechanism (see Sect. 2.5) to stop the motion. The SNN activity was recorded, and for clarity, we present in Fig. 9b only the spike activity of the most active neuron in one of the output populations for the index and thumb fingers.

4   Discussion

We presented proof of concept of a biologically inspired SNN control architecture (see Figs. 1 and 2) capable of learning and executing different types of grasp motions was developed and tested (see Fig. 7). With the hierarchy of a hand with finger networks motions are represented as synergies in the synaptic weights of the SNN reusing and combining motor primitives (individual finger movements). All the networks learn with the same supervised associative learning mechanism using STPD on grasp motions from human demonstration. We showed that the finger networks learn motion synergies by associating the proprioception and the fingertip target with joint changes, and that the hand network learns to coordinate the fingers generating the fingertip targets for each finger given the proprioception and the grasp type signal. After learning, the SNN was able to control both the simulation and the real robot hand. By using a sparse projection to high-dimensional space in the hand network and using winner-takes-it-all readout mechanism, we achieve notable noise reduction and stable control. Tactile feedback was incorporated into the finger networks to stop the motion on contact. This behavior can be used to adapt the motion to an object's shape.

In the future, we want to incorporate a muscle model for the SNN activation instead of the joint changes. The grasp type used in the hand network is currently an arbitrarily representation without semantic information. We will use this signal coming from higher brain areas, as the visual cortex [12], to represent grasp affordances. Following work will also include an implementation of the proposed method on neuromorphic hardware, i.e. SpiNNaker boards. This implementation will enable real-time execution, power efficiency and greater scalability.

Acknowledgments. The research leading to these results has received funding from the European Union Horizon 2020 Programme under grant agreement n.720270 (Human Brain Project SGA1).

References

1. Bernstein, N.A.: The co-ordination and regulation of movements (1967)
2. Bizzi, E., Cheung, V., d'Avella, A., Saltiel, P., Tresch, M.: Combining modules for movement. Brain Res. Rev. **57**(1), 125–133 (2008)
3. Bouganis, A., Shanahan, M.: Training a spiking neural network to control a 4-DoF robotic arm based on spike timing-dependent plasticity. In: IJCNN, pp. 18–23 (2010)
4. Chinellato, E., et al.: The Visual Neuroscience of Robotic Grasping, vol. 28 (2016)
5. Ciocarlie, M.T.: Low-dimensional robotic grasping: Eigengrasp subspaces and optimized underactuation. ProQuest Dissertations and Theses (2010)

6. Cutkosky, M.R.: On grasp choice, grasp models, and the design of hands for manufacturing tasks. IEEE Trans. Robot. Autom. **5**(3), 269–279 (1989)
7. d'Avella, A., Saltiel, P., Bizzi, E.: Combinations of muscle synergies in the construction of a natural motor behavior. Nat. Neurosci. **6**(3), 300–308 (2003)
8. Davison, A.P., Fragnac, Y.: Learning cross-modal spatial transformations through spike timing-dependent plasticity. J. Neurosci. **26**(21), 5604–5615 (2006)
9. Gütig, R., et al.: Learning input correlations through nonlinear temporally asymmetric Hebbian plasticity. J. Neurosci. **23**(9), 3697–3714 (2003)
10. Heppner, G.: schunk_svh_driver. http://wiki.ros.org/schunk_svh_driver
11. Ijspeert, A.J., et al.: Dynamical movement primitives: learning attractor models for motor behaviors. Neural Comput. **25**(2), 328–373 (2013)
12. Kaiser, J., et al.: Spiking convolutional deep belief networks. In: ICANN (2017)
13. Kleberg, F., et al.: Excitatory and inhibitory STDP jointly tune feedforward neural circuits to selectively propagate correlated spiking activity. Front Comput. Neurosci. (2014)
14. Maass, W.: Networks of spiking neurons: The third generation of neural network models. Neural Netw. **10**(9), 1659–1671 (1997)
15. Santello, M., Flanders, M., Soechting, J.F.: Postural hand synergies for tool use. J. Neurosci. **18**(23), 10105–10115 (1998)
16. Song, S., Miller, K.D., Abbott, L.F.: Competitive Hebbian learning through spike-timing-dependent synaptic plasticity. Nat. Neurosci. **3**(9), 919–926 (2000)
17. Sridharan, D., et al.: Selective disinhibition: a unified neural mechanism for predictive and post hoc attentional selection. Vision. Res. **116**, 194–209 (2015)
18. Srinivasa, N., et al.: Self-organizing spiking neural model for learning fault-tolerant spatio-motor transformations. IEEE Trans. Neural Netw. Learn. Syst. (2012)

Obstacle Avoidance by Profit Sharing Using Self-Organizing Map-Based Probabilistic Associative Memory

Daisuke Temma and Yuko Osana[✉]

Tokyo University of Technology, 1404-1, Katakura, Hachioji, Tokyo 192-0982, Japan
osana@stf.teu.ac.jp

Abstract. In this paper, we realize an action learning of obstacle avoidance by Profit Sharing using Self-Organizing Map-based Probabilistic Associative Memory (SOMPAM). In this method, patterns corresponding to the pairs of observation and action are memorized to the SOMPAM, and the brief degree is set to value of the rule. In this research robot learns with the aim of acquiring an action rule that can reach the goal point from the start point with as few steps as possible while avoiding collision with the obstacle. We use the reduced image of the image taken with the small camera mounted on the robot as observation. In the simulation environment reproducing the experimental environment, we confirmed that the learning converged to a state where it can reach the goal while avoiding obstacles with the minimum steps. Moreover, even in the real environment, it was confirmed that the robot can reach the goal while avoiding obstacles.

Keywords: Obstacle avoidance · Reinforcement learning · Associative memory

1 Introduction

Reinforcement learning is one of sub-areas in machine learning concerned with how an agent ought to take actions in an environment so as to maximize some notion of long-term reward [1]. Reinforcement learning algorithms attempt to find a policy that maps states of the world to the actions the agent ought to take in those states. Since the artificial neural network has flexible information processing ability and robustness for noise, some methods which realize reinforcement learning using artificial neural networks have been proposed [2–4].

In this paper, we realize an action learning of obstacle avoidance by Profit Sharing using Self-Organizing Map-based Probabilistic Associative Memory (SOMPAM) [4]. In this method, patterns corresponding to the pairs of observation and action are memorized to the SOMPAM [5], and the brief degree is set to value of the rule. In this research robot learns with the aim of acquiring an action rule that can reach the goal point from the start point with as few steps as possible while avoiding collision with the obstacle. We use the reduced image of the image taken with the small camera mounted on the robot as observation.

© Springer International Publishing AG 2017
A. Lintas et al. (Eds.): ICANN 2017, Part I, LNCS 10613, pp. 52–59, 2017.
https://doi.org/10.1007/978-3-319-68600-4_7

2   Realization of Profit Sharing by Self-Organizing Map-Based Probabilistic Associative Memory

Figure 1 shows the flow of the Profit Sharing [6] by Self-Organizing Map-based Probabilistic Associative Memory (SOMPAM) [4] which is used in this research. In this method, patterns corresponding to the pairs of observation and action are memorized to the SOMPAM [5], and the brief degree is set to value of the rule.

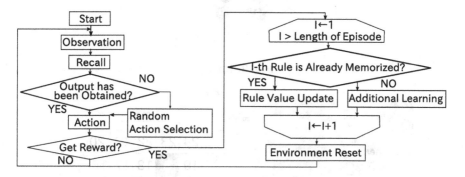

Fig. 1. Flow of profit sharing by SOMPAM.

3   Obstacle Avoidance by Profit Sharing Using SOMPAM

Here, we explain action learning of obstacle avoidance by Profit Sharing using Self-Organizing Map-based Probabilistic Associative Memory [4].

3.1   Robot

In this study, behavior learning is performed using a bipedal walking robot (Robovie-nano) as shown in Fig. 2. This robot has 15 servo motors. In Fig. 2, numbers 1 to 15 correspond to 15 servo motors, respectively. In addition, it carries a compact camera that can shoot 300,000 pixel movies and images on the shoulder.

3.2   Environment

In this research, the robot moves the environment where obstacles exist as shown in Fig. 3(a). The robot learns with the aim of acquiring an action rule that can reach the goal point from the start point with as few steps as possible while avoiding collision with the obstacle. In Fig. 3(a), the object B is a fixed obstacle that will not move from the place. The object A moves from the position of the

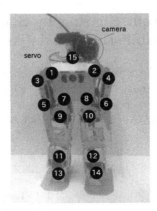

Fig. 2. Robot

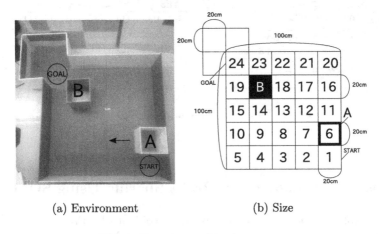

(a) Environment   (b) Size

Fig. 3. Experimental environment.

square of 6 shown in Fig. 3(b) by one step every two steps in the direction of the black arrow shown in Fig. 3(a). When reaching the end squares (6 or 10), the moving direction is changed in the opposite direction, and the object moves between 6 and 10.

3.3   Observation

In this research, we use the reduced image of the image taken with the small camera mounted on the robot as observation. The small camera can store images of bitmap format of 640×480 pixels. When using the image as observation, use a 8×6 reduced image as observation. Quantized RGB values in 15 levels are used as observations. Observation is 144 ($= 8 \times 6 \times 3$) dimensional data. In experiments in a real environment, in order to reduce the influence of noise, the average of five images shot by a camera reduced to 8×6 is used as observation.

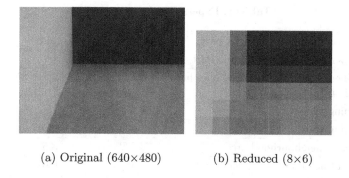

(a) Original (640×480)   (b) Reduced (8×6)

Fig. 4. Observation (Image).

In the environment used in this experiment, the image captured by the camera is very simple although it is affected by lighting, so it is reduced to 8×6. In the learning in simulation, observations are taken of all observation states that can be considered in the real environment by camera (Fig. 4).

3.4 Action

According to the observation, the robot selects one of the actions; (a) moving forward, (b) turning to the right, and (c) turning to the left.

4 Reward

One episode begins when the robot leaves the start point and ends when it reaches the goal point. The reward r is given by

$$r = \begin{cases} -0.1\tau - 0.01h + 10 & (\tau < 100) \\ 0 & \text{(otherwise)} \end{cases} \tag{1}$$

where τ is the number of steps from the start point to the goal point, and h is the number of contracts with walls, fixed or moving obstacles.

5 Computer Experiment Results

Here, we carried out experiments on action learning of obstacle avoidance by Profit Sharing using Self-Organizing Map-based Probabilistic Associative Memory under the conditions shown in Table 1. The results are shown below.

Table 1. Experimental conditions

The number of neurons in input part	N^{IN}	144
The number of neurons in output Part	N^{OUT}	1
The number of neurons in initial map layer ($N^{IN} = 144$)	$x_{max} \times y_{max}$	25×25
The learning time	T	75
The learning rate	α	0.01
Initial size of neighborhood area	δ^{ini}	3.5
Final size of neighborhood area	δ^{fin}	0.01
Thereshold for learning	θ^{L1}	1
Threshold for distance	θ^{L2}	0.3
Coeficient in threshold	a	10^{-6}
Minimum threshold in map layer	θ^R_{min}	0.99 (Simulation)
		0.7 (Robot)
Initial temperture	T_{ini}	10
Minimum temperture	T_{min}	0.005
Decay rate of temperture	γ	0.985
Initial value of rules	q_{ini}	0.001

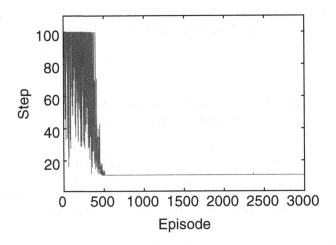

Fig. 5. Transition of the number of steps in simulation.

5.1 Learning in Simulation Environment

Figure 5 is the transition of the number of steps in the simulation environment. As shown in this figure, the robot reaches the goal within 100 steps after 400 trials. After 510 trials, the robot can reach the goal in eleven steps, which is the minimum steps of reaching the goal without colliding with obstacles.

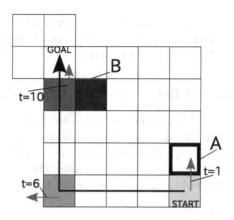

Fig. 6. Route in 3000th trail.

Table 2. Values of actions used at $t = 1,\ 6,\ 10$.

Time t	Observation	Action	Value of Rule		
			Forward	Right	Left
1		Left	-0.698998	0.001125	0.087205
6		Right	-0.441430	88.773337	0.001178
10		Forward	23237.301000	2.608582	1.108109

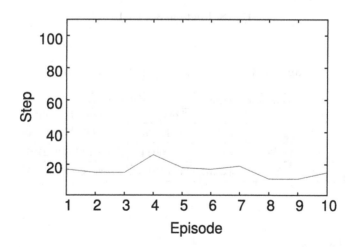

Fig. 7. Transition of the number of steps in experiment using robot.

Figure 6 shows the route that the robot moved in 3000th trail. Table 2 shows the values of actions taken into consideration for observation and action selection of $t = 1,\ 6,\ 10$ in the 3000th trial in simulation learning.

5.2 Experiment in Real Robot After Learning in Simulation

Figure 7 is the transition of the number of steps in the real environment using the robot after the learning in the simulation. As shown in this figure, the robot reaches the goal within 26 steps. Figure 8 shows the route that the robot moved in 8th trail. Table 3 shows the values of actions taken into consideration for observation and action selection of $t = 1,\ 6,\ 10$ in the 8th trial in simulation learning.

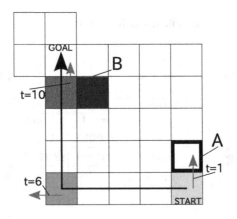

Fig. 8. Route in 8th trial.

Table 3. Values of actions used at $t = 1,\ 6,\ 10$.

Time t	Observation	Action	Value of Rule		
			Forward	Right	Left
1		Left	−0.427267	0.007061	1.389390
6		Right	2.326024	15.663851	0.282121
10		Forward	23305.101000	2.608582	1.108109

6   Conclusion

In this paper, we have realized an action learning of obstacle avoidance by Profit Sharing using Self-Organizing Map-based Probabilistic Associative Memory (SOMPAM). In this research robot learns with the aim of acquiring an action rule that can reach the goal point from the start point with as few steps as possible while avoiding collision with the obstacle. We use the reduced image of the image taken with the small camera mounted on the robot as observation. In the simulation environment reproducing the experimental environment, we confirmed that the learning converged to a state where it can reach the goal while avoiding obstacles with the minimum steps. Moreover, even in the real environment, it was confirmed that the robot can reach the goal while avoiding obstacles. The environment used in this experiment is very simple, but we would like to apply this method to a more complicated environment in the future.

References

1. Sutton, R.S., Barto, A.G.: Reinforcement Learning: An Introduction. The MIT Press, Cambridge (1998)
2. Shibata, K., Sakashita, Y.: Reinforcement learning with internal-dynamics-based exploration using a chaotic neural network. In: Proceedings of IEEE and INNS International Joint Conference on Neural Networks, Killarney (2015)
3. Koma, D., Osana, Y.: Profit sharing that can learn deterministic policy for POMDPs environments by Kohonen feature map associative memory. In: Proceedings of IEEE International Conference on System, Man and Cybernetics, Manchester (2013)
4. Katayama, T., Osana, Y.: Realization of profit sharing by self-organizing map-based probabilistic associative memory. In: Proceedings of International Conference on Artificial Neural Networks (2016)
5. Osana, Y.: Self-organizing map-based probabilistic associative memory. In: Proceedings of International Conference on Neural Information Processing, Kuching (2014)
6. Grefenstette, J.J.: Credit assignment in rule discovery systems based on genetic algorithms. Mach. Learn. **3**, 225–245 (1988)

An Ultra-Compact Low-Powered Closed-Loop Device for Control of the Neuromuscular System

Davide Polese[1($\boxtimes$)], Luca Pazzini[1($\boxtimes$)], Ignacio Delgado-Martínez[2($\boxtimes$)],
Luca Maiolo[1], Xavier Navarro[2], and Guglielmo Fortunato[1]

[1] Istituto per la Microelettronica e Microsistemi, Consiglio Nazionale delle Ricerche,
Via del Fosso del Cavaliere, 100, 00133 Rome, Italy
{davide.polese,luca.maiolo,guglielmo.fortunato}@cnr.it,
luca.pazzini@artov.imm.cnr.it
[2] Department of Cell Biology, Physiology and Immunology,
Institute of Neurosciences, Universitat Autònoma de Barcelona, Bellaterra, Spain
{ignacio.delgado,xavier.navarro}@uab.cat

Abstract. Neuroprosthetic interfaces require light-weighted and power-optimized systems that combine acquisition and stimulation together with a computational unit capable to perform on-line analysis for closed-loop control. Here, we present an ultra-compact and low-power system able to acquire from 32 channels and stimulate independently using both current and voltage. The system has been validated *in vivo* for rats in the recording of spontaneous and evoked potentials and peripheral nerve stimulation, and it was tested to reproduce the muscular activity involved in gait. This device has potential application in long-term clinical therapies for the restoration of limb control and it can become a development platform for closed loop algorithms in neuromuscular interfaces.

Keywords: EMG · Neuro-prosthetic · Motor prosthesis · Nerve stimulation · Closed-loop

1 Introduction

Motor neuroprostheses are typically used to replace muscle activation in spinal cord injuries or damages to the peripheral nervous system. Their action is through the application of short bursts of electrical charge, which generates an electrical field that triggers action potentials in the efferent neuromuscular system. The electrical activation must be precisely coordinated to resemble as closely as possible the normal neural mechanisms. For example, to assist walking, the stimulation is applied to the neuromuscular system of the leg so that muscle contraction is elicited at predetermined times, as it would be expected to occur in a normal gait cycle [3,14]. Such complex movements require automatic control systems, such closed-loop systems, that provide a certain stimulation pattern according to the state of the neuromuscular system and the requirements of that particular moment, without voluntary intervention [10].

Closed-loop systems are composed of three main elements: (1) recording and stimulation electrodes [4,12,15]; (2) a multichannel acquisition and stimulation

© Springer International Publishing AG 2017
A. Lintas et al. (Eds.): ICANN 2017, Part I, LNCS 10613, pp. 60–67, 2017.
https://doi.org/10.1007/978-3-319-68600-4_8

device [9,13]; and (3) a computational unit to perform closed-loop algorithms. These three elements generally are not integrated into a single device but rather are integrated into independent equipments, linked one to other. The result is generally an ensemble of heavy and bulky devices afflicted by communication delays that makes difficult the implementation of real-time closed-loop algorithms [8]. Such multi-device approach can have minor consequences for research purposes but has important limitations for clinical applications and in development of closed loop algorithms. When used in patients, the device should be compact to wear on but capable of efficient communication for low latency real-time operations. Thanks to the progress in microelectronics and miniaturization techniques, a wide variety of closed-loop neuroprosthetic devices have been proposed [11]. However, they are built using cutting-edge components, which may result too expensive for their implementation in therapeutic protocols.

Here we present an ultra-compact, low power, general purpose system for recording and stimulation of neuromuscular activity. The device is composed of an acquisition and a stimulation board intimately connected by high speed board-to-board communication. It incorporates a full closed-loop system: an acquisition board for amplification and digitalization of up to 32 channels at a combined sampling rate of 1 MHz, an integrated computational unit endowed of a Digital Signal Processor (DSP) and a highly precise stimulation board for independent voltage and current bipolar stimulation. The overall system consumption is less than 350 mW. The whole system weight is 30 g and is enclosed in a Faraday's cage of 68 × 45 × 1.5 mm to prevent environmental noise interference. The system was tested *in vivo* for the acquisition of spontaneous and evoked muscular activity and in the sequential activation of the muscles of the rat hind limb in order to simulate the walking movement. The results show that the system has the hardware capabilities to become a development platform for closed loop algorithms in neuromuscular interfaces.

2   System Architecture

The closed-loop neuroprosthetic system is composed of two logical subsystems: an acquisition and a stimulation part. In Fig. 1, a schematic representation of the system is presented. The two subsystems are developed onto two separate boards connected by a board-to-board high speed communication bus. This approach has two main advantages: (1) the modular approach allows an autonomous development for the two boards and make the device versatile for the different applications (2) it optimizes the space by stacking the two boards. This has allowed to contain the whole system in a 68 × 45 × 1.5 mm volume for a total weight of 30 g. The total power consumption is less than 350 mW.

2.1   Acquisition Board

The acquisition board functions as motherboard and handles the system power management from USB port supplying the stimulation board. The acquisition

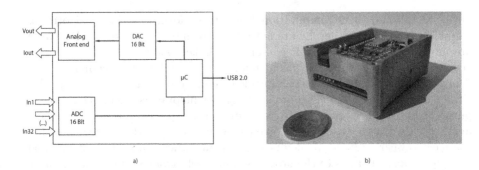

Fig. 1. (a) Schematic representation of the system showing the main components: the microcontroller (μC), the low noise analog to digital converter, the 16-bit digital to analog converter, and the analog front-end electronic of the stimulator. Communication of the system is done via USB. (b) Picture of the whole system, composed of the stacked boards, held in its case. A 1 euro coin is shown for size comparison.

board is endowed with a 32-input channels and a 200× gain. It contains a 16-bits analog to digital converter (ADC) by Intan Technology and a microcontroller (μC). The high- and low-pass filters can be adjusted in the range of 0.1 Hz-500 Hz and 100 Hz−20 kHz respectively on chip. The acquisition frequency can be arbitrary selected up to 1 MHz shared among the selected input channels and a blanking circuit is present to allow the input channels to be grounded during the stimulation in order to reduce the recovery time after stimulation. This flexibility makes the acquisition board suitable for different neurophysiology applications such as EMG, ENG, ECoG, ECG and EEG. On the other hand, the μC, in addition to managing the ADC, integrates a USB communication (High Speed 2.0) that permits the maximum data throughput of 16 *Mbit/s* of acquired data toward a PC. Other several general purpose I/O pins and standard communication protocols (I2C, UART, SPI) can be used to control external devices. In addition, the microcontroller is equipped with a DSP unit, which can be used to run detection algorithms and protocols for the stimulation board.

2.2 Stimulation Board

The stimulation board has two independent stimulation channels that permit bipolar local stimulation in voltage (± 2.35 V) and current (± 2.5 mA). The board is composed of a dual channel low noise 16 bit current DAC that is controlled by SPI from the underlying μC, and a dual channel low noise amplifier. Practically, the voltage output is obtained with a low noise op-amp in inverting configuration, whereas the current output is obtained using bipolar Howland current generator [7]. In this way, it is possible to generate a plethora of stimulation profiles, from pulse stimulation (down to 5 μs width) to arbitrary waveforms. The stimulation can be simultaneously performed with the recordings enabling the possibility of performing closed loop control algorithms.

2.3   Graphical User Interface

The system is controlled by a graphical user interface (GUI) developed in MAT-LAB (MathWorks, Inc. USA). The GUI allows controlling several parameters of the acquisition board (sampling frequency, acquisition channel, etc.) or of the stimulation board (waveform, amplitude, period, etc.). A real time data visualization is possible thanks to lab streaming layer library [1].

3   Experimental Results

The performance of the acquisition and stimulation subsystems were tested *in vivo* in adult Sprague Dawley rats. The tests consisted on the simultaneous recording of evoked and spontaneous muscular activity and the electrical activation of nerve and muscle action potentials.

3.1   Muscle Recording

Muscle activity was acquired from three muscles of the rat hind limb (gastrocnemius muscle, plantar interosseus muscle and tibialis anterior muscle) using subdermal steel needle electrodes in bipolar configuration. Spontaneous muscle activity was recorded for 20 s, before and after mechanical stimulation that has been applied at the corresponding paw for 20 s. The acquired signals have been filtered with a high pass Butterworth filter with cutoff frequency of 20 Hz to avoid motion artifacts [5]. The recorded signals are shown in Fig. 2a. It is possible to appreciate the signal amplitude increment during the mechanical stimulation.

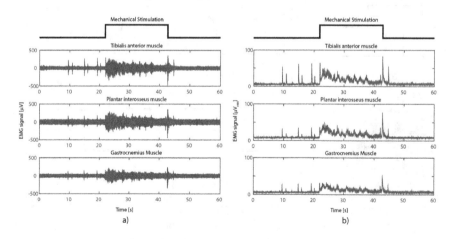

Fig. 2. (a) Spontaneous and induced muscular activity recorded from three different muscles of the rat hind limb. (b) Root mean square signal of spontaneous and induced muscular activity.

To further demonstrate the differences between evoked and spontaneous activity, the Root Mean Square of the recorded signals was calculated using a temporal window of 50 ms (Fig. 2b). As expected, mechanical stimulation evoked an increase in the signal power compared to the periods when only spontaneous activity was recorded. The previous data processing algorithm can be easily implemented into the μC firmware with very low latency between signal acquisition and stimulation feedback. Due to the hardware and firmware optimization, the latency can be reduced to be proportional to the acquisition time i.e. less than a 1 ms for acquisition frequency greater of 1 kHz. This latency value is lesser than the feasible latency achievable in a system composed of three different elements (acquisition system, PC and stimulation system) even only considering the standard communication latencies.

3.2   Sequential Muscle Stimulation

Bipolar stimulation of the quadriceps femoris muscle, biceps femoris muscle, tibialis anterior muscle, and gastrocnemius muscle was performed sequentially, in a timely pattern which resembled gait (Fig. 3a), using subdermal steel needles, using trains of pulses of 100 μs width at 20 Hz. To this purpose, two stimulation boards were synchronized together to supply two couples of stimulation channel outputs into the four muscles. The joint angles during the stimulation sequence were calculated from a video sequence at 30 fps using MATLAB (Fig. 3b). Using this setup, we were able to elicit independent stimulation of each muscle, leading to a leg movement similar to the one occurring during walking (Fig. 3c).

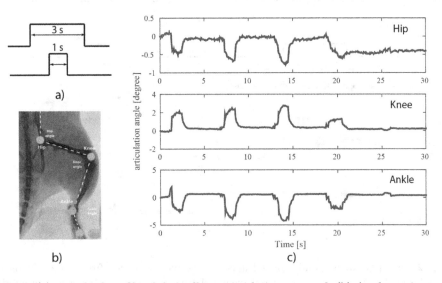

Fig. 3. (a) Temporal profile of the walking stimulation protocol. (b) A schematic representation of the rat hind limb is shown. In particular, the joint points and angles are highlighted. (c) Joint angles profiles during the experiment.

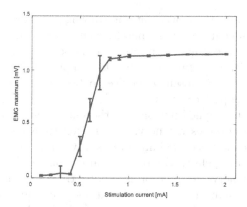

Fig. 4. Recruitment curve for tibialis anterioris muscle fibers after sciatic nerve stimulation.

3.3   Neuromuscular Stimulation and Recording

A train of biphasic current pulses of $100\,\mu$s width at $3\,$Hz was applied through the stimulation board to the sciatic nerve using steel needle electrodes while the acquisition board recorded the muscle activity from electrodes placed in four muscles of the hind limb of the rat (plantar interosseus muscle, tibialis anterior muscle, gastrocnemius muscle and biceps femoris muscle). The stimulation amplitude ranged from $100\,\mu$A to $2000\,\mu$A. The peak-to-peak amplitude of the resulting electrically evoked compound muscle action potential (CMAP) was measured and plotted against the corresponding stimulation strength to calculate a classical recruitment curve [6] (Fig. 4).

4   Discussion and Conclusion

An ultra-compact, low power, general purpose system for recording and stimulation of muscular activity is presented. Following a modular approach, the system is composed of two boards one for acquisition and system managing and a stimulation board connected by an high speed board-to-board connection everything hold in $68 \times 45 \times 1.5\,$mm of dimensions and $30\,$g of weight. These reduced dimensions, weight, combined with a low power consumption enable also the possibility the use in mobility.

The system was validated in acquisition and stimulation modes by *in vivo* experiments in rats. The acquisition board was able to successfully record spontaneous and mechanically-evoked EMG activity. Simple processing algorithms, such as the calculation of the RMS, was enough to show the muscle activity. This calculation can be incorporated in the DSP for on-line detection of muscle contraction for closed-loop control.

The stimulation board was able to provide independent muscle contraction in four different muscular groups. The pattern of stimulation was pre-programmed on the board to resemble the movement done during gait. However, by increasing the number of output channels, more muscles could be activated to achieve higher control. Additionally, the stimulation timing could be determined by the result of the processing algorithm contained in the DSP to provide better control. These characteristics enable the presented device to become a fruitful development platform for closed-loop algorithms.

Stimulation can be applied not only to the muscle but to the nerve as well. Newer motor neuroprotheses use nerve stimulation to achieve selective muscle control from a single interface, avoiding in this way extensive surgical procedures consisting on implanting electrodes to each target muscle [2]. Furthermore, the necessary charge for nerve stimulation is smaller than for muscle one, therefore saving battery. The compact size and reduced power consumption of our closed-loop device makes it very suitable for long-term, chronical, clinical applications.

References

1. Lab streaming layer. https://github.com/sccn/labstreaminglayer
2. Badia, J., Boretius, T., Andreu, D., Azevedo-Coste, C., Stieglitz, T., Navarro, X.: Comparative analysis of transverse intrafascicular multichannel, longitudinal intrafascicular and multipolar cuff electrodes for the selective stimulation of nerve fascicles. J. Neural Eng. 8(3), 036023 (2011)
3. Braz, G.P., Russold, M., Davis, G.M.: Functional electrical stimulation control of standing and stepping after spinal cord injury: a review of technical characteristics. Neuromodulation Technol. Neural Interface 12(3), 180–190 (2009)
4. Castagnola, E., Marrani, M., Maggiolini, E., Maita, F., Pazzini, L., Polese, D., Pecora, A., Maiolo, L., Fortunato, G., Fadiga, L., et al.: Recording high frequency neural signals using conformable and low-impedance ECoG electrodes arrays coated with PEDOT-PSS-PEG. In: Advances in Science and Technology, vol. 102, pp. 77–85. Trans Tech Publications (2017)
5. De Luca, C.J.: The use of surface electromyography in biomechanics. J. Appl. Biomech. 13(2), 135–163 (1997)
6. Durfee, W.K., MACLean, K.E.: Methods for estimating isometric recruitment curves of electrically stimulated muscle. IEEE Trans. Biomed. Eng. 36(7), 654–667 (1989)
7. Franco, S.: Design with Operational Amplifiers and Analog Integrated Circuits. Electrical and Computer Engineering. McGraw-Hill (2015)
8. Greenwald, E., Masters, M.R., Thakor, N.V.: Implantable neurotechnologies: bidirectional neural interfaces - applications and VLSI circuit implementations. Med. Biol. Eng. Compu. 54(1), 1–17 (2016)
9. Loi, D., Carboni, C., Angius, G., Angotzi, G.N., Barbaro, M., Raffo, L., Raspopovic, S., Navarro, X.: Peripheral neural activity recording and stimulation system. IEEE Trans. Biomed. Circuits Syst. 5(4), 368–379 (2011)
10. Mazurek, K.A., Holinski, B.J., Everaert, D.G., Stein, R.B., Etienne-Cummings, R., Mushahwar, V.K.: Feed forward and feedback control for over-ground locomotion in anaesthetized cats. J. Neural Eng. 9(2), 026003 (2012)
11. Nag, S., Thakor, N.V.: Implantable neurotechnologies: electrical stimulation and applications. Med. Biol. Eng. Compu. 54(1), 63–76 (2016)

12. Pazzini, L., Polese, D., Maiolo, L., Castagnola, E., Maggiolini, E., Zucchini, E., Marrani, M., Fortunato, G., Fadiga, L., Ricci, D.: Brain stimulation and recording with ultra-flexible pedot-cnt-coated micro-ecog electrode arrays. Brain Stimulation **10**(2), 478 (2017)
13. Pazzini, L., Polese, D., Marrani, M., Maita, F., Tort, N., Weinert, J.F., D'Andola, M., Maiolo, L., Pecora, A., Fortunato, G., et al.: A compact integrated system for neural signal acquisition and stimulation. In: B DEBATE - A Dialogue with the Cerebral Cortex: Cortical Function and Interfacing (Workshop), Barcelona, Spain, 29–30 April 2015
14. Ragnarsson, K.T.: Functional electrical stimulation after spinal cord injury: current use, therapeutic effects and future directions. Spinal Cord **46**(4), 255–274 (2008)
15. Xue, N., Sun, T., Tsang, W.M., Delgado-Martínez, I., Lee, S.-H., Sheshadri, S., Xiang, Z., Merugu, S., Gu, Y., Yen, S.-C., Thakor, N.V.: Polymeric C-shaped cuff electrode for recording of peripheral nerve signal. Sensors Actuators B Chem. **210**, 640–648 (2015)

Comparing Action Sets: Mutual Information as a Measure of Control

Sascha Fleer[✉] and Helge Ritter

Neuroinformatics Group, EXC Cognitive Interaction Technology (CITEC),
Bielefeld University, Bielefeld, Germany
{sfleer,helge}@techfak.uni-bielefeld.de
http://www.neuroinformatik.de

Abstract. Finding good principles to choose the actions of artificial agents like robots in the most beneficial way to optimize their control of the environment is very much in the focus of current research in the field of intelligent systems. Especially in reinforcement learning, where the agent learns through the direct interaction with the environment, a good choice of actions is essential. We propose a new approach that allows a predictive ranking of different action sets with regard to their influence on the learning performance of an artificial agent. Our approach is based on a measure of control that utilizes the concept of mutual information. To evaluate this approach, we investigate its prediction of the effectiveness of different sets of actions in "mediated interaction" scenarios. Our results indicate that the mutual information-based measure can yield useful predictions on the aptitude of action sets for the learning process.

Keywords: Reinforcement learning · Environment control · Q-learning · Mutual information · Mediated interaction learning · Physics-based simulation

1 Introduction

One of the bigger visions in the field of intelligent systems is to endow an artificial agent with the ability to solve human-level problems. To deal with such complicated tasks, the agent has to explore the learning domain autonomously by performing actions that affect the environment directly and learn from these effects. This important aspect is a distinct focus of reinforcement learning where the agent learns through the direct interaction with the environment [11]. To explore the terrain, the agent executes actions which alter its surroundings and lead to a feedback how much the chosen action benefits the agent in its current situation with respect to the primary learning goal. Therefore, actions play a crucial role in reinforcement learning as they determine how much control the agent has over the environment and by thus influence the effectiveness of exploration and learning.

This motivates the following question: are there general features that distinguish action sets that facilitate exploration, learning and control ("good" action

© Springer International Publishing AG 2017
A. Lintas et al. (Eds.): ICANN 2017, Part I, LNCS 10613, pp. 68–75, 2017.
https://doi.org/10.1007/978-3-319-68600-4_9

sets) from action sets for which exploration, learning and control is more difficult? Obviously, criteria to recognize such action sets would be of interest for designing interactive learning algorithms that are fast and efficient.

In the present paper, we consider this question for choosing a good action set for a reinforcement learning agent that has to learn a challenging "mediated interaction" task that can only be solved when the agent recognizes to use a "mediator object" as a tool to reach its goal. Using a simulation study with simulated physics, we present results that indicate that a simple, entropy-based measure can rank different possible action sets in a way that correlates well with the learning performance in the reinforcement learning task.

By defining actions relative to a coordinate system, we connect the choice of an action set with the choice of a coordinate system. In this way, we can use our approach also to rank different options for choosing a coordinate system that is "favorable" for the learning task at hand. Our findings are consistent with the expectation that "good" coordinate systems should be those that make uncertainty-reducing actions easy to express. For the task at hand, this turns out to be better achieved with "relational" instead of "absolute" coordinate choices.

In the next section we briefly anchor our notation to define action sets for a reinforcement learning agent and then describe our measure. Section 3 presents the learning domain, Sect. 4 reports the experiments and results and Sect. 5 provides the conclusion.

2   Comparing Action Sets: Mutual Information as a Measure of Control

The concept to maximize the information over the environment to gain more control is studied in various fields [5,12]. In our approach, the mutual information is employed to compare different action sets $\mathcal{A}$, defined by different sensorimotor coordinate systems that determine the agents motions. The ranking order is then used as a criteria for predicting the agents learning performance while using the respective action set.

Reinforcement learning is a class of machine learning algorithms for solving sequential decision making problems through maximization of a cumulative scalar reward signal [11]. It can be defined by the standard formulation of a Markov decision process $(\mathcal{S}, \mathcal{A}, P^{\mathcal{A}}, \mathcal{R}, \mathcal{S}_0)$, where $\mathcal{S}$ denotes the set of states and $\mathcal{A}$ the set of admissible actions. $P^{\mathcal{A}}$ is the set of transition matrices, one for each action $a \in \mathcal{A}$ with matrix elements $\mathcal{P}^a_{ss'} : \mathcal{S} \times \mathcal{A} \longrightarrow \mathcal{S}'$ specifying the probability to end up in state s' after taking action a when in state s. The probability to execute action a in state s can be defined as $\mathcal{P}^a_s$. Finally, $\mathcal{R} : \mathcal{S} \times \mathcal{A} \longrightarrow \mathbb{R}$ is a scalar valued reward function and $\mathcal{S}_0 \subseteq \mathcal{S}$ is the set of starting states.

If the agent induces a state transition from state $s \in \mathcal{S}$, the final state s' is within a subset of possible states $\mathcal{S}' \subseteq \mathcal{S}$. This can be described by the uncontrolled probability $\mathcal{P}_{ss'}$, which fulfills $\mathcal{P}_{ss'} = \sum_a \mathcal{P}^a_s \mathcal{P}^a_{ss'}$. To measure the uncertainty about the next state, the *entropy* [6,9] $\mathcal{H}_s(\mathcal{S}')$ of the current state s can be computed.

$$\mathcal{H}_s(\mathcal{S}') = -\sum_{s'\in\mathcal{S}'} \mathcal{P}_{ss'} \ln\left(\mathcal{P}_{ss'}\right) \tag{1}$$

By introducing surprise [2] (or self-information) which is defined as the negative logarithm of the probability, i.e. $-\ln(\mathcal{P}_{ss'})$, the entropy can be interpreted as the average surprise to end up in one of the possible states s' that can be reached within one transition step. Thus, a small entropy indicates a better prediction of s' while a large entropy implies a high uncertainty of the next state.

Additionally the *conditional entropy* [6] $\mathcal{H}_s(\mathcal{S}'|\mathcal{A})$ of state s can be computed. It measures the average surprise of state s to end up in a state s', conditioned on the actions $a \in \mathcal{A}$, resulting in

$$\mathcal{H}_s(\mathcal{S}'|\mathcal{A}) = -\sum_{a\in\mathcal{A}} \mathcal{P}_s^a \left[\sum_{s'\in\mathcal{S}'} \mathcal{P}_{ss'}^a \ln\left(\mathcal{P}_{ss'}^a\right)\right]. \tag{2}$$

The rate of influence enforced by the set of actions $\mathcal{A}$ on the uncontrolled transitions $\mathcal{P}_{ss'}$ of a state s is thus given by the difference of the state's entropy (1) and the conditional entropy (2) leading to

$$\mathcal{M}_s(\mathcal{S}',\mathcal{A}) = \mathcal{H}_s(\mathcal{S}') - \mathcal{H}_s(\mathcal{S}'|\mathcal{A}). \tag{3}$$

Equation (3) is known as the *mutual information* [6,9]. It measures the reduction of uncertainty of the final states $s' \in \mathcal{S}'$ due to the control of action set $\mathcal{A}$. The ranking order of the expected mutual information, which is (3) averaged over all available states $s \in \mathcal{S}$,

$$\mathcal{M}(\mathcal{S}',\mathcal{A}) = \mathbb{E}_{s\in\mathcal{S}}\left[\mathcal{M}_s(\mathcal{S}',\mathcal{A})\right] \tag{4}$$

turns out to be highly correlated with the learning performance of the reinforcement learning agent. Therefore, we propose to use the action set which leads to the lowest uncertainty of events within the domain and to select the coordinate system according to $\mathcal{A}^* = \text{argmax}_\mathcal{A}\mathcal{M}(\mathcal{S}',\mathcal{A})$.

This choice has the interpretation that the best coordinate system maximizes the expected mutual information (4).

3   Learning Domain

To compare different action sets using the entropy-based measure of control, we employ a 2D simulation world in which an agent has to solve a mediated interaction task. The world is illustrated in Fig. 1 and consists of an agent, a disc-shaped "target-object" and an L-shaped "mediator-object" ("tool"). The simulated learning domain further utilizes the open source Box2D physics engine [1] for interaction and collision handling.

The task of the agent is to bring the target-object into the shaded circle in the center ("goal area"). To this end, the agent can at each time step "pick" the target-object or the mediator-object and exert a (discretized) force/torque

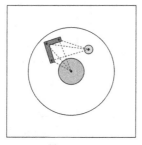 

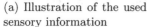

(a) Illustration of the used sensory information

(b)   An   "extension-of-reach" tool-using task

Fig. 1. The simulation world

at the chosen picking location. Picking locations (indicated by black dots in Fig. 1a) are discretized and fixed at the objects: the target-object offers a single picking location at its center, the mediator-object offers three picking locations, two at its ends and one in the middle. Furthermore, there is an additional picking location in the center of the domain which deals as an unbiased starting location for the agent and is further integrated to be an absorbing state that increases the stability of applied learning algorithms. However, the agent can only reach picking locations that lie inside the circular area. Therefore, when the target-object is outside the circle, the agent must first "discover" that the mediator-object can be used to extend the agent's reach beyond the circle boundary. We assume that the agent has a simple relational perception of the world state consisting of the six scalar distances between the three picking locations on the mediator-object and the center of the target-object, and the three distances of the picking locations and the domain's origin. They are visualized by the dotted lines in Fig. 1a. Additionally, the sensory representation encodes the agent's current picking choice. Learning occurs in discrete episodes, each episode being limited to 100 interaction-steps. If the agent is able to navigate the target object in the goal area, it receives a fixed reward of $R = 10$. The learning is handled by an ϵ-greedy Q-Learning algorithm with eligibility traces and linear function approximation [13]. To make the learned algorithm more stable, artificial noise is integrated into the system, that makes the agent execute a random action with a probability of 0.1. For performing and evaluating the learning process, the RLPy learning framework [3] is used. To adapt it to the specific needs of this work, it is extended by the presented learning domain and some additional functions.

4   Experiments

Six different coordinate systems (Fig. 2) were designed that exploit the different salient points within the learning domain (Fig. 1a). They are utilized by the agent as action sets $\mathcal{A}_i$ that define in which way the objects can be moved through the

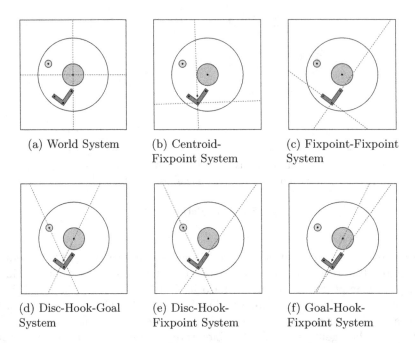

(a) World System

(b) Centroid-Fixpoint System

(c) Fixpoint-Fixpoint System

(d) Disc-Hook-Goal System

(e) Disc-Hook-Fixpoint System

(f) Goal-Hook-Fixpoint System

Fig. 2. Illustration of the different coordinate systems, representing the different action sets $\mathcal{A}_i$

environment. All coordinate systems, except Fig. 2a, are not fixed in the world but alter according to the objects positions.

The influence of each of these coordinate systems $\mathcal{A}_i$ – more precisely, its associated action set, as described in Sect. 2 – on the agent's learning performance is now compared with their ranking according to the mutual information measure $\mathcal{M}(\mathcal{S}, \mathcal{A}_i)$, introduced in (4). Estimating entropies from finite samples of probability densities can be a challenging problem and has been discussed in many works [8,10]. We here adopt the most basic approach to estimate the entropy [10]. The probability densities $\mathcal{P}^a_{ss'}$ and $\mathcal{P}^a_s$ used to compute $\mathcal{M}(\mathcal{S}, \mathcal{A}_i)$ are approximated by tessellating the agent's state space into $N = 10 \cdot 10^3$ Voronoi cells. In this space $200 \cdot 10^3$ tuples (s, a, s') were counted while the agent was performing a random walk. (1), (2) are then used to estimate the mutual information. For each coordinate system the results are averaged over 20 runs of the experiment while the standard deviation of the mean is used as the estimate of the error.

To this end, we consider three exemplary learning scenarios:

Single-Object Interaction Scenario. At the beginning of a learning episode, the positions of the mediator-object and the target-object are sampled from the uniform distribution over the simulation world inside the agent's interaction range (e.g. Fig. 1a). The agent now has to learn how to move the target-object into the goal area. After successfully solving the task instance or exceeding the limit of possible interaction-steps per episode, the task starts anew with different initial object positions that are again within the agents interaction range.

Mediated Interaction Scenario. This "extension-of-reach" scenario is structured like the first one, but the target-object is distributed *outside* the border of the agent's interaction range (e.g. Figure 1b). Now it is only possible for the agent to solve this task by learning to exploit the mediator-object as a tool to pull the target-object inside the agent's interaction range.

Mixed Interaction Scenario. The last scenario is a mixture of the **Single-Object-Interaction** and **Mediated-Interaction** task, where one of the mentioned scenarios is chosen at the beginning of each episode with equal probability.

To get a preferable general measure of the learning performance for every $\mathcal{A}_i$, each of them is utilized to learn the three presented learning scenarios. All scenarios were learned over $500 \cdot 10^3$ steps. We evaluate the learning performance for two kinds of linear function approximators, representing the sensor vector of the learning domain. The first, more efficient real valued representation is based on Gaussian radial basis functions (RBF) [4, 7]. The second is a simpler binary fixed sparse representation (FSR) [4].

For evaluating the efficiency of the learning processes, we depict the number of learning steps as a function of the average reward per episode $\langle R \rangle$ that is received by the agent. To compute $\langle R \rangle$, the learning performance under the current policy was evaluated over 100 episodes for each of the 25 evaluated data points. The results were then averaged over 20 distinct learning runs, where the standard deviation of the mean is used as the error.

As an example, Fig. 3 shows the agent's learning performance of the "Mediated Interaction Scenario" for the two used state representations. An optimal performance for solving the task is reached at $\langle R \rangle = 10$. In both plots, the learning performance is highly varying for each used coordinate system. Half of the coordinate systems achieve completely different results within the learning process for the two used state representations. Nevertheless there are 3 coordinate systems (see Fig. 2a, c and d) that lead to similar results. These coordinate systems include the two best ones and one with poor performance.

To evaluate the performance that takes all learned scenarios and state representations under consideration, the global reward $\mathcal{R}_{\text{global}}$ is defined as the sum over all $\langle R \rangle$, evaluated for the coordinate system $\mathcal{A}_i$. Table 1 now ranks the coordinate systems according to $\mathcal{R}_{\text{global}}$ and additionally lists the respective expected mutual information of all available states $\mathcal{M}(\mathcal{S}, \mathcal{A}_i)$. Although the two rankings are not exactly aligning, the coordinate system with the best and worst global reward can be clearly identified by using the mutual information. This two systems are the ones which performs best and worst in "all" evaluated scenarios. Three of the four not aligning frames are exactly the ones that behave diverse for the different kinds of scenarios and representations, as e.g. illustrated in Fig. 3. A further mentionable point is that the mutual information of similar constructed coordinate systems like Fig. 2b and c is also similar. The ranking is reliable within the facility of predicting the best action set. An efficient ranking

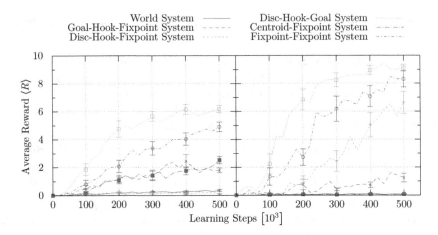

Fig. 3. Time course of the agent's average reward $\langle R \rangle$ of solving the "Mediated Interaction Scenario" using the different coordinate systems shown in Fig. 2. In the left plot, the sensor vector is represented by binary features while in the right plot the real-valued representation, based on RBFs, is used during learning.

Table 1. The ranking of the different movement frames according to R_{global}. The movement frames where the ranking of $\mathcal{M}(\mathcal{S}, \mathcal{A}_i)$ differs from the ranking of R_{global} are the ones between the "Disc-Hook-Goal System" and the "World System".

R_{global}	$\mathcal{M}(\mathcal{S}, \mathcal{A}_i)$	Coord. Systems $\mathcal{A}_i$ - Figure
1183.25 ± 36.3358	1.8147 ± 0.0020	Disc-Hook-Goal System - 2d
650.54 ± 38.2204	1.7786 ± 0.0028	Disc-Hook-Fixpoint System - 2e
547.015 ± 50.0568	1.7581 ± 0.0029	Fixpoint-Fixpoint System - 2c
471.995 ± 41.7003	1.8038 ± 0.0015	Goal-Hook-Fixpoint System - 2f
235.925 ± 23.3319	1.7645 ± 0.0032	Centroid-Fixpoint System - 2b
135.96 ± 9.23605	1.7364 ± 0.0028	World System - 2a

of the non-optimal sets might be hindered by the much larger space of solutions. It is further undermined by the strong dependence of the learning performance on the chosen set of parameters used by the learning algorithm. However, the ranking still provides some orientation for the non-optimal candidates.

5   Conclusion

In this work, we investigate the impact of action sets arising from different sensorimotor coordinate frames on the efficiency of learning mediated-interaction scenarios. Therefore the learning performance of different action sets were evaluated on solving different single-object and multi-object interaction tasks while using reinforcement learning methods. Additionally, the mutual information was computed for each action set which measures the reduction of uncertainty of the agent's next state due to the control of the used action set. After the empirical demonstration that different action sets lead to different learning performances, their performance ranking is compared with the ranking of their mutual information within the environment.

We find that the concept of mutual information, conditioned on the chosen action set, is well suited to predict the ranking of the general learning performance. Although these two rankings are not exactly aligning to each other, there are lots of similarities. In addition, the worst and the best action set can be clearly identified. Based on these findings, further investigations in this matter may lead to a better understanding of the relationship between the mutual information and the agent-environment interaction which can be used to guide the choice of actions within difficult learning scenarios.

Acknowledgments. This research/work was supported by the Cluster of Excellence Cognitive Interaction Technology 'CITEC' (EXC 277) at Bielefeld University, which is funded by the German Research Foundation (DFG).

References

1. Catto, E.: Box2d (2010). http://www.box2d.org
2. Friston, K.: The free-energy principle: a unified brain theory? Nat. Rev. Neurosci. **11**(2), 127–138 (2010)
3. Geramifard, A., Dann, C., Klein, R.H., Dabney, W., How, J.P.: Rlpy: a value-function-based reinforcement learning framework for education and research. J. Mach. Learn. Res. **16**, 1573–1578 (2015)
4. Geramifard, A., Walsh, T.J., Tellex, S., Chowdhary, G., Roy, N., How, J.P., et al.: A tutorial on linear function approximators for dynamic programming and reinforcement learning. Foundations and Trends®. Mach. Learn. **6**(4), 375–451 (2013)
5. Gottlieb, J., Oudeyer, P.Y., Lopes, M., Baranes, A.: Information-seeking, curiosity, and attention: computational and neural mechanisms **17**(11), 585–593 (2013)
6. Jones, D.S.: Elementary Information Theory. Oxford University Press, New York (1979)
7. Moody, J., Darken, C.J.: Fast learning in networks of locally-tuned processing units. Neural Comput. **1**(2), 281–294 (1989)
8. Paninski, L.: Estimation of entropy and mutual information. Neural Comput. **15**(6), 1191–1253 (2003)
9. Shannon, C.E., Weaver, W.: The mathematical theory of communication. Mathe. Gaz. **34**(310), 312 (1950)
10. Strong, S.P., Koberle, R., de Ruyter van Steveninck, R.R.: Entropy and information in neural spike trains. Phys. Rev. Lett. **80**(1), 197–200 (1998)
11. Sutton, R.S., Barto, A.G.: Introduction to Reinforcement Learning, vol. 135. MIT Press Cambridge, Cambridge (1998)
12. Tishby, N., Polani, D.: Information theory of decisions and actions. In: Cutsuridis, V., Hussain, A., Taylor, J. (eds.) Perception-Action Cycle. Cognitive and Neural Systems. Springer, New York (2010)
13. Watkins, C.J., Dayan, P.: Q-learning. Mach. Learn. **8**(3–4), 279–292 (1992)

Sensorimotor Prediction with Neural Networks on Continuous Spaces

Michaël Garcia Ortiz[(✉)]

SoftBank Robotics Europe - AI Lab, 43, rue du Colonel Pierre Avia,
75015 Paris, France
mgarciaortiz@softbankrobotics.com

Abstract. In the context of Developmental Robotics, we propose to learn how the sensations of a robot are modified by its action. Many theories of Artificial Intelligence argue that sensorimotor prediction is a fundamental building block of cognition. In this paper, we learn the sensorimotor prediction on data captured by a mobile robot equipped with distance sensors. We show that Neural Networks can learn the sensorimotor regularities and perform sensorimotor prediction on continuous sensor and motor spaces.

1   Introduction

State-of-the-art algorithms in Machine Learning, and more recently in Deep Learning [6], provide very powerful modules for perception [7] and action [15] for robotic systems. End-to-end skill learning [8] also demonstrated the feasibility of fully trainable architectures. However, these approaches rely heavily on extensive labeling of datasets [14], and expert design and fine-tuning of the learning algorithms. Applied to robotics, these approaches allow a certain level of skills in perception and action, but don't allow a robot to learn new concepts. The challenge of genuine artificial intelligence for robots remains: how can a robot learn how to perceive the world and learn to act in it by itself?

Current applications of Machine Learning for robotics are very far from how humans and animals learn. Babies, for example, don't have access to labeled information. In order to recognize objects, environments, or other persons, children build their own model of the world by interacting with it. Developmental robotic [2] proposes to take inspiration from animals and human intelligence. The goal is to identify the mechanisms that endow cognitive development, in order to allow robot to develop autonomously. We place ourselves in this context, where an agent has to learn, without prior knowledge or labels provided by the engineer, how to perceive its environment and how to act in it.

The agent senses its environment through sensors, and acts on its environment by controlling its motors. This sensorimotor loop is the only information about the world accessible to the agent. By learning how actions modify sensor values, the agent builds a model of its interaction with the world. This model can be used to predict future sensory states depending on motor commands,

© Springer International Publishing AG 2017
A. Lintas et al. (Eds.): ICANN 2017, Part I, LNCS 10613, pp. 76–83, 2017.
https://doi.org/10.1007/978-3-319-68600-4_10

in order to avoid undesirable states or reach desirable ones. Many fundamental [3,4,12] as well as practical [17] theories of intelligence and cognition argue that sensorimotor prediction is an elementary building block of cognition.

In this paper, we consider a robotic agent, endowed with distance sensors, moving in a fixed environment. We compare neural network architectures that can be used to learn sensorimotor prediction in the case of continuous sensor and motor spaces.

2 Related Works

Our approach differs from existing approaches by not using explicit vector quantization for the input and output space, which means that we perform prediction as regression and not classification. Additionally, the robot learns to control its sensorimotor space autonomously, without relying on features implemented by the designer.

In [18], the authors use a mobile robot navigating in a fixed environment. They use sensorimotor prediction as a forward model to perform prediction for an arbitrary motor program, in order to choose a sequence of actions that prevents the robot from colliding with obstacles. The speed of the robot is constant, but its direction can change. Their architecture relies on vector quantization for sensors, and context units that serve as a temporal internal representation that disambiguate situation and help the learning.

In [11], a sensorimotor prediction approach is used for navigation in the case of a simulated agent. The architecture presented uses a lot of prior knowledge: the sensorimotor prediction is based on already pre-processed features, and a predicting algorithm for each constituent of the environment. This is not compatible with a developmental approach, where the constituents of the environment are not known in advance but should be discovered.

In [10], the authors propose a computational model for sensorimotor contingencies and an algorithm for predicting future states of the sensors, in the case of a robot equipped with distance sensors, moving in a rectangular empty environment. The sensor values are quantized in 3 values, and the robot translates on 2 axis (no rotation). This work doesn't provide technical solutions to learning sensorimotor prediction in more complex (possibly continuous) spaces.

In [5], sensorimotor prediction is used as a forward model in order to control a robotic arm. The authors consider continuous sensor and motor spaces, and perform sensorimotor prediction on the configurations of the joint of the arm. Even if they showed robust online learning, the notion of multiple environmental element (such as walls and corners in our case) influencing this prediction is missing.

Even if the presented approaches are related to our work, the simplification of motor and sensor space (through vector quantization) doesn't guarantee that they can be used in more complex environments or with more complex sensors.

3   Presentation of the Approach

The agent acts in its environment through motors M_i that can be controlled by sending a motor command m_i, and it senses its environment through the sensors S_i receiving sensory signals s_i. At each timestep t, the agent sends a motor commands $m_i(t)$ and receives sensor values $s_i(t)$. The agent experiences sequences of $\{s(t), m(t)\}$, which are collected in order to learn a sensorimotor predictive model. The sensorimotor prediction is learned offline, and online incremental learning is not considered in this work. We focus on whether learning sensorimotor prediction can be achieved using standard neural networks, however, we will need to prove in future works that an incremental approach can be used, for the results to be used in a developmental robotics setting.

3.1   Prediction as a Regression Problem

Learning the sensorimotor prediction can be approached as a regression problem. The task of the regression algorithm is to learn the mapping. $(s(t), m(t) \rightarrow \Delta s(t+1))$ where $\Delta s(t+1) = s(t+1) - s(t)$. Our prediction algorithm is trained using neural network. We will propose several architectures in order to learn the sensorimotor prediction.

We predict the change in sensory values $\Delta s(t+1)$ instead of learning to predict the future value of the sensory input $s(t+1)$. Fundamentally, what interests us is to learn how motors affect sensors, so it makes sense to predict this change. On a more pragmatic level, by only predicting the change and not the raw value, we optimize the capacity of the neural network, and we avoid representing redundant information in the network. This is in line with the predictive coding approach [3,4].

Each architecture (illustrated in Fig. 1) is trained using gradient descent. For each training example, the inputs $((s(t), m(t))$ are used to formulate a prediction $\Delta s(t+1)_{pred}$ that we compare to the actual output $\Delta s(t+1)$. We compute the mean squared error as the average (over a batch of training samples) squared difference between the actual (desired) and the predicted output. We use this error signal to update the weights of the networks using gradient descent. Once the network is trained, we use it to perform prediction on a separate portion of the dataset and evaluate its prediction capabilities.

3.2   Neural Network Architectures for Sensorimotor Prediction

Feed Forward Neural Network. As a baseline for learning sensorimotor prediction, we propose to use a standard Feed-Forward Neural Network. The network takes as input a concatenation of $s(t)$ and $m(t)$. It is composed of several hidden layers of either sigmoid or rectifier linear units. The output layer is a linear layer connected to $s(t+1)$, and all the layers are fully connected.

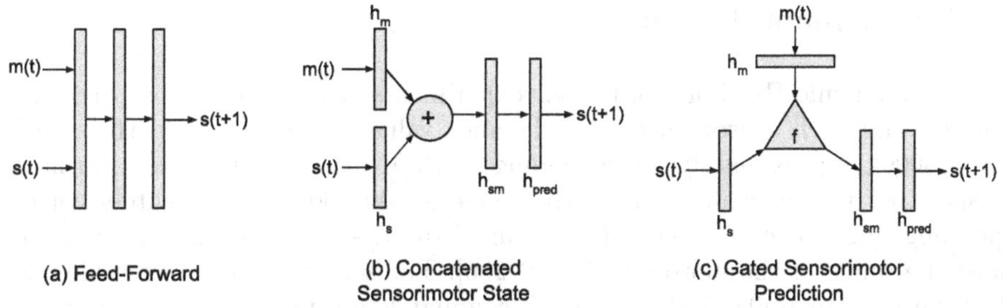

Fig. 1. Different architectures used for sensorimotor prediction

Concatenated Sensorimotor State. We want to compare the standard Feed-Forward architecture with an architecture where representations for sensors and motors are learned separately, and then concatenated to perform sensorimotor prediction. First, $s(t)$ is projected (fully connected) to a representation layer h_s, and similarly $m(t)$ is projected to a different representation layer h_m. h_s and h_m are concatenated and projected to a layer h_{sm}. This representation, supposed to represent the sensorimotor sate of the robot, is then projected to a prediction layer h_{pred}, which in turn is used to predict the output $s(t+1)$.

Gated Sensorimotor Prediction. As suggested in [16], gated interactions can be used to learn sensorimotor prediction. We take inspiration from Gated Neural Networks to propose an architecture where motors are influencing sensors through multiplicative gating interactions using factors. $s(t)$ is projected to a representation layer h_s, and $m(t)$ is projected to a representation layer h_m. h_s and h_m are then each projected on the factors f of the gating neural network. The factor activations are multiplied and fully connected to a representation layer h_{sm}, in turn projected to a prediction layer h_{pred} used to predict the output $s(t+1)$.

3.3   Long-Term Prediction

An important property of sensorimotor prediction is the capacity to predict future sensory states by simulating motor sequences. In order to predict multiple timesteps into the future, we propose to use the result of the sensorimotor prediction $\Delta s(t+1)$) at time $t+1$ to update the value of $s(t+1)$: $s(t+1) = s(t) + \Delta s(t+1)$. We can, in turn, perform sensorimotor prediction $(s(t+1), m(t+1) \rightarrow \Delta s(t+2))$.

This approach doesn't consider long-term dependencies, and we expect that it is not suitable to learn long-term predictions. However, we argue that it is sufficient to predict the immediate evolution of the sensor values depending on the motor sequence.

4   Experimental Setup

We use a Thymio-II robot [13] for our experiments. We use its 5 front distance sensors, and each sensor encodes a distance value as an integer in the range $[1500, 5000]$, approximately corresponding to $[13 \, cm, 0 \, cm]$. Motors are controlled in speed by integer commands in the range $[-500, 500]$, approximately corresponding to a range of speeds of $[-15 \, cm/s, 15 \, cm/s]$. For our experiments, we limit the range of the motors to $[-200, 200]$. The sensor values are rescaled as floats in the range $[0.0, 1.0]$ and motor commands are rescaled as floats in the range $[-1.0, 1.0]$. We control the robot using the library Aseba [9]. The frame rate is superior to $10 \, Hz$, and we interpolate the sensor readings at $5 \, Hz$. The environment of the robot is a rectangular empty maze of size 60×80 cm. Every 2 s, the robot picks randomly a new motor command (see Fig. 2(a)). We collected 40 sequences of 120 min each (around 1.4 million data points). We illustrated the sensations of the robot in Fig. 2(b).

The sensors are noisy, and the transfer function from sensor reading to actual distance is not linear. Additionally, these values depend on the reflective properties of the surface. The perception of what a wall or a corner is can't lie only in the values of the sensors, as these values change dramatically depending on their calibration, the surface, or their orientation. This highlights the pertinence of sensorimotor contingency theory [12], which states that the world imposes regularities on the way sensor values are changed by action, and that the mastering of these regularities is what constitutes perception.

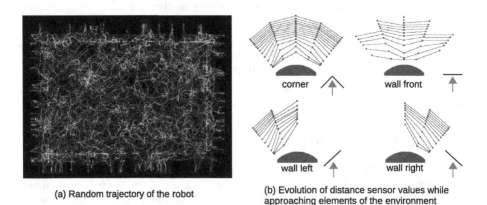

(a) Random trajectory of the robot

(b) Evolution of distance sensor values while approaching elements of the environment

Fig. 2. (a) Top-down visualization of the trajectory of the robot during one recorded sequence. (b) Sensor values of the robots captured while approaching different elements of the environment (illustrated with a black line for the environment and red arrow for the direction of the robot). Each line corresponds to a sensor reading at a certain distance from the element of the environment. The displacement of the robot between two consecutive lines is 0.5 cm. (Color figure online)

5   Experiments and Results

We use Tensorflow [1] to program our Neural Networks. We train the different architectures for 1 million iterations, with a batch size of 32 and a learning rate of 0.01, and we compute the average mean squared error of prediction over 100000 random samples from a separate dataset. For clarity, we display the MSE of the prediction multiplied by a factor 100.

Prediction Error for the Baselines. We compare different configurations of the baseline architecture presented in Sect. 3. The results are presented in Table 1. Rectifier Linear units are performing better than Sigmoid units. We suppose that it is because of the continuous nature of the mapping it tries to learn. In the following experiments, we will use Rectifier Linear Units.

Comparison of Structured Networks. We compare the two architectures that learn separate sensory and motor representations. We found that fixing the representation size of h_m to 3 is sufficient. We fixed the number of factors to 256 for the Gated sensorimotor prediction, and experimented with multiple sizes of h_s and h_{sm}. As we can see from Table 2, splitting the learning of sensors and motors doesn't improve the results. For equivalent size of the network, a standard Feed-Forward network with Rectifier Linear Units performs better than the network with separate learning of sensory representations. It might mean that the network benefits from very early sensorimotor representations.

Illustration of the Long-Term Prediction. We use an already trained model (Feed-Forward with 3 layers and 128 units per layer) to predict the future values of the sensors over multiple timesteps, depending on different motor commands. We can generate predictions of the change in the sensor space, and reconstruct future values of the sensors. The evolution of sensor values depending on the motor commands is presented in Fig. 3. One line correspond to one prediction, and we plot one prediction every 3 timestep. As can be observed, the chaining of prediction can be used to successfully predict the future values of the sensors depending on the motor commands.

Table 1. MSE for the baseline Feed-Forward neural networks

	Layer size	1 layer	2 layers	3 layers
Rectifier linear units	32	0.202	0.174	0.159
	64	0.187	0.159	0.149
	128	0.179	0.152	0.144
Sigmoid units	32	0.211	0.200	0.290
	64	0.210	0.199	0.247
	128	0.211	0.194	0.242

Table 2. MSE for the structured neural networks

		Size of h_{sm}					
		Concat. sensorimotor state			Gated sensorimotor state		
		32	64	128	32	64	128
Size of h_s	32	0.166	0.157	0.151	0.161	0.153	0.151
	64	0.164	0.156	0.150	0.158	0.154	0.149
	128	0.163	0.155	0.150	0.155	0.152	0.148

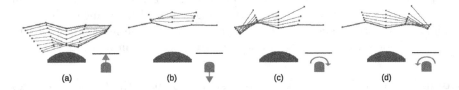

(a)   (b)   (c)   (d)

Fig. 3. Prediction across multiple timesteps, for different motor commands. The robot is facing a wall (bold line), and a trained model is used to predict the future sensory values depending on the motor commands. (a) corresponds to a movement forward, (b) to a movement backward, (c) to a rotation to the right and (d) to the left.

6   Conclusion

In this paper, we motivated the use of sensorimotor prediction in order for an autonomous robot to aquire knowledge about the regularities of interaction with its environment. We presented different neural architectures for this sensorimotor prediction, and showed that Feed-Forward Neural Networks with Rectifier Linear Units can be used to learn on continuous sensorimotor spaces. We also found that early sensorimotor representations might be beneficial to the overall learning, as learning sensor and motor separately appears to be detrimental to the overall quality of prediction. Finally, we showed that it was possible to chain the predictions in order to simulate future sensory values of the robot depending on its motor commands.

In future works, we want to investigate the use of predictive coding as a means to perform an efficient vector quantization on continuous sensory space. This predictive coding strategy will also be a way to transform our current framework into an incremental learning framework. Additionaly, we want to propose a probabilistic approach based on generative models. Another direction is to use the sensorimotor representations learned in the context of continuous sensorimotor prediction, and use them to predict discrete events, such as collisions. Another axis of development is the use of latent variables to represent the context of the robot in its environment. Finally, we want to investigate the possibility of using genetic algorithm to learn an efficient structure for sensorimotor prediction.

References

1. Abadi, M., et al.: TensorFlow: Large-scale machine learning on heterogeneous systems (2015). software available from tensorflow.org
2. Cangelosi, A., Schlesinger, M.: Developmental Robotics: From Babies to Robots. The MIT Press, Cambridge (2014)
3. Clark, A.: Whatever next? predictive brains, situated agents, and the future of cognitive science. Behav. Brain Sci. **36**(3), 181–204 (2013)
4. Friston, K.: The free-energy principle: a unified brain theory? Nat. Rev. Neurosci. **11**(2), 127–138 (2010)
5. Ghadirzadeh, A., Btepage, J., Kragic, D., Bjrkman, M.: Self-learning and adaptation in a sensorimotor framework. In: 2016 IEEE International Conference on Robotics and Automation (ICRA), pp. 551–558, May 2016
6. Goodfellow, I., Bengio, Y., Courville, A.: Deep Learning. MIT Press (2016)
7. Krizhevsky, A., Sutskever, I., Hinton, G.E.: Imagenet classification with deep convolutional neural networks. In: Pereira, F., Burges, C.J.C., Bottou, L., Weinberger, K.Q. (eds.) Advances in Neural Information Processing Systems 25, pp. 1097–1105. Curran Associates, Inc. (2012)
8. Levine, S., Finn, C., Darrell, T., Abbeel, P.: End-to-end training of deep visuomotor policies. J. Mach. Learn. Res. **17**(1), 1334–1373 (2016)
9. Magnenat, S., Rétornaz, P., Bonani, M., Longchamp, V., Mondada, F.: ASEBA: a modular architecture for event-based control of complex robots. IEEE/ASME Trans. Mechatron. **16**(2), 321–329 (2011)
10. Maye, A., Engel, A.K.: Extending sensorimotor contingency theory: prediction, planning, and action generation. Adapt. Behav. **21**(6), 423–436 (2013)
11. Möller, R., Schenck, W.: Bootstrapping cognition from behavior - a computerized thought experiment. Cogn. Sci. **32**(3), 504–542 (2008)
12. O'Regan, J., No, A.: A sensorimotor account of vision and visual consciousness. Behav. Brain Sci. **24**(05), 939–973 (2002)
13. Riedo, F., Chevalier, M.S.D., Magnenat, S., Mondada, F.: Thymio II, a robot that grows wiser with children. In: 2013 IEEE Workshop on Advanced Robotics and its Social Impacts (ARSO), pp. 187–193. IEEE (2013)
14. Russakovsky, O., Deng, J., Su, H., Krause, J., Satheesh, S., Ma, S., Huang, Z., Karpathy, A., Khosla, A., Bernstein, M., Berg, A.C., Fei-Fei, L.: ImageNet large scale visual recognition challenge. Int. J. Comput. Vision (IJCV) **115**(3), 211–252 (2015)
15. Schaal, S.: Dynamic movement primitives - a framework for motor control in humans and humanoid robotics. In: Kimura, H., Tsuchiya, K., Ishiguro, A., Witte, H. (eds.) Adaptive Motion of Animals and Machines. Springer, Tokyo (2006). doi:10.1007/4-431-31381-8_23
16. Sigaud, O., Droniou, A.: Towards deep developmental learning. IEEE Trans. Cogn. Dev. Syst. **8**(2), 99–114 (2016)
17. Sutton, R.S., Barto, A.G.: Introduction to Reinforcement Learning, 1st edn. MIT Press, Cambridge (1998)
18. Tani, J.: Model-based learning for mobile robot navigation from the dynamical systems perspective. IEEE Trans. Syst. Man Cybernetics Part B **26**(3), 421–436 (1996)

Classifying Bio-Inspired Model of Point-Light Human Motion Using Echo State Networks

Pattreeya Tanisaro[✉], Constantin Lehman, Leon Sütfeld, Gordon Pipa, and Gunther Heidemann

Institute of Cognitive Science, Osnabrück University, Osnabrück, Germany
pattanisaro@uni-osnabrueck.de

Abstract. We introduce a feature extraction scheme from a biologically inspired model using receptive fields (RFs) to point-light human motion patterns to form an action descriptor. The Echo State Network (ESN) which also has a biological plausibility is chosen for classification. We demonstrate the efficiency and robustness of applying the proposed feature extraction technique with ESN by constraining the test data based on arbitrary untrained viewpoints, in combination with unseen subjects under the following conditions: (i) lower sub-sampling frame rates to simulate data sequence loss, (ii) remove key points to simulate occlusion, and (iii) include untrained movements such as *drunkard's walk*.

Keywords: Echo state network · Motion capture · Motion recognition · Biological motion perception · Bio-inspired model

1 Introduction

Human motion recognition has a large variety of applications, for example, in safety and surveillance such as access control and congestion analysis, abnormal behavior detection [12], and in behavioral biometrics including gesture and posture recognition for human computer interaction (HCI) [11]. These applications employ different representations and recognition techniques; however, the representation and recognition methods are usually mutually reliant. As suggested in [7], the human motion representation can be categorized into two models: humanoid body model and humanoid image model. The humanoid body model uses structural representations from joint-positions of 2D or 3D points in space simulating point-light display. This point-light display can be seen as the model of a stick figure which can be used to estimate human body parts in the humanoid body model. The earliest application of using such point-light displays of motion patterns was introduced for studying biological motion recognition on human visual perception mechanisms [5]. The experiment reveals that the movement of 10–12 bright spots attached to human body parts is sufficient for humans to distinguish the actions. The point-light display of human motion has later been widely used for subsequent studies on human behavior in psychology and cognitive science because human motion also conveys information about emotions or mental states, personality traits and biological attributes [8,9,15].

© Springer International Publishing AG 2017
A. Lintas et al. (Eds.): ICANN 2017, Part I, LNCS 10613, pp. 84–91, 2017.
https://doi.org/10.1007/978-3-319-68600-4_11

Our objective in this study is to demonstrate the possibility of applying bio-logically inspired models for both feature representation and recognition of fuzzy human motion. This study was conducted using motion capture (MoCap) from the CMU MoCap database [1]. The 3D data was projected onto a 2D plane and transformed to screen coordinates simulating a 2D point-light video. Afterwards, the 2D coordinate-space of each video frame was enlarged or shrunk to fit inside a grid. This idea was inspired by human grid cells for the formation of environ-ment maps in the hippocampus. The receptive fields (RFs) resembling wavelets in the retina and primary visual cortex (V1) are generated inside the grid. With these techniques, we combined the trajectory-based approach from a kinematic structure of 2D point-lights with a pattern-based approach. The proposed feature extraction technique was tested under new angles of new subjects.

2   Temporal Pattern Classification Using an ESN

An ESN [4] is a type of RNNs of which the weights are left untrained. Only the output weights are trained for the desired target at the readout connection where no cyclic dependencies are created. The work of [10] presents an ESN as a framework for neurodynamical models of working memory. It illustrates ESN properties for storing, maintaining, retrieving and removing data that are similar to functions of the brain. A general ESN architecture is shown in Fig. 1.

Consider a discrete time neural network with input dimensionality N_u, neu-rons in the reservoir N_x, and output dimensionality N_y. Let $\boldsymbol{u}(t) \in \mathbb{R}^{N_u}$, $\boldsymbol{x}(t) \in \mathbb{R}^{N_x}$ and $\boldsymbol{y}(t) \in \mathbb{R}^{N_y}$ denote the vectors of input activities, internal state and output unit activity for time t respectively. Further, let $W_{in} \in \mathbb{R}^{N_x \times N_u}$, $W \in \mathbb{R}^{N_x \times N_x}$ and $W_{out} \in \mathbb{R}^{N_y \times N_x}$ denote the weight matrices for input connec-tions, internal connections, and output connections as seen in Fig. 1. In addition, the output might be back-coupled to the reservoir via weights $W_{fb} \in \mathbb{R}^{N_x \times N_y}$. The internal unit activities $\boldsymbol{x}$ in Fig. 1 are updated from time step $t-1$ to time t, where $t = 1, ..., T$, by

$$\boldsymbol{x}(t) = f(W_{in}\boldsymbol{u}(t) + W\boldsymbol{x}(t-1) + W_{fb}\boldsymbol{y}(t)) \tag{1}$$

$f(\cdot)$ is an activation function of the neurons, a common choice is $tanh(\cdot)$ applied element-wise. The *leaky integration rate* $\alpha \in (0, 1]$ is the leakage rate determining

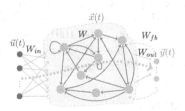

Fig. 1. Architecture of an ESN. The dashed lines denote the connections which are not compulsory.

the speed of the reservoir update dynamics. The update rule for the internal units is extended to

$$x_{leaky}(t) = (1 - \alpha)x(t - 1) + \alpha x(t). \tag{2}$$

If there are direct connections from the input $u(t)$ to the output layer, the output can be computed according to

$$y(t) = f_{out}\left(W_{out}[u(t); x(t)]\right), \tag{3}$$

where $[\cdot; \cdot]$ is a matrix concatenation and f_{out} is a nonlinear function. Accordingly, W_{out} now becomes $W_{out} \in \mathbb{R}^{N_y \times (N_x + N_u)}$. Typically, a simple linear regression is applied at the readout layer. Hence, Eq. (3) can be simplified to

$$y(t) = W_{out}[u(t); x(t)]. \tag{4}$$

The output class for testing the input sequences $u(t)$ is then computed by

$$\text{class}(u(t)) = \underset{k}{\text{argmax}} \left\{ \frac{1}{|\tau|} \sum_{t \in \tau} y_k(t) \right\} \tag{5}$$

where $y_k(t)$ is the corresponding output of class k, and τ is the length of time series of input $u(t)$.

3 Experimental Setup and Feature Representation

3.1 Dataset

Nine actions ($N_y = 9$) from the CMU MoCap database were chosen for the experiment. They were *bending* (i.e. subjects bend to pick up objects from the ground and sometimes put them over their heads), *boxing, golfing swing, jumping forward, marching, running, standing cross-crunch exercise* (written shortly as *crunching*), *standing side-twist exercise* (or *twisting*), and *walking*. The markers on MoCap were reduced to 15 representing the joints of a skeleton. Each training and test set consists of five videos of different subjects. For some actions such as *twisting* and *crunching*, there are only a few subjects, but the videos are long; therefore, we cut these long videos in order to obtain ten short videos. It is important to note that subjects in the training set are excluded from the test set. For the training set, we apply five camera angles $\{-90, -45, 0, 45, 90\}$ to each video. Three samples of these videos are shown in Fig. 2. For the test set, we use twenty-one angles in $\{-100, -90, ..., 90, 100\}$. Therefore, we have $9 \times 5 \times 5$ videos for training data, and $9 \times 5 \times 21$ videos for testing the recognition of new subjects and, from unseen camera angles.

3.2 Feature Representation

The 2D coordinates of each video frame were stretched to fit inside a 200×200 pixels grid as shown in Fig. 3(a). The grid has a fixed number of RFs producing

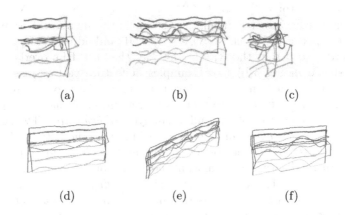

(a)   (b)   (c)

(d)   (e)   (f)

Fig. 2. Top: Three actions for 1.5 s (180 frames) at $-45°$. *Walking, running* and *marching* are shown in (a), (b) and (c), respectively. Bottom: The arbitrary views of corresponding trajectories of figures (a), (b) and (c) are extended in time-scale in a three dimensional space shown in (d), (e) and (f), accordingly.

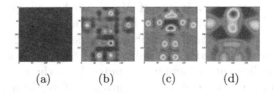

(a)   (b)   (c)   (d)

Fig. 3. Point-light figures with a diameter of 15 pixels at each joint. (a) The point-light is stretched and filled in the grid of 200×200 pixels. (b) The grid is mapped on the RFs of size $N_{RF} = 10 \times 10$ with a Marr wavelet of $\sigma = 10$. (c) $N_{RF} = 20 \times 20$, $\sigma = 10$ and (d) $N_{RF} = 10 \times 10$, $\sigma = 20$, where there are overlappings of the RFs in the setting. This setting is based on a preferred bio-inspired model.

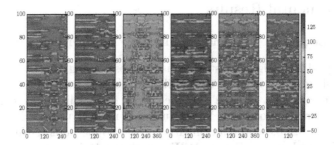

Fig. 4. The feature vectors $u(t)$ of six videos of different classes at $0°$ are shown from left to right: *golfing, bending, crunching, walking, marching* and *running*. The x-axis indicates the varying frame numbers of the video, whereas the y-axis has the fixed number of RFs.

an input feature vector $\boldsymbol{u}(t) \in \mathbb{R}^{N_{RF} \times N_F}$, where $N_{RF} = N_{RF_x} \times N_{RF_y}$ is the total number of RFs in a rectangular grid. N_F is the number of frames in a video. In our experiment, we chose $N_{RF} = 10 \times 10$ and adjusted the σ of Marr wavelet in order to design the RFs in the way that the RFs overlapped one another as shown in Fig. 3(b)–(d). Examples of feature vectors of six videos representing different actions are displayed in Fig. 4. The two leftmost figures are the *golfing* and *bending*, where there is no repetition of the action pattern. Next to them is the pattern of one and a half cycle of *crunching*. The last three images are *walking*, *marching* and *running* showing periodic patterns for about 2–3 cycles. The first 100 frames of the *golfing* and *bending* videos reveal very smooth patterns, indicating no significant movement of the agents in these two videos. This is typical for some actions such as *golfing*, *bending* and *jumping forward*. By contrast, actions such as *running*, *marching* and *walking* exhibit a very short onset of action and can complete one cycle in a very short time. In comparison, *running* is the shortest video with about 140 frames, while the other actions have an average in the range of 160–550 frames.

3.3   ESN Configurations

We set up a moderate reservoir size of $N_x = 500$ having sparsely connected neurons with 10% connectivity similar to [13]. The weight matrices, W and W_{in}, are random values uniformly distributed in the range $[-1, 1]$. The spectral radius $\rho(W)$ can be considered as the scaling factor of the weight matrix W. The desired spectral radius can be simply computed from the ratio of the desired value and the maximum of the absolute eigenvalues of weight matrix. For a long short-term memory network, [3] shows that the peak performance in the setup has the spectral radius set to one. The only parameter that would be varied in our experiment is the leaky rate (α), which can be regarded as a time warping of the input signal. All results in our experiment use the average of 4 runs of a randomly initialized ESN networks with the same configuration.

4   Experimental Results

4.1   Data Sequence Loss and Redundancy as Variations in Speed

We subsampled the original test data using subsampling factors of 1, 2, 4, 6, 8, and 10, whereas the training data still remained the same. The subsampling factor of 2 means that every 2nd frame of the data will be taken instead of each single frame (factor of 1). We evaluated our result using ESN with three leaky rates $\alpha = 0.1, 0.5$ and 0.9 comparing with two methods, 1-Nearest Neighbor (**1-NN**) and Random Forest (**RdF**) which use 15 joint-positions in videos obtained directly from MoCap **without RFs**. We used both a naive approach and a dimensionality reduction method to extract feature vectors for these two classifiers. The feature vectors for the naive approach are obtained by simply stacking all video frames on top of each other for training the classifiers. The voting majority of the frames in a target video is counted for the classification. For the dimensionality reduction method, the feature vectors are acquired from PCA employing three principal components in combination with 1-NN and RdF. Figure 5-Left shows the results of recognition rate using test data from twenty-one untrained angles with respect to data sequence loss by using a training factor of 1. Figure 5-Right shows the result of recognition rate using a training factor of 5 as a testing for data redundancy. Both figures reveal that the ESN with $\alpha = 0.9$ gives the best performance with robustness against data sequence loss and redundancy yielding a recognition rate of 95% even with large training and test subsampling factors. The good performance of ESN using $\alpha = 0.9$ which can handle the variations in speed might be explained by the behavior of a long short-term memory in ESN which is demonstrated in [3]. Classifying data in space using 1-NN as the naive approach also gains a stable outcome of about 80%. In contrast, classifying data in subspaces using PCA is sensitive to data sequence loss and only gains good outcomes when the frequencies of training and test data sequences are about the same.

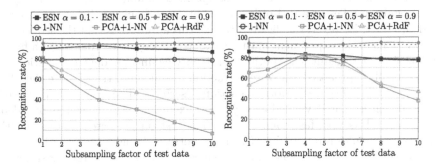

Fig. 5. Recognition rates from various classification approaches shown in y-axis. Subsampling factors of test data shown in x-axis. Left: Training factor of 1. Right: Training factor of 5.

4.2 Removing Key Points and Drunkard's Walks

We furthered the experiment by removing key points from the test data simulating occlusion from all frames in videos. Removing a *wrist* from a skeleton does not affect the recognition rate, while removing an *ankle* from a skeleton makes *running*, *crunching* and *walking* all mistaken as *marching*, which results in a recognition rate drop to 61%. Furthermore, we extended the test by having three new persons performing four trials simulating *drunkard's walk* from twenty-two untrained angles producing 92 test samples for *walking*, while the other actions remain the same. Two samples of *drunkard's walk* are shown in Fig. 6-Left. The confusion matrix in Fig. 6-Right reveals that *walking* is misclassified as *marching* for 20.7%. The closed trajectories of these two actions can be inspected from Fig. 2(c) and Fig. 6-Left.

	bend	box	golf	jump	march	run	crunch	twist	walk
bend	100	0	0	0	0	0	0	0	0
box	0	97.3	0	0	0	0	0.9	1.8	0
golf	0	0	100	0	0	0	0	0	0
jump	17.1	0	4.8	78.1	0	0	0	0	0
march	0	0	0	0	100	0	0	0	0
run	0	0	0	0	0	100	0	0	0
crunch	0	0	0	0	0	0	100	0	0
twist	0	0	0	0	0	0	1.9	98.1	0
walk	0	0	0	2.2	20.7	4.3	0	0	72.8

Fig. 6. Left: Two subjects perform *drunkard's walking*. Right: Confusion matrix of test samples by substituting *drunkard's walk* for *walk*.

4.3   Discussion of Related Work

One of the earliest promising methods for view-independent recognition of 3D MoCap was introduced by [6]. It applied a non-threshold recurrent plot by computing a similarity matrix of each joint as a sum of squared differences. The benefit of using this method is that the descriptors are stable across view changes. The recognition relies on a Bag-of-Features obtaining from the Histogram of Oriented Gradient. However, the disadvantage of this approach is that the sequences of all motions in the experiment must have an equal length in order to get a fixed window size for recognition. Another study on view-independent recognition of Mocap is [14]. It proposed a feature extraction technique to transform either 2D or 3D data into subspaces to form an action descriptor. The major advantage of this approach is that it yielded a very small fixed data size regardless of video length, as well as very fast computation. The test on projected motion in 2D achieves a recognition rate of 96.5% from 21 untrained angles for 10 actions and it is also very stable for the case of data sequence loss. Other interesting skeleton based action recognition approaches for 3D MoCap are for instance, [2,16]. They proposed and compared several deep recurrent neural network architectures with Long Short-Term Memory (LSTM) for classification. The tests were carried out using 65 classes of HDM05 MoCap yielding up to 96.92% and 97.25% recognition rate respectively. Nonetheless, the tests were only performed for one default view.

5   Conclusion

We have introduced a feature extraction scheme from a biologically inspired model by applying the concept of receptive field to point light patterns of human motion. Our proposed scheme in combination with ESN which presents itself as a good approximator, yields a good performance and robustness against variations of speed even when the trajectories of motions are fuzzy. This representation could be deployed for human motion classification based on optical flow obtained from standard videos, where the human pose estimation is infeasible. The designed ESN is generic in the sense that it is not specialized to human motion. It also shows a good prediction of the unseen data. Hence, application to other domains of articulated objects in motion is possible. Furthermore, new technologies such as the IBM TrueNorth chip have introduced a dedicated neuro-inspired hardware that allows modeling hundreds of thousands up to a million of neurons with very low energy. The ESNs, which offer very simple learning mechanisms, can be optimized by local learning rules that scale well even with very large systems. Therefore, ESN is a potential candidate for low energy systems that can be an integral part of sensor technology for the future.

References

1. CMU Graphics Lab: CMU Motion Capture Database. http://mocap.cs.cmu.edu/
2. Du, Y., Wang, W., Wang, L.: Hierarchical recurrent neural network for skeleton based action recognition. In: The IEEE Conference on Computer Vision and Pattern Recognition (CVPR), June 2015
3. Jaeger, H.: Long Short-Term Memory in Echo State Networks: Details of a Simulation Study. Technical Report, Jacobs University, Bremen, Germany, February 2012
4. Jaeger, H., Haas, H.: Harnessing nonlinearity: predicting chaotic systems and saving energy in wireless telecommunication. Science **304**(5667), 78–80 (2004)
5. Johansson, G.: Visual perception of biological motion and a model for its analysis. Percept. Psychophys. **14**(2), 201–211 (1973)
6. Junejo, I.N., Dexter, E., Laptev, I., Perez, P.: View-independent action recognition from temporal self-similarities. IEEE Trans. Pattern Anal. Mach. Intell. **33**(1), 172–185 (2011)
7. Kale, G.V., Patil, V.H.: A study of vision based human motion recognition and analysis. IJACI **7**(2), 75–92 (2016)
8. Livne, M., Sigal, L., Troje, N.F., Fleet, D.J.: Human attributes from 3D pose tracking. Comput. Vision Image Underst. (CVIU) (2012)
9. Miller, L.E., Saygin, A.P.: Individual differences in the perception of biological motion: Links to social cognition and motor imagery. Cognition **128**(2), 140–148 (2013)
10. Pascanu, R., Jaeger, H.: A neurodynamical model for working memory. Neural Netw. **24**(2), 199–207 (2011)
11. Rautaray, S.S., Agrawal, A.: Vision based hand gesture recognition for human computer interaction: a survey. Artif. Intell. Rev. **43**(1), 71 (2015)
12. Tanisaro, P., Schöning, J., Kurzhals, K., Heidemann, G., Weiskopf, D.: Visual analytics for video applications. Inf. Technol. **57**, 30–36 (2015)
13. Tanisaro, P., Heidemann, G.: Time series classification using time warping invariant echo state networks. In: 15th IEEE International Conference on Machine Learning and Applications (ICMLA) (2016)
14. Tanisaro, P., Mahner, F., Heidemann, G.: Quasi view-independent human motion recognition in subspaces. In: Proceedings of 9th International Conference on Machine Learning and Computing (ICMLC) (2017)
15. Troje, N.F., Sadr, J., Geyer, H., Nakayama, K.: Adaptation aftereffects in the perception of gender from biological motion. J. Vision **6**(8), 7 (2006)
16. Zhu, W., Lan, C., Xing, J., Zeng, W., Li, Y., Shen, L., Xie, X.: Co-occurrence feature learning for skeleton based action recognition using regularized deep lstm networks. In: Proceedings of the Thirtieth AAAI Conference on Artificial Intelligence, pp. 3697–3703 (2016)

A Prediction and Learning Based Approach to Network Selection in Dynamic Environments

Xiaohong Li[1], Ru Cao[1], Jianye Hao[2(⊠)], and Zhiyong Feng[2]

[1] School of Computer Science and Technology, Tianjin University, Tianjin, China
[2] School of Software, Tianjin University, Tianjin, China
jianye.hao@tju.edu.cn

Abstract. The heterogeneous property in the next generation wireless network arises challenges of network selection problem. Existing approaches are mainly implemented in static network environments while cannot handle unpredictable dynamics in practice. In this paper, we propose a prediction and learning based approach, which considers both the fluctuation of radio resource and the variation of user demand. The network selection scenario is modeled as a multiagent coordination problem, in which a population of rational agents compete to maximize their benefits with incomplete information (no prior knowledge of network bandwidth and other users' demands). Terminal users adaptively adjust their selections in response to the gradually or abruptly changing environment. The system is shown to converge to Nash equilibrium, which also turns out to be both Pareto optimal and socially optimal. Extensive simulation results show that our approach achieves significantly better performance compared with two existing approaches in terms of load balancing, user payoff and the overall bandwidth utilization efficiency.

1 Introduction

The next generation wireless network is envisioned as a heterogeneous network (HetNet) environment consisting of a variety of overlapping radio networks (e.g., WPAN, WLAN, WMAN) with various technologies [3]. Within the HetNet environment, there is an overwhelming growth in the number of terminal users and their varying bandwidth demands, meanwhile, network resource is limited and may change dynamically due to the interferences from intrinsic or extrinsic factors (noises, channel interferences, natural disturbances, etc.). How to achieve a good balance between increasing user demand and dynamically changing radio resource in multi-user, multi-provider HetNet environments is challenging.

To tackle this challenge, effective techniques are required to help select the most appropriate network from all available candidates to satisfy specific requirements. Commercial solutions usually involve rudimentary static network selection policies (e.g., always select the WLAN, always select the cheapest or the fastest network) [11]. However, varying network characteristics and user preferences are omitted, which may often result in lower quality of service (QoS). Many traditional methods in research literatures use multi-attribute decision making algorithms (e.g., SAW, TOPSIS, ELECTRE, AHP&GRA) to evaluate and rank

© Springer International Publishing AG 2017
A. Lintas et al. (Eds.): ICANN 2017, Part I, LNCS 10613, pp. 92–100, 2017.
https://doi.org/10.1007/978-3-319-68600-4_12

candidate networks in a preference order to guide the selection process [7]. This may cause congestion when all users connect the so-called "best" network. Learning based methods are promising candidate solutions to model the network selection problem. A channel selection and Routing approach is proposed in [1] which models the problem as Markov decision process to design the method of learning the best resource allocation policies. Q-learning is used in [12] to maximize the total reward in network selection decision. Reinforcement learning model is used in [6] to find the best strategy to maximise the reward function expressed in terms of call blocking and call dropping probabilities. Unfortunately, the above works suffer from the following two limitations: (1) requiring too much state information (the number of users, future bandwidth, etc.) as a prior, which is costly or impractical; (2) only focusing on the static resource without considering changing characteristics in practical environments.

To address the above problems, we model the network selection process as a multiagent coordination problem, in which a population of rational terminal users compete to select the "best" access networks to satisfy their varying demands with incomplete information (no prior knowledge of changing bandwidth and other users' demands) within a dynamic HetNet environment. Our approach is user-centric but does not require any central controller or additional communications between users. The only information available to users is the previous load and provided bandwidth of their connected networks. In addition, our approach is robust against failures of users: when they occasionally join or leave, the system can self-organize quickly and adapt to a newly created environment.

Simulation results show that the system guarantees convergence towards Nash equilibrium, which is also proved to be Pareto optimal and socially optimal. Extensive results demonstrate that our algorithm enables users to adaptively adjust their selections in response to the change of bandwidth, and it significantly outperforms either the learning or non-learning based approach in terms of load balance, user payoff and the overall bandwidth utilization efficiency.

2   Network Selection Problem Definition

In HetNet environments, radio resource may loss or be disturbed in transmission process by various factors (network topology, routers, base stations, noises, channel interferences, etc.) which greatly impact network performances [4,10]. Therefore, the available bandwidth of each base station allocated from its core network dynamically changes and is less than the nominal value due to many influence factors. In such dynamic environments, we assume that each user can only have access to the state information of the base station it connected from completed interactions and is lack of prior knowledge of any other networks or terminal users. The cooperation between the user and its connected base station is helpful and does not infringe upon any other's interest.

2.1 Multiagent Network Selection Model

In practice, each user makes independent decisions based on its local information only. However, actions taken by users influence the actions of others indirectly. Therefore, we model the problem as a multiagent coordination problem, in which a population of rational users located in the same or different service areas with no information about others learn to compete to maximize their payoffs given that available bandwidth varies dynamically. Formally, the multiagent network selection is modeled as a 6-tuple $<BS, B_k(t), U, b_i(t), A_i, P_i(t, \mathbf{a})>$, where:

- $BS = \{1, 2, ..., m\}$ is the set of available base stations (BS).
- $B_k(t)$ denotes the provided bandwidth of BS $k \in BS$ at time t.
- $U = \{1, 2, ..., n\}$ is the set of terminal users.
- $b_i(t)$ denotes the bandwidth demand of user $i \in U$ at time t.
- $A_i \subseteq BS$ is the finite set of actions available to user $i \in U$, and $a_i \in A_i$ denotes the action (i.e., selected base station) taken by user i.
- $P_i(t, \mathbf{a})$ denotes the expected payoff of user $i \in U$ by performing the strategy profile $\mathbf{a} = \{a_1, ..., a_i, ...a_n\} \in \times_{j \in U} A_j$ at time t.

There are n users competing for m base stations in the system. The detail definition of payoff based on the joint strategy profile $\mathbf{a}$ can be expressed as,

$$P_i(t, \mathbf{a}) = \frac{w_i(t, \mathbf{a})}{b_i(t)}, \quad w_i(t, \mathbf{a}) = \begin{cases} b_i(t), & \sum_j b_j(t) \leq B_{a_i}(t) \\ \frac{B_{a_i}(t) \cdot b_i(t)}{\sum_j b_j(t)}, & otherwise \end{cases} \tag{1}$$

where $w_i(t, \mathbf{a})$ is the perceived bandwidth (a theoretical value without considering the transmission loss) of user i at time t, and $j \in \{j \in U | a_j = a_i, a_j, a_i \in \mathbf{a}\}$ is the user who connect the same base station with user i.

2.2 Theoretical Analysis

Nash equilibrium (NE) is the most commonly adopted solution concept in game theory. Under a NE, no player can benefit by unilaterally deviating from its current strategy [11]. Underlying the multiagent network selection problem, a NE is reached when there is no overload on any base station (this situation is shown in later experiments). Under this condition, users' perceived bandwidth equals to their demands and all users' payoffs reach maximum. Therefore, no one is willing to change its strategy given that others' strategies are unchanged.

Definition 1. $\mathbf{a}^* \in \times_{i \in U} A_i$ is a Nash equilibrium if for all $k \in BS, \sum_j b_j(t) \leq B_k(t)$, where $j \in \{j \in U | a_j = k, a_j \in \mathbf{a}^*\}$.

However, a NE may not be desirable in general since it may not necessarily correspond to the maximization of the system-level payoff. Fortunately, any NE in our model is also Pareto optimal and socially optimal [11]. The two properties guarantee both the system's stability and system-level optimization.

Theorem 1. *Nash equilibrium, Pareto optimality and Social optimality are equivalent in the multiagent network selection problem.*

Proof. It can be deduced that if profile $\mathbf{a}^*$ is a NE, each user's payoff reaches maximum and cannot be further increased. Therefore, it's impossible to find another outcome under which no user's payoff is decreased while at least one user's payoff is strictly increased. This proves that $\mathbf{a}^*$ is Pareto optimal. In addition, $P_i(t, \mathbf{a}^*) = \max P_i(t, \mathbf{a}) \Rightarrow \sum_i P_i(t, \mathbf{a}^*) = \max \sum_i P_i(t, \mathbf{a}), \forall \mathbf{a} \in \times_{j \in U} A_j$. The sum of all users' payoffs reaching maximum means $\mathbf{a}^*$ is also socially optimal.

3   Multiagent Network Selection Strategy

A user's network selection strategy consists of two steps: selection and evaluation. In selection procedure, the user learns to choose the best candidate network to satisfy its special demand. Once the selection procedure is completed, evaluation procedure will be triggered to update its strategy.

3.1   Selection

Algorithm 1 summarizes the selection procedure for user $i \in U$. For each available base station $k \in BS$, the user checks whether it can satisfy its special demand (Lines 1–11). If the user sends a connection request to a base station with no historic information, which is the standard case at the beginning of the life-cycle, this unpredictable base station will be added in a spare list for a later decision. Otherwise, the user predicts the possible bandwidth and load on the base station. If the predicted load plus the demand is below the predicted bandwidth, this base station is added to the list of candidates (Lines 7–9). Then the user evaluates if any candidate base station is expected. There might be three cases. In the case where the list of candidate base stations predicted having adequate bandwidth available is not empty (Line 12), the "best network selection" is determined by the following policy: the base station with most expected free bandwidth is chosen as the most appropriate connection currently. In particular, in the case there is no available candidate, the user will randomly explore one from all unpredictable base stations and gather its state information (Line 17). There might be an exceptional case that no base station is generated from the algorithm (Line 19). In this case, the original base station is used and $flag$ is set into -1.

Each user maintains a historic information table $table_k = (h_0, ..., h_p), (0 \leq p < m)$ for each connected base station k. The table is composed of up to m items $h_j = (t_j, load_j, bw_j)$, comprising observed time t_j, load $load_j$ and bandwidth bw_j. The oldest item will be overwritten if already m items are recorded. Load prediction mechanism employs time series forecasting techniques to predict future load value based on records of this table. It involves three major steps:

- Create predictor set. Each user keeps a set of r predictors $P(A, k) = \{p_i | 1 \leq i \leq r\}$, which is created from some predefined set in evaluation procedure (following case 1), for each available base station k. Each predictor is a predictive function from a time series of historic loads to a predictive load value.
- Select active predictor. One predictor $p^A \in P$ is called active predictor, which is chosen in evaluation procedure (following case 2, 3), used in load prediction.
- Make prediction. Predict the possible load of the base station via the active predictor and the historic load records.

A similar prediction mechanism can also be adopted to bandwidth prediction.

3.2   Evaluation

Evaluation procedure introduced in Algorithm 2 is divided into three cases based on the selected base station.

Algorithm 1. Selection

```
 1: for all k ∈ BS do
 2:    if table_k = ∅ then
 3:       push k in unpredList
 4:    else
 5:       predLoad ←LoadPredict(p^A)
 6:       predBW ←BWPredict()
 7:       if predLoad + b_i ≤ predBW then
 8:          push k in candList
 9:       end if
10:    end if
11: end for
12: if candList ≠ ∅ then
13:    for all cand ∈ candList do
14:       availBW = predBW − predLoad
15:    end for
16:    seleBS ← argmax_{k∈BS}(availBW)
17: else if unpredList ≠ ∅ then
18:    seleBS ←random(unpredList)
19: else
20:    seleBS ← lastBS // stay at last BS
21:    flag = −1
22: end if
```

Algorithm 2. Evaluation

```
 1: if predictorSet = ∅ then
 2:    create predictorSet for seleBS
 3:    p^A ←random(predictordSet)
 4:    update(table_{seleBS})
 5: else if flag = −1 then
 6:    for all k ∈ BS do
 7:       delete h ∈ table_{seleBS} with a probability
 8:    end for
 9: else
10:    for all p ∈ predictorSet do
11:       predLoad ←LoadPredict(p)
12:       r_p = 1 − (|load−predload|)/load
13:       Q_p = (1 − α)Q_p + αr_p
14:    end for
15:    p^A ←BoltzmanExploration(predictordSet)
16:    //abruptly changing case
17:    if |B_{seleBS} − predBW| > Δ then
18:       clear(table_{seleBS})
19:    end if
20:    update(table_{seleBS})
21: end if
```

Case 1. If the selected base station is visited for the first time (Line 1), the user will create a new predictor set for this base station and record its load and bandwidth information into the corresponding record table. All predictors in the set are chosen randomly from a predefined set, hence users' predictor sets may be different from each other. The predefined set contains multiple types of forecasting functions which differ in window sizes (e.g., average method, linear regression, exponential smoothing, etc.) [2]. Different types of predictors are suitable for different situations and environments.

Case 2. If $flag = −1$, it implies that currently historical records recommended no appropriate base station (Line 5). In the case, some old records need to be removed from the table according to a probability distribution relative to their lifetime to get more up-to-date information for further predictions.

Case 3. The general situation is that the user switched to a previously visited base station. The evaluation mainly involves two aspects: assessing the performance of all predictors (Line 10) and dealing with the case of abruptly changing bandwidth (Line 17). The assessment of predictors is resorted to Q-learning. Specifically, Q-function in our approach is defined as the following equation,

$$Q_p(t) = (1 - \alpha)Q_p(t - 1) + \alpha r_p(t - 1), \qquad r_p = 1 - \frac{|load - predload|}{load}$$

where $p \in predictorSet$ denotes the predictor, $Q_p(t)$ is the Q-value of p, α is the learning rate, and r_p is the observed reward which denotes the predictive accuracy of p. The predictor which forecasted a more exact value receives a higher reward, else receives a lower reward.

In our approach, Boltzmann exploration mechanism [5] is adapted to explore the active predictor. The probability x_p of selecting predictor p is given by $x_p(t) = \frac{e^{Q_p(t)/T}}{\sum_k e^{Q_k(t)/T}}$, where the *temperature* $T > 0$ balances the tradeoff between exploration and exploitation.

The above process works well in the environment with static or gradually changing bandwidth. However, it is slightly different in abruptly changing case. When detecting that the difference between the observed bandwidth and predicted value of the base station in the last selection is larger than a threshold Δ, the user will consider it encounters abruptly changing environments (Line 17). At catastrophe points, all historic records are invalid and may mislead to inaccurate predictions in future. In order to eliminate the adverse influence and achieve rapid re-convergence, the record table should be cleared out. Then the latest information is added as the only valid record for a later prediction.

4   Performance Evaluation

Parameter settings of our simulated scenario are given in Table 1. We consider a variety of HetNet environments consisting of up to 900 users. On BS_0 and BS_1, the provided bandwidth changes gradually and abruptly. On BS_2, the provided bandwidth keeps static. All experimental results are averaged over 50 independent runs. We make comparisons with two existing multi-user network selection algorithms [8,9] in following aspects.

Table 1. Parameter settings

Access tech	Network rep	Base station	Max bandwidth	User demand
WLAN	Wi-Fi	BS_0	25 Mbps	32 kbps–128 kbps
WMAN	WiMAX	BS_1	50 Mbps	
CDMA Cellular Network	4G	BS_2	5 Mbps	

Load Balancing Analysis. Figure 1 depicts the load situations on the three base stations in static and dynamic environments. We observe that under our prediction and learning based algorithm (PLA), initially, all users randomly selecting their base stations results in high levels of overload or underload on different base stations. However after a few learning interactions, network bandwidth becomes well-utilized without being overloaded. Meanwhile, the load (i.e., total bandwidth demand) on each base station dynamically changes with the amount of provided bandwidth. This implies that the system converges to NE and achieves load balance among the three base stations. It is worth to note that the jitter on BS_2 is because users are trying to join or leave this base station in response to the abrupt changes on the other two base stations.

RAT selection algorithm (RATSA) [8] is similar to the best response, where the user always selects the network with maximum expected bandwidth allocated. Future provided bandwidth, user number on a base station and the number of past consecutive migrations are required as prior knowledge. A user switches its base station only if the value of allocated bandwidth from another base station divided by currently perceive bandwidth is higher than a given threshold η. For fair comparisons, we set $\eta = 1.5$ which gives RATSA the best performance. The comparative figure shows an unbalancing phenomena that too much unmet demand on BS_0 and BS_2, but too little utilization on BS_1 over some time. This indicates that users cannot sense the dynamic environment and adjust their strategies timely. We also simulate the network selection scenario using another Q-learning based approach (QLA) [9]. In QLA, it can be observed that users are trying to adapt to the changing environment. However, it takes a long time to get close to the varying bandwidth and cannot achieve complete load balance.

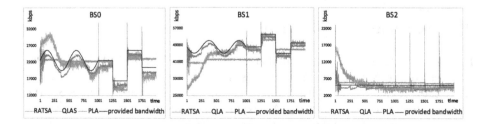

Fig. 1. Load situations on three base stations.

Convergence. In our approach, the system takes a learning phase to achieve convergence, i.e., when there is no overload on any base station (can be observed in Fig. 1), the system converges to Nash equilibrium, which is also Pareto optimal and socially optimal (Definition 1, Theorem 1). In gradually changing case, once it converges to equilibrium, the state sustains over time. We call it first-convergence and the average first-convergence time exponentially increases with the user number from 860 to 900. Specially, in abruptly changing case, when

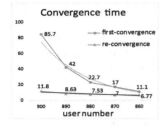

Fig. 2. Convergence time

Alg.	BW Utilization	Switching Rate	User Payoff
PLA	0.947379	0.007388	0.998231
RATSA	0.897151	0.000509	0.954789
QLA	0.902609	0.200071	0.957789

Fig. 3. Comparisons of average performances

encountering catastrophe points, the equilibrium is broken but re-converges in a number of steps. The average re-convergence time linearly varies with the number of users (see Fig. 2).

User Payoff, Switching Rate and Bandwidth Utilization. Comparison results of the three approaches in terms of average user payoff, switching rate and bandwidth utilization are presented in Fig. 3. We observe that over 2000 interactions, PLA outperforms RATSA in average user payoff and bandwidth utilization. The average switching rate of PLA is slightly higher because users are trying to switch their connections to respond to the dynamics to get higher payoffs in the initial phase and at catastrophe points. As for QLA, although we can sense it is trying hard to adapt to the dynamic environments, it gives bad performance of any of the three criteria compared to PLA.

5 Conclusions

In this paper, a prediction and learning based approach is presented to tackle the network selection problem with changing bandwidth in HetNet environments. The performance of the approach is investigated under various conditions and aspects. Extensive experimentations show that the system ideally converges to Nash equilibrium, which also turns out to be both Pareto optimal and socially optimal. Furthermore, our approach significantly outperforms state-of-the-art approaches in terms of load balance, user payoff and bandwidth utilization.

Acknowledgements. This work has partially been sponsored by the National Science Foundation of China (No. 61572349, No. 61272106), Tianjin Research Program of Application Foundation and Advanced Technology (No.:16JCQNJC00100).

References

1. Barve, S.S., Kulkarni, P.: Dynamic channel selection and routing through reinforcement learning in cognitive radio networks. In: IEEE International Conference on Computational Intelligence & Computing Research, pp. 1–7 (2012)
2. Brockwell, P.J., Davis, R.A.: Introduction to Time Series and Forecasting. STS. Springer, Cham (2016). doi:10.1007/b97391

3. Charilas, D.E., Panagopoulous, A.D.: Multiaccess radio network enviroments. IEEE Veh. Technol. Mag. **5**(4), 40–49 (2010)
4. Jain, K., Padhye, J., Padmanabhan, V.N., Qiu, L.: Impact of interference on multi-hop wireless network performance. Wireless Netw. **11**(4), 471–487 (2005)
5. Kianercy, A., Galstyan, A.: Dynamics of Boltzmann q learning in two-player two-action games. Phys. Rev. E **85**(4), 041145 (2012)
6. Kittiwaytang, K., Chanloha, P., Aswakul, C.: CTM-based reinforcement learning strategy for optimal heterogeneous wireless network selection. In: Computational Intelligence, Modelling and Simulation (CIMSiM), pp. 73–78. IEEE (2010)
7. Martinez-Morales, J.D., Pineda-Rico, U., Stevens-Navarro, E.: Performance comparison between madm algorithms for vertical handoff in 4G networks. In: Electrical Engineering Computing Science and Automatic Control (CCE), pp. 309–314. IEEE (2010)
8. Monsef, E., Keshavarz-Haddad, A., Aryafar, E., Saniie, J., Chiang, M.: Convergence properties of general network selection games. In: 2015 IEEE Conference on Computer Communications (INFOCOM), pp. 1445–1453. IEEE (2015)
9. Niyato, D., Hossain, E.: Dynamics of network selection in heterogeneous wireless networks: an evolutionary game approach. IEEE Trans. Veh. Technol. **58**(4), 2008–2017 (2009)
10. Perkins, D.D., Hughes, H.D., Owen, C.B.: Factors affecting the performance of ad hoc networks. In: IEEE International Conference on Communications, vol. 4, pp. 2048–2052 (2002)
11. Trestian, R., Ormond, O., Muntean, G.M.: Game theory-based network selection: solutions and challenges. IEEE Commun. Surv. Tutor. **14**(4), 1212–1231 (2012)
12. Xu, Y., Chen, J., Ma, L., Lang, G.: Q-learning based network selection for WCDMA/WLAN heterogeneous wireless networks. In: 2014 IEEE 79th Vehicular Technology Conference (VTC Spring), pp. 1–5. IEEE (2014)

Learning a Peripersonal Space Representation as a Visuo-Tactile Prediction Task

Zdenek Straka[1]([⊠]) and Matej Hoffmann[1,2]

[1] Department of Cybernetics, Faculty of Electrical Engineering, Czech Technical
University in Prague, Prague, Czech Republic
{straka.zdenek,matej.hoffmann}@fel.cvut.cz
[2] iCub Facility, Istituto Italiano di Tecnologia, Genoa, Italy

Abstract. The space immediately surrounding our body, or peripersonal
space, is crucial for interaction with the environment. In primate brains,
specific neural circuitry is responsible for its encoding. An important
component is a safety margin around the body that draws on visuo-tactile
interactions: approaching stimuli are registered by vision and processed,
producing anticipation or prediction of contact in the tactile modality. The
mechanisms of this representation and its development are not understood.
We propose a computational model that addresses this: a neural network
composed of a Restricted Boltzmann Machine and a feedforward neural
network. The former learns in an unsupervised manner to represent position and velocity features of the stimulus. The latter is trained in a supervised way to predict the position of touch (contact). Unique to this model,
it considers: (i) stimulus position and velocity, (ii) uncertainty of all variables, and (iii) not only multisensory integration but also prediction.

Keywords: Peripersonal space · Touch · RBM · Probabilistic population code · Visuo-tactile integration

1 Introduction

For survival, animals and humans have to be "aware" of their bodies and space
around them. This space is called peripersonal space (PPS) and is especially
important for safe interaction of an agent with the environment. PPS is the
space that extends the surface of the body. In the primate brain, there is neural
circuitry specialized on PPS representation, in particular bimodal neurons with
visuo-tactile receptive fields (e.g., [3]; [1] for a review) firing when some part
of the skin is stimulated or a visual stimulus is presented nearby. The PPS is
seemingly extended when a stimulus moves faster (e.g., [3]) and the direction of
the moving object (looming vs. receding) is also important for responses of the
PPS network [10]. Thus, position and velocity of the stimulus have to be considered. Moreover, there is evidence that the brain is able to combine different
sensory information in a statistically optimal manner ([2]; [5] for a computational
model), for which the brain must also encode uncertainty of sensory information.
The two modalities—visual and tactile—are presumably interacting in several

© Springer International Publishing AG 2017
A. Lintas et al. (Eds.): ICANN 2017, Part I, LNCS 10613, pp. 101–109, 2017.
https://doi.org/10.1007/978-3-319-68600-4_13

ways: (i) the correlations induced when the stimulus contacts the skin surface may facilitate learning and online adaptation of the PPS; (ii) the visual information is predictive of the tactile in both space and time—that is, an approaching stimulus that is perceived only visually facilitates the responses of neurons with tactile receptive fields at the expected contact location (e.g., [10]).

PPS learning—in a narrow sense of the visuo-tactile neurons' characteristics —can be viewed as a regression task: learning a functional relationship between a visual stimulus in space (position and velocity) and the expected contact location as perceived by the tactile modality. Training data is provided by approaching objects perceived visually and eventually contacting the skin. If uncertainty of the input is considered, we obtain a regression problem with errors in variables.

There are few computational models of PPS representation learning in the sense considered here (i.e., PPS as margin-of-safety rather than PPS as space within reach – see [1]). Magosso et al. [6] proposed a neural network that models unimodal (visual and tactile) and bimodal representations of an imaginary left and right body part, but focused on their interaction rather than learning and velocity was not considered. Roncone et al. [9], on a humanoid robot, developed a proxy for the visual receptive fields in a probabilistic sense (likelihood of contact) and showed that they can be learned from scratch from objects nearing and eventually contacting the skin. Velocity (or time to contact) was considered, but for both, position and velocity, the 3D space was collapsed to a single dimension. Neither of the models takes uncertainty of the inputs into account.

Our work departs from a neural network model based on a Restricted Boltzmann Machine (RBM) from [7] that enables integration of information from different modalities—there vision and proprioception, here position and velocity both derived from vision (the step of extracting these quantities from actual visual input is not addressed here). A probabilistic population code [5] is used to encode position and velocity as Gaussian distributions including uncertainty, which are then fed into the RBM model providing dimensionality reduction and feature extraction. However, the model is not able to make temporal predictions such as predicting the future state of one modality from the other modality. Thus, we extended the model by a feedforward neural network that takes the RBM hidden neurons as input and learns to predict a location on the body surface (covered by skin) that will be hit by a moving object based on the integrated representation of position and velocity of the object.

This article is structured as follows. The Materials and Methods section details input/output encoding and the RBM. This is followed by the Experiments and Results section where we describe learning and testing of the model. We close with a Conclusion and Discussion.

2   Materials and Methods

2.1   Input and Output Encoding

The input neurons use a "probabilistic population code" [5,7] to encode a measurement $\mathbf{x}$ and its uncertainty (determined by a gain g). A state (or "activation") $\mathbf{r}$ of the neuron population is sampled from the distribution

$$p(\mathbf{r}|\mathbf{x}, g, \mathbf{\Sigma}_t) = \prod_j Pois[r_j|gf_j(\mathbf{x})], \tag{1}$$

where $f_j(\mathbf{x}) = e^{-\frac{1}{2}(\mathbf{x}-\mathbf{c}_j)^T \mathbf{\Sigma}_t(\mathbf{x}-\mathbf{c}_j)}$ is a Gaussian function centered in the receptive field (RF) center $\mathbf{c}_j$ of the j-th neuron, the covariance matrix $\mathbf{\Sigma}_t$ is a constant diagonal matrix (for the given modality), with all diagonal elements having the same value (variance of the Gaussian function) that determines the width of the RF.

The state $\mathbf{r}$ of the neuron population can be interpreted as a normal distribution (we assume that the size of the neuron population is sufficiently large) $\mathcal{N}(\psi(\mathbf{r}), \overline{\mathbf{\Sigma}}(\mathbf{r}))$ [5, 7] where

$$\psi(\mathbf{r}) = \frac{\sum_i \mathbf{c}_i r_i}{\sum_i r_i} \tag{2}$$

is the mean and

$$\overline{\mathbf{\Sigma}}(\mathbf{r}) = \frac{\mathbf{\Sigma}_t}{\sum_i r_i} \tag{3}$$

is the covariance matrix. The matrix is diagonal, with all diagonal elements equal to the variance σ^2. Equations (2) and (3) are valid if we assume that a prior distribution $p(\mathbf{x})$ is uniform (for the Gaussian case see [7]). A relationship between g and the variance is $g \propto \frac{1}{\sigma^2}$ [5]. In what follows, instead of the covariance matrix (3), we will use η and call it *confidence* of a measurement, defined as follows:

$$\eta = \sum_i r_i \tag{4}$$

The confidence η fully determines the values of the covariance matrix (see the denominator in (3)). Note that $\eta \propto g \propto \frac{1}{\sigma^2}$. Thus, the decoded covariance σ^2 as the uncertainty of the measurement can always be determined from η.

For detailed information about neuron RF centers $\mathbf{c}_j^{pos}$, $\mathbf{c}_j^{vel}$, c_j^{tact} see [11].

2.2   Restricted Boltzmann Machine (RBM)

This part of the architecture is based on an RBM-like model from [7]. A Restricted Boltzmann machine is a generative model that consists of two layers with no intralayer connections and full interlayer connections [4, 12] (see Fig. 1 right). The input units (with state $\mathbf{r}$) are Poisson random variables that take nonnegative integer values according to (1). The hidden-layer units (with state $\mathbf{v}$) are binary. The input and hidden units have biases ($\mathbf{b}_r$, $\mathbf{b}_v$). The connection between both layers (weights $\mathbf{W}$) is undirected.

During learning, one population is given and the other is sampled. The units $\mathbf{v}$ (resp. $\mathbf{r}$) are sampled from Bernoulli (Poisson) distribution [4, 12]

$$p(\mathbf{v}|\mathbf{r}) = \prod_i Bern[v_i|\sigma(\{\mathbf{W}\mathbf{r} + \mathbf{b}_v\}_i)] \tag{5}$$

$$p(\mathbf{r}|\mathbf{v}) = \prod_j Pois[r_j|exp(\{\mathbf{W^T v} + \mathbf{b}_r\}_j)] \qquad (6)$$

The RBM was trained using one-step contrastive divergence [4].

3   Experiments and Results

We deploy our neural network architecture in a 2D scenario where objects are approaching a simulated skin surface (see Fig. 1 left). The performance of the learned representation is assessed, focusing on the precision and reliability of the predictions generated. Finally, we analyze how the PPS representation is modulated by stimulus speed. Complete code and parameters for all experiments is available online [11].

3.1   Peripersonal Space Representation Learning

Learning proceeds in two separate phases. The input variables are: (i) 2D stimulus position, $\mathbf{x}^{pos}$ (from the hypothetical "visual" modality), and (ii) stimulus velocity, $\mathbf{x}^{vel}$ – the change of position during a timestep $\mathbf{x}^{vel}(t) = \mathbf{x}^{pos}(t) - \mathbf{x}^{pos}(t-1)$. Both are encoded (using (1)) by the neural populations with states $\mathbf{r}^{pos}$ and $\mathbf{r}^{vel}$ respectively. The gains associated with the input variables, g^{pos}, g^{vel}, are uniformly generated from bounded intervals. First, the RBM is trained to represent this input space in an unsupervised fashion. Second, the tactile modality is added and learning proceeds in a supervised way to predict the contact location.

RBM Learning. The object positions $\mathbf{x}^{pos}(i), i \in \{1, 2, ..., N\}$ (N is the size of the training set) uniformly covered the space of the visual modality (see Fig. 1 left). The direction and magnitude of each velocity vector

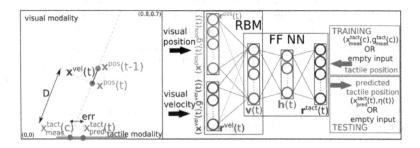

Fig. 1. Scenario and architecture. LEFT: 2D experimental scenario. Stimulus trajectory in orange; positions of stimulus at two different discrete time moments shown. "Skin" in green. **RIGHT:** Architecture of the neural network and illustration of training and testing (predicting) process. See text for details. (Color figure online)

$\mathbf{x}^{vel}(i), i \in \{1, 2, ..., N\}$ were uniformly generated from a bounded interval. For training of the RBM, we used the training set $U = \{[\mathbf{r}_U^{pos}(1), \mathbf{r}_U^{vel}(1)], [\mathbf{r}_U^{pos}(2), \mathbf{r}_U^{vel}(2)], ..., [\mathbf{r}_U^{pos}(N), \mathbf{r}_U^{vel}(N)]\}$, where $\mathbf{r}_U^{pos}(i)$ and $\mathbf{r}_U^{vel}(i)$ are obtained from $\mathbf{x}^{pos}(i)$ and $\mathbf{x}^{vel}(i)$ (using (1)). The RBM was trained using one-step contrastive divergence [4]. The main parameters of the learning were: $size(\mathbf{r}^{pos}) = 289$, $size(\mathbf{r}^{vel}) = 625$, $size(\mathbf{v}) = 150$, $g^{pos/vel} \in (12, 18)$, $\mathbf{x}^{vel} \in (-0.012, 0.012) \times (-0.012, 0.012)$ and the number of training epochs was 60 (for other parameters see [11]).

Feedforward Network Learning. The second phase of learning can be viewed as a regression task, with $\mathbf{x}^{pos}$ and $\mathbf{x}^{vel}$ as independent variables and x^{tact}, 1D position of the stimulation registered by the tactile modality, as the dependent variable (can be empty – no prediction). As before, all variables have their respective gains $g^{pos}, g^{vel}, g^{tact}$ (uniformly generated from bounded intervals) and are encoded using (1), giving $\mathbf{r}^{pos}, \mathbf{r}^{vel}$, and $\mathbf{r}^{tact}$. We will distinguish predicted value of the tactile position x_{pred}^{tact} and the measured value x_{meas}^{tact} that are used during training and testing.

Simulated looming objects follow trajectories that start at the top edge of a simulated space (dimensions chosen arbitrarily) and end at the bottom edge (see Fig. 1 left). The start and end of the trajectory and the object velocity are generated uniformly from bounded intervals. If the end of the trajectory falls in the region covered by the emulated "skin", the tactile modality is activated. The position of the stimulation object is recorded at discrete time moments (see the orange circles in Fig. 1 left).

The relationship between "visual" stimulation, $e(t)$, and tactile stimulation, $z(t)$, is formally described below. On contact of the object with "skin", the "connection" is strengthened if the tactile stimulation $x_{meas}^{tact}(c)$ follows the moment of "visual" stimulation at time t by at most Q timesteps. Formally, let $C \subset \{1, 2, .., M\}$ be the set of time moments when the tactile modality was activated, M size of the training set and Q an integer constant ("memory buffer size"). The set T consists of pairs $T = \{(e(1), z(1)), (e(2), z(2)), ..., (e(M), z(M))\}$, where $e(t) = (\mathbf{x}^{pos}(t), g^{pos}(t), \mathbf{x}^{vel}(t), g^{vel}(t))$ (independent variables with their gains) and $z(t) = (x_{meas}^{tact}(c), g_{meas}^{tact}(c))$ if $\exists c, c \in C$ that $t \in [c - Q, c]$, else $z(t)$ is empty.

For training of a feedforward neural network (FF NN), the set T will now be used to generate a set $S = \{(\mathbf{v}(1), \mathbf{r}^{tact}(1)), (\mathbf{v}(2), \mathbf{r}^{tact}(2)), ..., (\mathbf{v}(M), \mathbf{r}^{tact}(M))\}$, where $\mathbf{v}$ is the state of the RBM hidden layer and is sampled from the Bernoulli distribution (5) given $\mathbf{r} = [\mathbf{r}^{pos}, \mathbf{r}^{vel}]$, as obtained from $e(t)$. Then, $\mathbf{r}^{tact}(t)$ is obtained from a corresponding $z(t)$ – see Fig. 1 right. If $z(t)$ is empty, then $\mathbf{r}^{tact}(t)$ is a zero vector.

We used a standard two-layer feedforward neural network with sigmoid hidden neurons (state denoted $\mathbf{h}$) and linear output neurons (see Fig. 1 right). The training algorithm was scaled conjugate gradient backpropagation [8]. For the training we used MATLAB's Neural Network Toolbox. The main parameters of the learning were: $size(\mathbf{r}^{tact}) = 25$, $size(\mathbf{h}) = 20$, $Q = 70$, $g^{pos/vel/tact} \in (12, 18)$, $||\mathbf{x}^{vel}|| \in (0.005, 0.01)$ and the number of training epochs was 3369.

3.2 Peripersonal Space Representation Testing

The process of prediction is schematically illustrated in Fig. 1 right. The prediction is obtained from the feedforward neural network. An input $\mathbf{v}$ of the FF NN is obtained from the stimulus $(\mathbf{x}^{pos}, \mathbf{x}^{vel}, g^{pos}, g^{vel})$ in the same way as it is described in Sect. 3.1. From the output of the FF NN $\mathbf{r}^{tact}$ (to prevent negative activations and noise, we set to zero all r_j^{tact} that have smaller value than 1), we can get the predicted position $x_{pred}^{tact}(i) = \psi(\mathbf{r}^{tact}(i))$ and the confidence $\eta(i)$ (see Eqs. (2) and (4)). If all elements of a state $\mathbf{r}^{tact}$ are zeros, then no prediction is generated. The error of the prediction is $err = |x_{pred}^{tact} - x_{meas}^{tact}|$ (see Fig. 1 left). For testing we use x_{meas}^{tact} for the end point of the trajectory (even if it lies outside of the space covered by skin – cannot be "measured" by the tactile

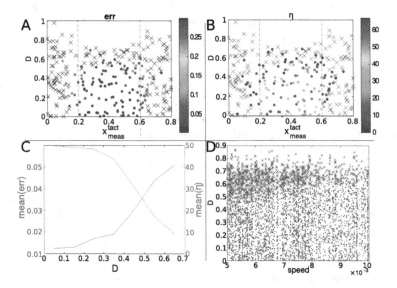

Fig. 2. Peripersonal space representation testing – touch prediction performance. **A: Dependence of error on distance D and end of the trajectory** $\mathbf{x}_{meas}^{tact}$. The color code encodes the error $|x_{meas}^{tact} - x_{pred}^{tact}|$ in actual vs. predicted contact location (for the meaning of the D, x_{meas}^{tact} and err see Fig. 1). The crosses denote that the prediction is not generated ($\mathbf{r}^{tact} = \mathbf{0}$). The area between the two dashed lines contains the stimuli that are followed by the tactile stimulation (x_{meas}^{tact} is on the skin). **B: Dependence of confidence on distance D and end of the trajectory $\mathbf{x}_{meas}^{tact}$.** The color code encodes the confidence (see (4)) of each prediction depending on D and x_{meas}^{tact}. **C: Dependence of error and confidence on D.** Only trajectories with end on the skin were used (the area between the dotted lines in A, B). Each value of the dependent variable is the mean of error or confidence for stimuli from a 0.1 wide area of D. Empty predictions were excluded. **D: Dependence of prediction on speed and distance D.** Each point represents a moving stimulus (with a known value of speed) at distance D from the end of trajectory. All stimuli were from trajectories that end on the skin. The stimuli for which predictions are empty are marked by a red cross, others are marked by a blue dot. (Color figure online)

modality). The stimuli for testing are obtained in the same way as for learning (see Sect. 3.1). The results are analyzed in the next section.

3.3   Analysis of the Results

The results are summarized in Fig. 2. Overall, the architecture has successfully coped with the task. We find that if the trajectory of the stimulus ends on the skin, the prediction error increases with the distance from the contact location, but the prediction confidence decreases. This is illustrated in aggregated form in Fig. 2C and in detail in Fig. 2A, B (in the latter, the testing set is reduced for visualization purposes). If the trajectory ends outside the skin ($x_{meas}^{tact} \notin [0.2, 0.6]$), there was no prediction ($\eta = 0$) or the confidence η had a low value (see Fig. 2A, B). This is desirable, as the lower confidence enables recognition of false and inaccurate predictions. It is also possible to see that the confidence was lower at the edges of the skin than in the central part.

In Fig. 2A and B, there seems to be a fuzzy but apparent border or threshold in distance, after which the generated predictions are empty or their confidence is low – around $D = 0.5$. This border is determined by buffer size Q, but, importantly, it is also modulated by speed of the stimulus. We analyzed this specifically in Fig. 2D: with higher speed, the empty predictions are generated farther from the skin, so the "border of the PPS" moves farther.

4   Conclusion and Discussion

The mechanisms of PPS representation and learning in biology are not fully understood. Arguably, PPS adaptation can be largely attributed to neuronal plasticity in the corresponding networks (probably fronto-parietal areas) through interaction with the environment. The contingencies between a visual stimulus looming to the body and tactile stimulation on contact of the object with the skin may constitute sufficient material for the development and continuous recalibration of the PPS representation.

To investigate this hypothesis, we proposed a neural network architecture that consists of two parts. The first network has two input populations, one encodes position of the "visual" stimulus, the other encodes velocity of the stimulus. Both of them also encode uncertainty of the stimuli. The information from the input layers is integrated by the hidden layer of an RBM. However, this model alone cannot make temporal predictions, so we extended it by a feedforward neural network with one hidden layer. This feedforward network is trained in a supervised manner to predict tactile stimulation.

We tested how the network after training can predict tactile stimulation given the "visual" position and velocity of a looming stimulus and found that: (i) the error of the prediction increased with the distance of the stimulus from the skin; (ii) the confidence of the prediction decreased with distance. The confidence was also low or zero if the trajectory of the stimulus ended outside the skin. These are expected and desired properties, thus verifying the suitability of our method.

Interestingly, our model reproduced the phenomenon of seeming PPS expansion pertaining to faster stimuli and predicts a hypothetical mechanism for this: for a given distance, there is an emergent cut-off speed, whereby slower stimuli do not induce any prediction of touch (and thus may not lead to PPS activation) but faster stimuli do.

In the future, we want to conduct a more detailed comparison with the properties of PPS in biology. In addition, it will be natural to add additional modalities next to vision and touch: (i) the auditory modality may provide additional information about the same stimulus, which in turn needs to be optimally integrated with vision; (ii) proprioception is mediating coordinate transformations for stimuli pertaining to the body. Finally, we want to test our model in a real scenario on a humanoid robot. These may require changes to the architecture presented here, such as possible recruitment of a convolutional neural network to process raw visual inputs, and—upon inclusion of additional modalities and hence dimensions to the task—transforming the RBM into a Deep belief network or adding more hidden layers to the FF NN.

Acknowledgement. Z.S. was supported by The Grant Agency of the CTU Prague project SGS16/161/ OHK3/2T/13. M.H. was supported by the Czech Science Foundation under Project GA17-15697Y and a Marie Curie Intra European Fellowship (iCub Body Schema 625727) within the 7th European Community Framework Programme. Base code for the RBM model was kindly provided by Joseph G. Makin [7].

References

1. Cléry, J., Guipponi, O., Wardak, C., Hamed, S.B.: Neuronal bases of peripersonal and extrapersonal spaces, their plasticity and their dynamics: knowns and unknowns. Neuropsychologia **70**, 313–326 (2015)
2. Ernst, M.O., Banks, M.S.: Humans integrate visual and haptic information in a statistically optimal fashion. Nature **415**(6870), 429–433 (2002)
3. Fogassi, L., Gallese, V., Fadiga, L., Luppino, G., Matelli, M., Rizzolatti, G.: Coding of peripersonal space in inferior premotor cortex (area f4). J. Neurophysiol. **76**(1), 141–157 (1996)
4. Hinton, G.E.: Training products of experts by minimizing contrastive divergence. Neural Comput. **14**(8), 1771–1800 (2002)
5. Ma, W.J., Beck, J.M., Latham, P.E., Pouget, A.: Bayesian inference with probabilistic population codes. Nat. Neurosci. **9**(11), 1432–1438 (2006)
6. Magosso, E., Zavaglia, M., Serino, A., Di Pellegrino, G., Ursino, M.: Visuotactile representation of peripersonal space: a neural network study. Neural Comput. **22**(1), 190–243 (2010)
7. Makin, J.G., Fellows, M.R., Sabes, P.N.: Learning multisensory integration and coordinate transformation via density estimation. PLoS Comput. Biol. **9**(4), e1003035 (2013)
8. Møller, M.F.: A scaled conjugate gradient algorithm for fast supervised learning. Neural Netw. **6**(4), 525–533 (1993)
9. Roncone, A., Hoffmann, M., Pattacini, U., Fadiga, L., Metta, G.: Peripersonal space and margin of safety around the body: learning visuo-tactile associations in a humanoid robot with artificial skin. PLoS ONE **11**(10), e0163713 (2016)

10. Serino, A., Noel, J.P., Galli, G., Canzoneri, E., Marmaroli, P., Lissek, H., Blanke, O.: Body part-centered and full body-centered peripersonal space representations. Sci. Rep. **5**, 18603 (2015)
11. Straka, Z., Hoffmann, M.: Supporting materials. https://github.com/ZdenekStraka/icann2017-pps
12. Welling, M., Rosen-Zvi, M., Hinton, G.E.: Exponential family harmoniums with an application to information retrieval. In: Proceedings of NIPS, vol. 4, pp. 1481–1488 (2004)

Learning Distance-Behavioural Preferences Using a Single Sensor in a Spiking Neural Network

Matt Ross[1(✉)], Nareg Berberian[1], André Cyr[1], Frédéric Thériault[2], and Sylvain Chartier[1]

[1] School of Psychology, University of Ottawa,
136 Jean-Jacques Lussier, Ottawa, ON K1N 6N5, Canada
{mross094,nberb062}@uottawa.ca
[2] Computer Science, Cégep du Vieux Montréal,
255 Ontario St E, Montreal, QC H2X 1X6, Canada

Abstract. Actions from autonomous agents demand adaptive rules rather than being hard coded. Contrary to using multiple pre-calibrated sensors, utilizing a single non-calibrated sensor in combination with neural elements could provide flexibility through learning, to effectively cope with changing environments. The objective of this study was to design an adaptive system with the potential capability of learning behavioural preferences in relation to distinct distances from a wall using only a single ultrasonic sensor. Using spike-timing dependent plasticity (STDP) as a learning mechanism in a spiking neural network (SNN), the agent displayed the correct behaviour and was successful in learning the desired behavioural preference at a medium distance. However, the agent treated far and close distances as ambiguous inputs from the sensory environment, despite the presentation of reinforcement cues during learning.

Keywords: Spiking neural networks · Spike timing dependent plasticity · Robotic simulation · Sensory calibration

1 Introduction

Brain-inspired artificial neural networks (ANNs) have proved their usefulness in modelling behavioural processes underlying biological phenomena [1]. With the advent of third generation ANNs, spiking neurons have been used as fundamental units that form a series of spikes. These trains of spikes have been observed in a wide range of biological models aimed for capturing neuronal dynamics more closely with respect to classic artificial neural networks, which operate via integer-valued inputs [1]. Spiking neural networks (SNNs) are particularly useful in bio-inspired robotic implementations, involving intelligent systems capable of converting data directly from sensors [2], doing recognition and detection tasks [3] among others [4]. Furthermore, SNNs are capable of performing realistic

© Springer International Publishing AG 2017
A. Lintas et al. (Eds.): ICANN 2017, Part I, LNCS 10613, pp. 110–118, 2017.
https://doi.org/10.1007/978-3-319-68600-4_14

learning tasks while demonstrating neural adaptation in different constraints commonly observed in biological neurons [5].

In this study, we aim to extend this line of research by implementing a SNN in a neurorobotic domain capable of detecting and associating external signals to desired behaviours. Contrary to using multiple pre-calibrated sensors, we explore the possibility of utilizing a single sensor that can be used to differentiate distances through an adaptive SNN. There are advantages of using a single non-calibrated sensor instead of multiple pre-calibrated sensors. First, a single sensor is more parsimonious versus an implementation that uses more sensors to explain the same underlying phenomena. Second, a non-calibrated component provides the system with greater versatility, because the network would possess a greater state space in transforming incoming signals. This would be hindered in the case of using multiple pre-calibrated sensors; as incoming signals are modulated before the system has time to process them, which is biologically implausible. Furthermore, non-calibrated sensors have a greater utility in a real-world robotic application, whereby afferent noisy signals are common denominators to all ultrasonic sensors. Hence, when the network receives noisy signals, the usage of multiple pre-calibrated sensors introduce false feedback, because multiple sensors in close proximity will interfere with one another, thus hindering the accuracy of the readouts. In addition, pre-calibrated sensors are more prone in failing to recover during a malfunction, resulting in inaccurate readings that are potentially irreversible. Given the advantages in using non-calibrated sensors, our work aims to design such adaptive system capable of learning behavioural preferences in relation to distinct distances from a stationary wall using a single ultrasonic sensor. This will be accomplished using the event-based phenomenon known as Spike-Timing Dependent Plasticity (STDP) [6], which was adapted as a learning algorithm in SNNs.

2   Methodology

2.1   The SIMCOG Environment and Parameters

Artificial intelligence simulator of cognition (SIMCOG) is used to easily design complex real-time SNN architectures that can be implemented in autonomous agents and then tested in a virtual world [7]. An unusual component in spiking neuron simulators is the transducers, as they usually accept a file input. In SIMCOG, this element represents the receptor component of the sensory neuron, whose main function is to convert one sensory modality into another [7]. In this simulation, this transformation involves taking input signals from the sensory environment using an ultrasonic sensor and converting them into spike trains. This transformation is analogous to sensory systems (i.e., visual, auditory) designed to convert incoming signals into electrical impulses. The parameters of individual neurons settled in SIMCOG include but are not limited to: a resting membrane potential (RMP), absolute refractory period (ARP), after-hyperpolarization (AH), as well as a post-synaptic potential multiplier

(PSP mul.; Table 1) [7]. Parameters of membrane potential are in a percentage scale mimicking a biological membrane potential variation in millivolt.

Table 1. Parameters of neurons in the SIMCOG environment.

Neuron	RMP	AH	ARP	PSPmul.
N-Far	53%	53%	10 cycles	1
N-Medium	43%	43%	15 cycles	1
N-Close	4%	4%	20 cycles	2
All other neurons	43%	36%	1 cycle	1

2.2 Architecture

The robot's controller consists of artificial neural units connected by synapses. Similar to standard leaky integrate-and-fire neuron models, our SNN model incorporates temporally ongoing inputs through the SNN [8]. In these neurons, when the membrane potential reaches a specific threshold, a spike is triggered. Spike emission is mediated by an electrical flux that is sent to the synapse. This signal is then transformed into a local excitatory or inhibitory synaptic current that is received by the targeted elements [9].

The simulation consists of a mobile 3-wheeled robot with four external sensors (ultrasonic, light, thermal, and vibration) and three LEDs (green, orange and red). The robot is in constant forward motion approaching a wall. This motion is mediated by the N-Motor neuron (Fig. 1), which uses a pacemaker property that emits spikes at a constant frequency in the absence of external input, thus activating the motors. Neuron N-S has a sensory transducer component that linearly converts distance information from the ultrasonic sensor to graded receptor potentials that serve as input to the network (Fig. 1) [10]. Hence, the distance-related sensory input signals are transformed into a linear percentage scale [0–100 scale]. Following the linear transformation, the timescale of sensory integration in the robotic domain varies non-linearly across time, a timescale of sensory integration that is similar to neural organisms. This non-linear dependence is mediated by the input and the current membrane potential state of the neuronal unit. Information is then sent to three neurons representing the far, medium, and close distances. These neurons have heterogeneously tuned parameters (Table 1), endowing each neuron to emit spikes at a preferred rate [9]. Hence, a single input spike train is transformed into three distinct spike trains, each operating at a given frequency range, thus mimicking the neural frequency preference as observed in bat echolocation [11].

Frequency-dependent signals get passed from these distance-encoding neurons to their respective interneurons, which serve two functions: (1) to continue propagating the information and (2) to inhibit the other two distance-encoding neurons. Each interneuron is connected to three action neurons (N-A:Red,

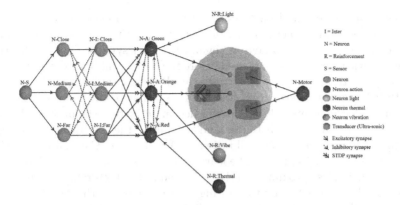

Fig. 1. SNN architecture of preferential action selection using reinforcement cues. (Color figure online)

N-A:Orange, N-A:Green). The strength of this connectivity is subject to modulation via the STDP learning rule [12]. The result of a STDP function is to increase the synaptic strength, if the presynaptic unit spikes before the postsynaptic unit. If the presynaptic spike occurs after the postsynaptic spike, then the inverse correlation leads to a decrease in synaptic strength [6]. Hence, the relative timing between the pre- and postsynaptic units is mediated by the competitive and stabilizing properties of STDP. The learning rule used for STDP is described by:

$$\Delta w = \alpha_{tpost-tpre} e^{tpost-tpre/\tau}. \tag{1}$$

where Δw is the change in synaptic strength, $\alpha = 1$ or -1, depending on the timing between pre- and post-synaptic spikes, and τ is the recovery time constant. When action neurons are activated, they will spike and turn on their respective coloured LED and inhibit the other two action neurons. These STDP synapses initially have lower connection strengths (20), compared to the other non-STDP synapses (50 or 100), making them unable to induce depolarization in any of the action neurons.

2.3 The Simulation

The simulation can be divided into two phases; a learning phase and a testing phase. The objective of the learning phase is to strengthen the STDP synapse between an interneuron and the desired action neuron in order to create a behavioural preference. The desired behavioural-distance preferences to be learned include the activation of: (1) the green LED at far distances, (2) the orange LED at medium distances, and (3) the red LED at close distances. This is accomplished by positively reinforcing the desired behaviour using one of three environmental cues (light, vibration, or thermal).

To learn the preference of activating the green LED at far distances, an external light cue is used. As the ultrasonic sensor becomes active, a light in the environment is emitted on top of the robot for 120 cycles ($\approx$53 msec. per cycle). The N-R: Light neuron fires in response to the light stimulus and is connected to the N-A: Green neuron via an excitatory synapse. This means that the presynaptic neuron (N-I: Far) fired before the N-R: Light neuron activates the postsynaptic action neuron (N-A: Green), thus leading to an increase in synaptic strength between the interneurons and the N-A: Green neuron via STDP.

A similar learning procedure is performed in activating the orange LED via neurons encoding medium distances and activating the red LED via neurons encoding close distances - using vibration (130 cycles) and thermal (250 cycles) as their respective cues (Fig. 1). The learning phase is complete after 500 cycles, as the robot is in close proximity to the wall. The wall is then removed and a new wall is placed ahead, whereby the testing phase begins. As the robot continues moving forward approaching the new wall during the last 600 cycles, we tested whether or not the robot has learned to encode far, medium and close distances in the absence of any environmental cues. If the robot has successfully learned the desired preferences, then distinct coloured LEDs illuminate within a range of the desired distances [13].

3   Results

The following results were obtained from a single trial that consisted of 1100 cycles. Provided that the architecture and parameter setup is held fixed, the data generated from the SIMCOG virtual environment remains consistent across multiple trials. The reliable results generated across multiple trials raises the importance in keeping parameters constant. Consequently, if the number of cycles is modified, the timing of reinforcement and STDP-dependent learning will change. This in turn will introduce dysynchronization in STDP weights, which results in a shift in the relative distances and hinder learning preferences.

The results are displayed into a series of graphs (see Fig. 2), where graphs A and B display sensor and transducer information. As the robot approaches the wall once during the learning phase and another during the testing phase, the capture value of the ultrasonic sensor rapidly increases as the echo has less distance to travel back to the sensor, resulting in a gradual increase in the stimulus force (graphic A). This information is then converted by the transducer (neuron N-S) into a constant neuronal spike pattern (black bars in graph B). This single input is sent to the distance encoding neurons, where it is separated into three distinct spike trains with different firing rates (graphs C-E). Ranges encoding for far, medium and close distances are relative labels given the total distance. The STDP learning rule adjusts weights according to the cycle at which the system has reached.

At the beginning of the learning phase of the simulation (cycles 0–120) a light is used to activate the N-A: Green action neuron, which causes an increase in the STDP coefficients from the interneurons for each distance (graphs F-H). However, the synapse between the N-I: Far and the N-A: Green action neuron reaches the highest STDP coefficient (93). These results are the same for cycles

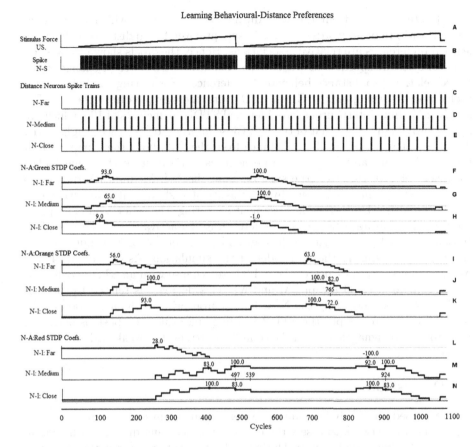

Fig. 2. Neural responses to incoming spike trains mediated by STDP across 1100 cycles. **A.** The amount of stimulus information (echoes of the wall) being captured by the ultrasonic sensor. **B.** Initial sensory information from the ultrasonic sensor converted into neuronal spikes. **C–E.** Transformations of the sensory information to distinct firing rates encoded by distance neurons. **F–N.** STDP coefficients between synapses connecting interneurons and action neurons.

120–250 where a vibration cue was used to activate the N-A: Orange action neuron, with the N-I: Medium neuron reaching an STDP coefficient of 100 (graphs I-K). For cycles 250–500 where a thermal cue was used to activate the N-A: Red action neuron, the N-I: Close neuron reaches an STDP coefficient of 100 (graphs L-N). However, the synapse between the N-I: Medium and the N-A: Red action neuron exceeds this STDP coefficient (reaching 100 compared to 83) from cycles 497–539, which is the last 13 cycles of the learning phase and the initial part of the testing phase whereby the robot is approaching the new wall (graphs M and N).

Successful learning is determined by maintaining the highest increase in the STDP coefficient for the synapse that connects the desired action at the appropriate distance from the wall during testing, within which there is no ground truth. In other words, changes in synaptic weights to distance-behavioral learned preferences are relative associations. Hence, the labels shown for a given range of cycle are specified in order to help delineate STDP weight changes associated relatively to distance-behavioral preferences. For testing the behavioural preference of turning on the Green LED, both the synapses from the N-I: Far and N-I: Medium interneurons have identical STDP coefficients of 100, which are significantly higher than that of the N-I: Close interneuron (−1; see graphs F-H). As the robot reaches a medium distance from the wall, both the synapses from the N-I: Medium and N-I: Close interneurons initially have the same STDP coefficient of 100. However, the synapse from the N-I: Medium interneuron is preferred as it remains stronger by decreasing at a slower rate (see cycle 765, graphs J and K). During the last segment of testing, the robot is in close proximity to the wall and the desired preference is the activation of the red LED. Initially the N-I: Close synapse has an STDP coefficient of 100, but progressively decreases during the remainder of the simulation. As of Cycle 924, the N-I: Medium synapse surpasses the N-I: Close synapse with an STDP coefficient of 100 compared to 83 (graphs M and N). This decrease is related to the N-I: Medium synapse activating the N-A: Red neuron prior to the activation of the N-I: Close neuron. As per the STDP learning rule, since the post- is activated prior to the pre-synaptic neuron the connection strength is weakened for the N-I: Close synapse.

4 Discussion

We have used the SIMCOG simulation environment in order to implement a spiking neural network to assess the capability of learning distance-behavioural preferences using a single sensor. During early stages of processing, the agent was presented with an equal opportunity to learn all actions (turning on coloured LEDs) at all distances from a stationary wall. Using three distinct external cues, the strength of synapses were modified via a STDP learning procedure, giving rise to a desired behaviour. Within the testing phase, all reinforcement cues were removed, allowing the agent to perform a particular action for a given distance. In the present study, the agent displayed correct behaviours, [13] and was successful in learning the preference of activating the orange LED at a medium distance. However, the agent treated far and close distances as ambiguous inputs from the sensory environment, despite the presentation of reinforcement cues during learning. The discrimination between far and close distances is clearly evident during the testing phase (see Graphs F and H; L and N). However, with regards to preference learning, we consider these two distances as ambiguous inputs due to the overlap of the strengths of the STDP coefficients for medium and far distance for the activation of the green LED, as well the strength of the STDP coefficients for medium and close distance for the activation of the red LED. We have conducted two additional simulations to show the progression of the hypothesis for using a single ultrasonic sensor to learn distance-behavioural preferences (one and two preferences), while maintaining the same architecture [14].

To account for this limitation, we provide suggestions that can be examined to achieve a better distinction between the preferred rates at which neurons are encoding sensory information linked to the distance ranges. First, a solution is to use multiple sensors each with their own transducer neuron fixed at dedicated specific ranges (i.e. T1 = 0–30 mm, T2 = 31–90 mm and T3 = 91–200 mm) to represent different distances, as in the visual cones in the retina [15]. This solution would allow for clear distinction between distances, but requires pre-calibrated sensors. Second, given the linear conversion of the distance information by the transducer, distinction of distances was treated more ambiguously. A logarithmic scale or using a non-linear function would allow for a more clear-cut distinction of the frequency range at which the US sensor is encoding information. It is noteworthy to mention that a follow-up of this paper aims at addressing these suggestions to better delineate the process of learning to differentiate between distances using a single sensor and then implement this behavioural adaptation in a real world robot. Our work also aims to generalize the learning function in other modalities such as with infra-red sensors.

5   Conclusion

In the present study, we explored the possibility of utilizing a single sensor that can be used to differentiate distances through an adaptive SNN. The agent displayed the desired behaviour and was successful in learning the preference of activating the orange LED at a medium distance. However, the agent treated far and close distances as ambiguous inputs from the sensory environment, despite the presentation of reinforcement cues during learning. We believe that based on the suggestions given, it is feasible to develop a SNN that uses heterogeneous transducers and neural parameters instead of pre-calibrated components to endow a SNN with adaptive capabilities. This simple simulation can be used as a precursor in developing adaptable networks that encompass neural plasticity with the ability to accommodate a wider range of distances.

References

1. Haykin, S.S.: Neural Networks and Learning Machines. 3rd edn. Prentice Hall (2009)
2. A Spiking Neural Network Alternative for the Analog to Digital Converter (2010)
3. Perez-Carrasco, J.A., Acha, B., Serrano, C., Camunas-Mesa, L., Serrano-Gotarredona, T., Linares-Barranco, B.: Fast vision through frameless event-based sensing and convolutional processing: application to texture recognition. IEEE Trans. Neural Networks **21**(4), 609–620 (2010)
4. Iakymchuk, T., Rosado-Muñoz, A., Guerrero-Martínez, J.F., Bataller-Mompeán, M., Francés-Víllora, J.V.: Simplified spiking neural network architecture and STDP learning algorithm applied to image classification. EURASIP J. Image Video Process. (4) (2015)
5. Izhikevich, E.: Simple model of spiking neurons. IEEE Trans. Neural Networks **14**(6), 1569–1572 (2003)

6. Bi, G.Q., Poo, M.M.: Synaptic modifications in cultured hippocampal neurons: dependence on spike timing, synaptic strength, and postsynaptic cell type. J. Neurosci. **18**(24), 10464–10472 (1998)
7. Cyr, A., Boukadoum, M., Poirier, P.: AI-SIMCOG: a simulator for spiking neurons and multiple animats' behaviours. Neural Comput. Appl. **18**(5), 431–446 (2009)
8. Cyr, A., Thériault, F.: Action selection and operant conditioning: a neurorobotic implementation. J. Robot. **2015**(6), 1–10 (2015)
9. Humphries, M.D., Gurney, K., Prescott, T.J.: Is there a brainstem substrate for action selection? Philosoph. Trans. R. Soc. B **362**, 1627–1639 (2007)
10. Cyr, A., Boukadoum, M., Thériault, F.: Operant conditioning: a minimal components requirement in artificial spiking neurons designed for bio-inspired Robot's controller. Front. Neurorobotics **8**(21), 1–13 (2014)
11. Wenstrup, J.J., Portfors, C.V.: Neural processing of target distance by echolocating bats: functional roles of the auditory midbrain. Neurosci. Biobehav. Rev. **35**(10), 2073–2083 (2011)
12. Caporale, N., Dan, Y.: Spike timing-dependent plasticity: a Hebbian learning rule. Annu. Rev. Neurosci. **31**, 25–46 (2008)
13. Ross, M.: Learning distance-behavioural preferences using a single sensor in a spiking neural network, April 2017. https://www.youtube.com/watch?v=TXPE-lbiK2c
14. Thériault, F.: Learning distance-behavioural preferences using a single sensor in a spiking neural network: supplementary material, May 2017. http://aifuture.com/res/2017-dist-learning/
15. Bryan Kolb, I.Q.W.: An Introduction to Brain and Behavior, 4th edn. Worth Publishers, New York (2014)

From Neurons to Networks

Towards an Accurate Identification of Pyloric Neuron Activity with VSDi

Filipa dos Santos, Peter Andras, and K.P. Lam[⊠]

School of Computing and Mathematics,
University of Keele, Newcastle-Under-Lyme, STAFFS ST5 5BG, UK
{f.dos.santos,p.andras,k.p.lam}@keele.ac.uk

Abstract. Voltage-sensitive dye imaging (VSDi) which enables simultaneous optical recording of many neurons in the pyloric circuit of the stomatogastric ganglion is an important technique to supplement electrophysiological recordings. However, utilising the technique to identify pyloric neurons directly is a computationally exacting task that requires the development of sophisticated signal processing procedures to analyse the tri-phasic pyloric patterns generated by these neurons. This paper presents our work towards commissioning such procedures. The results achieved to date are most encouraging.

Keywords: Duty cycle · Tri-phasic pyloric neural network · Voltage-sensitive dye imaging · Singular Spectrum Analysis · Dynamic phase detection

1 Introduction

In recent years, an optical recording technique based on voltage-sensitive dye imaging (VSDi) has become a practical means of simultaneously capturing the activities of multiple neurons in living tissues, providing a valuable tool for studying neural circuit connectivity and neuromodulation at the single cell level. This is exemplified by recent studies of the stomatogastric ganglion (STG) of the crab, *Cancer borealis* [1, 2]. In particular, the STG that contains the pyloric circuit in the crab stomatogastric nervous system, one of the two central pattern generators in the STG that are responsible for controlling the musculature of the digestive system. The pyloric rhythm (PR) controls the pylorus, which performs the mixing and filtering of food particles after chewing by the gastric mill inside of the crab stomach. Analytically, it is a classic model for motor pattern generation, where regular and predictable oscillatory activities of the participating neurons can be monitored and studied in vitro. In particular, a typical approach identifies neuron types participating in the PR by comparing the intracellular membrane potential oscillations and firing phases using extracellular captured activity patterns through the lateral ventricular nerve (lvn) [2–4].

This paper demonstrates the identification of pyloric neurons in the STG using the image/data obtained from the optical recordings with the VSDi approach described above without resorting to the difficult electrophysiological method of intracellular electrode recordings. Instead, the neural membrane potential oscillations in the STG were measured through the optically recorded intensity of the fluorescence produced by the voltage-sensitive dye (Di-4-ANEPPS) that was bath-applied to the STG exogenously.

© Springer International Publishing AG 2017
A. Lintas et al. (Eds.): ICANN 2017, Part I, LNCS 10613, pp. 121–128, 2017.
https://doi.org/10.1007/978-3-319-68600-4_15

Several key challenges had to be overcome. (1) The relatively low yield[1] of the potential-dependent fluorescence change (2–10%/100 mV) achieved by the Di-4-ANEPPS dye used in our study make the PR extraction from the recorded dye bath/images a complex signal processing task [5]. (2) The inherently tri-phasic PR monitored on the lvn by the activity of three distinct types of neurons; namely, lateral pyloric (LP, one cell) neuron, the pyloric constrictor (PY, 5 cells) neurons and the pyloric dilator (PD, two cells) neurons, is recorded as extracellular neuronal potentials (i.e. spikes) corresponding to the highly coordinated oscillatory activities of the participating neurons. As with most extracellular electrode recordings of neuronal activity, such recording is typically displayed in the form of high-frequency sequence or train of spikes (i.e. bursts). Consequently, robust signal processing methods are needed to identify the network activities at a single-cell level, to facilitate analysing these spike trains (e.g. burst and network burst detection) in order to decode the (three) characterising phases of the PR. (3) The timing lag between the optical and lvn recordings of the characteristic spike peaks for the participating neurons due to the axonal transmission delay between the ganglion and the extracellular recording site is unknown and dependent upon (a) the biological/STG sample, (b) the equipment ensemble and (c) the experiment setup.

Our work required the development of a computationally robust solution that would reliably detect and extract the PR from the simultaneous measurement of membrane potential changes in the pattern generating neurons described in (1) above. This problem is discussed in [5]. In this paper, we present our work toward addressing the outstanding challenges.

2   Duty Cycle of Component Neurons as Biometrics

In electrical engineering, it is commonly known that duty cycles (DCs) can be used to specify the percentage time of an active signal in an electrical device such as the power switch in a switching/mode power supply or, relevantly, the firing of action potentials by a living system such as a neuron[2]. In the biological context [6, 7], the relative phasing and DCs of the component neurons in a network are critically important for the generation of a specific behavior. Importantly, the ability of the pacemaker ensemble to maintain constant DC at different frequencies in the pyloric circuit of the STG could explain how the full network maintains fixed phase relationships at different frequencies [6]. To maintain fixed phase relationships, neurons must all begin to fire later in the cycle as the cycle period increases. As the pacemaker ensemble releases transmitters in a voltage-dependent fashion during the burst when the duration of the pacemaker burst increases, the time during which inhibitory transmitter is released is accordingly extended. This, in turn, retards the onset of a firing of the follower neurons inhibited by

---

[1] https://www.thermofisher.com/order/catalog/product/D1199 last accessed 2/4/2017.

[2] Broadly, the DC of a neuron is defined as the ratio of the duration of the oscillator burst to the cycle period.

the pacemaker network. Thus, the maintenance of constant phase in these follower neurons critically relies on the ability of the pacemaker ensemble to maintain a constant DC as frequency is changed. Recent studies on how pyloric neurons maintain their phase relationships with a relatively constant DC against temperature changes add further weight to such analysis [8].

2.1 Ratio of Harmonics (RH)

Computationally, the DC of a pyloric neuron can be defined as the percentage of the time, in each (pyloric) cycle, that the displayed waveform by the neuron is above its mean membrane potential. This enables studying of the waveform using the classical theory of Fourier/harmonics analysis. Specifically, any non-sinewave periodic waveform contains energy at harmonics of the fundamental frequency (f). This can be illustrated using a simple rectangular pulse wave/train as shown in Fig. 1 below, where the DC ($d = k/T$) is defined as the fraction of time when the amplitude (A) of the wave is positive. Here, the Fourier series coefficients (a_n and b_n) are computed by correlating the waveform, $x(t)$, with cosine and sine waves over a full period T (or $f = 1/T$). The results, described in most textbooks (e.g. [9]), are given in Eq. (1) which provides a complete description (based on the Fourier series expansion) of the harmonics (nf, $n = 1,2,...$) contained in $x(t)$. The latter can be used to characterize the pulse train and, in general, any periodic waveform[3]. In particular, the ratio of harmonics (RH), which has been used in recent years to measure symmetry, or relevantly, *rhythmicity*, as a defining characteristic in the investigation of the impact of various pathologies on locomotion [10], offers an amplitude independent measure of the periodic waveform of interest in this study; namely, $RH_{12} = a_2/a_1$ and $RH_{13} = a_3/a_1$, which are calculated as $\frac{\sin 2\pi d}{2\sin \pi d}$ and $\frac{\sin 3\pi d}{3\sin \pi d}$ respectively.

$$x(t) = Ad + \sum_{n=1}^{\infty} a_n \cos 2n\pi ft, \ where \ a_n = \frac{2A}{n\pi} \sin n\pi d \qquad (1)$$

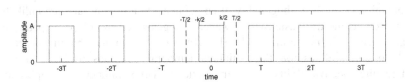

Fig. 1. An example pulse train $x(t)$ (blue) with a duty cycle (DC) calculated as the ratio of k/T. (Color figure online)

---

[3] NB. The b_n coefficients in this example are all zeros, as $x(t)$ is symmetrical at $t = 0$ without loss of generality.

3   Experimental Setup

Adult *Cancer pagurus* were obtained from Hodgkinson Fresh Fish, Manchester; they were kept in artificial seawater tanks (red sea salt, Red Sea) at 12–14 °C with 12 h light-dark cycle. The STG sample was prepared following the protocol described in [11] and was stained with Di-4-ANEPPS dye (Cambridge Bioscience, UK) and subsequently washed out using a saline flow.

The extracellular recording was executed on the lvn, with the resulting signal filtered and amplified by an AC differential amplifier before it was converted using Spike2 v8.07 (Power 1401, Cambridge Electronic Design, UK). The dyed STG was recorded using the MiCAM02 imaging system (SciMedia Ltd., Japan) simultaneously with the lvn recording. The optical data was extracted and exported using the BVAna imaging software (SciMedia Ltd., Japan) as a 3-D image stack written in CSV formatted spreadsheets, alongside a high-resolution image (HRI) of the sample. The HRI was used to identify neurons and select the pixels corresponding to the neurons as distinct regions of interest (ROIs). Signals corresponding to these ROIs were extracted from the 3-D stack in the form of 1-D time series data [5].

4   Signal Processing

To identify the pyloric neurons (PD, LP and PY) in the imaging data recorded from the dye-bathed STG, first we determined the three phases of the tri-phasic pyloric rhythm recorded on the lvn. This provided the discerning references with which the detected pyloric rhythm from the individual ROIs can be compared and analysed [5]. Here, so-called spike sorting techniques which were developed primarily to compare the waveforms of the individual spikes recorded extracellularly as "action potentials" of different neurons could be used [12]. However, while a detailed discussion or review on this approach is outside the scope of this paper, it should be noted that it is most difficult to identify the best algorithm with sufficient generality and also to define which spike sorter is the most appropriate given the task at hand [13]. In particular, the features-based approach that is primarily based on PCA and ICA to group spikes into clusters both rely on the orthogonality of components in a mixture and are unlikely to perform well, as the tri-phasic pyloric waveforms generated by the participating neurons are necessarily non-orthogonal [5]. Likewise, the template-based approach is unlikely to work well, as both the spatial and temporal variations displayed in the lvn would require the availability of an impractically large number of samples to be compared with the demonstrably noisy data obtained using the VSDi [5].

Our solution is formulated using the widely studied multi-resolution technique of time-frequency analysis to deconstruct the regular and predictable phasing of the pyloric activities recorded in the lvn [14]. Importantly, this is aided by the sequential Singular Spectrum Analysis (s-SSA) procedure, which we developed previously in [5] to extract the pyloric rhythm from the dye-bathed STG samples. As with the dye-bathed image/data, the SSA-based procedure removed much of the noise from the lvn whilst preserving selectively the pyloric frequency and, relevantly, its higher order harmonics. The effect on the resulting spectrogram is depicted the Fig. 2.

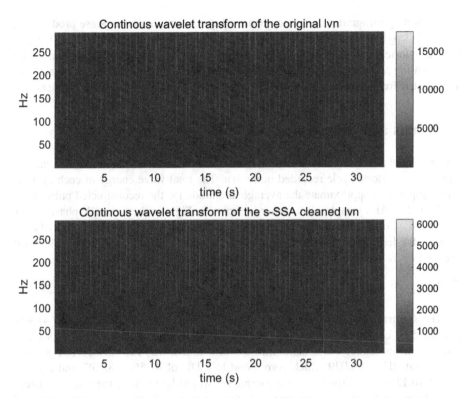

Fig. 2. Spectrograms generated with wavelet (Morse) based time-frequency decomposition. The improvement on clarity afforded to the frequency responses of the SSA processed lvn, particularly at the lower frequency bands, can be seen in bottom spectrogram. The colour bar accompanying each figure represents the amplitude computed by the continuous wavelet transform (CWT). (Color figure online)

The analytic Morlet wavelet, known for its superior time localization, was used to better localize the transients between individual phases of the pyloric rhythm from the relatively noise free recording on the lvn. This was achieved by selecting in the

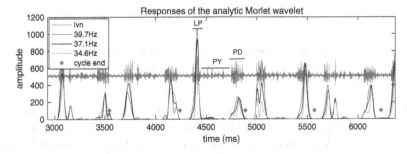

Fig. 3. Responses of the analytic wavelet in different frequency bands where the PY cycle is 'silenced'. The noise-free lvn is overlaid to demonstrate the accurate time localization of the transients between LP → PY and PY → PD cycles.

constructed spectrogram a frequency band, where the amplitude response produced in the PY-led pyloric cycle is significantly lower than that in either of the LP-led and PD-led pyloric cycle. This is illustrated in Fig. 3, where the noise-free version of the lvn recording and the end-of-cycle marker (*) are overlaid on the responses obtained in the selected frequency bands on which the PY-led cycles are effectively 'silenced'.

5   Results and Discussions

The transients of the PY bursts in each cycle obtained were used to reconstruct the PY phase of the pyloric cycle recorded in the lvn. The total wave energy of each cycle is also computed to approximate the average amplitude for the reconstructed pulse train; see Sect. 2.1. An example of the latter is shown in Fig. 4, where the PY phase/cycles were overlaid on the top of the lvn recording. Additionally, the duty cycle (DC) of each of these PY-led cycle/bursts were computed and their descriptive statistics calculated over the entire recording (32 pyloric cycles) are noted as follows:

$$DC_{mean} = 40.09\%, DC_{s.t.d.} = 6.61\%, DC_{min} = 26:02\% \text{ and } DC_{max} = 50.15\%$$

The spectral content of the reconstructed PY burst train (depicted in Fig. 4) was examined by computing the periodogram as shown in Fig. 5d, where the pyloric frequency and its higher order harmonics are also noted; $i.e.$, PR = 1.017 Hz, RH_{12} = 0.061 and $RH_{13} = 0.029$ which correspond to a DC of 41.5%, 38.75% and average DC of **40.13%** respectively. These parameters would be used, in the final validation step (described below), to compare with those obtained from the optically recorded dye-bathed data in the ground truth set. The results are summarised in Fig. 5a, b and c.

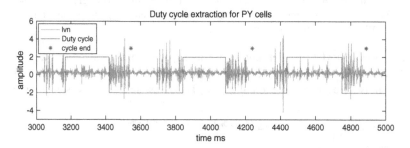

Fig. 4. Reconstruction of the PY burst train on the lvn recording (green background). The red asterisks are included to mark the end of each of the PD/burst cycle, to aid visual examination. (Color figure online)

The pyloric cycle of the three (known) PY cells taken from the dye bath was extracted using the previously described s-SSA procedure in [5]. Here, it should be noted that this s-SSA procedure was adjusted to enable extraction of the higher order harmonic components of the pyloric frequency from the individual PY neurons. A periodogram is then constructed for each of these (PY) neurons in order to measure respective harmonics and, relevantly, the harmonic ratios, RH_{12} and RH_{13} from which the respective DCs can be calculated as follows: $DC_{cell\_1} = \mathbf{39.5\%}$, $DC_{cell\_2} = \mathbf{39.9\%}$, $DC_{cell\_3} = \mathbf{38.1\%}$. These figures represent the averaged DC values corresponding to the RH_{12} and RH_{13} shown in each figure (a, b and c) for the respective cells (1, 2 and 3) in Fig. 5. Finally, the time delay between the optical and lvn recordings was computed using the Hilbert transform approach, whereby the instantaneous phase of the PY-cycle separate from each recording was obtained from the respective Hilbert spectra [15]. Here, the ability to effectively unpick the mono-frequency component of the pyloric rhythm by the s-SSA procedure developed in [5] was evident. The results are summarized in Fig. 6, where it is shown that the timing lag between the individual PY cell and the lvn maintains an expectedly constant mean phase shift of 3.34 radians (s.t. d = 0.24 rads).

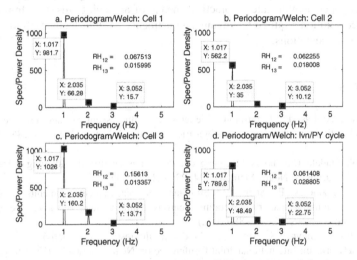

Fig. 5. Periodograms constructed for the individual cells (a, b and c) and the reconstructed PY burst (d), showing the pyloric frequency, 2nd and 3rd harmonics at 1.107 Hz, 2.035 Hz and 3.052 Hz respectively. The ratios of harmonics, RH_{12} and RH_{13} are also given in each case.

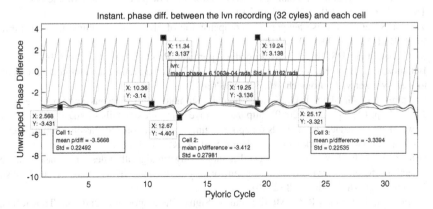

Fig. 6. Plots of the instantaneous phase shifts between the optical and lvn recordings obtained for the PY cells. The instantaneous phase changes of the lvn recording over the 32 pyloric cycles are also shown as a reference (green). (Color figure online)

6 Conclusions

The ability to locate circuit neurons and simultaneously record from them at single-cell resolution is fundamental to understanding the full-scale network behaviour of neural systems. In STG, the traditional method to identify pyloric neurons by intracellular recording can be challenging and VSDi, an optical recording technique which simultaneously measures the membrane potential of multiple neurons, offers a promising solution. However, analysing features of VSDi based recordings of these neurons in relation to the PR obtained on the lvn is an exacting task, requiring the development of sophisticated computational/signal processing techniques that aim to decode the intrinsically tri-phasic pattern of the PR. Using DC as a biologically meaningful biometric, this paper demonstrates a practical means of achieving this aim. Importantly, the proposed solution required few manual adjustments and thus lends itself to potential real-time implementations.

References

1. Stein, W., Andras, P.: Light-induced effects of a fluorescent voltage-sensitive dye on neuronal activity in the crab stomatogastric ganglion. J Neuro. Methods **188**, 290–294 (2010)
2. Stein, W., Städele, C., Andras, P.: Single-sweep voltage sensitive dye imaging of interacting identified neurons. J. Neuro Methods **194**, 224–234 (2011)
3. Städele, C., Andras, P., Stein, W.: Simultaneous measurement of membrane potential changes in multiple pattern generating neurons using voltage sensitive dye imaging. J. Neurosci. Methods **203**, 78–88 (2012)
4. dos Santos, F., Steyn, J.S., Andras, P.: Modelling the restoration of activity in a biological neural network. In: International Joint Conference on Neural Networks (IJCNN) (2016)
5. dos Santos, F., Andras, P., Lam, K.P.: A multi-resolution approach to the extraction of the pyloric rhythm. In: IEEE TSP, July, Barcelona (2017, to appear)
6. Harris-Warrick, R.M., et al.: Dynamic Biological Networks. MIT Press, Cambridge (1992)
7. Golowasch, J., Manor, Y., Nadim, F.: Recognition of slow processes in rhythmic networks. Trends Neurosci. **22**(9), 375–377 (1999)
8. Tang, L.S., et al.: Precise temperature compensation of phase in a rhythmic motor pattern. PLoS Biol. **8**(8), e1000469 (2010)
9. McClellan, J.H.: DSP First: A Multimedia Approach. Prentice Hall, London (1998)
10. Bellanca, J., Lowry, K., Van Swearingen, J., et al.: Harmonic ratios: a quantification of step to step symmetry. J. Biomech. **46**, 828–831 (2013)
11. Gutierrez, G., Grashow R.G.: Cancer borealis stomatogastric nervous system dissection. J. Vis. Exp. (25), p. 1207 (2009). http://www.jove.com/index/Details.stp?ID=1207
12. Lewicki, M.: A review of methods for spike sorting: the detection and classification of neural action potentials. Network Comput. Neural Syst. **9**, R53–R78 (1998)
13. Gibson, S., Judy, J.W., Markovic, D.: Technology-aware algorithm design for neural spike detection, feature extraction, and dimensionality reduction. IEEE Trans. Neural Syst. Rehabil. Eng. **18**(5), 469–478 (2010)
14. Akansu, A.N., Haddad R.A.: Multiresolution Signal Decomposition, 2nd edn. Transforms, Subbands, and Wavelets, AP (2000)
15. Hahn, S.: Hilbert Transforms in Signal Processing. Artech House Inc., Norwood (1996)

Interactions in the Striatal Network with Different Oscillation Frequencies

Jovana J. Belić[1,2(✉)], Arvind Kumar[1,2],
and Jeanette Hellgren Kotaleski[1,3]

[1] Department of Computational Science and Technology,
Royal Institute of Technology, Stockholm, Sweden
{belic,avkumar,jeanette}@kth.se
[2] Bernstein Center Freiburg, University of Freiburg, Freiburg, Germany
[3] Department of Neuroscience, Karolinska Institute, Stockholm, Sweden

Abstract. Simultaneous oscillations in different frequency bands are implicated in the striatum, and understanding their interactions will bring us one step closer to restoring the spectral characteristics of striatal activity that correspond to the healthy state. We constructed a computational model of the striatum in order to investigate how different, simultaneously present, and externally induced oscillations propagate through striatal circuitry and which stimulation parameters have a significant contribution. Our results show that features of these oscillations and their interactions can be influenced via amplitude, input frequencies, and the phase offset between different external inputs. Our findings provide further untangling of the oscillatory activity that can be seen within the striatal network.

Keywords: Corticostriatal network · Network oscillations · GABAergic transmission · Basal ganglia · Cortex

1 Introduction

The basal ganglia (BG) play a critical role in a variety of regular motor and cognitive functions. Striatum and subthalamic nucleus are the key sites for cortical inputs to the BG. Striatal GABAergic microcircuits in particular receive afferents from nearly all cortical areas. Therefore, it is important to understand how different components of the striatal network interact with each other and influence the striatal response to cortical inputs [1].

Population oscillations are an ubiquitous feature of many brain networks which may express a single or multiple oscillation frequencies and such oscillations are also modulated by the behavioral states [2]. Mutually interacting oscillations are often hypothesized to play an important role in information transmission and neural processing in terms of the integration of inputs [3, 4]. A wide range of oscillatory activity has also been reported to occur in the BG and in the associated regions of the cortex [5–7]. These oscillations may have an important role in both the normal and altered functions of the BG.

© Springer International Publishing AG 2017
A. Lintas et al. (Eds.): ICANN 2017, Part I, LNCS 10613, pp. 129–136, 2017.
https://doi.org/10.1007/978-3-319-68600-4_16

Striatal medium spiny neurons (MSNs; comprise about 95% of neurons in the striatum [8]) and fast spiking interneurons (FSIs; comprise 1–2% of striatal neurons [9]) are entrained to cortical oscillations in both awake and anaesthetized animals [10]. Previously we showed that FSIs play a prominent role in spreading input oscillations to the MSNs [11]. Here, we extended our earlier model to systematically study the interplay between different, externally induced striatal oscillations. We are particularly interested in the following two questions: (1) How are properties of the oscillatory driven MSNs influenced via a multiplicity of input-driven oscillations through FSIs? (2) How do different oscillatory-driven FSI populations transfer oscillations, and which parameters are crucial for the mutual frequency modulation? Therefore, we explored wide ranges of stimulation intensities, frequencies, and phases in order to manipulate the oscillatory properties of the striatal network. Our simulations show that features of these oscillations, including amplitude and frequency fluctuations, can be influenced by a change in the input intensities onto MSNs or FSIs and that these fluctuations are also highly dependent on the selected frequencies. Finally, our results show the influence that the phase offset between different cortical inputs have on modulating spectral characteristics of the network in the different frequency bands. These data suggest that several parameters can impact the interference between oscillatory signals within the striatal network.

2   Methods

Our model comprises two types of striatal neurons, MSNs and FSIs. We have chosen to use the simple leaky integrate-and-fire neuron model that lacks inherent oscillatory features and, therefore, all frequency responses are a direct outcome of network interactions. Subthreshold dynamics of the membrane potential $V_i(t)$ of a neuron i (i $\in$ {MSN, FSI}) is described by the following equation:

$$C \frac{d}{dt} V_i(t) + G_{rest}[V_i(t) - V_{rest}] = I_i(t), \tag{1}$$

where I_i is the total synaptic input current to the neuron, and C and G_{rest} denote the passive electrical cell properties, i.e. the capacitance and conductance of its membrane at rest (V_{rest}), respectively. When the membrane potential reaches a fixed spiking threshold, V_{th}, a spike is emitted and the membrane potential is reset to the resting value.

There are at least two main inhibitory circuits in the striatum that are activated by the cortical inputs and that control firing in MSNs [12]. The first is feedforward inhibition via population of FSIs, and the second is feedback inhibition from the axon collaterals of the MSNs themselves. We simulated a network encompassing neurons within the volume of the dendrites of one MSN (2800 MSNs and 56 FSIs). The connection probability between MSNs was equal to 0.18 [13] and from FSIs to MSNs was set to 0.2 (each MSN receives inhibitory inputs from 4–27 FSIs [14], and in this study we set an average value of 11).

Synaptic inputs were modelled by transient conductance changes using the alpha function such that:

$$g_{\tau}^{\mu} = \begin{cases} J_{\tau}^{\mu} \dfrac{t}{\tau_{\tau}} e^{1 - \frac{t}{\tau_{\tau}}} & for\ t \geq 0 \\ 0 & for\ t \leq 0 \end{cases}, \tag{2}$$

where $\mu \in \{MSN, FSI\}$, $\tau \in \{excitation, inhibition\}$, τ denotes the rise times for synaptic inputs, and J stands for the peak amplitude of the conductance transient ('strength' of the synapses). The parameter values for both MSNs and FSIs and more details about the model design can be found in [11].

Specific populations of neurons received sinusoidal current, corresponding to an external stimulation from other brain areas, given for neuron i as:

$$I_{i,ext}(t) = A_i \sin\left(C_{fi}t + \delta_i\right), \tag{3}$$

The amplitude of oscillations A_i depended on the selected neuron population and the driving frequency C_f. The sinusoidal input was present from the start of the simulation, and δ was a random starting phase in the $0° - 180°$ range. The background activity constrained MSNs to fire < 1 Hz and FSIs < 10 Hz.

Network activity in the population that consisted of MSNs was further evaluated by counting the overall spiking activity in time bins of 5 ms, which was equal to the number of active cells per time bin. Therefore, we estimated the spectrum of the population activity, directly from the spike trains, using the Fast-Fourier-Transform with the sampling frequency set to 200 Hz.

The values in different groups were compared using the Mann-Whitney U-test and a $p < 0.01$ was considered statistically significant.

We first studied the striatal network in the case when MSNs received oscillatory inputs at 40 Hz while FSIs were entrained to different frequencies (Fig. 1a). In the second case, half of the FSIs received oscillatory inputs at 40 Hz while the other half was oscillating at different frequencies (Fig. 1b). Lastly, each FSI was getting two oscillatory inputs (Fig. 1c). In two last scenarios, MSNs received only excitatory Poisson inputs (Fig. 1b and c).

All network simulations were written in the Python interface to NEST [15]. The dynamical equations were integrated at a fixed temporal resolution of 0.01 ms using the fourth order Runge-Kutta method. Simulations ran for 1 s and each explored scenario was repeated and averaged 10 times, yielding 10 trials.

3   Results

We developed a spiking network model of the corticostriatal network to investigate interactions in the striatal network with different oscillation frequencies. We conducted a series of simulations that varied the frequencies, amplitude intensities, and phase offsets of the oscillatory inputs to study their interplay and impact on the oscillation transfer to MSNs. Previously we have shown that FSIs can perform an important role in transferring particular cortical oscillations to the striatum [11]. The spectral peak in the

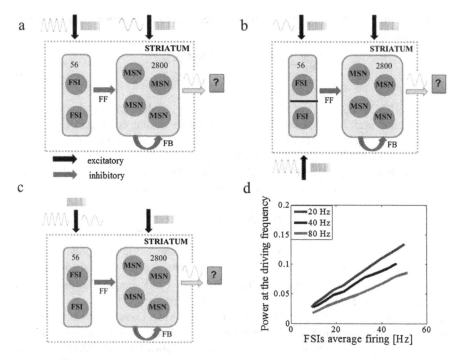

Fig. 1. Striatal network model and different oscillatory inputs. (**a**) Schematic of the network model of the striatum in the case when MSNs receive oscillatory inputs at the 40 Hz while FSIs are entrained to different frequencies. (**b**) Half of the FSIs receive oscillatory inputs at 40 Hz while the other half oscillates at different frequencies. (**c**) Each FSI gets two oscillatory inputs. In the last two scenarios, MSNs receive only excitatory Poisson inputs ($J_{exc}^{MSN} = 2.4$ nS). (**d**) Transfer of the external oscillations to the MSNs population depends on the driving frequency and FSIs' firing.

MSN population activity directly depended on the average firing of FSIs and the frequency of input oscillations (Fig. 1d). In this study, we first (Fig. 1a) investigated the response of the MSN network that received oscillatory inputs at 40 Hz (see Methods; average firing of MSNs was equal to 1.38 Hz when driven with the oscillatory inputs on the top of the background inputs), while FSIs were subjected to the range of different external frequencies. Varying the driving frequency alone of the FSI network (for a constant stimulation intensity; $A_{max}^{FSI} = 350$ pA) had a strong influence on the spectrum of the MSN population activity. Figure 2a details the power decrease in the case when FSIs were oscillating at different driving frequencies compared to the scenario when FSIs were not present (only values that were lower than the mean of all negative values are depicted). For all driving frequencies into FSIs, there was a noticeable decrease at the driving frequency of the MSNs. Power increase was also present (Fig. 2b; only values that were higher than the mean of all positive values are shown) and not only in the case of driving frequencies into FSIs. Components at the sum and absolute difference of the driving frequency into MSNs and driving frequencies into FSIs (sideband frequencies) have also emerged what indicates a plurality

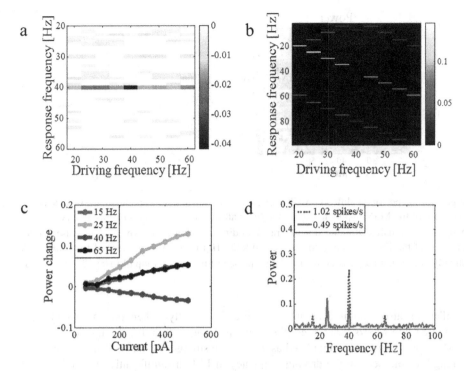

Fig. 2. Interplay between oscillatory inputs into MSNs and FSIs. (a) The power decrease of the MSN network that receives oscillatory inputs at 40 Hz (the referent network), while FSIs are subjected to the range of different external frequencies, indicated on the x-axes, and when compared to the scenario when FSIs are not present (only values that are lower than the mean of all negative values are depicted). (b) The power increase of the network explained in (a) and when compared to the scenario when FSIs are not present (only values that are higher than the mean of all positive values are shown). Components at the sum and absolute difference of the driving frequency into MSNs and driving frequencies into FSIs (sideband frequencies) are also present. (c) The influence of the stimulation intensity into FSIs on the power spectrum of the MSN population. As the value of A_{max}^{FSI} linearly increased, there is a prominent increase in the peak strength at the driving frequency into FSIs (25 Hz) and gradual decrease of the peak strength at the driving frequency into MSNs (40 Hz). The strengths of the sideband oscillations also exhibited increase (15 Hz and 65 Hz). (d) Change of A_{max}^{MSN} leads to a significant modulation of the peak at the driving frequency of MSNs.

of the network response. Further, we wanted to see how the peak frequencies change when stimulation intensity of oscillatory inputs was varied to both FSIs (Fig. 2c) and MSNs (Fig. 2d), in the case when driving frequency into FSIs was fixed to 25 Hz. First, we systematically varied the maximum input amplitude into FSIs (A_{max}^{FSI}), and recorded values at both driving frequencies and sideband frequencies. As the value of A_{max}^{FSI} linearly increased, we observed a gradual increase in the peak strength for the driving frequency into FSIs and at the same time a gradual decrease of the peak strength for the driving frequency into MSNs. The strengths of the sideband

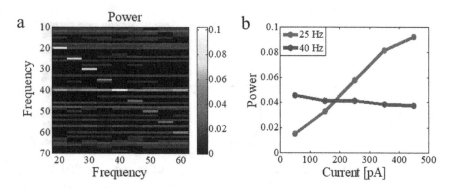

Fig. 3. Influence of the different oscillatory inputs into separated FSI populations. **(a)** The power spectrum of the MSN population when the first half of FSIs receives oscillatory inputs at 40 Hz and the second half is stimulated with a range of different frequencies. **(b)** A_{max}^{FSI} increase into the first half of the FSIs (driving frequency equal to 25 Hz) leads to an increase of the peak, while slightly decreasing the peak at the driving frequency of the other group (40 Hz; $J_{exc}^{MSN} = 2.4$ nS).

oscillations also exhibited an increase (Fig. 2c). Lastly, when the maximum input amplitude into MSNs was varied, the strength of the peak at the driving frequency of MSNs was significantly modulated as well as the strength of the sideband frequencies. Strength of the peak at the driving frequency of FSIs insignificantly changed (0.1135 vs. 0.1212, p > 0.5; Fig. 2d). In contrast, when the FSIs population was divided into two groups (Fig. 1b), the first receiving oscillatory inputs at 40 Hz and the second was stimulated with a range of different frequencies, the sideband oscillations were not present (Fig. 3a). The amplitude increase of the oscillatory inputs into the second half increased the peak in the power spectrum at its driving frequency (25 Hz), while slightly decreasing the peak at the driving frequency of the first group (Fig. 3b).

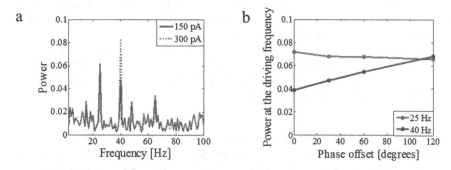

Fig. 4. Influence of the input amplitude and different phase offsets in the case when FSIs were stimulated with two independent oscillatory inputs at 25 Hz and 40 Hz. **(a)** An increase in the input amplitude for one of the inputs (40 Hz) significantly increases the peak strength compared to the baseline condition (when both inputs have the same $A_{max}^{FSI} = 150$ pA). **(b)** The phase offset between the two input signals shapes the spectral characteristics at the corresponding driving frequencies.

Finally, in the case when FSIs were stimulated with two independent oscillatory inputs at two different driving frequencies (25 Hz and 40 Hz; Fig. 1c), we observed that two parameters determined the strength of oscillations. First, an increase in the input amplitude for one of the inputs (40 Hz) increased significantly its strength compared to the baseline condition (when both inputs had the same $A_{max}^{FSI} = 150$ pA), and insignificantly decreased the strength of the observed oscillations for the other oscillatory input (Fig. 4a). Second, the phase offset between the two input signals was very important and shaped the spectral characteristics at the corresponding driving frequencies (Fig. 4b).

4   Conclusions

One of the most prominent features of the BG is their rich oscillatory activity that varies with the behavioral state [6]. Oscillations have also been observed at the level of individual MSNs firing and local field potential in the striatum of both awake and anaesthetized animals [5–7, 10]. First, the striatal oscillations are present in different frequency bands which might be important for normal neural processing. Second, it is quite likely that the experimentally observed oscillations in the striatum are in fact cortical oscillations transmitted by the cortico-striatal projections. Our previous work revealed that FSIs play a prominent role in spreading input oscillations to the MSNs [11]. However, in a more biologically plausible scenario the two different neuronal populations will also receive simultaneous oscillatory inputs at different frequencies. For instance, oscillatory inputs onto MSN population may be different from the oscillatory inputs onto FSI population. In this research, we extended our previous model substantially in order to further explore the interactions in the striatal network with different oscillation frequencies. Our results indicate that interactions between those frequencies depend on many stimulation parameters. We show that the features of these oscillations, including amplitude and frequency fluctuations, can be influenced by a change in the input intensities onto MSNs or FSIs and that these fluctuations are also highly dependent on the selected frequencies in addition to the phase offset between different cortical inputs. These data suggest that the striatum can exploit different parameters to impact the interference between oscillatory signals. Future work will explore the role of different frequency ranges and the mechanisms involved in their integration within and between different BG nuclei.

Acknowledgements. The research leading to these results has received funding from The European Horizon 2020 Framework Programme under grant agreement n°720270 (Human Brain Project SGA1); The Swedish Research Council; NIAAA (grant 2R01AA016022); Swedish e-Science Research Center; EuroSPIN – an Erasmus Mundus Joint Doctoral program.

References

1. Bolam, J.P., Hanley, J.J., Booth, P.A.C., Bevan, M.D.: Synaptic organisation of the basal ganglia. J. Anat. **196**, 527–542 (2000)
2. Herrmann, C.S., Murray, M.M., Ionta, S., Hutt, A., Lefebvre, J.: Shaping intrinsic neural oscillations with periodic stimulation. J. Neurosci. **36**, 5328–5337 (2016)
3. Canolty, R.T., Knight, R.T.: The functional role of cross-frequency coupling. Trends Cogn. Sci. **14**, 506–515 (2010)
4. Maris, E., Fries, P., van Ede, F.: Diverse phase relations among neuronal rhythms and their potential function. Trends Neurosci. **39**, 86–99 (2016)
5. Belić, J.J., Halje, P., Richter, U., Petersson, P., Hellgren Kotaleski, J.: Untangling cortico-striatal connectivity and cross-frequency coupling in L-DOPA-induced dyskinesia. Front. Syst. Neurosci. **10**, 1–12 (2016)
6. Boraud, T., Brown, P., Goldberg, J.A., Graybiel, A.M., Magill, P.J.: Oscillations in the basal ganglia: the good, the bad, and the unexpected. In: Bolam, J.P., Ingham, C.A., Magill, P.J. (eds.) The Basal Ganglia VIII. Advances in Behavioral Biology, vol. 56, pp. 1–24. Springer, New York (2005). doi:10.1007/0-387-28066-9_1
7. Berke, J.D.: Fast oscillations in cortical-striatal networks switch frequency following rewarding events and stimulant drugs. Eur. J. Neurosci. **30**, 848–859 (2009)
8. Oorschot, D.E.: Total number of neurons in the neostriatal, pallidal, subthalamic, and substantia nigral nuclei of the rat basal ganglia: a stereological study using the cavalieri and optical disector methods. J. Comp. Neurol. **366**, 580–599 (1996)
9. Tepper, J.M., Bolam, J.P.: Functional diversity and specificity of neostriatal interneurons. Curr. Opin. Neurobiol. **14**, 685–692 (2004)
10. Beatty, J.A., Song, S.C., Wilson, C.J.: Cell-type-specific resonances shape the responses of striatal neurons to synaptic input. J. Neurophysiol. **113**, 688–700 (2015)
11. Belić, J., Kumar, A., Hellgren Kotaleski, J.: Interplay between periodic stimulation and GABAergic inhibition in striatal network oscillations. PLoS ONE **12**(4), e0175135 (2017)
12. Tepper, J.M., Plenz, D.: Microcircuits in the striatum: striatal cell types and their interaction. Microcircuits: the interface between neurons and global brain function, pp. 127–148. The MIT Press, Massachusetts, Cambridge (2006)
13. Tepper, J.M., Koós, T., Wilson, C.J.: GABAergic microcircuits in the neostriatum. Trends Neurosci. **27**, 662–669 (2004)
14. Koós, T., Tepper, J.M.: Inhibitory control of neostriatal projection neurons by GABAergic interneurons. Nat. Neurosci. **2**, 467–472 (1999)
15. Gewaltig, M.O., Diesmann, M.: Nest (neural simulation tool). Scholarpedia **2**, 1430 (2007). doi:10.4249/scholarpedia.1430

Robot Localization and Orientation Detection Based on Place Cells and Head-Direction Cells

Xiaomao Zhou[1,2][✉], Cornelius Weber[2], and Stefan Wermter[2]

[1] College of Automation, Harbin Engineering University,
Nantong Street. 145, Harbin 150001, China
[2] Department of Computer Science, University of Hamburg,
Vogt-Kölln-Strasse. 30, 22527 Hamburg, Germany
{zhou,weber,wermter}@informatik.uni-hamburg.de
http://www.informatik.uni-hamburg.de/WTM

Abstract. Place cells and head-direction cells play important roles in animal navigation and have distinguishable firing properties in biology. Recently, a slowness principle has been argued as the fundamental learning mechanism behind these firing activities. Based on this principle, we extend previous work, which produced only a continuum of place and head-direction cells and mixtures thereof, to achieve a clean separation of two different cell types from just one exploration. Due to the unsupervised learning strategy, these firing activities do not contain explicit information of position or orientation of an agent. In order to read out these intangible activities for real robots, we propose that place cell activities can be utilized to build a self-organizing topological map of the environment and thus for robot localization. At the same time, the robot's current orientation can be read out from the head-direction cell activities. The final experimental results demonstrate the feasibility and effectiveness of the proposed methods, which provide a basis for robot navigation.

Keywords: Place cell · Head-direction cell · Slowness principle · Unsupervised learning · Robot localization

1 Introduction

Precise metric map building and pose detection are always convenient for robot navigation. During the last decades, various sensors [1] and approaches [2] have been proposed to build high-precision world representations and to detect the exact postures of a mobile agent. However, the necessity of using high-accuracy sensory information for navigation is still an open issue. Many animals present excellent navigational capabilities in various environments with limited sensing abilities compared to man-made sensors. For example, the human visual system cannot measure distance with an accuracy as a laser rangefinder does. Thus, the underlying mechanisms of visual processing should be a possible basis for successful navigations.

© Springer International Publishing AG 2017
A. Lintas et al. (Eds.): ICANN 2017, Part I, LNCS 10613, pp. 137–145, 2017.
https://doi.org/10.1007/978-3-319-68600-4_17

For animal navigation, findings of place cells [3], head-direction cells [4] and grid cells [5] in the hippocampus and entorhinal cortex can give some insights into how visual information is processed. In the hippocampus, certain neurons termed place cells have been found to become active when an animal reaches a certain position in the environment. Their firing activities are largely independent of the direction in open areas while displaying a certain degree of orientation-dependence in specific environmental structures for example, in linear tracks [6]. In contrast, head-direction cells are related to the direction of the animal's head. When the animal turns its head to a specific direction, these cells will fire significantly and their activities show a clear invariance to the position [7].

To model these firing activities computationally, the slowness principle [8] has been shown to be a candidate mechanism for learning. With a hierarchical structure, place cells or head-direction cells in a virtual rat were reproduced by processing its visual inputs only [9]. However, the strategy of changing movement patterns to generate different cell types was not plausible considering that, to get various cell types, an animal will not explore the same environment many times with different moving strategies. Note that this simple feed-forward model is memoryless and does not use recurrent circuitry for path integration.

In this paper, we propose a biologically plausible approach to generate place and head-direction cells simultaneously, in which an agent can produce different cell types from just one exploration. Then, we present a method of interpreting the encoded information. Considering that place cell activities encode positional information but in an implicit fashion, we bypass this problem by using a self-organizing network [10] to learn the relational structure of these activities in an unsupervised manner. By doing this, a topological map of the explored space is built for localization, which can be used for future navigation without explicit positional information. Based on head-direction cells which only fire when it comes close to their preferred direction, we calculate the agent's real-time orientation and estimate how much directional information is encoded in these activities in order to assess whether they contain sufficient information for navigation.

2   Experimental Setup and Methodologies

2.1   Experimental Set-Up

We use the RatLab simulator to generate our training data and to test our proposed approach [11]. RatLab provides an easy way to simulate a rat's random exploration in a variety of environments. It allows to change the environmental enclosures and textures, to place obstacles and to configure the moving strategies of the virtual rat. The rat's visual input during moving can be collected as training images to the Slow Feature Analysis (SFA) algorithm, in order to train place cells and head-direction cells. In this work, we use RatLab to replicate a real robot experiment.

2.2   Slow Feature Analysis

SFA is an unsupervised learning algorithm based on a slowness principle [8].
For raw sensory inputs, SFA intends to capture the slowly varying signals and
leave out quickly changing ones, such as trivial noise. In most cases, these slowly
varying features encode the underlying causes of input changes, which contain
the most descriptive statistical regularities.

Mathematically, the learning problem behind SFA can be described as follows: Given an I-dimensional input signal $x(t) = [x_1(t), x_2(t), \ldots, x_I(t)]$, find a
set of J real-valued input-output functions $g(t) = [g_1(t), g_2(t), \ldots, g_J(t)]$ such
that the output signal $y(t) = [y_1(t), y_2(t), \ldots, y_J(t)]^T$ with $y_j(t) = g_j(x(t))$ satisfies the criteria:

$$\Delta(y) = \langle \dot{y}_j^2 \rangle_t \quad is\ minimal \tag{1}$$

under three constraints:

$$\langle y_j \rangle_t = 0 \quad zero\ mean$$
$$\langle y_j^2 \rangle_t = 1 \quad unit\ covariance$$
$$\forall j' < j : \langle y_{j'} y_j \rangle_t = 0 \quad decorrelation$$

with $\langle \cdot \rangle$ and $\dot{y}$ indicating temporal averaging and the time derivative of y, respectively. Equation 1 expresses the primary objective of this optimization problem.
The first two constraints guarantee the output signals with meaningful information, instead of a trivial constant value. Decorrelation avoids uninteresting
solutions where different output signals encode the same information. In our
work, we implement SFA with a hierarchical architecture proposed in [11] to
learn place and head-direction cells from raw visual input.

2.3   Growing When Required Network

For the purpose of map building and localization, a self-organized Growing When
Required (GWR) network [10] learns a spatial map by extracting the important
topological relations of place cell activities during exploration. To map the input
space, GWR exerts a dynamic growing criterion and grows whenever the current
nodes cannot represent the input accurately. It can respond quickly to changes
in the input distribution by dynamically creating or deleting nodes and edges
during the learning process.

The GWR network starts with two random nodes n_1 and n_2 representing the
input space. For each iteration, the two best matching nodes s and t, determined
by the distance to the input, are first found and connected. Whenever s and t
fail to represent the current input sufficiently well, a new node will be added
halfway between them. The criterion of adding new nodes also relies on the
winning node's firing counter. The training will drive the weights of the winner
node and its neighbours to move towards the input and the rarely used nodes

will be deleted by an aging mechanism. The algorithm will keep iterating until meeting a stop criterion, such as performance behavior and network size.

3   Approach, Experimental Results and Discussion

3.1   Training with One Exploration

The training process and corresponding model configurations are illustrated in Fig. 1. Each network includes a hierarchical architecture containing three SFA layers and one ICA layer. Each SFA layer consists of a regular grid of SFA nodes which contain 30 or 40 output channels (cells) and act on a local receptive field, for example, the first layer has 63 × 9 SFA nodes working directly on the raw input images. On top of the SFA layers, one final ICA node performs a function of sparse coding on the raw SFA outputs to produce a more localized representation. We use 40 units in each SFA node for the head-direction cells outnumbering 30 units for the place cells to increase the precision of the orientation estimation (Sect. 3.3). For the training, during the *forward movement*, the robot changes its position continuously, while rotational information changes slowly. Obviously, the emerging slow features during forward movement compactly encode the robot's direction. Since SFA is sensitive to slowly varying signals, it will extract the directional information within this phase. Thus, the visual data from this moving period can be used for head-direction cell network training. Similarly, positional information will be a relatively slow signal during the robot's *turning movement* where directional information changes quickly. So we can use this phase to train the place cell network. This mechanism assumes that learning is modulated by behavior and, more specifically, that transitional and rotational motion can be differentiated to train different types of cells. This can in principle be supported by behavioral modulation of head-direction cells [12] and of place cells [13].

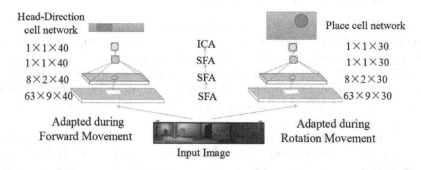

Fig. 1. Training place cell and head-direction cell networks in different phases of the same trajectory. Layers are trained sequentially from bottom to top.

Parts of the training results can be seen in Fig. 2. The learnt place cells only fire in a certain position in the environment (Fig. 2(a)) and they have little directional tuning, which means their activities are invariant to direction (Fig. 2(b)). Head-direction cells show little position preference (Fig. 2(c)), but they will be significantly active when it comes to their preferred direction (Fig. 2(d)).

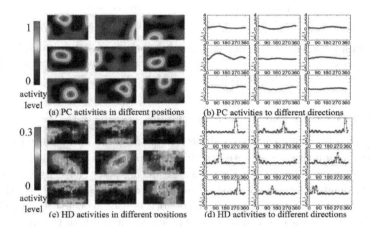

(a) PC activities in different positions   (b) PC activities to different directions

(c) HD activities in different positions   (d) HD activities to different directions

Fig. 2. Place cell activities and head-direction cell activities trained by the proposed approach (9 randomly chosen place cells are shown in (a) and (b), and 9 head-direction cells are shown in (c) and (d)).

In order to assess whether these two different cell types have obtained distinguishable firing properties, we adopt the concept of entropy. Assume a set of distributions using these activities as their probability values. For example, place cells have similar probabilities to be activated for different head directions. Their activities closely approximate a uniform random distribution and have a large entropy of direction H_{dir}. In contrast, head-direction activities are more peaked since they have large probability values for a certain direction, thus with a smaller entropy H_{dir}. The entropies are calculated by:

$$H_{dir} = -\sum_{\theta}^{dir} a_\theta \ln(a_\theta); \quad H_{pos} = -\sum_{i}^{pos} a_i \ln(a_i) \tag{2}$$

where a_θ represents normalized cell activity at direction θ averaged over positions, while a_i represents normalized cell activity at position i averaged over directions. Figure 3(b) shows that we obtain two cell types with clearly different properties using our proposed training. For comparison, Fig. 3(a) shows the training result of the existing model [9] which produces a continuum between place and head-direction cells, but not two distinct clusters.

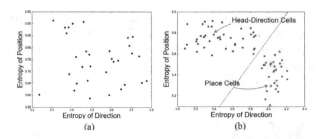

Fig. 3. Entropy analysis: (a) Training results from standard SFA, without knowledge to distinguish different cell types. (b) With our proposed training method, different cell types form two separate clusters.

3.2   Map Building Based on Place Cells

In our approach, we obtain place cell activities based on an unsupervised learning algorithm, which means these activities do not have a predefined relation to the agent's real-world position. However considering place cells' firing preference to different positions, collectively, these activities encode a certain environmental position. For spatial learning, a GWR network is used to capture the relationships of these activities and to build a topological map. Since the inputs to the GWR network are high-dimensional place cell activities, we use multidimensional scaling (MDS) [14] to visualize the map in two dimensions. Figure 4(a) shows that the trained GWR network represents the 2D topology of the agent's exploration area based on the place cells' activities. The robot's current position is represented by the winner neuron which has the weight vector closest to the input.

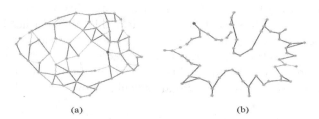

Fig. 4. (a) GWR result with input from a virtual rat's place cell activities in a square arena (rotation is caused by MDS). (b) GWR result based on the head-direction cell activities. The current state is represented by the winner node (red node). (Color figure online)

3.3   Orientation Detection Based on Head-Direction Cells

We applied the same analysis as in (Sect. 3.2) to the head-direction cell activities. Figure 4(b) shows that the trained GWR network captures the ring topology of a circular ground truth. However, due to the unsupervised learning, the head-direction cells' activation vector contains no predefined directional information.

In order to estimate the precision of the directional information lying in these activities, we use a simple vector sum process, based on knowledge of the real orientation. The principle behind the vector sum is that when the robot's current orientation is close to some head-direction cells' preferred direction, these cells will fire significantly and will dominate the sum result. However, in real scenarios, exploration may not fully cover all positions in the environment or perceive one position from different perspectives. We may have some head-direction cells with poor tuning, like Cell 2 in Fig. 5(a). So we assign to each cell k a reliability value R_k with a normalization as follows:

$$R_k = \left| \sum_{\theta}^{dir} a_\theta^k \right| \Big/ \sum_{\theta}^{dir} |a_\theta^k| \tag{3}$$

where a_θ^k is the activity vector of head-direction cell k to the direction of θ.

By doing this, more reliable head-direction cells (with clear direction preference) will contribute more to the vector sum than unreliable ones. The orientation sum vector v is calculated as follows:

$$v = \sum_{k}^{cells} (a^k R_k \sum_{\theta}^{dir} a_\theta^k) \tag{4}$$

where a^k denotes the activity of cell K and R_k represents its reliability value. $\sum_{\theta}^{dir} a_\theta^k$ approximates the activity vector of cell k to its preferred direction.

Figure 5(c) shows that, while the robot rotates its head, the real-time orientation can be reconstructed by these cells activities with a certain accuracy. The average error over all directions is $14.73°$ in our case.

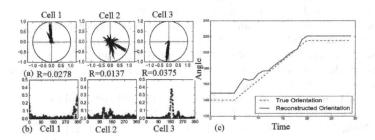

Fig. 5. (a) Head-direction cell activities to different directions. (b) Normalized head-direction cell activities to visualize their reliability R. (c) True and reconstructed robot orientation from 40 head-direction cell activities

4   Conclusion and Future Work

In this paper, we propose a method to train two distinct clusters of place cells and head-direction cells with SFA during just one exploration. The results showed that different cell types can emerge simultaneously with our proposed approach, using visual input and modulation from motion-related information. Using self-organised mapping and multidimensional scaling, we reconstructed a 2D area topology from the place cell activities and a 1D ring topology from the head-direction cell activities. With the head-direction cells, we obtained the agent's orientation by considering their firing preference to direction. Our experimental results demonstrate the potential of the proposed approach to provide fundamental information for robot navigation.

Obtaining of directional information allows future work of building a cognitive map, which has previously been done by using spatial information obtained from a ceiling camera [15]. The directional information of a link between neighboring GWR nodes, in our work, can be assigned based on the head-direction cell activities, without knowledge of the exact direction, and can be reused during path planning. Thus, a natural next step is to validate this work on a real robot platform, which may lead to a robust nature-inspired navigation system.

Acknowledgments. We thank Xiaolin Hu for feedback and acknowledge support from the German Research Foundation DFG, project CML (TRR 169).

References

1. Lobo, J., Marques, L., Dias, J., Nunes, U., de Almeida, A.T.: Sensors for mobile robot navigation. In: de Almeida, A.T., Khatib, O. (eds.) Autonomous Robotic Systems. Lecture Notes in Control and Information Sciences, vol. 236, pp. 50–81. Springer, London (1998). doi:10.1007/BFb0030799
2. Borenstein, J., Everett, R.H., Feng, L., Wehe, D.: Mobile robot positioning - sensors and techniques. J. Robotic Syst. **4**, 231–249 (1997)
3. Keefe, J.O., Burgess, N.: Geometric determinants of the place fields of hippocampal neurons. Nature **381**, 425–428 (1996)
4. Taube, J.S., Muller, R.U., Ranck, J.B.: Head-direction cells recorded from the postsubiculum in freely moving rats. I. Description and quantitative analysis. J. Neurosci. **10**, 420–435 (1990)
5. Moser, E.I., Kropff, E., Moser, M.B.: Place cells, grid cells, and the brain's spatial representation system. Annu. Rev. Neurosci. **31**, 69–89 (2008)
6. Dombeck, D.A., Harvey, C.D., Tian, L., Looger, L.L., Tank, D.W.: Functional imaging of hippocampal place cells at cellular resolution during virtual navigation. Nat. Neurosci. **13**, 1433–1440 (2010)
7. Sharp, P.E., Hugh, T.B., Jeiwon, C.: The anatomical and computational basis of the rat head-direction cell signal. Trends Neurosci. **24**, 289–294 (2001)
8. Wiskott, L., Sejnowski, T.J.: Slow feature analysis: unsupervised learning of invariances. Neural Comput. **14**(4), 715–770 (2002)
9. Franzius, M., Sprekeler, H., Wiskott, L.: Slowness and sparseness lead to place, head-direction, and spatial-view cells. PLoS Comput. Biol. **3**, 1605–1622 (2007)

10. Marsland, S., Shapiro, J., Nehmzow, U.: A self-organising network that grows when required. Neural Netw. **15**, 1041–1058 (2002)
11. Schönfeld, F., Wiskott, L.: RatLab: an easy to use tool for place code simulations. Front. Comput. Neurosci. **7**, 104–111 (2013)
12. Chen, L.L., Lin, L.H., Green, E.J., McNaughton, B.L.: Head-direction cells in the rat posterior cortex. Exp. Brain Res. **101**, 8–23 (1994)
13. Lu, X., Bilkey, D.K.: The velocity-related firing property of hippocampal place cells is dependent on self-movement. Hippocampus **20**, 573–583 (2010)
14. Borg, I., Groenen, J.F.: Modern Multidimensional Scaling: Theory and Applications. Springer, New York (2005). doi:10.1007/0-387-28981-X
15. Yan, W., Weber, C., Wermter, S.: Learning indoor robot navigation using visual and sensorimotor map information. Front. Neurorobotics **7**(15) (2013). doi:10.3389/fnbot.2013.00015

Algorithms for Obtaining Parsimonious Higher Order Neurons

Can Eren Sezener[1(✉)] and Erhan Oztop[2]

[1] Bernstein Center for Computational Neuroscience, Berlin, Germany
can@bccn-berlin.de
[2] Ozyegin University, Istanbul, Turkey
erhan.oztop@ozyegin.edu.tr

Abstract. Most neurons in the central nervous system exhibit all-or-none firing behavior. This makes Boolean Functions (BFs) tractable candidates for representing computations performed by neurons, especially at finer time scales, even though BFs may fail to capture some of the richness of neuronal computations such as temporal dynamics. One biologically plausible way to realize BFs is to compute a weighted sum of products of inputs and pass it through a heaviside step function. This representation is called a Higher Order Neuron (HON). A HON can trivially represent any n-variable BF with 2^n product terms. There have been several algorithms proposed for obtaining representations with fewer product terms. In this work, we propose improvements over previous algorithms for obtaining parsimonious HON representations and present numerical comparisons. In particular, we improve the algorithm proposed by Sezener and Oztop [1] and cut down its time complexity drastically, and develop a novel hybrid algorithm by combining metaheuristic search and the deterministic algorithm of Oztop [2].

1 Introduction

Higher Order Neurons (HONs), which we define in the next section, can represent Boolean functions (BFs) in a biologically plausible way, to which we also refer to as sign-representation. For a given n-variable BF, there are infinitely many HON representations with 2^n or less many monomials (product terms). To our knowledge there is no efficient algorithm (i.e. non-brute force) that produces HON representations with a guaranteed (small) margin off the theoretical optimal. However, a margin guarantee was given by Oztop [3] which led to the first deterministic algorithm that finds HON representations with at most 0.75×2^n monomials [2]. Later, Amano showed that almost all BFs can be sign-represented with less than 0.617×2^n monomials [4]. Recently, Sezener and Oztop developed a heuristic algorithm that obtains very compact (i.e. employing small number of monomials) sign-representations by taking advantage of the structure of the spectral coefficients [1]. With this algorithm it was possible to show that the analytical bound given by [3] is far from being tight, at least, for low dimensions. For instance, it was discovered that all 5-variable BFs can be represented with only 11 monomials whereas the theoretical results gave the bound of $0.75 \times 2^5 = 24$.

© Springer International Publishing AG 2017
A. Lintas et al. (Eds.): ICANN 2017, Part I, LNCS 10613, pp. 146–154, 2017.
https://doi.org/10.1007/978-3-319-68600-4_18

In this study[1], we improve the heuristic algorithm of Sezener and Oztop [1] to cut down the running time drastically, and give two direct applications of Genetic Algorithms (GAs) to sign representation. In addition, we develop a novel hybrid algorithm by combining GA search and the deterministic algorithm of Oztop [2] to find sign representations with lower densities. Finally, we compare these methods in terms of time efficiency and compactness of the representations found.

2   Representation of Boolean Functions

Spectral representation: For every BF f, there is a unique multilinear polynomial p_f that exactly interpolates f at all possible input combinations, which in particular, can be obtained by Lagrange Interpolation [3]:

$$p_f(x_1, x_2, \cdots, x_n) = \sum_{i=1}^{2^n} s_i \prod_{k \in S_i} x_k \text{ where } S_i \text{ runs over the powerset of}$$

$\{1, 2, .., n\}$.

This representation is called the spectral representation of f, and the coefficients (s_i) are referred as the spectral coefficients and are uniquely determined by Lagrange Interpolation for a given f. With a fixed ordering over the monomials (i.e. the products appearing in the expression of p_f), the spectral coefficients can be considered as a vector $\mathbf{s} \in \mathbb{R}^{2^n}$, and used to represent f. With this, we obtain two vector representations of a given BF: one is the spectrum $\mathbf{s}$ and the other is the natural binary vector $\mathbf{f}$ that is obtained by listing the function values for all variable assignments. With adoption of a suitable ordering[2], these two representations can be related by $\mathbf{f} = \mathbf{Ds}$ where $\mathbf{D}$ is the $2^n \times 2^n$ Sylvester-type Hadamard Matrix with columns representing the monomials evaluated at all possible input assignments taken in the adopted assignment order [5]. Due to the orthogonality of $\mathbf{D}$, the spectrum can be simply found by $\mathbf{s} = 2^{-n}\mathbf{Df}$. $\mathbf{D}$ is easy to construct recursively:

$$\mathbf{D}_0 = \begin{bmatrix} 1 \end{bmatrix} \text{ and } \mathbf{D}_{n+1} = \begin{bmatrix} \mathbf{D}_n & \mathbf{D}_n \\ \mathbf{D}_n & -\mathbf{D}_n \end{bmatrix} \text{ for } n > 0.$$

Higher Order Neuron / sign representation: We say that a polynomial p sign-represents a BF f, if and only if $f(x_1, x_2, \cdots, x_n) = \text{sign}(p(x_1, x_2, \cdots, x_n))$ for all $x_i \in \{-1, 1\}$. In vector notation this is expressed as $\mathbf{f} = \text{sign}(\mathbf{Da})$ where $\mathbf{a}$ is the vector of the coefficients of p. Hence, for a given BF f, all the sign-representations are characterized by $\mathbf{a} = 2^{-n}\mathbf{DY}_f\mathbf{k}$ with arbitrary $\mathbf{k} > \mathbf{0}$, where $\mathbf{Y}_f := diag(\mathbf{f})$. This is also called a Higher Order Neuron (HON) or a Sigma-Pi Neuron representation, which potentially captures the nonlinear operations of the dendrites [6].

---

[1] An earlier version of the paper was posted as arXiv:1504.01167.

[2] The vector is constructed as $[1, x_1, x_2, x_2x_1, x_3, x_3x_1, x_3x_2x_1, ..., x_n...x_2x_1]$. Assignments to $(x_1, x_2, x_3, ..., x_n)$ are ordered as (0's represent 1's and 1's represent -1's): $000...0, 100...0, 010...0, 110...0, ..., 111...1$.

Threshold Density: The minimum number of monomials that is sufficient to sign-represent a given BF f is called the *threshold density* of f.

Table 1 illustrates the HON representations found for the function $f_E = [-1, -1, -1, -1, -1, -1, 1, 1, -1, 1, -1, 1, -1, 1, 1, -1]$, which has a threshold density of 9 [1].

Table 1. HON representations of a 4-variable BFs obtained by different algorithms.

Algorithm	HON representation of f_E
3-Quarters	$-2 \cdot x_1 - 2 \cdot x_2 \cdot x_1 - 2 \cdot x_3 \cdot x_1 + 2 \cdot x_3 \cdot x_2 \cdot x_1 - 3 \cdot x_4 + 3 \cdot x_4 \cdot x_1$
	$-3 \cdot x_4 \cdot x_2 + 3 \cdot x_4 \cdot x_2 \cdot x_1 - 3 \cdot x_4 \cdot x_3 + 3 \cdot x_4 \cdot x_3 \cdot x_1$
	$+3 \cdot x_4 \cdot x_3 \cdot x_2 - 3 \cdot x_4 \cdot x_3 \cdot x_2 \cdot x_1$
L-Heuristic	$-x_2 \cdot x_1 - x_3 \cdot x_1 + x_3 \cdot x_2 \cdot x_1 - x_4 \cdot x_2 + x_4 \cdot x_2 \cdot x_1 - x_4 \cdot x_3$
	$+x_4 \cdot x_3 \cdot x_1 + x_4 \cdot x_3 \cdot x_2 - x_4 \cdot x_3 \cdot x_2 \cdot x_1$
B-Heuristic	$-2 \cdot x_2 \cdot x_1 - x_3 - x_3 \cdot x_1 + 2 \cdot x_3 \cdot x_2 - x_4 + 2 \cdot x_4 \cdot x_1 - x_4 \cdot x_2$
	$-2 \cdot x_4 \cdot x_3 + x_4 \cdot x_3 \cdot x_1 + x_4 \cdot x_3 \cdot x_2$

3 Algorithms for Sign-Representation

A series of sign-representation algorithms can be built based on the following useful result which we give without proof [1,2]:

Lemma 1. *Let* $\mathbf{Q}_f = diag(\mathbf{f})\mathbf{D}$, *and* $[\mathbf{A}, \mathbf{B}]$ *be an arbitrary partitioning of the columns of* $\mathbf{Q}_f$. *Then* $\exists \mathbf{k} > 0$ *such that* $\mathbf{k}^T \mathbf{B} = \mathbf{0}$ *if and only if* $\mathbf{a} = [\mathbf{A0}]^T \mathbf{r}$ *for some* $\mathbf{r} > 0$ *sign-represents* f, *i.e.* $\mathbf{Q}_f \mathbf{a} > 0$.

According to the above lemma, if we can find a $\mathbf{k} > 0$ such that $\mathbf{B}^T \mathbf{k} = \mathbf{0}$, it means that we can always 'eliminate' the monomials corresponding to $\mathbf{B}$. So a straightforward brute force algorithm to find this value can be given as:

Algorithm 1. A brute-force algorithm for finding the min density of f

---
1 Let $\mathbf{Q} = diag(\mathbf{f})\mathbf{D}$;
2 Enumerate all the column submatrices of $\mathbf{Q}$ as $\mathbf{B}_1, \mathbf{B}_2, ... \mathbf{B}_{2^{2^n}}$;
3 Set S as $\{\}$;
4 **for** $i = 1, 2, 3, \ldots, 2^{2^n}$ **do**
5   **if** $\exists \mathbf{k} > 0$, $\mathbf{k}^T \mathbf{B} = \mathbf{0}$ **then**
6   store (# of columns of $\mathbf{B}_i$) in S;

7 **return** $2^n - \max(S)$

Although the existence check in Line 5 can be done efficiently (e.g. by using Linear Programming methods), due to the super-exponential growth (with respect to n) of the number of column submatrices, the brute force solution is not feasible for investigating threshold densities of BFs with 6 or more variables. Since this problem is NP-hard, even with respect to the number of monomials (i.e., $N = 2^n$) [7], it is not likely that a deterministic algorithm that finds an optimal solution in subexponential time can be constructed. Therefore, we study heuristic algorithms, with the aim of finding near-optimal solutions (and optimal in some cases) in a fraction of the time required for the exhaustive search.

3.1   Structural heuristics for sign representation

The initial bounds for the threshold densities were obtained as $2^n - \sqrt{2^n} + 1$ see [8,9]. Later, an elementary proof was obtained establishing a significantly better bound on the threshold density as 0.75×2^n [3]. Based on this result, 3-Quarters algorithm with several variants were developed [2]. More recently Sezener and Oztop [1] gave a heuristic fast algorithm (L-Heuristic) that obtains HONs with low densities. This allowed the investigation of exact densities for low dimensions, and as a result the large gap between the theoretical bounds and the actual densities has been discovered. Unlike the brute-force method which checks the power set of monomials (2^{2^n} many) for a solution, the L-Heuristic only checks 2^n many subsets (see Algorithm 2). The logic is based on the intuition that some monomials are 'easier' to eliminate and as such it first attempts to eliminate the 'easy' monomials and then moves on to the harder ones. It does a single pass over the 2^n monomials and therefore is very efficient compared to the brute-force method which searches over 2^{2^n} subsets for possible solution.

Algorithm 2. L-Heuristic

---

1   $m = 1, E = \{\}$;
2   Sort the monomials using their absolute spectral coefficients as keys;
3   **while** $m < 2^n$ **do**
4   **if** *monomials from 1 to m that are not in E cannot be eliminated* **then**
5   add m to E;
6       $m = m + 1$;
7   **return** $2^n - cardinality\ of\ E$

In this study, we propose a modification to this algorithm (see Algorithm 3) to further reduce its running time. The idea is to change m (which controls how many monomials are to be eliminated) somewhat similar to binary search, rather than incrementing it by one at each trial (2^n many increments in total). With this change, the subroutine that checks for eliminability (e.g., via a LP routine) would be called $\log_2 2^n = n$ times in the worst case as opposed to 2^n times. This slight modification results in more than 100-fold increase in speed for 10-variable BFs.

Algorithm 3. B-Heuristic

---

1 $lo = 1$, $hi = 2^n - 1$;
2 Sort the monomials using their absolute spectral coefficients as keys;
3 **while** $lo \leq hi$ **do**
4      $m = floor((hi + lo)/2)$;
5   **if** *first m monomials can be eliminated* **then**
6          $lo = m + 1$;
7   **else**
8          $hi = m - 1$;

9 **return** m

In the results section, we show that this algorithm (B-Heuristic, see Algorithm 3) obtains HONs much faster than L-Heuristic and with less than 1 additional monomial on average for 4-variable BFs.

3.2   Metaheuristics for Sign Representation

In general, finding the minimal threshold density of a BF f is a combinatorial optimization problem. As such, it can be attacked by many metaheuristic algorithms. In this subsection, we present our investigations with Genetic Algorithms (GA) where we created two variants that search for solutions directly. Our initial intuition was that GAs would be successful and might even beat L- and B-heuristics described above. GAs seem to be suitable for obtaining low density sign-representations as we have a discrete optimization problem with multiple global minima and a large (discrete) parameter space (i.e. super exponential in the number of variables). In this section we present the direct applications of GAs to the problem; in the next section, we use GA in a more clever way to search in the arbitrary parameter space of the 3-Quarters algorithm that readily finds solutions with small number of monomials [2].

Subset-GA: Searching a Maximal Set of Monomials to Eliminate. Let **b** be an indicator binary vector of length 2^n to uniquely identify a submatrix $\mathbf{Q_b}$ of $\mathbf{Q}$ for elimination by having a 1 at position i to pick the ith column of $\mathbf{Q}$ (**b** in fact represents the elimination set E in Algorithms 1 and 2). Now, our goal is to find the **b** with the maximum number of 1's that indicates a $\mathbf{Q_b}$ that can be eliminated, which, thus ensures a solution due to Lemma 1 (where $\mathbf{Q_b}$ corresponds to **B** matrix in the lemma). We utilize the GA implementation of the MATLAB optimization toolbox with its default settings. The GA searches for genotypes (i.e. **b** vectors) with higher fitness values, which we defined as $\sum_{i=1}^{2^n}[b_i$ if $isEliminable(\mathbf{Q_b})$ else $0]$, where $isEliminable$ checks whether the columns of its argument can be annihilated by a positive vector (i.e., Line 5 of Algorithm 1). Intuitively, the GA tries to find the largest subset of monomials that are not 'needed' to sign-represent the BF under consideration.

K-GA: Generating Random Solutions. Instead of directly searching subsets that can be eliminated, one can generate random solutions by producing random positive **k** vectors based on the genotype. Because all the solutions are of the form $\mathbf{a} = 2^{-n}\mathbf{D}_n\mathbf{Y}_f\mathbf{k}$ with arbitrary $\mathbf{k} > \mathbf{0}$, we encode **k** as a vector composed of integers between 1 and k_{max}[3]; and again utilize MATLAB GA implementations to conduct the search.

The cardinality of $\mathcal{K} = \{\mathbf{k}|\mathbf{k} \in \mathbb{Z}_+^N$ and $\forall_i \, k_i \leq k_{max}\}$, where N is the number of monomials (i.e., 2^n), is $(k_{max})^N$. On the other hand, there are 2^N different configurations if one uses the subset-GA setting. Hence, for $k_{max} > 2$, the subset-GA search is conducted over a smaller space. The evaluation of the fitness values for a given genotype can be done in polynomial time with respect to N for both GAs once it is known that a solution is possible. The subset-GA needs to first check whether the selected subsets (bit negation of b) leads to a sign-representation. This check is cast as a linear programming problem with N variables and m constraints, which can be realized in $O(N^c)$ number of steps for a constant c by interior-point methods (in practice $c \approx 3.5$). The k-GA by default always generates sign-representation but to be able to evaluate the representation, it must be explicitly found. This can be done in $O(N^2)$ time as only a vector-matrix multiplication is needed to pass from **k** to monomial coefficients. In short, the subset-GA deals with a smaller search space, however it suffers from a higher worst-case time complexity. We present the performances of these two GAs as well as the aforementioned algorithms in the next section.

3.3 3Q-GA: Optimizing the Free Parameters of the 3-Quarters Algorithm

In the 3-Quarters Algorithm [2], there are several free parameters. Those parameters are selected arbitrarily in [2] since the algorithm guarantees solutions with $3/4 \cdot 2^n$ monomials or less, regardless of the value of the free parameters. However, a careful selection of these parameters may create more parsimonious solutions. An optimization on these free parameters is undertaken for the first time with this study. As a result, interesting and significant improvements have been obtained, which are presented in the next section. To this end, we utilized the GA implementation of MATLAB optimization toolbox as well.

3-Quarters is based on the fact that for a given n-variable BF f all the sign-representing vectors $\mathbf{a} = [\mathbf{wt}]^T$ can be obtained by arbitrary choices of row vectors $\alpha, \alpha', \beta, \beta'$ of appropriate size: $\mathbf{w^T} = (\alpha + \alpha')\mathbf{F} + (-\beta + \beta')\mathbf{G}$ and $\mathbf{t^T} = (-\alpha + \alpha')\mathbf{F} + (\beta + \beta')\mathbf{G}$ where $\mathbf{F}$ and $\mathbf{G}$ are $p \times 2^{n-1}$ and $q \times 2^{n-1}$ sized f-dependent fixed matrices. Depending whether $p > q$, either α, α' or β, β' vectors are set to **0.5**. This is the first freedom of choice since each component of those vectors can be independently set to any positive value. Once this is done, the next second freedom of choice pops out as $\mathbf{v} = (-\beta + \beta')$ if we have already determined α and α' in the previous step, or $\mathbf{v} = (-\alpha + \alpha')$ if we have already

---

[3] By inspection, we choose k_{max} as 5 and further constrain the space to odd-integers.

determined β and β' in the previous step. The details of the procedures and the mathematical justification can be found in [2].

What is important to see here is if $v_i \leq 0$ then $\beta_i = x_i + |v_i|, \beta'_i = x_i$ with $x_i > 0$ would satisfy $v_i = (-\beta_i + \beta'_i)$. On the other hand, if $v_i > 0$ then $\beta_i = x_i, \beta'_i = x_i + |v_i|$ with $x_i > 0$ would satisfy $v_i = (-\beta_i + \beta'_i)$. Here we just give the reasoning for the case of $v_i = (-\beta_i + \beta'_i)$, i.e. $p \leq q$, but the case for $v_i = (-\alpha_i + \alpha'_i)$, i.e. $p > q$, is exactly symmetrical. Thus the second freedom of choice is the selection of $\mathbf{x} > \mathbf{0}$ vector, which is of size 2^{n-1}. As in k-GA, we need to limit that maximum possible values for the components of $\mathbf{x} > \mathbf{0}$ and for both of (α, α') or (β, β') vector pairs. In our computations, we used the same constraints with k-GA. So the GA tuned these parameters by selecting from $\{1, 3, 5\}^{2^n}$ in order to increase the number of zeros in the $\mathbf{a} = [\mathbf{wt}]^{\mathbf{T}}$. It is worth reiterating that no matter what the GA finds, the number of zeros is guaranteed to be more than 0.25×2^n due to the 3-Quarters theorem [3]. Therefore, in this case, the search takes place in a 'nicer' region of the full search space.

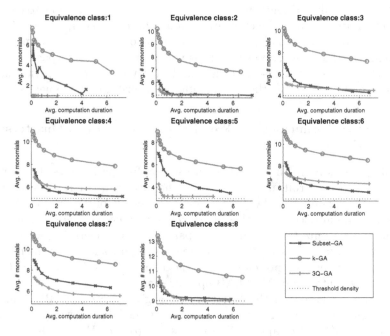

Fig. 1. Average number of monomials obtained for 4-variable BF equivalence classes. The x-axis denotes the average computation time of an algorithm to obtain the representations with y many monomials on the average (actual experimental data points are indicated with o, x and + markers). The horizontal dashed line indicates the ground truth of the threshold density for the particular problem class.

4   Results and Conclusion

We conducted numerical experiments by solving 4-variable BFs. It is possible to define several equivalence classes over the BFs with the minimum threshold density as an invariant [1]. Therefore it suffices to study a single member from each equivalence class to reason about all BFs. In Fig. 1, we separately present the average results for each equivalence class[4] of 4-variable BFs in order to assess the behavior of different algorithms on individual function classes. It should be noted that the 8th equivalence class is composed of only the so-called bent functions, which are conjectured to be the hardest BFs to be sign-represented in terms of number of monomials they require [1]. If the bent functions are in fact always the hardest functions, the best known upper bounds for the maximum threshold density of n-variable BFs can be obtained by simply finding threshold densities of bent functions. However, L and B-Heuristic are completely ineffective for representing bent functions because bent functions have flat spectrums, which make the heuristics equivalent to random search. On the other hand, It can be seen that both the subset-GA and 3Q-GA obtain close-to-perfect results for bent functions rather quickly. In particular, 3Q-GA seems to be the best for the bent function class. Therefore, GAs might be suitable for finding parsimonious representations for bent functions. The number of generations a GA runs determines the total running time of the program as well as the quality of its results. Because more generations usually mean better results, to get a better idea of their performance, we ran the GAs with different stopping conditions. Note that for B-Heuristic, L-Heuristic and 3-Quarters additional time is not beneficial, since they do not perform optimization until an iteration limit is reached, so in Fig. 1 their performances are shown as single points. Overall, we see that the L-Heuristic finds representations with the least number of monomials among all the studied algorithms. None of the GA based algorithms get close to the L-Heuristic even when they utilize 100-fold more CPU time. On the other hand, the B-Heuristic obtains similar results to the L-Heuristic, which is an impressive performance considering its very low time complexity. This makes, the B-Heuristic a good choice for studying very high dimensional BFs.

References

1. Sezener, C.E., Oztop, E.: Minimal sign representation of boolean functions: algorithms and exact results for low dimensions. Neural Comput. **27**(8) (2015)
2. Oztop, E.: Sign-representation of boolean functions using a small number of monomials. Neural Netw. **22**(7), 938–948 (2009)
3. Oztop, E.: An upper bound on the minimum number of monomials required to separate dichotomies of -1, 1^n. Neural Comput. **18**(12) (2006)
4. Amano, K.: New upper bounds on the average PTF density of boolean functions. In: Cheong, O., Chwa, K.-Y., Park, K. (eds.) ISAAC 2010. LNCS, vol. 6506, pp. 304–315. Springer, Heidelberg (2010). doi:10.1007/978-3-642-17517-6_28

---

[4] The same equivalence classes and numbering used in [1] is adopted.

5. Siu, K.Y., Roychowdhury, V., Kailath, T.: Discrete Neural Computation. Prentice Hall, Englewood Cliffs (1995)
6. Mel, B.W.: Information processing in dendritic trees. Neural Comput. **6** (1994)
7. Amaldi, E., Kann, V.: On the approximability of finding maximum feasible sub-systems of linear systems. In: Enjalbert, P., Mayr, E.W., Wagner, K.W. (eds.) STACS 1994. LNCS, vol. 775, pp. 521–532. Springer, Heidelberg (1994). doi:10. 1007/3-540-57785-8_168
8. Saks, M.E.: Slicing the hypercube. In: London Mathematical Society Lecture Note Series 187: Surveys in Combinatorics. Cambridge University Press (1993)
9. O'Donnell, R., Servedio, R.: Extremal properties of polynomial threshold functions. In: Eighteenth Annual Conference on Computational Complexity (2003)

Robust and Adaptable Motor Command Representation with Sparse Coding

Nobuhiro Hinakawa[1]([⊠]) and Katsunori Kitano[2]

[1] Graduate School of Information Science and Engineering, Ritsumeikan University,
1-1-1 Nojihigashi, Kusatsu, Shiga 5258577, Japan
h@cns.ci.ritsumei.ac.jp
[2] Department of Human and Computer Intelligence, Ritsumeikan University,
1-1-1 Nojihigashi, Kusatsu, Shiga 5258577, Japan
kitano@ci.ritsumei.ac.jp

Abstract. The advantages of using sparse coding to represent neural information have previously been suggested. It has been proposed for the neural information processing of sensory information, particularly visual information, but its role in processing motor information is poorly understood. In this study, therefore, we considered a motor-related system to determine the benefits of using sparse coding for motor command representation in terms of its energy cost, robustness against noise, and adaptability to damage. We compared the properties contributed by sparse coding and dense coding by simulating a task involving a reaching movement with a two-joint arm model. Our results showed that sparse coding was more beneficial than dense coding for each of the properties that we investigated, which suggests that it is worthy of study as a possible approach to representing the coding of motor-related information in the central nervous system.

Keywords: Sparse coding · Motor command · Reaching movement · Multi-joint arm

1 Introduction

In sparse coding, each item of information is represented by a small portion of neurons. It is more advantageous than the grandmother cell hypothesis and dense coding for neural information coding in terms of efficiency and robustness [1,2].

The use of sparse coding has been suggested for sensory information processing, especially in the visual cortex [3]. Little is known on its applicability to motor information processing, although a recent modeling study suggested that it can provide a contribution [4]. Our musculoskeletal system has a redundant structure; i.e., the number of muscles per joint is larger than the necessary and sufficient number required to manipulate the joint. This causes a severe problem in motor planning; in the case of a reaching movement, the trajectory of the endpoint (i.e., hand) from the starting point to the target point cannot be uniquely

© Springer International Publishing AG 2017
A. Lintas et al. (Eds.): ICANN 2017, Part I, LNCS 10613, pp. 155–162, 2017.
https://doi.org/10.1007/978-3-319-68600-4_19

determined. Because some constraints are required to determine a unique trajectory, most studies have considered kinematic or kinetic constraints to date [5]. On the other hand, it has been recently hypothesized that a constraint can be placed on neural information coding rather than on the kinematic or kinetic properties [6].

In this work, we examined using sparse coding to represent motor commands for a two-joint arm model [6] and compared it with dense coding in terms of efficiency and robustness.

2   Methods

2.1   Two-Joint Arm Model

We simulated the planar reaching movements of a two-joint (i.e., shoulder and elbow) arm model (Fig. 1a). The upper arm and forearm are controlled by six muscles [7]. These muscles are activated by the motor command $\boldsymbol{u}(t)$, where $u_i(t)(\geq 0)$ is the motor command for the ith muscle. The state of the arm is described by the vector of the two angles $\boldsymbol{\theta}(t) = (\theta_1(t), \theta_2(t))^T$, where $\theta_1(t)$ and $\theta_2(t)$ denote the angles of the shoulder and elbow, respectively. The torques for the angles are represented by $\boldsymbol{\tau}(t) = (\tau_1(t), \tau_2(t))^T$ and written as

$$\boldsymbol{\tau}(t) = AD\boldsymbol{u}(t), \tag{1}$$

where $A(2 \times 6)$ and $D(6 \times 6)$ are the constant moment arm and scaling matrices, respectively. With this, the dynamics of the arm can be described by the following equation of motion:

$$\ddot{\boldsymbol{\theta}}(t) = -M(\boldsymbol{\theta})^{-1}(C(\boldsymbol{\theta}, \dot{\boldsymbol{\theta}}) + B\boldsymbol{\theta} - \boldsymbol{\tau}), \tag{2}$$

where M is the inertia tensor and C denotes the centrifugal and Coriolis forces. The parameters of A, D, M, and C are assigned values determined in previous studies [6]. By using $\boldsymbol{\theta}(t)$, we can obtain the coordinate of the endpoint as $(x, y) = (l_1 \cos(\theta_1) + l_2 \cos(\theta_1 + \theta_2), l_1 \sin(\theta_1) + l_2 \sin(\theta_1 + \theta_2))$.

We chose a set consisting of a starting point and target point from 23 grid points on the horizontal plane of the reaching movement, which we termed a movement pattern. Hence, $23 \times 22 = 506$ patterns of reaching movements were supposed to be acquired with this arm model.

2.2   Motor Commands

It is hypothesized that the motor command for each muscle $u_i(t)$ can be determined by linearly combined basis functions that represent different temporal profiles of signals. Hence, the motor command for the ith muscle is represented by

$$u_i(t) = \sum_{j=1}^{3} \sum_{k=0}^{N_k} \omega_{ijk} \phi_j(t - kT) \quad (\omega_{ijk} \geq 0). \tag{3}$$

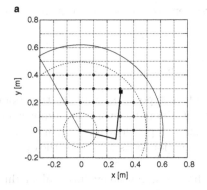 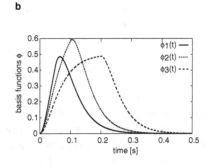

Fig. 1. Planar reaching movement task with a two-joint arm model. **a.** Coordinate of the reaching movement task. The shoulder of the two-joint arm is set to the origin $(x, y) = (0, 0)$ of the plane. The 23 grid points indicated by circles are candidates for the starting point and target point for the endpoint indicated by the filled square; hence, $23 \times 22 = 506$ movement patterns can be considered. **b.** Basis functions used to generate motor commands. Three types of temporal profiles are assumed; $\phi_1(t)$ rises and decays the fastest, whereas $\phi_3(t)$ is the slowest.

$\phi_j(t)$ represents the basis functions shown in Fig. 1b. kT is the discretized onset $(k = 0, 1, \cdots, N_k)$. T and N_k were set to 0.3 s and 1, respectively. $\boldsymbol{\omega} = (\omega_{ijk})$ is the coefficient vector ($6 \times 3 \times 2 = 36$ dimensions), which yields a time course of $\boldsymbol{u}(t)$. Therefore, in this model, motor planning corresponds to determining the appropriate vector $\boldsymbol{\omega}$.

2.3 Optimization of Motor Commands

Here, we formulate this exploration of $\boldsymbol{\omega}$ as an optimization problem. The reaching movement task requires the error between the target point and endpoint of the arm to be minimized. Therefore, the error function can be defined as

$$\text{Error}(\boldsymbol{\omega}; \boldsymbol{\kappa}) = \frac{1}{L+1} \sum_{l=0}^{L} \kappa_l |\boldsymbol{x}(t_l; \boldsymbol{\omega}) - \boldsymbol{x}_\mathrm{T}|^2, \qquad (4)$$

where $\boldsymbol{x}_\mathrm{T}$ is the coordinate of the target point. $t_0 \ (= 0.4 \ [\mathrm{s}])$ is the time for completion of a reaching movement, but it is not the beginning of the movement. The error should be evaluated even after the completion time because the endpoint should be kept at the target point for a while (i.e., until the end of the observation time $t_L = 0.8$ s). κ_l is the weight of the error at time l. Here, we increased the weights immediately after the completion time and at the end of the observation time.

We also introduced the following preference function to impose a constraint on the neural representation of motor commands $\boldsymbol{\omega}$:

$$\text{Preference}(\boldsymbol{\omega}; \boldsymbol{\lambda}) = \lambda_1 \sum_{ijk} \omega_{ijk} + \lambda_2 \sum_{ijk} \omega_{ijk}^2. \qquad (5)$$

Here, the first term is responsible for sparse representation, whereas the second term reduces the power.

Thus, the cost function is

$$\text{Cost}(\omega; \kappa, \lambda) = \text{Error}(\omega; \kappa) + \text{Preference}(\omega; \lambda). \tag{6}$$

The cost function depends on both the target point x_T and starting point (an initial condition) $x(0)$. This means that it differs for every set of movement patterns; i.e., we have to solve the optimization problem for each movement pattern. The vector that minimizes the cost function ω^* is defined as the optimal motor command for a movement pattern.

We solved the optimization problem with the differential evolution algorithm, which is a type of evolutional computation algorithm [8].

3   Results

3.1   Sparse vs. Dense Motor Command Representation

We first detected the optimal motor commands ω^* for 506 patterns of starting and target points in the sparse coding ($\lambda_1 \neq 0$) and the non-sparse (i.e., dense) coding ($\lambda_1 = 0$). Figure 2a shows typical examples of trajectories for the reaching movement under the two conditions. The trajectories commonly showed outwardly bell-shaped curves, although they tended to be long in the case of non-sparse coding. After the completion time ($t = 0.4$ s), the endpoint was retained in the vicinity of the target point, as confirmed by the short red lines. As shown in Fig. 2b, under the sparse condition only three or four elements took non-zero values for all of the movement patterns, whereas under the dense condition this was found to occur for almost all of the elements. Figure 2c shows the changes in torque $\int_0^T \dot{\tau}(t)^T \dot{\tau}(t)\, dt$ for the 506 movement patterns under the two conditions; the results suggest that reaching movements by sparse coding exhibited a smaller change in torque [5].

3.2   Robustness Against Noise

Second, we investigated the extent to which the representation of motor commands was robust against noise. We did this by adding uniform random noise to the optimal motor command vector ω^*. Each element of the vector ω^*_{ijk} was assumed to be $\omega^*_{ijk}(1 + \eta)$, where η was the uniform random number drawn from $[-0.05, 0.05]$ or $[-0.1, 0.1]$. Figure 3a shows the trajectories of a movement pattern generated by motor commands including noise. The locations of the endpoint at the completion time were scattered more widely with dense coding than with sparse coding, and the "bundle" of trajectories was thick with dense coding.

For 20 randomly sampled movement patterns, we obtained the distance error between the target point and endpoint at the end of observation (or simulation) time t_{end} ($= 0.8$ s), $|x(t_{\text{end}}) - x_T|$. We conducted 20 trials for each movement

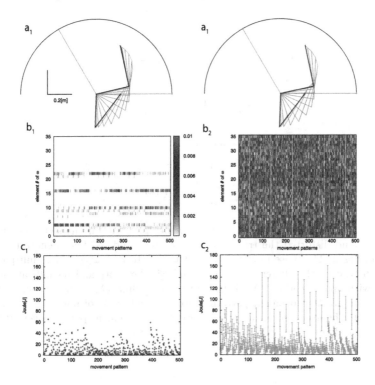

Fig. 2. Examples of endpoint trajectories and motor command representation. **a.** Trajectory generated by the optimal motor command for a set of starting (0.2, 0) and target (0.2, 0.4) points. While the green curve shows the endpoint trajectories until the completion time of the movement (0.4 s), the red lines show the fluctuations after the completion time. a_1 and a_2 indicate results obtained by sparse coding ($\lambda_1 \neq 0$) and dense coding ($\lambda_1 = 0$), respectively. **b.** Motor command representation for all of the movement patterns. The vertical line represents the optimal vector of 36 dimensions ω^* for a movement pattern. Similar to **a**, b_1 and b_2 indicate results obtained with sparse coding ($\lambda_1 \neq 0$) and dense coding ($\lambda_1 = 0$), respectively. **c** Changes in torque during reaching movements. Each point represents the change in torque for each movement pattern. Red and green points indicate the changes with sparse and dense coding, respectively. (Color figure online)

pattern and then averaged the errors over the trials. Figure 3b summarizes the results. Generally, sparse coding proved more robust against noise than dense coding for the two different levels of noise intensity.

3.3   Adaptation of the Motor Command System to Damage

Finally, we assumed the case where part of the motor system is damaged and the remaining part of the system reorganizes the motor command representation to compensate. Damage to the system was represented by forcing some of the elements of ω to be unavailable—i.e., by setting it to 0. After the damage, the

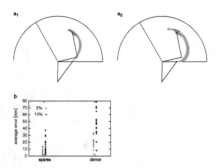

Fig. 3. Effect of noise on the accuracy of movements. **a.** Adding noise to the optimal motor command distorted the trajectories. The green and red lines denote the same as those in Fig. 2. The noise intensity was set to 0%–10% of $|\omega_{ijk}|$. The multiple lines indicate 20 trials with different noise patterns. Similarly, $\mathbf{a_1}$ and $\mathbf{a_2}$ indicate results obtained with sparse coding ($\lambda_1 \neq 0$) and dense coding ($\lambda_1 = 0$), respectively. **b.** Average errors for 20 movement patterns with different levels of noise intensity. Each dot represents the averaged error $|\boldsymbol{x}(t_L) - \boldsymbol{x}_{\mathrm{T}}|$ for a movement pattern over 20 trials. (Color figure online)

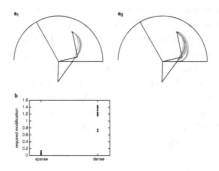

Fig. 4. Compensation for damage to the optimal motor command representation. Under the condition where some elements of $\boldsymbol{\omega}^*$ are forced to be unavailable, we examined the recovery of the motor command representation through re-optimization of the remaining elements. **a.** Trajectories after the recovery. The multiple green lines indicate trajectories for 20 trials. Similarly, $\mathbf{a_1}$ and $\mathbf{a_2}$ indicate results obtained with sparse coding ($\lambda_1 \neq 0$) and dense coding ($\lambda_1 = 0$), respectively. **b.** Required amounts of modification of $\boldsymbol{\omega}$ for 20 movement patterns. Each dot represents the sum of the amounts of modification $|\omega_{ijk}^{rec} - \omega_{ijk}^*|$ for a movement pattern. (Color figure online)

remaining available elements of ω were optimized to generate motor commands. Figure 4a shows the trajectories after this reorganization of the motor command representation. The green lines represent the acquired trajectories resulting from different patterns of damage (i.e., different combinations of unavailable elements). Although the trajectory variation was larger with dense coding, the reaching movement was achieved by both forms of coding even after damage.

We evaluated the cost of reorganization, i.e., the total amount of modification required by the motor commands. The cost was defined as the sum of the amounts of modification $\sum_{ijk} |\omega^{rec}_{ijk} - \omega^*_{ijk}|$, where ω^*_{ijk} and ω^{rec}_{ijk} are the values before and after recovery, respectively. As shown in Fig. 4b, sparse coding greatly reduced the cost in comparison to dense coding. When we considered relative changes of each motor command element, the average changes per element in both types of coding were almost on par. However, the averaged error to the target was smaller with sparse coding than with dense coding.

4 Discussion

As presented above, the torque driving the two-joint arm for reaching movements was successfully generated by motor commands with both sparse coding and dense coding. However, the motor command representation with sparse coding was found to be more beneficial than that with dense coding from the following viewpoints: (i) the signals required for muscle activation, the energy consumed by the muscles, and the total amount of torque change during a movement were greatly reduced; (ii) the target accuracy improved when commands were perturbed by noise; and (iii) the cost for reorganizing the motor command representation after partial damage to the motor system was greatly reduced. Thus, our results suggest that sparse coding for motor-related neural information processing is worthy of study. The other type of cost function, or endpoint variance, has been suggested to perform more appropriately [9]. Although this may cause a different result, the advantages of sparse coding itself should not be greatly influenced.

Meanwhile, the biological relevance of the model should be discussed, particularly with respect to the following two points. First, the neural substrates of the motor command ω and basis functions $\phi(t)$ need to be established. In the proposed model, ω represents direct signals of muscle forces rather than kinematic parameters, such as the direction of a reach. The primary motor cortex codes not only movement directions but also forces [10]. However, the sparse representation in the motor cortex has been not evident so far. Therefore, ω may be interpreted as the activity of a neural population in the spinal cord but not in the motor cortex. Based on such an hypothesis, $\phi(t)$ is a temporal pattern of synaptic currents activated by the spinal cord neurons. The other is the necessity for a method to obtain optimal motor commands ω^*. Here, we used an evolutional computation to obtain these commands, but this should preferably be achieved by using a method that can be implemented by synaptic plasticity, such as the BCM rule [11]. In future work, an important challenge will be incorporating more realistic details such as these into the present model.

References

1. Willshaw, D.J., Buneman, O.P., Longuet-Higgins, H.C.: Non-holographic associative memory. Nature **222**, 960–962 (1969)
2. Tsodyks, M.V., Feigelman, M.V.: Enhanced storage capacity in neural networks with low level of activity. Europhys. Lett. **6**, 101 (1988)
3. Olshausen, B.A., Field, D.J.: Emergence of simple-cell receptive field properties by learning a sparse code for natural images. Nature **381**, 607–609 (1996)
4. Takiyama, K.: Sensorimotor transformation via sparse coding. Sci. Rep. **5**, 9648 (2015). doi:10.1038/srep09648
5. Uno, Y., Kawato, M., Suzuki, R.: Formation and control of optimal trajectory in human multijoint arm movement. Biol. Cybern. **61**, 89–101 (1989)
6. Ikeda, S., Sakaguchi, Y.: Motor planning as an optimization of command representation. In: Proceedings of 48th IEEE Conference on Decision and Control (2009)
7. Katayama, K., Kawato, M.: Virtual trajectory and stiffness ellipse during multijoint arm movement predicted by neural inverse models. Biol. Cybern. **69**, 353–362 (1993)
8. Storn, R., Price, K.: Differential evolution - a simple and efficient heuristic for global optimization over continuous spaces. J. Global Optim. **11**, 341–359 (1997)
9. Harris, C.M., Wolpert, D.M.: Signal-dependent noise determines motor planning. Nature **394**, 780–784 (1998)
10. Kalaska, J.F., Cohen, D.A., Hyde, M.L., Prud'homme, M.: A comparison of movement direction-related versus load direction-related activity in primate motor cortex, using a two-dimenstional reaching task. J. Neurosci. **9**, 2080–2102 (1989)
11. Binenstock, E.L., Cooper, L.N., Munro, P.W.: Theory for the development of neuron selectivity: orientation specificity and binocular interaction in visual cortex. J. Neurosci. **2**, 32–48 (1982)

Translation-Invariant Neural Responses as Variational Messages in a Bayesian Network Model

Takashi Sano$^{(\boxtimes)}$ and Yuuji Ichisugi

The National Institute of Advanced Industrial Science and Technology (AIST),
Tokyo, Japan
{t.sano,y-ichisugi}@aist.go.jp

Abstract. In this paper, we propose the following interpretation: if a Bayesian network has acquired translation invariance in input images, its feedback messages from higher layers to lower layers can be interpreted as the response of complex cells in the visual system. To examine our proposal's validity, we trained a Bayesian network to acquire translation invariance using the standard belief propagation algorithm, and confirmed its feedback messages were translation invariant and thus they can be interpreted as the response of complex cells. Unlike previous studies, our model does not require specially prepared random variables. Furthermore, our model only uses the standard belief propagation algorithm. Therefore we believe that our model is more natural than the previous ones to integrate hierarchical Hubel-Wiesel architectures for the visual system, e.g. Hierarchical MAX models, and probabilistic graphical models.

Keywords: Visual cortex · Belief propagation · Bayesian network · Complex cells · Translation invariance

1 Introduction

Ranging from behavioral psychology to physiological experiments, probabilistic computation is strongly suggested as the fundamental computational principle of brain [1]. Especially for the visual cortex of mammals, probabilistic approaches are successfully employed to explain some extra-classical receptive field properties in the primary visual area (V1), for example, end-inhibition or context-dependent responses [2].

Most of the theories of vision are, however, based on non-probabilistic, feedforward neural networks [3,4]. Series of these studies originate from the finding of the simple and complex receptive fields [5]. In the primary visual area, both neurons that have the simple receptive fields and neurons that have the complex receptive fields are strongly tuned to their optimal orientations of stimuli (e.g. slit of light). For the position (or phase) of stimuli, however, simple cells have narrow, optimal positions, while complex cells respond relatively broad positions. This suggests that features extracted by simple cells are pooled by

© Springer International Publishing AG 2017
A. Lintas et al. (Eds.): ICANN 2017, Part I, LNCS 10613, pp. 163–170, 2017.
https://doi.org/10.1007/978-3-319-68600-4_20

complex cells. The neocognitron architecture [6] mimics these findings to build an object recognition model with a hierarchical feedforward neural network, in which convolutional feature extraction and max-pooling operation are repeated alternatingly. This kind of architecture, called convolutional neural networks or HMAX (Hierarchical MAX) models [3,4], is currently known to be the state-of-the-art visual recognition model.

These studies naturally lead us to the question; How can we integrate probabilistic models and the HMAX-like models? Although many probabilistic models are proposed for visual recognition tasks, most of them reproduce only responses of simple cells but not those of complex cells. For an exceptional example, convolutional deep belief networks (CDBNs) [7] consist of stacked restricted Boltzmann machines with special probabilistic pooling variables that correspond to complex cells. There are also models that are based on Bayesian networks in which variables for simple cells and complex cells are arranged in a way similar to the HMAX-model architecture [8]. In both cases, models of these types require special handling for complex-cell variables for model architecture building or for learning.

In this paper, we propose an alternative way to interpret simple cells and complex cells in probabilistic graphical models. Our approach is based on belief propagation, a bidirectional message propagation algorithm [9]. We point out that if a graphical model has successfully learned translation invariance in its higher levels, variational messages from those levels should have translation invariance. This means lower levels can receive translation invariant signals in feedback messages and therefore do not require special variables for complex-cells' behavior.

This paper is organized as follows; In the next section, we explain our approach to the integration of the graphical models and the HMAX models by comparing it to the previous attempts. To examine our idea, we performed an experiment by using a combination of a Bayesian network and the belief propagation algorithm. A preliminary of the experiment is given in Sect. 3, and results of the experiment appear in Sect. 4. Section 5 is devoted to describe the conclusion.

2   Related Work on Integration of Graphical Models and HMAX Models

A remarkable attempt to unify HMAX-like models and probabilistic graphical models is found in ref. [8]. The authors of ref. [8] propose the Bayesian network model that contains two kinds of random variables; one corresponds to simple cells, and the other to complex cells. Both cell types are trained so that each responds like the corresponding neuron type in HMAX models. The trained model successfully integrates bottom-up evidences and top-down predictions using belief propagation in a practical experiments.

However, their model has two disadvantages. The first one resides in the learning algorithm. In order to reproduce simple-cell like and complex-cell like responses, two different learning algorithms are used for the conditional probability tables. Furthermore, the learning algorithms are based on clustering, not on the maximal log-likelihood method.

The other one resides in the correspondence between the cells in model and the biological cells. In ref [8], the beliefs, or the marginal probabilities $BEL(x) = P(x|e)$, are compared to the biological simple and complex cell activities. However, if the belief propagation algorithm is executed in the cerebral cortex, the activities corresponding to the intermediate variables, such as the messages, should also be observed experimentally. It is not sufficient to model the biological neural activities only with the beliefs.

In this paper, we present a new view for modeling simple and complex cells. In a hierarchical graphical model, simple representations in lower levels can be combined and stored in higher levels as complex representations. Hence, the receptive fields of higher-level variables are broader and less sensitive to the position of stimuli than that of lower-level variables. In a variational inference, the effect of such broader receptive fields are initially observed in beliefs of higher-level variables, then sent to lower-level variables as messages. This mechanism leads us to the view that simple cells can be modeled by feedforward messages, and complex cells can be modeled by feedback messages.

Note that, with this view, we do not need special handling for translation invariant variables when we construct the graphical model that responses like HMAX models. We only need to train the graphical model so that it acquires translation invariance using a standard method, such as supervised learning, or unsupervised, slow-feature-analysis learning. Complex-cell like responses can be computed by using messages coming from higher levels in a variational inference. This is a new way to "integrate" graphical models and HMAX models. This viewpoint is explained in detail in the experiment section by using a simple, specific model and the belief propagation algorithm as an inference algorithm.

Before proceeding, let us compare our idea with the other related studies. Many models for the cerebral cortex with probabilistic graphical models are presented so far [10–14], but the emergence of complex-cell like responses is hardly addressed, except in Ref. [7,8].

The author of ref. [14] used hierarchical Bayesian network which has similar architecture to ours. The network was trained in an unsupervised manner with natural images. As a result, receptive fields similar to V1 and V2 cells were acquired by the model, and their details were carefully compared quantitatively to physiological experiments. The author concluded that the complex receptive fields could not be found.

From our point of view, we might give some explanations to this result. Firstly, in [14], cell activities were measured by the beliefs, or the marginal probabilities. As we mentioned above, if we execute a variational approximation in the model, we might find another type of responses in variational messages. Secondly, the author used unsupervised learning. If supervised learning had been used, the higher-level variables would have acquired broad receptive fields and would have shown complex-cell like responses.

In [11], the Bayesian network model was trained by a slow-feature-analysis like algorithm [15] to have the translation invariance. However, it was not clear whether there were responses corresponding to complex cells.

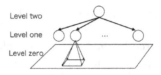

Fig. 1. Schematic representation of the Bayesian network in our experiment

3   Bayesian Network Model

3.1   Model Architecture

To model the visual system in the cerebral cortex, we introduce a hierarchical Bayesian network that mimics hierarchical structure of the dorsal stream of the visual cortex. The Bayesian network model has three layers. The level zero consists of N_0 binary variables $L_0 = \{L_{01}, \ldots, L_{0N_0}\}$. The level one consists of N_1 variables $L_1 = \{L_{11}, \ldots, L_{1N_1}\}$. The level two consists of one variable L_2. The level zero is used as the visible, input layer, while the level one and the level two are hidden layers.

Each level has rough correspondence to a part of visual area: the level zero corresponds to lateral geniculate nucleus (LGN), the level one to V1, and the level two to V2 and higher areas. The hierarchical structure of the model is shown in Fig. 1.

The joint probability distribution of the Bayesian network is given by

$$P(L_0, L_1, L_2) = \prod_{i=1}^{N_0} P(L_{0i}|\mathrm{pa}_i) \prod_{j=1}^{N_1} P(L_{1j}|L_2)P(L_2), \tag{1}$$

where $\mathrm{pa}_i \subset L_1$ denotes the set of parent variables of L_{0i}. The conditional probability tables, $P(L_{0i}|\mathrm{pa}_i)$, $P(L_{1j}|L2)$, and $P(L_2)$ are the model parameters.

3.2   Belief Propagation

Belief propagation [9] is an efficient algorithm for inference in probabilistic graphical models, exploiting graph structure to reduce the computational costs. In this study, we employ the max-product belief propagation algorithm, which gives maximum a posteriori (MAP) combination of the states in the model:

$$X^{\mathrm{MAP}} = \underset{X}{\mathrm{argmax}}\, P(X|e), \tag{2}$$

where X is the set of the hidden variables and e is the set of the visible variables with evidences given.

Generally, the max-product belief propagation algorithm gives an approximate MAP solution after sufficient iterative message passings. Since our model has a tree structure, however, the belief propagation gives the exact MAP solution in one cycle.

Because the set of message-update equations of the belief propagation algorithm is too lengthy, we no not describe its detail here. Instead, we give the key equation which connects the responses of beliefs in higher levels and the messages that are sent from a higher level to a lower level.

$$\pi_{L_{1j}}(L_2) = \prod_{k \neq j} \lambda_{L_{1k}}(L_2)P(L_2) \approx \text{BEL}(L_2), \tag{3}$$

where $\pi_{L_{1j}}(L_2)$ is the feedback message sent from the higher variable L_2 to the lower variable L_{1j}, $\lambda_{L_{1k}}(L_2)$ is the feedforward message sent from L_{1j} to L_2, and $\text{BEL}(L_2)$ is the belief of L_2. The approximation is justified if the number of the child variables of L_2 is large enough. This equation states how the feedback message $\pi_{L_{1j}}(L_2)$ is computed using the other messages and the conditional probability tables. As seen in the approximation, the feedback message $\pi_{L_{1j}}(L_2)$ behaves similar to the belief of L_2, $\text{BEL}(L_2)$. This means that if $\text{BEL}(L_2)$ responds translation invariantly, the feedback message $\pi_{L_{1j}}(L_2)$ also responds translation invariantly. This is the mathematical explanation of the translation invariant feedback messages in the belief propagation algorithm.

4   Simulation

4.1   Setup and Hyperparameters

We performed an experiment using a Bayesian network to concretely present our idea that translation invariant responses come from higher representations. The experiment consisted of two kinds of steps, i.e. the learning step and the recognition step.

The purpose of the learning step was to make the level-two variable learn translation invariant representations. For the sake of this, we used a supervised learning. We gave the translated images to the level-zero variables. Meanwhile, we gave the corresponding instruction signal to the level-two variable. Giving both the input and the instruction signal, the parameters in the model were updated so that the log-likelihood was maximized.

We used Gabor filters for the connections between the level-zero and the level-one variables instead of conditional probability tables. The Gabor filters were fixed throughout experiments, which means we only updated conditional probability table between level-one and two variables, $P(L_{1j}|L_2)$. This approximation is just for convenience and not essential. If one uses fully-probabilistic, maximal log-likelihood learning approach, one may obtain Gabor-filter like connection under an appropriate prior distribution [16]. With this approximation, the feedforward messages from the level-zero variables to the level-one variables were replaced by the convolutions of the image patches with the Gabor filters.

In the recognition step, we presented input signals in the level-zero variables. The hidden variables in the level one and level two were inferred with the belief propagation algorithm. We computed feedforward and feedback messages, as well as beliefs, as the responses of the model.

We used the following hyperparameters; The level zero had 16×16 binary variables, the level one had 4×4 variables each of which had 8 states corresponding to the 8 orientations of the Gabor filters (see below). The level two had one 4-state variable. Corresponding to the level-zero variables, an input image had 16×16 pixels. A level-one variable had 4×4 receptive field in level zero, and the level-two variable had also 4×4 receptive field in the level one. Throughout the network, there were no overlaps of receptive fields and therefore the model was tree-structured. Since the model was a tree, we used the belief propagation algorithm to get the exact MAP assignment in one cycle of iteration.

The Gabor filters employed to mimic the connections between the level zero and the level one were set by the parameters of $\gamma = 0.3, \sigma = 3.6$, and $\lambda = 4.6$ as in [4]. The angles were divided to eight directions by $\theta = 0, \pi/8, 2\pi/8, \ldots, 7\pi/8$, which consisted of the eight states of the level-one variables.

4.2   Results with Line Stimuli

We used horizontal line stimuli that covered the whole width of all level-one variables' receptive fields, namely, 16 pixels wide. In the learning step, we trained the model so that the sole level-two variable indicated the first state, out of the four possible states, whenever a horizontal line stimulus was presented regardless of its position. In the recognition step, we chose one level-one variable, L_1, and observed its two incoming messages $\lambda(L_1)$ and $\pi(L_1)$.

Figure 2 shows the state of $\lambda(L_1)$ that corresponds to the horizontal angle of the Gabor filter, and its equivalent of $\pi(L_1)$. $\lambda(L_1)$ responded more strongly when a line stimulus was presented in the receptive field of L_1 than when a line stimulus was presented out of the receptive field. On the other hand, $\pi(L_1)$ responded more equally concerning the position of the presented stimulus. With

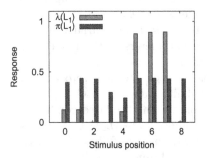
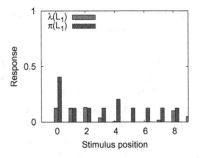

Fig. 2. Responses of the messages in the Bayesian network model. Horizontal axis indicates the position of presented horizontal stimuli, and vertical axis indicates the responses.

Fig. 3. Responses of the messages in the Bayesian network model. The same with Fig. 2, except that the presented stimuli are vertical.

these results, we can say that $\lambda(L_1)$ responds like simple cells and $\pi(L_1)$ responds like complex cells.

As a result of the supervised learning, the level-two variable predicted horizontal lines regardless of their positions. Since $\pi(L_1)$ was computed based on that prediction (Eq. (3)), it responded more equally concerning the position of the stimulus.

Figure 3 shows how the same state responded to the input stimuli that were rotated by 90°, namely, vertical stimuli. The responses of both $\lambda(L_1)$ and $\pi(L_1)$ were suppressed. This indicates that both responses were selectively tuned to their optimal orientation, namely, horizontal orientation. Since the model had not been trained to recognize vertical stimuli, the L_2 belief for vertical stimuli was uniform. Therefore, the $\pi(L_1)$ message in the feedback was weak.

5   Conclusion

We have shown that the biological neural responses can be interpreted as variational messages in a probabilistic graphical model. We have experimentally clarified this interpretation by using a Bayesian network and the belief propagation algorithm. We employed the standard supervised learning algorithm based on the maximal log-likelihood to obtain the translation invariance. The complex-cell like response in the level one was found in the computation of the feedback message from the higher level. Note that we do not need special architecture such as complex-cell random variables employed in the previous studies [7,8] to reproduce the complex-cell like response. We therefore consider that our interpretation gives a new way to integrate the HMAX-like models and graphical models for visual system.

We remark that our interpretation is not restricted to Bayesian network models or the belief propagation algorithm. Many variational inference algorithms, such as the mean-field algorithm, share the computation in which a prediction of a higher-level variable is sent as a feedback message to lower-level variables. This fact suggests that the feedback messages in many variational inference algorithms convey translation invariance if the graphical model has acquired translation invariance appropriately.

Although our model is presented for the concreteness of the interpretation and too simple to model the real cortex, we can find interesting correspondence with the experiments. Complex cells in V1 are mainly distributed in superficial layers (II, III) and in deep layers (V, VI) [17]. For complex cells in the deep layers, it is suggested that they receive feedback signals from higher areas [18]. This is consistent with our interpretation that feedback signals can be used to realize a translation invariant response. On the other hand, complex cells in the superficial layers are suggested to receive direct projections from simple cells in the same area [19]. The role of the superficial complex cells in a variational inference model is left for a future work.

Acknowledgments. The authors thank to Naoto Takahashi for careful reading of the manuscript. This paper is based on results obtained from a project commissioned by the New Energy and Industrial Technology Development Organization (NEDO).

References

1. Doya, K., Ishii, S., Pouget, A., Rao, R.P.N.: Bayesian Brain: Probabilistic Approaches to Neural Coding. MIT Press, Cambridge (2007)
2. Rao, R.P.N., Ballard, D.H.: Predictive coding in the visual cortex: a functional interpretation of some extra-classical receptive-field effects. Nat. Neurosci. **2**(1), 79–87 (1999)
3. LeCun, Y., et al.: Handwritten digit recognition with a back-propagation network. In: Proceedings of NIPS 1989, pp. 396–404 (1990)
4. Serre, T., et al.: Robust object recognition with cortex-like mechanisms. IEEE Trans. Pattern Anal. Mach. Intell. **29**(3), 411–426 (2007)
5. Hubel, D.H., Wiesel, T.N.: Receptive fields, binocular interaction and functional architecture in the cat's visual cortex. J. Physiol. **160**(1), 106–154 (1962)
6. Fukushima, K.: Neocognitron: a self-organizing neural network model for a mechanism of pattern recognition unaffected by shift in position. Biol. Cybern. **36**, 193–202 (1980)
7. Lee, H., Grosse, R., Ranganath, R., Ng, A.Y.: Unsupervised learning of hierarchical representations with convolutional deep belief networks. Commun. ACM **54**(10), 95–103 (2011)
8. Dura-Bernal, S., Wennekers, T., Denham, S.L.: Top-down feedback in an HMAX-like cortical model of object perception based on hierarchical Bayesian networks and belief propagation. PLoS ONE **7**(11), e48216 (2012)
9. Pearl, J.: Probabilistic Reasoning in Intelligent Systems: Networks of Plausible Inference. Morgan Kaufmann, San Francisco (1988)
10. Lee, T.S., Mumford, D.: Hierarchical Bayesian inference in the visual cortex. J. Opt. Soc. Am. A **20**(7), 1434–1448 (2003)
11. George, D., Hawkins, J.: A hierarchical Bayesian model of invariant pattern recognition in the visual cortex. In: Proceedings of IJCNN 2005, pp. 1812–1817 (2005)
12. Ichisugi, Y.: A cerebral cortex model that self-organizes conditional probability tables and executes belief propagation. In: Proceedings of IJCNN 2007, pp. 178–183 (2007)
13. Litvak, S., Ullman, S.: Cortical circuitry implementing graphical models. Neural Comput. **21**(11), 3010–3056 (2009)
14. Hosoya, H.: Multinomial Bayesian learning for modeling classical and nonclassical receptive field properties. Neural Comput. **24**(8), 2119–2150 (2012)
15. Wiskott, L., Sejnowski, T.J.: Slow feature analysis: unsupervised learning of invariances. Neural Comput. **14**(4), 715–770 (2002)
16. Olshausen, B.A., Field, D.J.: Emergence of simple-cell receptive field properties by learning a sparse code for natural images. Nature **381**(6583), 607 (1996)
17. Gilbert, C.D.: Laminar differences in receptive field properties of cells in cat primary visual cortex. J. Physiol. **268**(2), 391–421 (1977)
18. Sandell, J.H., Schiller, P.H.: Effect of cooling area 18 on striate cortex cells in the squirrel monkey. J. Neurophysiol. **48**(1), 38–48 (1982)
19. Martinez, L.M., Alonso, J.M.: Construction of complex receptive fields in cat primary visual cortex. Neuron **32**(3), 515–525 (2001)

Implementation of Learning Mechanisms on a Cat-Scale Cerebellar Model and Its Simulation

Wataru Furusho[1]([⊠]) and Tadashi Yamazaki[1,2]

[1] Graduate School of Informatics and Engineering,
The University of Electro-Communications, Chofu, Tokyo 182-8585, Japan
wf.yamazakilab@gmail.com
[2] Neuroinformatics Japan Center, RIKEN Brain Science Institute,
Wako, Saitama 351-0198, Japan

Abstract. We have built a large-scale spiking network model of the cerebellum with 1 billion neurons on a supercomputer previously. The model, however, did not incorporate synaptic plasticity such as long-term depression and potentiation at parallel fiber-Purkinje cell synapses. In this study, we implemented them on the model. To test the learning capability, as a benchmark, we carried out simulation of eye movement reflex called gain adaptation of optokinetic response (OKR). The present model successfully reproduced the increase of firing rate modulation of a Purkinje cell during simulated OKR training, resulting in the increase of OKR gain. The model completed a 6 s simulation within 4.4 s, suggesting realtime simulation even with the learning mechanisms. These results suggest that the present cerebellar model can now perform reservoir computing, a supervised learning machine for spatiotemporal signals, with very large reservoir composed of 1 billion neurons.

Keywords: Cerebellum · Network · Plasticity · Simulation · Realtime

1 Introduction

The cerebellum plays essential roles in realtime motor control and adaptation. The "small brain" occupies only 10% of the whole brain volume, but contains about 80% of neurons [1]. The functional role of the cerebellum is considered supervised learning, in which association between context and teacher signals conveyed respectively by mossy and climbing fibers (CF) is learned [2]. The functional module for the supervised learning is called a corticonuclear micro-complex (Fig. 1), which is composed of less than 10 types of neurons, and a number of microcomplexes are repeated throughout the cerebellar cortex so as to form the entire cerebellar network. Because of the clear relationship between the structure and function of the cerebellum, and its relatively simple structure than the cerebral cortex, the cerebellum seems an ideal candidate for computational modeling, especially implementing its neural circuit on computers.

© Springer International Publishing AG 2017
A. Lintas et al. (Eds.): ICANN 2017, Part I, LNCS 10613, pp. 171–178, 2017.
https://doi.org/10.1007/978-3-319-68600-4_21

Several models of the cerebellum have been built to date [2]. We have proposed that the cerebellum performs reservoir computing, a supervised learning algorithm for spatiotemporal signals [3]. We have implemented a large-scale, realistic cerebellar model on special hardware such as graphics processing units (GPU) [4,5]. Recently, we have extended the model to include 1 billion neurons, whose size is comparable to the entire cerebellum of a cat, and implemented on a supercomputer called "Shoubu" in Japan (submitted). The "cat-scale" cerebellar model runs in realtime, which means that computer simulation of the network dynamics of the cerebellum for 1 s completes within 1 s of the wall-clock time with a fine temporal resolution. The model, however, did not implement synaptic plasticity, so the model could not learn anything but exhibit only the dynamics.

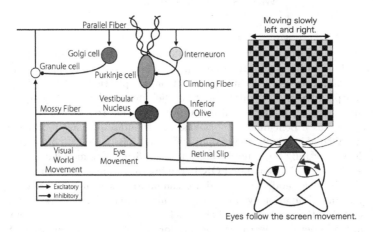

Fig. 1. Schematic of a corticonuclear microcomplex and its involvement for gain adaptation of optokinetic response (OKR) eye movement. A corticonuclear microcomplex consists of granule cells, Golgi cells, molecular layer interneurons such as stellate cells, Purkinje cells (PC), inferior olivary neurons, and vestibular nuclear neurons. Parallel fibers (PF) are axons of granule cells, and the climbing fiber (CF) is the axon of the inferior olive. A corticonuclear microcomplex is a 2-input and 1-output circuit. The inputs come from mossy fibers and the CF, and the output is generated by the vestibular nucleus. In OKR, the information of visual world's movement and slip of the retinal image are conveyed by mossy fibers and CF, respectively, and the vestibular nucleus provides the motor command to move eyes.

In this study, we implemented synaptic plasticity, specifically long-term depression (LTD) and potentiation (LTP) at parallel fiber (PF)-Purkinje cell (PC) synapses, which are thought as neuronal basis for cerebellar learning, on our cat-scale cerebellar model. To still achieve realtime simulation even with the plasticity, we used the PEZY-SC chip [6], the heart of the supercomputer Shoubu composed of 1,024 computational cores, efficiently. Specifically, we have invented a parallel reduction technique for calculation of PF-PC synaptic inputs, where each PC receives inputs from about 260,000 granule cells. As a benchmark, we carried out computer simulation of eye movement reflex mediated by the cerebellum called gain adaptation of optokinetic response (OKR), and confirmed that our cerebellar model exhibited qualitatively similar dynamics with our previous model. Moreover, thanks to the computational power of the PEZY-SC chip, the present model still ran in realtime. Furthermore, even if we increased the network size further while introducing more chips, the computational time did not increase so largely, suggesting a good weak-scaling property. These properties may allow us to use the present cerebellar model as an online supervised learning machine that requires realtime information processing.

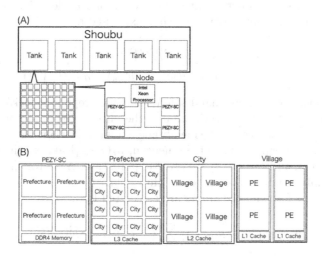

Fig. 2. Schematic of the Shoubu architecture. (A) General overview. Shoubu consists of 5 liquid immersion cooling tanks. Each tank contains 64 nodes, and each node is composed of 1 Xeon chip and 4 PEZY-SC chips. Therefore, Shoubu has 1,280 PEZY-SC chips and so 1.3 million cores. (B) Architecture of the PEZY-SC chip. The chip has a hierarchical structure. The chip consists of 4 functional blocks called Prefecture and a 32 GB global memory. Each Prefecture consists of 16 Cities and a 2 MB L3 cache. Each City consists of 4 Villages and a 64 KB L2 cache. Each Village consists of 4 processing elements (PE) or cores and two 8KB L1 caches. Each PE can issue 8 threads, so a chip can issue 8,192 threads simultaneously.

2   Methods

2.1   Overview of a Supercomputer Shoubu

In this study, we used a supercomputer Shoubu, which is developed by PEZY Computing K.K. and Exascaler Inc., and installed in RIKEN Advanced Center for Computing and Communication.

The architecture of Shoubu is shown in Fig. 2. Shoubu is composed of 1,280 manycore chips called PEZY-SC (Fig. 2A), and each PEZY-SC chip contains

1,024 cores (Fig. 2B). In total, Shoubu has 1.3 million cores that can work in parallel. To write a program running on a PEZY-SC chip, we use C language with PZCL library, which is a subset of OpenCL. To pull the performance of the chip out, we must think of the hierarchical structure and caches so as to reduce the number of accesses to the global memory as few as possible.

2.2   Overview of a Cerebellar Microcomplex Model

On a PEZY-SC chip, we implemented a model of the corticonuclear microcomplex (Fig. 3), which is composed of 1,048,576 granule cells, 1,024 Golgi cells, 32 interneurons, 32 PCs, an inferior olive, and a vestibular nucleus [5]. Each neuron is a leaky integrate-and-fire model, which is expressed by

$$c\frac{dV}{dt} = -g_{\text{leak}}(V(t) - E_{\text{leak}}) - g_{\text{ex}}(t)(V(t) - E_{\text{ex}})$$
$$- g_{\text{inh}}(t)(V(t) - E_{\text{inh}}) - g_{\text{ahp}}(t)(V(t) - E_{\text{ahp}}), \quad (1)$$

where the 4 terms of the right-hand side respectively represent leakage current, the current for excitatory synaptic inputs, the current for inhibitory synaptic inputs, and the current to reset the membrane potential V when the neuron fired. The variable c is a capacitance of the neuron, $g_x(x \in \{\text{leak}, \text{ex}, \text{inh}, \text{ahp}\} = \mathbb{S})$ are conductances, and $E_x(x \in \mathbb{S})$ are reversal potentials. A neuron makes a spike when the membrane potential exceeds a threshold.

Conductances for synaptic inputs are calculated by

$$g_{\{\text{ex,inh}\}}(t) = \bar{g}_{\{\text{ex,inh}\}} \sum_j w_j \int_0^t \alpha(t - s)\delta(s)ds, \quad (2)$$

where $\bar{g}_{\{\text{ex,inh}\}}$ is the peak conductance, j is an index number of a presynaptic neuron, w_j is a weight of the synaptic connection from the neuron j, α is a function for postsynaptic potentials, and δ represents the times at which neuron j made spikes. The differential equations were solved by the 2nd order Runge-Kutta method with temporal resolution of 1 ms.

In this study, we implemented LTD and LTP at PF-PC synapses to simulate cerebellar learning. The LTD decreases the weight of a synaptic connection when the PF and the CF innervating to the same PC are activated almost simultaneously. Specifically, we assumed that LTD is induced when a PF is activated 50 ms earlier than the CF activation as follows:

$$w_{\text{PC}i \leftarrow \text{PF}j}(t + \Delta t) = w_{\text{PC}i \leftarrow \text{PF}j}(t) - 0.05 w_{\text{PC}i \leftarrow \text{PF}j}(t) \sum_{\Delta s=0}^{50} \text{CF}(t)\text{PF}_j(t - \Delta s), \quad (3)$$

where $w_{\text{PC}i \leftarrow \text{PF}j}(t)$ represents the weight between PC i and PF j, $\text{PF}_j(t)$ and $\text{CF}(t)$ respectively represent the activity of PF j and the CF. $\text{PF}_j(t)$ and $\text{CF}(t)$ take 1 if PF j or the CF fired at t, and 0 otherwise. The constant 0.05 represents learning efficacy. On the other hand, LTP increases the weight when the PF is solely activated, which is implemented as follows;

$$w_{\text{PC}i \leftarrow \text{PF}j}(t + \Delta t) = w_{\text{PC}i \leftarrow \text{PF}j}(t) + 0.0005(w_{\text{init}} - w_{\text{PC}i \leftarrow \text{PF}j}(t))\text{PF}_j(t), \quad (4)$$

where the constant 0.0005 is the learning efficacy, and w_{init} represents the initial synaptic weight set at 1.0.

2.3   Implementation of Microcomplexes on Shoubu

We then implemented 1,280 microcomplexes on 1,280 PEZY-SC chips on Shoubu to build an entire cerebellar model. We virtually arranged the 1,280 chips on a two-dimensional sheet, and assigned one microcomplex to one chip. We connected PFs between neighboring chips so that PCs on a chip can receive inputs from PFs implemented on the other chips (Fig. 3). Eventually, we built a very large-scale model of the cerebellum composed of more than 1 billion spiking neurons, which is almost the same size of the whole cat cerebellum.

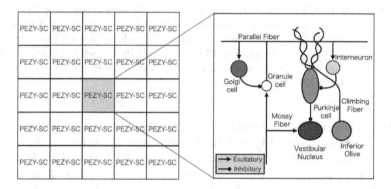

Fig. 3. Schematic of implementation of multiple microcomplexes on PEZY-SC chips. The 1,280 chips were arranged on a two-dimensional sheet, and for each chip, we implemented a microcomplex model. Neighbouring chips exchange spikes via PFs so as to build a large single network model rather than a collection of small models.

2.4   Parallel Reduction of Calculation of PF Synaptic Inputs to PCs

The most time consuming part of the simulation would be calculation of PF-PC synaptic inputs, because each PC receives excitatory inputs from 262,144 PFs with associated synaptic weights. The calculation is equal to the sum-of-product of the synaptic weights and PF spikes. To perform the calculation efficiently on the PEZY-SC chips, we focused on the hierarchical architecture of the chip.

Since there are 32 PCs on a chip, we calculate 4 PCs' inputs using 4 Prefectures at a time, and we repeat the procedure 8 times for 32 PCs. Figure 4 shows the procedure. In the first step, 262,144 values which are synaptic inputs from 262,144 PFs to a PC are assigned to each Prefecture, and these values are summed to 1,024 values by using 1024 threads of 256 cores in each prefecture. In the second step, 1,024 values are summed to 256 values by using the same

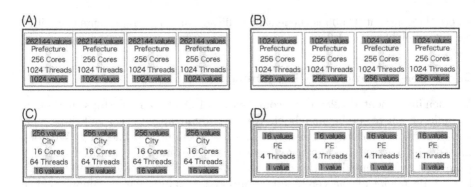

Fig. 4. Diagram for parallel reduction of calculation of synaptic inputs for PCs. A PC receives excitatory inputs from 262,144 PFs that need to be summed up. We calculate the inputs for each PC by each Prefecture, and repeat 8 times to complete 32 PCs. (A) 1st reduction: 262,144 float numbers are reduced to 1,024 numbers on each Prefecture. (B) 2nd reduction: 1,024 numbers are reduced to 256 values on each Prefecture. (C) 3rd reduction: 256 values are reduced to 16 values on a City in each Prefecture. (D) 4th reduction: 16 values are reduced to one value, which is the final result of the calculation, by using a core of each City.

prefecture. These values can be put in the L3 cache, and so they can be accessed by a City in the next step (Fig. 2B). In the third step, 256 values are summed to 16 values by using 64 threads of 16 cores in a City. Each thread reads 4 values and sums them, and then a thread in each core sums the result of the threads. These values are stored in the L2 cache, and so they can be accessed by a core in the next step. In the final step, 16 values are summed to the value by using 4 threads on a core, and we obtain the final result of a synaptic input from 262,144 PFs to a PC. In this way, all the above operations are made on the L3 cache. Because we do not need to access the slow global memory, the above calculation can be performed fast.

2.5   Simulation of the Cat-Scale Cerebellar Model

In order to examine whether our cat-scale cerebellar model works correctly, as a benchmark, we carried out computer simulation of OKR gain adaptation. OKR is a simple eye movement reflex in which our eyes follow the movement of the visual world to stabilize the retinal image. The amplitude of the eye movement, or gain, can be increased when the eyes are exposed continuously to moving visual inputs. The OKR gain adaptation is mediated by the cerebellum (Fig. 1). The information of the visual world movement is fed via mossy fibers, whereas the information of the slip of the retinal image via CFs, and the output of the vestibular nucleus represents the motor command to move the eyeball. Occurrence of a retinal slip induces LTD at active PFs at the time, and attenuates the activity of PCs. This in turn enhances the activity of the vestibular nuclear cell firing, resulting in OKR gain increase.

3   Results

We carried out computer simulation of OKR adaptation. We assumed that the
visual world moves horizontally, slowly and sinusoidally with the oscillation
period of 6 s, and the rotation is repeated for 100 cycles. We plotted the firing rates of a PC and a vestibular nuclear neuron at the 1st, 10th, and 100th
cycle in Fig. 5. The firing rate of a PC modulates out of the phase with the
simulated visual world movement due to the inhibition from molecular layer
interneurons, and the modulation amplitude increases during adaptation due to
LTD. On the other hand, the firing rate of a vestibular nuclear neuron modulates
in phase with the visual inputs, and the modulation amplitude increases due to
the disinhibition of PCs. Because the modulation amplitude of the vestibular
nuclear neuron represents the OKR gain, this result suggests that the OKR gain
increases by the adaptation training. These dynamical changes of the firing rates
are consistent with those in our previous model [7].

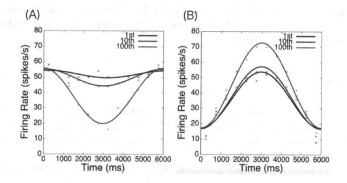

Fig. 5. Firing rate of a PC (A) and the vestibular nucleus (B) during simulation of
OKR adaptation in response to simulated optokinetic stimulus moving sinusoidally
with the oscillation period of 6 s. Horizontal axis represents time during one cycle of
the optokinetic stimulus movement, and the vertical axis the firing rate. Each point
represents the firing rate at each time point, and each line represents a cosine curve
fitted to these points. The three lines in different colors represent the results in 1st,
10th, and 100th cycles, respectively.

Moreover, the computer simulation for 1 cycle of 6 s completed in 4.4 s, suggesting that the computer simulation is carried out in realtime.

We also examined the weak-scale property, which indicates how the computational time changes as the number of neurons in a simulation and the number
of chips used in the simulation changed simultaneously. We changed the network
size as 4, 16, and 64 times larger while increasing the number of chips as 4, 16,
and 64. We found that the computational times for a 6 s simulation were 4.33,
4.45, and 4.54 s, respectively. This result suggests that the computational time
would not increase so largely even if we incorporate much more chips to built
much larger models.

4   Conclusion

In this study, we implemented synaptic plasticity of LTD and LTP at PF-PC synapses, which are thought as cerebellar learning mechanisms, on our cat-scale cerebellar model. Moreover, to achieve realtime simulation even with the plasticity, we invented a parallel reduction technique for calculation of PF-PC synaptic inputs. To demonstrate the learning capability, we carried out computer simulation of OKR gain adaptation, and successfully reproduced the neural dynamics in OKR adaptation. Furthermore, we obtained a good weak-scaling property. Even if we incorporate 100 times more chips to scale up the network size 100 times larger to build a human-scale cerebellum, the computational time for 6 s simulation would be less than 5 s, which is still faster than realtime. This result suggests that the present cerebellar model can be extended to human scale successfully while retaining online learning capability as a general supervised learning machine based on reservoir computing.

Acknowledgments. RIKEN Advanced Center for Computing and Communication kindly provided an account on Shoubu. Part of this study was supported by JSPS KAKENHI Grant Number 26430009.

References

1. Azevedo, F.A., Carvalho, L.R., Grinberg, L.T., Farfel, J.M., Ferretti, R.E., Leite, R.E., Filho, W.J., Lent, R., Herculano-Houzel, S.: Equal numbers of neuronal and nonneuronal cells make the human brain an isometrically scaled-up primate brain. J. Comp. Neurol. **513**, 532–541 (2009)
2. Ito, M.: The Cerebellum: Brain for the Implicit Self. FT Press, Upper Saddle River (2012)
3. Yamazaki, T., Tanaka, S.: The cerebellum as a liquid state machine. Neural Netw. **20**, 290–297 (2007)
4. Yamazaki, T., Igarashi, J.: Realtime cerebellum: a large-scale spiking network model of the cerebellum that runs in realtime using a graphics processing unit. Neural Netw. **47**, 103–111 (2013)
5. Gosui, M., Yamazaki, T.: Real-world-time simulation of memory consolidation in a large-scale cerebellar model. Frontiers in Neuroanatomy **10**(21), 1–10 (2016)
6. Aoyama, T., Ishikawa, K., Kimura, Y., Matsufuru, H., Sato, A., Suzuki, T., Torii, S.: First application of lattice QCD to Pezy-SC processor. Procedia Comput. Sci. **80**, 1418–1427 (2016)
7. Yamazaki, T., Nagao, S.: A computational mechanism for unified gain and timing control in the cerebellum. PLoS ONE **7**(3), e33319 (2012)

Neuromorphic Approach Sensitivity Cell Modeling and FPGA Implementation

Hongjie Liu[1], Antonio Rios-Navarro[2], Diederik Paul Moeys[1], Tobi Delbruck[1], and Alejandro Linares-Barranco[2(✉)]

[1] Institute of Neuroinformatics, ETHZ-UZH, Zurich, Switzerland
hongjie@ini.uzh.ch
[2] Robotic and Technology of Computers Lab, University of Seville, Sevilla, Spain
alinares@atc.us.es

Abstract. Neuromorphic engineering takes inspiration from biology to solve engineering problems using the organizing principles of biological neural computation. This field has demonstrated success in sensor based applications (vision and audition) as well in cognition and actuators. This paper is focused on mimicking an interesting functionality of the retina that is computed by one type of Retinal Ganglion Cell (RGC). It is the early detection of approaching (expanding) dark objects. This paper presents the software and hardware logic FPGA implementation of this approach sensitivity cell. It can be used in later cognition layers as an attention mechanism. The input of this hardware modeled cell comes from an asynchronous spiking Dynamic Vision Sensor, which leads to an end-to-end event based processing system. The software model has been developed in Java, and computed with an average processing time per event of 370 ns on a NUC embedded computer. The output firing rate for an approaching object depends on the cell parameters that represent the needed number of input events to reach the firing threshold. For the hardware implementation on a Spartan6 FPGA, the processing time is reduced to 160 ns/event with the clock running at 50 MHz.

Keywords: Neuromorphic engineering · Event-based processing · Address-Event-Representation · Dynamic Vision Sensor · Approach Sensitivity cell · Retina Ganglion Cell

1 Introduction

In [2], Münch et al. identified a ganglion cell type, the approach sensitivity cell (**AC**), in the mouse retina that is sensitive to approaching motion of objects. The detection of approaching motion elicits behaviors such as startle and protective motor responses in animals and humans. These responses are also important to predict collisions. This kind of function is also required in autonomous vehicles and robotics for obstacle avoidance. In [7], a time-to-contact algorithm in this kind of application based on event-based vision sensor [11] was reported. In this work, we report a more bio-inspired way of detecting approaching objects more efficiently, but also with more restrictions on the visual input.

© Springer International Publishing AG 2017
A. Lintas et al. (Eds.): ICANN 2017, Part I, LNCS 10613, pp. 179–187, 2017.
https://doi.org/10.1007/978-3-319-68600-4_22

The Dynamic Vision Sensor [1] (**DVS**) mimics the temporal dynamic responses of the retina by asynchronously outputting events signaling brightness changes. Every pixel works independently from others in such a way that when the detected brightness (log intensity) changes by more than a preset threshold from the pixel's memorized value of brightness, a spike is produced by that pixel in the sensor output. The communication protocol between event based sensors and other neuromorphic hardware is called the Address Event Representation (**AER**). The AER protocol encodes the x-y address of the pixel where the temporal change has surpassed the threshold and it transmits that address using an asynchronous handshake protocol. There are many promising applications in the literature that take advantage of this event-based processing concept, such as in [8] (one of the first) where DVS sensor output was connected to several convolutional event-based chips in parallel to detect particular objects, plus winner-take-all filters, to make it possible to move motors in order to follow one particular object in real time with sub-millisecond visual processing latencies. In [9], a spiking neural network is implemented in SpiNNaker [10] for DVS event processing to drive a mobile robot in a cognitive way.

This paper is structured as follows: the next section explains the AC biological model. Section 3 presents a software implementation of the model in Java, for the open-source jAER[1] project. Section 4 presents the hardware implementation of an AC on a field programmable gate array (**FPGA**) using a set of AER platform tools. Finally, Sects. 5 and 6 presents results and conclusions.

2   The Approach Sensitivity Cell Biological Model

In [2], it is reported that the AC receives excitatory and inhibitory inputs from small subunits. The excitatory inputs are from the so called OFF type subunits which respond to the decrease of brightness, and the inhibitory inputs are from the so called ON type subunits which respond to the increase of brightness. The ON and OFF type subunits cancel out each other when there is lateral motion. To be sensitive to approaching motion, the crucial point is that the cell **nonlinearly** integrates the potential of a broad area of ON-OFF subunits in its receptive field. The nonlinearity takes the form of an expansive function with a finite threshold. The thresholded responses of the subunits are summed into the AC (see Fig. 1). Because of this nonlinearity, weak global inhibitions will not cancel out local strong excitations, because the latter have stronger impact. The synaptic input to the AC is calculated as a weighted subtraction of the total ON and OFF units as in 1:

$$I_{net} = G_{off} * \sum V_{off} - G_{on} * \sum V_{on} \tag{1}$$

The membrane potential of the AC is calculated as 2:

$$dV_{mem} = I_{net} * dT \tag{2}$$

---

[1] jAER Open Source Project for real time sensory-motor processing for event-based sensors and systems. http://www.jaerproject.org/.

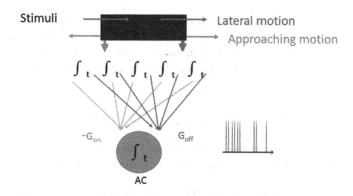

Fig. 1. Biological model of the Approach Sensitivity cell.

where dT is the inter-spike interval. To calculate the input of each subunit, the potential of each subunit is half rectified to perform non-linearity as described in [2].

3   The AC Software Implementation

Figure 2 shows the software model of the AC. One AC has been designed to have 8×8 subunits that process the input events in their receptive field in parallel. Each subunit has ON and OFF parts received from 16×16 pixels for a DVS128 sensor that has 128×128 pixels. Whenever an event with certain polarity (ON or OFF) is received in the receptive field of one subunit, the membrane potential of the ON or OFF subunit is updated. A threshold-linear nonlinearity is implemented for each subunit. All the subunits simultaneously and periodically decay. The decay time constant can be set to be tuned to a particular motion speed. The membrane potentials of all the OFF subunits are summed to provide the

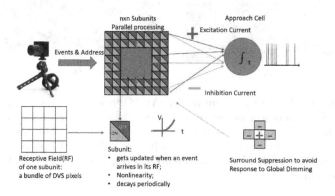

Fig. 2. Software implementation result of the Approach Sensitivity Cell.

excitation current to the AC ganglion cell; the potentials of all the ON subunits are summed to provide the inhibition current to the AC. An ON center - OFF surround subtract scheme is implemented to avoid the AC firing from global dimming of the environment. The potential of the center cell is calculated as in Eq. 3.

$$V_{centertoAC} = V_{center} - \frac{\sum V_{surround}}{n} \tag{3}$$

where n is the number of surrounding cells of the center cell; n can be 0, 2, 3, 4 depending on whether it is on the center, boarder or corner of the receptive field.

The membrane potential of the AC is calculated as in 2. It is compared either to a preset threshold voltage or a randomly generated number when Poisson firing mode is enabled. The AC fires when it is larger than the threshold at integrate-and-fire mode or a random number at Possion-fire mode. Important parameters for the AC Java model are the ON/OFF weight ratio, and the excitation strength. A parameter is also set for the maximum firing rate of the AC. Figure 3 shows the software implementation result of the AC in jAER. The object is a black cell phone. The phone is moved closer to the camera, causing it to apparently expand. The result corresponds to the working principle of the AC. The AC fires when the phone approaches (Fig. 3A), because there are more OFF events generated than ON events as the light intensity decreases on the expanding border. The AC is actively inhibited when the phone recedes, and the ON and OFF activities are balanced when it moves laterally (Fig. 3B).

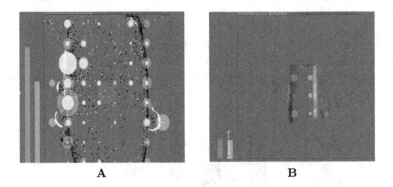

A   B

Fig. 3. Results of the Java software model. **A:** AC fires when object approaches **B:** AC doesn't fire when object movement is lateral. The red-yellow disk shows the OFF excitation while the green disk shows the ON inhibition. The blue disk shows the firing AC. The red and green bar on the left shows the total excitation and total inhibition respectively. Black/white dots represent respectively OFF/ON DVS events. (Color figure online)

4   Hardware Implementation

Figure 4 shows the state machine of the AC. The right branch shows the main state transition. Once receiving an event, after the potential of the subunit is updated (*OnEvent* or *OffEvent*), the input current of each subunit is calculated (*ComputeInputtoAC*). Then, the net current of all the subunits is computed (*ComputenetSynapticInput*). After receiving the input current, the AC updates its membrane potential state following the integrate-and-fire neuron model (*ComputeMembranState*). Then the membrane potential of the AC is compared to the threshold (*ComparetoIFThreshold*) to determine whether it should fire or not. The cell then goes back to *idle* state. The left branch of the state machine is the decay scheme. A global counter counts time that has passed. When the counter overflows, all the subunits decay by a shared programmable factor (*Decay*). If there is no event received, the cell stays in *idle* state.

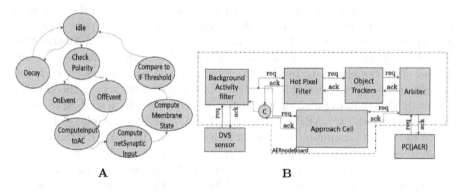

Fig. 4. Approach Sensitivity Cell hardware: **A:** State Machine. **B:** FPGA architecture

In [4], direct hardware integration of architectures for digital post-processing of DVS retina output was presented. The algorithms have the potential of lightweight, power-efficient, and fast retina processing that can be efficiently embedded inside a camera. This work reported the synthesis in a Spartan 6 platform a set of four object trackers - velocity estimation -pattern recognition systems described in VHDL in order to be used for demonstrators. This work was used as a starting point to integrate vision neural models, like [6], with the implementation of the Object Motion Cell functionality of the Retina Ganglion Cells. It is again used here for the AC.

The AC is implemented using the VHDL hardware description language in the Spartan6 1500FXT FPGA for the AERNode platform [3]. This AC implementation requires 4.5 K slice registers (2% of the FPGA), 11.2 K slice LUTs (12%) and 2 DSP blocks (1%). The AERNode platform allows multi-board communication with conventional parallel handshake AER chips, serial Low-Voltage Differential Signaling (LVDS) connections or robots control with the adequate motor interfaces. A daughter board based on an OpalKelly module,

Fig. 5. The hardware system setup.

called OKAERTool [5], is used for monitoring, sequencing, logging or playing events from and to the AERNode board. It is able to sequence events from its on-board DDR2 128MB SDRAM to the AERNode board and to monitor its output through USB2.0 in jAER. OKAERTool is used for debugging.

In this work we have implemented one AC in the FPGA to prove functionality. There are available resources in the FPGA to implement several ACs spread in different regions of the visual field if particular applications require that. The implementation is structured in two levels. The first level is called Mother Cell (**AC-MC**), which is ready to host one or many AC in different visual fields, together with the circuit to receive the corresponding parameters for each cell through an Serial Peripheral Interface (SPI) to the USB interface microcontroller on the OKAERTool. Figure 5 shows the testing scenario, where a DVS128 retina is connected to the OKAERTool merger. The OKAERtool is plugged to the AERNode, which is running the system showed in Fig. 4B. OKAERTool is configured to send to the AERNode the DVS128 output and to collect the output of the AERNode and send it to jAER through USB2.0. The output of the AERNode is configured to be the merge of the DVS128 after a Background-Activity-Filter in the FPGA, and the output of the AC. The USB2.0 output of the OKAER-Tool is connected to the NUC embedded computer, which is running jAER. This jAER is processing live incoming events and it is executing two processing filters: (1) the AC software model and (2) a simple algorithm to highlight the AC hw output in the screen.

5   Results

Figure 6A shows a snapshot of the combined results of the software and hardware implementations. The blue circle in the middle shows the software AC firing, while the red square shows the hardware AC firing when the object is approaching. Red and green bars on the left show an accumulated view of OFF and ON events respectively. Figure 6B shows a space-time view of the event data. The vertical dimension is the increasing timestamp while the horizontal dimensions are the (x, y) address of the pixel array. As time increases, the area of the blue dots (events) first decreases and then increases, indicating that the object first recedes (shrinks in the view) and then approaches (expands in the view). We can see the AC fires when the object approaches and does not fire when it recedes. Given this slow stimulation, the minimum inter-spike-interval (**ISI**) for each AC firing signal is 16.6 ms and the maximum is 75.7 ms. The average ISI is 31.2 ms. The latency to process one incoming event depends on the state machine. The clock of the FPGA runs at 50 MHz. The latency of the AC is 160 ns. It is the time difference between the input request to the AC and the output of the AC, measured using ChipScope embedded in the FPGA. Table 1 shows a comparison of the software and hardware performance in terms of latency and power. The software performance is measured in two types of PCs with very different resources. The software latency is measured by using the "measure filter performance" option in jAER.

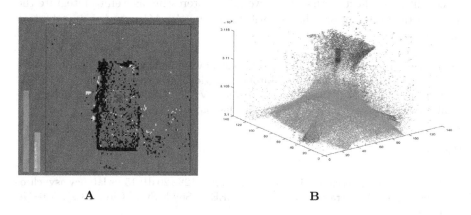

A   B

Fig. 6. A: Result of AC software and hardware implementation displayed in jAER viewer. **B:** 3-dimensional visualization of address-event and the AC firing, red stars shows the hardware AC firing, blue and green dots represent the excitatory (OFF) and inhibitory (ON) events respectively. (Color figure online)

Table 1. Performance table

	jAER (64 bit Intel NUC, 4 GB RAM, i54250U, 1.30 GHz)	jAER(64 bit PC, 16 GB RAM, i74770K, 3.50 GHz)	FPGA Xilinx Spartan6, 50 MHz
Latency	370 ns/ev at 0.2 Mev/s, at CPU load 5%	55 ns/ev at 0.2 Mev/s, at CPU load 3%	160 ns/ev at any event rate
Power	6.2 W static 6.2 W for running jAER 2.5 W	160 W	0.775 W static 0.05 W

6   Conclusions

This paper offers software and FPGA implementation of the AC model for real time detection of expanding dark objects. The FPGA implementation requires less than 0.8 W power and has a latency of 180 ns, which is smaller than that of the software approach, 370 ns on the embedded "Next Unit of Computing" Intel NUC computer. The software model running on a more powerful desktop PC takes 55 ns to process one event (on average) with a power consumption higher than 100 W. Future work will be focused on expanding from one AC to multiple ACs in order to infer the relative location of the approaching object. This will also solve the issue that multiple objects moving in opposite directions cancel out their effect to the AC. It would be interesting as well to integrate the AC with the OMC [6] or other algorithms where the AC serves as an attention mechanism.

Acknowledgments. This work has been partially supported by the Spanish government grant (with support from the European Regional Development Fund) COFNET (TEC2016-77785-P) and the European Project VISUALISE (FP7-ICT-600954). We thank Prof. Francisco Gomez-Rodriguez for his support.

References

1. Lichtsteiner, P., Posch, C., Delbrck, T.: A 128 x 128 120 dB 15 μs latency asynchronous temporal contrast vision sensor. IEEE J. Solid- State Circ. **43**(2), 566–576 (2008)
2. Münch, T.A., et al.: Approach sensitivity in the retina processed by a multifunctional neural circuit. Nat. Neurosci. **12**(10), 1308–1316 (2009)
3. Iakymchuk, T., et al.: An AER handshake-less modular infrastructure PCB with x8 2.5 Gbps LVDS serial links. In: 2014 IEEE International Symposium on Circuits and Systems (ISCAS). IEEE (2014)
4. Linares-Barranco, A., et al.: A USB3.0 FPGA event-based filtering and tracking framework for dynamic vision sensors. In: 2015 IEEE International Symposium on Circuits and Systems (ISCAS), pp. 2417–2420 (2015)
5. Rios-Navarro, A., et al.: A 20 Mevps/32 Mev event-based USB framework for neuromorphic systems debugging. In: 2016 Second International Conference on Event-based Control, Communication, and Signal Processing (EBCCSP). IEEE (2016)
6. Moeys, D.P., et al.: Retinal ganglion cell software and FPGA model implementation for object detection and tracking. In: 2016 IEEE International Symposium on Circuits and Systems (ISCAS). IEEE (2016)
7. Clady, X., et al.: Asynchronous visual event-based time-to-contact. In: Neuromorphic Engineering Systems and Applications 51. APA (2015)
8. Serrano-Gotarredona, R., et al.: CAVIAR: a 45k neuron, 5M synapse, 12G connects/s AER hardware sensory-processing-learning-actuating system for high-speed visual object recognition and tracking. IEEE Trans. Neural Netw. **20**(9), 1417–1438 (2009)

9. Denk, C., Llobet-Blandino, F., Galluppi, F., Plana, L.A., Furber, S., Conradt, J.: Real-time interface board for closed-loop robotic tasks on the SpiNNaker neural computing system. In: Mladenov, V., Koprinkova-Hristova, P., Palm, G., Villa, A.E.P., Appollini, B., Kasabov, N. (eds.) ICANN 2013. LNCS, vol. 8131, pp. 467–474. Springer, Heidelberg (2013). doi:10.1007/978-3-642-40728-4_59

10. Khan, M.M., et al.: SpiNNaker: mapping neural networks onto a massively-parallel chip multiprocessor. In: IEEE International Joint Conference on Neural Networks, 2008, IJCNN 2008. IEEE World Congress on Computational Intelligence. IEEE (2008)

11. Delbck, T., et al.: Activity-driven, event-based vision sensors. In: Proceedings of 2010 IEEE International Symposium on Circuits and Systems (ISCAS). IEEE (2010)

Brain Imaging

Event Related Potentials Reveal Fairness in Willingness-to-share

Alessandra Lintas[1]([✉]), Sarat Chandra Vysyaraju[2], Manon Jaquerod[1], and Alessandro E.P. Villa[1]

[1] NeuroHeuristic Research Group, University of Lausanne,
Quartier Dorigny, 1015 Lausanne, Switzerland
alessandra.lintas@unil.ch
[2] Department of Electrical Engineering, Columbia University,
New York, NY, USA
http://www.neuroheuristic.org

Abstract. Willingness-to-share is tested in an Ultimatum Game where the participants iteratively play a role of Proposer and Responder sharing a virtual amount of money. We test the hypothesis that brain activity associated with small *vs.* large share offered by the Proposer can be detected by event related potentials (ERPs). We observed that differences between wretched and prodigal offers in ERPs latencies, amplitudes and locations appeared along the antero-posterior midline at the time of Proposer's invite to make the offer, that is before the actual offer was made. Differences in ERPs associated with the offered amount of the share were localized at parietal areas when the offer was accepted. We discuss the outcome of these results for reward learning processes.

Keywords: EEG · Neuroeconomics · Reward circuit · Decision making

1 Introduction

In the "Theory of the Consumer" it is assumed that rational individuals maximize the consumption of real goods given a limited availability of nominal goods (money) [14,15]. According to Game Theory, the subgame perfect equilibrium in the Ultimatum Game (UG) occurs if the proposer offers the smaller possible amount (in order to save as much as possible), and the responder accepts any amount (because a small amount is better than nothing). Proposers tend to offer rather fair offers and responders tend to reject offers that are judged as unfair [1,16] despite this being an irrational behavior with respect to gain maximization [8,13]. This deviation from "rational" strategies that are suggested by game-theoretic analysis can be explained by the fact that humans being in a multi-stimulus and multi-target environment have been conditioned to act so. Such environment includes "irrational" concepts driven by emotions in decision making such as fairness and "social sharing" that involve the description of an emotional event by the person who experienced it to another person in a socially shared language [4,9]. A specific component, N2-P3, of the event related

© Springer International Publishing AG 2017
A. Lintas et al. (Eds.): ICANN 2017, Part I, LNCS 10613, pp. 191–198, 2017.
https://doi.org/10.1007/978-3-319-68600-4_23

potential (ERP) is associated with the activity in the Anterior Cingulate Cortex (ACC) generated by the conflict detection of willingness on honest and deceptive responses [19]. In the experimental framework of the Ultimatum Game Responders' behavior and brain activity have been extensively investigated, but Proposers' strategies received less attention. In a recent study, a specific negative wave (the medial frontal negativity) was selectively evoked in Proposer's ERP by the advantageous comparison to fair offers [17].

In the present study we test the hypothesis that wretched and prodigal amounts offered by the Proposers are driven by the activation of different brain circuits at the time of the offering invite. We present new findings that show that differences associated with the offered amount can be detected from the time of Proposer's invite to make an offer till the communication of Responder's acceptance of that offer. We discuss how the identification of the mechanisms associated with the perception of fairness may influence the concept of reinforcement learning.

2   Materials and Methods

Forty-eight healthy native French speakers, right-handed participants volunteered to participate in the study and provided written consent for their participation in line with the Declaration of Helsinki [18]. The Ultimatum Game (UG) is an anonymous, single-shot two-player game, in which the "Proposer" has a certain sum of money at his disposal and must propose a share to the "Responder" [7]. If the Responder accepts the proposal, the share is done accordingly. If the Responder refuses, both players end up with nothing. Participants were told to play the UG with virtual money trying to maximize their gain as much as possible. All had normal or corrected-to-normal vision, none reported a history of sustained head injury or neurological disease, and all were naive to the UG.

Figure 1 illustrates the experimental procedure along each Proposer's trial: The trial started (event at time 0) with the pressure of the spacebar of the computer keyboard. The participants maintained their gaze on the central fixation cross during a preparatory period of 2000 ms. At the end of this interval (event S), the invite message "Please, make your offer." appeared (in French) on the center of the display. By pressing a digit (event PT), from 1 to 9 on the numerical keypad, the Proposer selected the x amount of the offer, within a maximum allowed time of 10 seconds. This event was immediately followed by the display of the confirmation message "You offered x." (in French). The decision made by the other player (event PR) was conveyed to the proposer through a face diagram (smiley) that either smiled (offer accepted) or frowned (offer rejected) appearing on the center of the display. A new trial started by pressing the spacebar at least 1 second after the smiley. The sequence of the trials was self-paced by the participant, who played the role of Proposer for 3 blocks of 30 consecutive trials, alternated with 30 consecutive trials playing the role of Responder.

Event-related potentials (ERPs) triggered by events S, PT and PR were analyzed from recording sites Fz, Cz and Pz during all Proposer's trials, as

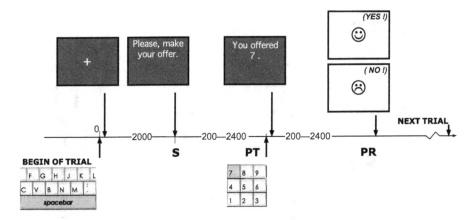

Fig. 1. Illustration of the ultimatum game task along one trial for the proposer. At proposer's invite (S): the participant received the invitation to offer an amount to the responder. At Proposer's choice (PT) the participant digitized the value of the amount offered to the responder on a numeric keypad. At Responder's decision (PR) the Proposer saw the display of the Responder's choice to accept (smiley emoticon, with a YES! message) or to reject (pouting emoticon, with a NO! message) the offer. Time intervals are in ms.

described elsewhere [5]. The trials were separated post-hoc, following Proposer's choice to offer a low (unfair or wretched, up 30% of the amount) or a high (fair or prodigal, more than 70% of the amount) share. Trials for wretched offers (values 1, 2, or 3) and prodigal offers (values 7, 8, or 9) were pooled together for each Participant. Then, in order to reduce the variability of the individual curves, we pooled the curves of 12 participants together. This means that eventually we obtained four grand average ERPs for each condition. Hence, the comparisons between mean values between two conditions were computed with Student's t-tests ($t(8)$), with N = 4 for each condition and a total degree of freedom df = 8.

3   Results

At the time of Proposer's invite (S), we observed differences in ERPs along the antero-posterior axis, as a function of the offer to come whether wretched or prodigal, with larger amplitudes and longer latencies in the frontal areas for prodigal *vs.* wretched offers (Fig. 2). Notice that prodigal offers elicit a positive wave at Fz immediately after the trigger onset, *i.e.* after receiving the invite to make an offer. The N2-P3 complex is a ERP component associated with the attentional load characterized by a negative wave immediately followed by a positive wave occurring approximately at a latency of 200 ms after the triggering event. Table 1 shows that N2 latencies tended always to be longer for prodigal offers at all sites along the midline, with a significance level below threshold for Fz (203 ± 4 ms and 173 ± 8 ms for prodigal and wretched offers, respectively;

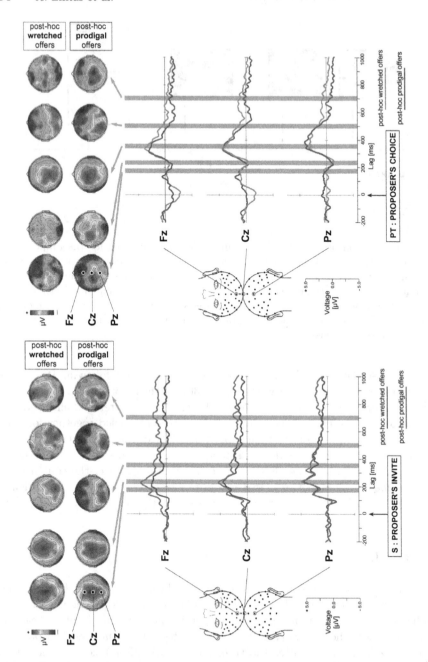

Fig. 2. Grand average ERPs at Fz, Cz, and Pz for trials corresponding to wretched and prodigal offers (separated post-hoc) triggered by Proposer's invite (S), when the Proposer received the invitation to offer an amount to the Responder (left panels) and by Proposer's choice (PT), when the proposer pressed the digit on the keypad corresponding to the offer made to the Responder (right panels). Upper panels show the topological maps of the ERPs at delays of 180, 220, 350, 500, and 700 ms after the trigger.

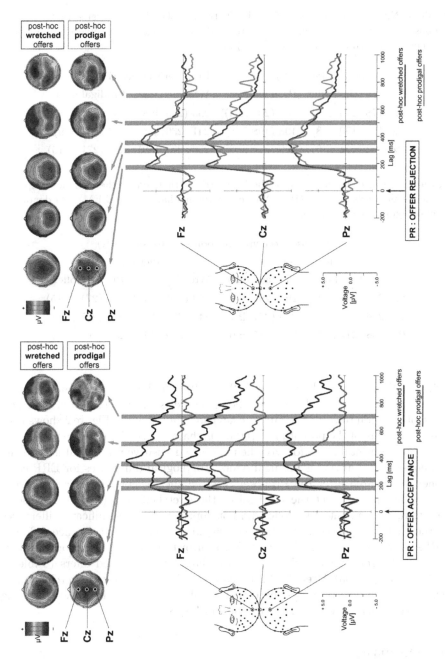

Fig. 3. Grand average ERPs at Fz, Cz, and Pz for trials corresponding to wretched and prodigal offers (separated post-hoc) triggered by the display of Responder's decision (PR), either acceptance of the offer (left panels), or rejection of the offer (right panels). Upper panels show the topological maps of the ERPs at delays of 180, 220, 350, 500, and 700 ms after the trigger.

Table 1. N2 peak latency [ms] of the ERPs trials evoked by Proposer's invite (S) and Proposer's choice (PT) calculated for wretched and prodigal trials separated post-hoc. We report the median (mean±SEM). (*) denotes a level of significance $p < 0.05$.

	Proposer's invite (S)		Proposer's choice (PT)	
	Wretched offer	Prodigal offer	Wretched offer	Prodigal offer
Fz	178 (173 ± 8)*	204 (203 ± 4)*	235 (235 ± 8)	237 (238 ± 8)
Cz	185 (190 ± 8)	198 (198 ± 5)	241 (239 ± 8)	224 (231 ± 9)
Pz	193 (191 ± 6)	199 (216 ± 22)	253 (257 ± 9)	269 (271 ± 15)

Table 2. N2 peak latency [ms] of the ERPs trials triggered by the feedback response of the Responder's decision (PR). We report the median (mean±SEM). (*) denotes a level of significance $p < 0.05$.

	Proposer receiving Responser's decision (PR)			
	Offer acceptance		Offer rejection	
	Wretched offer	Prodigal offer	Wretched offer	Prodigal offer
Fz	278 (273 ± 15)	293 (295 ± 15)	249 (254 ± 13)	267 (271 ± 15)
Cz	266 (259 ± 18)	270 (271 ± 13)	245 (256 ± 15)	269 (267 ± 11)
Pz	268 (272 ± 7)*	242 (245 ± 6)*	251 (259 ± 15)	261 (269 ± 9)

$t(8) = 3.517$, $p = .01$). The delay of 700 ms after the invite corresponds roughly at time when the cortical activity follows the decision of the selected offer and the motor action towards the numeric keypad is building up. Figure 2 shows that the topography of the potential at 700 ms is characterized by positive waves centered on the frontal areas for wretched offers and positive waves centered on the parieto-occipital areas for prodigal offers. Topological differences for ERP components appeared after the Proposer received the Responder's decision (event PR) to accept or reject the prodigal or the wretched offer (Fig. 3). In case of rejection, the amount of the offer did not appear to evoke significant differences in the ERP components. On the contrary, in case of offer acceptance different ERPs were evoked at all sites as a function of the wretched or prodigal offer. For the electrode Pz the N2 latency was larger for wretched offers (Table 2), $t(8) = 2.838$, $p = .03$) After the N2-P3 complex the acceptance of wretched offers evoked a large positivity that extended for about 1 second after the triggering event (the black curves in the left panels of Fig. 3).

4   Discussion

It is rationale to expect that in the Ultimatum Game the Proposer offers the smallest possible amount and the Responder accepts any amount. However, it is observed that Responders tend to reject an unfair offer, which is explained by a bias towards the maximization gain in UG associated with positive social factors like common ethical principles and friendship, but also negative factors as fear of the perceived consequences of having one's offer rejected, and guilt related to concerns for the opponents' outcomes [2,6,10].

The N2-P3 complex is associated with attentional load and in patients suffering of hyperactivity and attention deficit changes in response inhibition affect this ERP component [11]. In our study we observed that the activity in frontal areas developed immediately after the Proposer received the invite for prodigal offers 'to come': the waves are larger and N2 peaked later than at the other sites. Hence, it may suggest a broader network activity develops as soon as the Proposer expresses the willingness to offer a prodigal amount. The extension of that network might be associated with the mental expectations of offering a large share and the consequence of a lesser gain for oneself. Offers in bargaining are likely to be guided by the emotions that proposers anticipate when contemplating their offers [12]. Our study has shown that in case of acceptance of wretched offers, the ERPs waves evoked in the Proposer's brain are characterized by a larger amplitude and the latency of N2 peak is shorter than in the case of acceptance of prodigal offers. This is in agreement with the interpretation that an extended circuit is activated by the acceptance of wretched offers. Increased activity in dorsal ACC was recently reported in associated with higher expectation violations [3] and differences in the ERPs generated by unfair and fair offers were related to the Proposer's ACC activity while performing the UG [17].

Reinforcement learning has acquired popularity in the machine learning community. It is based on the assumptions, that under bounded rationality when learning process lead to near optimal decisions from the training experience, single-agent and multi-agent planning will lead to automated decision-making. The results of this study are coherent with the hypothesis that expectation and evaluation of the consequences of bargaining activate specific neural activity strongly associated with the willingness-to-share and the emotions that amplify it. The observation that brain circuits do not simply follow the rules of making a decision in a contextual scene so as to maximize some notion of cumulative reward should raise questions about how to integrate multidimensional components of a reward (e.g., the face-value of the amount, the social interaction, the emotions) which simply do not add up as assumed to be in a novel approach of machine learning.

Acknowledgments. The authors acknowledge the support by the Swiss National Science Foundation grant n. CR13I11_38032_1.

References

1. Cameron, L.A.: Raising the stakes in the ultimatum game: experimental evidence from Indonesia. Econ. Inq. **37**(1), 47–59 (1999)
2. Carver, C.S., Miller, C.J.: Relations of serotonin function to personality: current views and a key methodological issue. Psychiatry Res. **144**(1), 1–15 (2006)
3. Chang, L.J., Sanfey, A.G.: Great expectations: neural computations underlying the use of social norms in decision-making. Soc. Cogn. Affect. Neurosci. **8**(3), 277–284 (2013)

4. Chang, Y.H., Levinboim, T., Maheswaran, R.: The social ultimatum game. In: Guy, T.V., Kárný, M., Wolpert, D.H. (eds.) Decision Making with Imperfect Decision Makers. Intelligent Systems Reference Library, vol. 28. Springer, Heidelberg (2012). doi:10.1007/978-3-642-24647-0_6

5. Fiori, M., Lintas, A., Mesrobian, S., Villa, A.E.P.: Effect of emotion and personality on deviation from purely rational decision-making. In: Guy, V.T., Kárný, M., Wolpert, D. (eds.) Decision Making and Imperfection, pp. 129–161. Springer, Heidelberg (2013)

6. Gaertig, C., Moser, A., Alguacil, S., Ruz, M.: Social information and economic decision-making in the ultimatum game. Front. Neurosci. **6**, 103–103 (2012)

7. Güth, W., Schmittberger, R., Schwarze, B.: An experimental analysis of ultimatum bargaining. J. Econ. Behav. Organ. **3**(4), 367–388 (1982)

8. Henrich, J., Boyd, R., Bowles, S., Camerer, C., Fehr, E., Gintis, H., McElreath, R.: In search of Homo economicus: Behavioral experiments in 15 small-scale societies. Am. Econ. Rev. **91**(2), 73–78 (2001)

9. Lane, A., Luminet, O., Rimé, B., Gross, J.J., de Timary, P., Mikolajczak, M.: Oxytocin increases willingness to socially share one's emotions. Int. J. Psychol. **48**(4), 676–681 (2013)

10. Marchetti, A., Castelli, I., Harlé, K.M., Sanfey, A.G.: Expectations and outcome: the role of proposer features in the ultimatum game. J. Econ. Psychol. **32**(3), 446–449 (2011)

11. McLoughlin, G., Albrecht, B., Banaschewski, T., Rothenberger, A., Brandeis, D., Asherson, P., Kuntsi, J.: Electrophysiological evidence for abnormal preparatory states and inhibitory processing in adult ADHD. Behav. Brain. Funct. **6**, 66 (2010)

12. Nelissen, R.M.A., Leliveld, M.C., van Dijk, E., Zeelenberg, M.: Fear and guilt in proposers: Using emotions to explain offers in ultimatum bargaining. Eur. J. Soc. Psychol. **41**, 78–85 (2011)

13. Roth, A., Prasnikar, V., Okuno-Fujiwara, M., Zamir, S.: Bargaining and market behavior in Jerusalem, Ljubljana, Pittsburgh, and Tokyo: An experimental study. Am. Econ. Rev. **81**(5), 1068–95 (1991)

14. Samuelson, P.A.: A note on the pure theory of consumer's behaviour. Economica **5**, 61–71 (1938)

15. Samuelson, P.A.: Consumption theory in terms of revealed preference. Economica **15**, 243–253 (1948)

16. Slonim, R., Roth, A.E.: Learning in high stakes ultimatum games: an experiment in the Slovak Republic. Econometrica **66**(3), 569–596 (1998)

17. Wang, G., Li, J., Li, Z., Wei, M., Li, S.: Medial frontal negativity reflects advantageous inequality aversion of proposers in the ultimatum game: an erp study. Brain Res. **1639**, 38–46 (2016)

18. World Medical Association: World Medical Association Declaration of Helsinki. Ethical principles for medical research involving human subjects. Bull World Health Organ 79(4), 373–374 (2001)

19. Wu, H., Hu, X., Fu, G.: Does willingness affect the N2–P3 effect of deceptive and honest responses? Neurosci. Lett. **467**(2), 63–66 (2009)

Individual Identification by Resting-State EEG Using Common Dictionary Learning

Takashi Nishimoto[1]([✉]), Yoshiki Azuma[1,2], Hiroshi Morioka[3], and Shin Ishii[1,2]

[1] Kyoto University, Kyoto 606-8501, Japan
nishimoto-t@sys.i.kyoto-u.ac.jp
[2] ATR Cognitive Mechanisms Laboratories, Kyoto 619-0288, Japan
[3] ATR Neural Information Analysis Laboratories, Kyoto 619-0288, Japan

Abstract. Recently, a number of biometric methods to identify individuals based on personal characteristics, such as fingerprints and irises, have been developed. Individual identification based on electroencephalography (EEG) measurements is one of the safe identification techniques to prevent spoofing. In this study, we propose to employ common dictionary learning, which was formerly presented by Morioka *et al.* [1] aiming at performing subject-transfer decoding, for extracting features for EEG-based individual identification. Using the proposed method, though a classifier was trained based on the EEG signals during the selective spatial attention task, we found each test subject was almost perfectly identified out of 40 based on its resting-state EEG signals.

Keywords: Biometric authentication · Individual identification · Electroencephalography (EEG) · Dictionary learning and sparse coding · Resting-state brain activity

1 Introduction

To overcome the risk of the traditional trust-based authentication methods such as key or password which can be shared, duplicated, lost or stolen, biometric authentication has attracted much attention. To develop safer and more convenient authentication methods, various biometric features have been examined [2]. They are physical features such as fingerprints [3] and irises [4], and behavioral features such as voiceprints [5]. Some of these have been put into practical use, but how to make spoofing impossible is still an important problem.

Here, our particular interests are to use the brain as a biometric feature. Structurally and functionally, the brain has a higher confidentiality as compared

---

This study is originally presented in this manuscript. We previously submitted an abstract to a domestic technical meeting, but withdrew the submission so that we did not present the study at that meeting. The content page of the final meeting proceedings is attached below: http://www.ieice.org/ken/index/ieice-techrep-116-521-e.html.

© Springer International Publishing AG 2017
A. Lintas et al. (Eds.): ICANN 2017, Part I, LNCS 10613, pp. 199–207, 2017.
https://doi.org/10.1007/978-3-319-68600-4_24

to the other features described above. In the past, studies of individual identification using fMRI [6] or EEG [7,8] were presented. A study using fMRI succeeded in identifying individuals with a high accuracy of 99% [6], but there is a major problem that MRI is a large scale device. So are MEG and PET. In comparison to these, EEG can be measured with a simple device in a real environment.

Most studies of EEG-based individual identification required subjects to perform some tasks during which features were extracted for both training and test [7]. In this study, we employ to use resting-state brain activities for testing individual identification. The use of resting-state brain activities in biometric authentication is advantageous, because there is no need to impose special tasks on the users. However, identification would be difficult, because the extracted features may be unreliable due to the lack of task data. According to our framework, therefore, we measure EEG signals when a user is performing tasks and use them to register the user, but the same user would be identified based on his/her resting-state activities. This framework avoids imposing a complicated task at the scene of authentication. In particular, we use a selective spatial attention task for registration. A prior study of individual identification by resting-state EEG using a convolutional neural network identified 10 subjects with an accuracy of 88% [8], while we successfully identified all the 40 subjects.

In individual identification, we have to appropriately define the feature. In this study, we apply common dictionary learning, which was proposed by Morioka *et al.* for subject-transfer decoding [1], into individual identification.

2   Common Dictionary Learning and Individual Identification

2.1   Generative Model of Brain Activity Patterns

Figure 1 shows a generative model of brain activity patterns. This model was proposed by Morioka *et al.*, and was applied to the decoding of spatial attention task [1]. Based on this model, we analyzed EEG under the following assumptions.

(A1) Brain activity patterns can be expressed as a combination of a small number of spatial bases common across subjects and sessions.

(A2) Actual signals measuring the brain activities are deformed by subject-session-specific spatial transforms.

(A3) For the same subject, spatial transforms are consistent over different sessions.

2.2   Common Dictionary Learning

In the basic formulation of dictionary learning, a vector of measured signals $x_t \in \mathbb{R}^M$ at time t is represented by $x_t \approx D\alpha_t$, where $D = [d_1, ..., d_K] \in \mathbb{R}^{M \times K}$ is a dictionary whose column vectors d_k are called atoms and $\alpha_t \in \mathbb{R}^K$ is called a sparse code. We use an "overcomplete" dictionary ($K > M$). Dictionary

Common dictionary   Spatial transforms   Sparse codes   EEG signals

D Z_{ij} α_{ijt} x_{ijt}

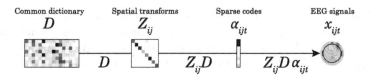

Fig. 1. A generative model of brain activity. A dictionary (spatial bases) common across subjects and sessions, D, is modulated by subject-session-specific spatial transforms Z_{ij}. At each time t, an EEG activity pattern x_{ijt} is represented as a linear combination of the transformed bases weighted by a sparse code α_{ijt}.

learning with overcomplete bases makes it possible to decompose signals into sparse factors, and has been applied to signal processing such as noise removal [9] and compressive sensing [10].

In this study, x_t presents measured brain activities. D is interpreted as the bases of spatial activity patterns (spatial bases), and α_t denotes the combination of a small number of spatial bases and their weights. The introduction of overcomplete dictionary enables us to analyze EEG based on assumption (A1).

Morioka *et al.* proposed a new dictionary learning method to transfer decoding [1]. According to that method, based on assumption (A2), subject-session-specific spatial transforms were introduced to deform the dictionary. Measured signals are then given by

$$x_{ijt} \approx Z_{ij}D\alpha_{ijt}, \tag{1}$$

where i, j, t are the indices for subjects, sessions, and time points, respectively, $x_{ijt} \in \mathbb{R}^M$ is a vector of measured signals, $Z_{ij} \in \mathbb{R}^{M \times M}$ is a matrix of a spatial transform, $D \in \mathbb{R}^{M \times K}$ is a dictionary, and $\alpha_{ijt} \in \mathbb{R}^K$ is a sparse code. Whereas the dictionary D is unique and shared over subjects and sessions, each spatial transform Z_{ij} is specific to the subject-session pair (i, j). Each spatial transform is assumed to be consistent during a session. The measured signal x_{ijt} is represented as a linear combination of a small number of bases in the deformed dictionary $Z_{ij}D$, and their weights are in total represented as the sparse code.

Since the combination of Z_{ij} and D is not unique in Eq. (1), Morioka *et al.* proposed the following optimization problem:

$$\min_{Z,D,A} \frac{1}{2} \sum_{i \in \mathcal{S}} \sum_{j \in \mathcal{S}_i} \sum_{t \in \mathcal{S}_{ij}} \{\|x_{ijt} - Z_{ij}D\alpha_{ijt}\|_2^2 + \lambda\|Z_{ij} - I\|_F^2\} \tag{2}$$

$$\text{s.t. } \forall i, j, t : \|\alpha_{ijt}\|_0 \leq L, \forall k \in \{1, \cdots, K\} : \|d_k\|_2 = 1,$$

where $i \in \mathcal{S}$, $j \in \mathcal{S}_i$ and $t \in \mathcal{S}_{ij}$ index subjects, sessions performed by subject i and time points in session j by subject i, respectively, and $Z = [Z_{ij}]$ and $A = [\alpha_{ijt}]$ are the spatial transforms and the sparse codes, respectively. $\lambda \geq 0$ is a regularization constant, $\|\cdot\|_p$ is the l_p norm, and $\|\cdot\|_F$ is the Frobenius norm. Introducing Z_{ij}, the factors derived from the difference between subjects and between sessions are removed from D and α_{ijt}. The regularization term in Eq. (2) plays a role to make each Z_{ij} similar to a unit matrix. This regularization is based on the assumption that even if the subjects or sessions are different, the spatial bases constituting the brain activity patterns are yet not much different.

A stochastic gradient descent algorithm [11] was performed to solve the optimization problem Eq. (2). See Morioka *et al.* [1] for more details.

2.3   Application to Individual Identification

In this study, we present an individual identification method based on easy-to-measure resting-state EEG data, in which Z_{ij} is regarded as individual features.

Proposed Method: Based on Spatial Transforms. In the proposed method, we use spatial transforms from multiple task sessions $Z_{ij}(i = 1, \cdots, I, j = 1, \cdots, J)$ to train the classifier, and spatial transforms from resting sessions $Z_{n0}(i = n, j = 0, 1 \le n \le I)$ to predict the subject label n. A feature vector for session j of subject i is given as

$$
\Delta_{ij} = \begin{pmatrix} \delta_{ij}^{11} \\ \delta_{ij}^{12} \\ \vdots \\ \delta_{ij}^{IJ} \end{pmatrix}
\tag{3}
$$

$$
\delta_{ij}^{i'j'} = \|Z_{ij} - Z_{i'j'}\|_F,
$$

where $\Delta_{ij} \in \mathbb{R}^{IJ}$ is a column vector of $\delta_{ij}^{i'j'} \in \mathbb{R}$, consisting of the distances of the spatial transform between every pair of subjects and sessions. Because the size of Z_{ij} ($M \times M$) is much larger than the number of pairs of subjects and sessions ($I \times J$), this feature representation has advantage to reduce the classifier's input dimensionality. When predicting a subject from a trained classifier based on Δ_{ij}, we use a feature vector of Eq. (3) but with $(i, j) = (n, 0)$, that means resting EEG activity.

Simpler Method: Based on Input Signals of Common Dictionary Learning. We also prepared a simple method without using the dictionary learning. In this method, Z_{ij} are replaced with the time average of the input x_{ijt}:

$$
\delta_{ij}^{i'j'} = \|x_{ij}^{mean} - x_{i'j'}^{mean}\|_F
\tag{4}
$$

$$
x_{ij}^{mean} = \frac{1}{T} \sum_t x_{ijt},
$$

where T represents the number of sample points in the session, (i, j).

Supplementary Method: Based on Sparse Codes. The proposed method is based on the idea that subject-specific information in EEG signals has been extracted to Z_{ij} through common dictionary learning. On the other hand, it is considered that the subject-specific information in sparse codes is less than in the raw data. To know how much subject information is included in sparse codes, therefore, we also examined the individual identification based on sparse codes. In this method, x_{ijt} in Eq. (4) is simply replaced with α_{ijt} to get a feature vector.

3   EEG Data Analysis

In this study, we used public EEG data measured by Morioka *et al.* and published by Advanced Telecommunications Research Institute International (ATR): http://biomark00.atr.jp/modules/xoonips/listitem.php?index_id=181.

We targeted data for 40 subjects whose data were successfully measured in both resting and task sessions. In the resting session, 5 min resting-state EEG activities were measured. In the task session, subjects performed a selective spatial attention task (attend-left or attend-right). Each task session includes 24 trials of 8 s task. Each subject completed one resting session and eight task sessions. EEG signals were measured at a sampling rate of 256 Hz with a 64-electrode cap that was configured according to the international 10–20 system.

The raw EEG data were passed through a band-pass filter(0.5–40 Hz) and re-referenced to a common average reference. Then, we performed time-frequency analysis using Morlet wavelets, and extracted power spectrum of 7 frequency bands, whose center frequencies were set $[4, 5.7, 8, 11.3, 16, 22.6, 32]$ Hz. After the wavelet analysis, the data were downsampled to 32 Hz and normalized for each time point and frequency, leading to $x_{ijt} \in \mathbb{R}^M$ in Eq. (2). The dimensionality M of x_{ijt} corresponded to the number of channels, 64.

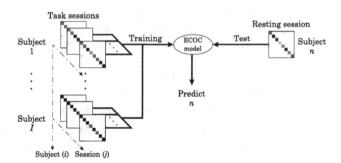

Fig. 2. Schematic diagram of the proposed multi-class classification problem. Spatial transforms of task sessions $Z_{ij}(i = 1, \cdots, I, j = 1, \cdots, J)$ were used for training, and spatial transform of resting session Z_{N0} was used for testing. The feature vectors were calculated based on the distance information between spatial transforms (Eq. (3)).

Figure 2 shows the outline of the individual identification by the proposed method. We evaluated how many subjects are successfully identified. The identification problem then became 40-class classification, for which we used an error correcting output code (ECOC) classifier. ECOC is a method to solve multiclass classification problems using multiple binary classifiers [12]. We performed an one-versus-the-rest classification with linear support vector machine classifiers. Individual identification accuracy was evaluated for each frequency band.

The common dictionary D and the ECOC classifier are learned only from the task data.

4   Results

Table 1 shows the individual identification accuracy by the proposed method. Columns (a1), (a2) and (a3) show the results of different measuring time for resting states (test), during 300, 60 and 30 s, respectively. Training data are common among (a1)–(a3). Column (a1) shows that we succeeded to identify all the 40 subjects for each of the 7 frequency bands. Notice that the chance level of 40-class classification is 2.5%. From (a2) and (a3), we can see that the performance gets worse as the resting-state signals for test become shorter.

Columns (b1)–(b3) show the results of the simpler method. The test data for (b1)–(b3) are the same as those for (a1)–(a3). Column (b1) shows the accuracy using five minutes EEG data with time-frequency analysis. In any of the frequency bands, it failed to identify 2 of 40 subjects. This difference clearly shows that the performance of individual identification has been improved by using the common dictionary learning.

Column (c) shows the results of the method using sparse codes α_{ijt}. The length of test data was 300 s. Although the performance was worse than that of the proposed method, it was indeed much higher than the chance level. This

Table 1. The results of individual identification. (a1)–(a3), (b1)–(b3) and (c) are respectively based on the proposed, simpler and supplementary methods. The test data length was as follows; (a1), (b1), (c): 300 s, (a2), (b2): 60 s, (a3), (b3): 30 s.

Frequency band [Hz]	(a1)	(a2)	(a3)	(b1)	(b2)	(b3)	(c)
4.0	100.0%	77.5%	58.25%	95.0%	89.0%	88.25%	92.5%
5.7	100.0%	79.0%	65.00%	95.0%	94.0%	91.50%	97.5%
8.0	100.0%	96.0%	72.00%	95.0%	91.0%	87.00%	95.0%
11.3	100.0%	95.5%	72.75%	95.0%	87.0%	81.00%	85.0%
16.0	100.0%	91.0%	77.75%	95.0%	94.5%	92.50%	92.5%
22.6	100.0%	93.0%	73.75%	95.0%	94.0%	91.75%	90.0%
32.0	100.0%	91.0%	73.00%	95.0%	91.5%	91.25%	92.5%
Number of samples	40	200	400	40	200	400	40

means that subject-specific information is extracted not only in spatial transforms but also in the remaining sparse codes.

5   Conclusion

We showed that highly accurate individual identification is possible using EEG data at resting states, which would be important for practical applications. The proposed method is based on the assumption that the spatial transform in common dictionary learning is consistent over sessions of the same subject. A prior study of individual identification by resting-state EEG identified 10 subjects with an accuracy of 88% [8]. On the contrary, we succeeded in identifying all the 40 subjects, so our result is encouraging. Since the number of subjects are still not enough for practical biometric authentication, verification with more subjects should be required.

We can also keep in mind that spatial transforms Z_{ij} contain not only the features of the spatial brain activity pattern itself but also the features of electrode position. In addition, human brain activity may change as time goes by. So it is desirable to measure and analyze brain activity over days, months, or years in order to confirm the influence of the electrode misalignment and to examine the robustness to the non-stationarity of brain activities.

Acknowledgments. We are grateful to ATR for providing the data used in this study.

Appendix: MDS of Spatial transforms Z_{ij}

Figure 3 displays multi-dimensional scaling (MDS) of Z_{ij} over all subjects (40) and sessions $(1 + 8)$ at the frequency band of 11.3 Hz. MDS presents the relative position in a low-dimensional space based on the distance information among data points (here, Z_{ij}), so that the more similar points are, the closer they are placed. We adopted the Frobenius norm between spatial transforms as distance information. Points are connected by colored lines if they are of a single subject. We can see that the points from a single subject (but different sessions) likely constitute a cluster, so that the distance between sessions of the same subject is shorter than that between different subjects regardless of session types. Considering the 2D-plot in Fig. 3 has some overlap due to the short of visualization dimensionality, these cluster structures are encouraging to make them use for subject identification. This result also shows the relevance of assumption (A3) that spatial transforms are consistent over different sessions of the same subject.

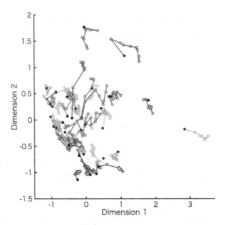

Fig. 3. Multi-dimensional scaling of spatial transforms Z_{ij} (11.3 Hz). Each point corresponds to a single session and points connected by colored lines are the spatial transforms of a single subject. Black and white points mean Z_{ij} of resting and task sessions, respectively. (Color figure online)

References

1. Morioka, H., Kanemura, A., Hirayama, J., Shikauchi, M., Ogawa, T., Ikeda, S., Kawanabe, M., Ishii, S.: Learning a common dictionary for subject-transfer decoding with resting calibration. NeuroImage **111**, 167–178 (2015)
2. Jain, A.K., Ross, A., Prabhakar, S.: An introduction to biometric recognition. IEEE Trans. Circ. Syst. Video Technol. **14**(1), 4–20 (2004)
3. Maltoni, D., Maio, D., Jain, A., Prabhakar, S.: Handbook of Fingerprint Recognition, 2 edn, pp. 25–31. Springer, Heidelberg (2009)
4. Wildes, R.P.: Iris recognition: an emerging biometrics technology. Proc. IEEE **85**(9), 1348–1363 (1997)
5. Roberts, W.J.J., Ephraim, Y., Sabrin, H.W.: Speaker classification using composite hypothesis testing and list decoding. IEEE Trans. Speech Audio Process. **13**(2), 211–219 (2005)
6. Finn, E.S., Shen, X., Scheinost, D., Rosenberg, M.D., Huang, J., Chun, M.M., Papademetris, X., Constable, R.T.: Functional connectome fingerprinting: identifying individuals using patterns of brain connectivity. Nat. Neurosci. **18**(11), 1664–1671 (2015)
7. Palaniappan, R., Mandic, D.P.: Biometrics from brain electrical activity: a machine learning approach. IEEE Trans. Pattern Anal. Mach. Intell. **29**(4), 738–742 (2007)
8. Ma, L., Minett, J.W., Blu, T., Wang, W.S.-Y.: Resting State EEG-based biometrics for individual identification using convolutional neural networks. In: 37th Annual International Conference of the IEEE Engineering in Medicine and Biology Society (EMBC), pp. 2848–2851 (2015)
9. Elad, M., Aharon, M.: Image denoising via sparse and redundant representations over learned dictionaries. IEEE Trans. Image Process. **15**(12), 3736–3745 (2006)

10. Patel, V.M., Chellappa, R.: Sparse Representations and Compressive Sensing for Imaging and Vision. Springer, Heidelberg (2013). doi:10.1007/978-1-84882-254-2
11. Mairal, J., Bach, F., Ponce, J.: Task-driven dictionary learning. IEEE Trans. Pattern Anal. Mach. Intell. **34**(4), 791–804 (2012)
12. Dietterich, T.G., Bakiri, G.: Solving multiclass learning problems via error-correcting output codes. JAIR **2**, 263–286 (1995)

Performance Comparison of Machine Learning Algorithms for EEG-Signal-Based Emotion Recognition

Peng Chen and Jianhua Zhang$^{(\boxtimes)}$

School of Information Science and Engineering,
East China University of Science and Technology, Shanghai 200237, China
zhangjh@ecust.edu.cn

Abstract. In this paper, we use the DEAP database to investigate emotion recognition problem. Firstly we use data clustering technique to determine four target classes of human emotional state. Then we compare two different feature extraction methods: one is wavelet transform and another is nonlinear dynamics. Furthermore, we examine the effect of feature reduction on classification performance. Finally, we compare the performance of four different classifiers, including *k*-nearest neighbor, naïve Bayesian, support vector machine, and random forest. The results show the effectiveness of Kernel Spectral Regression (KSR) and random forest based classifier for emotion recognition and analysis.

Keywords: Emotion recognition · Electroencephalogram (EEG) · Nonlinear dynamics · Wavelet transform · Feature extraction · Dimensionality reduction

1 Introduction

Human emotions can be identified by facial expressions, verbal language, nonverbal behavior, and physiological signals [1–3]. However, the first three kinds of emotion recognition methods are susceptible to the subjective influence of the subjects, that is, the subjects can deliberately disguise their emotions. The physiological signal is the human body spontaneously generated physiological phenomenon when the emotion occurs, so through the physiological signal for emotion recognition more objective and reliable [4]. EEG signals are produced by the central nervous system, and the response to affective changes is more real and rapid than other peripheral neurophysiological signals. EEG signals have been shown to be able to provide effective features corresponding to the emotional states [5, 6].

Feature extraction is an important part of emotion classification, and a variety of feature extraction methods are proposed in recent year [7]. Most of the studies on emotion recognition based on EEG signals directly extract the EEG signals after preprocessing without taking into account the role of the baseline (EEG signals recorded without the stimulation of the material), so our study takes into account the role of baseline in feature extraction, while comparing the differences when the baseline features are not applied. It is worth pointing out that the dimensionality reduction of features is not only beneficial in saving memory, increasing the speed of calculation,

© Springer International Publishing AG 2017
A. Lintas et al. (Eds.): ICANN 2017, Part I, LNCS 10613, pp. 208–216, 2017.
https://doi.org/10.1007/978-3-319-68600-4_25

but also improving the accuracy of classification greatly. Therefore, we compare the five methods of feature reduction. At the same time, compared with no dimension reduction. Moreover, we compare the effectiveness of four classifiers in emotion recognition, which are k-nearest neighbor (KNN), naive Bayes (NB), support vector machine (SVM), random forest (RF).

The paper is organized as follows: Sect. 2 introduce the emotion model of emotion recognition. Section 3 introduce the emotion data sets and methods we used. In Sect. 4, we present our experimental results and give some explanations and discussions on the results. Section 5 highlights the main conclusions of our study and the work for further research.

2 Emotion Model

Emotion is a group of the affective state of a human beings arising as a response to some interpersonal or other event. Different emotions have a crucial impact on self-motivation generation and decision-making. In general, there are two major approaches for describing emotions. One is discrete model. The point of view of this model is that there are some basic emotions, and other types of emotions are made up of basic emotional types. Weiner believes that happiness and sadness are the basic emotional types [8], while Kemper considers fear, anger, frustration, and satisfaction as the basic emotional type [9]. Based on Darwin's theory of evolution, Ekman puts forward six basic emotions [10]. The problem with this model is that there are still some disputes about the basic emotional types. The other model of emotion is dimensional model. Through this model, emotions can be determined by the position in the two-dimensional space. In other words, the dimensional model represent emotion through few independent dimensions on continuous scales. As shown in Fig. 1. The arousal dimension is used to describe the degree of emotion, from calm to excitement. The valence dimension is used to describe whether the emotion is positive or negative. In our study, we use dimensional model to identify our target emotion categories.

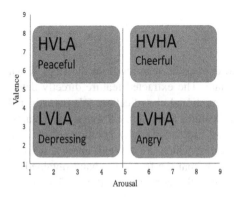

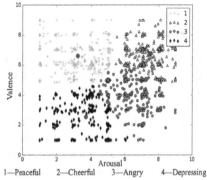

Fig. 1. A 2D emotional model   **Fig. 2.** *K*-means clustering result.

One of the main problems in emotion recognition is that different subjects may have different subjective emotional experiences for the same stimuli. Therefore, the number of emotional categories in the study of emotion recognition is usually relatively small, and many researches are focused on the classification of two categories, that is, positive and negative emotion. Many of the literature on the study of DEAP, their target emotion categories are divided by threshold [11]. We think that this method of determining the emotional labels is too simple, and with a lot subjectivity. In order to objectively determine the emotional class of the subjects in the two-dimensional emotional space, we carried out k-means clustering for the valence dimension and arousal dimension of the subjects' self-assessment. The final clustering results are shown in Fig. 2. We obtain the target emotion categories for each experiment by clustering the two dimensions of arousal and valence.

3   Data Acquisition and Preprocessing

3.1   DEAP Database and Data Preprocessing

In this research, we used DEAP as our research object [12]. Koelstra, Soleymani et al., who selected 40 pieces of music video as emotional material on the basis of emotional dimension model, and collected 32 subjects of physiological signals and facial video when watching 40 pieces of music video. Physiological signals have 40 channels, of which EEG signal have 32 channels, peripheral physiological signals have 8 channels. Here the EEG signals are used for emotion classification.

During the experiment, the EEG signals were sampled at 512 Hz and then down-sampled to 128 Hz. A band-pass frequency filter from 4.0 Hz to 45.0 Hz was applied. EOG artifacts were removed. The preprocessed EEG data contains 60 s data and a 3 s baseline data. In the follow-up we intend to discuss in two cases. For Case 1, we only extract feature from the 60 s EEG data when the subject was watching music videos. For Case 2, we also extract feature from 3 s baseline EEG data and 60 s EEG data, but the final features are formed by subtracting the 3 s baseline EEG feature from the 60 s EEG feature. The flowchart of emotional classification from EEG data is shown in Fig. 3.

3.2   Feature Extraction

The main purpose of feature extraction is to extract the features from the EEG signal that can significantly reflect the emotional state. The extracted feature directly determines the upper limit of the accuracy of the emotional classification. We investigated two EEG feature extraction methods: wavelet features and nonlinear dynamics features.

For the EEG signal of each channel, we use the wavelet coefficients of each sub-band to construct the three kinds of features, which are wavelet energy, wavelet energy ratio, and wavelet entropy. Table 1 show that the frequency band obtained by each level decomposition is roughly consistent with the rhythm of the EEG signal.

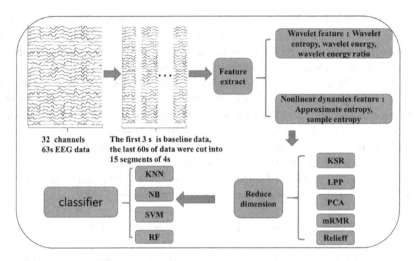

Fig. 3. The flowchart of EEG-based emotion recognition algorithm.

Table 1. Results of wavelet decomposition of EEG signals

Decomposition level	Frequency range (Hz)	EEG rhythm	Frequency range (Hz)
D1	32–64	Gamma	30–50
D2	16–32	Beta	13–30
D3	8–16	Alpha	8–13
D4	4–8	Theta	4–8
A5,D5	0–4	Delta	0.5–4

EEG is a very complex nonlinear signal. In recent years, nonlinear analytical methods have been widely used in the analysis of EEG signals [13–15]. Approximate entropy and sample entropy are important tools for quantifying the complexity of time series and studying the properties of time series. In this paper, we study the effectiveness of these two nonlinear dynamics methods to extract EEG signal features.

4   Data Analysis Results and Discussion

4.1   Comparison of 2 Feature Extraction and 6 Feature Reduction Algorithms

In order to investigate the impacts of baseline features on the final classification results, we extracted the wavelet features and nonlinear dynamics features in both cases using baseline features and without using baseline features. Case1 represents a situation where no baseline feature is used. Case2 represents a situation where baseline feature is used. To perform a more reliable classification process, we created a training set and a test set for each subject through a five-fold cross validation. We split the 60 s EEG data into 4-second fragment without overlapping. That is, the total number of instances for a subject is 40 * 15 = 600. The number of training set instances are 120 and the number of test set instances are 480 for each subject. The dimension of each sub-band after wavelet decomposition are 32 * 3 = 96, and the total feature dimension of all sub-band are 96 * 5 = 480. Approximate entropy and sample entropy feature dimensions are separately 32. The classifier we used is RF classifier because we will see that RF classifier is more accurate than KNN and NB, and is more efficient than SVM by discussing the classifier later. The parameters of each dimensionality reduction method are as follows: (1) The kernel type of KSR and LPP is Gaussian. (2) The regularization type of KSR is L2-norm regularizer, and the regularization parameter is 0.01. (3) The Nearest Neighborhood k of LPP is 5, and Euclidean distance is used. (4) The feature dimension of mRMR and Relieff respectively set to 20. (4) The features ratio of PCA is set to 0.98. (5) NDR means no feature reduction processing.

Table 2. Classification results based on wavelet-transform-extracted features in Case1 and Case 2.

Feature	Case	KSR	LPP	mRMR	Relieff	PCA	NDR
Delta	1	34.3 ± 4.9	38.3 ± 6.1	38.0 ± 5.7	38.2 ± 6.1	37.8 ± 6.0	40.3 ± 6.4
	2	**56.1 ± 9.9**	**59.6 ± 8.0**	**50.7 ± 7.3**	**51.8 ± 7.1**	**54.1 ± 9.9**	54.1 ± 6.5
Theta	1	36.5 ± 5.8	39.2 ± 6.0	41.1 ± 5.7	39.8 ± 5.8	37.6 ± 5.8	41.8 ± 6.1
	2	**55.7 ± 11.0**	**60.1 ± 8.2**	**51.6 ± 7.5**	**52.6 ± 8.6**	**55.5 ± 8.9**	55.5 ± 8.4
Alpha	1	38.8 ± 5.5	41.6 ± 5.8	40.5 ± 6.1	39.9 ± 6.1	39.8 ± 6.6	42.1 ± 5.7
	2	**63.2 ± 12.8**	**65.8 ± 8.9**	**55.4 ± 8.9**	**56.6 ± 9.5**	**58.7 ± 13.5**	58.7 ± 9.3
Beta	1	48.7 ± 8.4	52.1 ± 7.3	49.3 ± 8.1	49.3 ± 8.6	51.0 ± 8.6	50.8 ± 7.1
	2	**75.3 ± 11.5**	**79.6 ± 7.4**	**69.5 ± 8.6**	**68.6 ± 9.0**	**69.3 ± 17.8**	69.3 ± 8.5
Gamma	1	53.8 ± 8.7	57.7 ± 8.2	55.2 ± 8.7	55.4 ± 10.1	55.9 ± 9.1	56.4 ± 8.2
	2	**76.0 ± 10.6**	**82.0 ± 7.1**	**72.1 ± 8.9**	**71.6 ± 9.7**	**70.9 ± 18.2**	70.9 ± 9.2
All	1	44.6 ± 7.5	43.5 ± 6.3	46.4 ± 7.1	44.1 ± 7.9	44.1 ± 7.9	48.1 ± 6.5
	2	**63.0 ± 11.4**	**68.7 ± 8.8**	**56.6 ± 9.0**	**56.6 ± 9.8**	**58.2 ± 10.2**	58.2 ± 8.7

Table 3. Classification results based on ApEn and SampEn features in Case1 and Case 2.

Feature	Case	KSR	LPP	mRMR	Relieff	PCA	NDR
ApEn	1	38.6 ± 6.2	43.2 ± 5.4	43.3 ± 5.6	42.4 ± 5.1	43.5 ± 5.7	43.8 ± 5.7
	2	**89.9 ± 3.7**	**82.8 ± 4.1**	**75.7 ± 4.9**	**76.2 ± 5.1**	**82.9 ± 4.2**	78.7 ± 5.6
SampEn	1	42.3 ± 6.4	45.5 ± 6.1	45.0 ± 6.2	44.7 ± 6.3	46.4 ± 6.1	46.2 ± 5.7
	2	**87.5 ± 6.3**	**81.7 ± 6.8**	**74.7 ± 6.3**	**75.7 ± 6.2**	**81.1 ± 7.0**	77.4 ± 6.7
Both	1	45.4 ± 6.7	46.8 ± 6.1	45.1 ± 5.2	44.4 ± 5.4	46.7 ± 6.1	46.4 ± 5.6
	2	**92.8 ± 2.8**	**86.3 ± 6.6**	**75.2 ± 5.9**	**76.1 ± 5.7**	**83.8 ± 6.1**	77.4 ± 5.9

From Table 2, we can get the best classification accuracy when using the features of the gamma sub-band, followed by the beta sub-band features. This suggests that EEG signals most closely related to emotion are mainly distributed in the frequency band of gamma, beta, which is consistent with many existing findings in the literature [16, 17]. Secondly, in Case2, that is, when using the baseline feature, classification accuracy in any sub-band can be improved. Likewise, from Table 3, the accuracy of emotional classification have been greatly improved when considering the baseline features. Finally, we discuss the effectiveness of different methods to reduce the features dimension. In Case1, regardless of the use of wavelet features or nonlinear dynamic features, classification accuracy is very low, indicating that the upper limit of classification accuracy depends on the features. In Case2, when using the wavelet feature, LLP obtained the highest accuracy, the average classification accuracy of 32 subjects reached 82.0%, followed by KSR, which is 76.0%. However, KSR takes 0.614 s and LPP takes 1.256 s for single subject to reduce dimension, model training and test time. Similarly, in Case2, the KSR effect is the best when using approximate entropy and sample entropy. The average classification accuracy of 32 subjects is 92.8%, followed by LPP, which is 86.3%. In the Case of single subject, the model training and testing time were 0.388 s and 1.552 s when using KSR and LPP dimensionality reduction methods respectively. The total time of feature dimension reduction, training and testing the random forest model of the single subject in different features is shown in Table 4. We can see KSR outperforms other dimensionality reduction algorithms. Total1 represents the features of all sub-bands after wavelet decomposition. Total2 represents the features of approximate entropy and sample entropy. We can find KSR efficiency is much higher than other ways to reduce the dimension no matter what kind of feature extraction method. The computer configurations are as follows: Operating system is Window10 professional 64 bit, the processor is Intel Core i5-3230 M, and memory is DDR3, 8 G, 1600 MHz.

Table 4. The total computational time (sec.) required by 6 different feature reduction algorithms and RF model training and testing under different types of features.

Computing Time	KSR	LPP	mRMR	Relieff	PCA	NDR
Delta	**0.558**	1.25	1.48	2.33	0.799	3.713
Theta	**0.584**	1.168	1.498	2.354	0.799	3.498
Alpha	**0.564**	1.238	1.504	2.329	0.862	3.397
Beta	**0.552**	1.21	1.453	2.246	1.013	3.271
Gamma	**0.614**	1.256	1.44	2.245	1.146	3.395
All	**0.613**	1.257	3.21	3.309	0.899	7.189
ApEn	**0.4**	1.58	1.091	1.769	1.466	1.463
SampEn	**0.42**	1.559	1.092	1.641	1.394	1.49
Both	**0.388**	1.552	1.316	1.948	1.447	2.465

4.2   Comparison of 4 Types of Classifiers

One of our goals is to find a classifier that can perform well in the field of emotion classification. Combined with the previous conclusions, we investigated the effectiveness of each classifier in the case of four different classifiers using baseline features. The dimensionality reduction method is still the five dimensionality reduction methods mentioned earlier and the comparison of no dimensionality reduction (NDR). The results are shown in Figs. 4 and 5, respectively, where the results of Fig. 4 are based on wavelet-transform-extracted gamma sub-band features, the results of Fig. 5 are based on the features of nonlinear dynamics. The number of neighbors of the KNN classifier is set to six according to experience. SVM classifier uses the RBF kernel function, and for cost parameter C and the parameter γ, we choose the best combination of parameters using grid search algorithm: $C \in \{2^{-8}, 2^{-7}, \ldots 2^7, 2^8\}$ and $\gamma \in \{2^{-8}, 2^{-7}, \ldots 2^7, 2^8\}$. The parameters of the random forest are based on the experience value setting the number of decision trees: ntree = 500, the number of attributes mtry = , where m is the total number of attributes. From the two figures we can see, SVM and RF average classification accuracy is higher than KNN and NB. When the dimensionality reduction method is KSR, the accuracy of each classifier is very good, the difference is not great. Because SVM optimization process is relatively slow, and RF experience parameters can be used to get almost the same classification accuracy as SVM, which shows the RF in the emotion recognition of the superiority. Table 5 show the classification results of SVM and RF under different feature extraction and dimension reduction methods. It can be found that the classification accuracy of SVM is 92.8 in the combination of nonlinear dynamics features and KSR, and the classification accuracy of RF is 92.7, but the training time of the SVM is 15.49 s, and RF is 1.94 s for each subject. The former is about 8 times as long as the latter.

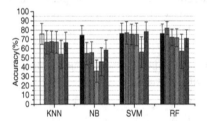

Fig. 4. Classification results of using wavelet features and 4 classifiers in Case 2.

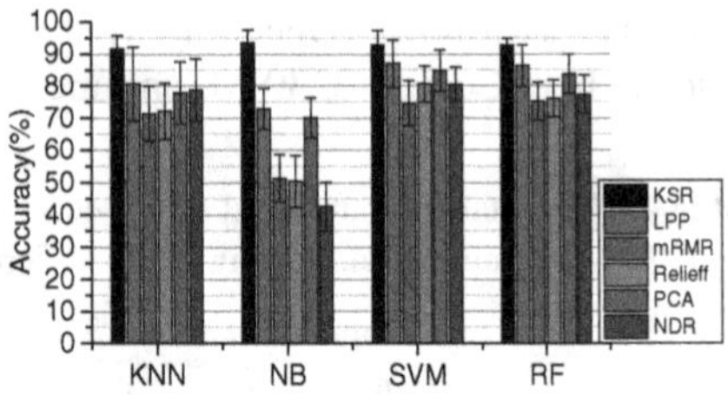

Fig. 5. Classification results of using ApEn and SampEn features and 4 classifiers in Case 2.

Table 5. Classification results of SVM and RF in Case 2. a: using gamma sub-band features. b: using ApEn and SampEn features.

Classifier	KSR	LPP	mRMR	Relieff	PCA	NDR
SVM (a)	76.2 ± 3.6	76.9 ± 3.9	75.3 ± 4.5	75.2 ± 4.4	56.1 ± 4.3	**78.1 ± 4.7**
RF (a)	76.0 ± 3.6	**82.0 ± 3.78**	72.1 ± 3.8	71.7 ± 4.3	57.1 ± 4.0	70.9 ± 4.0
SVM (b)	**92.8 ± 4.4**	86.8 ± 7.6	79.6 ± 7.1	80.5 ± 5.6	84.7 ± 6.5	80.4 ± 5.3
RF (b)	**92.7 ± 2.1**	86.3 ± 6.5	75.2 ± 5.9	76.1 ± 5.7	83.7 ± 6.1	77.3 ± 5.9

5   Conclusion

In this paper, we first compare Case 1 and Case 2 and find that the accuracy of classification can be significantly improved by taking into account the baseline data features, no matter wavelet transform or nonlinear dynamics approach is used for feature extraction. The comparative results show that nonlinear dynamic features lead to higher accuracy than wavelet-derived features. Further, approximate entropy and sample entropy are combined to extract the most salient features. It is shown that the EEG gamma-band features are more important than other frequency bands. It is also found that effective dimensionality reduction algorithm can not only speed up the classifier model training, but also improve the accuracy of the emotion classification. KSR is found to be the most effective among 5 dimensionality reduction algorithms under comparison. By comparing four types of classifiers, we find that the classification performance of random forest is better than KNN and NB and the parameters of SVM need to be optimized for better classification accuracy and the SVM is relatively inefficient computationally.

References

1. Petrushin, V.: Emotion in speech: recognition and application to call centers. In: Proceedings of Artificial Neural Networks in Engineering, vol. 710 (1999)
2. Anderson, K., Mcowan, P.W.: A real-time automated system for the recognition of human facial expressions. IEEE Trans. Syst. Man Cybern. Part B Cybern. 36(1), 96–105 (2006). A Publication of the IEEE Systems Man & Cybernetics Society
3. Yin, Z., Zhao, M., Wang, Y., Yang, J., Zhang, J.: Recognition of emotions using multimodal physiological signals and an ensemble deep learning model. Comput. Methods Programs Biomed. 140, 93–110 (2017)
4. Wang, X.W., Nie, D., Lu, B.L.: Emotional state classification from EEG data using machine learning approach. Neurocomputing 129, 94–106 (2014)
5. Petrantonakis, P.C., Hadjileontiadis, L.J.: A novel emotion elicitation index using frontal brain asymmetry for enhanced EEG-based emotion recognition. IEEE Trans. Inf. Technol. Biomed. 15(5), 737–746 (2011)
6. Li, X., Hu, B., Zhu, T., Yan, J., Zheng, F.: Towards affective learning with an EEG feedback approach. In: Proceedings of the First ACM International Workshop on Multimedia Technologies for Distance Learning. ACM (2009)
7. Jenke, R., Peer, A., Buss, M.: Feature extraction and selection for emotion recognition from EEG. IEEE Trans. Affect. Comput. 5(3), 327–339 (2014)
8. Weiner, B.: Attribution, emotion, and action (1986)
9. Kemper, T.D.: A Social Interactional Theory of Emotions. Wiley, New York (1978)
10. Ekman, P.: Basic Emotions. Handbook of Cognition and Emotion, vol. 98 (1999)
11. Zhang, Y., Ji, X., Zhang, S.: An approach to EEG-based emotion recognition using combined feature extraction method. Neurosci. Lett. 633, 152–157 (2016)
12. Koelstra, S., et al.: DEAP: A database for emotion analysis using physiological signals. IEEE Trans. Affect. Comput. 3(1), 18–31 (2012)
13. Zhang, C., Wang, H., Fu, R.: Automated detection of driver fatigue based on entropy and complexity measures. IEEE Trans. Intell. Transp. Syst. 15(1), 168–177 (2014)
14. Vijith, V.S., Jacob, J.E., Iype, T., Gopakumar, K., Yohannan, D.G.: Epileptic seizure detection using non-linear analysis of EEG. In: International Conference on Inventive Computation Technologies (ICICT), vol. 3. IEEE (2016)
15. Benzy, V.K., Jasmin, E.A., Koshy, R.C.: Approximate entropy and wavelet entropy based depth of anesthesia monitoring. In: 2015 International Conference on Control Communication & Computing India (ICCC). IEEE (2015)

16. Zheng, W.L., Lu, B.L.: Investigating critical frequency bands and channels for EEG-based emotion recognition with deep neural networks. IEEE Trans. Auton. Mental Dev. **7**(3), 162–175 (2015)
17. Zheng, W.: Multichannel EEG-Based emotion recognition via group sparse canonical correlation analysis. In: IEEE Transactions on Cognitive and Developmental Systems (2016)

Recurrent Neural Networks

A Neural Network Implementation
of Frank-Wolfe Optimization

Christian Bauckhage[1,2(✉)]

[1] B-IT, University of Bonn, Bonn, Germany
[2] Germany Fraunhofer IAIS, Sankt Augustin, Germany
`christian.bauckhage@iais.fraunhofer.de`

Abstract. We revisit the Frank-Wolfe algorithm for constrained convex optimization and show that it can be implemented as a simple recurrent neural network with softmin activation functions. As an example for a practical application of this result, we discuss how to train such a network to act as an associative memory.

1 Introduction

The Frank-Wolfe algorithm [7] is an efficient solver for constrained optimization problems of the general form

$$x^* = \operatorname*{argmin}_{x \in S} \; f(x) \tag{1}$$

where $S \subset \mathbb{R}^m$ is a compact convex set and $f : \mathbb{R}^m \to \mathbb{R}$ is a quadratic objective function. Since problems such as computing the distance to a convex hull, computing a minimum enclosing ball, or training a support vector machine are specific instances of (1), the Frank-Wolfe algorithm is of considerable interest in machine learning [4,9,12,14].

In this paper, we show that the Frank-Wolfe algorithm can be implemented as a simple recurrent neural network that is structurally equivalent to the well known echo state networks [8]. However, in contrast to echo state networks, the weight matrices that govern the dynamics of the internal states of the non-linear systems discussed in this paper can be adjusted to the problem at hand. We illustrate this by means of an example and discuss how to use a "Frank-Wolfe network" as an associative memory for pattern retrieval.

2 Frank-Wolfe Optimization via a Dynamical System

The Frank-Wolfe algorithm shown in Algorithm 1 is an iterative solver for the problem class in (1). Given an initial feasible guess $x_{t=0}$ as to the solution, the idea is to compute $s_t \in S$ that minimizes $s^T \nabla f(x_t)$ and to use sub-gradient updates $x_{t+1} = x_t + \gamma_t (s_t - x_t)$ where the learning rate $\gamma_t \in [0, 1]$ decreases over time. This guarantees that updates will never leave the feasible set and

© Springer International Publishing AG 2017
A. Lintas et al. (Eds.): ICANN 2017, Part I, LNCS 10613, pp. 219–226, 2017.
https://doi.org/10.1007/978-3-319-68600-4_26

Algorithm 1. Frank-Wolfe optimization for problems as in (1)

guess a feasible point $\boldsymbol{x}_0 \in S$
for $t = 0, \ldots, t_{\max}$ **do**
    determine $\boldsymbol{s}_t = \underset{\boldsymbol{s} \in S}{\operatorname{argmin}} \ \boldsymbol{s}^T \nabla f(\boldsymbol{x}_t)$
    update the learning rate $\gamma_t = \frac{2}{t+2}$
    update the current estimate $\boldsymbol{x}_{t+1} = \boldsymbol{x}_t + \gamma_t (\boldsymbol{s}_t - \boldsymbol{x}_t)$

---

the efficiency of the algorithm stems from the fact that it turns a quadratic optimization problem into a series of simple linear optimization problems. In fact, it can be shown that after t iterations the current estimate $\boldsymbol{x}_t$ is $O(1/t)$ from the optimal solution [4] which provides a convenient criterion for choosing the number $t_{\max}$ of iterations to be performed. For further details on the Frank-Wolfe algorithm and its properties, we refer to excellent review in [9].

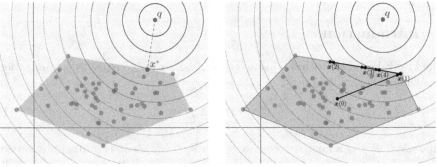

(a) illustration of the problem in Eq. (2)   (b) solution resulting from Eqs. (15),(16)

Fig. 1. Didactic example of the problem of minimizing a convex function over a compact convex set. (a) Given $X = \{\boldsymbol{x}_1, \ldots, \boldsymbol{x}_n\}$, the problem is to find $\boldsymbol{x}^*$ inside of the convex hull $H(X)$ that is closest to a query $\boldsymbol{q}$. Contour lines indicate the quadratic objective function $f(\boldsymbol{x}) = \|\boldsymbol{x} - \boldsymbol{q}\|^2$. (b) Trajectory of solutions computed by the non-linear dynamical system in (15) and (16) using $\beta = 1000$.

In order to provide an illustrative example for the following discussion, we will consider the "closest point in convex hull" problem (see Fig. 1a). Assuming a finite data set $X = \{\boldsymbol{x}_1, \ldots, \boldsymbol{x}_n\} \subset \mathbb{R}^m$, we want to find the point $\boldsymbol{x}^*$ inside of the convex hull $H(X)$ of X that is closest to a query point $\boldsymbol{q} \in \mathbb{R}^m$. Formally, this problem amounts to finding a solution to

$$\boldsymbol{x}^* = \underset{\boldsymbol{x} \in H(X)}{\operatorname{argmin}} \|\boldsymbol{x} - \boldsymbol{q}\|^2. \tag{2}$$

Since the objective function $f(\boldsymbol{x}) = \|\boldsymbol{x} - \boldsymbol{q}\|^2$ is quadratic and since by definition of the convex hull the feasible set $S = H(X)$ is compact and convex, the problem in (2) is indeed an instance of (1). However, to facilitate our discussion, we will rewrite it in a more general form.

Note that any $x \in H(X)$ can be expressed as a convex combination of the data in X. Collecting these in a data matrix

$$X = [x_1, x_2, \ldots, x_n] \in \mathbb{R}^{m \times n} \tag{3}$$

we thus can write $x = Xw$ where the coefficient vector $w \in \mathbb{R}^n$ is a vector that resides in the standard simplex

$$\Delta^{n-1} = \{w \in \mathbb{R}^n \mid \mathbf{1}^T w = 1 \wedge w \succeq \mathbf{0}\} \subset \mathbb{R}^n. \tag{4}$$

The problem in (2) can thus be cast as first finding an optimal coefficient vector w^* and second using it to determine x^*. Formally, this amounts to

$$w^* = \underset{w \in \Delta^{n-1}}{\operatorname{argmin}} \|Xw - q\|^2 \tag{5}$$

$$x^* = Xw^* \tag{6}$$

where the objective function $f(w) = \|Xw - q\|^2$ is again quadratic and the feasible set Δ^{n-1} is again compact and convex.

For the gradient of the new objective we have $\nabla f(w_t) \propto X^T X w_t - X^T q$ so that the Frank-Wolfe algorithm requires computing

$$s_t = \underset{s \in \Delta^{n-1}}{\operatorname{argmin}} s^T (X^T X w_t - X^T q) \tag{7}$$

where a feasible initial choice for the coefficient vector $w_{t=0}$ is given by $\frac{1}{n}\mathbf{1}$.

Clearly, the function on the right hand side of (7) is linear in s and needs to be minimized over a compact convex set. Since minima of a linear function over a compact convex set will necessarily be attained at a vertex of that set, the minimizer s_t of (7) must coincide with a vertex of Δ^{n-1}. On the other hand, the vertices of the standard simplex in $\mathbb{R}^n$ correspond to the standard basis vectors $e_i \in \mathbb{R}^n$, so that

$$s_t = \underset{i}{\operatorname{argmin}} e_i^T (X^T X w_t - X^T q) \tag{8}$$

$$\approx \sigma(X^T X w_t - X^T q) \tag{9}$$

where the non-linear, vector-valued function $\sigma(\cdot)$ denotes the well known *softmin* operator defined as

$$\sigma(z, \beta)_i = \frac{e^{-\beta z_i}}{\sum_j e^{-\beta z_j}} \tag{10}$$

for which we note that

$$\lim_{\beta \to \infty} \sigma(z, \beta) = e_i = \underset{j}{\operatorname{argmin}} e_j^T z. \tag{11}$$

Given the relaxed optimization step in (9), we can now rewrite the Frank-Wolfe updates for our problem as

$$\boldsymbol{w}_{t+1} = \boldsymbol{w}_t + \gamma_t\big(\boldsymbol{s}_t - \boldsymbol{w}_t\big) \tag{12}$$

$$= (1 - \gamma_t)\boldsymbol{w}_t + \gamma_t\boldsymbol{s}_t \tag{13}$$

$$\approx (1 - \gamma_t)\boldsymbol{w}_t + \gamma_t\boldsymbol{\sigma}\big(\boldsymbol{X}^T\boldsymbol{X}\boldsymbol{w}_t - \boldsymbol{X}^T\boldsymbol{q}\big). \tag{14}$$

But this is then to say that —by choosing an appropriate parameter β for the softmin function— the following non-linear dynamical system

$$\boldsymbol{w}_{t+1} = (1 - \gamma_t)\boldsymbol{w}_t + \gamma_t\boldsymbol{\sigma}\big(\boldsymbol{X}^T\boldsymbol{X}\boldsymbol{w}_t - \boldsymbol{X}^T\boldsymbol{q}\big) \tag{15}$$

$$\boldsymbol{x}_t = \boldsymbol{X}\boldsymbol{w}_t \tag{16}$$

mimics the Frank-Wolfe algorithm up to arbitrary precision and can therefore solve the problems in (2) or (5) and (6), respectively.

3   Discussion

The equivalence of the Frank-Wolfe algorithm and the non-linear dynamical system in (15), (16) is the main result of this paper. While we derived it by means of the example of the "closest point in convex hull" problem, it holds for any setting where the Frank-Wolfe algorithm applies. This is because both critical steps in our derivation, namely to express elements of a compact convex set in terms of convex combinations over prototypes and to approximate vector-valued *argmin* estimations in terms of *softmin* operators, are independent of the problem at hand.

From the point of view of neural network research, the system in (15), (16) is of interest because it is structurally equivalent to the governing equations of the simple recurrent architectures known as echo state networks [8].

In other words, we can think of this system in terms of a reservoir of n neurons whose synaptic connections are encoded in the matrix $\boldsymbol{X}^T\boldsymbol{X}$. Inputs are kept fixed over time and are weighted by $\boldsymbol{X}^T$. The linear readout is given by $\boldsymbol{X}$ and the learning rate γ_t assumes the role of the so called leaking rate. At each time t, the next internal state $\boldsymbol{w}_{t+1}$ of the network is a convex combination of the current state and a nonlinear softmin transformation of state and input. Since γ_t decays towards zero, states will stabilize and the output is guaranteed to approach a fixed point $\boldsymbol{x}^* = \lim_{t\to\infty}\boldsymbol{x}_t$.

What is further remarkable about the system in (15), (16) is that the weight matrices $\boldsymbol{X}^T\boldsymbol{X}$, $\boldsymbol{X}^T$, and $\boldsymbol{X}$ are given purely in terms of training data for the problem under consideration. On the one hand, this is reminiscent of traditional recurrent neural networks that realize associative memories [10,11,13]. On the other hand, this suggests training procedures based on prototype selection to improve system performance. Next, we will explore both these ideas.

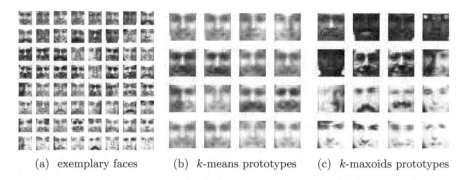

(a) exemplary faces   (b) k-means prototypes   (c) k-maxoids prototypes

Fig. 2. (a) examples of face images in the CBCL data base which illustrate the range of appearances. (b) k-means clustering produces prototypes which are the means of their clusters. (c) k-maxoids clustering yields prototypes that coincide with extremal data points and are therefore more distinct; in fact, one can prove that maxoids will necessarily be vertices of the convex hull of the given data [1].

4 Application: A Simple Associative Memory

The computations performed by a recurrent neural network whose dynamics are governed by the non-linear system in (15) and (16) can be thought of as an iterative process aimed at explaining a (possibly unknown) pattern q in terms of a convex combination

$$x^* = \sum_{i=1}^{n} w_i^* \, x_i \tag{17}$$

of known patterns $x_1, \ldots, x_n$. In other words, upon convergence, the process will have associated the new pattern q with the closest pattern x^* inside of the convex hull of the x_i. To further explore this idea, this section presents simple experiments with the CBCL database of face images[1].

The CBCL face database contains 2429 portraits of people each of size 19×19 pixels (see Fig. 2(a) for examples of the variety of images in this data set). We turn each of these images into a vector $x_i \in \mathbb{R}^{361}$ and *train* a recurrent neural network to act as an associative memory for these data.

A naïve approach in this regard would be to consider the entire data matrix $X = [x_1, \ldots, x_{2429}] \in \mathbb{R}^{361 \times 2429}$ of patterns in order to encode synaptic weights for the network. However, there is a better way.

Note that the convex hull $H(X)$ of any discrete data set X in any high dimensional space forms a polytope whose vertices $V(X)$ are given by a subset of X (see again the example in Fig. 1a). The key observation at this point is that any point in $H(X)$, that is any convex combination of points in X, can actually be written as a convex combination of the vertices in $V(X)$ only [15]. Since we

---

[1] http://www.ai.mit.edu/projects/cbcl.

always have that $V(X) \subseteq X \subset H(X)$, it would be sufficient and more efficient to form the weights of our associative memory only from those columns x_i in X that correspond to vertices of the data convex hull. Even though, for high dimensional data, it is computationally expensive to determine all the vertices of a convex hull [5], there are indeed several efficient algorithms to estimate a subset $\hat{V}(X)$ of $V(X)$ [2,3,6]; here, we resort to a particularly simple approach, namely the idea of k-maxoids clustering [1].

k-maxoids clustering can be understood as a variant of conventional k-means clustering, however, cluster prototypes are computed in terms of extremal data points rather than in terms of local means. Moreover, one can show that when a MacQueen-type online procedure is used to determine the prototypes, they will always correspond to vertices of the convex hull of the data at hand [1]. In our current context, this is of course a desirable property.

To illustrate this favorable behavior of k-maxoids clustering, we contrast it with conventional k-means clustering. Figure 2(b) shows 16 prototypes resulting from k-means clustering of the CBCL data. These represent average faces which are blurred to an extent that makes it difficult to discern characteristic features. The prototypes in Fig. 2(c), on the other hand, result from k-maxoids clustering and show clearly distinguishable visual characteristics. Since these prototypes coincide with actual data points which by design are maximally far apart, it is rather easy to identify them as faces of people of pale or dark complexion, of people wearing glasses, sporting mustaches, or having been photographed under varying illumination.

Prototype selection via k-maxoids clustering therefore provides a way of *learning* which patterns to encode in the weights of a recurrent associative memory network whose dynamics are governed by Eq. (15) and (16). We experimented with different choices of the number k of prototypes and found $k = 500$ to provide good performance. That is, an associative memory of only 500 neurons was found to produce good explanations of patterns which were not explicitly encoded in its weight matrices. Setting the initial state vector to $w_{t=0} = \frac{1}{n}\mathbf{1}$ and the soft-min parameter $\beta = 1000$, the iterative retrieval process was observed to converge after about $O(10)$ updates and always took mere milliseconds to compute.

Figure 3 provides an example as to the behavior of the system when confronted with a previously unseen query pattern. In this typical example, the

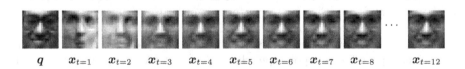

q $x_{t=1}$ $x_{t=2}$ $x_{t=3}$ $x_{t=4}$ $x_{t=5}$ $x_{t=6}$ $x_{t=7}$ $x_{t=8}$ $x_{t=12}$

Fig. 3. Example of an association process performed by the dynamical system in (15), (16). Given a query pattern q not explicitly encoded in its weight matrices, the network iteratively computes intermediate patterns x_t and, after 12 steps, converges to a result that resembles the query.

| query q |  |
| result x^* | |

Fig. 4. Examples of 9 query images and the corresponding associated patterns.

iterative computations of the network converged after 12 steps and yielded a pattern that closely resembles the query.

Figure 4 shows examples of undistorted and distorted query patterns and the corresponding results produced by the associative memory. Again, neither query pattern was explicitly encoded in the weights of the network. Nevertheless, the system was able to produce convincing results even in case of input images where large chunks of pixels were masked out. Again, the output of our recurrent network of 500 neurons stabilized after about $O(10)$ iterations and were obtained in mere milliseconds.

5   Conclusion

The Frank-Wolfe algorithm is an efficient optimization procedure that applies to a wide range of problems in machine learning. Our main contribution in this paper was to show that this algorithm can be implemented as a recurrent neural network.

The two crucial steps in our derivation were (1) to express elements of a compact convex set in terms of convex combinations of known points within that set and (2) to approximate *argmin* computations by means of *softmin* computations. This resulted in a non-linear dynamical system that is structurally equivalent to the system of equations governing the dynamics of echo state networks. In other words, the computations performed by the Frank-Wolfe algorithm can be understood as a form of reservoir computing.

As an application example of our result, we discussed the idea of using a "Frank-Wolfe network" as an associative memory. Exploiting the fact that points within the convex hull of a discrete high-dimensional data set can be expressed as convex combinations of extremal points or vertices of the data, we considered the use of k-maxoids clustering as a way of learning prototypical extremal patterns which were then encoded in the weight matrices of our network. Straightforward experimental results revealed that this simple approach is indeed well able to explain previously unseen patterns in terms of encoded ones.

Given the ideas and results brought forward in this paper, there are several directions for future work. Arguably the currently most interesting question that merits further exploration is how to combine several "Frank-Wolfe networks" into hierarchical architectures so as to establish a connection to the deep learning paradigm.

References

1. Bauckhage, C., Sifa, R.: k-Maxoids Clustering. In: Proceedings KDML-LWA (2015)
2. Bauckhage, C., Thurau, C.: Making archetypal analysis practical. In: Denzler, J., Notni, G., Süße, H. (eds.) DAGM 2009. LNCS, vol. 5748, pp. 272–281. Springer, Heidelberg (2009). doi:10.1007/978-3-642-03798-6_28
3. Civril, A., Magdon-Ismail, M.: On selecting a maximum volume sub-matrix of a matrix and related problems. Theore. Comput. Sci. **410**(47–49), 4801–4811 (2009)
4. Clarkson, K.: Coresets, sparse greedy approximation, and the Frank-Wolf algorithm. ACM Trans. Algorithms **6**(4) (2010)
5. de Berg, M., van Kreveld, M., Overmars, M., Schwarzkopf, O.: Computational Geometry. Springer, Heidelberg (2000)
6. Faloutsos, C., Lin, K.I.: FastMap: A fast algorithm for indexing, data-mining and visualization of traditional and multimedia datasets. In: Proceedings SIGMOD (1995)
7. Frank, M., Wolfe, P.: An algorithm for quadratic programming. Naval Research Logistics Quarterly **3**(1–2), 95–110 (1956)
8. Jäger, H., Haas, H.: Harnessing nonlinearity: predicting chaotic systems and saving energy in wireless communication. Science **304**(5667), 78–80 (2004)
9. Jaggi, M.: Revisiting frank-wolfe: projection-free sparse convex optimization. J. Mach. Learn. Res. **28**(1), I-427–I-435 (2013)
10. Kohonen, T., Oja, E., Lehtiö, P.: Storage and processing of information in distributed associative memory systems. In: Hinton, G., Anderson, J. (eds.) Parallel Models of Associative Memory. Laurence Earbaum Associates (1989). Chap. 4
11. Kosko, B.: Bidirectional associative memory. IEEE Trans. Systems Man Cybern. **18**(1) (1988)
12. Lacoste-Julien, S., Jaggi, M., Schmidt, M., Pletscher, P.: Block-coordinate frank-wolfe optimization for structural SVMs. In: Proceedings ICML (2013)
13. McClelland, J., Rummelhart, D.: Distributed memory and the representation of general and specific information. J. Exp. Psychol. Gen. **114**(2), 159–188 (1985)
14. Ouyang, H., Gray, A.: Fast stochastic frank-wolfe algorithms for nonlinear SVMs. In: Proceedings SDM (2010)
15. Ziegler, G.: Lectures on Polytopes. Springer, New York (1995)

Inferring Adaptive Goal-Directed Behavior Within Recurrent Neural Networks

Sebastian Otte[1][(✉)], Theresa Schmitt[1], Karl Friston[2], and Martin V. Butz[1]

[1] Cognitive Modeling Group, University of Tübingen,
Sand 14, 72076 Tübingen, Germany
sebastian.otte@uni-tuebingen.de
[2] The Wellcome Trust Centre for Neuroimaging, UCL,
12 Queen Square, London, UK

Abstract. This paper shows that active-inference-based, flexible, adaptive goal-directed behavior can be generated by utilizing temporal gradients in a recurrent neural network (RNN). The RNN learns a dynamical sensorimotor forward model of a partially observable environment. It then uses this model to execute goal-directed policy inference online. The internal neural activities encode the predictive state of the controlled entity. The active inference process projects these activities into the future via the RNN's recurrences, following a tentative sequence of motor commands. This sequence is adapted by back-projecting error between the forward-projected hypothetical states and the desired goal states onto the motor commands. As an example, we show that a trained RNN model can be used to precisely control a multi-copter-like system. Moreover, we show that the RNN can plan hundreds of time steps ahead, unfolding non-linear imaginary paths around obstacles.

Keywords: Recurrent neural networks · Long short-term memory · Neurorobotics · Robot control · Active inference · Goal-directed behavior

1 Introduction

Recently, it was shown that recurrent neural forward models can be used to compute the inverse kinematics of many-joint robot arms [12]. LSTM-like RNNs [6,10] were trained to estimate end-effector poses based on specified arm configurations. *back-propagation through time* (BPTT) was used to iteratively optimize a goal-oriented inverse mapping, that underwrites the goal-directed movement of the robot arm; essentially enacting the unfolding goal-directed optimization process. In this paper we extend this mechanism into a dynamic scenario, planning control trajectories dynamically through time.

In the motor control literature, direct inverse models [7] learn direct mappings from goal states to actions, which works only when the typically redundant inverse mappings are convex. Multiple forward-inverse models [15] as well as constraint Jacobians have been proposed for inverse redundancy resolution.

© Springer International Publishing AG 2017
A. Lintas et al. (Eds.): ICANN 2017, Part I, LNCS 10613, pp. 227–235, 2017.
https://doi.org/10.1007/978-3-319-68600-4_27

However, the results are always direct mappings from desired states to motor control commands, precluding online adaptations. Models that encode redundancies and resolve them on the fly are related to human motor control [1], but the requisite population-encoded spaces do not scale up to larger control spaces.

We show that dynamic active-inference-based processes, which are corollaries of the free-energy-based inference principle [3,5], implemented within RNNs, can generate suitable control commands when trajectory redundancies need to be resolved on the fly and even when more complex trajectories need to be found. The RNN learns a recurrent forward model, developing internal predictive encodings that reflect unobservable but inferable system dynamics. The resulting online active inference process projects neural activities into the future via the network recurrences, following a tentative sequence of motor commands. This sequence is adapted by back-projecting the error between the hypothetical and desired (goal-like) future system states onto anticipated motor commands, effectively inferring on the fly an action sequence that leads to the goal. Thus, the mechanism solves a sequential policy optimization problem. In exemplary multicopter-like simulations, we show that the approach can not only control dynamical systems with high precision, but even infer longer-term action sequences to circumnavigate obstacles.

2   Recurrent Anticipatory Neural Control Model

The RNN model consists of two main processing components. First, training the forward model, that is, learning a neural approximation of the dynamical system of interest. Second, inferring dynamic action sequences in order to generate adaptive goal-directed behavior in a continuous, dynamic control scenario.

2.1   Learning the Forward Model

Let us consider a simplified formulation of a discrete-time dynamical system. At a certain time step t the system is in a specific system state. Because we assume a dynamic, *partially observable Markov decision process* (POMDP) [13], the next system state is typically not deducible exactly from the current observables. Thus, we separate the system state into the perceivable state components $\mathbf{s}^t \in \mathbb{R}^n$ and the hidden state components $\boldsymbol{\sigma}^t \in \mathbb{R}^m$ Additionally, the system can be influenced via k control commands denoted by $\mathbf{x}^t \in \mathbb{R}^k$. The next system state $(\mathbf{s}^{t+1}, \boldsymbol{\sigma}^{t+1})$ is determined by

$$(\mathbf{s}^t, \boldsymbol{\sigma}^t, \mathbf{x}^t) \stackrel{\Phi}{\longmapsto} (\mathbf{s}^{t+1}, \boldsymbol{\sigma}^{t+1}), \tag{1}$$

where the mapping Φ models the forward dynamics of the system. Thus, the next system state depends on the current control inputs as well as, in principle, on the entire state history somehow encoded in the (hidden) system state components. The task of the forward model learner is to approximate the forward model Φ given the current state $\mathbf{s}^t$ and current control commands $\mathbf{x}^t$, as well as an internal memory encoding derived from the previous state information

$\{\mathbf{s}^0, \mathbf{s}^1, \ldots, \mathbf{s}^{t-1}\}$ and motor commands $\{\mathbf{x}^0, \mathbf{x}^1, \ldots, \mathbf{x}^{t-1}\}$. Learning proceeds by dynamically processing current state information and predicting the next state information. We propose to use LSTM-like RNNs [6] for this task because LSTMs can predict accurately and can associate even temporally dispersed input events, which is essential when learning forward models in POMDPs. Moreover, LSTMs provide stable gradients over long time periods, which is critically important when complex control trajectories are required.

2.2   Action Sequence Inference

Given a certain action sequence and an initial state, the RNN can predict a state progression that is expected when executing the imagined action sequence by means of the learned recurrent forward model. To effectively control the system, however, the inverse mapping is required, that is, an action sequence needs to be inferred to approach a desired goal-state (or follow a sequence of goal-states) from an initial state. In a stationary scenario, this can be accomplished by means of BPTT in combination with gradient descent, as shown, for example, in [12]. However, this principle cannot be directly projected into the temporal dynamic domain, because motor commands need to be executed sequentially and the commands are dynamically interdependent over time.

Our active inference procedure, sketched-out in Fig. 1, unfolds within the RNN system. At any point in "world" time t, the RNN has a certain internal neural activity reflecting the dynamical system's state, which the RNN recurrently updates given the current state and motor command signals. Additionally, the RNN maintains a preinitialized anticipated action sequence, that is, an *action policy*, and anticipated gradient statistics. At each world time step, the policy is (further) refined taking the actually encountered experiences into account. Currently, the anticipated action sequence has a fixed length, which corresponds to the actual temporal planning horizon T.

Based on the previous system state as well as the previous forward RNN hidden activations, that is, the recurrent context, the action policy is adapted by generating a sequence of error gradients. This is accomplished by projecting the predicted state progression into the future given the current action policy and back-projecting the discrepancy (quantified by the loss $\mathcal{L}$) between the predicted state and the desired goal-state (or sequence of goal states) in time using backpropagation through time (BPTT) [14]. As a result, the $\mathcal{L}$ is projected onto the action policy, thus updating it. During the forward-projection, the RNN is fed with its own state prediction. After back-projecting the error, the input gradient is computed via

$$\frac{\partial \mathcal{L}}{\partial x_i^{t'}} = \sum_{h=1}^{H} \left[\frac{\partial net_h^{t'}}{\partial x_i^{t'}} \frac{\partial \mathcal{L}}{\partial net_h^{t'}} \right] = \sum_{h=1}^{H} w_{ih} \delta_h^{t'}, \qquad (2)$$

where h indexes the hidden units after the input layer, $net_h^{t'}$ denotes the weighted sum of inputs (or *net input*) into unit h at time t', and t' with $t \leq t' \leq t + T$ is the running time index over the projected future sequence. Note that each gradient signal $\delta_h^{t'}$ recursively depends on the future $\delta_{h'}^{t'+1}$, $\delta_{h'}^{t'+2}$, $\ldots$, $\delta_{h'}^{t+T}$ signals,

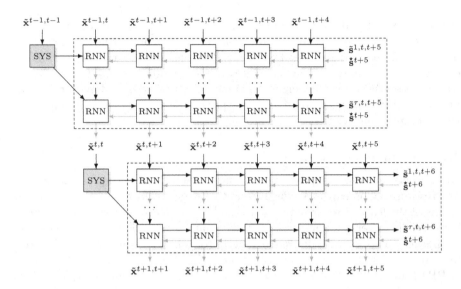

Fig. 1. The continuous action inference procedure. In each iteration, an optimization cycle (gray boxes) is performed, refining the anticipated actions. Within an optimization cycle the progression of the dynamical system is projected into the future (here $T = 5$ time steps ahead) and the discrepancy between the predicted state and the desired goal-state is back-projected via BPTT onto the individual motor commands of the policy. The black lines indicate context and information forward flow. The blue lines indicate gradient flow. $\tilde{\mathbf{x}}^{t',t''}$ refers to the action vector for time step t'' based on the context of world time step t'. Within the optimization cycle, $\tilde{\mathbf{s}}^{\tau,t',t''}$ refers to the state prediction for time step t'' based on the context of world time step t' in the τ-th optimization iteration, whereas $\mathring{\mathbf{s}}^{t''}$ refers to the desired system state for time step t''. (Color figure online)

which carry the gradient information back through time. For each world time step, the above procedure is repeated several times and embedded in a higher level optimization framework, for which we use Adam [8], which is more robust and usually faster than vanilla gradient descent with momentum. To move on to the next world time step, the first action of the refined sequence is executed (including system and RNN update) and the anticipated action sequence begins with its successor. The new last action is initialized with the previous last or a neutral action. The accumulated gradient statistics of Adam (first two moments) are retained to provide an uninterrupted continuation of the optimizer dynamics. As a result, the active inference mechanism can be applied seamlessly and a continuous, active inference process unfolds, generating goal-directed interactions with the environment while continuing to plan the next steps.

2.3   On the Relation to Active Inference and Free Energy

Conceptually, the current scheme inherits the important aspect of active inference; namely, casting the control problem in terms of planning as inference.

The crucial aspect of our scheme – that renders it a form of active inference – is that the control variables $x_i^{t'}$ are not deterministic states but random variables that are inferred online. This is necessarily the case because we consider control in the future – before it is realized. Effectively, this means that fictive policies are inferred under prior beliefs about outcomes. Crucially, this inference is updated online by assimilating outcomes to date, performing sequential policy optimization. In other words, instead of a fixed state-action policy, we infer policies online with the help of the learned forward model. On this view, our scheme is effectively minimizing a path integral of (free) energy, where the energy corresponds to the cost function $\mathcal{L}$. The goal can be regarded as a prior expectation about the path's endpoint, while the sum of squared errors measures the discrepancy between predicted and realized state-space trajectories. Formally speaking, this measure corresponds to the expected free energy under the policy in play – and the path integral approximates an Hamiltonian action.

3   Experiments

Our experiments are based on a simple dynamical system simulation of a multi-copter-like object, which we call *rocket ball*. The rocket ball is positioned in a rectangular environment with gravity. It has two propulsion units spread at a 45° angle from the vertical axis to both sides, inducing thrust forces in the respective direction. Each unit can be throttled within the interval $[0, 1]$.

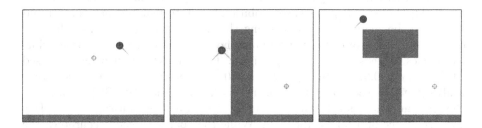

Fig. 2. Illustration of three rocket ball scenarios. The rocket ball (blue) has to reach the target (green). The red circle indicates the current position estimate predicted by the RNN. In free space (left), the rocket ball can approach the target directly. With a convex obstacle (center) a short detour is necessary. The concave obstacle case (right) requires a further ranging detour and, in addition, the local minima are more dominant. (Color figure online)

We considered three different scenarios, which are depicted in Fig. 2. In the free scenario, each target point can be approached directly somewhat linearly, while with increasingly complex obstacle constellations, reaching the goal state requires increasingly complex anticipatory behavior. For each scenario we trained an RNN with one hidden layer consisting of 16 LSTM blocks, which additionally provide block-wise gate-to-gate connections [10,11]. We also tried standard

RNNs, which, however, yielded significantly less accurate predictions and which could not be used for precise control.

At each time step a network is fed with the current position of the rocket ball as well as with the current action command (left and right thrust). The network output is the prediction of the position, the velocity, and the acceleration of the rocket ball for the next time step. In preliminary experiments it appeared that predicting the velocity and acceleration, while only signaling position information as input, forces the RNN to make more use of the recurrences (partially observable state). For all scenarios, we trained an RNN with 2 000 sequences each consisting of 200 time steps using stochastic sampling (no mini-batches) and Adam with default parameters (learning rate $\eta = 0.001$, first and second moment smoothing factors $\beta_1 = 0.9$, $\beta_2 = 0.999$). The training sequences were generated based on continuously randomly adjusted thrust values. All experiments were implemented using the JANNLab framework [9]. Note that the approach can in principle be implemented in an online-learning fashion, learning and exploiting the dynamics of the observed system concurrently.

3.1   Short-Term Inference

In free space, only short-term planning is required. The goal is to control the rocket ball such that it reaches the target as quickly and accurately as possible. We obtained the best performing controller by presenting the goal-state at each time-step during back-projection. Moreover, zero velocity and – to a lesser extent – zero acceleration in the goal-state is useful to suppress oscillations around the target. The best trade-off between robust goal state maintenance control and prospective behavior while approaching the target yielded a planning horizon of about 6–8 time steps. Shorter planning horizons increase overshooting, while longer ones decrease the control precision. To infer the action policy, we used Adam with $\eta = 0.01$ and $\beta_1, \beta_2 = 0.9$ and 30 iterations per active inference cycle. In all situations, the target was reached with a precision (RMSE) below 10^{-3} (the environment has a height of 2 units). Figure 3 depicts a short exemplary image sequence of a target approach. While the goal is reached accurately, the thrust is throttled down in anticipation of avoiding overshooting.

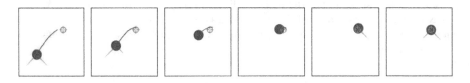

Fig. 3. Image sequence of the rocket ball approaching the target. The red line represents the actual imagined future state progression unfolded by the RNN. The length of the thrust expulsion indicates the respective force. (Color figure online)

3.2 Long-Term Inference

In order to handle the obstacle scenarios (cf. Fig. 2), it was necessary (i) to extend the planning horizon enabling the formation of more complex, indirect imaginary pathways towards the goal state and (ii) to present the goal-state only late in the future projection (here always only at the end of the planning horizon), which enables the RNN to anticipate sequences in which the state temporarily moves away from the target. We used Adam with a more aggressive learning rate of $\eta = 0.1$ but only one error projection per world time step.

Since long-term planning is fairly imprecise, we simultaneously used short-term planning, which assumes control once the distance to the target state is below a certain threshold. As a result, the rocket ball can reach the target with high precision when facing a convex and even a partially concave obstacle. Note, however, the goal reaching trajectories that evolve are only temporarily stable. They may collapse after some time as the inference process permanently searches for solutions that fulfill only the final state objective. At the moment no further constraints are added to the loss function.

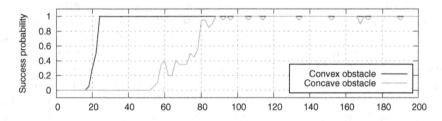

Fig. 4. Reaching the target (i.e. success probability) in the complex scenario depends on the scenario's complexity as well as on the planning horizon (x-Axis).

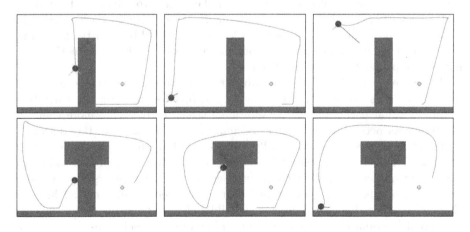

Fig. 5. Exemplar trajectories imagined by the RNN: while long term inference (120 steps) leads around the obstacle, short term inference (red) points towards the target. (Color figure online)

We systematically evaluated the required planning length by means of 20 random trials (the rocket ball is initially placed to the left of the obstacle and the target to the right of the obstacle) for several planning horizons. Figure 4 shows the fraction of trials in which the target was reached after 1 000 world time steps dependent on the set planning horizon. To provide an impression of the system's behavior, Fig. 5 shows six imaginary flight trajectories anticipated by the RNN.

4   Summary and Conclusion

We have shown that LSTMs, which learn a sensorimotor forward model in a dynamic control scenario, can generate active-inference-based, goal-directed action policies online. Active inference is accomplished by projecting neural activities into the future and back-projecting the error between the forward projections and currently desired goal states onto motor commands. The mechanism was even applicable for planning around obstacles more than hundred time steps into the future.

In should be noted that we could not achieve similar results with standard RNNs. Additionally, the usage of the Adam-based BPTT played an essential role in our system, particularly when unfolding long-term policies. Adam inherently stabilizes the gradient by smoothing it and by suppressing gradient fluctuations, dividing the gradient by its current variance estimate. As a result, the emerging policy tends to avoid uncertain regions of the gradient landscape, unfolding and adapting trajectory plans in a dynamically changing but stable manner. In other words, the mechanism attempts to achieve the extrinsic goal state while maintaining a stable trajectory, which is intrinsically motivated. Interestingly, expected free energy can also be decomposed into intrinsic and extrinsic values [4]. The extrinsic value corresponds to the degree to which goals or prior preferences are realized. In contrast, the intrinsic value scores the reduction in uncertainty about hidden or unobservable states afforded by a particular course of action. It should be explored further to which extent these two notions are indeed complementary or even identical.

Future work concerns adding suitable gradient optimization terms to the loss function, such as a term to minimize motor control effort to foster the generation of fully optimal paths. Moreover, additional scenarios involving more complex environments need to be evaluated to confirm the robustness of the approach. At the moment the system essentially learns control in only one dynamic system scenario. Thus, the grand challenge remains to extend this approach to hierarchical control scenarios, in which distinct sensorimotor controllers are necessary depending on the current event-based circumstances [2] and mutual interactions with other dynamical objects, possibly blending control responsibilities over event boundaries incorporating multiple temporal resolutions.

References

1. Butz, M.V., Herbort, O., Hoffmann, J.: Exploiting redundancy for flexible behavior: unsupervised learning in a modular sensorimotor control architecture. Psychol. Rev. **114**, 1015–1046 (2007)
2. Butz, M.V.: Towards a unified sub-symbolic computational theory of cognition. Fronti. Psychol. **7**(925) (2016)
3. Friston, K.: The free-energy principle: a rough guide to the brain? Trends Cogn. Sci. **13**(7), 293–301 (2009)
4. Friston, K., FitzGerald, T., Rigoli, F., Schwartenbeck, P., Pezzulo, G.: Active inference: a process theory. Neural Comput. **29**(1), 1–49 (2016)
5. Friston, K.J., Daunizeau, J., Kilner, J., Kiebel, S.J.: Action and behavior: a free-energy formulation. Biol. Cybern. **102**(3), 227–260 (2010)
6. Hochreiter, S., Schmidhuber, J.: Long short-term memory. Neural Comput. **9**(8), 1735–1780 (1997)
7. Jordan, M.I., Rumelhart, D.E.: Forward models: supervised learning with a distal teacher. Cogn. Sci. **16**, 307–354 (1992)
8. Kingma, D.P., Ba, J.L.: Adam: a method for stochastic optimization. In: 3rd International Conference for Learning Representations abs/1412.6980 (2015)
9. Otte, S., Krechel, D., Liwicki, M.: JANNLab neural network framework for Java. In: Poster Proceedings MLDM 2013, pp. 39–46. ibai-publishing, New York (2013)
10. Otte, S., Liwicki, M., Zell, A.: Dynamic cortex memory: enhancing recurrent neural networks for gradient-based sequence learning. In: Wermter, S., Weber, C., Duch, W., Honkela, T., Koprinkova-Hristova, P., Magg, S., Palm, G., Villa, A.E.P. (eds.) ICANN 2014. LNCS, vol. 8681, pp. 1–8. Springer, Cham (2014). doi:10.1007/978-3-319-11179-7_1
11. Otte, S., Liwicki, M., Zell, A.: An analysis of dynamic cortex memory networks. In: International Joint Conference on Neural Networks (IJCNN), pp. 3338–3345. Killarney, Ireland, Jul 2015
12. Otte, S., Zwiener, A., Hanten, R., Zell, A.: Inverse recurrent models – an application scenario for many-joint robot arm control. In: Villa, A.E.P., Masulli, P., Pons Rivero, A.J. (eds.) ICANN 2016. LNCS, vol. 9886, pp. 149–157. Springer, Cham (2016). doi:10.1007/978-3-319-44778-0_18
13. Sutton, R.S., Barto, A.G.: Reinforcement Learning: An Introduction (1998)
14. Werbos, P.: Backpropagation through time: what it does and how to do it. Proc. IEEE **78**(10), 1550–1560 (1990)
15. Wolpert, D.M., Kawato, M.: Multiple paired forward and inverse models for motor control. Neural Netw. **11**, 1317–1329 (1998)

Information Bottleneck in Control Tasks with Recurrent Spiking Neural Networks

Madhavun Candadai Vasu[✉] and Eduardo J. Izquierdo

Cognitive Science, School of Informatics and Computing, Indiana University,
Bloomington, USA
{madcanda,edizquie}@indiana.edu

Abstract. The nervous system encodes continuous information from the environment in the form of discrete spikes, and then decodes these to produce smooth motor actions. Understanding how spikes integrate, represent, and process information to produce behavior is one of the greatest challenges in neuroscience. Information theory has the potential to help us address this challenge. Informational analyses of deep and feed-forward artificial neural networks solving static input-output tasks, have led to the proposal of the *Information Bottleneck* principle, which states that deeper layers encode more relevant yet minimal information about the inputs. Such an analyses on networks that are recurrent, spiking, and perform control tasks is relatively unexplored. Here, we present results from a Mutual Information analysis of a recurrent spiking neural network that was evolved to perform the classic pole-balancing task. Our results show that these networks deviate from the *Information Bottleneck* principle prescribed for feed-forward networks.

Keywords: Spiking neurons · Evolutionary neural networks · Recurrent networks · Information theory · Information bottleneck

1 Introduction

Deep Learning systems have surpassed other algorithms and even humans at several tasks [1–4]. While their applications continue to grow, deep learning systems are still considered black-box optimization methods. One of the most vital features behind their success is their ability to extract relevant yet minimal information as it progresses into deeper and deeper layers [5]. This is an extension of *Rate Coding Theory* [6] presented as the *Information Bottleneck* principle [5,7]. The information bottleneck principle has been primarily focused on systems that are (a) feedforward, and (b) in an open-loop, decoupled from their environment.

Neuroscientists, on the other hand, have long been studying the principles behind encoding and representation of environmental information in neural activity using principles of information theory [9] and rate distortion theory [8]. Continuous variables from the environment are encoded as discrete spikes in the brain, which are then decoded to produce smooth continuous movement. Due to

© Springer International Publishing AG 2017
A. Lintas et al. (Eds.): ICANN 2017, Part I, LNCS 10613, pp. 236–244, 2017.
https://doi.org/10.1007/978-3-319-68600-4_28

experimental limitations, an informational analysis of a closed-loop brain-body-environment behaviour system is not yet feasible.

We take a radically different approach to understanding information flow in a behaviorally-functional agent. We artificially evolve embodied agents controlled by recurrent spiking neural networks to perform a task. For this paper, we focus on a non-Markovian version of the classical pole balancing task. Pole balancing has been explored quite extensively as a benchmark for control using neural networks [10,11]. With continuous states and actions, this task serves as an ideal setting to study the transformation of the continuous input information into spikes and then back to continuous action. While the typical task is Markovian, and thus too trivial for an informational analysis, it can easily be transformed into a non-Markovian task by making the available information to the agent limited. Our approach to pole balancing incorporates an agent-centric "visual" interface to the pole. Therefore, information that is typically available, like the pole's angle and angular velocity, the agent's position and velocity, are not fed directly to the network. Ultimately, the minimal nature of the task makes it tractable for an investigation of a recurrent network in a closed-loop task.

The parameters of the recurrent spiking neural network that balances the pole were optimized using an evolutionary algorithm. Evolving neural networks as opposed to hand-designing them allows maximum flexibility for exploring the parameter space. While evolutionary algorithms have been very commonly used in several fields [16], recently, they have been proven to be efficient for optimizing deep neural networks as well [14,15]. Moreover, due to the stochastic nature of the optimization, running the algorithm several times provides us with an ensemble of solutions that solve the problem. This allows the analysis of not just one solution but several to evaluate consistency of results.

The paper is organized as follows. In the first section we report on the agent, task, optimization technique, and analysis method. The section that follows presents an informational analysis for the best and top performing agents. In the last section we summarize the results.

2   Methods

Agent design. The agent lives in a 1-dimensional world with the pole attached to its center. Seven equidistant rays of "vision" with overlapping receptive fields spanning $36°$ provide it with sensory stimuli (Fig. 1A, B). The control network of the agent has three primary components: sensory units, spiking interneurons, and motor units. There is one sensory units per ray, which merely pass on the signal received from the rays. Sensory units are fully connected to N interneurons (here $N = 2$), modeled by Izhikevich spiking neuron model [13]. The model has 4 parameters per neuron and is governed by a two-dimensional system of ordinary differential equations [13]. Interneurons are recurrently connected (Fig. 1C).

Therefore, each interneuron receives weighted input from each sensory unit, S_i, and from other spiking interneurons, I_i, as follows:

$$S_i + I_i = \sum_{j=1}^{7} w_{ji}^s s_j + \sum_{j=1}^{N} w_{ji}^i o_i \qquad (1)$$

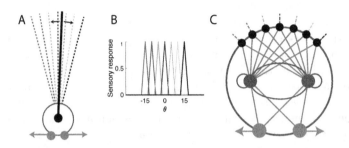

Fig. 1. Task set up and agent design. [A] The agent (gray circle) moves left/right along the horizontal axis (gray arrows) sensing the pole (black rod) through the seven vision rays (color dashed lines), with a range of 36 degrees. [B] Sensory rays have a linearly diffused receptive field from their centers and overlap at the edges with the receptive fields of adjacent rays. [C] The agent has 7 vision sensors (black) connected to two recurrent spiking interneurons (red) connected to two motor units (gray). (Color figure online)

where s_j is the input at the jth sensory unit, w_{ji}^s is the strength of the connection from the jth sensory unit to the ith spiking interneuron, w_{ji}^i is the strength of the recurrent connections from the jth to the ith spiking neuron, and o_i is the output of the neuron. The sign of all outgoing connections from an interneuron depends on its excitatory or inhibitory nature, as identified by a binary parameter. Finally, the layer of interneurons feeds into the two motor neurons, that has the following state equation:

$$\tau_m \dot{m}_i = -m_i + \sum_{j=1}^{N} w_{ji}^m \bar{o}_j \quad i = 1, 2 \qquad (2)$$

$$\bar{o}_j(t) = \frac{1}{h_j} \sum_{k=0}^{h_j} o_j(t - k) \qquad (3)$$

where m_i represents the motor neuron state, w_{ji}^m is the strength of the connection from the jth spiking interneuron to the ith motor neuron, $\bar{o}_j$ represents the firing rate code, the moving average over a window of length h_j for the output of spiking interneuron j. Finally, the difference in output between the motor neurons results in a net force that acts upon the agent, moving it along the track. The network was simulated using Euler integration with step size 0.01.

Pole balancing task design. The agent can move left/right to balance a pole for as long as possible. The pole-balancing task was implemented based on published descriptions [12]. The force from the agent, computed as the difference between motor unit outputs, affects the angular acceleration of the pole and acceleration of the agent. The physical parameters such as mass, length and coefficient of friction were all set as per the same reference. While typically pole-balancers receive as input the angle of the pole (θ), its angular velocity (ω), the agent's position (x) and velocity (v), our implementation was modified to only sense the pole through the sensory rays.

Evolutionary algorithm. The network was optimized using a real valued evolutionary algorithm. A solution was encoded by 38 parameters, including the intrinsic parameters of the Izhikevich neurons, the neuron-specific size of the window for estimating rate code, all connection weights (sensory-interneuron, interneuron-interneuron, interneuron-motor), and the time constant, bias and gain for the motor units. Parameters were constrained to certain ranges: connection strengths $\in [-50, 50]$; motor unit biases $\in [-4, 4]$; time-constants $\in [1, 2]$. The range of intrinsic parameters and the polarity of the outgoing weights from the inter-neuron depended on a binary inhibitory/excitatory neuron flag parameter in the genotype [13]. The population consisted of 100 individuals.

Fitness function. Performance was estimated by averaging over 16 trials, starting at pole angles θ_0 between $\pm 12°$, in increments of $3°$, and two initial angular velocities, $\omega_0 = \pm 0.001$. The fitness function to be maximized was $f = (\sum_{t=1}^{T} cos(\theta_t))/T$, where $T = 500\,s$ is the maximum duration of the run. The pole was considered balanced if it was within the sensory range of the agent. Also, the track length was fixed at 45 units, beyond which the trial was terminated.

Mutual information. The amount of information contained in one variable about another was estimated using Mutual Information (MI). We quantified the information that neurons contain about pole angle (θ), angular velocity (ω), agent position (x) and agent velocity (v) by calculating their probability distributions (using a binning method with each bin of width 0.01):

$$MI(N, X) = \sum_{n \in N} \sum_{x \in X} p(x, n) log \frac{p(x, n)}{p(x)p(n)} \qquad (4)$$

3   Results

Performance of evolutionary optimization. While pole balancing is a well-known benchmark, it was also a relatively easy task to optimize. The evolutionary algorithm found fairly good solutions (around 75% performance) at the very first random draw of the population. Figure 2A shows the performance of the best agent in every generation over time. Out of the 100 evolutionary runs, 99 converged to over 99% fitness with only two spiking interneurons.

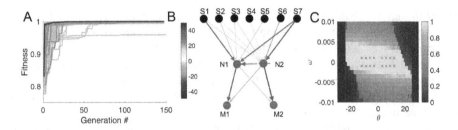

Fig. 2. Optimization performance. [A] Fitness of the best individual in the population vs. generations for 100 evolutionary runs. Best run in blue, top 10 in light blue and the rest in gray. [B] Network structure of the best agent. The width of the edges indicate the magnitude of the weights and are also color coded for polarity. The sensory units in black are identified as S1–S7, spiking interneurons N1, N2 in red and motor units M1, M2 in grey. [C] Generalization performance over a broader and finely grained set of initial conditions that were tested during evolution (marked by cross marks). (Color figure online)

Network structure and performance of the best agent. The network structure of the best agent from the 100 runs is shown in Fig. 2B. The behavioral traces of this agent on the 16 trials specified in the previous section are shown in Fig. 3A. This agent achieved a fitness of 99.4%. To test for generalization, its performance was evaluated on a finer and broader range of conditions, post-optimization (Fig. 2C): initial pole angle θ_0 in the range $[-45, 45]$ and initial pole angular velocity ω_0 in the range $[-0.01, 0.01]$. As can be seen, the agent generalizes well within and outside the region it was evolved on. Note that θ_0 that are beyond 18° on either side are beyond the range of the sensory rays.

Encoding of environmental variables. The different network elements that manipulate the input are shown in Fig. 3B. Sensory signals first act on neurons' potential. The neuron fires based on dynamics in its potential, which is then interpreted by its rate. The motor units then convert this discrete spike rate to smooth continuous movement. Note that a single neuron has three levels of informational content - continuous valued potential, binary spikes, and discrete spike rate codes. Figure 3C shows traces for the highlighted trial in Fig. 3A of the best agent. Although θ is the most directly available information, unlike the standard practice of directly providing it, the sensory rays provide an agent-centric perspective of θ. MI between each of the network elements with θ, see Fig. 3D, revealed that internal potential of neurons have relatively more information about θ than the spike rate and so does the motor units. Albeit only for one trial in one agent, this shows that the bottleneck does not always become narrow in control tasks. MI also reveals that indirect encoding of ω, x and v all happen in the very first stage of the network, neuron potential (black bars in Fig. 4). This can be attributed to the recurrent nature of connections between the interneurons and also their rather complex non-linear internal dynamics.

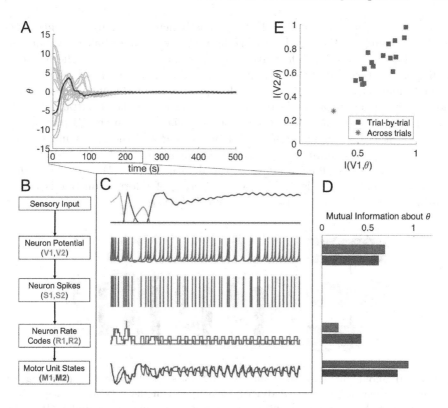

Fig. 3. Behavior of the best agent and one of its trials in detail. [A] Angle of the pole over time on 16 trials. One of the trials ($\theta_0 = -6°$ and $\omega_0 = 0.001$) is highlighted and explored further. [B] Information flowchart: from sensory input rays through the spiking inter-neuron layer, composed of 3 levels of processing (neuron potential, spiking activity and rate code), and then the motor units. [C] A sample trace for each of the components corresponding to each box in B from the trial highlighted in A. Each color in the first figure is matched with the sensory rays in Fig. 1. The blue and orange colors indicate interneurons 1 and 2 respectively. The green and brown traces corresponds to the left and right motor neurons respectively. [D] Mutual Information about the pole angle (θ) for the highlighted trial for each of the components. [E] Mutual information about θ in the neuron potential (V). A comparison between the trial-by-trial MI vs. the total MI across trials.

Analysis of the information bottleneck. All available information, as shown by MI in V, is not necessarily used in controlling movement, as shown by relatively lower information in R. To further study the bottleneck, we compared the amount of information contained in neuron potentials, V, versus the rate coded outputs of the neurons, R. Note that the spikes themselves do not have any information about the environment but, in fact, encode them in its rate. For each of the environmental variables a paired samples t-test was conducted with a significance threshold of $p < 0.05$. This revealed that there is a significant drop in the amount of information between V and R (Fig. 4) robustly across the top ten agents. This can be attributed to the loss due to the discretization of information available in V as spikes. However, the information in R is sufficient to perform the behavior with great accuracy and so this is in fact an efficient encoding of information. The minimal yet relevant information that is encoded in R is interpreted by the motor units. They integrate R from the interneurons and their outputs directly impact θ, ω, x and v and so this is where a deviation from the IB principle is expected. Statistical analyses of the MI between R and the motor units state, M, using the paired samples t-test yielded highly significant ($p \ll 0.05$) increase in information about all environmental variables in M (Fig. 4). This shows that the IB for control tasks is not always a filtering of information but is rather filtering followed by an expansion at the control layer.

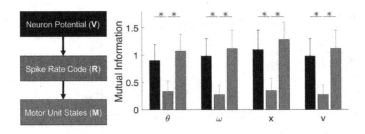

Fig. 4. MI about the four environmental variables: pole angle (θ), pole angular velocity(ω), agent position (x) and agent velocity (v) in the network elements: neuron potentials (V), rate coded outputs of neurons (R), and motor unit states (M). Paired samples t-test yielded highly significant ($p \ll 0.05$) differences between the information contained about θ, ω and v in V versus R and R versus M.

Context sensitive information encoding. From previous analysis, we know that components of the network encode information about the environment. But what information do they encode? Typically, when a neuron is said to encode information about a feature of the environment it is thought to be a consistent, context-independent code. To explore this idea further, we compared the MI the neuron potential has about the pole's angle $I(V,\theta)$ on a trial by trial basis to the information that same neuron has across all trials about the same feature of the environment on the best agent (Fig. 3E) and the top 10 agents. A one-sample t-test of the combined MI with the distribution of trial-by-trial MI values yielded a highly significant difference ($p \ll 0.05$). This means that the combined information is significantly lower than trial-by-trial information, and therefore that encoding is highly context-dependent across all evolved pole-balancers.

4   Discussion

In this paper, we have presented results from an information theoretic analysis of recurrent spiking neural networks that were evolved to perform a continuous control task: agent-centric non-Markovian pole balancing. Our results can be summarized as follows. First, networks with as few as two spiking neurons could be evolved to perform this task. Second, through the use of MI, we show that the spiking network encoded environmental variables of interest that were directly and indirectly available. Third, we show that the information bottleneck from the neuron potential to its firing rate is an efficient filtering/compression, which was followed by an increase in information at the control layer on account of their causal effect on the environment. This is a phenomenon that we expect to arise in control tasks in general, and plan to explore further with different tasks and types of networks. Perhaps, this can develop into an optimization method for neural network control. Finally, we show that the information encoded in the spiking neurons vary across trials, causing the across-trial combined information to be significantly lower. This can mean either that the same stimuli are encoded in different ways (redundancy) or that different stimuli are mapped on to the same encoding (generalization) or both. This warrants further analysis to understand the encoding in more detail and more interestingly, to understand how the context helps disambiguate the generalized representations during a trial.

References

1. Bengio, Y., Courville, A., Vincent, P.: Representation learning: a review and new perspectives. IEEE Trans. Pattern Anal. Mach. Intell. **35**(8), 1798–1828 (2013)
2. Krizhevsky, A., Sutskever, I., Hinton, G.E.: Imagenet classification with deep convolutional neural networks. In: Advances in Neural Information Processing Systems, pp. 1097–1105 (2012)
3. Mnih, V., Kavukcuoglu, K., Silver, D., Graves, A., Antonoglou, I., Wierstra, D., Riedmiller, M.: Playing atari with deep reinforcement learning. arXiv preprint arXiv:1312.5602 (2013)
4. Silver, D., Huang, A., Maddison, C.J., Guez, A., Sifre, L., Van Den Driessche, G., Schrittwieser, J., Antonoglou, I., Panneershelvam, V., Lanctot, M., Dieleman, S., Grewe, D., Nham, J., Kalchbrenner, N., Sutskever, I., Lillicrap, T., Leach, M., Kavukcuoglu, K., Graepel, T., Hassabis, D.: Mastering the game of Go with deep neural networks and tree search. Nature **529**(7587), 484–489 (2016)
5. Tishby, N., Pereira, F.C., Bialek, W.: The information bottleneck method. arXiv preprint physics/0004057 (2000)
6. Berger, T.: RateDistortion Theory. Encyclopedia of Telecommunications (1971)
7. Tishby, N., Zaslavsky, N.: Deep learning and the information bottleneck principle. In: Information Theory Workshop (ITW), pp. 1–5. IEEE (2015)
8. Simoncelli, E.P., Olshausen, B.A.: Natural image statistics and neural representation. Annu. Rev. Neurosci. **24**(1), 1193–1216 (2001)
9. Borst, A., Theunissen, F.E.: Information theory and neural coding. Nat. Neurosci. **2**(11), 947–957 (1999)
10. Pasemann, F., Dieckmann, U.: Evolved neurocontrollers for pole-balancing. In: Mira, J., Moreno-Díaz, R., Cabestany, J. (eds.) IWANN 1997. LNCS, vol. 1240, pp. 1279–1287. Springer, Heidelberg (1997). doi:10.1007/BFb0032588
11. Onat, A., Nishikawa, Y., Kita, H.: Q-learning with recurrent neural networks as a controller for the inverted pendulum problem (1998)

12. Barto, A.G., Sutton, R.S., Anderson, C.W.: Neuron-like adaptive elements that can solve difficult learning control problems. Behav. Process. **9**, 89 (1984)
13. Izhikevich, E.M.: Simple model of spiking neurons. IEEE Trans. Neural Networks **14**(6), 1569–1572 (2003)
14. Miikkulainen, R., Liang, J., Meyerson, E., Rawal, A., Fink, D., Francon, O., Raju, B., Shahrzad, H., Navruzyan, A., Duffy, N., Hodjat, B.: Evolving deep neural networks. arXiv preprint arXiv:1703.00548 (2017)
15. Salimans, T., Ho, J., Chen, X., Sutskever, I.: Evolution strategies as a scalable alternative to reinforcement learning. arXiv preprint arXiv:1703.03864 (2017)
16. De Jong, K.A.: Evolutionary Computation: A Unified Approach. MIT press, Cambridge (2006)

Neural Computation with Spiking Neural Networks Composed of Synfire Rings

Jérémie Cabessa[1]([✉]), Ginette Horcholle-Bossavit[2,3], and Brigitte Quenet[2,3]

[1] Laboratoire d'économie mathématique (LEMMA), Université Paris 2,
Panthéon-Assas, Paris, France
jeremie.cabessa@u-paris2.fr
[2] Équipe de Statistique Appliquée, PSL Research University,
ESPCI-ParisTech, Paris, France
[3] Neurophysiologie respiratoire expérimentale et clinique, Sorbonne Universités,
UPMC Université Paris 6, INSERM, UMRS1158, Paris, France

Abstract. We show that any finite state automaton can be simulated by some neural network of Izhikevich spiking neurons composed of interconnected synfire rings. The construction turns out to be robust to the introduction of two kinds of synaptic noises. These considerations show that a biological paradigm of neural computation based on sustained activities of cell assemblies is indeed possible.

Keywords: Neural computation · Izhikevich spiking neurons · Synfire rings · Finite state automata

1 Introduction

In neural computation, the issue of the computational capabilities of neural networks is of central importance.

In this context, it has early been observed that Boolean recurrent neural networks are computationally equivalent to finite state automata [1–3]. These results opened the way to studies about simulations of finite automata by neural network models, with the aim of improving the implementation of finite state machines on parallel hardwares [4]. Nowadays, the computational power of diverse neural models have been shown to range from the finite automaton degree [1–4], up to the Turing [5,6] or even to the super-Turing level [7,8].

But from a biological perspective, the following question naturally arises: can the implementation of abstract machines be extended to the context of (more) biological neural networks? In fact, in biological nets, information is more likely processed by cell assemblies rather than by isolated entities [9,10], "mental states" are most probably represented by sustained activities of such assemblies rather than by specific spiking configurations, single neural connections are unreliable, and neural nets are subjected to various mechanisms of plasticity [11].

Along these lines, a novel paradigm of neural computation based on Boolean networks composed of synfire rings [9,10,12] has recently been proposed [13]. In

© Springer International Publishing AG 2017
A. Lintas et al. (Eds.): ICANN 2017, Part I, LNCS 10613, pp. 245–253, 2017.
https://doi.org/10.1007/978-3-319-68600-4_29

this paper, we show that this paradigm can be extended to the context of more biological neural networks, in accordance with the approach pursued in [14]. More precisely, we prove that any finite state automaton can be simulated by some neural network of Izhikevich spiking neurons [15] composed of interconnected synfire rings [12]. Furthermore, the obtained network is robust to the introduction of two kinds of synaptic noises. Our construction is general and can be realized for any finite state automaton. These considerations intend to show that a biological paradigm of neural computation based on sustained activities of cell assemblies is indeed possible.

2   Finite State Automata and Boolean Recurrent Neural Networks

Boolean recurrent neural networks are computationally equivalent to finite state automata [1–3]. On the one hand, any Boolean neural network can be simulated by some finite state automaton, and on the other hand, any finite automaton can be simulated by some Boolean network.

In Minsky's original construction [3] (known to be not optimal), a finite automaton with n states and k input symbols is simulated by a Boolean network whose cells are organized in a $k \times n$ grid. The grid structure displays one row and one column of cells per input symbol and computational state of the automaton, respectively. The weighted synaptic connections are suitably chosen in such a way that, if the automaton and its corresponding network are working in parallel on a same input stream, then the cell of location (i, j) in the network's grid will produce a spike if and only if the automaton is currently receiving the i-th input symbol and visiting the j-th computational state. In this precise sense, the computation of the original automaton is simulated by the spiking pattern

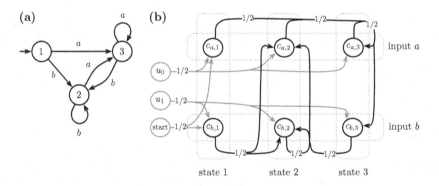

Fig. 1. Translation from a finite state automaton $\mathcal{A}$ (panel (a)) to an equivalent Boolean recurrent neural network $\mathcal{N}$ (panel (b)). The fact that $\mathcal{A}$ receives input a or b at time t is reflected by the input cells (u_0, u_1) of $\mathcal{N}$ taking values $(1, 0)$ or $(0, 1)$, respectively. The "start" cell spikes only at time $t = 0$ in order to initiate the dynamics.

Table 1. Simulation of automaton $\mathcal{A}$ of Fig. 1(a) by its corresponding network $\mathcal{N}$ of Fig. 1(b) and by its corresponding network of synfire rings $\mathcal{N}'$ of Fig. 3.

Inputs of $\mathcal{A}$	a	b	a	a	a	$\cdots$
States of $\mathcal{A}$	1	3	2	3	3	$\cdots$
Cell u_0 of $\mathcal{N}$	1	0	1	1	1	$\cdots$
Cell u_1 of $\mathcal{N}$	0	1	0	0	0	$\cdots$
Cell $start$ of $\mathcal{N}$	1	0	0	0	0	$\cdots$
Spiking cell of $\mathcal{N}$	$-$	$c_{a,1}$	$c_{b,3}$	$c_{a,2}$	$c_{a,3}$	$c_{a,3}$
Active synfire ring of $\mathcal{N}'$	$-$	$\mathbf{R_{a,1}}$	$\mathbf{R_{b,3}}$	$\mathbf{R_{a,2}}$	$\mathbf{R_{a,3}}$	$\mathbf{R_{a,3}}$

of the corresponding network. This translation from a given finite automaton to its corresponding Boolean network is illustrated in Fig. 1.

A parallel simulation of the automaton and corresponding Boolean network of Fig. 1 is illustrated in Table 1. We see that the consecutive input symbols i and computational states j of $\mathcal{A}$ are correctly reflected by the sequence of spiking cells $c_{i,j}$ of $\mathcal{N}$, with a time delay of 1.

3   Finite State Automata and Boolean Networks of Synfire Rings

An alternative way of simulating finite state automata by means of Boolean recurrent neural networks made up of interconnected synfire rings has rencently been proposed [13]. The general idea consists in replacing each cell $c_{i,j}$ of the Boolean network of Fig. 1(b) by a synfire chain that loops back in on itself – referred to as a *synfire ring* $R_{i,j}$ [12] – illustrated in Fig. 2(a). In this way, each computational state of the original automaton will no more correspond to the punctual activity of a specific cell, but rather to the sustained activity of a specific synfire ring, that will persist until the appearance of the next input.

In order to complete the construction, the transitions between the various synfire rings shall correspond precisely to those between the cells of the network of Fig. 1(b). For this purpose, each excitatory connection between cells $c_{i,j}$ and $c_{i',j'}$ (black connections of Fig. 1(b)) is replaced by a fibre of excitatory connections between the corresponding synfire rings $R_{i,j}$ and $R_{i',j'}$ which connects every cells of $R_{i,j}$ to every cells of $R_{i',j'}$ (all-to-all connections). In addition, each synfire ring is associating with a so-called "triangular structure", illustrated in Fig. 2(b). This structure ensures that, every time a specific synfire ring is activated, it will inhibit all other rings, in order to remain the only one active, as explained in Fig. 2(b). Finally, weights of the input, intra-ring and inter-ring connections need to satisfy the following conditions:

(C1) The sole activity of the inter-ring connections does not suffice to activate any of the synfire ring.

(C2) The combined activity of the input cell and inter-ring connections is sufficiently large to activate the targeted synfire ring.

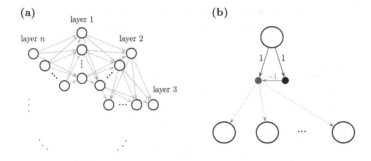

Fig. 2. (a) A synfire ring with n layers. Each cell of each layer is connected to all cells of the next layer. (b) The triangular structure associated to each synfire ring. Each large node represents a synfire ring and each little node represents a single cell. The two downward blue edges represent fibres of excitatory connections of weight 1 projecting from every cells of the upper ring to the blue and red units. The downward red edges represent fibres of sufficiently large inhibitory connections projecting from the red unit to every cells of the targeted synfire ring. If the upper ring fires at time t, it activates both red and blue cells at time $t + 1$. Consequently, from time $t + 2$ onwards, all other synfire rings, represented by the lower nodes, are inhibited via the red connections, and the red cell is also inhibited via the horizontal red connection. (Color figure online)

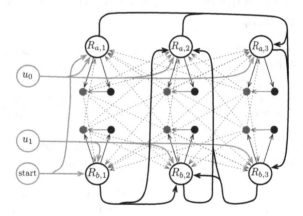

Fig. 3. Boolean recurrent neural network $\mathcal{N}'$ made up of interconnected synfire rings which simulates the automaton of Fig. 1(a). Each large node represents a synfire ring, as illustrated in Fig. 2(a). To each synfire ring is associated a triangular structure, as described in Fig. 2(b).

(C3) The inhibitory connections projecting from the triangular structures to the other synfire rings must be sufficiently negative to inhibit the total activity of the rings onto which they project.

The Boolean network of synfire rings associated to the automaton of Fig. 1 is illustrated in Fig. 3.

It was shown that every computation of the original automaton is correctly simulated by a corresponding sequence of sustained activities of synfire rings in the corresponding network [13]. More precisely, when the two systems are run in parallel on a same input stream, the synfire ring $R_{i,j}$ of the network – and only this one – will fire at a certain time step if and only if the automaton is currently receiving the i-th input symbol and visiting the j-th computational state. Moreover, the activity of that specific ring is self-sustained as long as no other input is received.

A parallel simulation of the automaton of Fig. 1(a) and its corresponding Boolean networks of synfire rings of Fig. 3 is illustrated in Table 1. We see that the consecutive input symbols i and computational states j of automaton $\mathcal{A}$ are correctly reflected by the sequence of active rings $R_{i,j}$ of network $\mathcal{N}'$.

The proposed construction can be applied to any finite state automaton. Consequently, the following result obtains [13]:

Theorem 1. *Any finite state automaton can be simulated by some Boolean neural network composed of interconnected synfire rings.*

4   Finite State Automata and Networks of Spiking Neurons

We show that the simulation of finite state automata by Boolean networks of synfire rings can be extended to the biological context of networks of spiking neurons.

More precisely, we consider a neural network made up of Izhikevich spiking neurons [15] with dimensionless parameters $a = 0.02, b = 0.2, c = -75, d = 0.4$ connected together by excitatory and inhibitory synapses with exponential decays of rates 0.3 and 0.2, respectively. The network contains the same architecture, i.e., the same input cells, synfire rings, and triangular structures as that of Fig. 3, but is subjected to a more complex dynamics defined by the differential equations of Izhikevich neurons [15]. Compared to the Boolean network of Sect. 3, the excitatory inter-rings connections needed to be considerably reduced (from 1.0 to 0.11), due to the combined activities of the neurons. The weight matrix of the network is given in Fig. 4 (left).

This network of spiking neurons was able to perfectly simulate the behavior of the automaton of Fig. 1(a), in the precise sense explained in Sect. 3. For instance, Fig. 5(a1) provides the raster plot of the network's activity where inputs $a, b, a,$ a, a are provided at regular intervals of 625 ms. We see that, according to the sequence of inputs received, the network's activity successively switches from the groups of neurons $4 - 21$ to $104 - 121$ to $24 - 41$ to $44 - 61$ and to $44 - 61$ again, which corresponds precisely to the successive activations of the synfire rings $R_{a,1}, R_{b,3}, R_{a,2}, R_{a,3}, R_{a,3}$, as expected by the simulation process described in Table 1. We repeated the simulations with different input streams and during longer times, and the simulation process was always correct. It is worth noting that the network's dynamics shows the emergence of a regular temporal structure

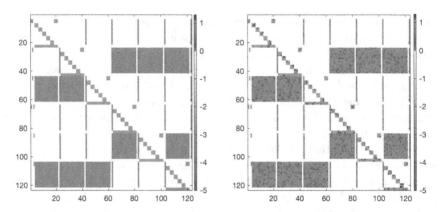

Fig. 4. Weight matrices of the network of Izhikevich neurons connected according to the architecture described in Fig. 3. The excitatory and inhibitory weights are expresses as percentages of the respective maximal synaptic strengths, set at 5.6 and 15.0. The left and right panel represent the matrix without and with the addition of synaptic noise, respectively. Neurons number 1, 2 and 3 are the *start*, u_0 and u_1 cells. Groups of neurons $4 - 21$, $24 - 41$, $44 - 61$, $64 - 81$, $84 - 101$ and $104 - 121$ represent the six synfire rings $R_{a,1}$, $R_{a,2}$, $R_{a,3}$, $R_{b,1}$, $R_{b,2}$ and $R_{b,3}$, respectively. Neurons $22 - 23$, $42 - 43$, $62 - 63$, $82 - 83$, $102 - 103$ and $122 - 123$ are the pairs of cells of the triangular structures associated to the six synfire rings. The blue regions represent the input and intra-ring connections; the green regions represent the inter-ring connections; the orange region are the inhibitory connections projecting from the triangular structures. (Color figure online)

induced by the synfire connectivity. Figure 5(a2) displays the synaptic current and membrane potential of neuron 10. We see that the neuron is spiking during the activation of the first synfire ring $R_{a,1}$. Afterwards, it remains quiet and endures the three successive massive inhibitions occurring at every switch of synfire ring activity.

Moreover, the simulation process turns out to be robust to the introduction of two kinds of synaptic noises. First, we perturbed the inter-ring, intra-ring and inhibitory connections with a centred Gaussian noise of about 10% of the original weights, as depicted in Fig. 4(left). The obtained noisy weight matrix is given in Fig. 4(right). Secondly, we introduced a dynamic synaptic noise (or membrane noise), by distorting the membrane current with a standard Gaussian noise at every updating step, as illustrated by the noisy black and magenta traces of Fig. 5(b2). Figure 5(b1) provides the raster plot of the network's activity subjected to these two kinds of synaptic noises, and shows that the simulation of the automaton is still correctly performed.

Besides, it is known that different kinds of neurons – e.g., Izhikevich thalamo-ortical (TC-IZH) [15], Izhikevich necortical regular-spiking (RS-IZH) [15], Izhikevich resonator (RZ-IZH) [15], exponential integrate-and-fire (RS-EIF) [16], multiple-timescale adaptive-threshold (RS-MAT) [17] – exhibit different properties in transmitting temporal information accurately and reliably when organized

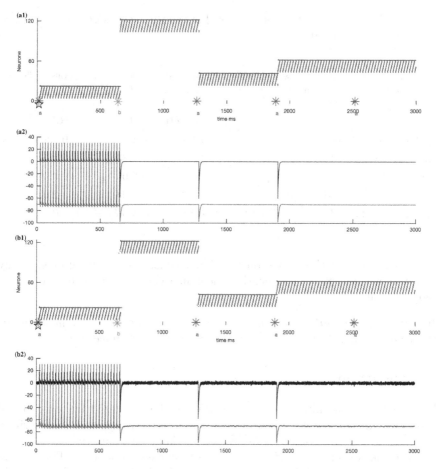

Fig. 5. (a1) Raster plot of the network's activity, when receiving the sequence of inputs a, b, a, a, a. **(b1)** Synaptic current (black) and membrane potential of neuron 10 (magenta) over time. **(a2)** Raster plot of the network's activity subjected to two kinds of synaptic noise, when receiving the sequence of inputs a, b, a, a, a. **(b2)** Synaptic current (black) and membrane potential of neuron 10 (magenta) over time, when the network is subjected to the two kinds of synaptic noises. (Color figure online)

either into simple chains [18] or into synfire chains [19]. Our network involves Izhikevich neurons whose dynamics resembles that of simple McCulloch and Pitts' cells. But by carefully tuning our synaptic connections, we were also able to correctly simulate the behavior of the finite automaton of Fig. 1(a) with networks of synfire rings composed of either TC-IZH or RS-IZH or RZ-IZH neurons (with dimensionless parameters $a = 0.02, b = 0.25, c = -65, d = 2$ or $a = 0.02, b = 0.2, c = -65, d = 8$ or $a = 0.1, b = 0.26, c = -65, d = 2$, respectively, cf. [18]), as well as with many other kinds of Izhikevich neurons. The synaptic weights of the networks composed of the three types of aforementioned neurons are given in Table 2.[1]

Table 2. Synaptic weights (s.w.) of three networks composed of three types of Izhikevich neurons, each of which correctly simulates the finite automaton of Fig. 1(a).

	TC-IZH	RS-IZH	RZ-IZH
Input s.w. (light blue Fig. 3)	0.45	1.11	0.1305
Intra-ring s.w. (grey Fig. 2(a))	0.8	1.83	0.8
Inter-ring s.w. (black Fig. 3)	0.049	0.09	0.02
Inhib. s.w. (dashed red Fig. 3)	-2.0	-6.0	-2.0
Triangle s.w. (dark blue & solid red Fig. 3)	1.0 & -1.1	1.0 & -2.0	1.0 & -1.1

Finally, note that the above construction is generic: it can be applied to any finite state automaton. Consequently, Theorem 1 can be extended to this more biological context.

Theorem 2. *Any finite state automaton can be simulated by some noisy neural network of Izhikevich spiking neurons composed of interconnected synfire rings.*

5   Conclusion

We showed that any finite state automaton can be simulated by some neural network of Izhikevich spiking neurons composed of interconnected synfire rings. Our construction turns out to be robust to two kinds of local synaptic noises as well as to the consideration of various types of Izhikevich neurons. This feature is based on the fact that the correctness of our simulation process does not rely on the processing of precise temporal information [18,19], but rather on simple activation and self-sustainability of specific synfire rings, which is a coarser feature. We however noticed that our construction turns out to be highly sensitive to global changes of the synaptic weights.

With these achievements, we do not intend to argue that brain computational processes really proceed via simulations of finite state automata in the very way that we described. Rather, our intention is to show that a bio-inspired paradigm of abstract neural computation based on sustained activities of neural assemblies is indeed possible, and potentially harnessable. As a consequence, biological neural networks should in principle be capable of simulating the abstract computational model represented by finite state automata, whether via the proposed paradigm, or via some other one.

For future work, we plan to extend these results to the Turing complete level of computation. Towards this purpose, the networks should be able to encode an

---

[1] For the case of RS-IZH neurons, the exponential decay's rate of the excitatory synapses has been changed from 0.3 to 0.4.

unbounded amount of information representing the possibly unbounded content of the Turing machine's infinite tape throughout the computational process. The biological plausibility of this feature is expected to be explored.

References

1. McCulloch, W.S., Pitts, W.: A logical calculus of the ideas immanent in nervous activity. Bull. Math. Biophys. **5**, 115–133 (1943)
2. Kleene, S.C.: Representation of events in nerve nets and finite automata. In: Shannon, C., McCarthy, J. (eds.) Automata Studies, pp. 3–41. Princeton University Press, Princeton (1956)
3. Minsky, M.L.: Computation: Finite and Infinite Machines. Prentice-Hall Inc., Englewood Cliffs (1967)
4. Siegelmann, H.T.: Recurrent neural networks and finite automata. Computat. Intell. **12**, 567–574 (1996)
5. Turing, A.M.: Intelligent machinery. Technical report, National Physical Laboratory, Teddington, UK (1948)
6. Siegelmann, H.T., Sontag, E.D.: On the computational power of neural nets. J. Comput. Syst. Sci. **50**(1), 132–150 (1995)
7. Siegelmann, H.T., Sontag, E.D.: Analog computation via neural networks. Theor. Comput. Sci. **131**(2), 331–360 (1994)
8. Cabessa, J., Siegelmann, H.T.: The super-Turing computational power of plastic recurrent neural networks. Int. J. Neural Syst. **24**(8), 1–22 (2014)
9. Abeles, M.: Local Cortical Circuits: An Electrophysiological Study. Studies of Brain Function, vol. 6. Springer, Heidelberg (1982)
10. Abeles, M.: Time is precious. Science **304**(5670), 523–524 (2004)
11. Abbott, L.F., Nelson, S.B.: Synaptic plasticity: taming the beast. Nat. Neurosci. **3**(Suppl), 1178–1183 (2000)
12. Zheng, P., Triesch, J.: Robust development of synfire chains from multiple plasticity mechanisms. Front. Comput. Neurosci. **8**, 66 (2014)
13. Cabessa, J., Masulli, P.: Emulation of finite state automata with networks of synfire rings. In: 2016 International Joint Conference on Neural Networks, IJCNN 2017, Anchorage, AK, USA, May 14–19, 2017 (2017, to appear)
14. Horcholle-Bossavit, G., Brigitte, Q.: Neural model of frog ventilatory rhythmogenesis. Biosystems **97**(1), 35–43 (2009)
15. Izhikevich, E.M.: Simple model of spiking neurons. IEEE Trans. Neur. Netw. **14**(6), 1569–1572 (2003)
16. Fourcaud-Trocmé, N., Hansel, D., van Vreeswijk, C., Brunel, N.: How spike generation mechanisms determine the neuronal response to fluctuating inputs. J. Neurosci. **23**(5), 11628–11640 (2003)
17. Kobayashi, R., Tsubo, Y., Shinomoto, S.: Made-to-order spiking neuron model equipped with a multi-timescale adaptive threshold. Front. Comput. Neurosci. **3**, 9 (2009)
18. Asai, Y., Guha, A., Villa, A.E.P.: Deterministic neural dynamics transmitted through neural networks. Neural Netw. **21**(6), 799–809 (2008)
19. Asai, Y., Villa, A.: Integration and transmission of distributed deterministic neural activity in feed-forward networks. Brain Res. **1434**, 17–33 (2012)

Exploiting Recurrent Neural Networks in the Forecasting of Bees' Level of Activity

Pedro A.B. Gomes[1], Eduardo C. de Carvalho[3], Helder M. Arruda[2],
Paulo de Souza[4], and Gustavo Pessin[2(✉)]

[1] Federal University of Pará, Belém, PA, Brazil
pedroabg@ufpa.br
[2] Instituto Tecnológico Vale, Belém, PA, Brazil
{helder.arruda,gustavo.pessin}@itv.org
[3] SENAI Institute of Innovation in Minerals Technologies, Belém, PA, Brazil
eduardo.isi@sesipa.org.br
[4] Data61, CSIRO, Sandy Bay, TAS, Australia
paulo.desouza@data61.csiro.au

Abstract. A third of the food consumed by humankind depends on bees' activities. These insects have a fundamental role in pollination and they are disappearing from the planet. An understanding of their behavior, discussed here from the point of view of their activity level, can help detect adverse situations and even improve the employment of bees in crops. In this work, several Recurrent Neural Networks' architectures, alternating topologies with GRU and LSTM structures, are evaluated in the task of forecasting bees' activity level based on the values of past levels. We also show how RNNs can improve its accuracy by evaluating how different input time windows impact on results.

Keywords: Recurrent Neural Networks · Gated recurrent unit · Long short-term memory · Forecasting · Bees · Pollination

1 Introduction

Bees are considered the most effective group of pollinating insects because they need the plants to obtain their food [9]. Unlike other groups of insects, both adult bees and their larvae and pupae feed exclusively on floral resources. In this way, to meet their food needs, bees visit a large variety of flowers by collecting pollen (source of protein) and nectar. Pollination activity is, therefore, an involuntary action of pollinators, but essential to plant life, which uses scents, colours and flavors to attract them [3]. Moreover, of all food consumed by mankind, it is estimated that 35% depends on bees' action [13]. This means that about a third of the food that people eat comes from these insects playing their role as pollinators.

However, in spite of the global growth of domesticated hives, the number of bees has been declining in the United States since the 1940s and in some European

© Springer International Publishing AG 2017
A. Lintas et al. (Eds.): ICANN 2017, Part I, LNCS 10613, pp. 254–261, 2017.
https://doi.org/10.1007/978-3-319-68600-4_30

countries since the 1960s [15]. According to [14], most of this population decline of bees comes from a combination of pesticides and fungicides that contaminates the pollen collected by bees to feed their hives. With these in mind, the importance of understanding bees' activities are clear. Thus, it is fundamental to study techniques that could be used to predict the condition of these insects. For example: (1) there are plants that offer male and female flowers at certain periods. If a beehive installed in an area records great movement during this period, it would be a strong indication that these bees would be pollinating in that crop; (2) if the agitation of the bees does not follow the level predicted, it may means that there is a change in the environment of the hive; (3) knowing the hours of highest recorded activity, it can be deduced the period which the plants near the hive are suitable for pollination.

In [1], other factors are also analyzed, such as the frequency of flight and its influence on the behavior of the swarm. In relation to animal behavior classification, [18] uses the machine learning algorithm K-means to separate the behavior of cows into two classes. Hence, the authors can discriminate when these animals are in a state of activity or inactivity. In the work of [12] the authors study how to train and use RNNs [17] for problems where data appears sequentially and have some dependence on previously trained data. In the article of [11], the recurrent unit structures for RNNs, GRUs and LSTMs are studied aiming sequential problems. Other approaches to understand bees behavior can be seen in the work by Chena and colleagues [4]. They employ image-based tracking while our approach uses a RFID tags. Using RFIDs allow us to identify each individual alone; it also works in any light condition.

With this in mind, this work aims to predict the level of activity of bees, which can be approached as a time-series forecasting problem. Here, RNNs will be employed to predict such behavior based on past levels of activity. Different architectures of RNNs will be evaluated, likewise different recurrent unit options. The remainder of this article is divided as follows: in Sect. 2 it is explained how the data were collected and how RNN models were created, tested and trained. The results are presented in Sect. 3 as well as more tests with different input time windows. Finally, Sect. 4 presents the conclusions and makes suggestions for future work.

2   Methods

2.1   Data Collect

The data collection phase was performed as part of the Microssensors project [19] where electronic tags were glued on bees to track its behavior and to improve the knowledge about these insects. Bees' movement data were obtained through the use of RFID (Radio-frequency identification) tags in eight hives, as shown in Fig. 1. In the period of 4 weeks, from August 1st to 31st, 2015, 1,280 bees had labels glued to the thorax, being 40 bees per week per hive, in 8 hives. Each time a tagged bee pass upon the RFID reader it records a movement. In the mentioned period, we recorded a total of 127,758 activities (approximately 100 activity records per bee during the data collection phase).

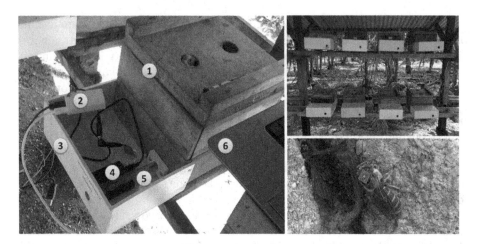

Fig. 1. Left: (1) *Melipona fasciculata* hive, (2) Intel Edison for antenna controlling and data storage, (3) PVC box for storing electronic items, (4) RFID reading antenna, (5) Plastic tube for bees' passage. Right-top: The 8 hives overview. Right-bottom: Bee with RFID tag attached to the chest.

Bees' level of activity is defined in this work as the total number of movements in a given hour, divided by the number of live bees at that time. In this way, the number ranges from 0.0 to approximately 2.0. Zero means no bee is performing activity; Two means that each bee is making two movements at that hour. On average, there were between 240 and 320 live bees per day during the experiment. The Fig. 2 shows part of the activity level time series.

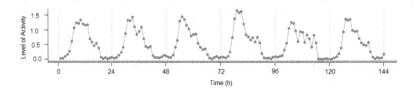

Fig. 2. Partial temporal series of bess' level of activity, from August 1st to 6th, 2015. Values per hour. The temporal series of bee activity presents the average number of activities performed by each active bee in the system.

2.2 The Model

Multi-layer Perceptron Artificial Neural Networks (ANNs) are a machine learning method that is based on a analogy on a brain's behavior. They are composed by simple processing units called neurons that are responsible for calculating mathematical functions. The neurons are organized in one or more layers and are interconnected by connections [2]. The architecture used in the neural network depends on the type of problem it proposes to solve. ANNs with only one layer are sufficient to solve linearly separable problems, while networks with more layers allow solving non-linear problems. Thus, the neural networks have been employed in many problems of prediction and interpolation of variables, as can be seen in [6,7].

In its turn, Recurrent Neural Networks (RNNs) are the family of neural networks specialized in sequential data processing, that is, a sequence of values $x(1), x(2), ..., x(T)$. In addition, recurrent networks are able to process much larger sequences than neural networks, which are not specialized in sequential data. Besides that, most RNNs can also process entries of varying sizes [8]. RNNs can be constructed in several ways, whereas almost any function can be considered a feed-forward neural network, basically any function that involves a recurrence can be considered a RNN. In general, the following equation represents the recurrence of the neural network: $h^{(t)} = f(h^{(t-1)}, x^{(t)}; \theta)$. Here, the term h indicate the hidden state at time step t, current moment. $h^{(t-1)}$ points all the calculations accumulated until the previous step. $x^{(t)}$ is the current input vector and θ is the set of shared parameters through time.

However, some conventional training algorithms such as *Back-Propagation Through Time*(BPTT) [20] and *Real-Time Recurrent Learning*(RTRL) [16], may have propagation problems with the error and the values of the previous instants along the structure, such as a high growth or disappearance of these values. To attenuate these situations, two architectures for the recurrent network unit are used: Long short-term memory (LSTM) [10] and Gated recurrent units(GRU) [5]. Both of these recurrent unit architectures are based on a *gate* structure. These, in their turn, control the amount of information entering the unit, the amount that will be stored and the information that will be passed to the next units. The two architectures have different gates that are trained together with the other network weights.

In order to investigate the best recurrent neural network topology for predicting the activity level of bees, three network arrangements were analyzed: (1) one hidden layer with 4 recurrent units, (2) two hidden layers with 2 recurrent units each, fully connected, and (3) four hidden layers with one unit each. All of them with an output layer. For each format, a different type of unit GRU or LSTM. Figure 3 shows these architectures. In this way, six models were generated: **GRU-4, GRU-2X2, GRU-1-1-1-1, LSTM-4, LSTM-2X2 e LSTM-1-1-1-1**.

2.3   Training and Testing

The models were evaluated through the Root Mean Square Error (RMSE) calculated by the formula:

$$RMSE = \sqrt{\frac{1}{n} \sum_{t=1}^{n} e_t^2}$$

where e is the difference between the value of the observed activity level and the one predicted by the model.

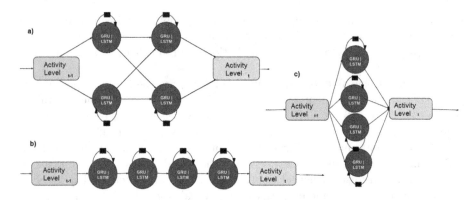

Fig. 3. Illustration of the created models. (a) Two hidden layers with two units each. (b) Four layers with one unit. (c) One layer with 4 units. All structures have one output layer and the recurrent units are GRU or LSTM, resulting in 6 models. The black square on arrows indicates the passage of time-steps.

The data were prepared in such a way that a two-column table was created, one with the activity level at time **t-1** (*feature*) and the other with the activity level at the instant **t** (*target*), one hour ahead. In other words, the models have the data of the first column as input and try to predict the activity level of the next instant. Finally, to train and test the networks, the data was shuffled and split into 70% for training and 30% for testing. So, to have more credibility in the results, each model was trained and tested 10 times.

3 Results

Because of the random initialization of the network's weights, each architecture was executed 10 times, as previously mentioned. Thus, the graph of Fig. 4 presents the error of each architecture, where each boxplot contains the values of the 10 runs. Therefore, it is observed that the best architecture was the **GRU-2x2**, obtaining a RSME mean of 0.214628, with a minimum of 0.207741.

Analysing the best execution from **GRU-2x2**, which has RMSE equal to 0.207741, it is observed by the Fig. 5 how the predicted values follow the observed values. This graph shows an observation of five days, in 120 h of activity level samples, sequentially in order as they were collected. The samples are from the 22nd to the 27th of August. It is observed that the predictions were able to match the observed values even at peak moments.

3.1 Increasing the Input Window

In an effort to improve the result of the forecast, a few more tests were made with the architecture **GRU-2x2**. However, the size of the input window was increased, in other words, different amounts of previous instants were tested to

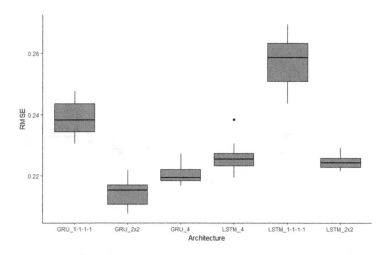

Fig. 4. Each box plot refers to an architecture and shows the RMSE of 10 executions.

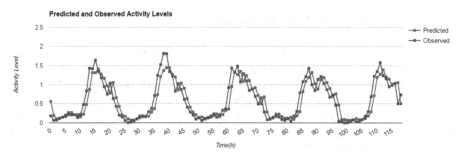

Fig. 5. Five days of observation and the correspondent forecast.

predict the next step, demanding the RNN's ability to keep useful information through time. The tests were set using 1, 6, 12, 24, 36, 48 and 60 instants of time before the predicted samples. The graph in Fig. 6 shows the errors of each configuration where each boxplot indicates 10 tests of that window size. This graph points out that the best setting is **t-24** indicating that a larger window does not always imply error reduction, see **t-36, t-48** and **t-60**. As defined in the Sect. 2, the activity level is calculated considering the total number of movements divided by the number of live bees at that period. Which means that, knowing the levels of the last 24 h, we can estimate, using the **GRU-2x2** model, its value at the current instant with a RMSE under 0.175. In other words, since the activity level ranged from 0.0 to 2.0, the mean error of this configuration was about 8%.

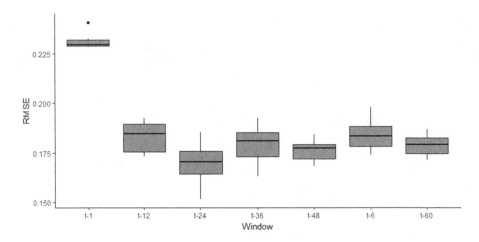

Fig. 6. GRU-2x2 model RMSE for each tested window size.

4   Conclusion and Future Work

In this work, six models of recurrent neural networks were analysed. The configurations were trained and tested with bees' activity level time series in order to forecast the level in the next instant. The model with the lowest RMSE was the **GRU-2x2** which has two hidden layers with two GRU recurrent units and an output layer with one neuron. In addition, the best model was trained with wider temporal window sizes, obtaining the minimum error of 0.171 when 24 past records were used, **t-24**.

Of course, a better understanding of bees' behaviour can contribute a lot to the environment and to our lives. In face of it, many future works can be elaborated. For example: (1) Analysis of bees' activity level using different species near a determined crop to indicate the most efficient pollination species for these plants, (2) Include climatic variables in the prediction, (3) Test larger architectures of RNNs, And (4) Use other machine learning methods to forecast bees' activity level.

References

1. Almeida, G.F.: Fatores que interferem no comportamento enxameatrio de abelhas africanizadas. Departamento de Biologia, Programa de Ps-Graduao em Entomologia (2008)
2. Braga, A., Ludemir, T., Carvalho, A.: Redes Neurais Artificiais: Teoria e Aplicaes. LTC editora (2000)
3. CETAPIS: Sem abelha sem alimento (2013). http://www.semabelhasemalimento.com.br/home/polinizacao
4. Chena, C., Yangb, E.C., Jianga, J.A., Lina, T.T.: An imaging system for monitoring the in-and-out activity of honey bees. Comput. Electron. Agric. **89**, 100–109 (2012)

5. Bahdanau, D., Cho, K., Bengio, Y.: Neural machine translation by jointly learning to align and translate. arXiv preprint arXiv:1409.0473 (2014)

6. Faiçal, B.S., Pessin, G., Filho, G.P., Carvalho, A.C., Gomes, P.H., Ueyama, J.: Fine-tuning of uav control rules for spraying pesticides on crop fields: An approach for dynamic environments. Int. J. Artif. Intell. Tools **25**(01), 1660003 (2016)

7. Furquim, G., Pessin, G., Faial, B.S., Mendiondo, E.M., Ueyama, J.: Improving the accuracy of a flood forecasting model by means of machine learning and chaos theory. Neural Comput. Appl. **27**, 1129–1141 (2015)

8. Goodfellow, I., Bengio, Y., Courville, A.: Deep Learning. MIT Press (2016). http://www.deeplearningbook.org

9. Gullan, P., Cranston, P.: Os insetos: um resumo entomolgico. Traduo de Sonia Hoenen, Roca (2008)

10. Hochreiter, S., Schmidhuber, J.: Long short-term memory. Neural Comput. **9**(8), 1735–1780 (1997)

11. Chung, J., Caglar Gulcehre, K.C., Bengio, Y.: Empirical evaluation of gated recurrent neural networks on sequence modeling. In: NIPS 2014 Deep Learning and Representation Learning Workshop (2014)

12. Martens, J., Sutskever, I.: Learning recurrent neural networks with hessian-free optimization. In: International Conference on Machine Learning, vol. 28, Bellevue, WA, USA (2011)

13. Message, D., Teixeira, E.W., Jong, D.D.: Polinizadores no Brasil: Contribuio e Perspectivas para a Biodiversidade, Uso Sustentvel, Conservao e Servios Ambientais. Editora da Universidade (2012)

14. Pettis, J.S., Lichtenberg, E.M., Andree, M., Stitzinger, J., Rose, R., van Engelsdorp, D.: Crop pollination exposes honey bees to pesticides which alters their susceptibility to the gut pathogen nosema ceranae. PLoS ONE (2013)

15. Potts, S.G., Roberts, S.P.M., Dean, R., Marris, G., Brown, M., Jones, R., Settele, J.: Declines of managed honey bees and beekeepers in europe. J. Apic. Res. **49**, 15–22 (2009)

16. Robinson, A.J., Fallside, F.: The utility driven dynamic error propagation network. Cambridge University Engineering Department (1987)

17. Rumelhart, D., Hinton, G., Williams, R.: Learning representations by back-propagating errors. Nature **323**, 533–536 (1986). http://www.nature.com/

18. Schwager, M., Anderson, D.M., Butler, Z., Rus, D.: Robust classification of animal tracking data. Comput. Electron. Agric. **56**(2007), 4659 (2006)

19. Souza, P., Williams, R.: Agent-based modeling of honey bee forager flight behaviour for swarm sensing applications. Environmental Modelling and Software (2017). (under review)

20. Werbos, P.J.: Generalization of backpropagation with application to a recurrent gas market model. Neural Netw. **1**, 339–356 (1987)

Inherently Constraint-Aware Control of Many-Joint Robot Arms with Inverse Recurrent Models

Sebastian Otte[1(⊠)], Adrian Zwiener[2], and Martin V. Butz[1]

[1] Cognitive Modeling Group, University of Tübingen,
Sand 14, 72076 Tübingen, Germany
sebastian.otte@uni-tuebingen.de
[2] Cognitive Systems Group, University of Tübingen,
Sand 1, 72076 Tübingen, Germany

Abstract. In a recent study, it was demonstrated that Recurrent Neural Networks (RNNs) can be used to effectively control snake-like, many-joint robot arms in a particular way: The inverse kinematics for control are generated using back-propagation through time (BPTT) on recurrent forward models that learned to predict the end-effector pose of a robot arm, whereby each joint is associated with a certain computation time step of the RNN. This paper further investigates this approach in terms of constraint-aware control. Our contribution is twofold: First, we show that an RNN can be trained to also predict the poses of intermediate joints within such an arm, and that these can consequently be included in the control-optimization objective as well, giving full control over the entire arm. Second, we show that particular components of the arm's target can be selectively switched on and off by means of "don't care" signals. This enables us to handle constraints inherently and on-the-fly, without the need of any outer constraint mechanisms, such as additional penalty terms. The experiments demonstrating the effectiveness of our methodology are carried out on a simulated three dimensional 40-joint robot arm with 80 articulated degrees offreedom.

Keywords: Recurrent neural networks · Long short-term memory · Neurorobotics · Robot control · Robot arm · Constraint handling

1 Introduction

Handling many-joint robot arms is usually challenging in terms of control and planning. Recently, it was shown that recurrent neural forward models can be used to compute the inverse kinematics of many-joint robot arms [14]. Specifically, variants of *Long Short-Term Memory* (LSTM) [8,12] were trained to estimate end-effector poses given specified arm configurations. The forward computation unfolds in a sequential manner, whereby the projection through each joint of the arm is computed via one recurrent iteration in the RNN. Thus, the

© Springer International Publishing AG 2017
A. Lintas et al. (Eds.): ICANN 2017, Part I, LNCS 10613, pp. 262–270, 2017.
https://doi.org/10.1007/978-3-319-68600-4_31

recurrences match the sequential nature of computing kinematic forward-chains and the LSTM structure provides highly accurate estimates. *Back-propagation through time* (BPTT) was used to iteratively optimize the goal-oriented inverse mapping, which induces the goal-directed movement of the robot arm; essentially enacting the unfolding goal-directed optimization process. From a computational neuroscience perspective this is closely linked to *active inference* in that action control is inversely inferred by the imagination of the future goal state [3–5].

Previous related approaches have implemented distributed mathematical models of the arm's local relative kinematics and induced control by means of the derivatives of the model [2,15]. In contrast, our approach learns the local relative kinematics by an RNN. Particularly, the combination of LSTMs and the application of BPTT during inference time allows flexible goal-directed arm control facing a much larger number of redundant joints. As shown previously [14], our RNN-based arm control approach scales well even for arms with up to 120 articulated degrees of freedom (DoF), training the forward model based on *stochastic gradient descent* (SGD) with momentum term.

Here, we focus on constraint-aware control. Originally, the recurrent forward model was trained to predict the pose of the end-effector only [14]. As a result, the output of intermediate computation steps reflects the internal representation of the developing end-effector pose estimate. An according analysis has shown that the intermediate outputs did not even approximately match the respective joint poses. Moreover, it appeared to be surprisingly difficult to learn when the network was forced to develop an internal representation that allows the prediction of all intermediate joint poses. For full control over the entire arm, however, it is essential to provide these intermediate poses – referred to as *pose chain* in the following – to enable the induction of joint-specific constraints and optimizations.

This paper tackles this issue by means of a more fine-granular learning setup as well as by using *Adam* [9] for training. Moreover, it is shown that all particular components of the entire pose chain can be selectively included or excluded (left free) from the optimization objective, where we call the latter a *"don't care"* signal. As a result, arm specific constraints can be formulated in work space easily and are inherently considered by the system on-the-fly and in an biological plausible, active-inference-like manner [3–5], without the need for preplanned trajectories or additional constraint-specific penalizations. The effectiveness of our modifications is demonstrated in several scenarios with a simulated 40-joint robot arm with 80 DoF.

2   Inverse Recurrent Model

To enable control via BPTT, an RNN is trained to approximate a forward model M, which maps a robot arm configuration state, that is, a sequence of angle vectors $\boldsymbol{\varphi}^j$, onto the corresponding pose chain:

$$\boldsymbol{\Phi} = \left(\boldsymbol{\varphi}^1, \ldots, \boldsymbol{\varphi}^n\right) \xmapsto{\mathrm{M}} \left({}_1^0\mathbf{A}, \ldots, {}_N^0\mathbf{A}\right), \tag{1}$$

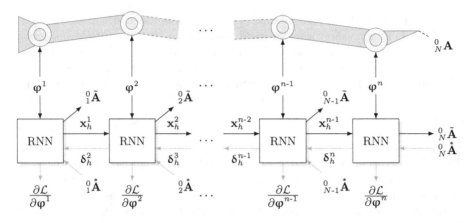

Fig. 1. Computing the inverse mapping using BPTT. An input sequence (the current state of the arm) is presented to RNN in a sequential manner, which produces and estimate of the pose chain. The discrepancy between the output and the desired pose chain is back-propagated through the network (blue lines) and mapped onto the input sequence. (Color figure online)

where $_j^0\mathbf{A} \in \mathbb{R}^{4\times4}$ refers to the reference frame transformation of the j-th joint and N denotes the end-effector frame. Each $_j^0\mathbf{A}$ can be decomposed into the joint's orientation, which is given by the orthonormal base $_j^0\mathbf{R} \in SO(3) \subset \mathbb{R}^{3\times3}$, and its translation, that is, its relative position, given by $_j^0\mathbf{p} \in \mathbb{R}^3$. Note that it is not necessary to explicitly model the lengths of the limbs as they can be inherently learned by means of trainable biases.

To calculate such a mapping with an RNN, each joint transformation is considered as a "computing time-step" in the RNN. Accordingly, the RNN requires only k input neurons, where k is the number of angles per joint – two in this paper. Thus, the computation is fully independent from the number of joints. The angle vectors $\boldsymbol{\varphi}^j$ are presented to the network in a sequential manner. As a result, the RNN is forced to use its recurrences to handle the repetitive character of computing chains of mostly very similar transformations [14]. After the RNN is trained on a sufficiently rich pool of training pairs, it is able to predict the pose chain of the arm given a sequence of angle vectors.

To control the arm, it is necessary to compute the inverse mapping, that is, an appropriate angle sequence given a desired pose chain. How this is achieved can best be explained by considering Fig. 1. First, the current arm configuration $\boldsymbol{\Phi}$ is processed by the RNN sequentially, producing corresponding pose chain estimates $(_1^0\tilde{\mathbf{A}}, \ldots, _N^0\tilde{\mathbf{A}})$. The discrepancies (loss) $\mathcal{L}$ between this estimated and the desired pose chain $(_1^0\overset{*}{\mathbf{A}}, \ldots, _N^0\overset{*}{\mathbf{A}})$ are back-propagated reversely through the unfolded RNN. The resulting input gradients are thus computed via

$$\frac{\partial \mathcal{L}}{\partial \varphi_i^j} = \sum_{h=1}^{H} \left[\frac{\partial net_h^j}{\partial \varphi_i^j} \frac{\partial \mathcal{L}}{\partial net_h^j} \right] = \sum_{h=1}^{H} w_{ih} \delta_h^j, \tag{2}$$

projecting the loss back onto the input sequence, where h indexes the hidden units and net_h^j denotes the weighted sum of inputs (or *net input*) into unit h at computation step j. Starting from any possible arm configuration, by following the negative gradient through the joint space in an iterative manner, a possible solution to the inverse mapping is generated. We thus update the joint angles in the following manner, which is essentially SGD with momentum:

$$\mathbf{\Phi}(\tau + 1) \longleftarrow \mathbf{\Phi}(\tau) - \eta \nabla_{\mathbf{\Phi}(\tau)} \mathcal{L} + \mu \left[\mathbf{\Phi}(\tau) - \mathbf{\Phi}(\tau - 1) \right], \tag{3}$$

where τ denotes the current iteration step, $\eta \in \mathbb{R}$ is a gradient scale factor (cf. learning rate in gradient descent learning), and the momentum is scaled with the rate $\mu \in \mathbb{R}$ (i.e., $\mu \approx 0.5$), which accelerates convergence when the gradient signal is weak. Independently of this tuning parameters, we also restrict the maximum update step size to regularize relatively high gradients, which results in a more uniform motion behavior.

As proposed previously [14], we also apply a target correction step, compensating the error of the forward model. This can be done when the real forward model is accessible during the optimization – for instance, by means of a mathematical formulation or a (visual) feedback mechanism. Instead of presenting the desired targets, encoded as vectors $\mathbf{z}^j \in \mathbb{R}^9$, we present "modified" versions $\tilde{\mathbf{z}}^j$ to the network when computing the loss. Let $\mathbf{u}^j \in \mathbb{R}^9$ be the true current pose and $\mathbf{y}^j \in \mathbb{R}^9$ the pose prediction of the RNN. We thus compute $\tilde{\mathbf{z}}^j$ with respect to a given $\mathbf{\Phi}$ as follows:

$$\tilde{\mathbf{z}}^j = \begin{bmatrix} \left[y_i^j + \gamma_1 (z_i^j - u_i^j) \right]_{1 \leq i \leq 3} \\ \left[y_k^j + \gamma_2 (z_k^j - u_k^j) \right]_{4 \leq k \leq 9} \end{bmatrix}, \tag{4}$$

where $\gamma_1, \gamma_2 \in [0, 1]$ are additional scaling factors, which scale the influence of the positional and the orientation discrepancy, respectively. This modification causes the RNN to converge towards the real target pose with high precision, effectively compensating for remaining forward model errors.

3   Selective Component Constraining

As formulated in the upper formalization, controlling the arm requires the presence of a full chain of desired poses with all associated components. Clearly this is impractical – especially for arms with lots of joints. It would be better if only particular components could be selectively included in the optimization process, while all other components should be optimized automatically. For instance, when moving a cup with a fluid in it, it is important to maintain a horizontal end-effector orientation, while the direction in the horizontal plain is not directly relevant. Previous studies have shown that such constraints can, for instance, be inferred by a programming by demonstration paradigm [1] or by means event boundary signal-oriented inference [7].

To enable the selective induction of constraints, we propose to use "don't care" signals, which we define as respective zero gradients in the unconstrained components. That is, don't cares do not induce any additional gradient signals to the backward pass, regardless of their forward pass estimates. As a result, full and arbitrarily selective control of the robot arm's behavior becomes possible.

4   Experimental Results

In this paper we focused on a simulated three dimensional 40-joint robot arm. Each joint can rotate along the x and the y axis, which is physically realizable easily. The entire arm thus has $2 \cdot 40 = 80$ DoF. For control, we used $\gamma_1 = 1.0, \gamma_2 = 0.1$ to equalize the magnitude of the position and orientation-induced gradients, as otherwise the orientation gradient would be numerically dominant.

Preliminary studies have shown that when training with SGD, it is difficult – for arms with 20+ joints even impossible – to learn to predict the poses of all intermediate joints (cf. Sect. 1). The following modifications ensured learning success: First, we dropped SGD and, instead, applied Adam [9], which is effectively more robust to gradient fluctuations and local minima, using the parameters $\beta_1 = 0.9, \beta_2 = 0.999$ (smoothing factors of the first two moment estimates) and a cautious learning rate of $\eta = 10^{-4}$. Second, we remodeled the training, into ten training episodes, which consisted of respective, randomly generated arm configurations, where the joint angle ranges were limited to 10%, 20%, 30% and so forth of the full range. The first nine sets contained 2 000 training examples, each, whereas the tenth set – in which the full angle ranges (here $\pm 45°$) are covered – contains 20 000 examples. In each training episode, 50 epochs were performed. The smallest possible amount of training data was not investigated.

The used RNN architecture consisted of two hidden layers with 24 LSTM blocks with intra-block connected gates [12]. This LSTM type is advantageous in regression tasks [13]. Each hidden block contained three inner cells and has variable biases for cells and gates, which is helpful when the computation involves spatial mappings [14]. Additionally, each hidden layer was not recurrently connected to itself, but both hidden layers were mutually fully connected. This was the best architecture discovered previously [14]. Our experiments have shown that this architecture, in combination with the training procedure detailed above, produces well performing RNNs reliably. All experiments were performed using the JANNLab neural network framework [11].

Figure 2 shows results when the task was to keep the end-effector pose horizontal, while approaching a certain target position. The was realized by presenting only the goal position and the upwards-orientation as targets, while the other components of the end-effector had assigned don't care signals. Figure 3 shows a related scenario, in which the goal was to follow an elliptic trajectory on a 2D vertical plane with the end-effector, while the orientation of the end-effector should remain horizontal. Again, the remaining components of the end-effector orientation are left free, as are all other components.

Figure 4 shows that it is also easily possible to fully fix the end-effector pose, while introducing targets to intermediate parts of the arm. In this example, the (x,y) position of the 20th joint was optimized, by following points on a virtual circle around the main axis of the arm.

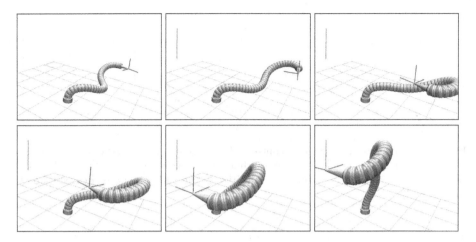

Fig. 2. This images sequence depicts the movement towards the target while an upright end-effector orientation is maintained (e.g. for handling fluids). The forward direction of the end-effector is assigned with a "don't care" signal, thus it is effectively ignored during the optimization, that is, the movement.

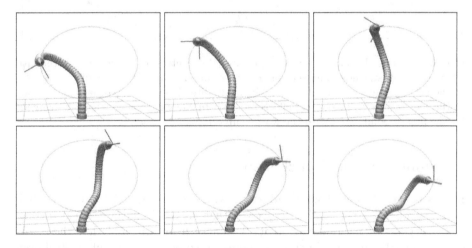

Fig. 3. Image sequence of a drawing/welding scenario. The target position for the end-effector tip moves along an elliptic trajectory on a 2D plane nearby the robot arm. The "forward" orientation of the target is fixed to the negative normal vector of the plane, while the "up" orientation is left free.

Finally, Fig. 5 demonstrates further possibilities of selective constraining joint components. Note that these kinds of constraints, and also those shown above, can be flexibly switched on and off on-the-fly, depending on the requirements of the current scenario or the current task.

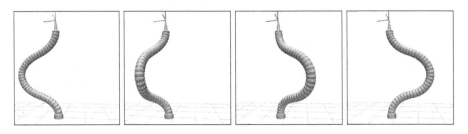

Fig. 4. Selective intermediate joint control. The x,y position of the 20th joint is defined following a circle around the main axis, while the end-effector pose is fixed. All other components of the arm (including the z position of the 20th joint) are left free ("don't care" signal).

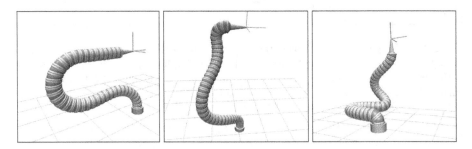

Fig. 5. Examples demonstrating intermediate joint control. In the left image the last 10 joints are constrained to have to same forward orientation as the end-effector target. In the center image the target of the "forward" direction of the sixth-last joint is set to the "up" direction of the end-effector target. In the right image, the "up" targets for the first 20 joints are set to the world's up direction (z-axis).

5   Summary and Conclusion

In this paper, we investigated and extended a procedure for RNN-based robot arm control [14]. Specifically, we showed that an RNN can be trained to predict the poses of intermediate joints within such an arm and that these can consequently be included in the controlling objective, enabling full control over all joints of an arm. Moreover, we showed that particular components of the arm's target can be selectively switched on and off by means of a "don't care" signal. This enabled us to handle constraints inherently and on-the-fly, without the need of any outer constraint mechanism, such as additional penalty terms. In several scenarios with a simulated three dimensional 40-joint robot arm, we demonstrated the effectiveness of our procedure.

The presented results underline the potential of this RNN-based approach for robot arm control. The approach is essentially inspired by an active inference [3–5] perspective on robot control, inferring motor commands by back-projecting error gradients between current and desired system states. We believe that similar techniques could be of practical interest for the novel field of continuum robots (c.f. e.g. [10]), for which precise and goal-directed control is still a major challenge.

Our future research will consider the addition of higher-level constraints, such as curvature optimization, by means of adding "constraint neurons", which will allow tuning the associated properties of the arm. Furthermore, we plan to include the dynamics of the arm as well, which requires extending the architecture in a multi-dimensional fashion [6]. Finally, we plan to combine this approach with options to project trajectory imaginations into the future, thus enabling trajectory optimization besides the current goal-directed arm state optimizations addressed in this paper.

References

1. Calinon, S., Guenter, F., Billard, A.: On learning, representing, and generalizing a task in a humanoid robot. IEEE Trans. Syst. Man Cybern. Part B Cybern. **37**(2), 286–298 (2007)
2. Ehrenfeld, S., Butz, M.V.: The modular modality frame model: continuous body state estimation and plausibility-weighted information fusion. Biol. Cybern. **107**, 61–82 (2013)
3. Friston, K.: The free-energy principle: a rough guide to the brain? Trends Cogn. Sci. **13**(7), 293–301 (2009)
4. Friston, K.: The free-energy principle: a unified brain theory? Nat. Rev. Neurosci. **11**(2), 127–138 (2010)
5. Friston, K., FitzGerald, T., Rigoli, F., Schwartenbeck, P., Pezzulo, G.: Active inference: a process theory. Neural Comput. **29**(1), 1–49 (2016)
6. Graves, A., Fernández, S., Schmidhuber, J.: Multi-dimensional recurrent neural networks. In: de Sá, J.M., Alexandre, L.A., Duch, W., Mandic, D. (eds.) ICANN 2007. LNCS, vol. 4668, pp. 549–558. Springer, Heidelberg (2007). doi:10.1007/978-3-540-74690-4_56
7. Gumbsch, C., Kneissler, J., Butz, M.V.: Learning behavior-grounded event segmentations. In: Papafragou, A., Grodner, D., Mirman, D., Trueswell, J.C. (eds.) Proceedings of the 38th Annual Meeting of the Cognitive Science Society, pp. 1787–1792. Cognitive Science Society, Austin (2016)
8. Hochreiter, S., Schmidhuber, J.: Long short-term memory. Neural Comput. **9**(8), 1735–1780 (1997)
9. Kingma, D.P., Ba, J.L.: Adam: A method for stochastic optimization. In: 3rd International Conference for Learning Representations abs/1412.6980 (2015)
10. Neumann, M., Burgner-Kahrs, J.: Considerations for follow-the-leader motion of extensible tendon-driven continuum robots. In: 2016 IEEE International Conference on Robotics and Automation (ICRA), pp. 917–923, May 2016
11. Otte, S., Krechel, D., Liwicki, M.: JANNLab neural network framework for Java. In: Poster Proceedings MLDM 2013, pp. 39–46. ibai-publishing, New York (2013)
12. Otte, S., Liwicki, M., Zell, A.: Dynamic cortex memory: enhancing recurrent neural networks for gradient-based sequence learning. In: Wermter, S., Weber, C., Duch, W., Honkela, T., Koprinkova-Hristova, P., Magg, S., Palm, G., Villa, A.E.P. (eds.) ICANN 2014. LNCS, vol. 8681, pp. 1–8. Springer, Cham (2014). doi:10.1007/978-3-319-11179-7_1

13. Otte, S., Liwicki, M., Zell, A.: An analysis of dynamic cortex memory networks. In: International Joint Conference on Neural Networks (IJCNN), pp. 3338–3345. Killarney, Ireland, July 2015

14. Otte, S., Zwiener, A., Hanten, R., Zell, A.: Inverse recurrent models – an application scenario for many-joint robot arm control. In: Villa, A.E.P., Masulli, P., Pons Rivero, A.J. (eds.) ICANN 2016. LNCS, vol. 9886, pp. 149–157. Springer, Cham (2016). doi:10.1007/978-3-319-44778-0_18

15. Schilling, M.: Universally manipulable body models - dual quaternion representations in layered and dynamic MMCs. Auton. Robots **30**, 399–425 (2011)

Neuromorphic Hardware

Accelerating Training of Deep Neural Networks via Sparse Edge Processing

Sourya Dey[✉], Yinan Shao, Keith M. Chugg, and Peter A. Beerel

Ming Hsieh Department of Electrical Engineering, University of Southern California,
Los Angeles, CA 90089, USA
{souryade,yinansha,chugg,pabeerel}@usc.edu

Abstract. We propose a reconfigurable hardware architecture for deep
neural networks (DNNs) capable of online training and inference, which
uses algorithmically pre-determined, structured sparsity to significantly
lower memory and computational requirements. This novel architecture
introduces the notion of edge-processing to provide flexibility and combines junction pipelining and operational parallelization to speed up
training. The overall effect is to reduce network complexity by factors
up to 30x and training time by up to 35x relative to GPUs, while maintaining high fidelity of inference results. This has the potential to enable
extensive parameter searches and development of the largely unexplored
theoretical foundation of DNNs. The architecture automatically adapts
itself to different network sizes given available hardware resources. As
proof of concept, we show results obtained for different bit widths.

Keywords: Machine learning · Neural networks · Deep neural networks · Sparsity · Online learning · Training acceleration · Hardware
optimizations · Pipelining · Edge processing · Handwriting recognition

1 Introduction

DNNs in machine learning systems are critical drivers of new technologies such
as natural language processing, autonomous vehicles, and speech recognition.
Modern DNNs and the corresponding training datasets are gigantic with millions
of parameters [14], which makes training a painfully slow and memory-consuming
experimental process. For example, one of the winning entries in the ImageNet
Challenge 2014 takes 2–3 weeks to train on 4 GPUs [16]. As a result, despite using
costly cloud computation resources, training is often forced to exclude large scale
optimizations over model structure and hyperparameters. This scenario severely
hampers the advancement of research into the limited theoretical understanding
of DNNs and, unfortunately, empirical optimizations remain as the only option.

Recent research into hardware architectures for DNNs has primarily focused
on inference only, while performing training *offline* [2,4,10,13,15,19]. Unfortunately, this precludes reconfigurability and results in a network incapable of
dynamically adapting itself to new patterns in data, which severely limits its

© Springer International Publishing AG 2017
A. Lintas et al. (Eds.): ICANN 2017, Part I, LNCS 10613, pp. 273–280, 2017.
https://doi.org/10.1007/978-3-319-68600-4_32

usability for pertinent real-world applications such as stock price prediction and spam filtering. Moreover, offline-only learning exacerbates the problem of slow DNN research and ultimately leads to lack of transparency at a time when precious little is understood about the working of DNNs.

There has been limited research into hardware architectures to support *online* training, such as [1,8,9]. However, due to the space-hungry nature of DNNs, these works have only managed to fit small networks on their prototypes. While other works [3,10–12,20] have proposed memory-efficient solutions for inference, none of them have addressed the cumbersome problem of online training. Therefore, a hardware architecture supporting online training and reconfiguration of large networks would be of great value for exploring a larger set of models for both empirical optimizations and enhanced scientific understanding of DNNs.

In this work, we propose a novel hardware architecture for accelerating training and inference of DNNs on FPGAs. Our key contributions are:

1. An architecture designed for FPGA implementation that can perform online training of large-scale DNNs.
2. A pre-defined, structured form of sparsity that starts off with an algorithmically deterministic sparse network from the very outset.
3. Edge-based processing – a technique that decouples the available hardware resources from the size and complexity of the network, thereby leading to tremendous flexibility and network reconfigurability.
4. Hardware-based optimizations such as operational parallelization and junction pipelining, which lead to large speedups in training.

The paper is organized as follows. Section 2 analyzes our proposed form of sparsity. Section 3 discusses our proposed technique of edge-based processing and interleaving, along with hardware optimizations. Then Sect. 4 presents hardware results and Sect. 5 concludes the paper.

2 Sparsity

The need for sparsity, or reducing the number of parameters in a network, stems from the fact that both the memory footprint and computational complexity of modern DNNs is enormous. For example, the well-studied DNN AlexNet [14] has a weight size of 234 MB and requires 635 million arithmetic operations only for feedforward processing [19]. Convolutional layers are sparse, but *locally connected*, i.e. the spatial span of neurons in a layer connecting to a neuron in the next layer is small. As a result, such layers alone are not suitable for performing inference and therefore need to be followed by fully-connected (FC) layers [14,16,18], which account for 95% of the connections in the network [19]. However, FC layers are typically over-parameterized [6,7] and tend to *overfit* to the training data, which results in inferior performance on test data. Dropout (deletion) of random neurons was proposed by [17], but incurs the disadvantage of having to train multiple differently configured networks, which are finally combined to regain the original full size network. Hashnet [3] randomly forced the same value on collections of weights, but acknowledged that "a significant number of nodes [get] disconnected from neighboring layers." Other sparsifying techniques such as pruning and quantization [11,12,20] first train the complete network, and then perform further computations to delete parameters, which increase the training time. In general, all of these architectures deal with the complete non-sparsified FC layers at some point of time during their usage cycle and therefore, fail to permanently solve the memory and complexity bottlenecks of DNNs.

Contrary to existing works, we propose a class of DNNs with *pre-specified sparsity*, implying that from the very beginning, neurons in a layer connect to only a subset of the neurons in the next layer. This means that the original network has a lower memory and computational complexity to begin with, and there are no additional computations to change the network structure. The degrees of *fan-out* and *fan-in* (number of connections to the next layer and from the previous layer, respectively) of each neuron are user-specified, and then the connections are algorithmically assigned. This ensures that no particular neuron gets disconnected, while the algorithm provides good *spatial spread* ensuring that activations from early layers can impact the output of the last layer.

As an example, consider MNIST digit classification over 5 epochs of training using a (784, 112, 10) network, i.e. there are 784 input, 112 hidden and 10 output neurons. If it is FC, the total number of weights is 88,928 (which is already less than other works such as [5]). Now suppose we preset the fan-out of the input and hidden neurons to 17 and 5, respectively. This leads to 13,888 total weights, implying that the overall network has 15% connectivity, or 85% sparsity. Figure 1 compares the performance of sparse networks, keeping all hyperparameters the same except for adjusting the learning rate to be inversely proportional to connectivity, which compensates for parameter reduction. Notice that 15% connectivity gives better performance than the original FC network. Moreover, 3% connectivity gives > 91% accuracy in 5 epochs, which is within 4% of the FC case. This leads us to believe that the memory and processor

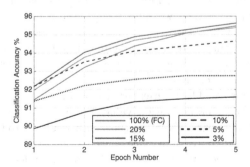

Fig. 1. Classification performance of a (784, 112, 10) network with varying connectivity percentage, trained for 5 epochs on the MNIST dataset.

requirements of FC layers in DNNs can be reduced by over 30x with minimal impact on performance.

3   Edge Processing and Interleaving

A DNN is made up of layers of interconnected neurons and the *junctions* between adjacent layers contain connections or *edges*, each having an associated *weight* value. The 3 major operations in a network are: (a) feedforward (FF), which primarily computes dot products between weights and the previous layer's activation values; (b) backpropagation (BP), which computes dot products between weights and the next layer's delta values and then multiplies them with derivatives of the previous layer's activations; and (c) update (UP), which multiplies delta values from the next layer with activation values from the previous layer to compute updates to the weights. Notice that the edges feature in all 3 operations, and this is where the motivation for our approach stems from.

We propose a DNN architecture which is processed from the point of view of its edges (i.e., weights), instead of its neurons. Every junction has a *degree of parallelism (DoP)*, denoted as z, which is the *number of edges processed in parallel*. All the weights in each junction are stored in a memory bank consisting of z memories. All the activation, activation derivative and delta values of each layer are also stored in separate memory banks of z memories each. The edges coming into a junction from its preceding layer are *interleaved*, or permuted, before getting connected to its succeeding layer. The interleaver algorithm is deterministic and reconfigurable. It serves to ensure good spatial spread and prevent regularity, thereby achieving a pseudo-random connection pattern. For example, if 4 edges come out of the first input neuron of the (784, 112, 10) network, they might connect to the 9th, 67th, 84th and 110th neuron in the hidden layer.

Figure 2a depicts a memory bank as a checkerboard, where each column is a memory. A single *cycle* of processing (say the nth) comprises accessing the nth cell in each of the z weight memories. This implies reading all z values from the same row (the nth), which we refer to as *natural order* access. Reading a row implies accessing weights of edges connected to consecutive neurons in the succeeding layer, since that's how they are numbered. Figure 2b gives an example where z is 6 and fan-in is 3. The interleaver determines which neurons in the preceding layer are connected to those z edges. For ideal spatial spread, these will be z different neurons. The interleaver algorithm is also designed to be *clash-free*, i.e. it ensures that the activation values of these z preceding neurons are stored in z different memories. Violating this condition leads to the same memory needing to be accessed more than once in the same cycle, i.e. a clash, which stalls processing. A consequence of clash-freedom and pseudo-random connection pattern is that the activation memories are accessed in *permuted order*, as shown in Fig. 2a, where there is only 1 shaded cell in each column.

Noting the significant data reuse between FF, BP and UP, we used *operational parallelization* to make all of them occur simultaneously. Since every

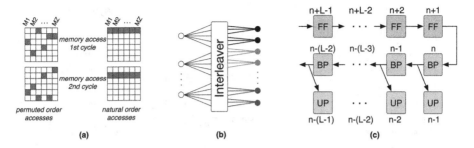

Fig. 2. (**a**): *Natural order* and *permuted order* access of memory banks. (**b**): reading $z = 6$ weights (corresponding to 2 succeeding layer neurons) in each cycle. (**c**): junction pipelining and operational parallelization in the whole network.

operation in a junction uses data generated by an adjacent junction or layer, we designed a *junction pipelining* architecture where all the junctions execute all 3 operations simultaneously on different inputs from the training set. This achieves a $3(L-1)$ times speedup, where L is the total number of layers. The high level view is shown in Fig. 2c. As an example, consider the (784, 112, 10) network. When the second junction is doing FF on input $n + 1$, it is also doing BP on the previous input n which just finished FF, as well as updating (UP) its weights from the finished BP results of input $n - 1$. Simultaneously, the first junction is doing FF on the latest input $n + 2$, BP on input $n - 1$, and UP using the BP results of input $n - 2$. Figure 3 shows the 3 simultaneous operations in more detail inside a single junction. Notice that the memories associated with layer parameters are both read from and written into during the same cycle. Moreover, the activation and its derivative memories need to store the FF results of a particular input until it comes back to the same layer during BP. Hence these memories are organized in queues. While this increases overall storage space, the fraction is insignificant compared to the memory required for weights. This problem is alleviated by using only 1 weight memory bank per junction for all 3 processes. Moreover, only 2 rows of this bank need to be accessed at a time, which makes efficient memory management techniques possible.

A key contribution of our architecture is that z can be set to any value depending on the area-speed tradeoff desired. z can be made small to process a large network slowly using limited hardware. For powerful FPGAs, z can be made large, which achieves tremendous increase in speed at the cost of a large number of multipliers. z can also be individually adjusted for each junction so that the number of clock cycles to process each junction is the same, which ensures an always full pipeline and no stalls. Thus, the size and complexity of the network is decoupled from the hardware resources available. Moreover, low values of connectivity alleviate challenges with weight storage for very large DNNs. Our architecture can be reconfigured to varying levels of fan-out and structured sparsity, which is neither possible in other online learning architectures such as [1,8,9], nor in architectures using forms of unstructured sparsity that suffer from

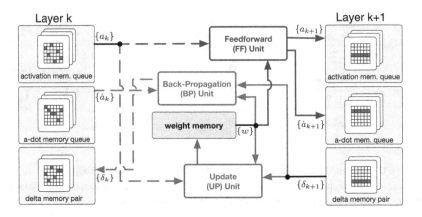

Fig. 3. Operational parallelization in a single junction between layers k and $k + 1$, showing natural and permuted order operations as solid and dashed lines, respectively.

the overhead of lookups and cache misses [18]. Thus, we achieve the ideal case of one-size-fits-all – an architecture that can adapt to a large class of sparse DNNs.

As a concrete example of speedup, consider the network formed by the FC layers of AlexNet. This has a (1728, 4096, 4096, 1000) neuron configuration and accounts for 6% of the computational complexity [14, 19]. Since the entire AlexNet takes 6 days to train on 2 GPUs for 90 epochs, we estimate that training only the FC network would take 0.36 days. The authors in [14] acknowledge the over-parameterization problem, so we estimate from the data for Fig. 1 that the same FC network with only 6% connectivity can be trained with minimal performance degradation. Using our architecture, modern Kintex Ultrascale FPGA boards will be able to support $z = 256$. This results in 4096 cycles being needed to train a junction, which, at a reasonable clock frequency of 250 MHz, processes each image through this sparse FC network in 16 μs. Training the network for the complete 1.2 million images over 90 epochs is estimated to take half an hour, which is a speedup of 35x over a single GPU.

4   Results

As proof of concept, we used Verilog Hardware Description Language to develop the register-transfer level (RTL) design for our hardware architecture, and simulated using the MNIST dataset for different fixed point bit widths. The neuron configuration is (1024, 64, 16) (we used powers of 2 for ease of hardware implementation and set the extra neurons to 0) and the fan-out for both junctions is 8, resulting in an 87% sparse network. The first and second junctions have $z = 512$ and $z = 32$, respectively. Figures 4a, b and c show histograms for the classification accuracy difference *"fixed point - floating point"* (i.e., more bars on the positive side indicate better fixed point performance). Figure 4d indicates that 10-bit fixed point (we used 3 integer bits and 7 fractional bits) for all network

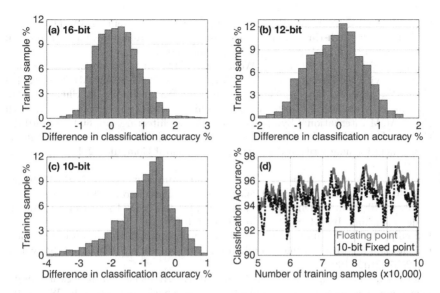

Fig. 4. (a), (b), (c): Classification accuracy difference histograms for 16-bit, 12-bit and 10-bit fixed point, respectively, with floating point. (d): Detailed comparison view of a portion of the network learning curves for 10-bit fixed point vs floating point.

parameters and computed values is sufficient to obtain classification performance very close to that of floating point simulations. The plots are for 10,000 training images over 10 epochs.

5   Conclusion and Future Work

This work presents a flexible architecture that can perform both training and inference of large and deep neural networks on hardware. Sparsity is preset, which greatly reduces the amount of memory and number of multiplier units required. A reconfigurable degree of parallel edge processing enables the architecture to adapt itself to any network size and hardware resource set, while junction pipelining and operational parallelization lead to fast and efficient performance. Our ultimate goal is to propel a paradigm shift from offline training on CPUs and GPUs to online training using the speed and ease of reconfigurability offered by FPGAs and custom chips. Future work would involve extension to other types of networks, tackling memory bandwidth issues, and extensive parameter space exploration to advance the limited theoretical understanding of DNNs.

References

1. Ahn, B.: Computation of deep belief networks using special-purpose hardware architecture. In: IJCNN-2014, pp. 141–148 (2014)

2. Chen, T., Du, Z., Sun, N., Wang, J., Wu, C., Chen, Y., Temam, O.: Diannao: a small-footprint high-throughput accelerator for ubiquitous machine-learning. In: ASPLOS-2014, pp. 269–284. ACM, New York (2014)
3. Chen, W., Wilson, J.T., Tyree, S., Weinberger, K.Q., Chen, Y.: Compressing neural networks with the hashing trick. In: ICML-2015, pp. 2285–2294. JMLR.org (2015)
4. Chen, Y., Luo, T., Liu, S., Zhang, S., He, L., Wang, J., Li, L., Chen, T., Xu, Z., Sun, N., Temam, O.: Dadiannao: a machine-learning supercomputer. In: 47th IEEE/ACM International Symposium on Microarchitecture, pp. 609–622 (2014)
5. Cireşan, D.C., Meier, U., Gambardella, L.M., Schmidhuber, J.: Deep, big, simple neural nets for handwritten digit recognition. Neural Comput. **22**(12), 3207–3220 (2010)
6. Cun, Y.L., Denker, J.S., Solla, S.A.: Optimal brain damage. In: NIPS-1989, pp. 598–605. Morgan Kaufmann Publishers Inc., San Francisco (1989)
7. Denil, M., Shakibi, B., Dinh, L., Ranzato, M., Freitas, N.D.: Predicting parameters in deep learning. In: NIPS-2013, pp. 2148–2156 (2013)
8. Eldredge, J.G., Hutchings, B.L.: Rrann: a hardware implementation of the back-propagation algorithm using reconfigurable FPGAs. In: IEEE ICNN-1994, vol. 4, pp. 2097–2102 (1994)
9. Gadea, R., Cerdá, J., Ballester, F., Mocholí, A.: Artificial neural network implementation on a single FPGA of a pipelined on-line backpropagation. In: ISSS-2000, pp. 225–230. IEEE Computer Society, Washington (2000)
10. Han, S., Liu, X., Mao, H., Pu, J., Pedram, A., Horowitz, M.A., Dally, W.J.: EIE: Efficient inference engine on compressed deep neural network. In: ISCA-2016, pp. 243–254 (2016)
11. Han, S., Mao, H., Dally, W.J.: Deep compression: compressing deep neural networks with pruning, trained quantization and huffman coding. In: ICLR-2016 (2016)
12. Han, S., Pool, J., Tran, J., Dally, W.: Learning both weights and connections for efficient neural network. In: NIPS-2015, pp. 1135–1143 (2015)
13. Himavathi, S., Anitha, D., Muthuramalingam, A.: Feedforward neural network implementation in FPGA using layer multiplexing for effective resource utilization. IEEE Trans. Neural Networks **18**(3), 880–888 (2007)
14. Krizhevsky, A., Sutskever, I., Hinton, G.E.: Imagenet classification with deep convolutional neural networks. In: NIPS-2012, pp. 1097–1105 (2012)
15. Sanni, K., Garreau, G., Molin, J.L., Andreou, A.G.: FPGA implementation of a deep belief network architecture for character recognition using stochastic computation. In: CISS-2015, pp. 1–5 (2015)
16. Simonyan, K., Zisserman, A.: Very deep convolutional networks for large-scale image recognition. CoRR abs/1409.1556 (2014). http://arxiv.org/abs/1409.1556
17. Srivastava, N., Hinton, G., Krizhevsky, A., Sutskever, I., Salakhutdinov, R.: Dropout: a simple way to prevent neural networks from overfitting. J. Mach. Learn. Res. **15**, 1929–1958 (2014)
18. Szegedy, C., Liu, W., Jia, Y., Sermanet, P., Reed, S., Anguelov, D., Erhan, D., Vanhoucke, V., Rabinovich, A.: Going deeper with convolutions. In: CVPR-2015, pp. 1–9 (2015)
19. Zhang, C., Wu, D., Sun, J., Sun, G., Luo, G., Cong, J.: Energy-efficient CNN implementation on a deeply pipelined FPGA cluster. In: ISLPED-2016, pp. 326–331. ACM, New York (2016)
20. Zhou, X., Li, S., Qin, K., Li, K., Tang, F., Hu, S., Liu, S., Lin, Z.: Deep adaptive network: an efficient deep neural network with sparse binary connections. CoRR abs/1604.06154 (2016). http://arxiv.org/abs/1604.06154

Unsupervised Learning Using Phase-Change Synapses and Complementary Patterns

Severin Sidler[1,2], Angeliki Pantazi[1(✉)], Stanisław Woźniak[1,2], Yusuf Leblebici[2], and Evangelos Eleftheriou[1]

[1] IBM Research – Zurich, Säumerstrasse 4, 8803 Rüschlikon, Switzerland
`agp@zurich.ibm.com`

[2] Microelectronic Systems Laboratory, EPFL, 1015 Lausanne, Switzerland

Abstract. Neuromorphic systems using memristive devices provide a brain-inspired alternative to the classical von Neumann processor architecture. In this work, a spiking neural network (SNN) implemented using phase-change synapses is studied. The network is equipped with a winner-take-all (WTA) mechanism and a spike-timing-dependent synaptic plasticity rule realized using crystal-growth dynamics of phase-change memristors. We explore various configurations of the synapse implementation and we demonstrate the capabilities of the phase-change-based SNN as a pattern classifier using unsupervised learning. Furthermore, we enhance the performance of the SNN by introducing an input encoding scheme that encodes information from both the original and the complementary pattern. Simulation and experimental results of the phase-change-based SNN demonstrate the learning accuracies on the MNIST handwritten digits benchmark.

Keywords: Neuromorphic systems · Phase-change devices · Unsupervised learning · Classification

1 Introduction

Neuromorphic computing is inspired by the distributed architecture of the human brain. This architecture offers parallel processing capabilities and high error tolerance, while consuming only 20 W of power. Neuromorphic systems are typically based on a Spiking Neural Network (SNN) model, in which computation relies on all-or-none spike-based communication between a large number of spiking neurons, which is energy-efficient given the temporal sparsity of the spikes arriving at the synapses. Nanoscale synapses can be realized using memristive properties of nanodevices, such as ones built using phase-change materials [1]. Using dense crossbar arrays of memristive elements enables massively parallel and highly area- and energy-efficient implementation, as the dynamics and the plasticity of the memristive synapses are used to realize both the memory and the distributed computing function of these systems.

In SNNs, a winner-take-all (WTA) mechanism is typically used to introduce competition between the neurons, which learn according to different variations

© Springer International Publishing AG 2017
A. Lintas et al. (Eds.): ICANN 2017, Part I, LNCS 10613, pp. 281–288, 2017.
https://doi.org/10.1007/978-3-319-68600-4_33

of the spike-timing-dependent plasticity (STDP) rule. The performance of SNNs trained in an unsupervised way using STDP rules has been studied extensively in simulations using the MNIST handwritten digits benchmark. As compared in [2], even though the best performance is achieved with supervised methods, the unsupervised approaches achieve good classification accuracies. In the context of memristive implementation of the synapses, the accuracy may be further affected due to the variability of the devices and the simplified implementation of the STDP mechanism. For instance, in a phase-change-based synapse implementation, the asymmetric conductance response is critical in the design of the synapse and the STDP learning rule [3,4]. In terms of the variability, even though there are several simulation studies demonstrating the effect [2], there is no experimental demonstration of the accuracies on the MNIST classification in an unsupervised SNN with memristive synapses.

In this work, we demonstrate the capabilities of an SNN architecture equipped with phase-change synapses. We evaluate different configurations of phase-change-based synaptic implementations along with the STDP-based learning rule. To enhance the SNN performance, we introduce a novel variant of the input encoding scheme. This variant encodes information in form of both the original and an additional complementary pattern. For the study of the phase-change-based SNN architecture, simulations using a matched model of the phase-change cells as well as experiments on a prototype neuromorphic hardware platform are performed. The unsupervised pattern learning capabilities are demonstrated on the MNIST handwritten digits recognition task.

2   Phase-Change Synapses

In the phase-change-based implementation of a synapse, the synaptic weight is stored in the phase configuration of the device and is altered through an application of a current pulse. Phase-change materials exhibit a large difference in resistivity between amorphous (high resistivity) and crystalline (low resistivity) phase. The transition from the amorphous phase to the crystalline phase is realized through the application of crystallizing pulses, which heat the material above the crystallization temperature and gradually alter the device conductance. This gradual characteristic offers incremental learning capability in a phase-change synapse. Figure 1(a) shows the conductance response after consecutive application of crystallizing pulses. In order to recreate the amorphous region, a higher amplitude current pulse is applied, which involves melting the phase-change material. The abrupt cutoff of the pulse causes the molten material to quench back to the amorphous phase. While the abrupt reset is tolerable in binary memory applications, it can become critical in phase-change synapses by instantly forgetting all the information that had been previously learned over a longer period of time. Besides the asymmetric conductance response, the phase-change synapses exhibit large variability. Figure 1 (b) shows a histogram of the cell conductances after application of 10 crystallizing pulses. It is important to study the impact of wide distribution of the synaptic weights during learning on the performance of the neuromorphic algorithm.

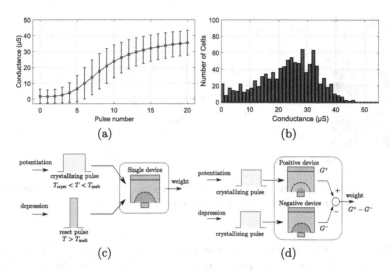

Fig. 1. Phase-change synapses: (a) Experimental conductance response as a function of the number of applied crystallizing pulses. (b) Histogram of the conductance response of 1000 devices after application of 10 crystallizing pulses. (c) Synapse realization using a single phase-change device per synapse. (d) Synapse realization using two phase-change devices in a differential configuration.

To characterize the impact of the synapse realization on the performance of an SNN, we evaluate two phase-change synapse configurations. In the first scheme, a single device per synapse is used and the learning mechanism is adapted to accommodate for the abrupt reset. The concept is illustrated in Fig. 1 (c) and described in detail in [3]. Here, a crystallizing pulse is used for potentiation, whereas a reset pulse reamorphizes the material at each depression event. This approach has a very simple implementation, although the disadvantage is that synapses easily forget the information and have to continuously relearn. In the second scheme, two devices are used in a differential way in the synapse implementation. The concept is illustrated in Fig. 1 (d) and described in detail in [5]. Here, the weight is encoded as the difference between a positively contributing conductance G^+ and a negatively contributing conductance G^-. In this way, the weight is increased by increasing the G^+ conductance whereas for the weight decrease the G^- conductance is increased. This approach has the advantage that the reset is no longer used during learning, although cyclic conductance rebalancing is required to avoid saturation of the G^+ and G^- conductances.

3   Neuromorphic System

A neuromorphic architecture with phase-change synapses is employed for MNIST classification. The task of the network is to recognize which digit is represented in the input and to classify it into one of the ten classes. In the first step, the

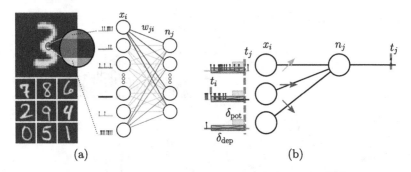

Fig. 2. Neuromorphic system: (a) SNN architecture for MNIST classification. (b) Learning mechanism with two timing windows.

network clusters the inputs in an unsupervised way, based on the similarity of appearance, and every neuron represents one cluster. In the second step, using the labels, every cluster is assigned to one class. Finally, the accuracy is defined based on the classification performance of the network. In this section, we describe the details of the SNN architecture and the classification procedure.

The network consists of a single layer with all-to-all synaptic connections, as shown in Fig. 2 (a). The input patterns consist of 28×28 pixel grayscale images that are presented to the network using a rate-encoding scheme. Specifically, the pixel intensity is linearly mapped to a spiking frequency. These frequencies are used as mean frequencies in random Poisson processes to generate the spike inputs, x_i. The architecture consists of 50 output neurons, n_j, implementing the leaky integrate-and-fire model. To introduce competition between the output neurons, a WTA mechanism is applied. The WTA scheme selects one winning neuron among all that cross the firing threshold. The selection is based on the difference between the respective membrane potential and the firing threshold. Furthermore, to ensure that all neurons participate in learning, the threshold voltages are adapted to their respective stimuli using homeostasis, similarly to [6].

For the learning mechanism, we used a modified version of the scheme presented in [6]. Two time windows are defined, δ_{pot} and δ_{dep}, as shown in Fig. 2 (b). When an output neuron n_j spikes at a time instant t_j, the corresponding synaptic weights are modified depending on the time t_i of their last input spike. If $t_j - t_i < \delta_{\mathrm{pot}}$, the synapse w_{ji} gets potentiated. In the case where, $t_j - t_i > \delta_{\mathrm{dep}}$, the synapse gets depressed. In all other cases, the synaptic weight remains unchanged. The introduction of two windows in the learning mechanism aims to reduce the number of the applied reset pulses, especially in the case of a phase-change synapse implemented with a single device.

Three phases were used to perform the MINST classification task:

– Training phase: During this phase, the samples from the training set are used as inputs. The synaptic weights are updated according to the learning mechanism and the thresholds are adjusted following the homeostasis rule.

– Validation phase: To assign a class to every neuron, the last 10000 samples from the training set are used. The network is executed with both learning mechanism and homeostasis deactivated. Based on the number of the firing events, every neuron is assigned to the class for which it spikes the most.
– Evaluation phase: During this phase, the test set from the MNIST database is used. Every input sample is classified to the class with the most output spikes and the classification accuracy is calculated.

4   Encoding Using Complementary Pattern

The input patterns in the neuromorphic architecture described in the previous section are presented in the form of spikes that carry a single bit of information. This is an inherent characteristic of SNNs, in which only the active information is used. In consequence, dark pixels are not distinguished from the absence of input. In rate-based artificial neural networks (ANNs), this issue is solved with the use of signed weights and inputs. Here, we propose to enhance the SNN network by encoding the input with information from a complementary pattern input, as presented in Fig. 3. For example, in the case of the MNIST image inputs, the complementary pattern inputs will simply encode the negative image. To apply this scheme, we double the number of input neurons as well as the number of synapses. The number of output neurons, along with their mode of operation in the SNN architecture, remains the same.

The proposed encoding scheme is beneficial in the case of synapses implemented with a single phase-change device. The benefits arise because two devices are used to represent the same information: one stores the original input and the other its complement. The number of devices are the same compared to the scheme with two phase-change devices per synapse but the implementation is simpler since there is no need for an additional mechanism for subtraction. Furthermore, there is no need for cyclic conductance rebalancing. Note that, the proposed approach is an input encoding scheme and can be implemented independently of the synapse configuration. Specifically, the input information from

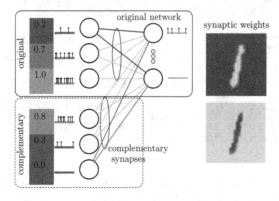

Fig. 3. Network architecture with complementary pattern inputs.

the complementary pattern could be beneficial for improving the performance of an SNN, especially for cases with high overlap between input patterns.

5   Simulation Results

The performance of the SNN architecture was evaluated for four different configurations. In the first configuration, the SNN was simulated with ideal synaptic weights. The weights were linear, bidirectional and bounded, but with an asymmetry between the potentiation and depression. This configuration provides the highest accuracy that can be reached with the specific network independent of synapse realization. The network reached a test set classification accuracy of 77.7%. The final weights are represented in Fig. 4 (a). The accuracy results are similar to the ones reported in the literature for similar network size [6]. As reported in that study, the performance of the network scales with the number of neurons.

Next, the synapse configuration with a single phase-change device per synapse was simulated. This is the simplest configuration with phase-change synapses. The synapses of the SNN were modelled using the experimentally measured phase-change conductance response for the potentiation. For the depression, the synapses were reset directly to the high resistance state. The simulation results yielded a test set accuracy of 55.55% and the weights are presented in Fig. 4 (b). Note that the simulation does not include device variability. Therefore, the significant drop in accuracy is attributed to the abrupt depression characteristics of the simulated phase-change synapses.

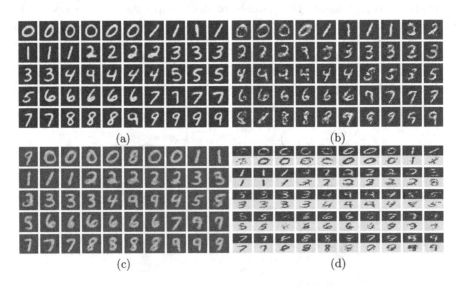

Fig. 4. Synaptic weights: (a) ideal synapse, (b) single phase-change device per synapse, (c) synapse with two phase-change devices in a differential configuration, (d) single phase-change device per synapse with complementary pattern encoding.

To avoid the impact of the asymmetric abrupt conductance response, the third synapse configuration used two phase-change devices per synapse in a differential configuration. We simulated the differential configuration scheme using the phase-change model and reached a test set accuracy of 73.73%. The reduction in the accuracy compared to the ideal synapse realization is due to the nonlinear response of the phase-change synapse. The final weights are presented in Fig. 4(c).

Finally, to evaluate the benefits of the complementary pattern scheme, we simulated the single-device phase-change synapse and we used a negative of the pattern as the complementary input. The final weights are presented in Fig. 4 (d). The simulation achieved a good test set accuracy of 68.61%. The complementary pattern provided an improvement of approximately 13% points over the simulation using a single phase-change device. Though, compared to the differential conductance configuration, there is a small reduction in performance. The main benefits here are from the simpler implementation and the fact that there is no need for cyclic conductance rebalancing operation. In terms of the stored information in the phase-change devices, the two schemes learn similar content. The difference is that in the differential configuration the stored information is a result of compound synapses' operation, whereas in the complementary pattern scheme it is induced by the additional inputs connected to the synapses.

6 Experimental Results

The performance of the phase-change SNN was further studied by experimentally realizing two network configurations. Specifically, the differential synapse approach was compared to the complementary pattern scheme implemented with a single-device synapse. The total number of phase-change devices is the same for both schemes. The hardware platform is described in detail in [7]. It consists of a prototype phase-change chip fabricated in 90 nm CMOS technology. The phase-change devices are of mushroom-type with doped $Ge_2Sb_2Te_5$ phase-change material. The phase-change devices implement the synapses of the SNN in hardware whereas the learning mechanism and the LIF neurons are emulated in software.

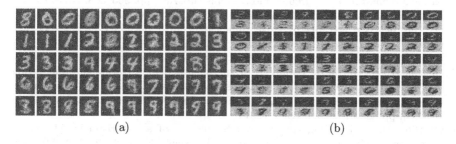

| (a) | (b) |

Fig. 5. Experimental results of synaptic weights: (a) synapse with two phase-change devices in a differential configuration, (b) single phase-change device per synapse with complementary pattern encoding.

The experimental weights for the differential synapse configuration and the complementary pattern approach with a single-device are shown in Fig. 5(a) and (b), respectively. The MNIST test set accuracy for the differential synapse is 68.14%. Due to the variability and imperfections of the phase-change devices, there is a reduction in the accuracy compared to the simulation, but the performance is good, especially considering the small size of the network. The complementary pattern with a single-device per synapse reached an accuracy of 59.20%. Given the simplicity of the scheme, the performance in the MNIST classification task is remarkably good. The proposed complementary pattern approach enabled performance improvement for the single-device per synapse configuration. Independently of the synapse configuration, additional benefits of the scheme are worth further investigation.

7   Conclusion

We demonstrated the learning capabilities of an SNN with phase-change synapses for the MNIST handwritten digits dataset. The impact on the classification accuracy of the asymmetric phase-change characteristics and the nonlinear conductance response was analyzed for four different network configurations. The differential synapse configuration achieved the highest accuracy which was further demonstrated with experimental results. Finally, we proposed an encoding scheme using complementary patterns and demonstrated the potential of this approach by substantially improving the performance of the simpler synapse design with a single device per synapse.

References

1. Kuzum, D., Jeyasingh, R.G.D., Lee, B., Wong, H.S.P.: Nanoelectronic programmable synapses based on phase change materials for brain-inspired computing. Nano Lett. **12**(5), 2179–2186 (2012)
2. Diehl, P.U., Cook, M.: Unsupervised learning of digit recognition using spike-timing-dependent plasticity. Front. Comput. Neurosci. **9** (2015)
3. Woźniak, S., Tuma, T., Pantazi, A., Eleftheriou, E.: Learning spatio-temporal patterns in the presence of input noise using phase-change memristors. In: IEEE International Symposium on Circuits and Systems (ISCAS), pp. 365–368. IEEE (2016)
4. Ambrogio, S., Ciocchini, N., Laudato, M., Milo, V., Pirovano, A., Fantini, P., Ielmini, D.: Unsupervised learning by spike timing dependent plasticity in phase change memory (PCM) synapses. Front. Neurosci. **10** (2016)
5. Burr, G., Shelby, R., di Nolfo, C., Jang, J., Shenoy, R., Narayanan, P., Virwani, K., Giacometti, E., Kurdi, B., Hwang, H.: Experimental demonstration and tolerancing of a large-scale neural network (165,000 synapses), using phase-change memory as the synaptic weight element. In: 2014 IEEE International Electron Devices Meeting (IEDM), pp. 29.5.1–29.5.4. IEEE (2014)
6. Querlioz, D., Bichler, O., Gamrat, C.: Simulation of a memristor-based spiking neural network immune to device variations. In: Neural Networks, IJCNN 2011, pp. 1775–1781. IEEE (2011)
7. Pantazi, A., Woźniak, S., Tuma, T., Eleftheriou, E.: All-memristive neuromorphic computing with level-tuned neurons. Nanotechnology **27**(35) (2016). 355205

Brain Topology and Dynamics

The Variational Coupled Gaussian Process Dynamical Model

Dmytro Velychko, Benjamin Knopp, and Dominik Endres[(✉)]

Department of Psychology, University of Marburg,
Gutenbergstr. 18, 35032 Marburg, Germany
dmytro.velychko@staff.uni-marburg.de,
{benjamin.knopp,dominik.endres}@uni-marburg.de

Abstract. We present a full variational treatment of the Coupled Gaussian Process Dynamical Model (CGPDM) with non-marginalized coupling mappings. The CGPDM generates high-dimensional trajectories from coupled low-dimensional latent dynamical models. The deterministic variational treatment obviates the need for sampling and facilitates the use of the CGPDM on larger data sets. The non-marginalized coupling mappings allow for a flexible exchange of the constituent dynamics models at run time. This exchange possibility is crucial for the construction of modular movement primitive models. We test the model against the marginalized CGPDM, dynamic movement primitives and temporal movement primitives, finding that the CGPDM generally outperforms the other models. Human observers can hardly distinguish CGPDM-generated movements from real human movements.

Keywords: Gaussian process · Variational methods · Movement primitives · Modularity

1 Introduction and Related Work

Planning and execution of human full-body movements is a formidable control problem for the brain. Modular movement primitives (MP) have been suggested as a means to simplify this control problem while retaining a sufficient degree of control flexibility for a wide range of task, see [4] for a review. 'Modular' in this context usually refers to the existence of an operation which allows for the combination of (simple) primitives into (complex) movements.

Technical applications of modular MPs have also been devised. For example in computer graphics, especially combined with dynamics models [7] and robotics, e.g. the dynamical MP (DMP) [9]. Each DMP is encoded by a canonical second order differential equation with guaranteeable stability properties and learnable parameters.

To lift the restriction of canonical dynamics, the Coupled Gaussian Process Dynamical Model (CGPDM) [17] learns both the dynamics mappings and their coupling for a given movement. The learning is accomplished in a Gaussian

© Springer International Publishing AG 2017
A. Lintas et al. (Eds.): ICANN 2017, Part I, LNCS 10613, pp. 291–299, 2017.
https://doi.org/10.1007/978-3-319-68600-4_34

process framework. The Gaussian process (GP) is a machine learning staple for classification and regression tasks. It can be interpreted as an abstraction of a neural network with a large, possibly infinite, hidden layer. Its advantages include theoretical elegance, tractability and closed-form solutions for posterior densities. It affords high flexibility but has poor (cubic) runtime scaling in the data set size. We improve this scaling with deterministic, sparse variational approximations using small sets of inducing points (IPs) and associated values [16] for each MP, resulting in the 'variational CGPDM' (vCGPDM). This yields a linear run-time dependence on the number of data points.

The CGPDM builds on the Gaussian process dynamical model (GPDM) [18], where a latent dynamics model is mapped onto observations by functions drawn from a GP. The GPDM can model the variability of human movements [15]. Sparse variational approximations have been developed for GPDM-like architectures [6] and even deep extensions thereof [11]. However, with the exception of the CGPDM, all these approaches have a 'monolithic' latent space(s) and thus lack the modularity of MPs. While deriving a variational approximation is not trivial, we expect it to avoid overfitting and yield a good bound on the marginal likelihood [2].

Our target application here is human movement modeling, but the vCGPDM could be easily applied to other systems where modularized control is beneficial, e.g. humanoid robotics [5].

We introduce the vCGPDM in Sect. 2. In Sect. 3, we first benchmark the vCGPDM against other MP models. Second, we determine the degree of human-tolerable sparseness in a psychophysics experiment. In Sect. 4 we propose future research.

2   The Model

A CGPDM is basically a number of GPDMs (the 'parts') run in parallel, with coupling between the latent space dynamics. See [17] for a graphical model representation. The model operates in discrete time $t = 0, \ldots, T$. For every part $i = 1, \ldots, M$ there is a Q^i-dimensional latent space with second-order autoregressive dynamics and inputs from the latent spaces of the other parts. Let $\boldsymbol{x}_t^i \in \mathbb{R}^{Q^i}$ be the state of latent space i at time t. Then

$$\boldsymbol{x}_t^i = \boldsymbol{f}^i(\boldsymbol{x}_{t-2}^1, \boldsymbol{x}_{t-1}^1, \ldots, \boldsymbol{x}_{t-2}^M, \boldsymbol{x}_{t-1}^M). \tag{1}$$

We chose a second-order model, because our target application is human movement modeling, and the literature indicates (e.g. [15]) that this is a good choice for this task. However, we note that this can be easily changed in the model. The latent states $\boldsymbol{x}_t^i$ give rise to D^i-dimensional observations $\boldsymbol{y}_t^i \in \mathbb{R}^{D^i}$ via functions $\boldsymbol{g}^i(.)$ plus isotropic Gaussian noise η_t^i

$$\boldsymbol{y}_t^i = \boldsymbol{g}^i(\boldsymbol{x}_t^i) + \eta_t^i \tag{2}$$

The functions $\boldsymbol{g}^i(.)$ are drawn from a GP prior with zero mean function and a suitable kernel. In a vCGPDM, the functions $\boldsymbol{f}^i(\ldots)$ are also drawn from a

GP prior with zero mean function, and a kernel that is derived with product-of-experts (PoE, [8]) coupling between the latent spaces of the different parts, as described by [17]: each part generates a Gaussian prediction about every part (i.e. including itself). Let $x_t^{i,j} = f^{i,j}(x_{t-2}^i, x_{t-1}^i)$ be the mean of the prediction of part i about part j at time index t, and $\alpha^{i,j}$ its variance. Following the standard PoE construction of multiplying the densities of the individual predictions and re-normalizing, one finds

$$
p(x_t^j | x_t^{:,j}, \alpha^{:,j}) = \frac{\exp\left[-\frac{1}{2\alpha^j} \left(x_t^j - \alpha^j \sum_i \frac{x_t^{i,j}}{\alpha^{i,j}} \right)^2 \right]}{(2\pi\alpha^j)^{\frac{Q^j}{2}}} \propto \prod_i \mathcal{N}\left(x_t^j | x_t^{i,j}, \alpha^{i,j} \right) \quad (3)
$$

where $\alpha^j = \left(\sum_i \alpha_{i,j}^{-1} \right)^{-1}$. It was shown in [17] that the individual predictions $x_t^{i,j}$ can be marginalized out in closed form. We will keep the individual predictions, because this allows us to couple a previously learned dynamics model for a part (including its predictions about the other parts) to any other dynamics model for the other parts, thus obtaining a modular MP model.

The form of Eq. 3 indicates the function of the coupling variances: the smaller a given variance, the more important the prediction of the generating part. When the $\alpha^{i,j}$ are optimized during learning, the model is able to discover which couplings are important for predicting the data, and which ones are not, see [17]. Put differently, if an $\alpha^{i,j}$ is small compared to $\alpha^{i' \neq i, j}$, then part i is able to make a prediction about part j with (relatively) high certainty. Furthermore, as demonstrated in [17], the $\alpha^{i,j}$ can be modulated after learning to generate novel movements which were not in the training data.

The basic CGPDM exhibits the usual cubic run time scaling with the number of data points, which prohibits learning from large data sets. We therefore developed a sparse variational approximation, following the treatment in [11,16]. We augment the model with IPs r^i and associated values v^i such that $g^i(r^i) = v^i$ for the latent-to-observed mappings $g^i(X^i)$ (referred to as 'LVM IPs' in the following), and condition the probability density of the function values of $g^i(X^i)$ on these points/values, which we assume to be a sufficient statistic. We apply the same augmentation strategy to reduce the computational effort for learning the dynamics mappings, which are induced by $z^{i,j}$ and $u^{i,j}$ (referred to as 'dynamics IP').

Key assumption of the vCGPDM: To obtain a tractable variational posterior distribution q over the latent states $x_t^i = (x_{t,1}^i, \ldots, x_{t,Q^i}^i)$, we choose a distribution that factorizes across time steps $0, \ldots, T$, parts $1, \ldots, M$ and dimensions $1, \ldots, Q^i$ within parts, and assume that the individual distributions are Gaussian:

$$
q(x_0^1, \ldots, x_T^M) = \prod_{t=0}^{T} \prod_{i=1}^{M} \prod_{q=1}^{Q^i} q(x_{t,q}^i) \; ; \quad q(x_{t,q}^i) = \mathcal{N}(\mu_{t,q}^i, \sigma_{t,q}^{2,i}). \quad (4)
$$

This approximation assumption is clearly a gross simplification of the correct latent state posterior. However, it allows us to make analytical progress: a free-energy evidence lower bound, ELBO (see Eq. 8 of [16] and Eq. S20 in the online supplementary material[1]) can now be computed in closed form if we choose the right kernels for the GPs. We opt for an ARD (automatic relevance detection) squared exponential kernel [3] for every part-i-to-j prediction GP:

$$k^{i,j}(\boldsymbol{X}, \boldsymbol{X}') = \exp\left(-\frac{1}{2}\sum_q^{Q^i} \frac{(\boldsymbol{X}_q - \boldsymbol{X}'_q)^2}{\lambda_q^{i,j}}\right). \tag{5}$$

and a radial basis function kernel for the latent-to-observed mappings. The computations yielding the ELBO are lengthy (and error-prone) but straightforward. The details can be found in Sect. 2 of the online supplementary material. Whether our simplistic approximation assumption (Eq. 4) is useful depends on the data, but at least for human movement it seems appropriate (see Sect. 3).

3 Results

We implemented the model in `Python 2.7` using the machine-learning framework `Theano` [1] for automatic differentiation to enable gradient-based maximization of the ELBO with the `scipy.optimize.fmin_l_bfgs_b` routine [10]. Latent space trajectories were initialized with PCA.

While the sparse approximations in the vCGPDM greatly reduce the memory consumption of the model, they might also introduce errors. Also, our fully factorized latent posterior approximation (Eq. 4) might be too simple. We tried to quantify these errors in a cross-validatory model comparison, and in a human perception experiment.

3.1 Human Movement Data

Comparisons were carried out on human movement data. We recorded these data with a 10-camera PhaseSpace Impulse motion capture system, mapped them onto a skeleton with 19 joints and computed joint angles in angle-axis representation, yielding a total of 60 degrees of freedom. The actors were instructed to walk straight with a natural arm swing, and to walk while waving both arms. Five walking-only and four walking+waving sequences each were used to train the models.

3.2 MAP Is Worse Than Variational Approximation

To check how the predictive quality is affected by our sparse variational approximation, we conducted a comparison by five/four-fold cross-validation of the following models for walking/walking+waving. Our cross-validation score is the kinematics mean squared error (MSE), computed after dynamic time warping

---

[1] Available at http://uni-marburg.de/wk8Vf or from the authors.

[14] of trajectories generated by initializing the model to the first two frames of a held-out trial onto the complete held-out trial: (1) a GPDM with maximum-a-posteriori (MAP) estimation of the latent variables [18], called MAP GPDM in Fig. 1. (2) a fully marginalized two-part (upper/lower body) CGPDM with MAP estimation of the latent variables [17], called MAP CGPDM U+L. (3) Their variational counterparts, vCGPDM U+L and vGPDM. We experimented with # LVM IPs= 4, ..., 30, and # dynamics IPs = 2, ..., 30. The MSE optima were near 10–15 IPs for both. All latent spaces were three-dimensional. (4) Temporal movement primitives (instantaneous linear mixtures of functions of time) [5]. We used up to 10 primitives, the MSE optimum was located at ≈6. (5) Dynamical movement primitives (DMP) [9]. We used between 1–50 basis functions, the lowest MSE was found at ≈15.

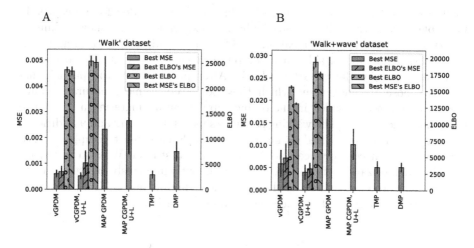

Fig. 1. Model comparison results. Shown is the average squared kinematics error on held-out data after dynamic time warping (MSE) and the variational lower bound on the model evidence (ELBO), where available. Error bars are standard errors of the mean. **A**: walking dataset. **B**: walking+waving dataset. For model descriptions and further details, see text.

The results are plotted in Fig. 1. Generally, all models perform better on the walking only dataset, than on walking+waving. This might be due to the latter being a more complex movement, as can be seen in the movie modular_primitives.avi in the online supplementary material. Of all tested models, the 2-part vCGPDM performs best in terms of MSE. It is significantly better than the full-capacity (no IPs) MAP models, i.e. the development of a variational approximation which needs to store only ≈10 IPs rather than ≈10^4 data points was well worth the effort. Furthermore, note that the Best ELBO's MSE (i.e. the MSE at the maximum of the ELBO w.r.t the #IPs) is a fairly good predictor of the best MSE, which indicates that our simple variational approximation is useful for model selection via ELBO. Further evidence for this is shown in Fig. 1 of Sect. 4 in the online supplementary material: we plotted MSE vs. ELBO for the vCGPDM U+L, symbols indicate different # LVM IPs. The negative correlation between MSE and ELBO is clearly visible. Furthermore, timing results for the vCGPDM can be found in Sect. 5 of the supplement, confirming the theoretical expectations of linear learning time scaling in the data set size for the vCGPDM.

Note that the vCGPDM U+L outperforms the vGPDM particularly on the 'walking+waving' dataset. This shows the usefulness of having modular, coupled dynamics models when the (inter)acting (body)parts execute partially independent movements. A visual demonstration of that modularity can be found in the video `modular_primitives.avi` in the online supplementary material.

3.3   A Small Number of IPs Is Enough to Fool Human Observers

Next, we investigated the number of inducing points needed for perceptually plausible movements with a psychophysical experiment: We showed human observers ($n = 31$, 10 male, mean age: $23.8 \pm 3.5a$) videos of natural and artificial movements side-by-side on a computer screen. The artificial movements were generated by the vCGPDM U+L. After presentation, the participants had to choose the movement which they perceived as more natural. Examples of stimuli are provided in the online supplementary material in the movie `example_stimuli.mov` The walking sequences used for training and 9 additional walking sequences were used as natural stimuli. Each subject completed 1170 trials in randomized sequence, judging all artificial stimuli. We also tested for stimulus memorization effects via catch trials with previously unused natural movements in the last quarter of the experiment, finding none. All experimental procedures were approved by the local ethics commission.

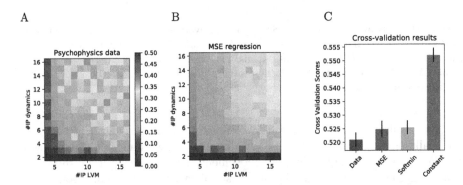

Fig. 2. Perceived naturalness of the model, as a function of the number of inducing points (#IP) **A**: Rate of perceiving vCGPDM-generated stimulus as more natural than natural stimulus, averaged across all participants. **B**: Regression of data in panel A, MSE as regressor and logistic sigmoid as psychometric function. **C**: Regression model comparison with 107-fold cross-validation. Softmin and MSE perform comparably well. Both are close to optimal.

Results are shown in Fig. 2, A: we computed the frequency f_{gen} of choosing the vCGPDM-generated movement across all subjects as a function of the number of dynamics IPs and the number of LVM IPs. At best, we might expect f_{gen} to approach 0.5 when the generated movements are indistinguishable from the natural ones. We fitted those data with a logistic sigmoid $\frac{1}{1+\exp(a \cdot r(.)+c)}$ and a Bernoulli observation model, using two different regressor functions $r(.)$: a soft-minimum between the number of IPs and the MSE. Panel B shows the fit of f_{gen} with MSE, panel C shows 107-fold crossvalidation results for the two regressors, using the average negative log-probability on the held-out data as score. Error bars are standard deviations. 'Constant' is the constant regressor, any other regressor should predict better. 'Data' uses the data mean of the individual #IP combinations as a predictor, and constitutes a lower bound on the cross validation score.

Clearly, f_{gen} increases with the number of IPs, approaching (but not quite reaching) 0.5 for a sufficiently large number of IPs, this is true for the MSE regression, too. Hence, MSE is a good predictor of perceptual performance. Furthermore, a rather small number of IPs is sufficient for modeling this data. This allows for compactly parametrized MPs.

4   Conclusion

We developed a full variational approximation of the CGPDM, the vCGPDM, which obviates the need for sampling the latent space trajectories [6]. We demonstrated that the vCGPDM with a small number of IPs performs better than the full-capacity CGPDM with a MAP approximation to the latent states, and that the vCGPDM is also able to outperform other contemporary MP models, most likely due to its learnable dynamics. Next, we showed that it produces perceptually believable full-body movements. While perceptual evaluations of full and sparse GPDM-like models [15] have been done before, we are the first to investigate systematically the number of IPs of all model components required for perceptual plausibility. Furthermore, we showed that the MSE and the number of IPs can be used to predict average human classification performance almost optimally. This indicates that the model selection process on large databases of training movements for the model could possibly be automated.

We are now in a position to learn a large library of movements with a CGPDM, and study its compositionality. This is possible due to the compact representation of each MP. Instead of direct connections between parts in the vCGPDM, it is also conceivable to embed the parts into a hierarchical architecture, like [15]. While the vCGPDM is suitable when the number of parts is relatively small (computational complexity $\mathcal{O}(T * M * (M * \#IP)^3)$ per optimization iteration), a hierarchical architecture might enable more computational savings for many parts. A further direction of future research are *sensorimotor* primitives, i.e. MPs that can be conditioned on sensory input [11–13] which we will implement by adding sensory predictions to the latent-to-observed mappings.

Acknowledgements. DFG-IRTG 1901 'The Brain in Action', DFG-SFB-TRR 135 project C06. We thank Olaf Haag for help with rendering the movies, and Björn Büdenbender for assistance with MoCap.

References

1. Bastien, F., Lamblin, P., Pascanu, R., Bergstra, J., Goodfellow, I.J., Bergeron, A., Bouchard, N., Bengio, Y.: Theano: new features and speed improvements. In: Deep Learning and Unsupervised Feature Learning NIPS Workshop (2012)
2. Bauer, M., van der Wilk, M., Rasmussen, C.: Understanding probabilistic sparse Gaussian process approximations. Technical report, arXiv:1606.04820 (2016)
3. Bishop, C.M.: Pattern Recognition and Machine Learning (Information Science and Statistics). Springer, New York (2006)
4. Bizzi, E., Cheung, V., d'Avella, A., Saltiel, P., Tresch, M.: Combining modules for movement. Brain Res. Rev. **57**(1), 125–133 (2008)
5. Clever, D., Harant, M., Koch, K.H., Mombaur, K., Endres, D.M.: A novel approach for the generation of complex humanoid walking sequences based on a combination of optimal control and learning of movement primitives. Rob. Aut. Sys. **83**, 287–298 (2016). doi:10.1016/j.robot.2016.06.001
6. Frigola, R., Chen, Y., Rasmussen, C.: Variational Gaussian process state-space models. In: Ghahramani, Z., Welling, M., Cortes, C., Lawrence, N., Weinberger, K. (eds.) Advances in NIPS, vol. 27, pp. 3680–3688 (2014)
7. Giese, M.A., Mukovskiy, A., Park, A.-N., Omlor, L., Slotine, J.-J.E.: Real-time synthesis of body movements based on learned primitives. In: Cremers, D., Rosenhahn, B., Yuille, A.L., Schmidt, F.R. (eds.) Statistical and Geometrical Approaches to Visual Motion Analysis. LNCS, vol. 5604, pp. 107–127. Springer, Heidelberg (2009). doi:10.1007/978-3-642-03061-1_6
8. Hinton, G.E.: Products of experts. In: Proceedings of ICANN 1999, vol. 1, pp. 1–6 (1999)
9. Ijspeert, A.J., Nakanishi, J., Hoffmann, H., Pastor, P., Schaal, S.: Dynamical movement primitives: learning attractor models for motor behaviors. Neu. Comp. **25**(2), 328–373 (2013)
10. Jones, E., Oliphant, T., Peterson, P., et al.: SciPy: Open source scientific tools for Python (2001). http://www.scipy.org/. Accessed 9 Oct 2015
11. Mattos, C.L.C., Dai, Z., Damianou, A., Forth, J., Barreto, G.A., Lawrence, N.D.: Recurrent Gaussian processes. Technical report, arXiv:1511.06644 (2016)
12. Paraschos, A., Daniel, C., Peters, J., Neumann, G.: Probabilistic movement primitives. In: Burges, C., Bottou, L., Welling, M., Ghahramani, Z., Weinberger, K. (eds.) Advances in NIPS, vol. 26, pp. 2616–2624 (2013)
13. Pastor, P., Kalakrishnan, M., Righetti, L., Schaal, S.: Towards associative skill memories. In: IEEE-RAS International Conference on Humanoid Robots, pp. 309–315 (2012)
14. Sakoe, H., Chiba, S.: Dynamic programming algorithm optimization for spoken word recognition. IEEE Trans. Acoust. Speech Sig. Proc. **26**(1), 43–49 (1978)
15. Taubert, N., Christensen, A., Endres, D., Giese, M.: Online simulation of emotional interactive behaviors with hierarchical Gaussian process dynamical models. In: Proceedings of the ACM SAP, pp. 25–32. ACM (2012)
16. Titsias, M.K., Lawrence, N.D.: Bayesian Gaussian process latent variable model. In: Proceedings of the 13th AISTATS, pp. 844–851 (2010)

17. Velychko, D., Endres, D., Taubert, N., Giese, M.A.: Coupling Gaussian process dynamical models with product-of-experts kernels. In: Wermter, S., Weber, C., Duch, W., Honkela, T., Koprinkova-Hristova, P., Magg, S., Palm, G., Villa, A.E.P. (eds.) ICANN 2014. LNCS, vol. 8681, pp. 603–610. Springer, Cham (2014). doi:10. 1007/978-3-319-11179-7_76

18. Wang, J.M., Fleet, D.J., Hertzmann, A.: Gaussian process dynamical models for human motion. IEEE Trans. Pattern Anal. Mach. Intell. **30**(2), 283–298 (2008)

q-Maximum Entropy Distributions and Memory Neural Networks

Roseli S. Wedemann[1]($\boxtimes$) and Angel R. Plastino[2,3]

[1] Instituto de Matemática e Estatística, Universidade do Estado do Rio de Janeiro,
Rua São Francisco Xavier 524, Rio de Janeiro, RJ 20550-900, Brazil
`roseli@ime.uerj.br`
[2] CeBio, Universidad del Noroeste de la Provincia de Buenos Aires,
UNNOBA-Conicet, Roque Saenz Peña 456, Junin, Argentina
`arplastino@unnoba.edu.ar`
[3] Centro Brasileiro de Pesquisas Físicas (CBPF), Rua Xavier Sigaud 150,
Rio de Janeiro, RJ 22290-180, Brazil

Abstract. q-Maximum Entropy (q-MaxEnt) distributions optimizing the S_q, power-law entropic functionals are at the core of the nonextensive thermostatistical formalism. This formalism has been increasingly applied to the description of diverse complex systems in physics, biology, economics, and other fields. Previous work on computational neural models for mental phenomena, such as neurosis, creativity, and the interplay between consciousness and unconsciousness, suggests that q-MaxEnt distributions may be relevant for the study of neural models for these processes. Evidence for q-MaxEnt distributions arises in connection with models of associative memory, which constitute a key ingredient in the theoretical analysis of the alluded mental phenomena. In the present contribution, we compare two possible dynamical mechanisms leading to q-MaxEnt distributions in memory neural networks, when these are modeled by linear or non-linear deformed Fokker-Planck equations. Our joint analysis of these two formalisms (that have been treated separately in the literature) allow us to identify some general features of these approaches that clarify and differentiate their underlying physical basis.

Keywords: Mental functions · Memory · Nonextensive thermostatistics · S_q entropies · q-maximum entropy distributions

1 Introduction

Human memory is central to several of the complex mental processes, both normal and pathological, studied by psychiatry, psychoanalysis and neuroscience [1–3]. According to a standard assumption made in neuroscience, (associative) memory is encoded in the architecture of the brain's neural network. In this regard, a line of research that we have been developing in recent years [4–7] concerns the development of neuronal network models, aimed at investigating an associative memory approach to aspects of neurosis, creativity, and the

© Springer International Publishing AG 2017
A. Lintas et al. (Eds.): ICANN 2017, Part I, LNCS 10613, pp. 300–308, 2017.
https://doi.org/10.1007/978-3-319-68600-4_35

interaction between consciousness and unconsciousness. In these works, to simulate memory retrieval, both the standard Boltzmann Machine (BM) [8] and the Tsallis-Stariolo Generalized Simulated Annealing (GSA) [9] have been used. In the latter case, a statistical analysis of the avalanches generated during the retrieval process, indicated the presence of q-Maximum Entropy (q-MaxEnt), power-law distributions, typical of scenarios where the nonextensive thermostatistics applies [7]. Interestingly, these theoretical results are consistent with recent experimental data on the distribution of the time duration and spatial reach of signal propagation (captured by fMRI images) during brain stimulation. These findings stimulated us to discuss, in the present work, possible dynamical mechanisms generating the aforementioned q-MaxEnt distributions in memory neural networks. The dynamical scenarios we shall consider are based upon two types of Fokker-Planck equations (FPE), one of them linear, and the other one nonlinear. The present considerations may also be relevant in connection with other recent works applying ideas from generalized thermostatistics to models in neuroscience, such as their application to the Haken-Kelso-Bunz model [10], or to neural network models for the learning of new words [11].

In previous efforts [4–7], where we have studied mental processes related to memory, we have simulated the memory retrieval mechanism by recourse to the BM [8], and to its q-statistical generalization, the GSA algorithm [9]. These schemes for simulating pattern retrieval are based on two different implementations of the simulated annealing (SA) process. In both cases, the transition probabilities between different states of the net depend on a temperature parameter T that is gradually lowered by an appropriate annealing schedule. We considered a network with N nodes, each node i having a discrete state S_i in $\{-1, 1\}$. The synaptic weights ω_{ij} between nodes i and j were assumed to be symmetric: $\omega_{ij} = \omega_{ji}$. This condition guarantees the existence of an energy function, $E(\{S_i\}) = -(1/2)\sum_{ij}\omega_{ij}S_iS_j$, such that the attractors of the memory retrieval process (the SA scheme), corresponding to the memories stored in the net, are given by the minima of the (multidimensional) energy landscape determined by $E(\{S_i\})$. The GSA transition probabilities [9], which concern us here because they lead to q-exponential distributions, are

$$P_{GSA}(S_i \rightarrow -S_i) = [1 + (q-1)(E(\{-S_i\}) - E(\{S_i\}))/T]^{\frac{1}{1-q}} . \qquad (1)$$

For $q \rightarrow 1$, the BM rule is recovered. When transitions between states follow the GSA scheme, the system tends to evolve from the current state to a later state of lower energy, although energy may increase at some intermediate steps, allowing the escape from local minima. The GSA scheme constitutes a natural dynamics, leading to q-exponential distributions, for neural networks with states described by discrete variables [5,7]. Here we discuss two dynamical mechanisms based on different versions of the FPE, which can generate q-exponential distributions for neural networks described by continuous variables. As an illustration, we calculated these distributions for a simple two neuron circuit, with a typical activation function. We show that the explicit comparison of these alternative approaches elucidates and differentiates essential features, of the concomitant physical mechanisms, that have not been clearly perceived when they were considered separately in the literature.

2   Nonextensive Thermostatistical Formalism

The nonextensive thermostatistics and its diverse applications constitute nowadays a flourishing field of research [12–15]. This theoretical framework is based on the nonadditive, power-law entropy measure

$$S_q[\mathcal{P}] = \frac{1}{q-1} \int (\mathcal{P} - \mathcal{P}^q)\, d^N \boldsymbol{X}\,, \tag{2}$$

evaluated on a probability density $\mathcal{P}(\boldsymbol{X})$ (with $\boldsymbol{X} \in \Re^N$) and characterized by the real, entropic index q. The standard Boltzmann-Gibbs (BG) logarithmic entropy, $S_{BG} = S_1 = -\int \mathcal{P}\ln \mathcal{P} d^N \boldsymbol{X}$, can be regarded as a particular instance of S_q, corresponding to the limit $q \to 1$. Central to the nonextensive thermostatistics is the q-exponential function

$$\exp_q(x) = \begin{cases} [1 + (1-q)x]^{\frac{1}{1-q}}\,, & \text{for } 1 + (1-q)x > 0\,, \\ 0\,, & \text{for } 1 + (1-q)x \leq 0\,. \end{cases} \tag{3}$$

This function arises naturally in constrained optimization problems based on the entropic functional S_q [12]. Here we will use an alternative notation for q-exponentials: $\exp_q(x) = [1 + (1-q)x]_+^{1/(1-q)}$.

Current research work on the applications of the nonextensive thermostatistical formalism involves scientists from diverse fields, including physics, biology, and economics. Among the most explored applications, we can mention nonequilibrium (or meta-equilibrium) states of systems endowed with long-range interactions [13,14], nonlinear dynamical systems with weak chaos [15], and systems described by power-law, nonlinear Fokker-Planck (NLFP) equations [16–19]. q-MaxEnt distributions fit very well experimental data in diverse areas, and they have also been observed in many numerical simulations of complex systems [12,13]. Systems described by NLFP equations should be highlighted, because they constitute the area of application of nonextensive thermostatistics which is most developed, from the analytical point of view, and where the dynamical origin of the q-MaxEnt distributions is better understood [18,19].

3   Fokker-Planck Dynamics, q-MaxEnt, and Neural Networks

In the absence of random perturbations (noise), the continuous neural network can be regarded as a continuous deterministic dynamical system, whose dynamical state at a given time is described by a set of N phase space variables

$\{X_1, X_2, \cdots, X_N\}$. These state variables evolve in time according to a set of coupled ordinary differential equations,

$$dX_i/dt = G_i(X_1, X_2, \cdots X_N), \quad i = 1, \ldots, N, \tag{4}$$

which in self-explanatory vector notation can be recast as $\frac{d\boldsymbol{X}}{dt} = \boldsymbol{G}(\boldsymbol{X})$, where $\boldsymbol{X}, \boldsymbol{G} \in \Re^N$. This means that the evolution of the system's state, which is represented by the vector $\boldsymbol{X}$, is given by the phase space flux associated with the vectorial field $\boldsymbol{G}$. This is the basic framework for the study of continuous neural networks [8]. A continuous analogue of the McCulloch-Pitts neural model can be formulated, having continuous state variables that evolve in time according to a set of coupled, ordinary differential equations. The net input to neuron i is then $u_i = \sum_j \omega_{ij} V_j$, where V_j is the output signal from neuron j, and ω_{ij} are the synaptic weights. One possible updating rule for the V_i [8] is

$$dV_i/dt = [-V_i + g(u_i)]/\tau_i = G_i(V_1, V_2, \ldots), \tag{5}$$

where τ_i are suitable time constants, and $g(u)$ is an appropriate activation function that saturates for large values of $|u|$, such as a sigmoid or $\tanh(u)$.

The equations of motion (4) govern the motion of one individual realization of a dynamical system, that evolves from one given set of initial conditions. For instance, they describe the evolution of a neural network starting from given initial conditions. In practice, when dealing with complex dynamical systems of high dimensionality, it is often convenient not to focus on one instance of the system's evolution, but rather to study the evolution of a statistical ensemble of copies of the system, that start from different initial conditions. Indeed, this is one of the main ideas behind statistical mechanics. An intriguing example of the application of the ensemble approach to the dynamics of continuous neural networks has been discussed in [20]. According to the ensemble procedure, instead of following the evolution of one realization of the system, governed by the Eq. (4), one studies the behavior of a time-dependent probability density $\mathcal{P}(X_1, \cdots, X_N, t)$, that describes the evolution of the aforementioned statistical ensemble. This probability density obeys the Liouville equation $(\partial \mathcal{P}/\partial t) + \boldsymbol{\nabla} \cdot (\mathcal{P} \boldsymbol{G}) = 0$, which is a continuity equation in phase space. Here $\boldsymbol{\nabla} = (\partial/\partial X_1, \ldots, \partial/\partial X_N)$ is the N-dimensional $\boldsymbol{\nabla}$-operator. If the evolution is nondeterministic, the effects of noise can be taken into account by recourse to an extra diffusion-like term in the above continuity equation, leading to the celebrated FPE

$$(\partial \mathcal{P}/\partial t) - D\nabla^2 \mathcal{P} + \boldsymbol{\nabla} \cdot (\mathcal{P} \boldsymbol{G}) = 0, \tag{6}$$

where D is the diffusion coefficient and the last term on the left hand side is usually called the *drift* term. Accordingly, we shall refer to $\boldsymbol{G}$ as the *drift* field. If, for some potential function $W(\boldsymbol{X})$, one has that $\boldsymbol{G} = -\boldsymbol{\nabla}W$, then the phase space flow $\boldsymbol{G}$ always goes "downhill" in the landscape given by W. This is the case for the continuous neural networks we consider here (the flow is not strictly in the direction of $-\boldsymbol{\nabla}W$, but always has a positive projection long this direction). In the Hopfield model, the potential function, given by

$$W = -\frac{1}{2}\sum_{ij}\omega_{ij}V_iV_j + \sum_i \int_0^{V_i} g^{(-1)}(V)dV \,, \tag{7}$$

is often referred to as the "energy function" and denoted by H [8]. Through the rest of this work, except where explicitly stated otherwise, we shall keep the notation $\boldsymbol{X}$ for the state variables and W for the potential function.

The FPE (6) admits a stationary solution of the BG form,

$$\mathcal{P}_{BG} = Z^{-1}\exp\left[-W(\boldsymbol{X})/D\right], \tag{8}$$

where $Z = \int \exp\left[-\frac{1}{D}W(\boldsymbol{X})\right]d^N\boldsymbol{X}$ is a normalization constant. Here we assume that the shape of the potential function $W(\boldsymbol{X})$ is such that the integral defining Z converges. The probability density $\mathcal{P}_{BG}$ maximizes the entropy S_{BG}, under the constraints imposed by normalization and the mean value $\langle W\rangle = \int WP\,d^N\boldsymbol{X}$, of the potential function W.

3.1 Fokker-Planck Equations as Roads to q-Statistics in Memory Neural Networks: Two Approaches

We now discuss and compare two possible mechanisms leading to q-exponential distributions in memory neural networks, respectively based on two types of deformed FPE's. We want to model stable properties of complex systems, such as the stored memory states in neural networks. Therefore, we focus on stationary solutions to the FPE (which satisfy $\partial P/\partial t = 0$), of the q-exponential form

$$\mathcal{P}_q = A[1 - (1-q)\beta W(\boldsymbol{X})]_+^{\frac{1}{1-q}} \,, \tag{9}$$

where A and β are constants to be determined. Illustrations of this stationary probability density are given in Fig. 1, for a two-neuron circuit. Notice that,

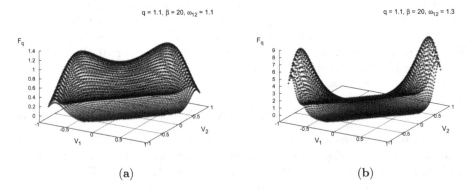

(a)   (b)

Fig. 1. The (unnormalized) q-exponential stationary distribution (9) for a two-neuron circuit, as a function of V_1, V_2. $q = 1.1$, $\beta = 20$, in (a) $\omega_{12} = 1.1$, and in (b) $\omega_{12} = 1.3$. For both cases, $g(V) = \tanh(V)$ in (7).

as the connection strength becomes stronger, the two neurons tend to have simultaneous firing or non-firing states. Now we consider the Stariolo deformed FPE [21], based on an effective potential $\tilde{W}$, and the NLFP equation endowed with a power-law nonlinearity in the diffusion term [16,19]. Let us briefly review these two proposals.

The Stariolo effective potential approach - This was historically the first proposal for a stochastic dynamics leading to *q*-exponential distributions [21]. Stariolo proposed the linear FPE, replacing the potential W by the effective potential $\tilde{W} = (q-1)^{-1}D\ln\left[1 + (q-1)W/D\right]$. The linear FPE (6), with this effective potential, has a stationary solution of the form (9), which is a *q*-exponential of the original potential W.

The NLFP equation approach - This proposal is based on the NLFP equation,

$$(\partial \mathcal{P}/\partial t) - D\nabla^2 \left(\mathcal{P}^{2-q}\right) + \boldsymbol{\nabla} \cdot (\mathcal{P}\boldsymbol{G}) = 0\,. \tag{10}$$

The *q*-exponential ansatz (9) is a stationary solution of (10), provided that $A = [(2-q)\beta D]^{1/(q-1)}$. Both the Stariolo deformed FPE and the NLFP Eq. (10) reduce to the standard linear one (6), in the limit $q \to 1$. In that limit, the *q*-exponential stationary solution (9) reduces to the BG one (8), with $\beta = 1/D$. Both the Stariolo and the NLFP equation are continuity equations and, therefore, preserve the normalization of the density $\mathcal{P}$.

3.2 Comparison of the Stariolo and the NLFP Equation Approaches

In spite of sharing the same *q*-exponential stationary solution, the Stariolo and NLFP approaches differ from each other in interesting ways. The Stariolo approach modifies only the deterministic part of the network dynamics. It does not introduce any deformation in the diffusion term, which describes the effects of noise. The new (deterministic) equations of motion are of the form

$$dX_i/dt = [1 + (1/D)(q-1)W]^{-1}\,G_i(X_1, X_2, \cdots X_N)\,, \quad i = 1, \ldots, N\,, \tag{11}$$

with $G_i = \partial W/\partial X_i$. This deformation implies a non-local effect in the deterministic part of the network's dynamics. Indeed, each component of the phase space flux is re-scaled by a factor $[1 + (1/D)(q-1)W]^{-1}$ that depends, through $W(X_1, \ldots, X_N)$, on the global state of the network. However, the general pattern of the phase space flux is not modified, since each component of the flux is re-scaled by the same factor. Another important aspect of the Stariolo proposal that becomes manifest when contrasting it with the NLFP approach, is that the implied deformation on the deterministic part of the network dynamics depends on features of the stochastic component. In fact, the Stariolo deformation explicitly involves the diffusion parameter D, which characterizes the effects of noise in the FPE. That is, even though the Stariolo proposal modifies only the deterministic part, this deformation depends explicitly on properties of the stochastic part of the dynamics. This is a general feature exhibited by attempts at obtaining q-exponential distributions from the linear FPE: the needed modifications of the deterministic and the stochastic parts of the dynamics become intertwined. The Stariolo FPE inherits from the standard FPE the H-theorem, $(d/dt)(S_{BG}[\mathcal{P}] - \langle \tilde{W} \rangle / D) \geq 0$, with equality achieved only for the stationary solution. This implies that the stationary solution is a density that maximizes the BG entropy, under the constraints of normalization and the mean value of the effective potential $\tilde{W}(\boldsymbol{X})$.

Let us now consider the NLFP equation. In this case, the deformation of the standard FPE occurs only in the diffusion term. The drift term (associated with the original deterministic evolution law of the network) is not modified. This constitutes a deep difference between the Stariolo and the NLFP approaches. In the NLFP case the deformation is restricted to the diffusion term. By changing the value of the diffusion parameter, we can obtain different q-MaxEnt stationary distributions having different temperature parameters, but always for the same potential W, *which is independent of D*. Therefore, the flux in phase space due to the drift field is also independent of D. The diffusion and the drift terms in the NLFP equation, even though they obviously act together, have structures that remain independent of each other. The NLFP approach to q-statistics seems, then, less contrived than alternative approaches based on linear deformations of the standard FPE. The power-law NLFP equation complies with the H-theorem, $(d/dt)(S_q[\mathcal{P}] - \langle W \rangle / D) \geq 0$, with equality corresponding to the stationary density. This means that the stationary solution maximizes the S_q entropy, under the constraints of normalization and the mean value of the network potential $W(\boldsymbol{X})$.

With regards to the origins of the nonlinearity, it is worth stressing that spatial disorder, long-range interactions, or long-time memory effects do not, per se, lead to nonlinear Fokker-Planck equations. Fundamental evolution equations for probability densities have to be linear. However, it is possible to introduce a nonlinear diffusion term to the FPE to describe a physical density of interacting particles (as opposed to a probability density) so that the nonlinearity is an effective description of the interactions [19]. It is not clear if this interpretation can be applied to neural networks. Nonlinear evolution equations can also arise as approximate descriptions of more fundamental linear ones. A detailed analysis of this last possibility for neural networks is beyond the scope of this brief contribution, but certainly deserves further scrutiny.

4   Conclusions

Concepts from the nonextensive thermostatistical formalism have been applied by various researchers to neural network models in neuroscience. Motivated by these efforts, we have discussed and compared two possible dynamical mechanisms, based on deformed FPE's, that generate q-exponential distributions in neural networks. Our present joint analysis of these mechanisms allowed us to identify some relevant features of these approaches that are difficult to appreciate when they are treated independently. The Stariolo proposal is more conservative, in the sense that it keeps the linear structure of the FPE. However, to maintain linearity, one must pay the price of deforming in a non-local way the drift field characterizing the deterministic part of the network dynamics. An important fact transpiring from our work is that any deformed linear Fokker-Planck equation leading to q-MaxEnt stationary distributions must have a temperature dependent (β-dependent) drift field. That is, the drift deformation is highly intertwined with features of the diffusion component, which describes the effects of noise. On the other hand, within the NLFP approach, one modifies solely the diffusion term, in a fashion that is independent of the particular features of the drift field. Different values of the diffusion constant then lead to different stationary q-MaxEnt distributions, with different temperature parameters. Both the Stariolo and the NLFP proposals have pros and cons but, our analysis suggests that the NLFP one is more consubstantial with q-thermostatistics.

Acknowledgments. We acknowledge financial support from the Brazilian National Research Council (CNPq), the Rio de Janeiro State Research Foundation (FAPERJ) and the Brazilian agency which funds graduate studies (CAPES). RSW is grateful for the kind hospitality of the Universidad Nacional del Noroeste de la Prov. de Buenos Aires (particularly, to the UNNOBA Sede CABA), where part of this work was written.

References

1. Kandel, E.: Psychiatry, Psychoanalysis, and the New Biology of Mind. American Psychiatric Publishing Inc., Washington D.C., London (2005)
2. Cleeremans, A., Timmermans, B., Pasquali, A.: Consciousness and metarepresentation: a computational sketch. Neural Netw. **20**, 1032–1039 (2007)
3. Taylor, J.G.: A neural model of the loss of self in schizophrenia. Schizophr. Bull. **37**(6), 1229–1247 (2011)
4. Carvalho, L.A.V., Mendes, D.Q., Wedemann, R.S.: Creativity and delusions: the dopaminergic modulation of cortical maps. In: Sloot, P.M.A., Abramson, D., Bogdanov, A.V., Dongarra, J.J., Zomaya, A.Y., Gorbachev, Y.E. (eds.) ICCS 2003. LNCS, vol. 2657, pp. 511–520. Springer, Heidelberg (2003). doi:10.1007/3-540-44860-8_53
5. Wedemann, R.S., Donangelo, R., Carvalho, L.A.V.: Generalized memory associativity in a network model for the neuroses. Chaos **19**, 015116-(1–11) (2009)
6. Wedemann, R.S., Carvalho, L.A.V.: Some things psychopathologies can tell us about consciousness. In: Villa, A.E.P., Duch, W., Érdi, P., Masulli, F., Palm, G. (eds.) ICANN 2012. LNCS, vol. 7552, pp. 379–386. Springer, Heidelberg (2012). doi:10.1007/978-3-642-33269-2_48
7. Siddiqui, M., Wedemann, R.S., Jensen, H.: Avalanches and Generalized Memory Associativity in a Network Model for Conscious and Unconscious Mental Functioning. arxiv:1704.02741 (2017)
8. Hertz, J.A., Krogh, A., Palmer, R.G. (eds.): Introduction to the Theory of Neural Computation. Lecture Notes, vol. I. Perseus Books, Cambridge (1991)
9. Tsallis, C., Stariolo, D.A.: Generalized simulated annealing. Phys. A **233**, 395–406 (1996)
10. Frank, T.D.: On a nonlinear master equation and the haken-kelso-bunz model. J. Biol. Phys. **30**, 139–159 (2004)
11. Khordada, R., Rastegar Sedehi, H.R.: Application of different entropy formalisms in a neural network for novel word learning. Eur. Phys. J. Plus **130**, 246:1–246:10 (2015)

12. Tsallis, C.: Introduction to Nonextensive Statistical Mechanics, Approaching a Complex World. Springer, New York (2009)
13. Tsallis, C.: The nonadditive entropy S_q and its applications in physics and elsewhere: some remarks. Entropy **13**, 1765–1804 (2011)
14. Brito, S., da Silva, L.R., Tsallis, C.: Role of dimensionality in complex networks. Nature Sci. Rep. **6**, 27992:1–27992:8 (2016)
15. Tirnakli, U., Borges, E.P.: The standard map: From Boltzmann-Gibbs statistics to Tsallis statistics. Nature Sci. Rep. **6**, 23644:1–23644:8 (2016)
16. Franck, T.D.: Nonlinear Fokker-Planck Equations: Fundamentals and Applications. Springer, Berlin (2005)
17. Malacarne, L.C., Mendes, R.S., Pedron, I.T., Lenzi, E.K.: N-dimensional nonlinear Fokker-Planck equation with time-dependent coefficients. Phys. Rev. E **65**, 052101:1–052101:10 (2002)
18. Schwämmle, V., Nobre, F.D., Curado, E.M.F.: Consequences of the H theorem from nonlinear Fokker-Planck equations. Phys. Rev. E **76**, 041123:1–041123:8 (2007)
19. Andrade Jr., J.S., da Silva, G.F.T., Moreira, A.A., Nobre, F.D., Curado, E.M.F.: Thermostatistics of overdamped motion of interacting particles. Phys. Rev. Lett. **105**, 260601:1–260601:4 (2010)
20. Yana, H., Zhaoa, L., Hu, L., Wang, X., Wang, E., Wang, J.: Nonequilibrium landscape theory of neural networks. PNAS **10**(45), E4185–E4194 (2013)
21. Stariolo, D.A.: The Langevin and Fokker-Planck equations in the framework of a generalized statistical mechanics. Phys. Lett. A **185**, 262–264 (1994)

Adaptively Learning Levels of Coordination from One's, Other's and Task Related Errors Through a Cerebellar Circuit: A Dual Cart-Pole Setup

Martí Sánchez-Fibla$^{(\boxtimes)}$, Giovanni Maffei, and Paul F.M.J. Verschure

SPECS, Technology Department, Universitat Pompeu Fabra,
Carrer de Roc Boronat 138, 08018 Barcelona, Spain
{marti.sanchez,giovanni.maffei,paul.verschure}@upf.edu
http://www.specs.upf.edu

Abstract. Behavioral and theoretical studies have shown that during joint action in an interpersonal skilled activity, like carrying an object collaboratively, anticipation is required to further improve the precision in the realization of the task. We model this task as a dual cart pole setup, and we provide a computational basis of how this anticipation can be realized at different levels: anticipating errors originating from the agent's body control, errors related to the global task and errors derived from the anticipation of the other's actions. We model computationally the control loops of the agents as an interplay of feedback and feedforward components and we base the latter on previous research on the cerebellar circuit network. Our results confirm experimentally that anticipating the error in the task including inputs extracted from the behavior of the other, further improves precision in the realization.

Keywords: Social sensorimotor contingencies · Anticipation · Cerebellar circuit · Forward/Feedback control · Dual cart pole setup

1 Introduction

The realization of a skilled activity requires anticipation possibly realized as an interplay of feedback and feedforward components [14]. Anticipation is necessary because of the delays of the sensory feedback (up to 100 milliseconds in the case of the visual modality): to be able to guide the initial part of a movement of an action in a skilled task, sensory feedback is still not available at that moment (thus the need for feedforward control). These delays can increase even further in the case of an interpersonal coordination task [14], where the consequences of our actions can have an effect on the other. Being able to attend, anticipate and adapt to the other's actions are key factors in the coordination of joint action [5].

M. Sánchez-Fibla and G. Maffei—Contributed equally.

P.F.M.J. Verschure—Is also with ICREA Institució Catalana de Recerca i Estudis Avançats, Passeig Lluís Companys 23, E-08010 Barcelona.

© Springer International Publishing AG 2017
A. Lintas et al. (Eds.): ICANN 2017, Part I, LNCS 10613, pp. 309–316, 2017.
https://doi.org/10.1007/978-3-319-68600-4_36

Consider the example of two persons that need to carry together a table with objects on top to a target position: they need to maintain the table in an horizontal position while maintaining balance when moving and being able to anticipate the other's movements not to be uncoordinated.

In the following we contribute to the modelling of the presented task by means of two self-balancing cart pole agents that are linked by an object of variable elasticity[1] (see Fig. 1).

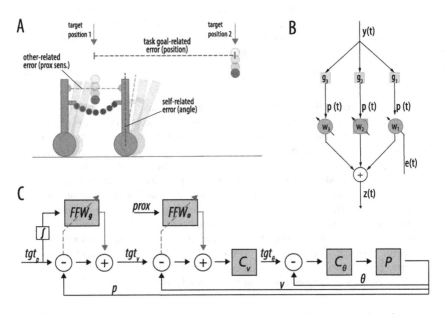

Fig. 1. Setup, control neural network and architecture. A. Dual cart pole robotic setup with two cart-pole agents facing each other and attached by an elastic chain. The agents have the goal of moving together to target positions (1 and 2) which alternate in time. B. Cerebellar circuit based on an adaptive filter neural network [4]. C. Feedfoward feedback architecture. The cascade PID feedback controller is shown as the main pipeline with the two feedforward components based on the network shown in B.

We also contribute to the computational modelling of how the task is implemented in the brain. Following [14] we model the control loops of the agents as nested feedback/feedforward loops that relate to errors originating from: the control of the agent body, from task related errors and from predicting the other. The anticipatory components are implemented based on the cerebellar circuitry presented in [4].

We propose a computational and neurobiologically plausible substrate for joint action. We provide as well experimental results of the benefits of monitoring the other agent to improve coordination, just as hypothesised in [12]

---

[1] The simulation has been implemented by the authors in python with pybox2d and can be download from https://github.com/santmarti/PythonRobot2DSim.

where monitoring and prediction are identified as the minimal components of an architecture supporting joint action. We address the question of what are the mechanisms supporting precise temporal coordination of actions [9], by assessing the additional precision achieved in the presented interpersonal coordination task by modelling and quantifying the contribution of the anticipatory loops related to the prediction of actions of others.

When performing a multi-agent sensorimotor coordination task (as the one just presented) different errors have to be taken into account:

1. Errors derived from the agent's own state: optimizing the posture for the realization of the joint action
2. Task related errors: e.g., if a furniture has to be carried maintaining its horizontal position (so that objects on top don't fall).
3. Resulting errors of the predictions involving other's actions: so that others intentions are anticipated or compensated as quickly as possible.

We start coupling the two agents with one feedback loop each. This first level translates task goals (target position of the agents) into a velocity and the feedback loops bring velocity and angle of the agents to zero, so that posture is controlled, and the own errors can be minimized (1). Given the parametrization of the simulation, the task can be performed using only feedback, but collisions and interactions among the agents affect performance severely. We then add an adaptive feedforward loop relating to the realization of the task which anticipates task related errors (2) as the one derived from under/overshooting the target position due to control delays. We finally show experimentally that the anticipation loop based on predicting the actions of the other (3), extracted from its own actions and the distance to the other, further improves the efficiency and precision in the realization of the task.

2 Methods

2.1 Setup

For the modelling of the task (carrying together an object to a desired location), we depart from the cart pole (inverted pendulum) setup often used as an approximation of posture and well known in the machine learning community. We implement a cart pole agent using library pybox2d (see github link in the intro for source code). The agent has one degree of freedom in its wheel, implemented as the so called revolution joint (joint of pybox2d library, basically a motor with torque). Each agent has a distance sensor in the upper part of his body which is implemented as a ray cast in the physics library (from a point and a direction vector in the body, the distance to the first colliding body is returned).

The setup is then constituted by two cart pole agents facing each other and attached by an elastic chain implemented as sequence of spheres linked by a distance joint.

2.2 Task

The task is composed of two goals: a local and a global one. Each agent has the personal goal of balancing while performing the global task. The chosen global task is an adaptation of a position reference tracking task for two agents (see Fig. 1). The target position of both agents switches from two different positions every ten seconds (see target positions in Fig. 1A). Both agents, each equipped with a different controller, have the common goal of reaching a target position, which is communicated as an additional input to the system, eliminating the problem of having to attend to it.

The agents need to collaborate if they want to perform the task efficiently and without losing balance as the chain causes indirect instabilities. The task is a collaborative motor task with multiples sources of error.

2.3 Architectures

The behavior of both agents is driven by a control scheme composed of coupled feedback and feedforward controllers (see Fig. 1). The feedback controller is in charge of adjusting the velocity and the angle of the agent according to a desired target position based on sensory feedback. On the other hand, the feedforward controllers are in charge of issuing sensory predictions (following the counter-factual predictive control, CFPC scheme [3]) with the goal to minimize a given error by acting in anticipation.

The feedback controller is implemented as a cascade PID composed by: a module setting a desired angular position (tgt_θ) that minimizes the error in velocity, and, a module generating a motor response (u) modifying the state of the plant to minimize the angular error and consequently the error in velocity (see Fig. 1C). A desired position is achieved by setting a desired velocity (tgt_v) as the difference between target (tgt_p) and current position (p).

Each feedforward controller module is implemented as a neural network consistent with cerebellar physiology and anatomy [1] (Fig. 1B), that expands an input $y(t)$ into a set of 100 gaussian bases (g). The output (z) of a single adaptive module is obtained as a weighted linear combination the bases vectors p. The weight vector (W) is updated according to a variation of the Widrow-Hoff rule such that: $w_j(t) = \beta e(t) p_j(t)$, where β (=10) is the learning rate, δ (=200 ms) accounts for the anticipatory delay and e is the error function. Importantly the two feedforward modules are identical in the implementation but differ in the nature of the error they minimize. FFW_g acquires a prediction useful to minimize a goal related error (i.e. position) associated with a change in target position. As such the input is defined as $y_{ffwg} = \int tgt_p$ and its error signal is defined as $e_{ffwg} = p_{tgt} - p$. Finally, the output (z_{ffwg}), representing a prediction of the error in position, is linearly integrated with the input to the descending reactive module C_v and processed as an anticipatory change in target velocity.

Differently, FFW_o acquires a prediction useful to minimize an error in velocity elicited by the distance to the other agent. Its input is defined as $y_{ffwo} = H(x_{prox})$, with $y = 1$ for $x_{prox} > 0.4$ and $y = 0$ otherwise, while its error signal is defined as $e_{ffwo} = v_{tgt} - v$. Finally, the output (z_{ffwo}), representing a prediction of the error in velocity, is linearly integrated with the current error in velocity and further transformed into a desired angular position by C_v.

3   Results

We run experiments where the agents have to minimize the displacement from a target goal position in two conditions: first, by learning to anticipate the target goal related error (ffGoal, ffG for short, condition in Fig. 3C legend, where only the feedforward goal component is activated) and second, by learning to anticipate simultaneously the goal related and the other related error (ffMixed, ffM for short, condition in Fig. 3C legend where both feedforward components are activated).

We start checking the performance of the agents engaged in the collaborative sensory-motor task by describing the performance of the feedback controller alone (Fig. 2A). Here, the error in position (red shaded) is due to the control latencies introduced by the physical properties of the plant, responsible for delays and overshooting, and by the interaction of the two agents introducing oscillations when colliding. A minimization of the first source of error is achieved by enabling the FFW_g module. After a number of repetitions a feedforward signal encoding a position error prediction (Fig. 2B) is issued with enough anticipation to trigger a corrective movement before the actual error is perceived (Fig. 3A, B black solid line). At the end of the experimental session the original error in position is reduced by approximately 40% (Fig. 3C, black solid and dashed lines).

Importantly, an ulterior increase in performance is achieved by enabling the FFW_o. This module learns over time to issue an anticipatory prediction of the velocity error introduced by the collision with the partner in response to its proximity (Fig. 2C). As a result, the agents progressively increase their ability

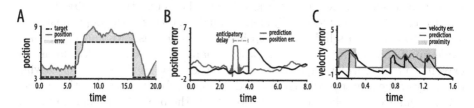

Fig. 2. Feedback and feedforward results. **A**. Results of the feedback controller alone for one of the agents. The curve shows the position of one agent with respect to the target reference which switches position every ten seconds. **B**. Predictive response signal of the first feedforward component FFW_g at the moment where the reference target changes. It can be observed that a predictive anticipatory signal is generated after 8 trials. **C**. Response signal of the second feedforward component FFW_o component that issues a response predictive signal (green solid line) every time the proximity sensor is activated (green shaded area). (Color figure online)

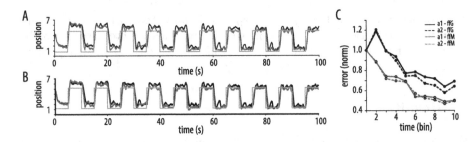

Fig. 3. Comparison between experimental conditions. **A.** Agent one results for the two conditions denoted ffG (black solid line) and ffM (green solid line), referring to the goal and mixed conditions (ffG and ffM respectively). **B.** Agent two results for the two conditions as in A. **C.** Learning curves of both agents for both conditions: ffG (only goal feedforward component activated) and ffm (both goal and proximity feedforward components activated). Legend refers to: agent one/ffG condition (a1-ffG), agent one/ffM condition (a1-ffM), and similarly for agent two. (Color figure online)

to react to the collision before it is perceived (see Fig. 3A, B green solid lines). Learning to predict the effects of the action of the other has a beneficial effect on performance by reducing the initial error by a total of 55% (15% addition to FFW_g alone, see Fig. 3C).

4   Discussion

We study the computational basis of sensorimotor contingencies (SMCs) involved in the realization of joint action during a skilled activity. We characterize social SMCs in a truly collaborative sensorimotor coordination task. The task itself (carrying something together to a target) has been proposed as a prototypical example of collaborative task with a common goal 90 years ago by Allport in his seminal book "social psychology" as credited in [9]. We have modeled the task by two cart pole agents linked by an object. We used different types of objects to be able to control levels of physical linking. Available objects in the implementation are: (1) two rigid bars linked by a spring of variable elasticity and (2) a chain made up of spheres linked by a join with variable elasticity. This feature is not exploited in the current paper and we leave the study of the effects of varying elasticity of the object to the agent coordination for future work. For the current experiments we have chosen to use option (2) as the problem of balancing while moving together becomes more challenging. We observed that when using a rigid bar the two agents became more linked and balance easily.

In the following we place our research in the context of related social cognition literature. We go beyond the approach of the "perceptual crossing" task where social sensorimotor contingencies can only be characterized by the dynamics of the interaction when the two agents cross [2] and where no joint task exists truly, only the derived goal of distinguishing the other. The "perceptual crossing tasks" is more related to the distinction of self and other.

In [13] the fact that adaptation is driven linearly or proportionally to an error is discussed, but the proposed Bayesian model that processes the relevance of the error is applied to a single source of error. Here different sources of error are taken simultaneously into account and being applied to a social collaborative task.

As discussed in [14], a social joint task that we address here deals in reality with a more complex types of anticipation. Fully predicting the consequences of actions may need to include an internal model (feedforward/anticipatory component) of the other. We don't deal with this fact in the paper as each agent only considers the subjective distance to the other and does not take into account any additional aspect as: weight estimation, strength assessment or even physiological state of the other. We leave this aspect as future work and we foresee interesting experiments that could be done: interchange partner in the task and reassess convergence of efficiency; make an agent more active than the other and look at coupling and turn taking behaviours. In fact, in this paper, we are interested in the pure perceptual anticipatory nature of a joint coordination task without considering communication aspects between agents; as we did in [6] for maximizing probability presence estimation within a group in occluded environments; or like they do in [11] for coordinating autonomous crossing vehicles in junctions.

The proposed architecture could be the basis to model and explain the neurophysiological basis of anticipatory aspects involved in social interaction, based on the cerebellar circuitry. It can also shed light into explaining experimental data of behavioral experiments like the lifting and balancing task presented in [7].

5   Conclusion

Wolpert et al. [14], investigate theoretically the role of the interplay of feedback/feedforward components in social interaction. We propose and test experimentally a computational biologically plausible architecture for joint action supporting anticipation and monitoring of self, other and task related errors. We base the computational modeling of adaptive loops in the cerebellar circuitry [4] which has been proposed as a plausible substrate of the neurophysiological cerebellar circuit and has been identified to be crucial for anticipatory action [1], and its malfunctions and deficits have also been pointing to possible causal factors of complex disorders like autism [8,10].

Acknowledgment. This work was supported by socSMC-641321H2020-FETPROACT-2014, INSOCO-DPI2016-80116-P and ERC-2013-ADG-341196.

References

1. Dean, P., Porrill, J., Ekerot, C.F., Jörntell, H.: The cerebellar microcircuit as an adaptive filter: experimental and computational evidence. Nat. Rev. Neurosci. **11**(1), 30–43 (2010)
2. Di Paolo, E.A., Rohde, M., Iizuka, H.: Sensitivity to social contingency or stability of interaction? Modelling the dynamics of perceptual crossing. New Ideas Psychol. **26**(2), 278–294 (2008)
3. Herreros, I., Arsiwalla, X., Verschure, P.: A forward model at Purkinje cell synapses facilitates cerebellar anticipatory control. In: Advances in Neural Information Processing Systems, pp. 3828–3836 (2016)
4. Herreros, I., Verschure, P.F.: Nucleo-olivary inhibition balances the interaction between the reactive and adaptive layers in motor control. Neural Netw. **47**, 64–71 (2013)
5. Keller, P.E., Novembre, G., Hove, M.J.: Rhythm in joint action: psychological and neurophysiological mechanisms for real-time interpersonal coordination. Phil. Trans. R. Soc. B **369**(1658) (2014)
6. Moulin-Frier, C., Sanchez-Fibla, M., Verschure, P.F.: Autonomous development of turn-taking behaviors in agent populations: a computational study. In: 2015 Joint IEEE International Conference on Development and Learning and Epigenetic Robotics (ICDL-EpiRob), pp. 188–195. IEEE (2015)
7. Pezzulo, G., Iodice, P., Donnarumma, F., Dindo, H., Knoblich, G.: Avoiding accidents at the champagne reception. Psychol. Sci., 095679761668301 (2017). doi:10.1177/0956797616683015
8. Schmitz, C., Martineau, J., Barthélémy, C., Assaiante, C.: Motor control and children with autism: deficit of anticipatory function? Neurosci. Lett. **348**(1), 17–20 (2003)
9. Sebanz, N., Bekkering, H., Knoblich, G.: Joint action: bodies and minds moving together. Trends Cogn. Sci. **10**(2), 70–76 (2006)
10. Stins, J.F., Emck, C., de Vries, E.M., Doop, S., Beek, P.J.: Attentional and sensory contributions to postural sway in children with autism spectrum disorder. Gait Posture **42**(2), 199–203 (2015)
11. Sukhbaatar, S., Szlam, A., Fergus, R.: Learning multiagent communication with backpropagation. arXiv preprint arXiv:1605.07736 (2016)
12. Vesper, C., Butterfill, S., Knoblich, G., Sebanz, N.: A minimal architecture for joint action. Neural Netw. **23**(8), 998–1003 (2010)
13. Wei, K., Körding, K.: Relevance of error: what drives motor adaptation? J. Neurophysiol. **101**(2), 655–664 (2009)
14. Wolpert, D.M., Doya, K., Kawato, M.: A unifying computational framework for motor control and social interaction. Philos. Trans. R. Soc. B Biol. Sci. **358**(1431), 593–602 (2003)

Weighted Clique Analysis Reveals Hierarchical Neuronal Network Dynamics

Paolo Masulli[✉] and Alessandro E.P. Villa

NeuroHeuristic Research Group, University of Lausanne,
Quartier Dorigny, 1015 Lausanne, Switzerland
{paolo.masulli,alessandro.villa}@unil.ch
http://www.neuroheuristic.org

Abstract. A biologically-plausible simulation of a neuronal network is studied as its topology is shaped by its activity by means of an encoding of its connectivity structure as a directed clique complex. Specially defined invariants of this mathematical structure, including the information about synaptic strength, are introduced and show how the initial topology of a network and its evolution during the simulation are tightly inter-related with the dynamical activity.

Keywords: Recurrent neural dynamics · Graph topology · Directed clique complex · Synfire chain · Synaptic plasticity

1 Introduction

Brain imaging techniques have raised the possibility that brain networks are organized following scale-free [5] or small-world diagrams [1]. A well known hallmark of the anatomical organization of brain circuits in all species is the hierarchical topology of neural modules [2,8]. This observation suggests that the neural substrate for the functional integration of specialized neural operations, which form the basis of cognition, may require hierarchical modularity. Hence, patterns of spontaneous activity associated with functional connectivity patterns suggest that structural networks determine the operations characteristic of functional networks, as revealed by the relations between topology and activity [6,15,17]. An extension of time integration from external input modules (appropriate for sensory processing) to higher hierarchical levels (exhibiting persistent activity suitable for decision-making and working memory) of associative areas is likely to produce progressively extended timescales along the modular hierarchy [3,4,14]. In the olfactory system, for example, the relative roles of feedforward (FF), feedback (FB) and inter-module horizontal (H) connections within the same hierarchical level suggest the possibility to gain insight into effective connectivity on the basis of self-organization of structural and functional connectivity [18].

A natural way to mathematically encode a network is the notion of directed graph – a set of nodes connected by arcs with a fixed direction. This structure

© Springer International Publishing AG 2017
A. Lintas et al. (Eds.): ICANN 2017, Part I, LNCS 10613, pp. 317–325, 2017.
https://doi.org/10.1007/978-3-319-68600-4_37

allows for mathematical constructions yielding a topological space, which can in turn be studied with the powerful toolbox of algebraic topology, such as the directed clique complex which we introduced previously [12,13]. In the present study we study the relations between topology and dynamics on a biologically inspired hierarchical network simulation with a high number of cells and a structure of connectivity that is spontaneously shaped by the network's dynamical evolution. The current model is based on leaky integrate-and-fire neurons and features developmental phases, including apoptosis at the early developmental stage, Spike Timing Dependent Plasticity (STDP) and coherent external input patterns. We consider two hierarchical levels of processing modules and two different topologies depending on their reciprocal pattern of connections within and between successive hierarchical levels. We used a modular and flexible simulation framework, based on the system JNet [16]. By studying new topological invariants based on the weight of the connections, we gain new insight into the relations between dynamics, network topology and self-organization of functional networks.

2   Methods

2.1   Topology and the Directed Clique Complex

We consider a finite directed weighted graph $G = (V, E)$ with vertex set V and edge set E with no self-loops and no double edges, and denote with N the cardinality of V. Let W be the $|V| \times |V|$ matrix with positive entries defining the weights of the edges in the graph: W_{ij} is the weight of the edge from node n_i to node n_j, or 0 if they are not connected. Associated to G, we can construct its *(directed) clique complex* $K(G)$, which is the directed simplicial complex [7] given by $K(G)_0 = V$ and

$$K(G)_n = \{(v_0, \ldots, v_n) \colon (v_i, v_j) \in E \text{ for all } i < j\} \quad \text{for } n \geq 1. \quad (1)$$

In other words, an n-simplex contained in $K(G)_n$ is a directed $(n + 1)$-clique or a completely connected directed subgraph with $n + 1$ vertices. An n-simplex is an object of dimension n and consists of $n + 1$ vertices.

By definition, a directed clique (or a simplex in our complex) is a fully-connected directed sub-network: this means that the nodes are ordered and there is one source and one sink in the sub-network, and the presence of the directed clique in the network means that the former is connected to the latter in all the possible ways within the sub-network, as illustrated by Fig. 1A.

The *weight* of a clique is defined as the sum of the weights of all the graph edges belonging to the clique.

2.2   The Neuronal Network Simulator JNet

We simulated a multi-module neuronal network using the expandable framework named JNet, which was developed and maintained within our research group [16].

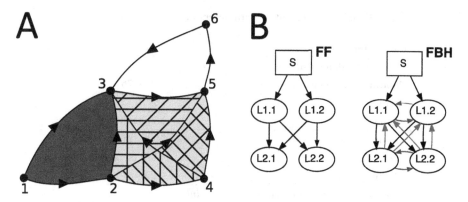

Fig. 1. (A) Example of cliques. The directed clique complex of the represented graph consists of a 0-simplex for each vertex and a 1-simplex for each edge. The shaded area (123) represents a 3-clique and the area (2345) is the only 4-clique in this example. (B) The feedforward (FF) and feedback with horizontal connections (FBH) arrangements of hierarchical network modules in the simulations. L1.x: hierarchical level 1; L2.x: hierarchical level 2.

Each network module was simulated by a 2D lattice of 76×76 leaky integrate-and-fire neuronal models that includes 80% of excitatory neurons and 20% of inhibitory neurons, whose main parameters are summarized in Table 1. Each simulation has a global clock and a time step variable t that ranges from 0 to 10^6 in unitary increments.

The overall structure of the network features one sensory module **S**, which is the only one to receive an external stimulus, and a two hierarchical levels processing modules, with two modules at each level **L1.1–L2.2** (Fig. 1B). The **FF** model is a feedforward network without horizontal connections. The **FBH** model also includes feedback and horizontal connections. Note that the inter-module connections are actually fibres of multiple synapses, as explained further below. This simulation features a number of important bio-inspired processes [10] that affect the connectivity within a neural module, namely synaptogenesis, cell death, spike timing dependent plasticity (STDP) and synaptic pruning. During the synaptogenesis, each cell establishes a pattern of projections, avoiding self-connections, but so that each neuron can project to other excitatory or inhibitory cells, following a 2-dimensional Gaussian probability distribution. This process is randomized and runs independently for each cell of either type and for each network module. Connections have an intensity (weight), which is an integer in the set $\{1, 2, 4\}$. At the beginning, all the weights are set to 2, and they evolve during the simulation increasing or decreasing as a consequence of STDP.

During synaptogenesis, inter-module connections are also established. They model the long-distance synapses in the brain. In each network module, an input and an output layer are defined. The output layers of each module are connected to the input layers of the target modules, according to the topology that is adopted (Fig. 1B). The inter-module out-degree of an output cell is chosen to

Table 1. Main initial parameters of the simulation.

Parameter	Unit	Value
Network modules features		
Module dimensions		76 × 76
Neurons		5776
Projections		890000
Input neurons		900 (processing)
		450 (sensory)
Output neurons		450
External stimulation of the sensory module		
Start	Time step	6144
Amplitude	mV	1.9
Stimulus duration	Time step	512
Pause between stimuli	Time step	1024
Background activity		
Background stimulus amplitude	mV	1.90 (processing)
Background stimulus amplitude	mV	3.80 (sensory)
Background stimulus frequency	1/time step	.3
Plasticity and apoptosis		
Apoptosis start	Time step	0
Apoptosis end	Time step	767
STDP start	Time step	768
Excitatory cells		
Proportion	%	80
PSP	mV	0.92
Inhibitory cells		
Proportion	%	20
PSP	mV	−1.64

be proportional to the intra-module out-degree, i.e., if a cell project to other k cells within its module, it will project to a fixed fraction ρk of input cells of each of the downstream modules. After the initial stage of synaptogenesis, no new projections are added to the network.

There are two types of cell death: "apoptosis" or programmed cell death – which is active during the initial part of the network evolution – and "necrotic cell death", which occurs when neurons do not establish enough connections, either because of an anomalous development or because of synaptic pruning, occurring at any stage after the developmental phase [9]. Apoptosis reflects the biological process of massive synaptic pruning associated with cell death occurring during early stages of neural development, right after the initial excessive and to some extent diffusive synapse generation [11].

2.3   External Stimulation and Background Activity

The input layer of the sensory module **S** receives an external input which is activated for the first time at $t = 6144$. The input pattern is formed by a basis stimulus of the duration of 10 time steps, which is repeated 52 times with each repetition slightly modified with the introduction of a jitter. At each time step, an average number of 4% of the input cells receives an input. The entire pattern – truncated to the duration of 512 time steps – is applied to the input layer. Afterwards, there is a pause of 1024 time steps, during which no input is applied to the network, and then the input pattern is applied again, until the end of the simulation. All the modules in the network are subject to a background noise activity, which is active for the entire duration of the simulation. The background activity is applied as an extra input potential of fixed amplitude (see Table 1) at a given random Poisson distributed times, with fixed average frequency for each neuron. All parameters have been chosen in accordance with those determined in [10,16], adjusting for the network size when appropriate.

2.4   The Topological Invariants of the Simulated Network

The jNet network modules described above are naturally modelled as directed weighted graphs, allowing us to construct the directed clique complex and the topological invariants. To be able to consistently compare clique weights, we normalise connection weights by dividing their value (an integer in $\{1, 2, 4\}$) by the maximum possible weight, namely 4. This way, the weights of connections in the graph are in the interval $[0, 1]$.

In our analysis we consider two simply defined invariants of the directed clique complex:

- The **number of** m**-cliques** (($m - 1$)-simplices), for a fixed integer $m \geq 0$, which is defined as the cardinality of the set $K(G)_m$.
- The **weighted number of** m**-cliques** (($m - 1$)-simplices), for a fixed integer $m \geq 0$, which is defined as the sum of the weights of all directed cliques of dimension m in the graph.

Notice that to make the calculation of the directed clique complex computationally feasible we introduced a *quadrant technique*. We split each network module into 4 quadrants and computed the complex on each quadrant (removing the connections in-between different quadrants). This reduces the number of cliques, but we concentrate on low-dimensional cliques whose quantity is not significantly affected by this reduction and we can average the results on all the quadrants of modules lying at the same hierarchical level.

3   Results

As we observed in our earlier work with a different type of simulations [12,13], the clique invariants are a predictor of network activity, since they are able to detect at an early stage of a simulation whether a given network will have a high or low activation during the simulation. Here we compared the topological invariants with the average activity of the network. This is computed as the number of active (spiking) neurons at a given instant averaged *over the entire duration of the simulation*. This quantity is computed *a posteriori* at the end of each simulation. We computed the correlation of such averaged activity with the topological invariants of the networks at different moments of the simulation on $N = 50$ different simulations (different initializations of the random seed), half with **FF** and half with **FBH** (Table 2).

Table 2. Activity and topology. Pearson's correlation coefficients of the average activity of the network at different time steps of the simulation, following with the number of 2-simplices and the number of weighted 2-simplices. L1: hierarchical level 1, L2: hierarchical level 2. *ns*: $p \geq 0.05$, *: $p < 0.05$, **: $p < 0.01$, ***: $p < 0.001$.

Time step	No. 2-simplices				No. weighted 2-simplices			
	FF		FBH		FF		FBH	
	L1	L2	L1	L2	L1	L2	L1	L2
1500	*ns*	*ns*	*ns*	*ns*	*ns*	*ns*	*ns*	*ns*
160000	*ns*	*ns*	*ns*	*ns*	.362*	.402*	*ns*	*ns*
320000	.511***	*ns*	.399**	*ns*	.607***	.604***	.512***	.484**
500000	.758***	.612***	.670***	.612***	.836***	.674***	.755***	.606***
1000000	.875***	.487***	.843***	.582***	.920***	.548***	.856***	.604***

We notice that, for the **FF** network architecture, the number of weighted 2-simplices has a significant positive correlation with the network activity already from $t = 160000$ in both hierarchical levels, while the non-weighted invariant is significantly correlated only from $t = 320000$ and only in the first level. This means that the weighted invariants are a better predictor of network activity. In the **FBH** network architecture, both non-weighted and weighted invariants are correlated with the activity at a later stage of the simulation (respectively from $t = 500000$ and $t = 320000$ for correlation in both levels), but still the weighted invariants show a better performance (earlier prediction). In a general sense, the weighted invariants show higher correlation coefficients with the activity with respect to the non-weighted ones at all times, suggesting that they are indeed better indicators of high activity.

Figure 2 shows an example of low- and high-activity **FBH** level 1 network modules: even though the two represented networks have the same architecture, because of different initialisation they evolved to two different topologies.

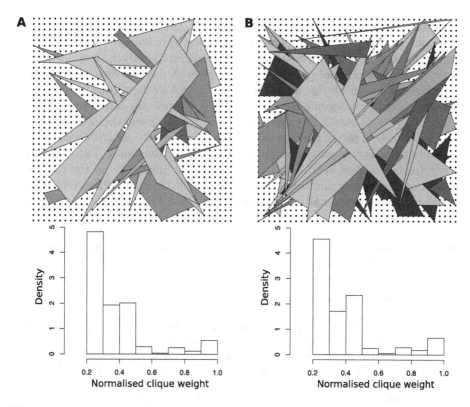

Fig. 2. Comparison of the weighted cliques at time $t = 320000$ of the simulations in two different network modules. The figures show the 3-cliques in the two networks (i.e. 2-simplices in the directed clique complex), and the color reflects their weight (darker cliques have higher weight). Both figures are network modules in level 1 of two simulations with topology FBH. Figure **A** (random seed $r = 5694$) has an average activity of 7.18 and a weighted 3-cliques invariant of 57.3. Figure **B** (random seed $r = 7385$) has average activity 11.65 and a weighted 3-cliques invariant of 68.9. For readability of the figure, only cliques having a maximum connection length of 10 units in the grid are drawn. We observe that network **B** presents a higher number of cliques and of higher weight. This appears evident as well when looking at the bar plots of the normalised clique weight distribution for the two networks (lower panel). Network **A** has more low-weight cliques, whereas network **B** is characterised by a higher number of high-weight cliques. (Color figure online)

The network in Fig. 2A is characterised by a lower number of weighted cliques, which is higher for the one in Fig. 2B. This example fits with our result that the number of weighted cliques is a predictor for a network's activation.

4   Discussion

We proposed the notion of directed clique complex as an indicator of network activity [12], showing that it encodes the information about brain connectivity in the form of topological space. In the current study we have extended the simulation in order to include plausible biological processes shaping the structural connectivity of networks two orders of magnitude larger than our initial study. An improved topological invariant that takes into account the strength of synapses shows that the initial structural topology is a good predictor of network's activity at specific hierarchical levels, despite the much greater complexity of the dynamical processes shaping the topology and the activity in our new simulations. The networks studied here are generated as grids with a random initial connection and are only shaped by their dynamics. This paves the way to further studies in which we shall analyze in greater detail the topology of spontaneously occurring connectivity patterns in relation with precise time-related patterns of external stimulation fed at the entrance of the hierarchical organization of neural modules.

Acknowledgments. This work was partially supported by the Swiss National Science Foundation grant CR13I1-138032.

References

1. Bassett, D.S., Bullmore, E.T.: Small-world brain networks revisited. Neuroscientist **23**(5), 499–516 (2016). doi:10.1177/1073858416667720
2. Bonson, G.: The hierarchical organization of the central nervous system: implications for learning processes and critical periods in early development. Behav. Sci. **10**, 7–25 (1965)
3. Chaudhuri, R., Knoblauch, K., Gariel, M.A., Kennedy, H., Wang, X.J.: A large-scale circuit mechanism for hierarchical dynamical processing in the primate cortex. Neuron **88**(2), 419–431 (2015)
4. Del Prete, V., Martignon, L., Villa, A.E.: Detection of syntonies between multiple spike trains using a coarse-grain binarization of spike count distributions. Network **15**(1), 13–28 (2004)
5. Eguiluz, V.M., Chialvo, D.R., Cecchi, G.A., Baliki, M., Apkarian, A.V.: Scale-free brain functional networks. Phys. Rev. Lett. **94**(1), 018102 (2005)
6. Freeman, W.J.: Neural networks and chaos. J. Theor. Biol. **171**, 13–18 (1994)
7. Hatcher, A.: Algebraic Topology. Cambridge University Press, Cambridge (2002)
8. Hilgetag, C.C., Hütt, M.T.: Hierarchical modular brain connectivity is a stretch for criticality. Trends Cogn. Sci. **18**(3), 114–115 (2014)
9. Hutchins, J.B., Barger, S.W.: Why neurons die: cell death in the nervous system. Anat. Rec. **253**(3), 79–90 (1998)
10. Iglesias, J., Villa, A.E.: Recurrent spatiotemporal firing patterns in large spiking neural networks with ontogenetic and epigenetic processes. J. Physiol. Paris **104**(34), 137–146 (2010). Neural Coding
11. Innocenti, G.M.: Exuberant development of connections, and its possible permissive role in cortical evolution. Trends Neurosci. **18**(9), 397–402 (1995)
12. Masulli, P., Villa, A.E.P.: The topology of the directed clique complex as a network invariant. Springer Plus **5**, 388 (2016)
13. Masulli, P., Villa, A.E.P.: Dynamics of evolving feed-forward neural networks and their topological invariants. In: Villa, A.E.P., Masulli, P., Pons Rivero, A.J. (eds.) ICANN 2016. LNCS, vol. 9886, pp. 99–106. Springer, Cham (2016). doi:10.1007/978-3-319-44778-0_12

14. Park, H.J., Friston, K.: Structural and functional brain networks: from connections to cognition. Science **342**(6158), 1238411 (2013)
15. Tannenbaum, N.R., Burak, Y.: Shaping neural circuits by high order synaptic interactions. PLoS Comput. Biol. **12**(8), 1–27 (2016)
16. Shaposhnyk, V., Villa, A.E.: Reciprocal projections in hierarchically organized evolvable neural circuits affect EEG-like signals. Brain Res. **1434**, 266–276 (2012)
17. Stam, C.J., Reijneveld, J.C.: Graph theoretical analysis of complex networks in the brain. Nonlinear Biomed. Phys. **1**(1), 3 (2007)
18. Yang, W., Sun, Q.Q.: Hierarchical organization of long-range circuits in the olfactory cortices. Physiol. Rep. **3**(9), e12550 (2015)

Why the Brain Might Operate Near the Edge of Criticality

Xerxes D. Arsiwalla[1]([✉]) and Paul Verschure[1,2]

[1] Synthetic Perceptive Emotive and Cognitive Systems (SPECS) Lab,
Center of Autonomous Systems and Neurorobotics,
Universitat Pompeu Fabra, Barcelona, Spain
x.d.arsiwalla@gmail.com

[2] Institució Catalana de Recerca i Estudis Avançats (ICREA), Barcelona, Spain

Abstract. Would operating near criticality provide any functional benefit to the brain? In this paper we show that near critical dynamics is necessary for efficient information integration. The latter is quantified by a dynamical complexity measure Φ, which aims to capture the amount of information generated by a networked dynamical system as a whole over and above that generated by the sum of its parts when the system transitions from one dynamical state to another. This formulation is based on the Kullback-Leibler divergence between the multi-variate distribution on the set of network states versus the corresponding factorized distribution over its parts. Using Gaussian distributions, we compute Φ for several network topologies. Our formulation applies to weighted networks with stochastic dynamics. We first compute Φ for artificial networks and then for the human brain's connectome network. In all case we find that operating near the edge of criticality leads to high integrated information.

Keywords: Network dynamics · Complexity measures · Information theory

1 Introduction

Complex systems displaying critical behavior have played a vital role in statistical physics for investigating scaling properties (via the renormalization group) and phase transitions [16]. However, whether biological systems such as the brain really operate at criticality is still an open question [17,24]. More recent evidence, in fact, suggests that the brain might be operating, not at criticality, but near criticality [15]. In this paper, we try to argue why this might actually be beneficial for global information integration in the brain. To quantify the latter, we use "Integrated Information", a dynamical complexity measure (often denoted as Φ), which was first introduced in neuroscience as a complexity measure for neural networks, and by extension, as a possible correlate of consciousness itself [23]. It is defined as the quantity of information generated by a network as a whole, due to its causal dynamical interactions, and one that is over and above the

© Springer International Publishing AG 2017
A. Lintas et al. (Eds.): ICANN 2017, Part I, LNCS 10613, pp. 326–333, 2017.
https://doi.org/10.1007/978-3-319-68600-4_38

information generated independently by the disjoint sum of its parts. As a complexity measure, Φ seeks to operationalize the intuition that complexity arises from simultaneous integration and differentiation of the network's structure and dynamics. The interplay of integration and differentiation generates information that is highly integrated yet diversified, thus coding for complex cognitive and behavioral states. Following initial proposals [22,23], several approaches have been developed to compute integrated information [1,5–8,10,12,20] (see [2] for another application of an entropy measure). In this paper, we consider stochastic network dynamics with continuous state variables as this is appropriate for modeling realistic neural networks that generate time-series data. We want to study the relationship between the information integrated by these networks and the couplings that parametrize their topology and dynamics. Our main finding is that tuning the dynamical operating point of a network near the edge of criticality leads to high integrated information. We show these computations for both, toy model examples as well as the human connectome network [19].

2   Methods

We consider complex networks with stochastic dynamics. The state of each node is given by a continuous random variable pertaining to a Gaussian distribution. For many realistic applications, Gaussian distributed variables are fairly reasonable abstractions. The state of the network $\mathbf{X_t}$ at time t is taken as a multivariate Gaussian variable with distribution $\mathbf{P_{X_t}}(\mathbf{x_t})$. $\mathbf{x_t}$ denotes an instantiation of $\mathbf{X_t}$ with components x_t^i (i going from 1 to n, n being the number of nodes). When the network makes a transition from an initial state $\mathbf{X_0}$ to a state $\mathbf{X_1}$ at time $t = 1$, observing the final state generates information about the system's initial state. The information generated equals the reduction in uncertainty regarding the initial state $\mathbf{X_0}$. This is given by the conditional entropy $\mathbf{H}(\mathbf{X_0}|\mathbf{X_1})$. In order to extract that part of the information generated by the system as a whole, over and above that generated individually by its irreducible parts, one computes the relative conditional entropy given by the Kullback-Leibler divergence of the conditional distribution $\mathbf{P_{X_0|X_1=x'}}(\mathbf{x})$ of the system with respect to the joint conditional distributions $\prod_{k=1}^{n} \mathbf{P_{M_0^k|M_1^k=m'}}$ of its irreducible parts [6]. Denoting this as Φ, we have

$$\Phi(\mathbf{X_0} \rightarrow \mathbf{X_1} = \mathbf{x'}) = D_{KL}\left(\mathbf{P_{X_0|X_1=x'}} \middle\| \prod_{k=1}^{n} \mathbf{P_{M_0^k|M_1^k=m'}}\right) \tag{1}$$

where state variables $\mathbf{X_0}$ and $\mathbf{X_1}$ can be decomposed as a direct sum $\mathbf{X_0} = \bigoplus_{k=1}^{n} \mathbf{M_0^k}$ and $\mathbf{X_1} = \bigoplus_{k=1}^{n} \mathbf{M_1^k}$ respectively. To have a measure that is independent of any particular instantiation of the final state $\mathbf{x'}$, we average Eq. (1) with respect to final states to obtain

$$\langle\Phi\rangle(\mathbf{X_0} \rightarrow \mathbf{X_1}) = -\mathbf{H}(\mathbf{X_0}|\mathbf{X_1}) + \sum_{k=1}^{n} \mathbf{H}(\mathbf{M_0^k}|\mathbf{M_1^k}) \tag{2}$$

This is the definition of integrated information that we will use [6]. The state variable at each time $t = 0$ and $t = 1$ follows a multivariate Gaussian distribution $\mathbf{X_0} \sim \mathcal{N}(\bar{\mathbf{x}}_0, \mathbf{\Sigma}(\mathbf{X_0}))$ and $\mathbf{X_1} \sim \mathcal{N}(\bar{\mathbf{x}}_1, \mathbf{\Sigma}(\mathbf{X_1}))$ respectively. The generative model for this system is equivalent to a multi-variate auto-regressive process [11]

$$\mathbf{X_1} = \mathcal{A}\mathbf{X_0} + \mathbf{E_1} \tag{3}$$

where $\mathcal{A}$ is the weighted adjacency matrix of the network and E_1 is Gaussian noise. Taking the mean and covariance respectively on both sides of this equation, while holding the residual independent of the regression variables gives

$$\bar{\mathbf{x}}_1 = \mathcal{A}\bar{\mathbf{x}}_0 \qquad \mathbf{\Sigma}(\mathbf{X_1}) = \mathcal{A}\mathbf{\Sigma}(\mathbf{X_0})\mathcal{A}^{\mathbf{T}} + \mathbf{\Sigma}(\mathbf{E}) \tag{4}$$

In the absence of any external inputs, stationary solutions of a stochastic linear dynamical system as in Eq. (3) are fluctuations about the origin. Therefore, we can shift coordinates to set the means $\bar{\mathbf{x}}_0$ and consequently $\bar{\mathbf{x}}_1$ to the zero. The second equality in Eq. (4) is the discrete-time Lyapunov equation and its solution will give us the covariance matrix of the state variables. The conditional entropy for a multivariate Gaussian variable was computed in [12]

$$\mathbf{H}(\mathbf{X_0}|\mathbf{X_1}) = \frac{1}{2}n\log(2\pi e) - \frac{1}{2}\log\left[\det \mathbf{\Sigma}(\mathbf{X_0}|\mathbf{X_1})\right] \tag{5}$$

and depends on the conditional covariance matrix. Substituting in Eq. (2) yields

$$\langle \varPhi \rangle (\mathbf{X_0} \to \mathbf{X_1}) = \frac{1}{2}\log\left[\frac{\prod_{k=1}^{n} \det \mathbf{\Sigma}(\mathbf{M_0^k}|\mathbf{M_1^k})}{\det \mathbf{\Sigma}(\mathbf{X_0}|\mathbf{X_1})}\right] \tag{6}$$

In order to compute the conditional covariance matrix we make use of the identity (proof of this identity for the Gaussian case was demonstrated in [11])

$$\mathbf{\Sigma}(\mathbf{X}|\mathbf{Y}) = \mathbf{\Sigma}(\mathbf{X}) - \mathbf{\Sigma}(\mathbf{X}, \mathbf{Y})\mathbf{\Sigma}(\mathbf{Y})^{-1}\mathbf{\Sigma}(\mathbf{X}, \mathbf{Y})^{\mathbf{T}} \tag{7}$$

Computing $\mathbf{\Sigma}(\mathbf{X_0}, \mathbf{X_1}) = \mathbf{\Sigma}(\mathbf{X_0})\,\mathcal{A}^{\mathbf{T}}$ and using the above identity, we get

$$\mathbf{\Sigma}(\mathbf{X_0}|\mathbf{X_1}) = \mathbf{\Sigma}(\mathbf{X_0}) - \mathbf{\Sigma}(\mathbf{X_0})\,\mathcal{A}^{\mathbf{T}}\,\mathbf{\Sigma}(\mathbf{X_1})^{-1}\mathcal{A}\,\mathbf{\Sigma}(\mathbf{X_0})^{\mathbf{T}} \tag{8}$$

$$\mathbf{\Sigma}(\mathbf{M_0^k}|\mathbf{M_1^k}) = \mathbf{\Sigma}(\mathbf{M_0^k}) - \mathbf{\Sigma}(\mathbf{M_0^k})\,\mathcal{A}^{\mathbf{T}}\big|_{k}\,\mathbf{\Sigma}(\mathbf{M_1^k})^{-1}\mathcal{A}\big|_{k}\,\mathbf{\Sigma}(\mathbf{M_0^k})^{\mathbf{T}} \tag{9}$$

the conditional covariance for the whole system and that for its parts respectively. The variable $\mathbf{M_0^k}$ refers to the state of the kth node at $t = 0$ and $\mathcal{A}\big|_k$ denotes the (trivial) restriction of the adjacency matrix to the kth node. Note, that for linear multi-variate systems, a unique fixed point always exists. We want to find stable stationary solutions of this system. In that regime, the multi-variate probability distribution of states approaches stationarity and the covariance matrix converges, such that $\mathbf{\Sigma}(\mathbf{X_1}) = \mathbf{\Sigma}(\mathbf{X_0})$ (here $t = 0$ and $t = 1$ refer to time-points after the system has converged to its fixed point). Then the discrete-time Lyapunov equations can be solved iteratively for the stable covariance matrix $\Sigma(\mathbf{X_t})$. For networks with symmetric adjacency matrix and independent Gaussian noise, the solution takes a particularly simple form

$$\Sigma(\mathbf{X_t}) = \left(1 - \mathcal{A}^2\right)^{-1} \Sigma(\mathbf{E}) \tag{10}$$

and for the parts, we have

$$\Sigma(\mathbf{M_0^k}) = \Sigma(\mathbf{X_0})\big|_{\mathbf{k}} \tag{11}$$

given by the restriction of the full covariance matrix on the kth component. Note that Eq. (11) is not the same as taking Eq. (10) on the restricted adjacency matrix as that would mean that the kth node has been explicitly severed from the rest of the network. In fact, Eq. (11) is the variance of the kth node while it is still part of the network and $\langle \Phi \rangle$ yields the amount of information that is still greater than that of the sum of these connected parts. Inserting Eqs. (8), (9), (10) and (11) into Eq. (6) yields $\langle \Phi \rangle$ as a function of network weights for symmetric networks[1].

3   Results

Using the framework described above, we compute $\langle \Phi \rangle$ for 6 networks shown in Fig. 1. Each network has an 8 dimensional adjacency matrix with bi-directional weights (our computations works as well with directed graphs). We compute $\langle \Phi \rangle$ as a function of network weights, which we keep as free parameters. For simplicity, we set all weights to a single parameter, the global coupling strength g. $\langle \Phi \rangle$ as a function of g is computed for stationary solutions of the system. The results are shown in Fig. 2. These results show that irrespective of topology, all

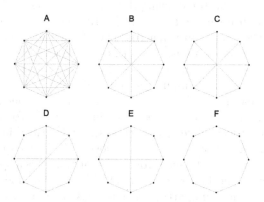

Fig. 1. Graphs of 6 networks, from the most densely connected (A) to the least (F).

---

[1] For the case of asymmetric weights, the entries of the covariance matrix cannot be explicitly expressed as a matrix equation. However, they may still be solved by Jordan decomposition of both sides of the Lyapunov equation.

these networks approach a pole at some value of g, near which, $\langle \Phi \rangle$ for that network is extremely high. We have checked that the location of the pole is precisely the critical point after which the largest eigenvalue of the network slips outside of the radius of stability. Figure 2 also shows an ordering of $\langle \Phi \rangle$ profiles based on topology, that is, the most densely packed networks occupy a small region of allowed values of g, while while the least densely connected networks have $\langle \Phi \rangle$ profiles that spread across broader intervals of g.

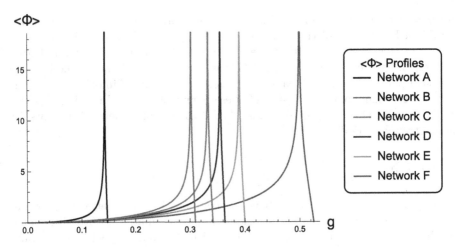

Fig. 2. $\langle \Phi \rangle$ profiles showing an ordering, for the most densely connected network on the left to the least on the right.

Next we apply our formulation to compute the integrated information of the human cerebral connectome, using data acquired from high-resolution T1-weighted diffusion spectrum imaging (DSI) [19]. The left-hand side of Fig. 3 shows the 998 × 998 connectivity matrix. The 998 network nodes (ROIs) represent cortical neural populations. Network edges denote weighted fiber counts between populations, amounting to about 15,000 weighted bi-directional connections. Note that we now compute $\langle \Phi \rangle$ for real network weights and g serves as a global scaling parameter. To simulate brain dynamics, one may chose from among a variety of possible models, discussed in [3,4,9,18]. To run these simulations, one may use customizable tools such as those described in [13,14,21]. The simplest model among the ones mentioned above is the linear stochastic Wilson-Cowen model. In fact, it can be seen from [18] that Eq. (3) is a special case of the discrete-time limit of the linear stochastic Wilson-Cowen model. This justifies the use of Eq. (3) for modeling attractor dynamics. The brain's state of spontaneous activity or resting-state is identified as the attractor of these models. This corresponds to stable stationary solutions of the system, which is the regime in which we compute $\langle \Phi \rangle$ in bits as a function of the scaling g. Our results are shown in the red profile in Fig. 4. Further, in order to contrast this result with a null model, we also rewired the edges of the connectome network randomly,

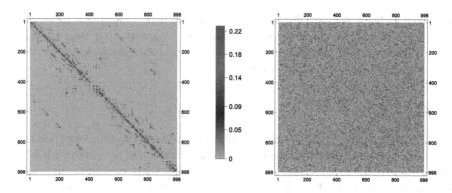

Fig. 3. Data from human cerebral white matter fiber tracts from 998 cortical voxels. The connectivity matrix on the left is a weighted matrix with the color-bar (in the middle) indicating connection strengths. The randomized matrix on the right is obtained by randomly shuffling positions of weights from the connectivity matrix. (Color figure online)

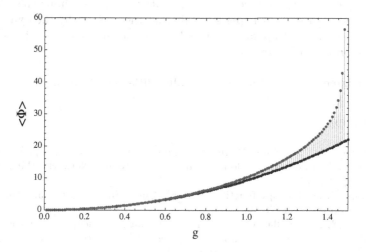

Fig. 4. $\langle \Phi \rangle$ for the human brain (shown as red points) as a function of global scaling parameter g, compared to $\langle \Phi \rangle$ for the randomized network (shown as blue points). Stationary solutions exist up to g = 1.49, the critical point of the data network. (Color figure online)

while preserving the magnitude of the weights. This generates the randomized data matrix shown on the right-hand side of Fig. 3. We also compute $\langle \Phi \rangle$ for this matrix. The resulting profile is the blue curve in Fig. 4. For extremely small couplings, the two networks are indistinguishable with respect to $\langle \Phi \rangle$, however, as g grows, the architecture of the brain's network turns out to perform better at integrating information than its randomized counterpart. More importantly, what Fig. 4 shows is that $\langle \Phi \rangle$ for the 998 dimensional connectome follows the same trend as that of the profiles shown in Fig. 2, namely, that near the critical coupling $g = 1.49$, integrated information of the brain network dramatically increases upon approaching criticality.

4   Discussion

In this paper we have implemented an information-theoretic complexity measure $\langle \Phi \rangle$ and applied it to compute the integrated information of networks with linear stochastic dynamics. We found poles in $\langle \Phi \rangle$ at criticality, leading to high information integration near the edge of criticality. This implies that it is not only the network's topology that determines how much information it can integrate, but also its dynamical operating point. As a matter of fact, operating near the edge of criticality leads to a sharp increase in $\langle \Phi \rangle$, irrespective of network topology. $\langle \Phi \rangle$ taken as a proxy for a system's information processing capacity, implies that operating near criticality is favorable for efficient information processing. These conclusions reconcile with recent evidence that resting-state dynamics of brain networks operate just at the edge of a bifurcation [15]. Combining this observation with the results of our paper suggests that the reason why the dynamics of the human brain might operate at the edge of criticality is in order to facilitate efficient information integration.

Acknowledgments. The CDAC project (ERC-2013-ADG 341196).

References

1. Arsiwalla, X.D., Verschure, P.: Integrated information for large complex networks. In: The 2013 International Joint Conference on Neural Networks (IJCNN), pp. 1–7, August 2013
2. Arsiwalla, X.D.: Entropy functions with 5D Chern-Simons terms. J. High Energy Phys. **2009**(09), 059 (2009)
3. Arsiwalla, X.D., Betella, A., Bueno, E.M., Omedas, P., Zucca, R., Verschure, P.F.: The dynamic connectome: a tool for large-scale 3D reconstruction of brain activity in real-time. In: ECMS, pp. 865–869 (2013)
4. Arsiwalla, X.D., Dalmazzo, D., Zucca, R., Betella, A., Brandi, S., Martinez, E., Omedas, P., Verschure, P.: Connectomics to semantomics: addressing the brain's big data challenge. Procedia Comput. Sci. **53**, 48–55 (2015)
5. Arsiwalla, X.D., Moulin-Frier, C., Herreros, I., Sanchez-Fibla, M., Verschure, P.F.: The morphospace of consciousness. arXiv preprint arXiv:1705.11190 (2017)
6. Arsiwalla, X.D., Verschure, P.: Computing information integration in brain networks. In: Wierzbicki, A., Brandes, U., Schweitzer, F., Pedreschi, D. (eds.) NetSci-X 2016. LNCS, vol. 9564, pp. 136–146. Springer, Cham (2016). doi:10.1007/978-3-319-28361-6_11
7. Arsiwalla, X.D., Verschure, P.F.M.J.: High integrated information in complex networks near criticality. In: Villa, A.E.P., Masulli, P., Pons Rivero, A.J. (eds.) ICANN 2016. LNCS, vol. 9886, pp. 184–191. Springer, Cham (2016). doi:10.1007/978-3-319-44778-0_22

8. Arsiwalla, X.D., Verschure, P.F.: The global dynamical complexity of the human brain network. Appl. Netw. Sci. **1**(1), 16 (2016)

9. Arsiwalla, X.D., Zucca, R., Betella, A., Martinez, E., Dalmazzo, D., Omedas, P., Deco, G., Verschure, P.: Network dynamics with brainX3: a large-scale simulation of the human brain network with real-time interaction. Front. Neuroinformatics **9**(2) (2015)

10. Balduzzi, D., Tononi, G.: Integrated information in discrete dynamical systems: motivation and theoretical framework. PLoS Comput. Biol. **4**(6), e1000091 (2008)

11. Barrett, A.B., Barnett, L., Seth, A.K.: Multivariate granger causality and generalized variance. Phys. Rev. E **81**(4), 041907 (2010)

12. Barrett, A.B., Seth, A.K.: Practical measures of integrated information for time-series data. PLoS Comput. Biol. **7**(1), e1001052 (2011)

13. Betella, A., Bueno, E.M., Kongsantad, W., Zucca, R., Arsiwalla, X.D., Omedas, P., Verschure, P.: Understanding large network datasets through embodied interaction in virtual reality. In: Proceedings of the 2014 Virtual Reality International Conference, VRIC 2014, pp. 23:1–23:7. ACM, New York (2014)

14. Betella, A., Cetnarski, R., Zucca, R., Arsiwalla, X.D., Martínez, E., Omedas, P., Mura, A., Verschure, P.: BrainX3: embodied exploration of neural data. In: Proceedings of the 2014 Virtual Reality International Conference, VRIC 2014, pp. 37:1–37:4. ACM, New York (2014)

15. Deco, G., Ponce-Alvarez, A., Mantini, D., Romani, G.L., Hagmann, P., Corbetta, M.: Resting-state functional connectivity emerges from structurally and dynamically shaped slow linear fluctuations. J. Neurosci. **33**(27), 11239–11252 (2013)

16. Domb, C.: Phase Transitions and Critical Phenomena, vol. 19. Academic Press, London (2000)

17. Eguiluz, V.M., Chialvo, D.R., Cecchi, G.A., Baliki, M., Apkarian, A.V.: Scale-free brain functional networks. Phys. Rev. Lett. **94**(1), 018102 (2005)

18. Galán, R.F.: On how network architecture determines the dominant patterns of spontaneous neural activity. PLoS ONE **3**(5), e2148 (2008)

19. Hagmann, P., Cammoun, L., Gigandet, X., Meuli, R., Honey, C.J., Wedeen, V.J., Sporns, O.: Mapping the structural core of human cerebral cortex. PLoS Biol. **6**(7), 15 (2008)

20. Oizumi, M., Albantakis, L., Tononi, G.: From the phenomenology to the mechanisms of consciousness: integrated information theory 3.0. PLoS Comput. Biol. **10**(5), e1003588 (2014)

21. Omedas, P., Betella, A., Zucca, R., Arsiwalla, X.D., et al.: Xim-engine: a software framework to support the development of interactive applications that uses conscious and unconscious reactions in immersive mixed reality. In: Proceedings of the 2014 Virtual Reality International Conference, VRIC 2014, pp. 26:1–26:4. ACM, New York (2014)

22. Tononi, G., Sporns, O.: Measuring information integration. BMC Neurosci. **4**(1), 31 (2003)

23. Tononi, G., Sporns, O., Edelman, G.M.: A measure for brain complexity: relating functional segregation and integration in the nervous system. Proc. Natl. Acad. Sci. **91**(11), 5033–5037 (1994)

24. Zucca, R., Arsiwalla, X.D., Le, H., Rubinov, M., Verschure, P.F.M.J.: Scaling properties of human brain functional networks. In: Villa, A.E.P., Masulli, P., Pons Rivero, A.J. (eds.) ICANN 2016. LNCS, vol. 9886, pp. 107–114. Springer, Cham (2016). doi:10.1007/978-3-319-44778-0_13

Interactive Control of Computational Power in a Model of the Basal Ganglia-Thalamocortical Circuit by a Supervised Attractor-Based Learning Procedure

Jérémie Cabessa[1] and Alessandro E.P. Villa[2]([⊠])

[1] Laboratoire d'économie Mathématique (LEMMA),
Université Paris 2 – Panthéon-Assas,
4, Rue Blaise Desgoffe, 75006 Paris, France
[2] NeuroHeuristic Research Group, University of Lausanne,
Quartier UNIL-Dorigny, 1015 Lausanne, Switzerland
avilla@unil.ch
http://www.neuroheuristic.org

Abstract. The attractor-based complexity of a Boolean neural network refers to its ability to discriminate among the possible input streams, by means of alternations between meaningful and spurious attractor dynamics. The higher the complexity, the greater the computational power of the network. The fine tuning of the interactivity – the network's feedback output combined with the current input stream – can maintain a high degree of complexity within stable domains of the parameters' space. In addition, the attractor-based complexity of the network is related to the degree of discrimination of specific input streams. We present a novel supervised attractor-based learning procedure aimed at achieving a maximal discriminability degree of a selected input stream. With a predefined target value of discriminability degree and in the absence of changes in the internal connectivity matrix of the network, the learning procedure updates solely the weights of the feedback projections. In a Boolean model of the basal ganglia-thalamocortical circuit, we show how the learning trajectories starting from different configurations can converge to final configurations associated with same high discriminability degree. We discuss the possibility that the limbic system may play the role of the interactive feedback to the network studied here.

Keywords: Boolean recurrent neural networks · Learning · Attractors · Plasticity · Interactivity · Basal ganglia-thalamocortical circuit · Limbic system

1 Introduction

Attractor dynamics or quasi-attractor dynamics have been associated to perceptions, thoughts and memories, and the chaotic itinerancy between those with

© Springer International Publishing AG 2017
A. Lintas et al. (Eds.): ICANN 2017, Part I, LNCS 10613, pp. 334–342, 2017.
https://doi.org/10.1007/978-3-319-68600-4_39

sequences in thinking, speaking and writing [1–3]. Specific spike trains – time series defined by the epochs of neuronal discharges – were experimentally shown to be associated with such (chaotic) attractor dynamics [4–8]. Moreover, experimental neurophysiological studies suggest that spatiotemporal patterns of discharges repeating more often than expected by chance may be associated to processing and coding of information in the brain, in particular in association with specific behaviors [9–14]. Spatiotemporal patterns have also been observed in simulations of nonlinear dynamical systems [15,16] as well as in simulations of large scale neuronal networks [17]. Hence, the correlation between attractor dynamics and recurrent spatiotemporal patterns of discharges has been suggested as an alternative model to synfire chains [3,9,18]. Neural coding of perceptual and contextual information may be performed by underlying attractor dynamics, with the advantage of implicit transmission and storage of memory traces in the network connectivity [19].

We introduced an *attractor-based complexity* measure for Boolean recurrent neural networks, which refers to the ability of the networks to discriminate among their possible input streams, by means of alternations between meaningful and spurious attractor dynamics [18,20,21]. This complexity measure is assumed to be related to some aspects of the computational capabilities of Boolean neural networks. It was applied to study the attractor dynamics of a Boolean model of the basal ganglia-thalamocortical circuit [18]. In this model, the attractor dynamics and its associated complexity measure are highly sensitive to local and global modifications of the coupling strength between network's nodes. The fine tuning of synaptic weights, global threshold and interactive feedback can maintain a high degree of complexity within stable domains of the parameters' space [22,23].

In this study, we first show that the attractor-based complexity of a Boolean network is related to the *discriminability degree* of specific input streams. We present a supervised attractor-based learning procedure aimed at achieving a maximal *discriminability degree* of a selected input stream. This procedure updates the *interactive weights* – the feedback projections which are combined with the external input – according to a target value of attractor-based complexity. We illustrate this learning procedure on a Boolean model of the basal ganglia-thalamocortical circuit. This circuit is known to be crucially involved in the processing and coding of information in the brain [24,25]. We discuss the possibility that the role of interactivity played by the modifiable feedback projections might correspond to the functional connectivity of the limbic system [26].

2   Attractor-Based Complexity of Boolean Recurrent Neural Networks

We briefly summarize the theoretical background exposed in detail in [18]. Any recurrent neural network $\mathcal{N}$ composed of Boolean integrate-and-fire (IF) units can be simulated by a corresponding finite state automaton $\mathcal{A}(\mathcal{N})$, and vice versa. The nodes of $\mathcal{A}(\mathcal{N})$ correspond to the different states (i.e., the spiking configurations) of $\mathcal{N}$. There exists a transition from node i to node j labelled by u in $\mathcal{A}(\mathcal{N})$ if and only if $\mathcal{N}$ switches from state i to state j when receiving input u. Accordingly, the possible *dynamics* of a given network $\mathcal{N}$ correspond to the different *paths* in the graph of the associated automaton $\mathcal{A}(\mathcal{N})$.

Let us consider the Boolean network $\mathcal{N}$ of the basal ganglia-thalamocortical circuit (Fig. 1A) and its connectivity matrix [18] together with its corresponding finite automaton $\mathcal{A}(\mathcal{N})$ (Fig. 1B). Each node of the automaton represents a specific state of the network. For instance, node 384 corresponds to firing activity exclusively in the units representing the thalamus and superior colliculus (SC). If input $u = 0$ is received, which corresponds to unit 'IN' being not active, then the automaton switches from node 384 to node 223, which corresponds to activity in the units representing the thalamus, the thalamic reticular nucleus (NRT), the

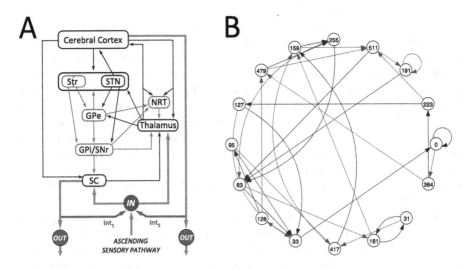

Fig. 1. A. Simplified Boolean model of the basal ganglia-thalamocortical circuit. Each brain area is represented by a single Boolean unit: superior colliculus (SC), Thalamus, thalamic reticular nucleus (NRT), Cerebral Cortex, the striatopallidal and the striatonigral components of the striatum (Str), the subthalamic nucleus (STN), the external part of the pallidum (GPe), and the output nuclei of the basal ganglia formed by the GABAergic projection neurons of the intermediate part of the pallidum and of the substantia nigra pars reticulata (GPi/SNR). We consider also the inputs (IN) from the ascending sensory pathway and the efferent outputs (OUT). The excitatory pathways are labeled in blue and the inhibitory ones in orange. We considered a closed-loop model with a recurrent connection from the efferent output to the input unit via 'interactive' connections int_1 and int_2. **B.** Finite automaton associated to the Boolean model of the basal ganglia-thalamocortical circuit. Each node of the automaton is a state of the circuit. There is a blue or red transition from node i to node j if and only if the network switches from state i to state j when receiving input 0 or 1, respectively. The cycles in the automaton correspond to the attractors of the network. (Color figure online)

pallidum (both internal GPi and external GPe parts), the striatum (Str), the subthalamic nucleus (STN) and the cerebral cortex. If the next input is $u = 1$, which corresponds to unit 'IN' being active, then the automaton switches from node 223 switches to node 511, which corresponds to firing activity in all units of the circuit. And so on, with each distinct node corresponding to a distinct unique activity pattern in the circuit.

According to this construction, the *attractors* of $\mathcal{N}$ – i.e., those dynamics which eventually become trapped into the repetition of a same set of states – correspond to the *cycles* in the graph of $\mathcal{A}(\mathcal{N})$. The set of attractors of network $\mathcal{N}$ can therefore be computed effectively, by constructing the associated automaton $\mathcal{A}(\mathcal{N})$ and listing the cycles of this latter. Note that any *periodic attractor* of $\mathcal{N}$ will necessarily elicit some recurrent *spatiotemporal pattern of discharges* which corresponds to the set of states visited periodically.

In this context, we introduced an *attractor-based measure of complexity* [18], which corresponds to the translation of a refined automata-theoretic notion [27] to the Boolean neural network context. Formally, suppose that $\mathcal{N}$ is a Boolean network provided with a classification of all of its attractors according to their meaningfulness – i.e., an attractor is classified as meaningful or spurious depending on the meaningfulness of its composing states (see [18] for more details). The *attractor-based complexity* of $\mathcal{N}$ is the integer n associated to a maximal sequence of cycles $\mathcal{C} = (C_0, \ldots, C_n)$ of $\mathcal{A}(\mathcal{N})$ – i.e., of attractors of $\mathcal{N}$ – which satisfies:

- C_i is included in C_{i+1}, for $i = 0, \ldots, n-1$; (1)
- C_i and C_{i+1} have opposite meaningfulness, for $i = 0, \ldots, n-1$. (2)

Conditions (1) and (2) state that the complexity measure is related to sequences of attractors that are included one into the next and of alternating meaningfulness. The general idea behind this complexity measure is that the meaningful and spurious attractors of a network are interpreted as the dynamical behaviors encoding the "acceptance" or "rejection" of the continual input received. Hence, a switch from one attractor to another of opposite meaningfulness corresponds to a moment when the network shifts from an "acceptance" to a "rejection" (or vice-versa) of its continual input. Accordingly, the attractor-based complexity of the network refers to its ability to discriminate between its input streams, by means of alternations between meaningful and spurious attractor dynamics [18]. This feature has been argued to be related to the computational power of the network (cf. [18] and Sect. 4).

The Boolean network of Fig. 1A has an attractor-based complexity of 6 with its connectivity matrix described elsewhere [18]. This value is highly dependent from both local and global variations of the synaptic strengths [22,23]. In fact, small perturbations of the connectivity weights and firing threshold might lead to completely distinct associated automata (with completely different cycle structures), and therefore, to very different attractor-based complexities. Furthermore, the interactive feedback (Fig. 1A, weights int_1 and int_2) plays a key role in the regulation of the network's attractor-based complexity. The parameter space defined by the variations of int_1 and int_2 shows the existence of *stable domains* characterized by same values of the network's complexity, as illustrated by the different colored areas of Fig. 2.

Note that short input streams would induce the network's dynamics to visit only few (or no) attractors. By contrast, longer input streams will necessarily bring the network's dynamics into multiple successive attractors. For any such long input stream s, let $C_s = (C_0, \ldots, C_n)$ be a corresponding sequence of attractors visited by the network receiving input s (note that C_s is not unique). We will say that s is *discriminated* by C_s whenever C_s satisfies the above conditions (1) and (2). Accordingly, the *discriminability degree* of s, denoted as $d^*(s)$, is the largest number of attractor alternations that can be found in a sequence C_s which discriminates s. In other words, s has a *discriminability degree* of k if s is discriminated by some sequence $C_s = (C_0, \ldots, C_k)$, but by no larger sequence $C'_s = (C_0, \ldots, C_l)$ with $l > k$. Notice that by definition, if some input stream s has a discriminability degree of k in $\mathcal{N}$, then the attractor-based complexity of

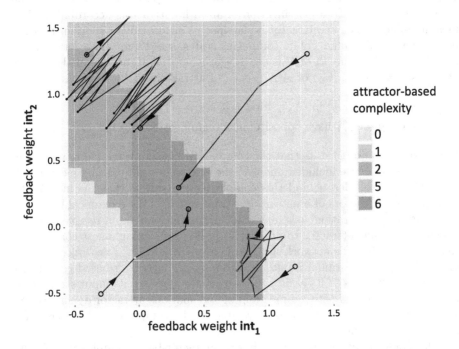

Fig. 2. Illustration of four trajectories of the attractor-based learning procedure. The color scale indicates the attractor-based complexity of the network of Fig. 1 as a function of its two interactive weights, with an optimal domain of complexity 6. Each trajectory describes a specific learning procedure updating the interactive weights at each step. The start and end points of the trajectories are the initial and final values of the interactive weights, and the intermediate points correspond to the successive updates of the weights achieved by the learning procedure. (Color figure online)

$\mathcal{N}$ is at least k (since $\mathcal{A}(\mathcal{N})$ contains at least the sequence $C_s = (C_0, \ldots, C_{k-1})$ discriminating s).

In the sequel, we will consider a specific input stream $\bar{s}$ having discriminability degree 6 for the circuit of Fig. 1A. Due to limited space available, we do not provide here the full description of that input.

3 Attractor-Based Learning

We consider a learning task consisting in the discrimination of a selected perceptual input fed into the basal ganglia-thalamocortical circuit via the ascending sensory pathway. The optimal learning is achieved if the dynamics associated with the reading of that perceptual input reaches the largest discriminability degree (in the sense of Sect. 2). In summary, the *attractor-based learning* procedure defined here performs updating of the network's weights with the aim of achieving a maximal discriminability degree of a selected input stream s. In our case, we assume that the connectivity matrix of the circuit is fixed and that the learning procedure only modifies the feedback weights int_1 and int_2 (Fig. 1A). The updating of the weights int_1 and int_2 depends on whether the network's dynamics induced by the given input stream s visits mainly spurious or meaningful attractors, and on the number of alternations between such attractors. The learning procedure is supervised in the sense that a target value for the discriminability degree is set at the begin.

More precisely, let s be an input stream, let w_k for $k = 1, \ldots, N$ be the modifiable weights of the network, and let N^* be the target value of the discriminability degree of s. Let C_s be a sequence of attractors visited by the network reading input s, and such that C_s contains a maximal subsequence that discriminates s. Let also $m_s \in \{-1, 1\}^{len(C_s)}$ be the "meaningfulness of C_s", simply defined as: $m_s(i) = -1$ if $C_s(i)$ is spurious and $m_s(i) = 1$ if $C_s(i)$ is meaningful. Finally, let $d^*(s)$ be the current discriminability degree of s. If the discriminability degree $d^*(s) < N^*$, the weights w_k are updated according to the following rule:

$$f(w_k) = w_k + step \cdot \frac{-sum(m_s)}{len(m_s)} \cdot \left(1 + \frac{len(m_s) - d^*(s)}{len(m_s)}\right) + \epsilon$$

where $sum(m_s)$, $len(m_s)$ are the sum and length of m_s, ϵ is a uniform noise in the range $[-0.1, 0.1]$, and $step = 0.3$. Note that if the reading of s induces a sequence C_s of only spurious (resp. of only meaningful) attractors, then $d^*(s) = 0$ and $|sum(m_s)| = len(m_s)$, and thus an update of maximal amplitude $f(w) = w + 2 \cdot step + \epsilon$ (resp. $f(w) = w - 2 \cdot step + \epsilon$) ensues. In words, the weight's update is increased when the number of alternations and the discriminability degree are lower (i.e., $|sum(m_s)|$ is high and $d^*(s)$ is small). The learning procedure based on this updating rule is given in Algorithm 1.

We illustrate this learning procedure in the case of the neural circuit presented in Sect. 2. For this purpose, we have considered $\bar{s}$ as the selected input

---

Algorithm 1. Attractor-based learning procedure

Require: input stream s; initial weights w_1, w_2; target discriminability degree N^*
1: compute $d^*(s)$
2: **while** $d^*(s) < N^*$ **do**
3:     $w_k \leftarrow f(w_k)$, for $k = 1, \ldots, N$ weights' updating
4:     compute $d^*(s)$ for the network with updated weights w_k, for $k = 1, \ldots, N$
5: **end while**
6: **return** w_k, for $k = 1, \ldots, N$

---

stream (cf. Sect. 2) and set the target discriminability degree to $N^* = 6$. We analyzed the learning procedure over the parameter space defined by the interactive weights int_1 and int_2 in the range $[-0.5, 1.5]$ by steps of 0.1 (Fig. 2). For each point in this space, we simulated the procedure from this point and followed its trajectory until it stopped. In the majority of the simulations (427/441), the procedure converged to novel interactive weights such that $d^*(\bar{s}) = N^* = 6$. Notice that during the procedure, the update of the weights int_1 and int_2 tended to be on the same direction (both increased or both decreased), which favored trajectories with angles between $30°$ and $60°$.

4 Discussion

We have introduced an attractor-based learning procedure which modifies the modifiable weights of a network in order to achieve the optimal discrimination of a selected input stream. In our simplified model of the basal ganglia-thalamocortical circuit, we showed that interactive weights can be updated to reach a high level of discriminability of a given input stream, and in turn, to drive the dynamics of the network to a basin of attractions with a high level of complexity. Hence, the higher the level of discriminability, the larger the sequence of attractors visited by the dynamics, and accordingly, the larger amount of spatiotemporal patterns, and the higher the storage capacity of dynamic memories. We suggest that this correlation between attractor-based complexity and storage capacity of dynamic memories also prevails in real brain networks. Experimental evidence for bump attractor dynamics underlying spatial working memory has been provided by data from oculomotor delayed response tasks in awake behaving monkeys [28]. This study shows that persistent activity reinforcement is associated with a continuous prefrontal representation of memorized space, which is in agreement with other experimental data showing the emergence of recurrent spatiotemporal firing patterns associated with persistent activity in the inferotemporal cortex of behaving monkeys [11]. Hence, despite the oversimplification of our model (e.g. the brain probably is not behaving as a boolean network), the attractor-based complexity defined here may be considered an indicator of some aspects of the computational capabilities of neural networks.

General forms of synaptic plasticity and interactive architecture play a crucial role in regulating and controlling the computational and dynamical capabilities of Boolean neural networks [22,23]. In the brain, the role assumed by the feedback might be played by the connections to and from the limbic system [26]. Such interaction reflects a dynamic adaptation to the learning situation. Dysfunctions of synaptic plasticity and functioning of the hippocampal formation and basal ganglia-thalamocortical loops may lead to impairment of learning, memory, and attention evoked by sleep deprivation.

References

1. Skarda, C.A., Freeman, W.J.: How brains make chaos in order to make sense of the world. Behav. Brain Sci. **10**, 161–173 (1987)
2. Tsuda, I.: Chaotic itinerancy as a dynamical basis of hermeneutics of brain and mind. World Futures **32**, 167–185 (1991)
3. Villa, A.E.P.: Empirical evidence about temporal structure in multi-unit recordings. In: Miller, R. (ed.) Time and the Brain. Conceptual Advances in Brain Research, vol. 3, pp. 1–61. CRC Press, London (2000)
4. Mpitsos, G.J., Burton, R.M., Creech, H.C., Soinila, S.O.: Evidence for chaos in spike trains of neurons that generate rhythmic motor patterns. Brain Res. Bull. **21**(3), 529–38 (1988)
5. Hoppensteadt, F.C.: Intermittent chaos, self-organization, and learning from synchronous synaptic activity in model neuron networks. Proc. Natl. Acad. Sci. U.S.A. **86**(9), 2991–2995 (1989)
6. Celletti, A., Villa, A.E.P.: Low-dimensional chaotic attractors in the rat brain. Biol. Cybern. **74**(5), 387–393 (1996)
7. Villa, A.E.P., Tetko, I.V., Celletti, A., Riehle, A.: Chaotic dynamics in the primate motor cortex depend on motor preparation in a reaction-time task. Cah. Psychol. Cogn. **17**, 763–780 (1998)
8. Segundo, J.P.: Nonlinear dynamics of point process systems and data. Int. J. Bifurcat. Chaos **13**(08), 2035–2116 (2003)
9. Abeles, M.: Local Cortical Circuits: An Electrophysiological Study. Studies of Brain Function, vol. 6. Springer, New York (1982)
10. Vaadia, E., Bergman, H., Abeles, M.: Neuronal activities related to higher brain functions-theoretical and experimental implications. IEEE Trans. Biomed. Eng. **36**(1), 25–35 (1989)
11. Villa, A., Fuster, J.: Temporal correlates of information processing during visual short-term memory. Neuroreport **3**(1), 113–116 (1992)
12. Vaadia, E., Haalman, I., Abeles, M., Bergman, H., Prut, Y., Slovin, H., Aertsen, A.: Dynamics of neuronal interactions in monkey cortex in relation to behavioural events. Nature **373**(6514), 515–518 (1995)
13. Prut, Y., Vaadia, E., Bergman, H., Haalman, I., Slovin, H., Abeles, M.: Spatiotemporal structure of cortical activity: properties and behavioral relevance. J. Neurophysiol. **79**(6), 2857–2874 (1998)
14. Villa, A.E.P., Tetko, I.V., Hyland, B., Najem, A.: Spatiotemporal activity patterns of rat cortical neurons predict responses in a conditioned task. Proc. Natl. Acad. Sci. U.S.A. **96**(3), 1106–1111 (1999)
15. Asai, Y., Villa, A.E.: Reconstruction of underlying nonlinear deterministic dynamics embedded in noisy spike trains. J. Biol. Phys. **34**(3–4), 325–340 (2008)
16. Asai, Y., Villa, A.: Integration and transmission of distributed deterministic neural activity in feed-forward networks. Brain Res. **1434**, 17–33 (2012)

17. Iglesias, J., Villa, A.E.: Recurrent spatiotemporal firing patterns in large spiking neural networks with ontogenetic and epigenetic processes. J. Physiol. Paris **104**(3–4), 137–146 (2010)
18. Cabessa, J., Villa, A.E.P.: An attractor-based complexity measurement for boolean recurrent neural networks. PLoS ONE **9**(4), e94204 (2014)
19. Masulli, P., Villa, A.E.P.: The topology of the directed clique complex as a network invariant. Springerplus **5**, 388 (2016)
20. Cabessa, J., Villa, A.E.P.: The expressive power of analog recurrent neural networks on infinite input streams. Theor. Comput. Sci. **436**, 23–34 (2012)
21. Cabessa, J., Villa, A.E.P.: Expressive power of first-order recurrent neural networks determined by their attractor dynamics. J. Comput. Syst. Sci. **82**, 1232–1250 (2016)
22. Cabessa, J., Villa, A.E.P.: Attractor-based complexity of a boolean model of the basal ganglia-thalamocortical network. In: 2016 International Joint Conference on Neural Networks (IJCNN), pp. 4664–4671. IEEE, July 2016
23. Cabessa, J., Villa, A.E.P.: Attractor dynamics driven by interactivity in boolean recurrent neural networks. In: Villa, A.E.P., Masulli, P., Pons Rivero, A.J. (eds.) ICANN 2016. LNCS, vol. 9886, pp. 115–122. Springer, Cham (2016). doi:10.1007/978-3-319-44778-0_14
24. Nakahara, H., Amari Si, S., Hikosaka, O.: Self-organization in the basal ganglia with modulation of reinforcement signals. Neural Comput. **14**(4), 819–844 (2002)
25. Guthrie, M., Leblois, A., Garenne, A., Boraud, T.: Interaction between cognitive and motor cortico-basal ganglia loops during decision making: a computational study. J. Neurophysiol. **109**(12), 3025–3040 (2013)
26. Leblois, A., Boraud, T., Meissner, W., Bergman, H., Hansel, D.: Competition between feedback loops underlies normal and pathological dynamics in the basal ganglia. J. Neurosci. **26**(13), 3567–3583 (2006)
27. Wagner, K.: On ω-regular sets. Inf. Control **43**(2), 123–177 (1979)
28. Wimmer, K., Nykamp, D.Q., Constantinidis, C., Compte, A.: Bump attractor dynamics in prefrontal cortex explains behavioral precision in spatial working memory. Nat. Neurosci. **17**(3), 431–439 (2014)
29. Packard, M.G., Goodman, J.: Factors that influence the relative use of multiple memory systems. Hippocampus **23**(11), 1044–1052 (2013)
30. Lintas, A.: Discharge properties of neurons recorded in the parvalbumin-positive (pv1) nucleus of the rat lateral hypothalamus. Neurosci. Lett. **571**, 29–33 (2014)
31. Atallah, H.E., Frank, M.J., O'Reilly, R.C.: Hippocampus, cortex, and basal ganglia: insights from computational models of complementary learning systems. Neurobiol. Learn Mem. **82**(3), 253–267 (2004)
32. Perrig, S., Iglesias, J., Shaposhnyk, V., Chibirova, O., Dutoit, P., Cabessa, J., Espa-Cervena, K., Pelletier, L., Berger, F., Villa, A.E.P.: Functional interactions in hierarchically organized neural networks studied with spatiotemporal firing patterns and phase-coupling frequencies. Chin. J. Physiol. **53**(6), 382–395 (2010)

Synaptic Plasticity and Learning

Model Derived Spike Time Dependent Plasticity

Melissa Johnson[⊠] and Sylvain Chartier

University of Ottawa, Ottawa, ON K1N 6N5, Canada
mjohn140@uottawa.ca

Abstract. When developing learning rules, many researchers develop the rules based on biological findings outside of their network, not with the properties of their network. This means that there is a discontinuity between the network and the learning rule. This paper proposes to search within the network itself for properties that display learning rule characteristics. Within the bidirectional associative memory neural network, the transmission function works both as a node, and through mathematical analysis, displays properties similar to learning. The results of this analysis are used to create a learning rule. Using a presynaptic spike train on a postsynaptic neuron model, the derivative of the node equation successfully displays both potentiation and depression that is adjusted based on spike time. The results also show the importance of repetition in achieving long term synaptic weight changes that have an effect on the postsynaptic neuron. The simulation shows a new way to explore spike time dependent plasticity and is a step towards creating a network with the full benefits of using spiking neurons.

Keywords: STDP · Learning · Potentiation · Depression

1 Introduction

Spiking neural networks (SNNs) theoretically are at least as powerful, if not more so, than other artificial neural networks (ANNs), and they are more efficient, requiring fewer neurons for similar tasks [1]. Therefore, it is no surprise that new SNNs are being developed and traditional ANNs are being converted into SNNs. While SNNs should be an improvement over previous ANNs, within long term memory, there is an issue: researchers still do not know how spikes create memories [2]; there is no clear learning rule for SNNs [3, 4]!

It is known that long term memory is created using spike time dependent plasticity (STDP) [5] but not exactly how. This paper approaches creating a learning rule in a novel, yet still biologically inspired, way. Specifically, while it is unknown how STDP works, logically STDP has to be a property of the neurons and how they are connected. Therefore, instead of using a STDP learning rule that was fitted to biological findings, the learning rule is derived from the neural model itself, including the STDP properties. This allows for a cleaner network that explains how STDP occurs from its internal properties. The main purpose of this paper is to show that such network properties can be found and used for learning via STDP.

© Springer International Publishing AG 2017
A. Lintas et al. (Eds.): ICANN 2017, Part I, LNCS 10613, pp. 345–353, 2017.
https://doi.org/10.1007/978-3-319-68600-4_40

2 Spiking Neural Network

While this paper does not deal with a fully implemented neural network, all the concepts used are based off of the bidirectional associative memory (BAM) ANN created by [6]. The final goal is to develop a general long term memory model that encompasses both rate base and time dependent encodings.

In BAM, the transmission function is a modified Verhulst equation:

$$\frac{dz}{dt} = \left(1 - z^2\right)z \tag{1}$$

It should be noted though, that the modified Verhulst equation is a specific example of a cubic equation:

$$\frac{dz}{dt} = \alpha(z - y_1)(z - y_2)(z - y_3) \tag{2}$$

where $\alpha = -1$, and the y-intercepts, y_1, y_2, and y_3 equal -1, 0, and 1 respectively. The benefit of the general cubic form over the specific equation shown in Eq. 1 is that the general equation allows stable points to occur at the researcher's discretion and allows the researcher to determine the depth of the curve, giving the researcher more control over the function. The sign of the parameter α plays an important role in the cubic equation as it determines if the function is positive or negative which in turn determines which fixed points are stable and how the graph flows (see Fig. 1).

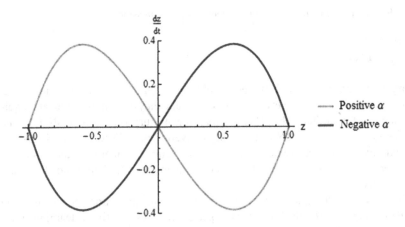

Fig. 1. Positive and negative cubic functions with z-intercepts at -1, 0, and 1.

Transmission functions, such as the one in Eq. 2, are normally displayed as differential equations. To solve these equations, the common practice is to use Euler's method to approximate the solution. For Eq. 2, this approximation yields the function:

$$f(z) = z + \alpha\,\delta(z - y_1)(z - y_2)(z - y_3) \tag{3}$$

where δ is a small constant term. In the BAM architecture, the above equation defines the transmission function, as long as the variable α is negative. In a SNN, the transmission function is replaced with a related spiking neural model, or node. Because the main goal is to have the learning rule be related to how the node works with minimal changes to the network, it follows that both the node and the learning rule should be related to the above equation.

2.1 Neural Model

Nonlinear integrate and fire models are both popular to use and have properties such as spike latency, bi-stability, and threshold variability [7, 8]. The two most common nonlinear integrate and fire models are the quadratic and the exponential models [4] with the quadratic model being an easier model to analysis and use but the exponential model being more biologically accurate.

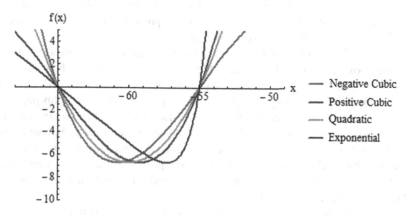

Fig. 2. Both cubic equations, the quadratic equation, and the exponential equation set with the same x-intercepts and local minimum.

Figure 2 shows that the curve of the positive cubic equation pattern falls between the exponential and quadratic equations. This implies that with a few minor modifications, similar to those used for the quadratic function, the cubic function can become another nonlinear integrate and fire model. Mathematically, the cubic integrate and fire (CIF) is described as:

$$\frac{dv}{dt} = f(v) = \alpha(v - u_1)(v - u_2)(v - u_3) + RI(t) \tag{4}$$

where v is the current voltage, α is a constant that affects the rheobase, u_1, u_2, and u_3 are fixed points, R is the input resistance, typically set to 1, and $I(t)$ is input at time t. Each presynaptic-postsynaptic neuron has its own synaptic weight, w, therefore for each neuron k, the input is:

$$I_k(t) = \sum w_{j,k} S_j(t) \tag{5}$$

where $w_{j,k}$ is the weight between the jth and k^{th} neurons, and $S_j(t)$ represents the incoming voltage of the jth presynaptic neuron. Approximating the integral of Eq. 4, with input from Eq. 5 via Euler's method yields the neural model:

$$v_i(t+1) = \delta\left(\alpha(v_i(t) - u_1)(v_i(t) - u_2)(v_i(t) - u_3) + \sum_j w_{j,i} S_j(t)\right) + v_i(t) \tag{6}$$

The parameter δ is a small constant. The resting potential is u_2 and the neuron is said to spike if the voltage, v, reaches some threshold, Θ, where $\Theta > u_3$. Note that Eqs. 3 and 6 are the same equation if there is no input; if $S_j(t) = 0$ for all j.

2.2   STDP

The most common form of learning for SNNs is Hebbian/Anti-Hebbian pair based STDP [9, 10]. Logically, STDP should be an innate property of the neurons, therefore in SNNs, this property should be based on the neural model.

Neural models are generally defined by an ordinary differential equation (ODE) as seen in the above equations. First order ODEs describe the velocity; how fast is the voltage moving at time t and in what direction. Second order ODEs describe the acceleration: how is the velocity changing at time t. The main concept of this paper is to capitalize on the interplay between these two characteristics of membrane voltage to create a learning rule. While Eq. 4 does not have the explicit time component that is needed, Eq. 6 does. In fact, Eq. 6 has the original ODE, time change component, and the current voltage. Therefore, the differentiation equation of Eq. 6 yields results that display how the acceleration of the membrane potential relates to the time needed to calculate the change of the membrane potential.

Input is a complication to the derivative though, because it is related to time in a completely unknown way. For simplicity, it is assumed that there is no input; this assumption is valid because the learning rule is applied after a spike occurs, during hyperpolarization when input has minimal effect.

The derivative of Eq. 6 displays interesting properties that can be exploited for learning. Calculating where the function changes behaviour with regard to δ and solving for voltage produces two equations using the time difference, or the small constant δ, to retrieve voltage slope. These equations are used to calculate change in the synaptic weight. The equations need to be offset by the rheobase so that large time differences do not produce any weight changes. Of the two equations, one is used for

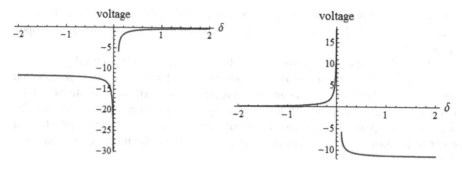

Fig. 3. Two functions produced by the derivative of Eq. 6, set to 0, solved for voltage, adjusted by the rheobase to center around 0 mV.

depression and the other for potentiation, which form that basis of STDP in this paper. These equations, visually shown in Fig. 3, mathematically are:

$$if \, \Delta > 0$$

$$\frac{2\alpha\Delta u_1 + 2\alpha\Delta u_2 + 2\alpha\Delta u_3 + \sqrt{(-2\alpha\Delta u_1 - 2\alpha\Delta u_2 - 2\alpha\Delta u_3)^2 - 12\alpha\Delta(1 + \alpha\Delta u_1 u_2 + \alpha\Delta u_1 y_3 + \alpha\Delta u_2 u_3)}}{6\alpha\Delta} - Rb$$

$$if \, \Delta < 0 \tag{7}$$

$$\frac{2\alpha\Delta u_1 + 2\alpha\Delta u_2 + 2\alpha\Delta u_3 - \sqrt{(-2\alpha\Delta u_1 - 2\alpha\Delta u_2 - 2\alpha\Delta u_3)^2 - 12\alpha\Delta(1 + \alpha\Delta u_1 u_2 + \alpha\Delta u_1 y_3 + \alpha\Delta u_2 u_3)}}{6\alpha\Delta} - Rb$$

where Δ is the presynaptic spike time minus the postsynaptic spike time and Rb is the rheobase of the model. Relating Eq. 7 to Fig. 3, when Δ is positive, or the presynaptic spike occurs after the postsynaptic spike, the left hand diagram is used to decrease synaptic weight. If Δ is negative, or the postsynaptic spike comes first, the right hand diagram is used to increase synaptic weight. By setting Eq. 7 equal to H(Δ) the final learning rule is:

$$w(t+1) = Max(w) \qquad If \, w(t) \geq Max(w)$$
$$10^{-15} \qquad\qquad If \, w(t) \leq 0 \tag{8}$$
$$w(t+1) = w(t) + w(t) * H(\Delta) \qquad else$$

There are two conditions shown in Eq. 8: a maximum and a minimum value. To avoid uncontrolled synaptic activity due to extremely large weights [10], the weights require a defined maximum value. In addition, weights can never equal 0 otherwise extinction occurs.

3 Simulation

For all simulations: u_1, u_2, and u_3, are set to -75, -65, and -55 respectively while $\alpha = 0.1$ and $\delta = 0.01$. The threshold, θ, is set to -50 mV although a spike is guaranteed to happen some point after the voltage passes -55 mV. The node used is the CIF neural model as described in Eq. 6 and the learning rule used is described in Eq. 8. Time windows of 20 ms are used for pre- and postsynaptic spike interactions as found in previous studies [3, 11, 12]. The synaptic weight between the pre- and postsynaptic spike starts at 1.

The goal of these simulations is to confirm that such a neural related property as found in the CIF model will successfully allow weight changes to produce potentiation and depression between the pre- and postsynaptic neuron. All the simulations contain input in the form of a spike train that is used by a single postsynaptic CIF model. For depression, the postsynaptic neuron has input unrelated to the presynaptic spike train in order to produce spiking at specific time intervals before the presynaptic spike train fires.

3.1   Simulation 1: Potentiation

When constant input is applied, without neural adaptation, the postsynaptic neuron should display an increase of spiking over time [13]. To confirm the increased spike frequency, a spike train with the constant input of 1 mV is used, and the resulting postsynaptic spikes are recorded over a time of 500 ms.

Results
The postsynaptic neuron displays an increase in spike frequency over time with the small constant input (see Fig. 4, left). This increased spike frequency is tied to an increase of synaptic weight. The synaptic weight increases in a non-linear fashion the closer together the pre- and postsynaptic spikes occur (see Fig. 4, right). A single spike does not account for this increase in synaptic strength though; at the input of 1 mV, 3 to 4 spikes are be needed to make a significant enough change in weight to speed up the spike response.

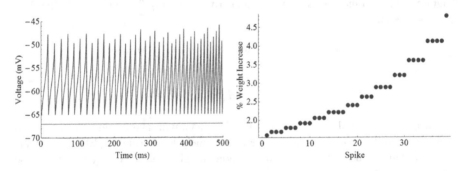

Fig. 4. Left: postsynaptic spikes with a constant input of 1 mV over 500 ms. Right: percentage of weight increase per spike

3.2   Simulation 2: Depression

Depression requires the postsynaptic neuron to fire before the presynaptic neuron. Therefore the simulation forces the postsynaptic neuron to fire before the input spike train fires. In this simulation, the input voltage is 17 mV which is enough to force the postsynaptic to spike with the default synaptic weight of 1. The postsynaptic neuron automatically spikes 25 ms into the simulation and then fires every 30 ms for the next 375 ms. The presynaptic input also fires every 30 ms, but it fires either 5 or 10 ms after the postsynaptic spike and continues to fire for the full 500 ms simulation; sending two extra spikes to the postsynaptic neuron.

Results

The input train successfully causes the postsynaptic neuron to fire initially but over time the presynaptic neuron loses efficacy. The synaptic weight decreases quicker when there is 5 ms between spikes compared to 10 ms (see Fig. 5). The difference in weight decrease is most pronounced at the end of the simulation when just the spike train input is passed into the postsynaptic neuron. At the 5 ms time difference, the input is no long able to induce a postsynaptic spike. Yet, with an increase in time (10 ms), the input can still cause a spike but that postsynaptic spike is delayed.

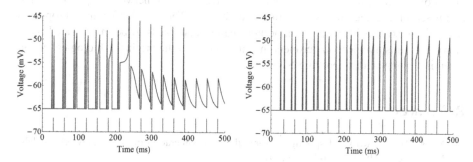

Fig. 5. Depression when a presynaptic spike occurs after a postsynaptic spike. On the left, there is 5 ms between pre- and postsynaptic spikes. On the right, 10 ms between pre- and postsynaptic spikes. Red vertical lines show when the presynaptic train fires; blue is the postsynaptic membrane voltage. (Color figure online)

4   General Discussion

The two simulations show that the learning rule successfully produces STDP in both potentiation and depression. The weight changes are affected in a non-linear manner, dependent on the difference in time between the pre- and postsynaptic spike.

While changing synaptic weights is a necessary feature of STDP, an interesting observation is the requirement of repetition to produce any noticeable results in the postsynaptic spike patterns. For the weights shown in Fig. 4, a spike train of 3 or 4 postsynaptic spikes occur before the weight change causes spike timing change. This also occurs in depression – the postsynaptic spikes that are the result of the presynaptic input occur at the same time intervals for the first few spikes before slowing down; although the voltage of those first few spikes does change.

It has been noted that the paired input does not account for the repetition needed for long term potentiation, therefore other models, such as the triplet model have been developed [14]. Yet here it shows that even with just paired input, repetition is still very important for any significant potentiation or depression between pairs. Biologically, repeated bursts are more effective for long term potentiation [15], not the constant input used here, but because these neurons do not have adaption, these results may still display similar repetition requirements. Future simulations of the network should include adaptation and multiple presynaptic spike trains.

While matching to biological data may be important in some cases, the fact that it is unknown how that data is derived should also be considered when creating SNNs. These networks have their own individual nodes and proprieties which should, and can, be used to create efficient SNNs that are easy to understand and interpret. The goal of SNNs is to improve upon the results obtained from traditional non-spiking ANNs, and this might be better achieved by harvesting known properties of network itself.

While this paper does use biological inspiration, it does not create a biological model of the brain. Instead, it uses an SNN to create its own network inspired learning rule based on the neuron's acceleration and velocity. The fact that learning properties can and do exist in SNNs is an important feature that needs to be investigated more thoroughly; this may lead to pertinent information about the origins of biological action potentials along with improving SNNs.

References

1. Maass, W.: Networks of spiking neurons: the third generation of neural network models. Neural Netw. **10**(9), 1659–1671 (1997)
2. Brader, J., Senn, W., Fusi, S.: Learning real-world stimuli in a neural network with spike-driven synaptic dynamics. Neural Comput. **19**(11), 2881–2912 (2007)
3. Markram, H., Gerstner, W., Sjöström, P.J.: A history of spike-timing-dependent plasticity. Front. Syn. Neurosci. **3**, 4 (2011)
4. Gerstner, W., Kistler, W.M., Naud, R., Paninski, L.: Neuronal Dynamics: From Single Neurons to Networks and Models of Cognition. Cambridge University Press, Cambridge (2014)
5. Nicoll, R.A.: A brief history of long-term potentiation. Neuron **93**(2), 281–290 (2017)
6. Chartier, S., Boukadoum, M.: A bidirectional heteroassociative memory for binary and grey-level patterns. IEEE Trans. Neural Netw. **17**(2), 385–396 (2006)
7. Mihalaş, Ş., Niebur, E.: A generalized linear integrate-and-fire neural model produces diverse spiking behaviors. Neural Comput. **21**(3), 704–718 (2009)
8. Izhikevich, E.M.: Which model to use for cortical spiking neurons? IEEE Trans. Neural Netw. **15**(5), 1063–1070 (2004)
9. Gerstner, W.: Spiking Neuron Models: Single Neurons, Populations, Plasticity. Cambridge University Press, Cambridge, New York (2002)
10. Abbott, L.F., Nelson, S.B.: Synaptic plasticity: taming the beast. Nat. Neurosci. **3**, 1178–1183 (2000)
11. Zhang, L.I., Tao, H.W., Holt, C.E., Harris, W.A., Poo, M.: A critical window for cooperation and competition among developing retinotectal synapses. Nature **395**(6697), 37–44 (1998)

12. Bliss, T.V.P., Lømo, T.: Long-lasting potentiation of synaptic transmission in the dentate area of the anaesthetized rabbit following stimulation of the perforant path. J. Physiol. **232** (2), 331–356 (1973)
13. Bi, G., Poo, M.: Synaptic modifications in cultured hippocampal neurons: dependence on spike timing, synaptic strength, and postsynaptic cell type. J. Neurosci. **18**(24), 10464–10472 (1998)
14. Pfister, J.-P., Gerstner, W.: Triplets of spikes in a model of spike timing-dependent plasticity. J. Neurosci. **26**(38), 9673–9682 (2006)
15. Douglas, R.M., Goddard, G.V.: Long-term potentiation of the perforant path-granule cell synapse in the rat hippocampus. Brain Res. **86**(2), 205–215 (1975)

Online Representation Learning with Single and Multi-layer Hebbian Networks for Image Classification

Yanis Bahroun[✉] and Andrea Soltoggio

Computer Science Department, Loughborough University,
Loughborough, Leicestershire, UK
{y.bahroun,a.soltoggio}@lboro.ac.uk

Abstract. Unsupervised learning permits the development of algorithms that are able to adapt to a variety of different datasets using the same underlying rules thanks to the autonomous discovery of discriminating features during training. Recently, a new class of Hebbian-like and local unsupervised learning rules for neural networks have been developed that minimise a *similarity matching* cost-function. These have been shown to perform sparse representation learning. This study tests the effectiveness of one such learning rule for learning features from images. The rule implemented is derived from a nonnegative classical multidimensional scaling cost-function, and is applied to both single and multi-layer architectures. The features learned by the algorithm are then used as input to an SVM to test their effectiveness in classification on the established CIFAR-10 image dataset. The algorithm performs well in comparison to other unsupervised learning algorithms and multi-layer networks, thus suggesting its validity in the design of a new class of compact, online learning networks.

Keywords: Classification · Competitive learning · Feature learning · Hebbian learning · Online algorithm · Neural networks · Sparse coding · Unsupervised learning

1 Introduction

Biological synaptic plasticity is hypothesized to be one of the main phenomena responsible for human learning and memory. One mechanism of synaptic plasticity is inspired by the Hebbian learning principle which states that connections between two units, e.g., neurons, are strengthened when they are simultaneously activated. In artificial neural networks, implementations of Hebbian plasticity are known to learn recurring patterns of activations. The use of extensions of this rule, such as Oja's rule [9] or the Generalized Hebbian rule, also called Sanger's rule [15], have permitted the development of algorithms that have proved particularly efficient at tasks such as online dimensionality reduction. Two important properties of brain-inspired models, namely competitive learning [14] and sparse

© Springer International Publishing AG 2017
A. Lintas et al. (Eds.): ICANN 2017, Part I, LNCS 10613, pp. 354–363, 2017.
https://doi.org/10.1007/978-3-319-68600-4_41

coding [10] can be performed using Hebbian and anti-Hebbian learning rules. Such properties can be achieved with inhibitory connections, which extend the capabilities of Hebbian rules beyond simple extraction of the principal component of input data. The continuous and local update dynamics of Hebbian learning also make it suitable for learning from a continuous stream of data. Such an algorithm can take one image at a time with memory requirements that are independent of the number of samples.

This study employs Hebbian/anti-Hebbian learning rules derived from a similarity matching cost-function [12] and applies it to perform online unsupervised learning of features from multiple image datasets. The rule proposed in [12] is applied here for the first time to online features learning for image classification with single and multi-layer architectures. The quality of the features is assessed visually and by performing classification with a linear classifier working on the learned features. The simulations show that a simple single-layer Hebbian network can outperform more complex models such as Sparse Autoencoders (SAE) and Restricted Boltzmann machines (RBM) for image classifications tasks [3]. When applied to multi-layer architectures, the rule learns additional features. This study is the first of its kind to perform multi-layer sparse dictionary learning based on the similarity matching principle developed in [12] and to apply it to image classification. A preliminary draft of this paper has been made available on arXiv repository [2].

2 Hebbian/anti-Hebbian Network Derived from a Similarity Matching Cost-Function

The rule implemented by the Hebbian/anti-Hebbian network used in this work derives from an adaptation of Classical MultiDimensional Scaling (CMDS). CMDS is a popular embedding technique [4]. Unlike most dimensionality reduction techniques, e.g. PCA, the CMDS uses as input the matrix of similarity between inputs to generate a set of embedding coordinates. The advantage of MDS is that any kind of distance or similarity matrix can be analyzed. However, in its simplest form, CMDS produces dense features maps which are often unsuitable when considered for image classification. Therefore an adaptation of the CMDS introduced recently in [12] is used to overcome this weakness. The model implemented is a nonnegative classical multidimensional scaling that has three properties: it takes a similarity matrix as input, it produces sparse codes, and can be implemented using a new biologically plausible Hebbian model. The Hebbian/anti-Hebbian rule introduced in [12] is given as follows: for a set of inputs $x^t \in \mathbb{R}^n$ for $t \in \{1, \ldots, T\}$, the concatenation of the inputs defines an input matrix $X \in \mathbb{R}^{n \times T}$. The output matrix Y of encodings is an element of $\mathbb{R}^{m \times T}$ that corresponds to a sparse overcomplete representation of the input if $m > n$, or to a low-dimensional embedding of the input if $m < n$. The objective function proposed by [12] is:

$$Y^* = \arg\min_{Y \geq 0} \| X'X - Y'Y \|_F^2 \tag{1}$$

where F is the Frobenius norm and $X'X$ is the Gram matrix of the inputs which corresponds to the similarity matrix. Solving Eq. 1 directly requires storing $Y \in \mathbb{R}_+^{m \times T}$ which increases with time T making online learning difficult. Thus instead an online learning version of Eq. 1 is expressed as:

$$(y^T)^* = \underset{y^T \geq 0}{\arg\min} \|X'X - Y'Y\|_F^2. \tag{2}$$

The components of the solution of Eq. 2, found in [12] using coordinate descent, are:

$$(y_i^T)^* = \max\left(W_i^T x^T - M_i^T (y^T)^*, 0\right) \quad \forall i \in \{1, \ldots, m\}, \tag{3}$$

where

$$W_{ij}^T = \frac{\sum\limits_{t=1}^{T-1} y_i^t x_j^t}{\sum\limits_{t=1}^{T-1} (y_i^t)^2}; \quad M_{ij}^T = \frac{\sum\limits_{t=1}^{T-1} y_i^t y_j^t}{\sum\limits_{t=1}^{T-1} (y_i^t)^2} 1_{i \neq j}. \tag{4}$$

W^T and M^T can be found using the recursive formulations:

$$W_{ij}^T = W_{ij}^{T-1} + \left(y_i^{T-1}(x_j^{T-1} - W_{ij}^{T-1} y_i^{T-1})\Big/\hat{Y}_i^T\right) \tag{5}$$

$$M_{ij \neq i}^T = M_{ij}^{T-1} + \left(y_i^{T-1}(y_j^{T-1} - M_{ij}^{T-1} y_i^{T-1})\Big/\hat{Y}_i^T\right) \tag{6}$$

$$\hat{Y}_i^T = \hat{Y}_i^{T-1} + (y_i^{T-1})^2. \tag{7}$$

W^T (green arrows) and M^T (blue arrows) can be interpreted respectively as feedforward synaptic connections between the input and the hidden layer and lateral synaptic inhibitory connections within the hidden layer. The weight matrices are of fixed sizes and updated sequentially, which makes the model suitable for online learning. The architecture of the Hebbian/anti-Hebbian network is represented in Fig. 1.

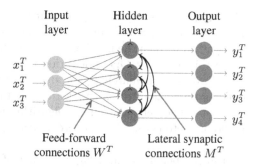

Fig. 1. Hebbian/anti-Hebbian network with lateral connections derived from Eq. 2. (Color figure online)

3 A Model to Learn Features from Images

In the new model presented in this study, the input data vectors $(x^1, \ldots, x^T)$ are composed of patches taken randomly from a training dataset of images. For every new input x^t presented, the model first computes a sparse post-synaptic activity y^t. Second, the synaptic weights are modified based on local Hebbian/anti-Hebbian learning rules requiring only the current pre- post-synaptic neuronal activities. The model can be seen as a sparse encoding followed by a recursive updating scheme, which are both well suited to solve large-scale online problems.

A multi-class SVM classifies the pictures using output vectors obtained by a simple pooling of the feature vectors, Y^*, obtained for the input images from the trained network. In particular, given an input image, each neuron in the output layer produces a new image, called a feature map, which is pooled in quadrants [3] to form 4 terms of the input vector for the SVM.

3.1 Multi-layer Hebbian/anti-Hebbian Neural Network

In the proposed approach, layers of Hebbian/anti-Hebbian network are stacked similarly to the Convolutional DBN [5], and Hierarchical K-means. In the multi-layer Hebbian/anti-Hebbian network, both the weights of the first layer and second layer are continuously updated. Unlike other CNNs, the non-linearity used in each layer is not only due to the positivity constraint, but to the combination of a rectified linear unit activation function and of interneuronal competition. This model combines the powerful architecture of convolutional neural networks using ReLU activation with interneuronal competition, while all synaptic weights are updated using online local learning rules. In between layers, a 2×2 average pooling is used to downsample the feature maps.

3.2 Overcompleteness of the Representation and Multi-resolution

As part of the evaluation of the new model, it is important to assess its performance with different sizes (m) of the hidden layers. If the number of neurons exceeds the size of the input $(m > n)$, the representation is called overcomplete. Overcompleteness may be beneficial, but requires increased computation, particularly for deep networks in which the number of neurons has to grow exponentially in order to keep this property. One motivation for overcompleteness is that it may allow more flexibility in matching the output structure with the input. However, not all learning algorithms can learn and take advantage of overcomplete representations. The behaviour of the algorithm is analysed in the transition between undercomplete $(m < n)$ and overcomplete $(m > n)$ representations.

Although the model might benefit from a large number of neurons, from a practical perspective an increase in the number of neurons is a challenge for such models due to the number of operations required in the coordinate descent. In order to limit the computational cost of training a large network while still benefiting from overcomplete representations, this study proposes to train simultaneously three single-layer neural networks, each of them having different receptive field sizes ($4 \times 4, 6 \times 6$, and 8×8 pixels). Thus, a variation of the model tested here is composed of three different networks. This architecture of parallel networks with different receptive field sizes requires less computational time and memory than a model with only one receptive field size and the same total number of neurons, because the synaptic weights only connect neurons within each neural network. This model will be called multi-resolution in the following.

3.3   Parameters and Preprocessing

The architecture used here has the following tunable parameters: the receptive field size (n) of the neurons and the number of neurons (m). These parameters are standard to CNNs but their influence on this online feed-forward model needs to be investigated.

For computer vision models, understanding the influence of input preprocessing is of critical importance for both biological plausibility and practical applicability. Recent findings [1], confirm partial decorrelation of the input signal in the retinal ganglion cells. The influence of input decorrelation by applying whitening will be investigated.

4   Results

The effectiveness of the algorithm is assessed by measuring the performance on an image classification task. We acknowledge that classification accuracy is at best an implicit measure evaluating the performance of representation learning algorithms, but provides a standardised way of comparing them. In the following, single and multi-layer Hebbian/anti-Hebbian neural networks combined with the standard multi-class SVM are trained on the CIFAR-10 dataset [6].

4.1   Evaluation of the Single-Layer Model

A first experiment tested the performance of the model with and without whitening of the input data. Although there exist Hebbian networks that can perform online whitening [11], an offline technique based on singular value decomposition [3] is applied in these experiments. Figure 2a and b show the features learned by the network from raw input and whitened input respectively. The features learned from raw data (Fig. 2a) are neither sharp nor localised filters and just slightly capture edges. With whitened data (Fig. 2b), the features are sharp, localised, and resemble Gabor filters, which are observed in the primary visual cortex [10].

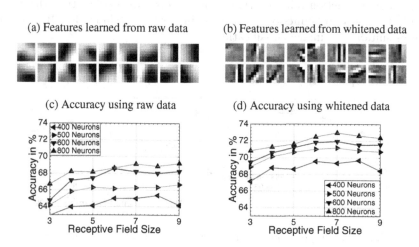

(a) Features learned from raw data   (b) Features learned from whitened data

(c) Accuracy using raw data   (d) Accuracy using whitened data

Fig. 2. Sample of features learned from raw (2a) and whitened input (2b). Classification accuracy with raw (2c) and whitened input (2d).

In a second set of experiments, the performance of the network was tested for varying receptive field sizes (Fig. 2c–d) and varying network sizes (400, 500, 600, and 800 neurons). The results show that the performance peaks at a receptive field size of 7 pixels and then begins to decline. This property is common to most unsupervised learning algorithms [3], showing the difficulty of learning spatially extended features. Figures 2c and d also show that for every configuration, the performance of the algorithm is largely and uniformly improved when whitening is applied to the input.

4.2   Comparison to State-of-the-Art Performances and Online Training

Various unsupervised learning algorithms have been tested on the CIFAR-10 dataset. Spherical K-means, in particular, proved in [3] to outperform autoencoders and restricted Boltzmann machines, providing a very simple and efficient solution for dictionary learning for image classification. Thus, spherical K-means is used here as a benchmark to evaluate the performance of the single-layer network. As with other unsupervised learning algorithms, increasing the number of output neurons to reach overcompleteness also improved classification performance (Fig. 3a). Although the single-layer neural network has a higher degree of sparsity than the K-means proposed in [3] (results not shown here), they appear to have the same performance in their optimal configurations (Fig. 3a).

The classification accuracy of the network during training is shown in Fig. 3b. The graph (Fig. 3b) suggests that the features learned by the network over time help the system improve the classification accuracy. This is significant because it demonstrates for the first time the effectiveness of features learned with a Hebb-like cost-function minimisation. It is not obvious a priori that the online optimisation of a cost-function for sparse similarity matching (Eq. 2) produces features suitable for image classification.

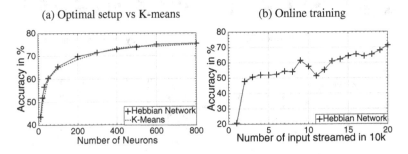

Fig. 3. (a) Proposed model vs K-means, (b) Classification accuracy

As shown in Table 1, the multi-resolution network outperforms the single resolution network and K-means algorithm [3], reaching 80.42% accuracy on the CIFAR-10. The multi-resolution model shows better performance, while requiring less computation and memory than the single resolution model. It also outperforms the single layer NOMP [7], sparse TIRBM [16], CKN-GM and CKN-PM [8], which are more complex models. It was outperformed only by combined models or models with three layers or more. The results reported in Table 1 were averaged over multiple training and testing. The classification accuracy did not deviate by more than ±0.17% for the single resolution and ±0.13% for the multi-resolution networks.

4.3   Evaluation of the Multi-layer Model

A single resolution, double-layer neural network with different numbers of neurons in each layer was trained similarly to the single-layer network in the previous section. In Table 2, ϕ_1 and ϕ_2 correspond respectively to the features learned by the first and second layer. The results show that ϕ_2 alone are less discriminative

Table 1. Comparison of the single-layer network with unsupervised learning algorithms on CIFAR-10.

Algorithm	Accuracy
Single-layer, single resolution (4 k neurons)	**79.58% (± 0.17%)**
Single-layer, multi-resolution (3×1.6 k neurons)	**80.42% (± 0.13%)**
Single-layer K-means [3] (4 k neurons)	79.60%
Multi-layer K-means [3] (3 layers, >4 k neurons)	82.60%
Convolutional DBN [5]	78.90%
Sparse TIRBM [16] (4 k neurons)	80.10%
TIOMP-1/T [16] (combined transformations, 4 k neurons)	82.20%
Single layer NOMP [7] (5 k neurons)	78.00%
Multi-layer NOMP [7] (3 Layers, >4 k neurons)	82.90%
Multi-layer CKN-GM [8]	74.84%
Multi-layer CKN-PM [8]	78.30%
Multi-layer CKN-CO [8] (combining CKN-GM & CKN-PM)	82.18%

Table 2. Classification accuracy for a two-layer network.

		#Neurons layer 2				
		50	100	200	400	800
100 Neurons layer 1	ϕ_2	54.9%	59.7%	64.7%	68.7%	71.5%
	$\phi_1 + \phi_2$	67.2%	68.1%	69.9%	72.4%	73.8%
200 Neurons layer 1	ϕ_2	55.8%	60.6%	65.3%	70.3%	72.7%
	$\phi_1 + \phi_2$	69.9%	70.8%	71.9%	73.7%	75.1%

than ϕ_1 as indicated in Fig. 3a. However, when combined $(\phi_1 + \phi_2)$ the model achieves better performance than each layer considered separately. Nevertheless, the preliminary results indicate that the sizes of the two layers unevenly affect the performance of the network. A future test may investigate if a multi-layer architecture can outperform the largest shallow networks. The accuracies in Table 2 are averaged over 7 runs that delivered consistent results with a standard deviation less than 0.2%. Further tests on smaller datasets might help determine if this robustness can be attributed to the model or to the SVM.

5   Conclusion

This work proposes single and multi-layer neural networks that exploit Hebbian/anti-Hebbian rules to learn features for image classification. The networks are trained on the CIFAR-10 image dataset prior to feeding a linear classifier. The model successfully learns online more discriminative representations of the data when the number of neurons and the number of layers increase. The overcompleteness of the representation is critical for learning relevant features. The results show that a minimum unsupervised learning time is needed to optimise the network leading to better classification accuracy. Finally, one key factor in improving image classification is the appropriate choice of the receptive field size used for training the network.

Such findings prove that neural networks can be trained to solve problems as complex as sparse dictionary learning with Hebbian learning rules, delivering competitive accuracy compared to other encoder, including deep neural networks. This makes deep Hebbian networks attractive for building large-scale image classification systems. The competitive performances on the CIFAR-10 suggests that this model can offer an alternative to batch trained neural networks. Ultimately, thanks to its bio-inspired architecture and learning rules, it also stands as a good candidate for memristive devices [13]. Moreover, if a decaying factor is added to the proposed model that might result in an algorithm that can deal with complex datasets with temporal variations of the distributions.

References

1. Abbasi-Asl, R., Pehlevan, C., Yu, B., Chklovskii, D.B.: Do retinal ganglion cells project natural scenes to their principal subspace and whiten them? arXiv preprint arXiv:1612.03483 (2016)
2. Bahroun, Y., Soltoggio, A.: Online representation learning with multi-layer Hebbian networks for image classification tasks. arXiv preprint arXiv:1702.06456 (2017)
3. Coates, A., Lee, H., Ng, A.Y.: An analysis of single-layer networks in unsupervised feature learning. In: AISTATS 2011, vol. 1001 (2011)
4. Cox, T.F., Cox, M.A.: Multidimensional Scaling. CRC Press, Boca Raton (2000)
5. Krizhevsky, A., Hinton, G.: Convolutional deep belief networks on CIFAR-10. Unpublished manuscript 40 (2010)
6. Krizhevsky, A., Hinton, G.: Learning multiple layers of features from tiny images (2009)
7. Lin, T.h., Kung, H.: Stable and efficient representation learning with nonnegativity constraints. In: Proceedings of the 31st International Conference on Machine Learning, ICML 2014, pp. 1323–1331 (2014)
8. Mairal, J., Koniusz, P., Harchaoui, Z., Schmid, C.: Convolutional kernel networks. In: Advances in Neural Information Processing Systems, pp. 2627–2635 (2014)
9. Oja, E.: Neural networks, principal components, and subspaces. Int. J. Neural Syst. 1(01), 61–68 (1989)
10. Olshausen, B.A., et al.: Emergence of simple-cell receptive field properties by learning a sparse code for natural images. Nature 381(6583), 607–609 (1996)
11. Pehlevan, C., Chklovskii, D.: A normative theory of adaptive dimensionality reduction in neural networks. In: Advances in Neural Information Processing Systems, pp. 2269–2277 (2015)
12. Pehlevan, C., Chklovskii, D.B.: A Hebbian/Anti-Hebbian network derived from online non-negative matrix factorization can cluster and discover sparse features. In: 2014 48th Asilomar Conference on Signals, Systems and Computers, pp. 769–775. IEEE (2014)

13. Poikonen, J.H., Laiho, M.: Online linear subspace learning in an analog array computing architecture. In: CNNA 2016 (2016)
14. Rumelhart, D.E., Zipser, D.: Feature discovery by competitive learning. Cogn. Sci. **9**(1), 75–112 (1985)
15. Sanger, T.D.: Optimal unsupervised learning in a single-layer linear feedforward neural network. Neural Netw. **2**(6), 459–473 (1989)
16. Sohn, K., Lee, H.: Learning invariant representations with local transformations. In: Proceedings of the 29th International Conference on Machine Learning, ICML 2012, pp. 1311–1318 (2012)

Building Efficient Deep Hebbian Networks for Image Classification Tasks

Yanis Bahroun[1]([✉]), Eugénie Hunsicker[2], and Andrea Soltoggio[1]

[1] Department of Computer Science, Loughborough University,
Loughborough, Leicestershire, UK
{y.bahroun,a.soltoggio}@lboro.ac.uk
[2] Department of Mathematics, Loughborough University,
Loughborough, Leicestershire, UK
e.hunsicker@lboro.ac.uk

Abstract. Multi-layer models of sparse coding (deep dictionary learning) and dimensionality reduction (PCANet) have shown promise as unsupervised learning models for image classification tasks. However, the pure implementations of these models have limited generalisation capabilities and high computational cost. This work introduces the Deep Hebbian Network (DHN), which combines the advantages of sparse coding, dimensionality reduction, and convolutional neural networks for learning features from images. Unlike in other deep neural networks, in this model, both the learning rules and neural architectures are derived from cost-function minimizations. Moreover, the DHN model can be trained online due to its Hebbian components. Different configurations of the DHN have been tested on scene and image classification tasks. Experiments show that the DHN model can automatically discover highly discriminative features directly from image pixels without using any data augmentation or semi-labeling.

Keywords: Sparse coding · Dimensionality reduction · Hebbian/Anti-Hebbian learning · Multidimensional Scaling · Biologically plausible learning rules

1 Introduction

When applied to supervised learning tasks, deep neural networks trained using back-propagation dominate the field of machine learning in terms of performances on benchmarks. However, such networks often under-perform standard techniques when the number of labelled data available is relatively small. Unsupervised learning, on the contrary, enables the development of algorithms able to adapt to a variety of different unlabeled data sets. For unsupervised learning, a variety of algorithms and principles exist, one of which is the Hebbian principle, stating that in human learning, the connections between two neurons are strengthened when simultaneously activated. Despite the apparent vagueness of this principle, the authors of [20] argue in their work that if rigorously

© Springer International Publishing AG 2017
A. Lintas et al. (Eds.): ICANN 2017, Part I, LNCS 10613, pp. 364–372, 2017.
https://doi.org/10.1007/978-3-319-68600-4_42

expressed, this principle could be the key to major advances in machine learning. We explicitly express here two important aspects of Hebbian learning that will be used in this work: (1) to be Hebbian, a learning rule should employ only the local information contained in the activities of pre-synaptic and post-synaptic neurons; (2) such learning rules should depend only on the correlation between the activities of these neurons. These two properties of the Hebbian principle are also part of the more general concept of local learning presented in [2].

The work presented here focuses on two unsupervised learning methods, namely, sparse coding and dimensionality reduction. In addition to being powerful statistical learning models, those methods also proved successful at modelling biological signal processing [9,12]. In this work we have made use of a novel approach [15,16] that implements both sparse coding and dimensionality reduction by means of a unique principle called *similarity matching*. The minimization of the cost-functions associated, based on Classical Multidimensional Scaling (CMDS) [8], led to trainable neural networks using Hebbian/anti-Hebbian rules.

The work presented here is motivated by two main goals. The first goal is to implement a network for online learning using only feed-forward and lateral connections. The second is to demonstrate that the proposed architecture successfully combines Convolutional Neural Networks (CNN) structure, PCANet [5] and deep sparse coding. In particular, the intent of this work was not to outperform neural networks trained on back-propagation but to evaluate a novel bio-inspired online unsupervised model performing feature extraction for image classification. To achieve these two goals, this study introduces a new type of network called Deep Hebbian Network (DHN) that combines, within one architecture, stages of overcomplete sparse coding and dimensionality reduction based on the *similarity matching* principle. The performance of the DHN is evaluated on indoor scene classification (MIT-67) and image classification (CIFAR-10) tasks.

2   Similarity Matching: A Unifying Framework for Building Efficient Deep Hebbian Networks

The rules implemented in the proposed model derive from adaptations of CMDS. CMDS generates a set of coordinates in a different Euclidean space where the solution is an optimal embedding minimizing the changes to the distances between data points [8]. The formulation of CMDS is given as follows: for a set of inputs $x^t \in \mathbb{R}^n$ for $t \in \{1, \ldots, T\}$, the concatenation of the inputs defines an input matrix $X \in \mathbb{R}^{n \times T}$. The output matrix Y of embeddings is an element of $\mathbb{R}^{m \times T}$. The objective function of CMDS is:

$$Y^* = \arg\min_{Y \in \mathcal{C}} \|X'X - Y'Y\|_F^2. \tag{1}$$

where F is the Frobenius norm, $X'X$ is the Gram matrix of the inputs, which combines the information of similarity and norm of the vectors, and the space $\mathcal{C}$ encodes the constraints, which depend on the problem to solve. Classically, this method has been used to accomplish dimensionality reduction, and $m < n$.

However, it can be adapted to achieve sparse coding. This work focuses on two online versions of CMDS, which leads to non-trivial neural implementations and Hebbian learning rules.

2.1   Hebbian/Anti-Hebbian Learning for Similarity Matching

To achieve dimensionality reduction and sparse coding, two different sets of constraints are considered for building the DHN. First, let us assume that the outputs are constrained to be non-negative and of dimension greater than the input dimension, and $(m > n)$ i.e. $\mathcal{C} = \{Y \in \mathbb{R}_+^{m \times T} | m > n\}$. Such constraints correspond to a sparse coding model [16], which optimal solution will be noted Y_{SC}^*. Second, if the input dimension is greater than the output dimension, $(n > m)$ and $\mathcal{C} = \{Y \in \mathbb{R}^{m \times T} | m < n\}$, it corresponds to a dimensionality reduction model [15], which optimal solution will be noted Y_{DR}^*. In particular, these two optimization problems can be expressed as:

$$Y_{SC}^* = \underset{Y \in \mathbb{R}_+^{m \times T}, \ m > n}{\arg\min} \|X'X - Y'Y\|_F^2 \ , \ Y_{DR}^* = \underset{Y \in \mathbb{R}^{m \times T}, \ m < n}{\arg\min} \|X'X - Y'Y\|_F^2. \quad (2)$$

Online learning versions of the problems in Eq. 2 are expressed as:

$$(y_{SC}^T)^* = \underset{y^T \in \mathbb{R}_+^m, \ m > n}{\arg\min} \|X'X - Y'Y\|_F^2 \ , \ (y_{DR}^T)^* = \underset{y^T \in \mathbb{R}^m, \ m < n}{\arg\min} \|X'X - Y'Y\|_F^2, \quad (3)$$

where the inputs are considered as a sequence. When a new element, x^T, is presented to the model, an output, y^T, is generated while keeping the previous y^ts unchanged. The components of the solutions of Eq. 3 found in [15,16] using coordinate descent are:

$$(y_{i,SC}^T)^* = \max\left(W_i^T x^T - M_i^T y^T, 0\right), \ (y_{i,DR}^T)^* = W_i^T x^T - M_i^T y^T \quad (4)$$

$$\text{with} \quad W_{ij}^T = \frac{\sum_{t=1}^{T-1} y_i^t x_j^t}{\sum_{t=1}^{T-1} (y_i^t)^2}; \quad M_{ij}^T = \frac{\sum_{t=1}^{T-1} y_i^t y_j^t}{\sum_{t=1}^{T-1} (y_i^t)^2} 1_{i \neq j} \quad \forall i \in \{1, \ldots, m\}. \quad (5)$$

W^T and M^T can be found using recursive formulations:

$$W_{ij}^T = W_{ij}^{T-1} + \left(y_i^{T-1}(x_j^{T-1} - W_{ij}^{T-1} y_i^{T-1})\right) \Big/ \hat{Y}_i^T \quad (6)$$

$$M_{ij \neq i}^T = M_{ij}^{T-1} + \left(y_i^{T-1}(y_j^{T-1} - M_{ij}^{T-1} y_i^{T-1})\right) \Big/ \hat{Y}_i^T \quad (7)$$

$$\hat{Y}_i^T = \hat{Y}_i^{T-1} + (y_i^{T-1})^2. \quad (8)$$

The matrices W^T and M^T are sequentially updated using only the relationship between x^{T-1} and y^{T-1}, which are analogous to pre and post-synaptic activities, thus satisfying the Hebbian principle. The learning dynamic of M^T is called anti-Hebbian since the connections between neurons are reduced when activated simultaneously. In both cases the weight matrices W^T and M^T can be interpreted respectively as feed-forward synaptic connections and lateral synaptic inhibitory connections (Fig. 1). The main difference between the two models is in the use of a rectified linear unit (ReLU) on the sparse coding problem.

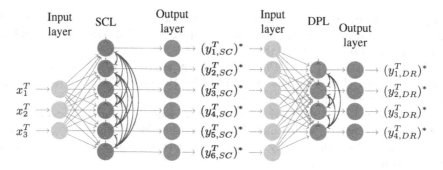

Fig. 1. Network implementing successively sparse coding and dimensionality reduction

3   Deep Hebbian Network

A DHN is defined here as a combination of three basic layers: a Sparse Coding Layer (SCL), a Depth Pooling Layer (DPL), and a Spatial Pooling Layer (SPL). The different layers can be stacked in various manners to construct a variety of DHNs. Figure 2 shows a graphical representation of such a network with 2 layers.

3.1   Feature Extraction by Sparse Coding: Simple Cell Inspiration

The SCL performs the encoding of local patches using competitive learning modeled by lateral synaptic inhibitions. The choice of layer for extracting features is inspired by the simple cells of the visual cortex V1. It has been proved that overcomplete sparse coding reproduces important tuning properties of those cells [12].

As part of the evaluation of the DHN it is important to assess its performance as a function of the number of SCLs and of the number of neurons in each of those layers. As in an earlier work [1], the sparse coding layers considered perform overcomplete representations of the input data with more output neurons than input neurons, $(m > n)$, as expressed in Eq. 3. Overcompleteness in the SCL was chosen because it may allow for more flexibility in matching the output structure to the inputs [12].

3.2 Dimensionality Reduction and Pooling: Complex Cells Inspiration

The model in [1] suffered from the fact that the number of neurons exponentially increases with the number of layers. A key idea in the proposed DHN architecture is to overcome this problem by using dimensionality reduction techniques to reduce the input sizes of the successive SCLs.

Depth Pooling: The DPL performs an online low-dimensional embedding of the data using the *similarity matching* principle. The DPL reduces the number of feature maps before feeding the following SCL.

The introduction of the DPL is inspired by the work of [9], which showed that visual spatial pooling can be learned by Principal Components analysis (PCA) based techniques, reproducing the tuning properties of V1 complex cells. A similar idea, in a supervised learning setup, can be found in the inception layer proposed by [20], which includes a dimensionality reduction stage. Other less bio-inspired dimensionality reduction models, e.g. autoencoders [21], can also be used.

Spatial Pooling: A standard spatial pooling technique is used in this model to reduce the width and height of the feature maps produced after convolution. The max-pooling operation is used after SCL, and no spatial pooling is performed after DPL.

4 Experiments and Results

The results presented here measure the performance of the DHN on classification tasks. A multi-class Support Vector Machine (SVM) [7] classifies the pictures using output vectors obtained by a simple pooling of the feature vectors, Y^*_{SC}, obtained for the input images from the trained network. In particular, given an input image, each neuron in the SCLs produces a new image, called a feature map, which is pooled in quadrants to form 4 terms of the input vector for the SVM as shown in Fig. 2. The linear SVM has been widely used when evaluating the efficiency of unsupervised learning model, on the benchmarks presented below. Although the use of nonlinear classifiers could increase the accuracy, such increase could not be attributed to the efficiency of the DHN.

4.1 Datasets and Preprocessing

Two datasets are used for evaluating the performance of the features learned by the DHN. The first dataset was the standard benchmark used for indoor scene recognition, the MIT Scene Indoor 67 (MIT-67) [18], which contains 67 indoor categories, with a total of 15620 images. In the following, only 80 images from each class were used for training, and 20 for testing. The second dataset was the

CIFAR-10 [10], which contains 50,000 training and 10,000 test images of 32×32 color images of 10 different classes.

Prior to feeding the DHN, basic preprocessing is performed on the inputs, namely brightness and contrast normalization, and whitening. Although online versions of such techniques [15] exist, offline preprocessing is performed in this study to enable a fairer comparison to other unsupervised learning models. A study on the influence of the whitening on the performance of single-layer Hebbian networks is proposed in [1]. The images contained in the MIT-67 are of different resolutions. In order to train and test the DHN on a consistent set of images, the images of the MIT-67 were resized to $100 \times 100 \times 3$, size of the smallest image on the dataset.

4.2   Evaluation of DHN

For both datasets, tests were performed on DHNs with up to 5 layers as indicated in the schema in Fig. 2.

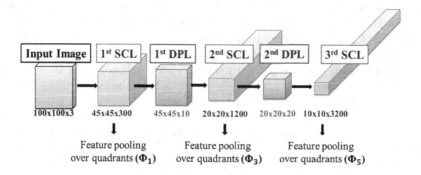

Fig. 2. DHN with convolutional architecture trained on the MIT-67 dataset.

Understanding the Impact of the Number of Neurons in SCLs and DPLs: The results reported in Fig. 3a clearly shows that the performance of the DHN combining the features from the 1st and 2nd SCL, noted $(\Phi_1 + \Phi_3)$, consistently outperforms Φ_1 and Φ_3 alone, which is also confirmed in Fig. 3b. Figure 3a shows a monotonic increase of classification accuracy with the number of neurons in the 2nd SCL, again confirmed in Fig. 3b. However, the influence of the number of neurons in the 1st DPL on the classification accuracy is more subtle. It appears in Fig. 3b that there exists an optimal number of neurons for that layer, which is around 15 neurons. An explanation of this phenomenon is the fact that DPL learns a low-dimensional linear subspace in which part of the information might be lost if the dimension is too small. Reciprocally, if the embedding space is too big, the following SCL is unable to learn an appropriate representation as in the naive multi-layer sparse coding model proposed in [1].

(a) Classification accuracy as a function of the number of neurons in the 2nd SCL for different sizes of the 1st DPL (10, 20, and 30 neurons) and using either only Φ_1 or Φ_3 or both.

(b) Classification accuracy as a function of the number of neurons in the 1st DPL for different sizes of the 2nd SCL (200 and 800 neurons) and using either only Φ_1 or Φ_3 or both.

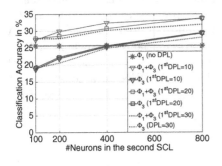
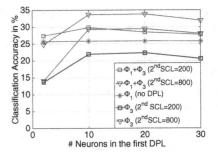

Fig. 3. Classification accuracy of different 3-layer DHN on the MIT-67 dataset.

Impact of the Number of Layers: Table 1 shows that the classification accuracy of a DHN increases when using features from more layers on the MIT-67 dataset. The features extracted from Φ_5 appear beneficial in the MIT-67 but not so in the CIFAR-10. The highest classification accuracy on the MIT-67, 41.4%, is reached when the features of the three SCLs are combined ($\Phi_1 + \Phi_3 + \Phi_5$). For the CIFAR-10 however, the highest accuracy, 79.1%, is achieved using only the features from the 1st and 2nd SCL ($\Phi_1 + \Phi_3$).

This discrepancy is likely due to the difference in sizes of the images used, 32×32 pixels and 100×100 pixels. Such results support the utility of using convolutional architecture and depth pooling, which enables the DHN to successfully exploit both local and global discriminative information, which are necessary for addressing scene recognition problems.

Table 1. Classification accuracy when using features from different layers of the DHN on the MIT-67 and CIFAR-10. The features extracted by the DHN are used to train a linear SVM. $\Phi_1 + \Phi_3 + \Phi_5$ denotes the concatenation of features from the three SCLs.

	Features used in the Linear SVM for the classification				
	Φ_1 (300 Neurons)	Φ_3 (1200 Neurons)	Φ_5 (3200 neurons)	$\Phi_1 + \Phi_3$	$\Phi_1 + \Phi_3 + \Phi_5$
MIT-67	28.5 %	32.4 %	35.1 %	37.8 %	**41.4%**
CIFAR-10	72.2%	76.6%	61.6%	**79.1%**	74.5%

Comparison to Other Models: On the MIT-67, the DHN shows higher accuracy than the PCANet [5], Deformable Parts models (DPM), Spatial Pyramid Matching (SPM) [13] and Reconfigurable Models (RBoW) [14], as reported in Table 2. It reaches similar accuracy to Hierarchical Matching Pursuit trained on RGB images (HMP-RGB) [3]. However, the combined model

(DPM+Gist+SPM) [13] and the Multipath-HMP (M-HMP) [4] still outperform the DHN. Improvements of the architecture of the DHN inspired by the M-HMP may enable it to capture richer features at different scales.

Although on the CIFAR-10 the performance of the DHN are comparable to the single-layer Hebbian (SLH) introduced in [1], it does so with half of the neurons used in the single layer in [1], which increases further its computational and memory efficiency.

Table 2. Evaluation of the DHN against other unsupervised models on (a) MIT-67 and (b) CIFAR-10.

(a) Classification accuracy on the MIT-67

Algorithm	Accuracy
DHN ($\Phi_1 + \Phi_3 + \Phi_5$)	**41.4 %**
SPM [13]	34.4 %
PCANet [5]	34.7 %
RBoW [14]	37.9 %
HMP - RGB [3]	41.8 %
DPM+Gist+SPM [13]	43.1 %
M-HMP [4]	51.2 %

(b) Classification accuracy on the CIFAR-10

Algorithm	Accuracy
DHN ($\Phi_1 + \Phi_3$)	**79.1 %**
Sparse RBM	72.4 %
PCANet [5]	78.7 %
Single-layer Hebbian [1]	79.6 %
Multi-layer K-means [6]	82.0 %
TIOMP-1/T [19]	82.2 %
Multi-Layer NOMP [11]	82.9 %

5 Conclusion

This work introduces the first multi-layer Hebbian network, called DHN, which combines sparse coding and dimensionality reduction. It is the first time a Hebbian network has shown competitive performance at unsupervised features learning for image classification tasks. When evaluated on indoor scene recognition, the DHN achieves higher accuracy than many algorithms, e.g. RBoW. Although the model does not reach the highest accuracy on those benchmarks, it has the major advantage of being trainable online, making it an excellent candidate for learning from unbounded streams of data.

The power and memory efficiency of the architecture proposed might also prove particularly useful for mobile and embedded computing. Recent work [17] already explores potential hardware devices implementing similar principles to those used in the DHN. Although the DHN proves competitive when compared to unsupervised models, it does not compare to models using back-propagation. Future work will explore the introduction of supervision in the form of local learning rules [2] in the DHN.

References

1. Bahroun, Y., Soltoggio, A.: Online representation learning with single and multi-layer Hebbian networks for image classification tasks. In: Lintas, A., Rovetta, S., Verschure, P.F.M.J., Villa, A.E.P. (eds.) ICANN 2017, Part I. LNCS, vol. 10613, pp. 354–363. Springer International Publishing, Cham (2017)

2. Baldi, P., Sadowski, P.: A theory of local learning, the learning channel, and the optimality of backpropagation. Neural Netw. **83**, 51–74 (2016)
3. Bo, L., Ren, X., Fox, D.: Hierarchical matching pursuit for image classification: architecture and fast algorithms. In: NIPS, vol. 1, p. 6 (2011)
4. Bo, L., Ren, X., Fox, D.: Multipath sparse coding using hierarchical matching pursuit. In: Proceedings of the IEEE Conference on Computer Vision and Pattern Recognition, pp. 660–667 (2013)
5. Chan, T.H., Jia, K., Gao, S., Lu, J., Zeng, Z., Ma, Y.: PCANet: a simple deep learning baseline for image classification? IEEE Trans. Image Process. **24**(12), 5017–5032 (2015)
6. Coates, A., Ng, A.Y.: Selecting receptive fields in deep networks. In: Advances in Neural Information Processing Systems, pp. 2528–2536 (2011)
7. Cortes, C., Vapnik, V.: Support-vector networks. Mach. Learn. **20**(3), 273–297 (1995)
8. Cox, T.F., Cox, M.A.: Multidimensional Scaling. CRC Press, Boca Raton (2000)
9. Hosoya, H., Hyvärinen, A.: Learning visual spatial pooling by strong PCA dimension reduction. Neural Comput. **28**, 1249–1264 (2016)
10. Krizhevsky, A., Hinton, G.: Learning multiple layers of features from tiny images (2009)
11. Lin, T.H., Kung, H.: Stable and efficient representation learning with nonnegativity constraints. In: Proceedings of the 31st International Conference on Machine Learning, ICML 2014, pp. 1323–1331 (2014)
12. Olshausen, B.A., Field, D.J.: Sparse coding with an overcomplete basis set: a strategy employed by V1? Vision. Res. **37**(23), 3311–3325 (1997)
13. Pandey, M., Lazebnik, S.: Scene recognition and weakly supervised object localization with deformable part-based models. In: 2011 IEEE International Conference on Computer Vision (ICCV), pp. 1307–1314. IEEE (2011)
14. Parizi, S.N., Oberlin, J.G., Felzenszwalb, P.F.: Reconfigurable models for scene recognition. In: 2012 IEEE Conference on Computer Vision and Pattern Recognition (CVPR), pp. 2775–2782. IEEE (2012)
15. Pehlevan, C., Chklovskii, D.: A normative theory of adaptive dimensionality reduction in neural networks. In: Advances in Neural Information Processing Systems, pp. 2269–2277 (2015)
16. Pehlevan, C., Chklovskii, D.B.: A Hebbian/anti-Hebbian network derived from online non-negative matrix factorization can cluster and discover sparse features. In: 2014 48th Asilomar Conference on Signals, Systems and Computers, pp. 769–775. IEEE (2014)
17. Poikonen, J.H., Laiho, M.: Online linear subspace learning in an analog array computing architecture. In: Proceedings of the 16th International Workshop on Cellular Nanoscale Networks and their Applications (CNNA) (2016)
18. Quattoni, A., Torralba, A.: Recognizing indoor scenes. In: IEEE Conference on Computer Vision and Pattern Recognition, CVPR 2009, pp. 413–420. IEEE (2009)
19. Sohn, K., Lee, H.: Learning invariant representations with local transformations. In: Proceedings of the 29th International Conference on Machine Learning, pp. 1311–1318 (2012)
20. Szegedy, C., Liu, W., Jia, Y., Sermanet, P., Reed, S., Anguelov, D., Erhan, D., Vanhoucke, V., Rabinovich, A.: Going deeper with convolutions. In: Proceedings of the IEEE Conference on Computer Vision and Pattern Recognition, pp. 1–9 (2015)
21. Zhang, S., Wang, J., Tao, X., Gong, Y., Zheng, N.: Constructing deep sparse coding network for image classification. Pattern Recogn. **64**, 130–140 (2017)

Automatic Recognition of Mild Cognitive Impairment from MRI Images Using Expedited Convolutional Neural Networks

Shuqiang Wang[1]([envelope]), Yanyan Shen[1], Wei Chen[2], Tengfei Xiao[3],
and Jinxing Hu[1]

[1] Shenzhen Institutes of Advanced Technology, Chinese Academy of Sciences,
Shenzhen, China
sq.wang@siat.ac.cn
[2] Department of Diagnostic Radiology, Wake Forest University,
Winston-salem, USA
[3] School of Data and Computer Science, Sun Yat-sen University,
Guangzhou, China

Abstract. Few studies have focused on the potential of applying deep learning algorithms into magnetic resonance imaging (MRI) for automatic recognition of subjects with mild cognitive impairment (MCI). In this work, we propose the expedited convolutional neural networks involving Tucker decomposition to recognize MCI using MRI images. We employ transfer learning and data augmentation to deal with limited training data. The effect of Tucker decomposition on saving computational time is discussed. The experimental results show that the proposed model outperforms the previous methods. The expedited convolutional neural networks can provide a good guidance for the applications of deep learning in real-world classification with large training dataset.

Keywords: Expedited convolutional neural network · Mild cognitive impairment · Tucker decomposition · Magnetic resonance imaging

1 Introduction

Mild cognitive impairment (MCI) is a syndrome defined as cognitive decline greater than expected for an individual's age and education level but that does not interfere notably with activities of daily life. It indicates an intermediate state between Alzheimers disease (AD) and healthy aging. For each year, about 10–15% of patients with MCI develop dementia while only 1–2% of healthy controls develop dementia [1,2]. Thus, MCI is often seen as a feasible aim for the early detection of Alzheimers disease. The detection of MCI is playing an important role in understanding of AD and AD drug development. However, the existing tools for the detection of MCI and AD, such as the CERAD [3], often take too much time and cost. Moreover, the objectivity of CERAD is contentious.

© Springer International Publishing AG 2017
A. Lintas et al. (Eds.): ICANN 2017, Part I, LNCS 10613, pp. 373–380, 2017.
https://doi.org/10.1007/978-3-319-68600-4_43

In this work, we propose a method of combining magnetic resonance imaging (MRI) together with deep learning tools to automatically recognize MCI. Deep learning can be seen as an improvement of artificial neural networks, including more hidden layers that allow higher levels of abstraction and advanced predictions from a rich supply of data [4]. It is a growing trend in general data analysis and has been termed one of the 10 breakthrough technologies of 2013. Nowadays, deep learning is becoming a leading machine-learning tool in the general imaging and computer vision domains [5–8].

In particular, convolutional neural networks (CNNs) have presented outstanding effectiveness on medical image computing problems and made a lot of improvement for computer-aided detection [9]. Roth et al. [10] employed convolutional neural networks to improve three existing CAD systems for the recognition of colonic polyps on CT colonography, sclerotic spine metastases on body CT and enlarged lymph nodes on body CT. Dou et al. [11] used 3D CNN and weighted MRI scans to detect cerebral microbleeds. They address developed predictions with their 3D CNN compared to various classical and 2D CNN approaches. Sirinukunwattana et al. [12] employed CNNs to detect nuclei in histopathological images. In their work, they take small patches as input and model the output as a high peak in the vicinity of the center of each nucleus and flat elsewhere. Anthimopoulos et al. [13] employed CNNs to detect patterns of interstitial lung diseases from 2D patches of chest CT scans. Their results show that CNNs can outperform existing methods that use hand-crafted features. However, there is a big challenge for applying deep learning into medical images. The deep learning can only benefit from large amounts of training data while it is difficult in medical area. The reasons are mainly due to high cost and privacy issues [9,14].

In the current work, we propose an expedited convolutional neural network by involving tensor decomposition for classification of MCI and control subject. We employ transfer learning and data augmentation to deal with limited training data. The rest of this paper is organized as follows. In Sect. 2, the expedited convolutional neural networks are proposed, and the schemes for dealing with limited training data are given. The experimental results are presented in Sect. 3. Finally, Sect. 4 gives conclusions and future work.

2   Methods

2.1   Proposed Expedited Convolutional Neural Networks

Compared with the general CNNs, the architecture of our proposed tensor deep neural network mainly contains two aspects: (1) in each convolutional layer, decomposing its kernel and the training samples using Tucker decomposition [15], (2) Fine-tuning the entire networks using backpropagation. In the following, we first review the Tucker decomposition.

Tucker decomposition decomposes a tensor into a core tensor, multiplied by a matrix along each mode. The core tensor usually serves as the relationship/interaction between the modes. Let $\mathcal{X} \in R^{I_1 \times I_2 \times \cdots \times I_M}$ be a tensor and $\mathcal{X}$ can be written as:

$$\mathcal{X} = \mathcal{G} \times_1 A^{(1)} \times_2 \cdots \times_M A^M = [\mathcal{G}; A^{(1)}, A^{(2)}, \cdots, A^{(M)}] \tag{1}$$

We call the Eq. (1) the Tucker decomposition of tensor "$\mathcal{X}$" with r-rank, where $\mathbf{r} = (r_1, \cdots, r_d)$, $\mathcal{G} \in R^{r_1 \times r_2 \times \cdots \times r_d}$ is a core tensor, and $A^{(k)} \in R^{r_k \times I_k}$ is the factor matrix along to the kth mode, and the notation $\times_k$ is the k-mode multiply operation.

In the proposed model, the units within CNN are organized as a sequence of third-order tensors with two spatial dimensions and the third dimension corresponding to different "channels". The convolutional kernel and the corresponding training sample are decomposed respectively using Tucker decomposition before the convolution operation. The architecture of the proposed expedited convolutional neural networks is shown in Fig. 1.

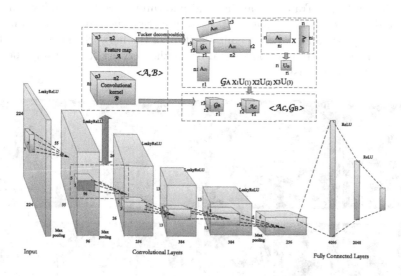

Fig. 1. Architecture of the proposed CNN for MCI recognition

The proposed networks consist nine layers including the input and output. There are five alternating convolutional and pooling layers followed by two fully connected layers and output layer. In convolutional layers, we employ five different filters to get feature maps. In this work, we choose Leaky-ReLU as activation functions. Leaky-ReLU can solve the dying ReLU problem that the tendency of ReLU for keeping a neuron constantly inactive as may happen after a large gradient update. In pooling layers, we employ max pooling. We choose max pooling due to the following two reasons: (1) By deleting non-maximal values, it can reduce computation for upper layers. (2) It provides a form of translation invariance and is a "smart" way of reducing the dimensionality of intermediate representations.

2.2   Schemes for Dealing with Limited Training Data

Deep learning enables highly representative features that have been demonstrated to be a very strong and robust representation in many application domains. However, it only can benefit from large amounts of training data. A key challenge in applying deep convolutional neural networks is that sufficient training data are not always available in medical images. In this work, we employ two schemes to deal with this issue: (1) Data augmentation enables generating new training data from a smaller data set such that the new data set represents the real-world data one may see in practice. Augmentation can extract as much information from data as possible. In this work, we employ the following data augmentation techniques: brightness augmentation, horizontal and vertical shifts, shadow augmentation and flipping. One example of data augmentation is shown in Fig. 2. (2) Transfer learning and fine tuning: we first employ different medical dataset or natural image dataset to pre-train the proposed CNN model. We take the pre-trained model as initialization of the network. Then, we further conduct supervised training on several or all the network layers using the new medical data for the task.

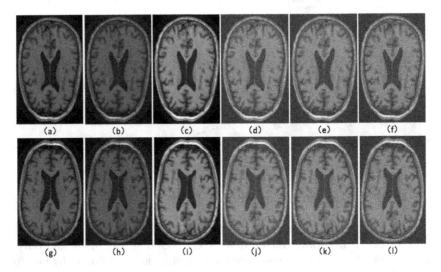

Fig. 2. Data augmentation for MRI image of MCI. (a) is an original image and (b)–(l) are the images generated by data augmentation.

3   Experiment and Results

3.1   Datasets

In this work, we employ the MRI dataset from the Alzheimers Disease Neuroimaging Initiative (ADNI) database (http://adni.loni.usc.edu/methods/mri-analysis/adni-standardized-data/). The selected dataset includes serial brain MRI scans from 400 individuals with MCI (age: 74.8 ± 7.4 years, 257 Male/143 Female), and 229 healthy elderly controls (age: 76.0 ± 5.0 years, 119 Male/110 Female). Subjects were scanned at screening and followed up at 6, 12, 18 (MCI), 24, and 36 months (MCI and normal). For more details, please refer to Ref. [16]. After data augmentation, we obtain 8000 images including 4000 images of MCI and 4000 images of healthy control. We extract 5000 images for training, 1500 images for validation, 1500 images for testing.

3.2 Evaluation

The proposed CNN model is evaluated by a train-validation-test scheme. The actual training of the method is carried-out on the training set, while the validation set is used for fine tuning the hyper-parameters; the overall performance of each system is assessed on the test set. The performance of the proposed model is evaluated by F-score and accuracy. F-score is given by

$$\text{F-score} = \frac{2 \text{precision} \times \text{ recall}}{\text{precision} + \text{recall}},$$

where

$$\text{precision} = \frac{\text{samples correctly classified as c}}{\text{samples classified as c}}$$

and

$$\text{recall} = \frac{\text{samples correctly classified as c}}{\text{samples of class c}}.$$

The accuracy is given by

$$\text{Accuracy} = \frac{\text{correctly classified samples}}{\text{total number of samples}}.$$

3.3 Implementation

The proposed method was implemented using the Theano [17] framework. All the experiments are performed on a computer with Intel(R) Core(TM) i5-4200M CPU @2.50 GHz, GPU NVIDIA GeForce Titan X, and 64 GB of RAM.

3.4 Results

We first demonstrate the effects of pre-training and data augmentation on classification MCI and control subjects. The experimental results are shown in Table 1. LIDC [18] dataset is employed for Pre-training-1 and OASIS [19] dataset is used for Pre-training-2. The best performance with accuracy of 90.6%, recall of 92.8% and F-score of 89.4% is given by the proposed CNNs combining with Pre-training and data augmentation, while the proposed CNNs without any tuning options produce the lowest F-score of 72.8%, accuracy of 74.3%, recall of 74.7% and precision of 71.1%. From Table 1, the following findings can be given: (1) The proposed CNNs combining with pre-training outperform the proposed CNNs

Table 1. Performance of the proposed model with different tuning options.

Model tuning	F-Score (%)	Accuracy (%)	Recall (%)	Precision (%)
No pre-training & no augmentation	72.8	74.3	74.7	71.1
No Pre-training & augmentation	80.2	80.9	81.4	79.0
Pre-training-1 & no augmentation	81.7	82.1	80.8	82.6
Pre-training-2 & no augmentation	83.5	84.2	85.4	81.7
Pre-training-1 & augmentation	87.1	88.8	86.5	87.7
Pre-training-2 & augmentation	89.4	90.6	92.8	87.2

combining with data augmentation. This is mainly because the proposed model can learn more features using different kinds of datasets in the pre-training stage. (2) The effect of transfer learning is influenced by the dataset employed for pre-training. The proposed CNNs combining with pre-training using OASIS dataset outperform the proposed CNNs combining per-training using LIDC dataset.

Table 2. Comparison of the proposed CNNs with previous methods.

Methods	F-Score (%)	Accuracy (%)	Recall (%)	Precision (%)
Wee et al. [20]	81.1	81.5	82.3	79.9
Liu et al. [21]	78.6	79.1	81.5	75.9
Wolz et al. [22]	82.1	82.5	83.7	80.6
Our methods	89.4	90.6	91.2	87.7

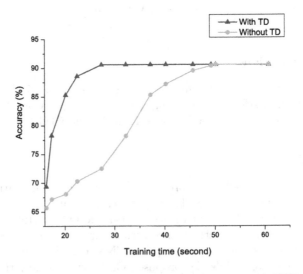

Fig. 3. Testing accuracy versus training time for the proposed CNNs with/without Tucker decomposition. TD is short for Tucker decomposition.

Table 2 shows the comparison of the proposed model with previous methods. It can be seen that our proposed CNNs perform best in classification of MCI with accuracy of 90.6%, recall of 91.2%, precision of 87.7% and F-score of 89.4%, while the best previous method produces an accuracy of 82.5%, a recall of 83.7%, a precision of 83.6% and a F-Score of 82.1%. Figure 3 shows the effect of Tucker decomposition on training time. From Fig. 3, it can be seen that Tucker decomposition can shorten the training time without loss of testing accuracy. In this work, the employed medical dataset is relatively small. Therefore, it seems that the effect of involving Tucker decomposition takes subtler forms. However, it is not a trivial if the dataset of training is large.

4 Conclusion

In this work, we propose the expedited convolutional neural networks for the automatic diagnosis of MCI using MRI images. To address the problem of limited labeled data, we introduce transfer learning and data augmentation into the proposed model. The experimental results demonstrate that the proposed model outperforms the previous methods. In future work, we will focus on the application of the proposed model in classification with large training dataset.

Acknowledgment. This work was supported by Shenzhen Basic Research Projects (Grant No. JCYJ 20160531184426303 and JCYJ 20150401150223648), National Natural Science Foundations of China (Grants No. 61502473 and No. 61503368), and Natural Science Foundation of Guangdong Province (Grant No. 2014A030310154 and No. 2016A030313176).

References

1. Bischkopf, J., Busse, A., Angermeyer, M.C.: Mild cognitive impairment–a review of prevalence, incidence and outcome according to current approaches. Acta Psychiatr. Scand. **106**, 403–414 (2002)
2. Reese, L.C., Laezza, F., Woltjer, R., et al.: Dysregulated phosphorylation of Ca2+/calmodulin-dependent protein kinase II-α in the hippocampus of subjects with mild cognitive impairment and Alzheimers disease. J. Neurochem. **119**, 791–804 (2011)
3. Mirra, S.S., Heyman, A., McKeel, D., et al.: The consortium to establish a registry for Alzheimer's disease (CERAD) part II, standardization of the neuropathologic assessment of Alzheimer's disease. Neurology **41**, 479–486 (1991)
4. LeCun, Y., Bengio, Y., Hinton, G.: Deep learning. Nature **521**, 436–444 (2015)
5. Ciodaro, T., Deva, D., De Seixas, J.M., et al.: Online particle detection with neural networks based on topological calorimetry information. J. Phys. Conf. Ser. **368**, 012030 (2012)
6. Turaga, S.C., Murray, J.F., Jain, V., et al.: Convolutional networks can learn to generate affinity graphs for image segmentation. Neural Comput. **22**, 511–538 (2010)

7. Tompson, J., Goroshin, R., Jain, A., et al.: Efficient object localization using convolutional networks. In: Proceedings of the IEEE Conference on Computer Vision and Pattern Recognition, pp. 648–656 (2015)

8. Taigman, Y., Yang, M., Ranzato, M.A., et al.: Deepface: closing the gap to human-level performance in face verification. In: Proceedings of the IEEE Conference on Computer Vision and Pattern Recognition, pp. 1701–1708 (2014)

9. Greenspan, H., van Ginneken, B., Summers, R.M.: Guest editorial deep learning in medical imaging: overview and future promise of an exciting new technique. IEEE Trans. Med. Imaging 35, 1153–1159 (2016)

10. Roth, H., Lu, L., Liu, J., et al.: Improving computer-aided detection using convolutional neural networks and random view aggregation. IEEE Trans. Med. Imaging 35, 1170–1181 (2016)

11. Dou, Q., Chen, H., Yu, L., et al.: Automatic detection of cerebral microbleeds from MR images via 3D convolutional neural networks. IEEE Trans. Med. Imaging 35, 1182–1195 (2016)

12. Sirinukunwattana, K., Raza, S.E.A., Tsang, Y.W., et al.: Locality sensitive deep learning for detection and classification of nuclei in routine colon cancer histology images. IEEE Trans. Med. Imaging 35, 1196–1206 (2016)

13. Anthimopoulos, M., Christodoulidis, S., Ebner, L., et al.: Lung pattern classification for interstitial lung diseases using a deep convolutional neural network. IEEE Trans. Med. Imaging 35, 1207–1216 (2016)

14. He, K., Zhang, X., Ren, S., et al.: Deep residual learning for image recognition. In: Proceedings of the IEEE Conference on Computer Vision and Pattern Recognition, pp. 770–778 (2016)

15. Kolda, T.G., Bader, B.W.: Tensor decompositions and applications. Soc. Ind. Appl. Math. Rev. 51, 455–500 (2009)

16. Wyman, B.T., Harvey, D.J., Crawford, K., et al.: Standardization of analysis sets for reporting results from ADNI MRI data. Alzheimer's Dement. 9, 332–337 (2013)

17. Bastien, F., Lamblin, P., Pascanu, R., et al.: Theano: new features and speed improvements. arXiv preprint arXiv:1211.5590 (2012)

18. Armato, S.G., McLennan, G., Bidaut, L., et al.: The lung image database consortium (LIDC) and image database resource initiative (IDRI): a completed reference database of lung nodules on CT scans. Med. Phys. 38, 915–931 (2011)

19. Marcus, D.S., Wang, T.H., Parker, J., et al.: Open access series of imaging studies (OASIS): cross-sectional MRI data in young, middle aged, nondemented, and demented older adults. J. Cogn. Neurosci. 19, 1498–1507 (2007)

20. Wee, C.Y., Yap, P.T., Shen, D.: Prediction of Alzheimers disease and mild cognitive impairment using cortical morphological patterns. Hum. Brain Mapp. 34, 3411–3425 (2013)

21. Liu, X., Tosun, D., Weiner, M.W., Schuff, N.: Locally linear embedding (LLE) for MRI based Alzheimers disease classification. Neuroimage 83, 148–157 (2013)

22. Wolz, R., Julkunen, V., Koikkalainen, J., et al.: Multi-method analysis of MRI images in early diagnostics of Alzheimers disease. PLoS ONE 6, e25446 (2011)

Interplay of STDP and Dendritic Plasticity in a Hippocampal CA1 Pyramidal Neuron Model

Ausra Saudargiene[1,2(✉)], Rokas Jackevicius[2], and Bruce P. Graham[3]

[1] Neuroscience Institute, Lithuanian University of Health Sciences,
Kaunas, Lithuania
ausra.saudargiene@lsmuni.lt
[2] Department of Informatics, Vytautas Magnus University, Kaunas, Lithuania
[3] Division of Computing Science and Mathematics, School of Natural Sciences,
University of Stirling, Stirling, UK

Abstract. Synaptic plasticity in hippocampal CA1 pyramidal neurons is accompanied and shaped by dendritic plasticity, the long-lasting and region-specific alteration of the biophysical properties of voltage-gated dendritic ion channels. Down-regulation of A-type potassium current I_A, observed after long-term potentiation induction, boosts the amplitude of somatic back-propagating action potentials and the associated calcium concentration in dendritic spines, increases the amplitude of the excitatory postsynaptic potentials and promotes synaptic integration. Using a detailed computational model of a CA1 pyramidal cell and a spike-timing-dependent synaptic plasticity (STDP) protocol we found that suppression of A-type potassium current I_A leads to the increased dendritic excitability converting long-term depression to long-term potentiation in proximal synapses and supporting fast Hebbian plasticity in distal synapses on a hippocampal CA1 pyramidal neuron.

Keywords: Spike-timing-dependent synaptic plasticity · Dendritic plasticity · A-type Potassium Current I_A

1 Introduction

Biological neurons store memories not only in their synapses, but also in the biophysical properties of dendritic ion channels. Long-term spike-timing-dependent synaptic plasticity (STDP) refers to the synaptic ability to modify its strength depending on the temporal order of presynaptic and postsynaptic activity: if the presynaptic spike precedes the postsynaptic spike within a short time window, the synapse undergoes long-term potentiation (LTP), and it exhibits long-term depression (LTD) if the temporal order is reversed [2]. Physiological experiments show that induction of long-term synaptic plasticity is followed by a local increase in dendritic excitability in CA1 pyramidal neurons [4,8,9,11]. Specifically, LTP is accompanied by a region-specific and long-lasting down-regulation of A-type

© Springer International Publishing AG 2017
A. Lintas et al. (Eds.): ICANN 2017, Part I, LNCS 10613, pp. 381–388, 2017.
https://doi.org/10.1007/978-3-319-68600-4_44

potassium current I_A that leads to the boosted amplitude of the somatic back-propagating action potentials (bAPs), elevated calcium levels in dendrites and dendritic spines, increased amplitude of the excitatory postsynaptic potentials and enhanced synaptic integration [4]. Decreased I_A allows effective backpropagation of somatic action potentials into the distal dendrites and promotes LTP induction in distal synapses [3].

In this study we analyzed the influence of dendritic plasticity on the properties of synaptic plasticity in a hippocampal CA1 pyramidal neuron using a computational modeling approach. We assumed that LTP was induced at synapses on proximal apical dendrites of a CA1 pyramidal neuron and suppressed A-type potassium current I_A in proximal dendritic region. We modeled synaptic weight changes in proximal stratum radiatum (SR) and distal lacunosum-moleculare (SLM) spines of a CA1 pyramidal neuron, applying a classical STDP stimulation protocol. The results show that I_A - mediated dendritic plasticity enhances learning in the CA1 pyramidal neuron.

2   Methods

2.1   Model of CA1 Pyramidal Neuron

We use a detailed compartmental model of CA1 pyramidal neuron [7] with the spines on the proximal SR dendrite and distal SLM dendrite 98 μm and 324 μm from the soma, respectively (Fig. 1). The model includes a leak current, somatic/axonic and dendritic Hodgkin-Huxley-type sodium and potassium currents, proximal and distal A-type potassium currents, m-type potassium current, a mixed conductance hyper polarization-activated h-current, low-voltage-activated T-type calcium current, somatic and dendritic high-voltage-activated R-type currents, somatic and dendritic high-voltage-activated L-type currents, two types of Ca^{2+}-dependent potassium currents (a slow afterhyperpolarization current and a medium afterhyperpolarization current), and a persistent sodium current. Full details of the model are given in [7]. Spines contain the same ion channels as their parent dendrites. Spine head diameter and length equal 0.5 μm, spine neck diameter is 0.2 μm and length is 1 μm. Dendritic spines express AMPA and NMDA receptor-gated synaptic channels modeled via a conventional double exponential function, including Mg^{2+} block for NMDA channels. Peak AMPA synaptic conductance is 1.5 μs, and peak NMDA synaptic conductance is 0.003 μs.

The stimulation protocol consists of the presynaptic action potential at the SR spine or SLM spine paired with a burst-like doublet of somatic action potentials [10], schematically shown in Fig. 1. Postsynaptic action potentials in doublets are spaced 10 ms apart. T denotes a temporal difference between the presynaptic and a second postsynaptic action potential: if the presynaptic action potential precedes a second postsynaptic potential, T is positive; if the temporal order is reversed, T is negative. T values are set to -10 ms and 10 ms. Stimulation consists of 100 pairings at 5 Hz and lasts 20 s as in experimental study [10].

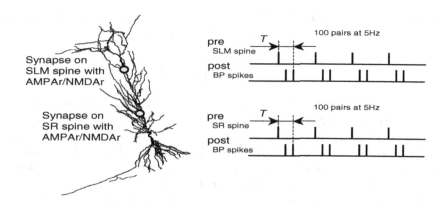

Fig. 1. Compartmental model of a CA1 pyramidal neuron [7] with the added AMPA/NMDA receptor-gated channels on the proximal stratum radiatum (SR) and distal lacunosum-moleculare (SLM) spines, and schematic illustration of the stimulation protocols. Presynaptic action potential at the SR spine and SLM spine is paired with a burst-like doublet of somatic action potentials spaced 10 ms apart. T denotes a temporal difference between the presynaptic and a second postsynaptic action potential and is set to -10 ms and 10 ms.

2.2 Synaptic and Dendritic Plasticity in a CA1 Pyramidal Neuron Model

Synaptic modifications are driven by the intracellular calcium concentration in the SR and SLM spines. Calcium concentration in spines is modelled as [1]:

$$\frac{d[Ca^{2+}]}{dt} = -\frac{I_{Ca}}{2Fd18} + \frac{[Ca^{2+}]_0 - [Ca^{2+}]}{\tau_{Ca}}, \tag{1}$$

where $[Ca^{2+}]$ is the calcium concentration in a spine, I_{Ca} is the calcium current into the spine, $[Ca^{2+}]_0 = 0.1\,\mu m$ is the resting calcium concentration in a spine, factor 18 reflects the influence of the endogenous buffers [1], $\tau_{Ca} = 15$ ms is the time constant of calcium concentration decay [1], F is the Faraday constant, $d = 0.1\,\mu m$ is the depth of dendritic shell.

Synaptic efficacy variable ρ is described by a differential equation [5]:

$$\tau\frac{d\rho}{dt} = -\rho(1-\rho)(\rho_0-\rho) + \gamma_p(1-\rho)\Theta([Ca^{2+}]-\theta_p) - \gamma_d\rho\Theta([Ca^{2+}]-\theta_d) + Noise(t), \tag{2}$$

where $[Ca^{2+}]$ is the instantaneous calcium concentration in a spine, $\rho_0 = 0.5$ is unstable ρ state, $\gamma_p = 400$ is the rate of increase in ρ, $\gamma_d = 100$ is the rate of decrease in ρ, $\theta_p = 0.8$ is the LTP threshold, $\theta_d = 0.24$ is the LTD threshold, Θ is the the Heaviside function, $Noise(t)$ is an activity-dependent noise term (not implemented), $\tau = 100$ s is the time constant of ρ changes.

In SR and SLM spines ρ is set to the DOWN and to the UP states ρ_{DOWN} and ρ_{UP} to represent either an initially unpotentiated or a potentiated synapse.

Transitions from the DOWN to the UP or from the UP to the DOWN states trigger positive or negative synaptic weight change [5]:

$$\Delta\omega = -1 + \frac{((1-U)\beta + D(1-\beta)) + b(U\beta + (1-D)(1-\beta))}{\beta + (1-\beta)b}, \qquad (3)$$

where U is the probability of ρ_{DOWN} transition from the DOWN state to the UP state, D is the probability of ρ_{UP} transition from the UP state to the DOWN state, $\beta = 0.7$ is the fraction of synapses in the DOWN state, $b = 5$ is the synaptic strength of the UP/DOWN state. Initially, $U = 0$ and $D = 0$; during learning $U =$ becomes 1 when ρ_{DOWN} increases and crosses the 0.5 threshold; $D = 1$ when ρ_{UP} decreases and crosses the 0.5 threshold.

The numerical simulations of the compartmental model of a CA1 pyramidal neuron were performed in NEURON [6].

3   Results

Presynaptic action potential at a SR spine, paired with a doublet of postsynaptic action potentials at $T = -10$ ms and $T = 10$ ms, leads to LTD and LTP as observed in physiological experiments [10] (Fig. 2). If the presynaptic action potential follows the second postsynaptic spike by $T = -10$ ms (Fig. 2a), calcium concentration in a SR spine reaches 1.8 μm (Fig. 2b) and leads to synaptic efficacy variable ρ transition from the UP state to the DOWN state (Fig. 2c, black line) and negative synaptic weight change, i.e. LTD induction (Fig. 2d). If the presynaptic action potential precedes the second postsynaptic spike by $T = 10$ ms (Fig. 2e), calcium concentration in a SR spine increases up to 2.2 μm (Fig. 2f) and forces synaptic efficacy variable ρ to transit from the DOWN state to the UP state (Fig. 2g, gray line) leading to the positive weight change, i.e. LTP induction (Fig. 2h).

The experiments were repeated under the influence of the enhanced local excitability of the proximal apical dendrites of a CA1 pyramidal neuron (Fig. 3g). The voltage of half-maximal inactivation for A-type potassium current was hyperpolarised from −63 mV to −69 mV, and maximal conductance of A-type potassium channel was down-scaled by a factor of 0.2 in the SR apical dendrites up to 121 μm from the soma to account for the experimentally observed increase in the amplitude of bAPs and dendritic calcium concentration. For $T = -10$ ms, calcium levels in a SR spine are elevated up to 2.2 μm (Fig. 3b), synaptic efficacy variable ρ performs transition from the DOWN state to the UP state (Fig. 3c, gray line) and leads to the positive synaptic weight change and LTP induction (Fig. 3d). For $T = 10$ ms, calcium in a SR spine reaches higher values of 3.1 μm (Fig. 3f) and induces LTP (Fig. 3g, h).

Similar stimulation protocol was applied for the distal SLM spine: presynaptic action potential at a SLM spine was paired with a doublet of postsynaptic somatic action potentials at $T = -10$ ms and $T = 10$ ms. In control conditions, synaptic modifications are not induced for $T = -10$ ms (not shown); a SLM synapse is depressed for $T = 10$ ms (Fig. 4a–d) as the bAPs are too weak to

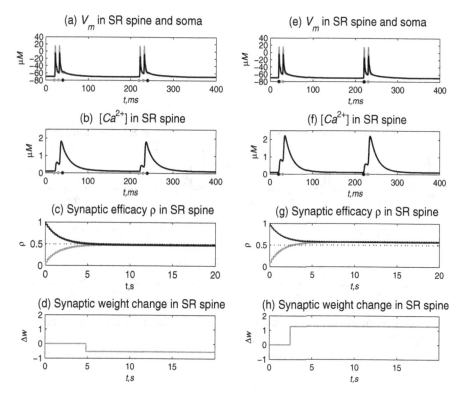

Fig. 2. Membrane potential, calcium concentration, synaptic efficacy and synaptic weight change in a proximal SR spine for $T = -10$ ms (a)–(d) and $T = 10$ ms (e)–(h) in control conditions. (a, e) Membrane potential in a proximal SR spine (black line) and soma (gray line) during two pre-post pairings. Postsynaptic action potentials are generated at 20 ms and 30 ms; 220 ms and 230 ms (gray dots). Every second postsynaptic action potential in a burst is used as a reference point for T definition. Presynaptic action potential is induced at 40 ms and at 240 ms for $T = -10$ ms; at 20 ms and at 220 ms for $T = 10$ ms (black dots). (b, f) Calcium concentration in a proximal SR spine during two pre-post pairings. (c, g) Synaptic efficacy ρ: initially in DOWN state - gray line; initially in UP state - black line. (d, h) Synaptic weight change: (d) for $T = -10$ ms LTD is induced; (h) for $T = 10$ ms LTP is induced.

invade distal dendritic regions and effectively open NMDA receptor-gated channels that mediate strong calcium current, necessary for LTP. If A-type potassium current is down-regulated, bAPs, paired with the SLM synaptic input, induce dendritic spikes for $T = -10$ ms (not shown) and for $T = 10$ ms (Fig. 4e, black line). Dendritic spikes open NMDA receptor-gated channels and contribute to the elevation of intracellular calcium concentration in a SLM spine via voltage-gated calcium channels. Calcium concentration reaches $37\,\mu$m and causes fast LTP (Fig. 4g, black line; h).

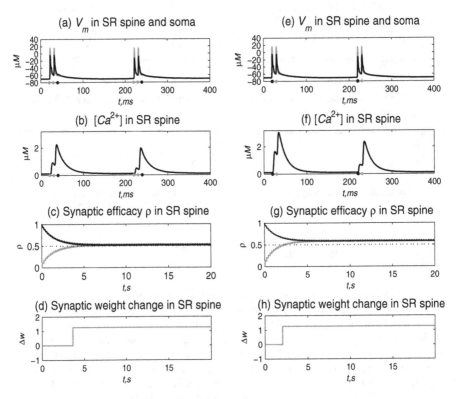

Fig. 3. Membrane potential, calcium concentration, synaptic efficacy and synaptic weight change in a proximal SR spine for $T = -10\,\mathrm{ms}$ (a)–(d) and $T = 10\,\mathrm{ms}$ (e)–(h) in conditions of enhanced local excitability of proximal dendritic region. (a, e) Membrane potential in a proximal SR spine (black line) and soma (gray line) during two pre-post pairings. Stimulation protocol as in Fig. 2. (b, f) Calcium concentration in a proximal SR spine during two pre-post pairings. (c, g) Synaptic efficacy ρ initially in DOWN state - gray line; initially in UP state - black line. (d, h) Synaptic weight change: (d) for $T = -10\,\mathrm{ms}$ LTP is induced; (h) for $T = 10\,\mathrm{ms}$ LTP is induced.

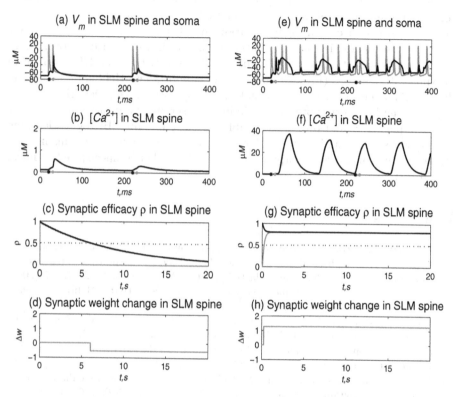

Fig. 4. Membrane potential, calcium concentration, synaptic efficacy and synaptic weight change in a distal SLM spine for $T = 10$ ms in control conditions (a)–(d) and in conditions of enhanced local excitability of proximal dendritic region (e)–(h). (a, e) Membrane potential in a distal SLM spine (black line) and soma (gray line) during two pre-post pairings. Presynaptic action potential is induced at 20 ms and at 220 ms (black dots). In control conditions (a), the postsynaptic action potentials are generated at 20 ms and 30 ms; 220 ms and 230 ms (gray dots), every second postsynaptic action potential is used as a reference point for T definition. In conditions of enhanced dendritic excitability (e), back-propagating action potentials paired with the distal synaptic input induce dendritic spikes that propagate to the soma and cause somatic action potentials. (b, f) Calcium concentration in a distal SLM spine during two pre-post pairings. (c, g) Synaptic efficacy ρ initially in DOWN state - gray line; initially in UP state - black line. (d, h) Synaptic weight change: (d) LTD is induced; (h) fast LTP is induced.

4   Conclusions

Long-lasting region-specific down-regulation of A-type potassium current I_A is an important factor of synaptic plasticity in hippocampal CA1 pyramidal neuron as it boosts the amplitude of the somatic back-propagating action potentials and the associated calcium concentration in SR spines, and creates favorable conditions for dendritic spike generation in distal SLM dendritic regions. Simulation results show that suppression of I_A acts as a switch from LTD to LTP in proximal SR synapses (Figs. 2d and 3d) and supports fast Hebbian plasticity in distal SLM spines due to dendritic spike initiation (Fig. 4e, h). Dendritic plasticity, following long-term potentiation induction, serves as a positive feedback for synaptic plasticity and promotes reliable and fast learning. Biological learning rules might serve as an inspiration for more efficient learning algorithms in spiking neural networks, neuromorphic computing and other brain-inspired artificial neural systems.

References

1. Badoual, M., Zou, Q., Davison, A.P., Rudolph, M., Bal, T., Fregnac, Y., Destexhe, A.: Biophysical and phenomenological models of multiple spike interactions in spike-timing dependent plasticity. Int. J. Neural Syst. **16**(2), 79–97 (2006)
2. Bi, G., Poo, M.: Synaptic modification by correlated activity: Hebb's postulate revisited. Annu. Rev. Neurosci. **24**, 139–166 (2001)
3. Chen, X., Yuan, L., Zhao, C., Birnbaum, S., Frick, A., Jung, W., Schwarz, T., Sweatt, J., Johnston, D.: Deletion of Kv4.2 gene eliminates dendritic A-type K+ current and enhances induction of long-term potentiation in hippocampal CA1 pyramidal neurons. J. Neurosci. **26**(47), 12143–12151 (2006)
4. Frick, A., Magee, J., Johnston, D.: LTP is accompanied by an enhanced local excitability of pyramidal neuron dendrites. Nat. Neurosci. **7**(2), 126–135 (2004)
5. Graupner, M., Brunel, N.: Calcium-based plasticity model explains sensitivity of synaptic changes to spike pattern, rate, and dendritic location. Proc. Natl. Acad. Sci. U.S.A. **109**(10), 3991–3996 (2012)
6. Hines, M., Carnevale, N.: The NEURON simulation environment. Neural Comput. **9**(6), 1179–1209 (1997)
7. Poirazi, P., Brannon, T., Mel, B.: Arithmetic of subthreshold synaptic summation in a model CA1 pyramidal cell. Neuron **37**, 977–987 (2003)
8. Sjostrom, P.J., Hausser, M.: A cooperative switch determines the sign of synaptic plasticity in distal dendrites of neocortical pyramidal neurons. Neuron **51**(2), 227–238 (2006)
9. Wang, Z., Xu, N.L., Wu, C.P., Duan, S., Poo, M.M.: Bidirectional changes in spatial dendritic integration accompanying long-term synaptic modifications. Neuron **37**(3), 463–472 (2003)
10. Wittenberg, G.M., Wang, S.S.: Malleability of spike-timing-dependent plasticity at the CA3-CA1 synapse. J. Neurosci. **26**(24), 6610–6617 (2006)
11. Xu, J., Kang, N., Jiang, L., Nedergaard, M., Kang, J.: Activity-dependent long-term potentiation of intrinsic excitability in hippocampal CA1 pyramidal neurons. J. Neurosci. **25**(7), 1750–1760 (2005)

Enhancements on the Modified Stochastic Synaptic Model: The Functional Heterogeneity

Karim Ellatihy[✉] and Martin Bogdan

Computer Engineering Department, Universität Leipzig, 04109 Leipzig, Germany
kellaithy@informatik.uni-leipzig.de
http://www.informatik.uni-leipzig.de

Abstract. This study is a "morphosis" of the presented modified stochastic synaptic model (MSSM) with major validations using evidences from a number of clinical as well computational studies addressing the general question of copying the dynamics of synaptic transmission. The MSSM represents a, relatively, complex model-compilation of the synaptic connecting process with a focus on copying the relevant biophysical details in order to capture to the computational capacity of biological neural circuitry. The use of MSSM in large scale simulations has been mainly challenged due to the heavy mathematical functional execution, and more importantly due its sensitivity to high ($>60\,\mathrm{Hz}$) input firing rates. The presented analysis addresses both aspects with slightly new implementation of the model. It shows that the new understanding about vesicles dynamics helps the MSSM to present a richer repertoire of dynamics and meets the required functional synaptic heterogeneity.

Keywords: Stochastic synapses · Functional heterogeneity · Vesicle release

1 Introduction

This study revisits the, previously presented, modified stochastic synaptic model (MSSM) using evidences from a number of clinical as well computational studies addressing the general question of copying the dynamics of synaptic transmission. The MSSM represents relatively a complex compilation of the synaptic process with a focus on copying the relevant biophysical details in order to capture to the computational capacity of biological neural circuitry [5,6] while being computationally inexpensive.

The use of MSSM in large scale simulations has been mainly challenged due to the heavy mathematical functional execution [9], and more importantly due its sensitivity to high input firing rates [7]. The presented analysis addresses both aspects.

The current version of MSSM has a main setback which is the sensitivity to input firing rates outside the window of 10–50 Hz. Specifically, with stimuli featuring e.g. relatively high firing rates the synaptic response undergoes an

© Springer International Publishing AG 2017
A. Lintas et al. (Eds.): ICANN 2017, Part I, LNCS 10613, pp. 389–396, 2017.
https://doi.org/10.1007/978-3-319-68600-4_45

irreversible state of either facilitation or depression. In a network simulation, this effect drives the network into synchrony, i.e. synchronous firing. This might be a needed behavior; as this ability enables the network to feature what is known as "system neural states"; which led to introducing the concept of temporal finite state machines (tFSM) and the synaptic energy with its relation to neural information processing [7,8]. Mathematically, one may describe the collective behavior of the model as a hyper-attractor with input-dependent minima.

For the model to avoid transforming into an attractor, a second level of rate-adaptive response is needed. This was the case in modeling visual cortex data as reported in [5], where MSSM has successfully modeled the synaptic transmission of the input stimuli. The model was able to predict the recorded output in the visual cortex with a hit-rate of 92%.

The recent work of [3] has discussed the concept of synaptic functional heterogeneity and its relation to the dynamics controlling the process of vesicles release at he presynaptic site. This is strongly supported by number of biological studies e.g. [1] where there is a clear correlation between the dynamics of vesicles pool rebuilding and synaptic transmission.

The analysis at hands investigates the possibility of using a different internal coupling mechanism between the concentration of released neurotransmitter in the cleft and the probability of release from the presynaptic terminal. The introduced coupling mechanism overcomes the limitation of the current MSSM and its sensitivity to the input firing rates. The simulation shows how this new implementation allows the modeling of a more heterogeneous neural activity. Moreover, this work uses a new script developed with the Brian2 library [11] on Python. This new approach shows a significant enhancement in the simulation overheads which opens new avenues for large scale simulations.

2   The Model

2.1   Basic Synaptic Model: The Modified Stochastic Synaptic Model

The modified stochastic synaptic model (MSSM) introduced in [6] models the coupling between the presynaptic and post synaptic activities. The term "stochastic" acknowledges the probabilistic nature of vesicles release upon the arrival of an action potential on the presynaptic terminal. However, the model uses a deterministic approach to model this nature [10].

Thus, $P(t_i)$ models the probability that the ith spike in a presynaptic spike train $\sum_i \delta(t - t_i)$ (input spikes) triggers the release of a vesicle at time t_i at the synapse. The involved probability-of-release is modeled as:

$$P(t) = 1 - \exp(-C(t) \cdot V(t)) \tag{1}$$

which is governed by two counteracting intrinsic mechanisms: facilitation and depression. Facilitation reflects the calcium concentration in the presynaptic neuron, $C(t)$, while depression represents the effect of the concentration of ready-to-release vesicles in the presynaptic terminal, $V(t)$. The model reads [4,5]:

$$\frac{dC}{dt} = \frac{(C_o - C)}{\tau_C} + \alpha \cdot \sum_i \delta(t - t_i), \tag{2}$$

$$\frac{dV}{dt} = \frac{(V_o - V)}{\tau_V} - P(t) \cdot \sum_i \delta(t - t_i), \tag{3}$$

$$\frac{dN_t}{dt} = max(0, -\frac{dV}{dt}) + (\frac{N_{to} - N_t}{\tau_{N_t}}), \tag{4}$$

$$\tau_{E_{psp}} \frac{dE_{psp}}{dt} = -E_{psp} + k_{epsp} \cdot N_t, \tag{5}$$

A schematic simulation mapping of the state parameters in the presynaptic part (Eqs. 1–3) is illustrated in Fig. 1.

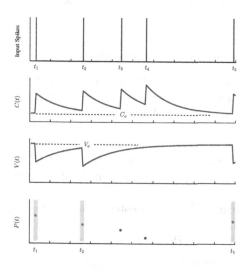

Fig. 1. The presynaptic dynamics of MSSM. Schematic illustration of the time evolution of the state parameters from top $C(t)$ (second panel), $V(t)$ (third panel) and $P(t)$ in the last panel.

In Eq. 2, the intracellular calcium concentration starts at C_o. It is raised incrementally by each stimulus impulse, approximated herein by a Dirac Delta function $\delta(t - t_i)$. The impact of each stimulus impulse to the intracellular calcium concentration is equal to the product of calcium gain (calcium current), α, caused by action potential and set to 0.095. Once the stimulus sequence ends, $C(t)$ decays with time constant τ_C toward C_o. $C(t)$ represents, in an abstract way, the intrinsic synaptic processes of synaptic facilitation [6]. In Eq. 3, $V(t)$ is the expected number of vesicles of neurotransmitter molecules in the ready-for-release pool at time instant t. V_o is the maximum number of vesicles that can be stored in the pool. In a similar fashion to $C(t)$, $V(t)$ follows first-order nonlinear differential equations with a time constant τ_V.

Still in the synaptic cleft, N_t determines the concentration of the released neurotransmitter in the synaptic cleft, Eq. 4. This concentration can be estimated by tracing the amount of vesicles of neurotransmitter that remains in the presynaptic neuron, $V(t)$, over time. Each quantum of neurotransmitter is stored in one synaptic vesicle. The concentration of neurotransmitter in the synaptic cleft is meant to be the corresponding concentration of quanta of neurotransmitter. Hence, in Eq. 4 we use here a first-order nonlinear differential equation similar in nature to Eq. 2. The incremental raise in this case is then the decrease in the concentration of vesicles (first term). The drift term (second term) allows the value of N_t to decay, in case of no input, to a minimum accepted concentration N_{to} with a decay time constant τ_{N_t}. This decay reflects the biological cleaning action (or complete removal) of the neurotransmitter from the cleft. As the binding process of neurotransmitter in the post synaptic membrane induces $EPSP$, it is calculated as in Eq. 5; where τ_{epsp} is a decay time constant and k_{epsp} is a scaling factor.

2.2   Revision of Probability Representation

In [8], the synaptic weight of the MSSM was presented as $w = C \cdot V \cdot N_t$. In [2], it has been shown that the synaptic terminals can individually adjust their neurotransmitter release probability dynamically through local feedback regulation. This suggests that the N_t can be used as a feedback mechanism for regulating the release process via altering $P(t)$ from Eq. 1 and following Eq. 3. The synaptic weight can be viewed then as $w = (C \cdot V) \cdot N_t$ where the neurotransmitter dynamics modulate the combined quantity of facilitation and depression.

Hence, in the revisited MSSM presented here $P(t)$ representation is changed from Eq. 1 to be:

$$P(t) = 1 - \exp(-w) \qquad (6)$$

where the rest of the MSSM remains unchanged.

This alteration in the P representation allows the synaptic model to have local feedback mechanism of the current synaptic state without the need of an external rate-response adaptation to be implemented. Moreover, the effect of changing the profile of calculating the $P(t)$ influences mainly the depressive sub-process represented of $V(t)$. This might be viewed as an enhanced local inhibition mechanism that keeps the model away from transforming into an the dynamics of an attractor.

3   Simulation Results and Discussion

In all below simulations, the network setup is recurrent with three groups of neurons with 10 neurons each. The first two are used as input ones feeding activity to the third one. One of the input groups feeds only excitatory input while the second feeds only inhibitory ones (by changing the sign of the E_{psp}). The third (output group) feeds its excitatory activity back to the input inhibitory group. All synaptic connections are modeled using the MSSM either with the standard implementation or the new presented one in the first and second subsections respectively. This configuration uses 300 synapses among the three neuron groups.

Neuronal representation is implemented using standard leaky integrate-and-fire neurons from the Brian2 library with a membrane relaxing time constant $\tau_m = 15$ ms. Neurons were stimulated with spontaneous background activity (white Gaussian-noise) controlled via the noise standard deviation parameter σ. Only the input neuron groups are activated with the background noise, σ for the third group is set to Zero. The simulation epoch is 1 s with $dt = 1$ ms. The simulation duration was between 6–7 s.

3.1 Standard MSSM Approach

Figure 2 illustrates the simulation results with using the standard definition of $P(t)$ of Eq. 1. The noise level set to simulate an input at a firing rate of 30–40 Hz.

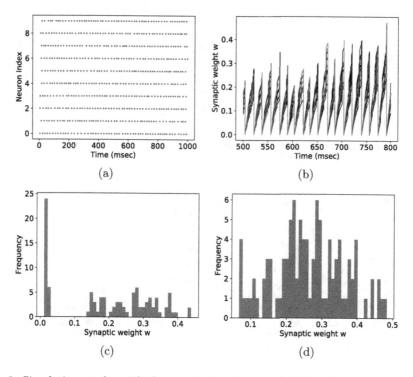

(a)   (b)

(c)   (d)

Fig. 2. Simulation results with the standard definition of $P(t)$ with simulation epoch of 1 s. (a) Neuronal activity of output neurons group. (b) Zoom in of the time evolution of synaptic weights, from the excitatory synaptic group from input neurons to output ones. (c) and (d) Histograms of the synaptic weights w of two different synaptic groups: Inhibitory from input to output and excitatory from output to input respectively.

As mentioned above in the introduction of this work, the network under such conditions undergoes a rhythmic activity as shown in Fig. 2(a); this is the spiking activity of the output neurons group (third one). If the simulation continues, the firing rate shall increase and stays in synchrony. The network "maintains" this level of activity till the input changes its temporal features.

Figure 2(b) zooms in on the evolution of the synaptic weights w of the excitatory synaptic connections from input to output neuron groups. It can be shown that there is steady incremental increase in the overall synaptic weights as time evolves which leads to the mentioned synchronous activity. For the sake of simplicity and in order to show the courses of the synaptic weights for the 300 synaptic connections, Fig. 2(c) and (d) illustrates the histograms of the synaptic weights of the three different synaptic groups.

3.2 Heterogeneity and New Representation of $P(t)$

The results reported in Figs. 3 and 4 are simulated using the new presented definition of $P(t)$ as in Eq. 6. The two figure groups represent two main settings

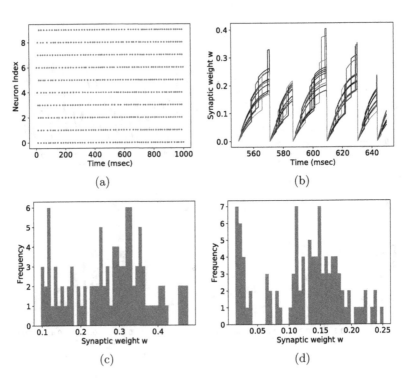

Fig. 3. (a) – (d) Simulation results with the new definition of $P(t)$ with simulation epoch of 1 s at *low* noise level. (a) Neuronal activity of output neurons group. (b) Zoom in of the time evolution of the excitatory synaptic group from input neurons to output ones. (c) and (d) Histograms of the synaptic weights w from two synaptic groups: Inhibitory from input to output and excitatory from output to input respectively.

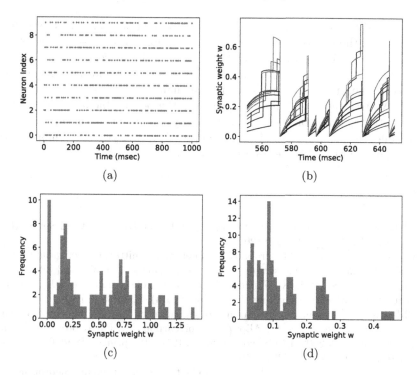

Fig. 4. Simulation results with the standard definition of $P(t)$ with simulation epoch of 1 s at *high* noise level. (a) Neuronal activity of output neurons group. (b) Zoom in of the time evolution of the excitatory synaptic group from input neurons to output ones. (c) and (d) Histograms of the synaptic weights w of two different synaptic groups: Inhibitory from input to output and excitatory from output to input respectively

of noise level that are assigned to stimulate the network with corresponding input firing rate below 20 Hz and above 60 Hz respectively.

By comparing the firing patterns from the Figs. 3(a) and 4(a) on one hand to the one from Fig. 2(a), it is obvious that even at low input firing rate the network is able to reach a different level of complex firing pattern rather than synchronous firing. This is supported by the evolution of the synaptic weights shown in Fig. 3(b) and 4(b). The synaptic efficacy does not show a continuous trending as shown before with the standard definition of P.

The histograms of the all synaptic weights shows more aggregation towards lower synaptic weights, even with the higher noise level as seen in Fig. 4(c) and (d). These histograms gives an indication of the functional heterogeneity expected from the MSSM. The shifts within the range of low synaptic weights to the mid-ranges across the three different groups of synapses is a clear indication that the new representation adds to the capacity of the synaptic model to capture wider range of dynamics. It remains to be seen, how this added capacity can be quantified and modulated to target specific patterns of dynamics.

The duration for each of these simulations needed only 7 s, this represents a factor of 7 vs. the real simulated time of 1 s. The former approach using Matlab (from MathWorks) would require a factor >300 as discussed in [9].

The new implementation presented here pretenses a significant enhancement over the former used methodology in two main aspects. First, it empowers the MSSM with more plausibility in copying the needed biophysical nature of the synaptic transmission. Second, and equally important, by using the Brian2 library and the new optimized implementation with Python it enhances the readiness of the MSSM to be used in large scale simulations.

References

1. Alabi, A.A., Tsien, R.W.: Synaptic vesicle pools and dynamics. Cold Spring Harb. Perspect. Biol. **4**(8), a013680 (2012)
2. Branco, T., Staras, K.: The probability of neurotransmitter release: variability and feedback control at single synapses. Nat. Rev. Neurosci. **10**, 373–383 (2009)
3. Chamberland, S., Tóth, K.: Functionally heterogeneous synaptic vesicle pools support diverse synaptic signalling. J. Physiol. **594**(4), 825–835 (2016)
4. El-Laithy, K., Bogdan, M.: Synchrony state generation in artificial neural networks with stochastic synapses. In: Alippi, C., Polycarpou, M., Panayiotou, C., Ellinas, G. (eds.) ICANN 2009. LNCS, vol. 5768, pp. 181–190. Springer, Heidelberg (2009). doi:10.1007/978-3-642-04274-4_19
5. El-Laithy, K., Bogdan, M.: Predicting spike-timing of a thalamic neuron using a stochastic synaptic model. In: ESANN Proceedings, pp. 357–362 (2010)
6. El-laithy, K., Bogdan, M.: Synchrony state generation: an approach using stochastic synapses. J. Artif. Intell. Soft Comput. Res. **1**, 17–26 (2011)
7. El-Laithy, K., Bogdan, M.: Temporal finite-state machines: a novel framework for the general class of dynamic networks. In: Huang, T., Zeng, Z., Li, C., Leung, C.S. (eds.) ICONIP 2012. LNCS, vol. 7664, pp. 425–434. Springer, Heidelberg (2012). doi:10.1007/978-3-642-34481-7_52
8. El-Laithy, K., Bogdan, M.: Synaptic energy drives the information processing mechanisms in spiking neural networks. Math. Biosci. Eng. **11**(2), 233–256 (2014)
9. Hoffmann, J., El-Laithy, K., Güttler, F., Bogdan, M.: Simulating biological-inspired spiking neural networks with OpenCL. In: Diamantaras, K., Duch, W., Iliadis, L.S. (eds.) ICANN 2010. LNCS, vol. 6352, pp. 184–187. Springer, Heidelberg (2010). doi:10.1007/978-3-642-15819-3_23
10. Maass, W., Zador, A.M.: Dynamic stochastic synapses as computational units. Neural Comput. **11**, 903–917 (1999)
11. Stimberg, M., Goodman, D., Benichoux, V., Brette, R.: Equation-oriented specification of neural models for simulations. Front. Neuroinf. **8**, 6 (2014)

Multicompartment Simulations of NMDA Receptor Based Facilitation in an Insect Target Tracking Neuron

Bo Bekkouche[1](✉), Patrick A. Shoemaker[2], Joseph Fabian[3], Elisa Rigosi[1], Steven D. Wiederman[3], and David C. O'Carroll[1]

[1] Department of Biology, Lund University, Lund, Sweden
bo.bekkouche@biol.lu.se
[2] Computational Science Research Center, San Diego State University, San Diego, USA
[3] Adelaide Medical School, The University of Adelaide, Adelaide, Australia

Abstract. Computational modelling of neurons on different scales provides not only methods to explore mechanisms observed in vivo but also for testing hypotheses that would be impossible physiologically. In this paper we present initial computational analysis of insect lobula small target motion detector (STMD) neurons. We simulate a multicompartment model in combination with a bioinspired model for front-end processing. This combination of different simulation environments enables a combination of scale and detail not possible otherwise. The addressed hypothesis is that facilitation involves N-methyl-D-aspartate (NMDA) synapses which map retinotopically onto the dendritic tree of the STMD neuron. Our results show that a stronger response (facilitation) is generated when using continuous visual stimuli as opposed to random jumps. We observe two levels of facilitation which may be involved in selective attention.

Keywords: Computational neuroscience · Simulation · Model · Multicompartment · Bioinspired · Facilitation · Small target motion detection · Selective attention

1 Introduction

The small target motion detection (STMD) neurons of the insect lobula (Fig. 1) are activated by small moving targets and ignore large features [12,13]. They show an interesting form of short-term plasticity called facilitation that has been linked to selective attention [4,13,18]. The STMDs can be subdivided into many subtypes depending on excitability, direction sensitivity and the size of the receptive field [11].

The N-methyl-D-aspartate receptor (NMDAR) is a post-synaptic receptor subtype found in some glutamatergic synapses (GS). GS are widely expressed in the insect brain (as in mammals) and NMDARs are expressed in the medulla and lobula of the optic lobe in the fruitfly *Drosophila melanogaster* [3,7,16]. A recent

© Springer International Publishing AG 2017
A. Lintas et al. (Eds.): ICANN 2017, Part I, LNCS 10613, pp. 397–404, 2017.
https://doi.org/10.1007/978-3-319-68600-4_46

study also shows that *D. melanogaster* may possess neurons that are functionally similar to STMDs [8]. We thus make the assumption that NMDA synapses are expressed on dragonfly STMD neurons, although direct evidence for this has yet to be obtained. One hypothesis [14] is that facilitation involves NMDA synapses at the outputs of local 'elementary detectors' for object motion which map retinotopically onto the input dendritic tree of the wide-field STMD neuron. Due to lack of good anatomical data for STMD neurons, previous attempts to simulate this mechanism have been based on a different neuron subtype [14]. In this paper, we investigated properties of the facilitation mechanism using newly obtained 3D reconstruction of the morphology in a dragonfly binocular STMD neuron, BSTMD1, which has been implicated as a key input neuron to higher order STMD neurons that express a sophisticated form of selective attention [4].

The input dendrites for BSTMD1 are distributed across a tree-like structure (Fig. 1B) that we assume maps inputs from small-field columnar input neurons. Such retinotopy has not yet been confirmed in the dragonfly lobula neurons, however calcium imaging from other species supports retinotopical mapping in optic lobe neurons at a similar level of the visual processing [6,17]. Despite the lack of direct evidence for the mechanisms that we have tested here, a main aim of this study was to build and test a framework of modelling tools enabling combined bioinspired models for input processing (the retinotopic elements) and biophysically plausible simulations of small target tracking in the wide-field integration neurons of the insect visual system believed to be the site at which competitive selection is first generated.

2   Simulation Environment and Model Construction

Our model consists of two major blocks: an array of small-field retinopically organized 'elementary small target motion detectors' (ESTMDs), and a wide-field integrator taking synaptic input from the ESTMD array via NMDA synapses.

We reconstructed the input dendritic tree of an intracellularly labelled dragonfly binocular STMD neuron, BSTMD1 [4] using confocal microscope imagery (Fig. 1). The reconstructed dendritic tree (Fig. 1C) is dissimilar from the one previously used in [14] (Fig. 1D). The image set was reconstructed in neuTube [5] and exported to .swc format describing 3D coordinates, connectivity and radius of the compartments. This morphological model consists of electrical nodes (compartments) built by resistors and capacitors representing the electrical properties of a specific piece of the neuron. We then implemented the model in the NEURON simulator [10] under Python. We then inserted passive membrane properties (non-spiking) and NMDA receptor inputs. We placed one NMDA synapse at each compartment (1757 compartments total) in order to capture morphological variation. Synaptic input for targets moving through the receptive field was generated using a bioinspired ESTMD model [1] implemented in MATLAB (Fig. 1E). This model provided a simulation of the outputs of small-field, retinotopically organized neurons selective for small target motion.

The NEURON model is based on the following equation:

$$C_m dV_m/dt = I_{syn} - I_{pas}.\tag{1}$$

(Membrane capacitance: $C_m = 1F/\text{cm}^2$) where I_{pas} is the current due to passive properties:

$$I_{pas} = g_{pas}(V_m - E_{pas}),\tag{2}$$

(Membrane conductivity: $g_{pas} = 100 S/\text{cm}^2$, Passive reversal potential: $E_{pas} = -70\,\text{mV}$) and I_{syn} is the externally induced current (in this protocol due to NMDA synapses):

$$I_{syn} = \frac{a[g_{max}(e^{-t/\tau_2} - e^{-t/\tau_1})(V_m - E_{syn})]}{(1 + \frac{Mg}{3.57}e^{-0.062V_m})},\tag{3}$$

(Synaptic reversal potential $E_{syn} = 0$, magnesium concentration $Mg = 1mM$, normalized maximum conductance $g_{max} = 1$, rising time constant $\tau_1 = 4\,\text{ms}$, falling time constant $\tau_2 = 42\,\text{ms}$). The variable a is chosen so that the maximum value of the synaptic conductance $(I_{syn}/(V_m - E_{syn}))$ matches g_{max}. More information about this synapse can be found in: [2]. A weight of 0.01 was used on all inserted synapses. The characteristics of the NMDA synapse is illustrated in Fig. 2A and B. The passive membrane variable values were taken from: [14] and the default NMDA variable values were used.

The experimental protocols are illustrated in Fig. 2C and D. An image set (500 images) with a small square moving at random (Fig. 2D) or from the bottom to the top of the image (Fig. 2C) in 500 ms (1000 Hz) was generated. The subsampled pixel values generated by the ESTMD model are then used to calculate the probability of an NMDA synapse receiving an input impulse. The further away a pixel is from a particular synapse the lower chance of spiking. $Probability = pixelValue(1 - distance/maxDistance)$, where maxDistance is set equal to the diagonal of the subsampled image (original: 292×219 pixels, subsampled: 49×37 pixels). The probability is then trialed 2048 times (since pixelValue is a very low value) in a binomial random distribution function (binornd). $doSpike = binornd(2048, Probability)$. This value can be thought of as a weight to control number of inputs generated. Each NMDA synapse receives between 300–600 spikes during the 500ms simulation. The small target is generated in a coordinate system with high resolution and then saved in a lower resolution image (292×219) corresponding to 0.1 pixels. The target is thus never in a single pixel (although there is always a main pixel with the highest intensity) resulting in a smooth movement by up to 4 pixels with varying intensity.

The bioinspired front-end ESTMD model used in this study [1] was originally based on a parametric model previously shown to provide a quantitatively good match to the tuning properties of dragonfly STMD neurons [15]. This model was recently shown to provide high computational efficiency for robotics simulations [1]. In this study we utilize this computational efficiency to repeat many simulations to generate synaptic inputs which are more realistic than simply generating input from a single point moving in the receptive field.

The bioinspired ESTMD model is described in Fig. 1E and is essentially a set of mathematical functions that takes a matrix (image) as input and generates an output image. In the early visual processing box the green channel is extracted, blurred and subsampled followed by a temporal and spatial bandpass filters to mimic the photoreceptors and lamina of the insect optic lobe and reject redundancy from the image [4]. The next brain region is the medulla in which

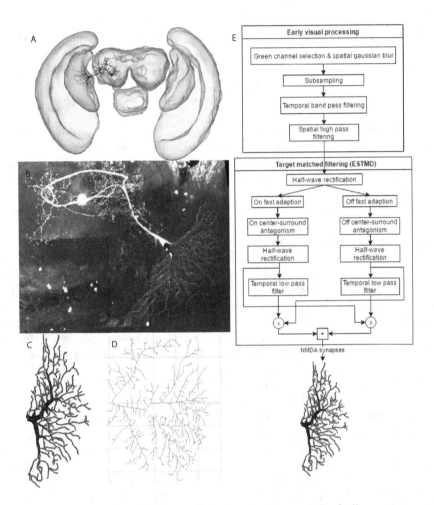

Fig. 1. 3D reconstruction of a dragonfly brain showing medulla (yellow outer parts) followed by the lobula complex (orange) and the location of the BSTMD1 neuron. B. Reconstruction of BSTMD1 dendritic tree superimposed on a Maximum Intensity Projection of the confocal image stack. Only one dendritic tree was reconstructed to mimic the setup in [14]. C. Morphology of BSTMD1 as implemented in NEURON. D. Morphology of HSE neuron used in [14]. E. Illustration of ESTMD model from [1] (MATLAB) connected to BSTMD1 model (NEURON simulator [10]). (Color figure online)

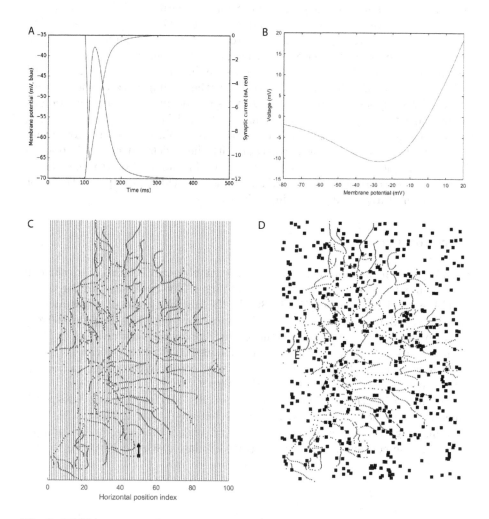

Fig. 2. NMDA synapse characteristics without weight of 0.01. A. Impulse response showing membrane potential (blue) and synaptic current (red). B. Plot of the function $\frac{V_m - E_{syn}}{(1 + \frac{Mg}{3.57} e^{-0.062 V_m})}$ from Eq. 3 to illustrate the membrane potential dependence of the macroscopic NMDAR current (shown as voltage). The units are mV, rather than current, which does not matter since it is the shape of the dependence that is being illustrated. C and D. Illustration of the experimental protocols. The red dots represent the dendritic compartments which have been given one NMDA synapse each. To improve the illustrator visibility, the size of the target is around 10 times larger than the actual target used in the input images. C. The continuous experimental setup where blue lines show the vertical trajectories on which the small target (black square) travels (in the direction of the black arrow) with 500 steps. D. The random experimental setup showing an example of 500 random positions. (Color figure online)

we believe that the elementary STMD (ESTMD) is situated. Here the response to brightening events ('ON') and dimming events ('OFF') are separated into different parallel pathways by half-wave rectification of the input signal (with inversion of the negative phases). In the ESTMD model, movement of a contrasting feature is assumed to consist of a stimulus that triggers either an ON or OFF detector in one half of the pathway (the leading edge of the feature) followed by an opposite sign stimulus with a short delay at the same location as the trailing edge passes. A low-pass temporal filter delays the signals from each partially rectified detector so that a non-linear (multiplicative) correlator within the ESTMD compares each delayed signal with the undelayed signal of opposite sign. Combination of this 'feature template' with fast adaptation (to reject background texture) and center-surround antagonism provides a sharp selectivity for small, moving targets within the input images.

3   Simulation Results

Fig. 3A shows the membrane potential of 200 simulations (500 ms) of continuous or random patterns of activation by a small target. The curves are similar to the ones observed in [14] shown in Fig. 3C. In the random protocol, illustrated in Fig. 2D, a random position is generated at each time step (1ms/step for 500 ms) to which the target is moved, and the x-axis (horizontal position) in Fig. 3B is the index of the trial number (one trial includes 500 random positions). In the continuous protocol the target moves from the bottom of the image to the top in a straight vertical line, as illustrated in Fig. 2C.

Around 30% of the continuous trajectories (Fig. 3B) had a stronger response indicating that the number of synapses affected was higher in those paths and the remaining 70% had a weaker response yet higher than the random jumps. Repeating the continuous experiment (two simulation sets with 100 horizontal

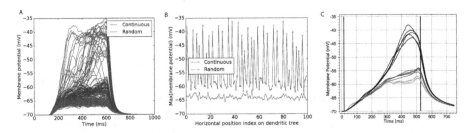

Fig. 3. A. Simulation of a single BSTMD1 model with passive properties showing the effects of continuous vs random trajectory movement (a small square moving on vertical line or random position). B. Maximum membrane potential from A plotted against horizontal position (meaning position of vertical trajectory line from left to right in Fig. 1B). C. Figure from [14] similar to A but black indicates continuous trajectory mid-gray indicates random with short trajectories and light gray indicates random positions.

positions each resulting in 100 paired measurements) resulted in a standard deviation of 1.51 mV for the difference between the max values. Hence, the variance is due to differential activation of synapses along each vertical trajectory and not mainly due to random chance.

4   Discussion and Conclusions

The variation within the membrane potential curves is higher in the novel STMD simulations (Fig. 3A, B) compared to the previous model (Fig. 3C) which may be due to differences in statistical method for spatial distribution of the synaptic inputs. If the difference cannot be explained by different algorithms, then it might be the morphology of the neuron. The differences (high and low membrane potential) between continuous curves (Fig. 3A) is not due to random chance (standard deviation = 1.51 mV) but instead reflect the morphology of the neuron. The differences could potentially create heterogeneity in neural network activity enabling a winner takes all algorithm to select one out of multiple equally salient moving targets. Although this is an important and bold conclusion, it remains speculative. The negative conductance slope shown in Fig. 2B (around -80 to -30 mV on x-axis), characteristic for NMDA synapses (due to magnesium block), is the reason for the amplifying effect [9] seen in some of the continuous response curves. Consecutive synaptic input at a near location will be more effective than one at a distant (random) location because the pre-pulse can build on the response of the post-pulse. The implication of the negative slope of the NMDA conductance is that as long as the membrane potential is within the negative slope region, depolarization will have more effect along the buildup. Random locations at the dendritic tree will most likely be too far away to allow for buildup of enough membrane potential.

In conclusion, we have shown that using the new STMD morphology with NMDA based facilitation, the neuron can discriminate between continuous and random small target motion. A more in-depth analysis of how the synaptic spatial distribution correlates with trajectory path is needed to precisely explain the results. The developed computational model and simulation method provides a tool to further investigate these and other mechanisms in the insect optic lobe.

The method of combining simulation environments and computational models with different abstraction levels enables a unique combination of scale and detail not otherwise possible. We believe this approach is important to understand the brain and its underlying mechanisms.

References

1. Bagheri, Z.M., Wiederman, S.D., Cazzolato, B.S., Grainger, S., Carroll, D.C.O.: Performance of an insect-inspired target tracker in natural conditions. Bioinspiration Biomim. **12**(2) (2017)
2. Baker, J.L., Perez-Rosello, T., Migliore, M., Barrionuevo, G., Ascoli, G.A.: A computer model of unitary responses from associational/commissural and perforant path synapses in hippocampal CA3 pyramidal cells. J. Comput. Neurosci. **31**(1), 137–158 (2011)
3. Daniels, R.W., Gelfand, M.V., Collins, C.A., DiAntonio, A.: Visualizing glutamatergic cell bodies and synapses in Drosophila larval and adult CNS. J. Comp. Neurol. **508**(1), 131–152 (2008)
4. Dunbier, J.R., Wiederman, S.D., Shoemaker, P.A., O'Carroll, D.C.: Facilitation of dragonfly target-detecting neurons by slow moving features on continuous paths. Front. Neural Circ. **6**, 1–11 (2012)
5. Feng, L., Zhao, T., Kim, J.: neuTube 1.0: a new design for efficient neuron reconstruction software based on the SWC format. eNeuro **2**(1), 1–10 (2015). doi:10.1523/ENEURO.0049-14.2014
6. Hopp, E., Borst, A., Haag, J.: Subcellular mapping of dendritic activity in optic flow processing neurons. J. Comp. Physiol. A Neuroethol. Sens. Neural Behav. Physiol. **200**(5), 359–370 (2014)
7. Karuppudurai, T., Lin, T.Y., Ting, C.Y., Pursley, R., Melnattur, K.V., Diao, F., White, B.H., Macpherson, L.J., Gallio, M., Pohida, T., Lee, C.H.: A hard-wired glutamatergic circuit pools and relays UV signals to mediate spectral preference in drosophila. Neuron **81**(3), 603–615 (2014)
8. Keles, M.F., Frye, M.A.: Object-detecting neurons in drosophila. Curr. Biol. **27**, 1–8 (2017)
9. Lazarewicz, M.T., Ang, C.W., Carlson, G.C., Coulter, D.A., Finkel, L.H.: Analysis of NMDA-dependent voltage bistability in thin dendritic compartments. Neurocomputing **69**(10), 1025–1029 (2006)
10. Hines, M.L., Carnevale, N.T.: The NEURON simulation environment. Neural Comput. **9**(6), 1179–1209 (1997)
11. Nordström, K., O'Carroll, D.C.: Small object detection neurons in female hoverflies. Proc. R. Soc. B-Biol. Sci. **273**(1591), 1211–1216 (2006)
12. Nordström, K., Barnett, P.D., O'Carroll, D.C.: Insect detection of small targets moving in visual clutter. PLoS Biol. **4**(3), 0378–0386 (2006)
13. Nordström, K., Bolzon, D.M., O'Carroll, D.C.: Spatial facilitation by a high-performance dragonfly target-detecting neuron. Biol. Lett. **7**(4), 588–92 (2011)
14. Shoemaker, P.: Multicompartment simulations of NMDA receptor-based facilitation in insect visual neurons. In: Proceedings of the 2011 7th International Conference on Intelligent Sensors, Sensor Networks and Information Processing, ISSNIP 2011, pp. 85–90 (2011)
15. Wiederman, S.D., Shoemaker, P.A., O'Carroll, D.C.: A model for the detection of moving targets in visual clutter inspired by insect physiology. PLoS ONE **3**(7), 1–11 (2008)
16. Xia, S., Chiang, A.S.: NMDA receptors in Drosophila (2009)
17. Zhu, Y., Gabbiani, F.: Fine and distributed subcellular retinotopy of excitatory inputs to the dendritic tree of a collision-detecting neuron. J. Neurophysiol. **115**, 3101–3112 (2016). doi:10.1152/jn.00044.2016
18. Wiederman, S.D., Fabian, J.M., Dunbier, J.R., O'Carroll, D.C.: A predictive focus of gain modulation encodes target trajectories in insect vision. eLife, **6** (2017)

Neural Networks Meet Natural and Environmental Sciences

On the Estimation of Pollen Density on Non-target Lepidoptera Food Plant Leaves in Bt-Maize Exposure Models: Open Problems and Possible Neural Network-Based Solutions

Francesco Camastra$^{(\boxtimes)}$, Angelo Ciaramella, and Antonino Staiano

Department of Science and Technology, University of Naples Parthenope,
Centro Direzionale Isola C4, 80143 Naples, Italy
camastra@ieee.org,
{angelo.ciaramella,antonino.staiano}@uniparthenope.it

Abstract. Sometimes, mathematical modelling in ecology requires approximation assumptions, on the model at hand, in order to meet domain constraints, thus making the mathematical construction unrealistic. To this end, the paper analyzes a model representing the Bt-maize pollen density on non-target Lepidoptera food plant leaves by a differential equation. The exact solution of the differential equation is provided, showing that the solution behavior, when the time goes to infinity, does not vanish, differently from what assumed in the model, consequently undermining the theoretical model soundness. In order to solve this drawback, the paper proposes a neuro-fuzzy model capable to obtain a robust pollen density estimate directly from data, thus avoiding unnecessary and unfeasible model approximations.

1 Introduction

A potential risk, associated with the cultivation of insect-resistant transgenic maize, containing Bt toxin, is represented by the Bt pollen consumption of herbivorous butterfly larvae [1–3]. Maize is pollinated by wind and during flowering can be deposited large amounts of pollen on more varieties of plants that inhabit the surrounding soil. In such conditions it is very likely the chance of ingesting toxic pollen by butterfly larvae. In the last years, some mathematical models for estimating the effects of Bt-maize [4–9] on non-target Lepidoptera were published. In all these models it is crucial modelling the pollen density on leaves of non-target Lepidoptera food plant.

In this work, the only model [8] representing (and computing) the pollen density on food leaves by an analytical mathematical model is discussed, showing why its theoretical soundness is undermined. In order to solve this drawback, a neuro-fuzzy model is introduced, that can provide reliable estimates of the pollen density on leaves of food plants.

In the remainder, the work is organized as follows: In Sect. 2 the computation of pollen density on food plant leaves is discussed; Sect. 3 describes the

© Springer International Publishing AG 2017
A. Lintas et al. (Eds.): ICANN 2017, Part I, LNCS 10613, pp. 407–414, 2017.
https://doi.org/10.1007/978-3-319-68600-4_47

neuro-fuzzy approach for the estimation of the pollen density on food plants; Finally, some conclusions are drawn in Sect. 4.

2 Estimation of Pollen Density on Food Plant Leaves

In the last years, several mathematical models [4–9] have been proposed for the estimation of Bt-maize effects on non-target Lepidoptera. Among them, Holst et al.'s model [8] is the only one that analytically estimates the pollen density on food plant leaves. Therefore, in this section the focus is on the description of the pollen density modelling given in [8]. Prior to begin with the analysis, it is worth pointing out that the goal of the discussion is merely the mathematical correctness of the model proposed in [8] and not its biological nor ecological implications (see [10]).

The pollen exposure is represented by means of pollen concentration in the environment. In particular, for Inachis io larvae, pollen exposure is represented by average pollen density, measured in cm^{-2}, on the leaves of the food plant. According to Kawashima et al. [11], pollen deposition rate can be described by a parabolic curve through the pollination period. The integral of the parabolic curve yields the accumulated deposition. Nonetheless, pollen deposited on food plant leaves could be lost after deposition, especially during rain [12,13]. Therefore, in [8], pollen loss on plant leaves is represented by the following differential equation:

$$\frac{dN}{dt} = at^2 + bt + c - \epsilon N, \tag{1}$$

where N is pollen density and t is time, measured in cm^{-2} and in days, respectively, ϵ is *loss rate* namely, relative amount of pollen lost per day, and a, b, c are the coefficients of the parabola, properly estimated.

The authors in [8] stated that "*the equation (1) was integrated and re-parameterized to predict average pollen density on leaves (N)*", also showing that the average pollen density achieves a maximum at a given value N_{peak} and decreasing to zero when time $t \to \infty$.

However, it is worth observing here that Eq. (1) is an *inhomogeneous linear differential equation of first order* and, therefore, it can be exactly solved [14]. Indeed, an inhomogeneous linear differential equation of first order has the form:

$$\frac{dN}{dt} = u(t)N + v(t), \tag{2}$$

whose general solution is:

$$N(t) = e^{\int_\alpha^t u(x)dx}[K + \int_\beta^t v(x)e^{-\int_\alpha^x u(s)ds}dx], \tag{3}$$

where $K \in \mathbb{R}$, and α, β are values that must be properly choosen, fixed to zero for the sake of convenience.

In order to fulfill Eq. (2), the following conditions must hold:

$$u(t) = -\epsilon \qquad\qquad v(t) = at^2 + bt + c. \qquad (4)$$

Substituting Eqs. (4) in (3), the solution of the differential Eq. (1) is given by:

$$N(t) = e^{-\epsilon t}[K + \int_0^t (ax^2 + bx + c)e^{\epsilon x}dx]$$

$$= Ke^{-\epsilon t} + e^{-\epsilon t}[e^{\epsilon x}\frac{a(2 - 2x\epsilon + x^2\epsilon^2) + \epsilon(c\epsilon + b(-1 + x\epsilon))}{\epsilon^3}]_0^t$$

$$= \frac{a}{\epsilon}t^2 + (-\frac{2a}{\epsilon^2} + \frac{b}{\epsilon})t + (\frac{2a}{\epsilon^3} + \frac{c}{\epsilon} - \frac{b}{\epsilon^2}) + (K - \frac{2a - b\epsilon + c\epsilon^2}{\epsilon^3})e^{-\epsilon t} \quad (5)$$

where $K \in \mathbb{R}$.

It's straightforward verifying that the limit of pollen density $N(t)$, when $t \to \infty$, is not 0 as stated in [8], rather:

$$\lim_{t\to\infty} N(t) = \left\{ \begin{array}{l} \frac{c}{\epsilon} \quad \text{if } a = b = 0 \\ +\infty \text{ if } (a > 0) \text{ or } (a = 0 \wedge b > 0) \\ -\infty \text{ if } (a < 0) \text{ or } (a = 0 \wedge b < 0) \end{array} \right\} \qquad (6)$$

The degenerate case $a = b = 0$ has no practical interest, since the parabola $v(t) = at^2 + bt + c$ reduces to a constant line, i.e., $v(t) = c$. In all other cases, pollen density $N(t)$ goes to infinity when time $t \to \infty$. Figure 1 shows the plot of function $N(t)$.

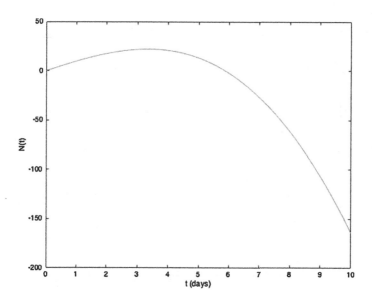

Fig. 1. The plot of the function $N(t)$, setting $a = -1$, $b = 1$, $c = 10$, $K = 0$, $\epsilon = 0.1$

Since the density of the pollen, in a reliable ecological model, has to go to zero when time goes to infinity, this latter improper (mathematical) assumption has been introduced in [8] in order to meet the ecological domain requirement. Nonetheless, it is clear that the differential Eq. (1) cannot correctly model the pollen density on food plants. Therefore, the problem of properly modelling the pollen density on food plant leaves remains open.

3   A Neuro-Fuzzy Approach to Model Pollen Density on Food Plant

As previously discussed, there are several critical points for properly modelling the pollen density on food plant leaves. The main drawback is the use of an analytic distribution curve that has not generalization properties. A more realistic and effective estimation could be obtained by considering real data. To this end, we propose an alternative approach. Let us suppose, as an example, to work with five simulated unevenly sampled estimations of $N(t)$ ($x_1, \ldots, x_5$), for clarity, plotted in Fig. 2. Specifically, we consider a 20 days simulated $N(t)$ distribution from Eq. 5. The unevenly sequences $x_1, \ldots, x_5$ are obtained randomly extracting 10 points from the simulated $N(t)$ and adding a Gaussian noise. From this distributions, a neuro-fuzzy approach [15] could be used to infer a more robust pollen density estimation. Concretely, by focusing on the example, a special type of neuro-fuzzy model, namely, a Fuzzy Relational Neural Network (FRNN) [16] has been adopted. FRNN is based on a fuzzy relational IF-THEN reasoning scheme and it can be defined by using different t-norms and t-conorms (here

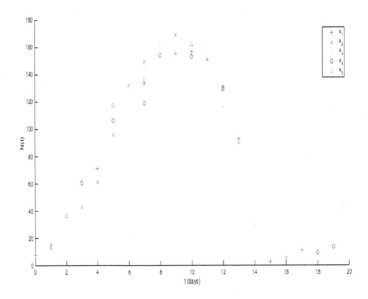

Fig. 2. Five realistic sampled $N(t)$ densities.

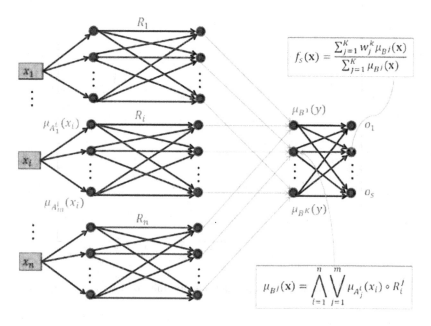

Fig. 3. Fuzzy Relational Neural Network model.

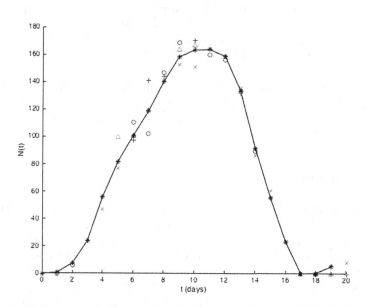

Fig. 4. FRNN pollen density estimation.

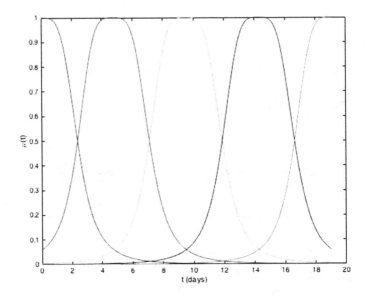

Fig. 5. Membership functions obtained by FRNN.

Lukasiewicz norms are used). The FRNN schema is visualized in Fig. 3. The model is composed by three steps, namely,*fuzzification, relational rule composition* and *defuzzification*. For the fuzzification phase, several different fuzzy sets could be adopted. Here, we use 5 generalized bell curve membership functions (see Fig. 5). To estimate the parameters of the model, both Back-Propagation and recursive Pseudoinverse matrix techniques are used. Figure 4 depicts a realistic pollen density estimation obtained when applying FRNN to unevenly sampled distributions $x_1, \ldots, x_5$.

Moreover, the estimated density and the memberships turn out to be very useful when used in a fuzzy inference model (e.g., IF-THEN rules) to accomplish a Fuzzy Decision System for a more robust Environmental Risk Assessment, as discussed in [17,18].

4   Conclusions

In this paper, it has been analyzed a mathematical model representing the Bt-maize pollen density on non-target Lepidoptera food plant leaves. The exact solution of the differential equation of the model has been provided, also showing that the solution behaviour, when the time goes to infinity, does not vanish, differently from what stated for the model proposed in [8]. In this way, the model theoretical soundness is undermined. To solve the drawback, it has been proposed a neuro-fuzzy model capable to get reliable density estimates directly from data, and avoiding unnecessary and unfeasible model approximations. In the next future, we're planning to launch a campaign for collecting Bt-maize pollen density on food plant leaves, in order to experimentally validate the proposed approach.

Acknowledgments. This work was funded by *Sostegno alla ricerca individuale per il triennio 2015-17* project of University of Naples Parthenope and supported by *Gruppo Nazionale per il Calcolo Scientifico (GNCS-INdAM)*.

References

1. Mendelsohn, M., Kough, J., Vaituzis, Z., Matthews, K.: Are bt crops safe? Nat. Biotechnol. **21**, 1003–1009 (2003)
2. Banks, H.T., Banks, J.E., Joyner, S.L., Stark, J.D.: Dynamic models for insect mortality due to exposure to insecticides. Math. Comput. Model. **48**, 316–332 (2008)
3. Sanvido, O., Romeis, J., Bigler, F.: Environmental change challanges decision-making during post-market environmental monitoring of transgenic crops. Transgenic Res. **20**, 1191–1201 (2011)
4. Perry, J., Devos, Y., Arpaia, S., Bartsch, D., Gathmann, A., Hails, R., Kiss, J., Lheureux, K., Manachini, B., Mestdagh, S., Neemann, G., Ortego, F., Schiemann, J., Sweet, J.: A mathematical model of exposure of non-target lepidoptera to bt-maize pollen expressing cry1ab within europe. Proc. R. Soc. B Biol. Sci. **277**, 1417–1425 (2010)
5. Lang, A., Brunzel, S., Dolek, M., Otto, M., Thei, B.: Modelling in the light of key parameters: a call to exercise caution in field prediction of bt-maize effects. Proc. R. Soc. B Biol. Sci. **278**, 980–981 (2011)
6. Perry, J.N., Devos, Y., Arpaia, S., Bartsch, D., Gathmann, A., Hails, R., Kiss, J., Lheureux, K., Manachini, B., Mestdagh, S., Neemann, G., Ortego, F., Schiemann, J., Sweet, J.: The usefulness of a mathematical model of exposure for environmental risk assessment. Proc. R. Soc. B Biol. Sci. **278**, 982–985 (2011)
7. Perry, J.N., Devos, Y., Arpaia, S., Bartsch, D., Ehlert, C., Gathmann, A., Hails, R.S., Hendriksen, N.B., Kiss, J., Messean, A., Mestdagh, S., Neemann, G., Nuti, M., Sweet, J.B., Tebbe, C.C.: Estimating the effects of cry1f bt-maize pollen on non-target lepidoptera using a mathematical model of exposure. J. Appl. Ecol. **49**, 29–37 (2012)
8. Holst, N., Lang, A., Lovei, G., Otto, M.: Increased mortality is predicted of inachis io larvae caused by bt-maize pollen in european farmland. Ecol. Model. **250**, 126–133 (2013)
9. Camastra, F., Ciaramella, A., Staiano, A.: A note on some mathematical models on the effects of bt-maize exposure. Environ. Ecol. Stat. **21**(3), 477–485 (2014)
10. Perry, J.N., Arpaia, S., Bartsch, D., Birch, A., Devos, Y., Ehlert, C., Gathmann, A., Gathmann, A., Gennaro, A., Kiss, J., Messean, A., Mestdagh, S., Nuti, M., Sweet, J.B., Tebbe, C.C.: No evidence requiring change in the risk assessment of inachis io larvae. Ecol. Model. **268**, 103–122 (2013)
11. Kawashima, S., Matsuo, K., Du, M., Takahashi, Y., Inoue, S., Yonemura, S.: An algorithm for estimating potential deposition of corn pollen for environmental assessment. Environ. Biosaf. Res. **3**, 197–207 (2004)

12. Pleasants, J., Hellmich, R., Dively, G., Sears, M., Stanley-Horn, D., Mattila, H.: Corn pollen deposition on milkweeds in and near cornfields ? Proc. Natl. Acad. Sci. **98**, 11919–11924 (2001)

13. Lang, A., Ludy, C., Vojtech, E.: Dispersion and deposition of bt-maize pollen in field margins. J. Plant Dis. Prot. **111**, 417–428 (2004)

14. Korn, G.A., Korn, T.A.: Mathematical Handbook for Scientists and Engineers. Dover Publications, New York (2000)

15. Petrosino, A., Staiano, A.: A neuro-fuzzy approach for sensor network data cleaning. In: Apolloni, B., Howlett, R.J., Jain, L. (eds.) KES 2007. LNCS (LNAI), vol. 4694, pp. 140–147. Springer, Heidelberg (2007). doi:10.1007/978-3-540-74829-8_18

16. Ciaramella, A., Tagliaferri, R., Pedrycz, W., Di Nola, A.: Fuzzy relational neural network. Int. J. Approx. Reason. **41**(2), 146–163 (2006)

17. Camastra, F., Ciaramella, A., Giovannelli, V., Lener, M., Rastelli, V., Staiano, A., Staiano, G., Starace, A.: Tera: a tool for the environmental risk assessment of genetically modified plants. Ecol. Inform. **24**, 186–193 (2014)

18. Camastra, F., Ciaramella, A., Giovannelli, V., Lener, M., Rastelli, V., Staiano, A., Staiano, G., Starace, A.: A fuzzy decision system for genetically modified plant environmental risk assessment using mamdani inference. Expert Syst. Appl. **42**(3), 1710–1716 (2015)

Short Papers

Neural Networks for Adaptive Vehicle Control

J. Kaste[(✉)], J. Hoedt[(✉)], K. Van Ende[(✉)], and F. Kallmeyer[(✉)]

Volkswagen AG, Group Research, Berliner Ring 2, 38436 Wolfsburg, Germany
{jonas.kaste,jens.hoedt,kristof.van.ende,felix.kallmeyer}@volkswagen.de

Abstract. With increasing computational performance and the possibility to collect huge amounts of training data, Machine Learning approaches gain a lot of interest in the automotive community [1]. To process all the given information and enable an accurate and convenient driving experience, a robust control strategy is required for autonomous vehicles. Recent work on vehicle control at the limit of handling has shown good results for ensuring trajectories precisely under complex conditions [2]. In terms of changing conditions, deviations from the controller operating point, for example damages or inaccurate modeled systems, might cause a heavy decrease in control performance. To overcome those issues, it is possible to combine classic model based control approaches with learning algorithms [4]. To evaluate the potential of artificial neural networks in addition to a model based control approach the present study investigates different topologies and training methods for iteratively trained neural networks in the closed control loop. The neural network is implemented in a cascaded lateral controller, to compensate remaining control errors in yaw motion and lateral deviation.

The objective is to decrease the control errors, learning the dependencies between vehicle dynamic parameters and model errors and to show the potential of artificial neural networks to increase control performance over time. Related to [3] the potential for increased robustness in case of heavy error intrusion (e.g. steering angle offset) is investigated for an autonomous vehicle at the limit of handling. The achieved results are promising in terms of fast recovery and precise trajectory following, after a steering angle offset up to 90°. During the tests the observed long time stability indicated potential for further investigations regarding memory based approaches e.g. recurrent networks.

Keywords: Autonomous driving · Online training · Adaptive control

References

1. Prokhorov, D.: Computational Intelligence in Automotive Applications. Springer-Verlag, Heidelberg (2008)
2. Kritayakirana, K.M.: Autonomous vehicle control at the limit of handling. Ph.D. thesis, Stanford University (2012)
3. Schnetter, P., Kaste, J., Krueger, T.: Advanced sliding mode online training for neural network flight control applications. (AIAA 2015-1323) (2015)
4. Urnes, J.: Intelligent flight systems: Progress and potential of this technology. In: Aviation Safety Technical Conference (2007)

© Springer International Publishing AG 2017
A. Lintas et al. (Eds.): ICANN 2017, Part I, LNCS 10613, p. 417, 2017.
https://doi.org/10.1007/978-3-319-68600-4

Brain–Computer Interface with Robot-Assisted Training for Neurorehabilitation

Roman Rosipal[1(✉)], Natália Porubcová[2], Peter Barančok[3], Barbora Cimrová[3], Michal Teplan[1], and Igor Farkaš[3]

[1] Institute of Measurement Science, Slovak Academy of Sciences, Bratislava, Slovakia
{roman.rosipal,michal.teplan}@savba.sk
[2] EuroRehab, S.r.o., Bratislava, Slovakia
nataliaporubec@gmail.com
[3] Faculty of Mathematics, Physics and Informatics, Comenius University
in Bratislava, Bratislava, Slovakia
peter.barancok@gmail.com, {barbora.cimrova,igor.farkas}@fmph.uniba.sk
http://www.um.sav.sk/projects/BCI-RAS/

Abstract. To improve upper limb neurorehabilitation in chronic stroke patients, we apply new methods and tools of clinical training and machine learning for the design and development of an intelligent system allowing the users to go through the process of self-controlled training of impaired motor pathways. We combine the brain–computer interface (BCI) technology with a robotic splint into a compact system that can be used as a robot-assisted neurorehabilitation tool.

First, we use the mirror therapy (MT) which represents a mental process where an individual rehearses a specific limb movement by reflecting the movements of the non-paretic side in the mirror as if it were the affected side. This step is not used for improving the motor functions only, but also for identification of subject's specific electroencephalogram (EEG) oscillatory elemental patterns or "atoms" associated with imagery or real hand movements. We estimate these EEG atoms using a multiway analysis, specifically the parallel factor analysis (PARAFAC) for modeling. Using the data from a longitudinal case study, we will report statically significant effects of the MT on the modulation of sensorimotor EEG atoms of a patient with chronic upper limb impairment due to a stroke.

Second, we introduce the BCI-based robotic system operating on the principle of the motor imagery and incorporating a reward-based physical movement of the impaired upper limb. The novelty of this approach lies in the design of the control protocol which uses spatial and frequency weights of the previously estimated sensorimotor atoms during the MT sessions. By projecting the recorded EEG onto the spatial and frequency weights, one-dimensional time scores of the atoms are computed. Getting under the empirically preset threshold of the scores triggers the robotic splint which executes the physical movement with the impaired hand (up and down). We will report analytical and clinical results of three patients with different severity of the upper limb impairment due to a stroke and different lengths of the proposed neurorehabilitation training.

Keywords: Brain–computer interface · Robotic arm · Multiway analysis

© Springer International Publishing AG 2017
A. Lintas et al. (Eds.): ICANN 2017, Part I, LNCS 10613, p. 418, 2017.
https://doi.org/10.1007/978-3-319-68600-4

Unsupervised Learning of Factors of Variation in the Sensory Data of a Planar Agent

Oksana Hagen[1]($\boxtimes$) and Michaël Garcia Ortiz[2]($\boxtimes$)

[1] AI Lab, Softbank Robotics Europe and Plymouth University, Plymouth, UK
oksana.hagen@softbankrobotics.com
[2] AI Lab, Softbank Robotics Europe, Plymouth, UK
mgarciaortiz@softbankrobotics.com

Abstract. An autonomous agent needs means to perceive the outside world by interpreting its sensory data. In many cases it is not possible to provide the agent with the detailed description of everything it may encounter. So it has to build useful explanations of the world by itself, using only its own data.

In the case of a real robot with a set of IR sensors, which operates in a rectangular room, we assume that sensory data can be explained using a finite number of factors of variation. We propose to build a generative model of the observed data, where the finite number of probabilistic latent variables z contributes to the observed data distribution $P(x)$. To infer the latent distribution z we use a variational auto-encoder (VAE) [2]. It has been previously demonstrated in [1] that by manipulating the ratio β between reconstruction and latent loss of the model it is possible to recover the disentangled factors of variation in visual data.

We show, that VAE can efficiently learn to model noisy data distribution from a real robot using a redundant set of latent variables, while simultaneously building sparse representation and extracting meaningful structure from the data. We illustrate in Fig. 1, that the latent variables learned are indeed disentangled by showing how their variation influences the generated samples.

Keywords: Generative models · Representation learning · VAE

Fig. 1. Samples generated by varying two latent variables: each line corresponds to one generated sample with respect to change of one of the latent variables; each plot corresponds to the change in the second latent variable. These variables independently encode distance and angle of the wall.

© Springer International Publishing AG 2017
A. Lintas et al. (Eds.): ICANN 2017, Part I, LNCS 10613, pp. 419–420, 2017.
https://doi.org/10.1007/978-3-319-68600-4

References

1. Higgins, I., Matthey, L., Pal, A., Burgess, C., Glorot, X., Botvinick, M., Mohamed, S., Lerchner, A.: beta-VAE: learning basic visual concepts with a constrained variational framework. In: ICLR (2017)
2. Kingma, D.P., Welling, M.: Auto-encoding variational bayes. In: ICLR (2014)

State Dependent Modulation of Perception Based on a Computational Model of Conditioning

Jordi-Ysard Puigbò[1,2(✉)], Miguel Angel Gonzalez-Ballester[2,3(✉)], and Paul F.M.J. Verschure[1,3(✉)]

[1] Laboratory of Synthetic, Perceptive, Emotive and Cognitive Science (SPECS), DTIC, Universitat Pompeu Fabra (UPF), Barcelona, Spain
jordiysard@gmail.com
[2] Laboratory for Simulating, Imaging, and Modeling of Biological Systems (SIMBIOsys), DTIC, Universitat Pompeu Fabra (UPF), Barcelona, Spain
[3] Catalan Research Institute and Advanced Studies (ICREA), Barcelona, Spain

Abstract. The embodied mammalian brain evolved to adapt to an only partially known and knowable world. The adaptive labeling of the world is critically dependent on the neocortex which in turn is modulated by a range of subcortical systems such as the thalamus, ventral striatum and the amygdala. A particular case in point is the learning paradigm of classical conditioning where acquired representations of states of the world such as sounds and visual features are associated with predefined discrete behavioral responses such as eye blinks and freezing. Learning progresses in a very specific order, where the animal first identifies the features of the task that are predictive of a motivational state and then forms the association of the current sensory state with a particular action and shapes this action to the specific contingency. This adaptive feature selection has both attentional and memory components, i.e. a behaviorally relevant state must be detected while its representation must be stabilized to allow its interfacing to output systems. Here we present a computational model of the neocortical systems that underlie this feature detection process and its state dependent modulation mediated by the amygdala and its downstream target, the nucleus basalis of Meynert. Specifically, we analyze how amygdala driven cholinergic modulation switches between two perceptual modes [1], one for exploitation of learned representations and prototypes and another one for the exploration of new representations that provoked these change in the motivational state, presenting a framework for rapid learning of behaviorally relevant perceptual representations. Beyond reward-driven learning that is mostly based on exploitation, this paper presents a complementary mechanism for quick exploratory perception and learning grounded on the understanding of fear and surprise.

Reference

1. Angela, J.Y., Dayan, P.: Uncertainty, neuromodulation, and attention. Neuron **46**(4), 681–692 (2005)

© Springer International Publishing AG 2017
A. Lintas et al. (Eds.): ICANN 2017, Part I, LNCS 10613, p. 421, 2017.
https://doi.org/10.1007/978-3-319-68600-4

Optimal Bases Representation for Embodied Supervised Learning

Ivan Herreros[1]([✉]), Xerxes D. Arsiwalla[1]([✉]), and Paul Verschure[1,2]

[1] Synthetic Perceptive Emotive and Cognitive Systems (SPECS) Lab,
Center of Autonomous Systems and Neurorobotics, Universitat Pompeu Fabra,
Barcelona, Spain
ivanherreros@gmail.com
[2] Institució Catalana de Recerca i Estudis Avançats (ICREA), Barcelona, Spain

Abstract. Standard implementations of supervised learning for time-series predictions are disembodied, meaning that the learning system does not affect the predicted events. However, in the case of embodied systems which learn to act in a supervised manner, predictions may lead to actions that change the forecasted events. For instance, in classical conditioning, blinking to a predicted air-puff changes its physical consequences in the sensory channels. Hence, optimal learning requires taking into account the dynamics of the process by which the learning agent can act on those events [1]. Here we formalize this problem as learning a linear combination of basis signals in order to drive the output of a dynamical system along a desired trajectory. Accordingly, we show that, in contrast to standard supervised learning schemes, wherein the optimal bases for learning are those which are maximally de-correlated, in embodied supervised learning the optimal bases are those that maximally de-correlate their effects on the system's output.

Keywords: Supervised learning · Adaptive control · Embodied agents · Cerebellum

Acknowledgments. This work has been supported by the European Research Council's CDAC project: "The Role of Consciousness in Adaptive Behavior: A Combined Empirical, Computational and Robot based Approach" (ERC-2013-ADG 341196).

Reference

1. Herreros, I., Arsiwalla, X., Verschure, P.: A forward model at Purkinje cell synapses facilitates cerebellar anticipatory control. Adv. Neural Inf. Process. Syst. 3828–3836 (2016)

© Springer International Publishing AG 2017
A. Lintas et al. (Eds.): ICANN 2017, Part I, LNCS 10613, p. 422, 2017.
https://doi.org/10.1007/978-3-319-68600-4

The Effects of Neuronal Diversity on Network Synchronization

Aubin Tchaptchet$^{(\boxtimes)}$ and Hans Albert Braun

Institute of Physiology, Philipps University of Marburg, Marburg, Germany
tchaptch@students.uni-marburg.de, braun@staff.uni-marburg.de

Abstract. We are examining the synchronization characteristics of a net of gap junction coupled neurons under the particular assumption that the network is composed of diversity of individual Hodgkin-Huxley type neurons with randomized parameter values as implemented in the virtual Sim-Neuron laboratories (www.virtual-physiology.com, see also [1]). Uniform distributions of basic parameters, like ion concentrations or half activation values, lead to distributions of different shape of the dynamically relevant ion currents.

With the chosen randomization values there are typically around 80% of the neurons in the steady state while the others are periodically firing with different firing rates in a broad range of about 10 to 200 Hz leading in an uncoupled array to seemingly irregular firing with tiny fluctuations in the field potential. Introducing gap-junction coupling with $I_c = g_c(V - V_n)$ tends to synchronize the spiking of the individual neurons but, in contrast to a homogeneous net, a certain spike timing variability always remains. Some previously spiking neurons disappear some others are coming up while the majority of the neurons will mostly remain silent.

At high coupling strengths, the intervals between spike-generation can be considerably lengthened which may be due to the strengthening of repolarizing bias currents from the silent neurons slowing down the depolarization of the spontaneously active neurons. This can even lead to a completely silent net. In some other nets, at a certain coupling strength, more and more neurons are recruited to fire until only a few silent neurons remain. Such opposite effects may essentially depend on the rheobase and, on the size of the neurons of which the network is composed.

These data demonstrate that the experimentally well known neuronal diversity can be a relevant factor in determining neuronal network synchronization and therefore, beyond the mostly examined coupling strength, should also be considered in network simulations. Which parameters, or combinations of them, are the relevant determinants of the network behavior shall be systematically examined in future simulations.

Keywords: Randomness · Pattern · Field potential

Reference

1. Tchaptchet, A., Postnova, S., Finke, C., Schneider, H., Huber, M.T., Braun, H.A.: Modeling neuronal activity in relation to experimental voltage-/patch-clamp recordings. Brain Res. **1536**, 159–167 (2013)

© Springer International Publishing AG 2017
A. Lintas et al. (Eds.): ICANN 2017, Part I, LNCS 10613, p. 423, 2017.
https://doi.org/10.1007/978-3-319-68600-4

Temporal Regions for Activity Recognition

João Paulo Aires[(✉)], Juarez Monteiro, Roger Granada, Felipe Meneguzzi,
and Rodrigo C. Barros

Faculdade de Informática, Pontifícia Universidade Católica do Rio Grande do Sul,
Av. Ipiranga, 6681, Porto Alegre, RS 90619-900, Brazil
{joao.aires.001,juarez.santos,roger.granada}@acad.pucrs.br,
{felipe.meneguzzi,rodrigo.barros}@pucrs.br

Abstract. Recognizing activities in videos is an important task for
humans, since it helps the identification of different types of interactions
with other agents. To perform such task, we need an approach that is
able to process the frames of a video and extract enough information in
order to determine the activity. When dealing with activity recognition
we also have to consider the temporal aspect of videos since activities
tend to occur through the frames. In this work, we propose an approach
to obtain temporal information from a video by dividing its frames into
regions. Thus, instead of classifying an activity using only the information from each image frame, we extract and merge the information from
several regions of the video in order to obtain its temporal aspect. To
make a composition of different parts of the video, we take one frame of
each region and either concatenate or take the mean of their features. For
example, consider a video divided into three regions and each frame containing ten features, the resulting vector of a concatenation will contain
thirty features, while the resulting vector of the mean will contain ten
features. Our pipeline includes pre-processing, which consists of resizing
images to a fixed resolution of 256×256; Convolutional Neural Networks,
which extract features from the activity in each frame; region divisions,
which divides each sequence of frames of a video into n regions of the
same size; and classification, where we apply a Support Vector Machine
(SVM) on the features from the concatenation or mean phase in order
to predict the activity. Experiments are performed using The DogCen-
tric Activity dataset [1] that contains videos with 10 different activities
performed by 4 dogs, showing that our approach can improve the activity recognition task. We test our approach using two networks *AlexNet*
and *GoogLeNet*, increasing up to 10% of precision when using regions to
classify activities.

Keywords: Neural networks · Convolutional neural networks · Activity
recognition

References

1. Iwashita, Y., Takamine, A., Kurazume, R., Ryoo, M.S.: First-person animal activity
recognition from egocentric videos. In: ICPR 2014 (2014)

© Springer International Publishing AG 2017
A. Lintas et al. (Eds.): ICANN 2017, Part I, LNCS 10613, p. 424, 2017.
https://doi.org/10.1007/978-3-319-68600-4

Computational Capacity of a Cerebellum Model

Robin De Gernier[1]([✉]), Sergio Solinas[2], Christian Rössert[3], Jonathan Mapelli[4],
Marc Haelterman[1], and Serge Massar[1]

[1] Université libre de Bruxelles, Brussels, Belgium
rdegerni@ulb.ac.be
[2] University of Sassari, Sassari, Italy
[3] École polytechnique Fédérale de Lausanne, Lausanne, Switzerland
[4] Universitá degli Studi di Modena E Reggio Emilia, Modena, Italy

Abstract. Linking network structure to function is a long standing issue in the neuroscience field. An outstanding example is the cerebellum. Its structure was known in great detail for decades but the full range of computations it performs is yet unknown. This reflects a need for new systematic methods to characterize the computational capacities of the cerebellum. In the present work, we apply a method borrowed from the field of machine learning to evaluate the computational capacity and the working memory of a prototypical cerebellum model.

The model that we study is a reservoir computing rate model of the cerebellar granular layer in which granule cells form a recurrent inhibitory network and Purkinje cells are modelled as linear trainable readout neurons. It was introduced by [2, 3] to demonstrate how the recurrent dynamics of the granular layer is needed to perform typical cerebellar tasks (e.g. : timing-related tasks).

The method, described in detail in [1], consists in feeding the model with a random time dependent input signal and then quantifying how well a complete set of functions (each function representing a different type of computation) of the input signal can be reconstructed by taking a linear combination of the neuronal activations. We conducted simulations with 1000 granule cells. Relevant parameters were optimized within a biologically plausible range using a Bayesian Learning approach. Our results show that the cerebellum prototypical model can compute both linear functions - as expected from previous work -, and - surprisingly - highly nonlinear functions of its input (specifically, up to the 10th degree Legendre polynomial functions). Moreover, the model has a working memory of the input up to 100 ms in the past. These two properties are essential to perform typical cerebellar functions, such as fine-tuning nonlinear motor control tasks or, we believe, even higher cognitive functions.

Keywords: Cerebellum · Computational capacity · Reservoir computing

© Springer International Publishing AG 2017
A. Lintas et al. (Eds.): ICANN 2017, Part I, LNCS 10613, pp. 425–426, 2017.
https://doi.org/10.1007/978-3-319-68600-4

References

1. Dambre, J., Verstraeten, D., Schrauwen, B., Massar, S.: Information processing capacity of dynamical systems. Sci. Rep. 2(514) (2012)
2. Rössert, C., Dean, P., Porrill, J.: At the edge of chaos: how cerebellar granular layer network dynamics can provide the basis for temporal filters. PLoS Comput. Biol. **11**(10), e1004515 (2015)
3. Yamazaki, T., Tanaka, S.: Neural modeling of an internal clock. Neural Comput. **17**(5), 1032–1058 (2005)

The Role of Inhibition in Selective Attention

Sock Ching Low[1], Riccardo Zucca[1], and Paul F.M.J. Verschure[1,2(✉)]

[1] SPECS, Universitat Pompeu Fabra, Barcelona, Spain
{sockching.low,riccardo.zucca,paul.verschure}@upf.edu
[2] Institució Catalana de Recerca i Estudis Avançats (ICREA), Barcelona, Spain
https://www.specs.upf.edu

Abstract. The phenomenon of attending to a stimulus is at the neuronal level usually assumed to mean an increase in excitation of the neurons representing that stimulus and or its underlying features. This is strongly influenced by the notion that attention works like a spot light. Increased neuronal activity is not only observed in the presence of an attended stimulus [7], but such an increased activity has been also found in the absence of the stimulus as long as it is expected to be present [4]. It is thus demonstrated that attention can be affected by both bottom-up information from the environment, and top-down typically information considered to originate in the prefrontal cortex (PFC). This bottom-up/top-down interaction results in a selection of stimuli to attend to [5]. In the case of visual information, there are established pathways in the human brain that allow for excitatory influences from the frontal cortices on the input processing pathways of the thalamus [1, 2]. However, other puzzling attentional effects, such as inattentional blindness, exist and seem to contradict this mechanism. A complementary view on attention is the concept of the Validation Gate (VG) [6]. It posits that through both excitation and inhibition, predicted features can be downregulated to increase sensitivity to novelty. The same aforementioned pathways could also allow for such indirect inhibition of input to the thalamus via the thalamic reticular nucleus (TRN) [9–11]. Here, we investigate the viability of this thalamocortical substrate by computationally modelling it with a network consisting of four distinct populations of spiking neurons: specific and non-specific nuclei of the thalamus, the thalamic reticular nucleus, and a cortical map [3, 8]. We validate the model using an experimental protocol in which the network has to attend to a region of interest (ROI). Only stimuli appearing within the ROI is task-relevant. We show that in the absence of PFC influence, the modelled cortical map exhibits activity proportional to the size of the stimulus. However, PFC activity can bias the cortical response through a marked decrease in activity in response to stimuli outside of the ROI and a slight increase for that within the ROI. This modulatory effect ensures that stimuli within the ROI consistently elicit stronger activation than those outside of it, regardless of size. Our results thus provide support for the mechanism of inhibitory attention with the TRN as its hub.

Keywords: Selective attention · Thalamocortical system · Computational models

© Springer International Publishing AG 2017
A. Lintas et al. (Eds.): ICANN 2017, Part I, LNCS 10613, pp. 427–428, 2017.
https://doi.org/10.1007/978-3-319-68600-4

References

1. Behrens, T.E.J., Johansen-Berg, H., Woolrich, M.W., Smith, S.M.: Wheeler-Kingshott, C.A.M., Boulby, P.A., Barker, G.J., Sillery, E.L., Sheehan, K., Ciccarelli, O., Thompson, A.J., Brady, J.M., Matthews, P.M.: Non-invasive mapping of connections between human thalamus and cortex using diffusion imaging. Nature Neurosci. 6(7), 750–757 (2003)

2. Gollo, L.L., Mirasso, C., Villa, A.E.: Dynamic control for synchronization of separated cortical areas through thalamic relay. Neuroimage 52(3), 947–955 (2010)

3. Izhikevich, E.M.: Simple model of spiking neurons. IEEE Trans. Neural Netw. 14(6), 1569–1572 (2003)

4. Kastner, S., Pinsk, M.A., De Weerd, P., Desimone, R., Ungerleider, L.G.: Increased activity in human visual cortex during directed attention in the absence of visual stimulation. Neuron 22(4), 751–61 (1999)

5. Kastner, S., Ungerleider, L.G.: Mechanisms of visual attention in the human cortex. Ann. Rev. Neurosci. 23, 315–341 (2000)

6. Mathews, Z., Cetnarski, R., Verschure, P.: Visual anticipation biases conscious decision making but not bottom-up visual processing. Front. Psychol. 6 (2015)

7. Watanabe, M., Cheng, K., Murayama, Y., Ueno, K., Asamizuya, T., Tanaka, K., Logothetis, N.: Attention but not awareness modulates the BOLD signal in the human V1 during binocular suppression. Science 334(6057), 829–831 (2011)

8. van Wijngaarden, J.B.G., Zucca, R., Finnigan, S., Verschure, P.F.M.J.: The impact of cortical lesions on thalamo-cortical network dynamics after acute ischaemic stroke: a combined experimental and theoretical study. PLOS Comput. Biol. 12(8), e1005048 (2016)

9. Wimmer, R.D., Schmitt, L.I., Davidson, T.J., Nakajima, M., Deisseroth, K., Halassa, M.M.: Thalamic control of sensory selection in divided attention. Nature (2015)

10. Zikopoulos, B., Barbas, H.: Prefrontal projections to the thalamic reticular nucleus form a unique circuit for attentional mechanisms. J. Neurosci. 26(28), 7348–7361 (2006)

11. Zikopoulos, B., Barbas, H.: Circuits for multisensory integration and attentional modulation through the prefrontal cortex and the thalamic reticular nucleus in primates. Rev. Neurosci. 18(6), 417–38 (2007)

Stochasticity, Spike Timing, and a Layered Architecture for Finding Iterative Roots

Adam Frick[1] and Nicolangelo Iannella[2(✉)]

[1] School of Electrical and Electronic Engineering, The University of Adelaide,
Adelaide, Australia
adam.frick@adelaide.edu.au

[2] School of Mathematical Sciences, University of Nottingham, Nottingham, UK
https://www.researchgate.net/profile/Nicolangelo_Iannella,
http://www.nottingham.ac.uk/mathematics/people/nicolangelo.iannella
nicolangelo.iannella@nottingham.ac.uk

Abstract. The human brain and human intelligence has come a long way having evolved the ability to do many things including solving difficult mathematical problems and understanding complex operations and computations. How these abilities are implemented within the brain is poorly understood, but typically tackled by asking what type of computations networks of neurons are capable of? Previous studies have shown how both artificial neural networks (based upon MultiLayer Perceptrons MLPs) and networks of (biologically inspired) spiking neurons can solve single tasks efficiently, such as character recognition or nonlinear function approximation [1, 5, 6]. There are, however, many nontrivial yet important industrial and physical problems that rely upon computations based on iteration and composition. There have been rare demonstrations of neural networks solving multiple tasks simultaneously but the few available examples have shown they are able to solve functional equations. This exemplifies the likelihood that the computational power of neural populations has been under estimated and their true capabilities are far greater than than previously thought. Significantly, previous studies have shown that the solution to a particular class of functional equations, called the functional iterative root or half-iterate, is attainable using MLPs and is continuous in nature [3, 4]. Methods which employ networks of spiking neurons have, til now, shown that piecewise continuous solutions are obtainable [2]. Here, we demonstrate that taking advantage of the stochastic or probabilistic nature of spike generation and population coding, spiking neural networks can learn to find solutions to iterative root that are continuous in nature. Specifically, we show how plasticity, the stochastic nature of neuronal spike generation, and population coding allows spiking neural networks to find solutions to functional equations, like the iterative root of monotonically increasing functions, in a continuous manner. Significantly, our work expands the foundations of neural-based computation by demonstrating a nontrivial underlying computational principle: *robustness through uncertainty*.

© Springer International Publishing AG 2017
A. Lintas et al. (Eds.): ICANN 2017, Part I, LNCS 10613, pp. 429–430, 2017.
https://doi.org/10.1007/978-3-319-68600-4_57

Keywords: Spiking neural network · Functional equations · Iterative root · Artificial intelligence

References

1. Iannella, N., Back, A.: A spiking neural network architecture for nonlinear function approximation. Neural Netw. **14**, 933–939 (2001)
2. Iannella, N., Kindermann, L.: Finding iterative roots with a spiking neural network. Inform. Proc. Lett. **95**, 545–551 (2005)
3. Kindermann, L., Georgiev, P.: Modelling iterative roots of mappings in multidimensional spaces. In: Proceedings of the 9th International Conference on Neural Information Systems, pp. 2655–2659 (2002)
4. Kindermann, L.: Computing iterative roots with neural networks. In: The 5th International Conference on Neural Information Systems, pp. 713–715 (1998)
5. Maass, W.: Fast sigmoidal networks via spiking neurons. Neural Comput. **9**, 279–304 (1997)
6. Sanger, T.D.: Probability density methods for smooth function approximation and learning in populations of tuned spiking neurons. Neural Comput. **10**, 1567–1586 (1998)

Matching Mesoscopic Neural Models to Microscopic Neural Networks in Stationary and Non-stationary Regimes

Lara Escuain-Poole[✉], Alberto Hernández-Alcaina, and Antonio J. Pons

Department of Physics, Universitat Politècnica de Catalunya–BarcelonaTech,
Barcelona, Spain
lara.escuain@upc.edu

Abstract. A whole group of mesoscopic neural models, often called neural mass models, reflect the averaged activity of networks of thousands of neurons. A general statistical approach may be taken to reduce the complex microscopic dynamics to that described by these very simple mesoscopic models. The approach is limited, however, to situations where the input that feeds the microscopic network does not vary in time. This condition limits the general validity of mesoscopic models. In particular, the parameters that result from the derivation of the mesoscopic model are valid only in stationary regimes and, therefore, in transient regimes they cannot be well defined. This limitation raises reasonable doubts about the validity of the dynamical description of networks of mesoscopic models, where the output of one mesoscopic model becomes the input of others. In this work, we explore the variation in time of these mesoscopic parameters when the inputs of the microscopic neural networks which they aim to characterize are not stationary. By using Kalman filtering techniques we estimate the evolution of these parameters in both stationary and non-stationary regimes. By doing this, we match the description of a mesoscopic model to that of a neural network. Our results show that this matching is possible in stationary regimes, but in some non-stationary regimes, memory effects appear which are not accounted for in the standard mesoscopic derivation.

Keywords: Mesoscopic neural models · Microscopic neural networks · Scale bridging · Non-stationary regimes

© Springer International Publishing AG 2017
A. Lintas et al. (Eds.): ICANN 2017, Part I, LNCS 10613, p. 431, 2017.
https://doi.org/10.1007/978-3-319-68600-4

Hyper Neuron - One Neuron
with Infinite States

Shabab Bazrafkan$^{(\boxtimes)}$, Joseph Lemley, and Peter Corcoran

National University of Ireland, Galway, Galway, Ireland
{s.bazrafkan1,peter.corcoran}@nuigalway.ie
http://www.c3imaging.org

Abstract. Neural networks learn by creating a decision boundary. The
shape and smoothness of the decision boundary is ultimately determined by the activation function and the architecture. As the number of
neurons in an artificial neural network increase to infinity, the decision
function becomes smooth. A network with an infiniete number of neurons is impossible to implement with finite resources, but the behavior
of such a network can be modeled to an arbitrary degree of precision
by using standard numerical techniques. We named the resulting model
Hyper Neuron.

A flexible characteristic function controlling the rate of variations in
the weights of these neurons is used. The Hyper Neuron does not require
any assumptions about the parameter distribution. It utilizes a numerical methodology that contrasts with previous work (such as infinite
neural networks) which relies on assumptions about the distribution.

In the classical model of a neuron, each neuron has a single state and
output which is determined by an input, the weights, and the bias. Consider a neuron with more than one distinct output for the same input.
A layer made from an infinite number of these neurons can be modeled as a single neuron with an infinite number of states and an infinite
weight field. This kind of neuron is called a "Hyper Neuron" indicated
by symbol ʮ. Now consider the independent variable $\mathbf{x}$ where the Hyper
Neuron is defined over it i.e., the function ʮ$(\mathbf{x})$ is defined over the space
$\mathbf{x} \in \mathbb{R}^N$ To model the data in such a way that it represents the target
distribution, we use weighted inputs and non-linearity functions, where
the weights are not vectors but instead are multidimensional functions
$f_{ch}^{k,k+1}(\mathbf{x_k}, \mathbf{x_{k+1}}; \mathbf{p_{k+1}})$ which define the weight field between two Hyper
Neurons when the input is given by another Hyper Neuron. This func-
tion is simplified as $f_{ch}^{i_k,k+1}(\mathbf{x_{k+1}}; \mathbf{p_{k+1}})$ when the input is a feature
space or a conventional layer. In these equations k is the previous layer,
$k + 1$ is the layer with the Hyper Neuron, i_k is the ith element in the
previous layer and $\mathbf{p}$ represents parameters of the weight field function.

Hyper Neurons follow naturally from numerical models involving an
infinite number of conventional neurons in a single layer and the associated weight fields are described by characteristic functions. To validate
this idea, experiments were performed that used sinusoidal functions for

© Springer International Publishing AG 2017
A. Lintas et al. (Eds.): ICANN 2017, Part I, LNCS 10613, pp. 432–433, 2017.
https://doi.org/10.1007/978-3-319-68600-4

the weight fields, because they allowed rapid changes due to the inclusion of their frequency as a parameter that the network learned from the input data. A comparison between the proposed model and a conventional model containing up to 7 neurons was performed.

Keywords: Artificial neural networks · Numerical modeling · Infinite neural networks

Sparse Pattern Representation in a Realistic Recurrent Spiking Neural Network

Jesús A. Garrido$^{(\boxtimes)}$ and Eduardo Ros$^{(\boxtimes)}$

Department of Computer Architecture and Technology, CITIC-UGR,
University of Granada, Granada, Spain
{jesusgarrido,eros}@ugr.es

Abstract. The reliability of brain learning strongly depends on the quality of spatio-temporal pattern representation. However, the way neuronal mechanisms contribute to generate distinguishable representations remains largely unknown. In this sense, sparse codes combine the representational capacity of dense codes and the accuracy of learning with local codes. The most representative structure of sparse coding in the nervous system is the cerebellum since it accounts in its input layer with around 50 billion granule cells (which represent half of the neurons in the brain). Each granule cell receives input, on average, from only 4 mossy fibers [2].

In this work we have reproduced a 100um-length cube of the cerebellar input layer according to experimental data of neuronal density, electrical properties of neurons, connectivity constraints and dendritic length. The network was equipped with leaky integrate and fire neurons with adaptive threshold, since this neuron model has shown very effective in pattern transmission [1]. The input layer has been stimulated with four overlapping current patterns and oscillations in theta-frequency band (8 Hz) as previously presented in [3]. By connecting the resulting activity of the granule cells to a single-layer perceptron we have assessed the quality of pattern representation.

The perceptron obtained 97 percent of pattern recognition accuracy in the test subset. Both recurrent inhibition and adaptive threshold contributed to keep granule cell activity sparse, while theta-band frequency oscillations at the input enabled synchronization between successive neuronal layers.

Keywords: Pattern representation · Recurrent networks · Oscillations · Cerebellum

References

1. Asai, Y., Villa, A.E.: Integration and transmission of distributed deterministic neural activity in feed-forward networks. Brain Res. **1434**, 17–33 (2012)

© Springer International Publishing AG 2017
A. Lintas et al. (Eds.): ICANN 2017, Part I, LNCS 10613, pp. 434–435, 2017.
https://doi.org/10.1007/978-3-319-68600-4

2. Cayco-Gajic, A., Clopath, C., Silver, R.A.: Sparse synaptic connectivity is required for decorrelation and pattern separation in feedforward networks, p. 108431 (2017). bioRxiv
3. Garrido, J.A., Luque, N.R., Tolu, S.: Oscillation-driven spike-timing dependent plasticity allows multiple overlapping pattern recognition in inhibitory interneuron networks. Int. J. Neural Syst. **26**, 1650020 (2016)

Gender Differences in Spontaneous Risky Decision-Making Behavior: A Hyperscanning Study Using Functional Near-Infrared Spectroscopy

Mingming Zhang[1(✉)], Tao Liu[2], Matthew Pelowski[3], and Dongchuan Yu[1(✉)]

[1] Key Laboratory of Child Development and Learning Science,
Ministry of Education, Research Center for Learning Science, Southeast University,
Nanjing, China
{230149278,dcyu}@seu.edu.cn
[2] Department of Marketing, School of Management, Zhejiang University,
Hangzhou, China
125319321@qq.com
[3] Department of Basic Psychological Research and Research Methods,
Faculty of Psychology, Vienna University, Vienna, Austria
mattpelowski@yahoo.com

Abstract. Previous studies have demonstrated that genders tend to show different behavioral and neural patterns in risky decision-making situations. These studies, however, mainly focused on intra-brain mechanisms in single participants. To examine neural substrates underlying risky decision behaviors in realistic, interpersonal interactions, the present study employed a functional near-infrared spectroscopy (fNIRS) hyperscanning technique to simultaneously measure pairs of participants' frontotemporal activations in a face-to-face gambling card-game. This resulted in two main findings: The intra-brain analysis revealed higher activations in the orbitofrontal cortex (OFC), the medial prefrontal cortex (mPFC) and the posterior superior temporal sulcus (pSTS) in cases involving decisions carrying higher, versus more conservative, risk. This aligns with previous literature, indicating the importance of the mentalizing network in such decision-making tasks. Second, while both males and females showed interpersonal neural synchronization (INS) in their dlPFC in both risky and conservative decisions, as well as in the pSTS for females. Furthermore, females also showed INS in their mPFC in conservative decisions. The inter-brain analysis suggests that males and females may have different strategies in risky decision tasks. Males may make a risky decision depending on their non-social cognitive ability, and females may use their social cognitive ability to yield a choice. To our best knowledge, the present study is the first to investigate the interbrain processing of risky decision-making behavior in real face-to-face interactions. The implications of this outcome are also discussed for the general topics of human interaction and two-person neuroscience.

Keywords: Gender differences · Risky decision-making · Hyperscanning · fNIRS · Interpersonal neural synchronization

© Springer International Publishing AG 2017
A. Lintas et al. (Eds.): ICANN 2017, Part I, LNCS 10613, p. 436, 2017.
https://doi.org/10.1007/978-3-319-68600-4

An Implementation of a Spiking Neural Network Using Digital Spiking Silicon Neuron Model on a SIMD Processor

Sansei Hori[1(✉)], Mireya Zapata[2], Jordi Madrenas[2], Takashi Morie[1], and Hakaru Tamukoh[1]

[1] Graduate School of Life Science and Systems Engineering,
Kyushu Institute of Technology, Kitakyushu, Japan
hori-sansei@edu.brain.kyutech.ac.jp, {morie,tamukoh}@brain.kyutech.ac.jp
[2] Department of Electronics Engineering, Universitat Politécnica de Catalunya,
Barcelona, Spain
{mireya.zapata,jordi.madrenas}@upc.edu

Abstract. We implement a digital spiking silicon neuron (DSSN) [1] in a single instruction multiple data (SIMD) processor. The SIMD processor is a scalable, reconfigurable, and real-time spiking neural network emulator based on field programmable gate arrays [2]. We implement the DSSN model in the SIMD processor for the first time. The behavior of the membrane potential of one neuron based on the DSSN model is shown in Fig. 1. The operation results of the SIMD processor with 16-bit fixed-point operation are compared with software simulation results based on 64-bit floating-point operation. From the results, it is concluded that the SIMD processor successfully emulated the behavior of the membrane potential. In addition, a full-connection network consisting of 100 neurons is simulated in a software using fixed-point binary numbers to evaluate the bit width for the SIMD processor. In this experiment, the network stores two patterns selected from [1]. In the recall phase, the first pattern with noise is given to this network to recall the pattern. Experimental results show that the network with 16-bit fixed-point numbers, each of which includes a 12-bit fraction, a 3-bit integer, and a 1-bit sign, successfully recalled the input pattern as shown in Fig. 2. Here, M_u is a recall rate [1]. From this result, a large DSSN network simulation on the SIMD processor is promising.

Keywords: SNN · DSSN · SIMD processor · FPGA

© Springer International Publishing AG 2017
A. Lintas et al. (Eds.): ICANN 2017, Part I, LNCS 10613, pp. 437–438, 2017.
https://doi.org/10.1007/978-3-319-68600-4

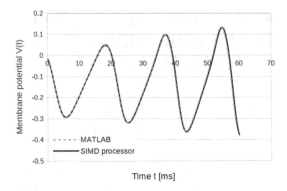

Fig. 1. Membrane potential.

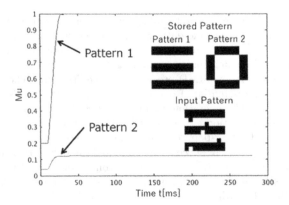

Fig. 2. Results of recall.

References

1. Li, J., Katori, Y., Kohno, T.: An FPGA-based silicon neuronal network with selectable excitability silicon neurons. Front. Neurosci. **6**, 183 (2012)
2. Zapata, M., Madrenas, J.: Synfire chain emulation by means of flexible SNN modeling on a SIMD multicore architecture. In: International Conference on Artificial Neural Networks, pp. 365–373. Springer (2016)

Hardware Implementation of Deep Self-organizing Map Networks

Yuichiro Tanaka$^{(\boxtimes)}$ and Hakaru Tamukoh$^{(\boxtimes)}$

Kyushu Institute of Technology, Kyushu, Japan
tanaka-yuichiro@edu.brain.kyutech.ac.jp, tamukoh@brain.kyutech.ac.jp
http://www.brain.kyutech.ac.jp/tamukoh/

Abstract. We aim to develop a recognition system of high accuracy and low power consumption by designing a digital circuit for deep neural networks (DNNs), and by implementing the circuit on field programmable gate arrays (FPGAs). DNNs include numerous multiply operations, whereas FPGAs include a limited number of multipliers. We aim to reduce the number of multiply operations generated by the algorithms within DNNs. Deep self-organizing map networks (DSNs) [1] are DNNs comprising self-organizing maps (SOMs) [2] as shown in Fig. 1. A hardware-oriented algorithm for SOMs has been proposed herein [3]. The algorithm represents SOMs by replacing multiply operations with bitshift operations. DSNs that include only a few multiply operations can then be represented by employing the algorithm. In this paper, we propose a hardware-oriented algorithm and a hardware architecture for DSNs. The hardware-oriented algorithm reduces multiply operations and exponential functions in a computation of SOM Module as shown in Fig. 1. In addition, we confirm that the algorithm does not worsen performance of DSN by a software simulation. Figure 2 shows error rates of DSN during learning MNIST Dataset [4]. The performance of the proposed algorithm achieve comparable results to the conventional algorithm. We also describe a DSN comprising three layers by Verilog-HDL as shown in Fig. 1, and implement it on a Xilinx Vertex-6 XC6VLX240T FPGA. Experimental results showed that the proposed DSN circuit estimates a label of an input image in $2\,\mu s$ while the software implemented using an Intel Core i5-3470 (3.20 GHz) CPU estimates it in about 1 ms. Thus the hardware is 500 times faster than the software. Its logic utilization is shown in Table 1.

Keywords: Deep neural networks · Self-organizing maps · FPGAs

Table 1. Logic Utilization of DSN circuit

	Used	Utilization
Number of Slice Registers	26803	8%
Number of Slice LUTs	47830	31%
Number of Block RAM/FIFO	136	32%
Number of DSP48E1s	544	70%

© Springer International Publishing AG 2017
A. Lintas et al. (Eds.): ICANN 2017, Part I, LNCS 10613, pp. 439–441, 2017.
https://doi.org/10.1007/978-3-319-68600-4

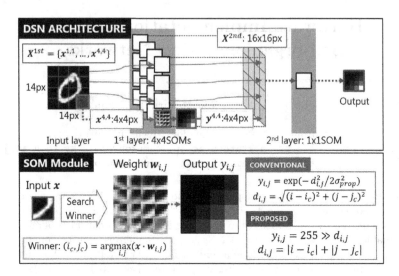

Fig. 1. Architecture and hardware-oriented algorithm of DSN

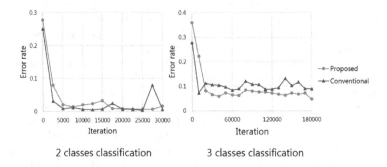

Fig. 2. Error rates of DSN during learning MNIST Dataset

References

1. Shinozaki, T., Naruse, Y.: A novel learning method with feedforward supervisory signal. In: The 28th Annual Conference of the Japanese Society for Artificial Intelligence (2014)
2. Kohonen, T.: Self-organized formation of topologically correct feature maps. Biol. Cybern. **43**, 59–69 (1982)

3. Tamukoh, H., Horio, K., Yamakawa, T.: Fast learning algorithms for self-organizing map employing rough comparison WTA and its digital hardware implementation. IEICE Trans. Electron. **E87-C**(11), 1787–1794 (2004)
4. LeCun, Y., Bottou, L., Bengio, Y., Haffner, P.: Gradient-based learning applied to document recognition. Proc. IEEE **86**(11), 2278–2324 (1998)

A Model of Synaptic Normalization and Heterosynaptic Plasticity Based on Competition for a Limited Supply of AMPA Receptors

Jochen Triesch[(✉)]

Frankfurt Institute for Advanced Studies, Goethe University,
Frankfurt am Main, Germany
triesch@fias.uni-frankfurt.de

Abstract. Simple models of Hebbian learning exhibit an unconstrained growth of synaptic efficacies. To avoid this unconstrained growth, some mechanism for limiting weights needs to be present. There is a long tradition of addressing this problem in neural network models using synaptic normalization rules. A particularly interesting normalization rule scales synapses multiplicatively such that the sum of a neuron's afferent exctiatory synaptic weights remains constant. One attractive feature of such a rule, next to its conceptual simplicity, is that in combination with Hebbian mechanisms it can give rise to lognormal-like weight distributions as observed experimentally. While such a normalization mechanism is not considered implausible, its link to neurobiology has been tenuous. A full understanding of such synaptic plasticity arguably requires the development of models that capture its complexities at the molecular level. Inspired by recent findings on the trafficking of neurotransmitter receptors across a neuron's dendritic tree, I propose a mathematical model of synaptic normalization and homeostatic heterosynaptic plastictiy based on competition between a neuron's afferent excitatory synapses for a limited supply of AMPA receptors.

In the model, synapses on the dendritic tree of a neuron compete for a limited supply of AMPA receptors, which are produced and distributed across the dendritic tree and stochastically transition into and out of receptor slots in the synapses, or simply disintegrate at a low rate. Using minimal assumptions, the model produces fast multiplicative normalization behavior and leads to a homeostatic form heterosynaptic plasticity as observed experimentally. If the production rate of AMPA receptors is controlled homeostatically, the model also accounts for slow multiplicative synaptic scaling. Thus, the model offers a parsimonious and unified account of both fast normalization and slow scaling processes, which it both predicts to act multiplicatively. It therefore supports the use of such

© Springer International Publishing AG 2017
A. Lintas et al. (Eds.): ICANN 2017, Part I, LNCS 10613, pp. 442–443, 2017.
https://doi.org/10.1007/978-3-319-68600-4

rules in neural network models. Because of its simplicity and analytical tractability, the model provides a convenient starting point for the development of more detailed models of the molecular mechanisms underlying different forms of synaptic plasticity.

Keywords: Heterosynaptic plastictiy · Synaptic scaling

Acknowledgment. I thank C. Tetzlaff, A.-S. Hafner, E. Schuman, and the Quandt Foundation.

Hebbian Learning Deduced
from the Stationarity Principle Leads
to Balanced Chaos in Fully Adapting
Autonomously Active Networks

Claudius Gros[1]([✉]), Philip Trapp[1], and Rodrigo Echeveste[2]

[1] Institute for Theoretical Physics, Goethe University Frankfurt, Frankfurt, Germany
gros@itp.uni-frankfurt.de
[2] CBL, Department of Engineering, University of Cambridge, Cambridge, UK

Neural information processing includes the extraction of information present in the statistics of afferent signals. For this, the afferent synaptic weights w_j are continuously adapted, changing in turn the distribution $p_\theta(y)$ of the post-synaptic neural activity y, which is in turn dependent on parameters θ of the processing neuron. The functional form of $p_\theta(y)$ will hence continue to evolve as long as learning is ongoing, becoming stationary only when learning is completed. This stationarity principle can be captured by the Fisher information

$$F_\theta = \int p_\theta(y) \left(\frac{\partial}{\partial \theta} \ln \left(p_\theta(y) \right) \right)^2 dy, \qquad \frac{\partial}{\partial \theta} \rightarrow \sum_j w_j \frac{\partial}{\partial w_j}$$

of the neural activity with respect to the afferent synaptic weights w_j. The learning rules derived from the stationarity principle are self-limiting [1], performing a standard principal component analysis with a bias towards a negative excess Kurtosis [2].

For large autonomous networks of continuous-time rate-encoding neurons, respecting Dale's law and whose synapses evolve under these plasticity rules, plus synaptic pruning, we find: (a) The continuously ongoing adaption of all synaptic weights leads to a homeostatic self-regulation of the typical magnitude of the synaptic weights

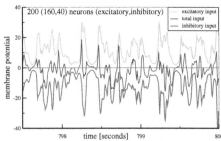

and of the neural activities. (b) The system settles into autonomously ongoing chaotic neural activity (the usual starting point for learning of coherent patterns of activity [3]) in which the excitatory and inhibitory inputs tend to balance each other. (c) Short-term synaptic plasticity stabilizes the balanced state.

© Springer International Publishing AG 2017
A. Lintas et al. (Eds.): ICANN 2017, Part I, LNCS 10613, pp. 444–445, 2017.
https://doi.org/10.1007/978-3-319-68600-4

References

1. Echeveste, R., Gros, C.: Generating functionals for computational intelligence: the fisher information as an objective function for self-limiting hebbian learning rules. Front. Robot. AI **1**, 1 (2014)
2. Echeveste, R., Eckmann, S., Gros, C.: The fisher information as a neural guiding principle for independent component analysis. Entropy **17**, 3838–3856 (2015)
3. Sussillo, D., Abbott, L.F.: Generating coherent patterns of activity from chaotic neural networks. Neuron **63**(4), 544–557 (2009)

A Granule-Pyramidal Cell Model for Learning and Predicting Trajectories Online

Mehdi Abdelwahed[1,2], Ihor Kuras[1,2], Artem Meltnyk[1,2], and Pierre Andry[1,2(✉)]

[1] ETIS UMR 8051, Université Paris Seine, Cergy, France
{mehdi.abdelwahed,pierre.andry}@ensea.fr
[2] ENSEA, CNRS, Université Cergy-Pontoise, Cergy, France

Abstract. In this poster, we outline a NN model for trajectories learning and prediction *online*, i.e. to learn without knowing the future of the trajectory. Our model is based on the idea that a trajectory can be learned and recognized by chunks. Each chunk is learned by a prediction unit (PU). Hence, our problem can be divided in two parts: (1) how a PU can learn and recognize online a given chunk as a temporal category; and (2) how a global architecture allow the competition of many prediction units to provide the prediction of the whole trajectory thru time. The current poster aims at showing how (1) is feasible online providing details about tuning parameters, geometric scaling, time scaling, generalization, and starts to investigate possible mechanims for (2), from ART internal competition to synchronization with the external environment. Central to our model, one PU is based on a self-conditionning Widrow Hoff rule for synapses connecting many granule cells (GC) that act as temporal gaussian filters of time, with one pyramidal cell (PC) learning sensory-motor trajectories. One novelty of such PU is the use of a random spacing of the learning through time and result in an efficient gradient descent while allowing a limited number of presentations of the input (Fig. 1).

We have tested the PU on (1) handwritted letters with a graphic tablet and (2) a hydraulic humanoid robot for mass discrimination that lacks a low level information about the oil pressure level (no direct return about the joint's effort). We show that mass discrimination is possible by comparing the robot's arm trajectories with the prediction of the movement with different mass.

Keywords: Spectrum generator · Granular cells · Cerebellum model · Adaptive resonance theory · Motor trajectory

© Springer International Publishing AG 2017
A. Lintas et al. (Eds.): ICANN 2017, Part I, LNCS 10613, pp. 446–447, 2017.
https://doi.org/10.1007/978-3-319-68600-4

tested	predicted		
	a	b	c
a	38.92	59.77	59.44
b	74.36	58.43	82.62
c	40.93	49.87	24.48

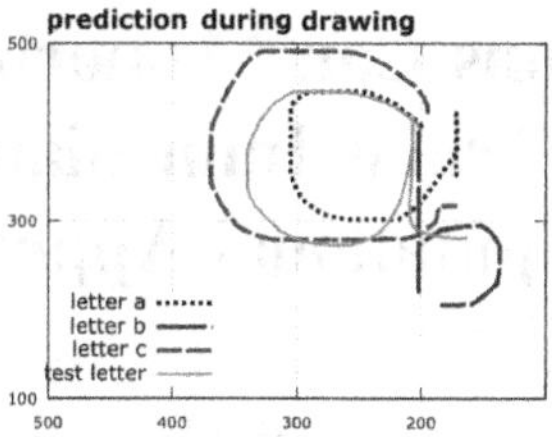

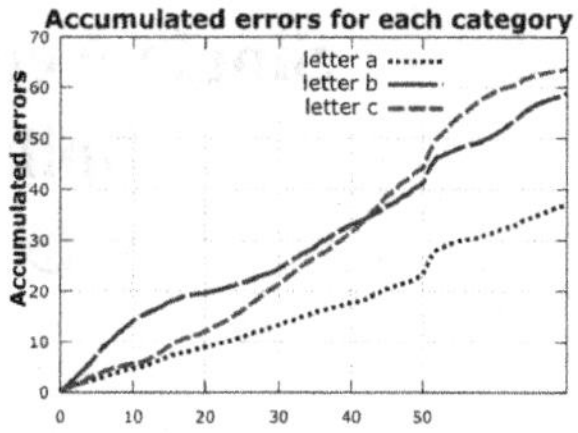

Fig. 1. Online evolution of the prediction and error accumulation of 3 categories of handwritten letters.

Single Neurons Can Memorize Precise Spike Trains Immediately: A Computational Approach

Hubert Loeffler[⊠]

Independent Scholar, Bregenz, Austria
loeffler.hubert@outlook.com

Abstract. Neuronal oscillations build the basis of the presented computational model of memory of temporally precise spike trains. In particular, subthreshold membrane potential oscillations (SMOs) of neuronal units enable a conversion of temporal properties of an input into spatial ones by phase coding [1, 2]. Since the excitability of units varies over time based on different phases of SMO, the input spikes activate different units at different time points. For the storage, the connections to the spatially distributed active units are enhanced by spike timing-dependent plasticity (STDP). When the spatial distribution is realized by different branches of a single neuron, the memory of the entire spike train is located by the input connections to this neuron. At this local level, plasticity changes emerge by dendritic spiking. As the prototype model was simulated via a spiking neuronal network, a spike burst from the input unit could exactly recall every randomly generated temporal input spike train. The time span of the memory is limited by the duration of unchanged oscillations between encoding and recall. This memory could act as working memory by replacing sustained activity. For now, the model combining oscillations and learning mechanisms is only a theoretical realization of the memory of precise spike trains. However, it complements the so-called ReSuMe-models as a kind of implicit memory of spike trains by learning associations between input and desired output spike trains [e.g. 3].

Keywords: Temporally precise spike trains · Phase coding · Oscillations · Working memory

References

1. Nadasdy, Z.: Information encoding and reconstruction from the phase of action potentials. Front. Syst. Neurosci. **3**, Article 6 (2009). doi:10.3389/neuro.06.006.2009.d
2. Maris, E., Fries, P.: Diverse Phase Relations among Neuronal Rhythms and Their Potential Function. Trends Neurosci. (2016). doi:10.1016/j.tins.2015.12.004
3. Ponulak, F., Kasinski, A.: Supervised learning in spiking neuronal networks with ReSuMe: sequence learning, classification, and spike shifting. Neuronal Comput. **22**(2), 467–510 (2010)

© Springer International Publishing AG 2017
A. Lintas et al. (Eds.): ICANN 2017, Part I, LNCS 10613, p. 448, 2017.
https://doi.org/10.1007/978-3-319-68600-4

Learning Stable Recurrent Excitation in Simulated Biological Neural Networks

Michael Teichmann$^{(\boxtimes)}$ and Fred H. Hamker

Department of Computer Science, Technische Universität Chemnitz,
Chemnitz, Germany
{michael.teichmann,fred.hamker}@informatik.tu-chemnitz.de

Abstract. Recurrent excitation is required to model advanced effects of cortical processing, e.g. attentional feedback within the visual cortex. However, recurrent processing allows an exponential growth of activities with time. We use a minimal model with two excitatory and two inhibitory neurons to illustrate under which conditions recurrent excitation can be stable. In our solution recurrent inhibition balances the recurrent excitation: Recurrent excitation, returned from the second excitatory neuron to the first, is routed in parallel to the inhibitory interneuron connected to the first excitatory neuron. This parallel routing of excitatory feedback onto excitatory and inhibitory neurons is also found as a general principle in the cortex [1].

We use this principle in a large-scale network implementing the layers 4 and 2/3 of the visual areas V1 and V2. Each layer consists of excitatory and inhibitory neurons with neuroscientifically grounded connectivity (delay 1 ms). The cortico-cortical feedback projects from V2-L2/3 to both neuron types in V1-L2/3 [2]. Excitatory synapses are learned with an improved version of our Hebbian learning rule [3], able to learn V1 complex-cells as well as simple-cells. Inhibitory synapses are learned with an anti-Hebbian rule [4]. The network is trained on natural scenes, five times longer as required for convergence. The neurons learned proper receptive fields and achieve good recognition accuracy, tested on COIL-100. The feedback mechanism leads to balanced modulation of activities in the different layers without any exponential amplifications. In the top layer, where feedback emanates, rate activity slightly increases for the neuron's preferred stimuli. Thus, parallel feedback onto excitatory and inhibitory circuit parts enables stable networks while providing the demanded modulation properties of feedback.

Keywords: Recurrent excitation · Hebbian learning

References

1. Isaacson, J.S., Scanziani, M.: How inhibition shapes cortical activity. Neuron **72**(2), 231–243 (2011)
2. Douglas, R.J., Martin, K.C.: Neuronal circuits of the neocortex. Annu. Rev. Neurosci. **27**, 419–51 (2004)

© Springer International Publishing AG 2017
A. Lintas et al. (Eds.): ICANN 2017, Part I, LNCS 10613, pp. 449–450, 2017.
https://doi.org/10.1007/978-3-319-68600-4

3. Teichmann, M., Wiltschut, J., Hamker, F.H.: Learning invariance from natural images inspired by observations in the primary visual cortex. Neural Comput. **24**(5), 1271–1296 (2012)
4. Wiltschut, J., Hamker, F.H.: Efficient coding correlates with spatial frequency tuning in a model of V1 receptive field organization. Vis. Neurosci. **26**(1), 21–34 (2009)

Speech Emotion Recognition: Recurrent Neural Networks Compared to SVM and Linear Regression

Leila Kerkeni[1,2(✉)], Youssef Serrestou[1], Mohamed Mbarki[2],
Mohamed Ali Mahjoub[2], Kosai Raoof[1], and Catherine Cleder[3]

[1] Acoustics Laboratory,University of Maine, Orono, USA
kerkeni.leila@gmail.com
[2] Laboratory of Advanced Technology and Intelligent Systems, Sousse, Tunisia
[3] Research Centre for Education, University of Nantes, Nantes, France

Abstract. Emotion recognition in spoken dialogues has been gaining increasing interest all through current years. A speech emotion recognition (SER) is a challenging research area in the field of Human Computer Interaction (HCI). It refers to the ability of detection the current emotional state of a human being from his or her voice. SER has potentially wide applications, such as the interface with robots, banking, call centers, car board systems, computer games etc. In our research we are interested to how, emotion recognition, can top enhance the quality of teaching for both of classroom orchestration and E-learnning. Integration of SER into aided teaching system, can guide teacher to decide what subjects can be taught and must be able to develop strategies for managing emotions within the learning environment. In linguistic activity, from student's interaction and articulation, we can extract information about their emotional state. That is why learner's emotional state should be considered in the language classroom. In general, the SER is a computational task consisting of two major parts: feature extraction and emotion machine classification. The questions that arise here: What are the acoustic features needed for a most robust automatic recognition of a speaker's emotion? Which methods is most appropriate for classification? How the database used influence the recognition of emotion in speech? Thus came the idea to compare a RNN method with the basic method (LR) [1] and the most widely used method (SVM). Most of previously published works generally use the berlin database. In this work we use another database. To our knowledge the spanish emotional database has never been used before. In recent years in speech emotion recognition, many researchers [2] proposed important speech features which contain emotion information and many classification algorithms. The aim of this paper is to compare firstly differents approachs that have proven their efficiency for emotions recognition task. Then to propose an efficient solution based on combination of these approachs. For classification, Linear regression (LR), Support vector machine (SVM) and Recurrent neural network (RNN) classifiers are used to classify seven different emotions present in the German and Spanish databases. The explored features

© Springer International Publishing AG 2017
A. Lintas et al. (Eds.): ICANN 2017, Part I, LNCS 10613, pp. 451–453, 2017.
https://doi.org/10.1007/978-3-319-68600-4

included: mel-frequency cepstrum coefficients (MFCC) [2] and modulation spectral features (MSFs) [3]. Table 1 show the recognition rate for each combination of various features and classifiers for Berlin and Spanish databases. The overall experimental results reveal that the feature combination of MFCC and MS has the highest accuracy rate on both Spanish emotional database using RNN classifier 90,05% and Berlin emotional database using LR 82,41%. These results can be explained as follows: LR classifier performed better results with feature combination of MFCC and MS for both databases. And under the conditions of limited training data (Berlin database), it can have a very good classification performance compared to other classifiers. A high dimension can maximize the rate of LR. As regarding the SVM method, we found the same results as these presented in [3]. The MS is the most appropriate features for SVM classifier. To improve the performance of SVM, we need to change the model for each types of features. To the spanish database, the feature combination of MFCC and MS using RNN has the best recognition rate 90.05%. For Berlin database, combination both types of features has the worst recognition rate. That because the RNN model having too many parameters (155 coefficients in total)and a poor training data. This is the phenomena of overfitting. The performance of SER system is influenced by many factors, especially the quality of samples, the features extracted and classification algorithms. Nowadays, a lot of uncertainties are still present for the best algorithm to classify emotions and what features influence the recognition of emotion in speech. To extract the more effective features of speech, seek for an efficient classification techniques and enhance the emotion recognition accuracy is our future work. More work is needed to improve the system so that it can be better used in classroom orchestration.

Keywords: Speech emotion recognition · Recurrent neural networks · SVM · Linear regression · MFCC · Modulation spectral features.

Table 1. Recognition results using RNN, SVM and LR classfiers based on Berlin and Spanish databases

Dataset	Feature	RNN (%)	SVM (%)	LR (%)
Berlin	MS	66.32	63.30	60.70
	MFCC	69.55	56.60	67.10
	MFCC+MS	58.51	59.50	75.90
Spanish	MS	82.30	77.63	70.60
	MFCC	86.56	70.69	76.08
	MFCC+MS	**90.05**	68.11	82.41

References

1. Naseem, I., Togneri, R., Bennamoun., M.: Linear regression for face recognition. IEEE Trans. Pattern Anal. Mach. Intell. **32** (2010)
2. Surabhi, V., Saurabh, M.: Speech emotion recognition: a review. IRJET **03** (2016)
3. Wua, S., Falk, T.H., Chan, W.Y.: Automatic speech emotion recognition using. Speech Commun. **53**, 768–785 (2011)

Pelagic Species Identification by Using a PNN Neural Network and Echo-Sounder Data

Ignazio Fontana[1]([✉]), Giovanni Giacalone[1], Angelo Bonanno[1],
Salvatore Mazzola[1], Gualtiero Basilone[1], Simona Genovese[1],
Salvatore Aronica[1], Solon Pissis[5], Costas S. Iliopoulos[5], Ritu Kundu[5],
Antonino Fiannaca[2], Alessio Langiu[2], Giosue' Lo Bosco[3,4], Massimo La Rosa[2],
and Riccardo Rizzo[2]

[1] IAMC-CNR, Capo Granitola, Torretta Granitola, Italy
{ignazio.fontana,giovanni.giacalone,angelo.bonanno,salvatore.mazzola,
gualtiero.basilone,simona.genovese,salvatore.aronica}@cnr.it
[2] ICAR-CNR, Palermo, Italy
{antonino.fiannaca,alessio.langiu,massimo.rosa,
riccardo.rizzo}@icar.cnr.it
[3] DMI, Universita' Degli Studi di Palermo, Palermo, Italy
giosue.lobosco@unipa.it
[4] Dipartimento SIT, IEMEST, Palermo, Italy
[5] King's College, Strand, London, UK
{solon.pissis,costas.iliopoulos,ritu.kundu}@kcl.ac.uk

Abstract. For several years, a group of CNR researchers conducted acoustic surveys in the Sicily Channel to estimate the biomass of small pelagic species, their geographical distribution and their variations over time. The instrument used to carry out these surveys is the scientific echo-sounder, set for different frequencies. The processing of the back scattered signals in the volume of water under investigation determines the abundance of the species. These data are then correlated with the biological data of experimental catches, to attribute the composition of the various fish schools investigated. Of course, the recognition of the fish schools helps to produce very good results, that is very close to the truth about the abundances associated with the various species. In this work, only the acoustic traces of biological monospecific catches, exclusively of two species of pelagic fish. The ecograms where pre-processed using various software tools [1, 2]. For this work, the potential fish schools are detected and isolated using the SHAPES algorithm in Echoview. At the end of the pre-processing phase, the signals are labelled using the two species of pelagic fish: Engraulis encrasicolus and Sardina pilchardus. These labelled signals were used to train a Probabilistic Neural Network (PNN) [3].

Keywords: Probabilistic neural networks · Pelagic species identification · Classification

© Springer International Publishing AG 2017
A. Lintas et al. (Eds.): ICANN 2017, Part I, LNCS 10613, pp. 454–455, 2017.
https://doi.org/10.1007/978-3-319-68600-4

References

1. De Robertis, A., Higginbottom, I.: A post-processing technique to estimate the signal-to-noise ratio and remove echosounder background noise. ICES J. Mar. Sci. **64**, 1282–1291 (2007)
2. Swartzman, G., Brodeur, R., Napp, J., Walsh, D., Hewitt, R., Demer, D., Hunt, G., Logerwell, E.: Relating spatial distributions of acoustically determined patches of fish and plankton: data viewing, image analysis, and spatial proximity. Can. J. Fish. Aquat. Sci. **56**(S1), 188–198 (1999). doi:10.1139/f99-206
3. Specht, D.F.: Probabilistic neural networks. Neural Netw. **3**(1), 109–118 (1990)

The Impact of Ozone on Crop Yields by Combining Multi-model Results Through a Neural Network Approach

A. Riccio[1(✉)], E. Solazzo[2], and S. Galmarini[2]

[1] Department of Science and Technology, Università degli Studi di Napoli "Parthenope", Naples, Italy
angelo.riccio@uniparthenope.it
[2] EC/DG-Joint Research Center, Ispra, Italy
{efisio.solazzo,stefano.galmarini}@ec.europa.eu

Abstract. Field experiments have demonstrated that atmospheric ozone can damage crops, leading to yield reduction and a deteriorating crop quality [3]. The availability of regional scale air pollution models allows one to combine modeled ozone fields, exposure-response functions, crop location and growing season, to obtain regional estimates of crop losses. Since 2008 the Air Quality Model Evaluation International Initiative (AQMEII) coordinated by the EC/Joint Research Center and the US EPA has worked toward knowledge and experience sharing on air quality modeling in Europe and North America [1]. Within this context multi-model ensemble has been exercised proving to be very instrumental for a number of applications (e.g. [2]).

In this work we explore the capabilities of neural networks to combine model results and improve ozone predictions, under current and future scenarios, over the European region. The ability of neural networks to account for both nonlinear input-output relationships and interactions between inputs has made them popular in areas where model interpretation is of secondary importance to predictive skill. The possibility to improve the predictive capabilities of the existing models has fundamental implications both on the model forecasting ability necessary to sketch future scenarios and on legislation to regulate the impact of air quality.

Keywords: Ozone · Crop losses · Ensemble modeling · AQMEII

References

1. Rao, S.T., Galmarini, S., Puckett, K.: Air quality model evaluation international initiative (AQMEII): advancing the state of the science in regional photochemical modeling and its applications. Bull. Am. Meteorol. Soc. **92**(1), 23–30 (2011)
2. Riccio, A., Ciaramella, A., Giunta, G., Galmarini, S., Solazzo, E., Potempski, S.: On the systematic reduction of data complexity in multimodel atmospheric dispersion ensemble modeling. J. Geophys. Res.: Atmos. **117**(D5) (2012)
3. Van Dingenen, R., Dentener, F.J., Raes, F., Krol, M.C., Emberson, L., Cofala, J.: The global impact of ozone on agricultural crop yields under current and future air quality legislation. Atmos. Environ. **43**(3), 604–618 (2009)

© Springer International Publishing AG 2017
A. Lintas et al. (Eds.): ICANN 2017, Part I, LNCS 10613, p. 456, 2017.
https://doi.org/10.1007/978-3-319-68600-4

Artificial Neural Networks for Fault Tollerance of an Air-Pressure Sensor Network

Salvatore Aronica[1], Gualtiero Basilone[1], Angelo Bonanno[1], Ignazio Fontana[1], Simona Genovese[1], Giovanni Giacalone[1], Alessio Langiu[3], Giosué Lo Bosco[2(✉)], Salvatore Mazzola[1], and Riccardo Rizzo[3]

[1] IAMC, CNR, Campobello di Mazara, TP, Italy
[2] DMI, Università Degli Studi di Palermo, Palermo, PA, Italy
giosue.lobosco@unipa.it
[3] ICAR, CNR, Palermo, PA, Italy

Abstract. A meteorological tsunami, commonly called *Meteotsunami*, is a tsunami-like wave originated by rapid changes in barometric pressure that involve the displacement of a body of water. This phenomenon is usually present in the sea cost area of Mazara del Vallo (Sicily, Italy), in particular in the internal part of the seaport canal, sometimes making local population at risk. The Institute for Coastal Marine Environment (IAMC) of the National Research Council in Italy (CNR) have already conducted several studies upon meteotsunami phenomenon. One of the project has regarded the creation of a sensors network composed by micro-barometric sensors, located in 4 different stations close to the seaport of Mazara del Vallo, for the purpose of studying meteotsunami phenomenon. Each station sends all the measurements to a collecting one that elaborates them with the purpose of identifying the direction and speed of pressure fronts. Unfortunately, four stations provide the minimum amount of data necessary to a reliable characterization of pressure fronts so that the failure of only one is a serious issue. Such failures regard blackouts, connection loss, hardware failures or maintenances. In this context we have developed a fault tolerance system that is based on neural networks. A feed forward neural network i is associated with each station i, and is trained to predict its measurements using as inputs the ones of the other three station j with $j \neq i$. In the normal condition, the collecting station receives the measurements from each station. In the case of failure of only one station k, the related neural network k can be used to predict the missing measurements. We have conducted preliminary experiments using a two layer feed forward neural network with sigmoid and linear activation functions for the hidden and output layer respectively. In order to simulate failures, we have removed group of data from each station measurements that follow inside a fixed temporal range. The related networks have been used to predict the missing measurements, and the mean square error (MSE) from the real measured value has been computed as performance index. The very low values of obtained MSE lead to the suggestion of a certain effectiveness of the proposed system.

Keywords: Meteotsunami · Pressure sensors · Neural networks

© Springer International Publishing AG 2017
A. Lintas et al. (Eds.): ICANN 2017, Part I, LNCS 10613, p. 457, 2017.
https://doi.org/10.1007/978-3-319-68600-4

Modelling the Impact of GM Plants and Insecticides on Arthropod Populations of Agricultural Interest

Alberto Lanzoni[(✉)], Edison Pasqualini, and Giovanni Burgio

Dipartimento di Scienze Agrarie - Entomologia,
Alma Mater Studiorum-Università di Bologna, Bologna, Italy
{alberto.lanzoni2,edison.pasqualini,giovanni.burgio}@unibo.it

Abstract. Matrix population models (MPM) are nowadays not widely used to simulate arthropod population dynamics with applications to risk assessment. However, an increasing body of studies are prompting the finding of optimization techniques to reduce uncertainty in matrix parameters estimation. Indeed, uncertainty in parameters estimates may lead to significant management implications. Here we present two case studies where MPM are used for assessing the potential impact of genetically modified (GM) plants on beneficial insect species (the coccinellid *Adalia bipunctata*) and for evaluating spider mites (the two-spotted spider mite *Teranychus urticae*) resurgence after insecticide application. In both studies the data obtained, consisting of population time series, were used to generate a stage-classified projection matrix. The general model used to simulate population dynamics consists of a matrix containing (i) survival probabilities (the probability of growing and moving to the next stage and the probability of surviving and remaining in the same stage), and (ii) fecundities of the population. Most of the methods utilized for estimate the parameter values of stage-classified models rely on following cohorts of identified individuals [1]. However in these studies the observed data consisted of a time-series of population vectors $n(t)$, for $t = T_0, T_1, \ldots, T_n$, where individuals are not distinguished. The relationship between the observed data and the values of the matrix parameters that produced the series involves an estimation process called inverse problem. The set of parameters that minimize the residual between the collected data and the model output for the two studies presented here was estimated using the quadratic programming method [2]. The set of estimated parameters for the *A. bipunctata Rhopalosiphum maidis* maize tritrophic system model supports the hypothesis that GM maize does not negatively influences *A. bipunctata* population growth in the tritrophic system studied [3]. Otherwise, in the case of the two-spotted spider mite resurgence, some insecticides, namely etofenprox, deltamethrin and betacifluthrin, fostered a higher mite population growth than the untreated control. This was principally due to higher adult fecundity and egg fertility, clearly explained by Life Table Response Experiments, performed starting from estimated matrices, indicating a likely trophobiotic effect. A variety of inverse modelling approaches have been applied to demographic models other than

© Springer International Publishing AG 2017
A. Lintas et al. (Eds.): ICANN 2017, Part I, LNCS 10613, pp. 458–459, 2017.
https://doi.org/10.1007/978-3-319-68600-4

quadratic programming. Bayesian approaches [4] and evolutionary algorithms, such as Genetic Algorithms [5] have also been used for inverse modelling and parameters fitting. In order to find a better model fit for the observed stage class distributions on two case studies, we would like to explore Neural Networks or more generally machine learning possibilities in finding a set of parameter values that successfully describes observed data.

Keywords: Matrix population model · Inverse problem · Parameter estimate · *Adalia bipunctata* · Ecological risk assessment Teranychus urticae · Spider mites resurgence

References

1. Caswell, H.: Matrix Population Models. John Wiley & Sons, Ltd (2001)
2. Wood, S.N.: Obtaining birth and mortality patterns from structured population trajectories. Ecol. Monogr. **64**(1), 23–44 (1994)
3. Lanzoni, A.: Evaluation of the effects of Bt-maize on non target insects using a demographic approach. Ph.D. dissertation thesis, Alma Mater Studiorum Università di Bologna (2016)
4. Gross, K., Ives, A.R., Nordheim, E.V.: Estimating fluctuating vital rates from time-series data: a case study of aphid biocontrol. Ecology **86**(3), 740–752 (2005)
5. Cropper, W.P., Holm, J.A., Miller, C.J.: An inverse analysis of a matrix population model using a genetic algorithm. Ecol. Inf. **7**(1), 41–45 (2012)

Deep Neural Networks for Emergency Detection

Emanuele Cipolla$^{(\boxtimes)}$, Riccardo Rizzo, and Filippo Vella

Institute for High-Performance Computing and Networking, National Research
Council of Italy (ICAR-CNR), Rende, Italy
{Emanuele.Cipolla,Riccardo.Rizzo,Filippo.Vella}@icar.cnr.it

Abstract. The increasing deployment of sensor networks has resulted in an high availability of geophysical data that can be used for classification and predictions of environmental features and conditions. In particular, detecting emergency situations would be desirable to reduce damages to people and things. In this work we propose the use of a deep neural network architecture to detect pluvial-flood emergencies, building upon and extending our previous works [1, 2] in which we gathered a large set of rain measures coming from a sensor and surveillance network deployed in the last decade in the Italian region of Tuscany and built a database of verified emergency events using a manually annotated set of resources found on the World Wide Web.

We used a stacked LSTM [3] network to classify 4-day-long sequences (the measures for a given day and the three days prior) of pluvial measurements gathered from the whole set of stations belonging to Servizio Idrogeologico Regionale in Tuscany. After empirical tests, we chose two 2 LSTM layers with 256 outputs each for the hidden part of the network. Using multiple layers we exploit the abstraction power for pattern recognition in time sequences that has been previously recognized for LSTMs: lower layers are able to detect the most significant variations, while the higher ones use these patterns to spot emergency events.

As they are very infrequent, a balanced subset of quiet days has to be considered to build a binary classifier to avoid overfitting. To increase the number of relevant true examples we performed a linear interpolation of existing sequences, generating 10 new examples for each original one. After training the network using 560 examples, we tested its performance using 1276 sequences. We had 131 true positives, 1074 true negatives, 64 false positives and 7 false negatives.

This leads to a precision of 0.67 and a recall of 0.95, so the F_1-score is 0.79. Accuracy is also high (0.94). We are planning to train this network on a bigger dataset, and then perform transfer learning to have an overall better classifier.

Keywords: LSTM · Neural network · Rain · Flood · Emergency · Deep learning

References

1. Cipolla, E., Maniscalco, U., Rizzo, R., Vella, F.: Analysis and visualization of meteorological emergencies. J. Ambient Intell. Humanized Comput. **8**(1), 57–68 (2017)

© Springer International Publishing AG 2017
A. Lintas et al. (Eds.): ICANN 2017, Part I, LNCS 10613, pp. 460–461, 2017.
https://doi.org/10.1007/978-3-319-68600-4

2. Cipolla, E., Rizzo, R., Stabile, D., Vella, F.: A tool for emergency detection with deep learning neural networks. In: Proceedings of the 2nd Internatinal Workshop on Knowledge Discovery KDWeb 2016 (2016)
3. Hochreiter, S., Schmidhuber, J.: Long short-term memory. Neural Comput. **9**(8), 1735–1780 (1997). http://dx.doi.org/10.1162/neco.1997.9.8.1735

Author Index

Printed in the United States
by Bookmasters

Printed in the United States
By Bookmasters